THIRD EDITION

WITHDRAWN

Readings in
LABOR ECONOMICS AND LABOR RELATIONS

LLOYD G. REYNOLDS
Yale University

STANLEY H. MASTERS
State University of New York at Binghamton

COLLETTE H. MOSER
Michigan State University

PRENTICE-HALL, INC., *Englewood Cliffs, New Jersey 07632*

Library of Congress Cataloging in Publication Data

Readings in labor economics and labor relations.

Includes bibliographical references.
1. Labor economics—Addresses, essays, lectures.
2. Industrial relations—Addresses, essays, lectures.
I. Reynolds, Lloyd George, (date)   . II. Masters,
Stanley H., (date)   . III. Moser, Collette, (date)
IV. Title: Labor economics and labor relations.
HD4901.R389 1982   331   81-23362
ISBN 0-13-761577-9   AACR2

Editorial/production supervision and interior design by *Barbara Grasso*
Original text cover design by *Dawn Stanley,* adapted by *Anne T. Bonanno*
Manufacturing buyer: *Edward O'Dougherty*

Burgess
HD
4901
R389
1982
c. 1

Printed in the United States of America

10 9 8 7 6 5 4 3 2 1

ISBN 0-13-761577-9

PRENTICE-HALL INTERNATIONAL, INC., *London*
PRENTICE-HALL OF AUSTRALIA PTY. LIMITED, *Sydney*
PRENTICE-HALL OF CANADA, LTD., *Toronto*
PRENTICE-HALL OF INDIA PRIVATE LIMITED, *New Delhi*
PRENTICE-HALL OF JAPAN, INC., *Tokyo*
PRENTICE-HALL OF SOUTHEAST ASIA PTE. LTD., *Singapore*
WHITEHALL BOOKS LIMITED, *Wellington, New Zealand*

Contents

II INDUSTRIAL RELATIONS

Preface

The literature of labor economics is rich and varied. In the past, graduate students generally were exposed to this literature, gaining a sense of its historical development, the controversies in the field, and the frontiers of current research. In recent years, the literature has become increasingly specialized and technical so that broad exposure for students is less frequent. The undergraduate usually has access to original literature only indirectly through a textbook, in which knowledge about labor economics necessarily appears more authoritative than it actually is.

Because we believe that students can benefit by reading the original works of leading scholars in labor economics and industrial relations, we have tried to assemble as rich a menu as possible. The general organization follows that of Reynolds's *Labor Economics and Labor Relations,* but the readings in this volume could form a useful supplement to any labor text.

In addition to setting high quality standards, we have sought to include selections that would achieve a balanced coverage of both labor economics and industrial relations and of the important topics within each area. We have also attempted to represent different points of view on major issues.

Two other editorial principles have governed the content of the book. First, we have edited selections to avoid unnecessary mathematical equations and technical arguments. On the other hand, we have retained fairly long excerpts where they are needed to give the full flavor of the author's thought.

In making revisions for this edition, our primary objective has been to add selections that reflect recent developments in the field of labor economics. A new unit has been added on protective legislation; the sections on labor supply, unemployment, and inflation have been substantially revised; and new selections have been added in all areas.

Lloyd G. Reynolds
Stanley H. Masters
Collette H. Moser

I

LABOR MARKETS

Labor Market Theory and Practice

The operation of markets, in which buyers and sellers exchange commodities or services at a price, is central to the study of economics. The hiring of labor at a specified price (wage rate) is a market transaction. Economists have always recognized, however, that a worker selling labor is in a position far different from a shoe merchant selling shoes.

One difference is that the worker delivers himself or herself as part of the bargain. So, in choosing among occupations, the agreeableness or disagreeableness of the work is an important consideration. The worker will also consider such things as the cost of training for the occupation, the chances of success in it, and the regularity of employment. Given full information and freedom of choice, the market will operate to equalize not the wage rate for different occupations, but the occupations' total attractiveness to workers on the margin of decision. Jobs that cost much to learn, involve disagreeable work, or offer only irregular employment will pay a higher wage to offset these disadvantages.

3

These principles were first stated two hundred years ago in Adam Smith's *Wealth of Nations*. It is a mark of Smith's genius that later writers have not been able to improve very much on his original statement. We should note also that Smith recognized the important restrictions on free choice that existed in his day, which prevented the market from equalizing the advantages of different occupations.

Alfred Marshall, the great Cambridge University economist of the period 1880–1920, analyzed labor markets in a way that, while consistent with Smith, goes beyond him in several respects. He noted, first, that workers differ in efficiency. Thus, a competitive labor market will not equalize the wage rates of workers in the same occupation, but rather will equalize the ratio of their wage rates to their efficiency—what Marshall termed their *efficiency earnings*. He then proceeded to explore several "peculiarities" in the operation of labor markets. Of these, the most interesting are:

1. Parents who invest in the education and training of their children do not receive the future monetary rewards. Parents in the lower occupational grades, he thought, will have neither the resources nor the foresight to invest much in training; this is an important factor perpetuating inequality from generation to generation.

2. Workers are under greater pressure than employers to conclude an employment bargain quickly because they must have income to live. This fact, Marshall believed, placed them at a bargaining disadvantage and tended to drive down wages. This provides an argument for trade union organizations to "equalize bargaining power."

3. Since training for the higher occupations takes a long time, supply responds only slowly to changes in earnings. Thus, at any moment the market for such occupations is likely to be out of equilibrium. The "long run," in which competition would equalize the total attractiveness of occupations, must be interpreted as a long period of calendar time.

In recent years labor economists have devoted much attention to the effect of human capital on wage rates. Investments in human capital are costs incurred to increase future earnings and productivity by improving health, education, and training. The theory of human capital is developed in the selection from Gary Becker's pioneering book, *Human Capital—A Theoretical and Empirical Analysis*.

A worker's wage rate is determined partly by the worker's human capital and the supply and demand for the specific skills he or she has obtained. Although wage differentials are affected by these market forces, they are also affected by what workers and employers consider to be customary and fair. A worker, especially one who has spent many years with an employer, compares his or her wage more with that of co-workers than with what the worker might earn with some new employer. Moreover, there are often wide differences in wage rates for similar jobs in different firms, especially if the firms are in different industries. John Dunlop discusses these issues and shows why such differentials are not transitory and should not be dismissed as "imperfections."

Nonmarket forces may be more important in the market for labor than many other markets, in part because information and mobility are often more limited in the labor market. The information sources available to workers and employers can be divided into two channels: formal, such as local offices of the state employment service, and informal, such as tips from friends and relatives. Economists concerned with improvement of information have tended to urge greater use of formal channels. Albert Rees, on the basis of research in the Chicago labor market, points out that informal channels have certain advantages to both employers and workers and often work better than has been supposed. He suggests that formal information networks may be most useful for specialized managerial, professional, and technical jobs, where matching vacancies and applicants may require search over a wide geographical area.

Restrictions on free choice of occupation have concerned economists from Adam Smith to the present. Clark Kerr argues that, instead of the complete open market of pure competition, actual labor markets are highly compartmentalized ("Balkanized") by employer and union rules. In unionized craft occupations, entrance to the market occurs only via the union. In manufacturing industries, workers are hired from the outside only at a few "ports of entry" to the company. Most jobs are filled by promotion from inside—the "internal" labor market—with seniority the dominant principle. This channeling of labor mobility by institutional rules, Kerr argues, makes actual wage decisions quite different from those pictured in simple supply-demand models. Although these restrictions on mobility are viewed as market "imperfections" by some economists, they are quite consistent with the interest of most workers in job security—an issue that is addressed in our section on the labor movement.

Peter Doeringer and Michael Piore describe how the low-wage labor market functions and how it differs from other labor markets. In addition to lower pay, there are generally poorer working conditions, less job security, and little chance for promotion. Still, such a labor market serves the needs of some workers and firms.

The low-wage labor market includes a disproportionate number of blacks and women, partly as a result of discrimination. Kenneth Boulding discusses the concept of discrimination, with emphasis on three of its sources—monopoly power, personal prejudice, and role prejudice.

Most college graduates obtain reasonably well-paid, secure positions. Nevertheless the job market for college graduates has undergone a marked downturn in the past decade, with demand falling relative to supply. The changes that have occurred and their social implications are discussed by Richard Freeman.

1

The Wealth of Nations

Adam Smith

Adam Smith, *The Wealth of Nations* (Edinburgh: Adam & Charles Black, 1853).

Of Wages and Profit in the Different Employments of Labour and Stock

The whole of the advantages and disadvantages of the different employments of labour and stock must, in the same neighbourhood, be either perfectly equal or continually tending to equality. If in the same neighbourhood, there was any employment evidently either more or less advantageous than the rest, so many people would crowd into it in the one case, and so many would desert it in the other, that its advantages would soon return to the level of other employments. This at least would be the case in a society where things were left to follow their natural course, where there was perfect liberty, and where every man was perfectly free both to choose what occupation he thought proper, and to change it as often as he thought proper. Every man's interest would prompt him to seek the advantageous and to shun the disadvantageous employment.

Pecuniary wages and profit, indeed, are everywhere in Europe extremely different, according to the different employments of labour and stock. But this difference arises partly from certain circumstances in the employments themselves, which either really, or at least in the imaginations of men, make up for a small pecuniary gain in some, and counterbalance a great one in others; and partly from this policy of Europe, which nowhere leaves things at perfect liberty.

The particular consideration of those circumstances and of that policy will divide the chapter into two parts.

PART I

Inequalities Arising from the Nature of the Employments Themselves

The five following are the principal circumstances which, so far as I have been able to observe, make up for a small pecuniary gain in some employments, and counterbalance a great one in others: First, The agreeableness or disagreeableness of the employments themselves; Secondly, The easiness and cheapness, or the difficulty and expense of learning them; Thirdly, The constancy or inconstancy of employment in them; Fourthly, The small or great trust which must be reposed in those who exercise them; and, Fifthly, The probability or improbability of success in them.

First, the wages of labour vary with the ease or hardship, the cleanliness or dirtiness, the honourableness or dishonourableness of the employment. Thus in most places, take the year round, a journeyman tailor earns less than a journeyman weaver. His work is much easier. A journeyman weaver earns less than a journeyman smith. His work is not always easier, but it is much cleanlier. A journeyman blacksmith, though an artificer, seldom earns so much in twelve hours as a collier, who is only a labourer, does in eight. His work is not quite so dirty, is less dangerous, and is carried on in day-light, and above ground. Honour makes a great part of the reward of all honourable professions. In point of pecuniary gain, all things considered, they are generally underrecompensed, as I shall endeavour to show by and by. Disgrace has the contrary effect. The trade of a butcher is a brutal and an odious business; but it is in most places more profitable than the greater part of common trades. The most detestable of all

employments, that of public executioner, is, in proportion to the quantity of work done, better paid than any common trade whatever. . . .

Disagreeableness and disgrace affect the profits of stock in the same manner as the wages of labour. The keeper of an inn or tavern, who is never master of his own house, and who is exposed to the brutality of every drunkard, exercises neither a very agreeable nor a very creditable business. But there is scarce any common trade in which a small stock yields so great a profit.

Secondly, the wages of labour vary with the easiness and cheapness, or the difficulty and expense of learning the business.

When any expensive machine is erected, the extraordinary work to be performed by it before it is worn out, it must be expected, will replace the capital laid out by it, with at least the ordinary profits. A man educated at the expense of much labour and time to any of those employments which require extraordinary dexterity and skill, may be compared to one of those expensive machines. The work which he learns to perform, it must be expected over and above the usual wages of common labour, will replace to him the whole expense of his education, with at least the ordinary profits of an equally valuable capital. It must do this too in a reasonable time, regard being had to the very uncertain duration of human life, in the same manner as to the more certain duration of the machine.

The difference between the wages of skilled labour and those of common labour is founded upon this principle. . . .

Thirdly, the wages of labour, in different occupations vary with the constancy or inconstancy of employment.

Employment is much more constant in some trades than in others. In the greater part of manufactures, a journeyman may be pretty sure of employment almost every day in the year that he is able to work. A mason or bricklayer, on the contrary, can work neither in hard frost nor in foul weather, and his employment at all other times depends upon the occasional calls of his customers. He is liable, in consequence, to be frequently without any. What he earns, therefore, while he is employed, must not only maintain him while he is idle, but make him some compensation for those anxious and desponding moments which the thought of so precarious a situation must sometimes occasion. Where the computed earnings of the greater part of manufacturers, accordingly, are nearly upon a level with the day wages of common labourers, those of masons and bricklayers are generally from one half more to double those wages. Where common labourers earn four and five shillings a week, masons and bricklayers frequently earn seven and eight; where the former earn six, the latter often earn nine and ten; and where the former earn nine and ten, as in London, the latter commonly earn fifteen and eighteen. No species of skilled labour, however, seems more easy to learn than that of masons and bricklayers. Chairmen in London, during the summer season, are said sometimes to be employed as bricklayers. The high wages of those workmen, therefore, are not so much the recompense of their skill, as the compensation for the inconstancy of their employment.

A house carpenter seems to exercise rather a nicer and more ingenious trade than a mason. In most places, however, for it is not universally so, his day-wages are somewhat lower. His employment, though it depends much, does not depend so entirely upon the occasional calls of his customers; and it is not liable to be interrupted by the weather. . . .

Fourthly, the wages of labour vary according to the small or great trust which must be reposed in the workmen.

The wages of goldsmiths and jewellers are everywhere superior to those of many other workmen, not only of equal, but of much superior ingenuity; on account of the precious materials with which they are intrusted.

We trust our health to the physician; our fortune, and sometimes our life and reputation, to the lawyer and attorney. Such confidence could not safely be reposed in people of a very mean or low condition. Their reward must be such, therefore, as may give them that rank in the society which so important a trust requires. The long time and the great expense which must be laid out in their education, when combined with this circumstance, necessarily enhance still further the price of their labour. . . .

Fifthly, the wages of labour in different employments vary according to the probability or improbability of success in them.

The probability that any particular person shall ever be qualified for the employment to which he is educated, is very different in different occupations. In the greater part of mechanic trades, success is almost certain; but very uncertain in the liberal professions. Put your son apprentice to a shoemaker, there is little doubt of his learning to make a pair of shoes: but send him to study the law, it is at least twenty to one if ever he makes such proficiency as will enable him to live by the business. In a perfectly fair lottery, those who draw the prizes ought to gain all that is lost by those who draw the blanks. In a profession where twenty fail for one that succeeds, that one ought to gain all that should have been gained by the unsuccessful twenty. The counsellor at law who, perhaps, at near forty years of age, begins to make something by his profession, ought to receive the retribution, not only of his own so tedious and expensive education, but of that of more than twenty others who are never likely to make any thing by it. How extravagant soever the fees of counsellors at law may sometimes appear, their real retribution is never equal to this. . . .The lottery of the law, therefore, is very far from being a perfectly fair lottery; and that, as well as many other liberal and honourable professions, are, in point of pecuniary gain, evidently under-recompensed.

Those professions keep their level, however, with other occupations, and, notwithstanding these discouragements, all the most generous and liberal spirits are eager to crowd into them. Two different causes contribute to recommend them. First, the desire of the reputation which attends upon superior excellence in any of them; and, secondly, the natural confidence which every man has, more or less, not only in his own abilities, but in his own good fortune.

To excel in any profession, in which but few arrive at mediocrity, is the most decisive mark of what is called genius or superior talents. The public admiration which attends upon such distinguished abilities, makes always a part of their reward; a greater or smaller in proportion as it is higher or lower in degree. It makes a considerable part of that reward in the profession of physic; a still greater perhaps in that of law; in poetry and philosophy it makes almost the whole. . . .

The five circumstances above mentioned, though they occasion considerable inequalities in the wages of labour and profits of stock, occasion none in the whole of the advantages and disadvantages, real or imaginary, of the different employments of either. The nature of those circumstances is such, that they make up for a small pecuniary gain in some, and counterbalance a great one in others.

In order, however, that this equality may take place in the whole of their advantages or disadvantages, three things are requisite, even where there is the most perfect freedom. First, the employments must be well known and long established in the neighbourhood; secondly, they must be in their ordinary, or what may be called their natural state; and, thirdly, they must be the sole or principal employments of those who occupy them.

First, this equality can take place only in those employments which are well known, and have been long established in the neighbourhood.

Where all other circumstances are equal, wages are generally higher in new than in old trades. When a projector attempts to establish a new manufacture, he must at first entice his workmen from other employments by higher wages than they can either earn in their own trades, or than the nature of his work would otherwise require, and a considerable time must pass away before he can venture to reduce them to the common level. Manufactures for which the demand arises altogether from fashion and fancy, are continually changing, and seldom last long enough to be considered as old established manufactures. Those, on the contrary, for which the demand arises chiefly from use or necessity, are less liable to change, and the same form or fabric may continue in demand for whole centuries together. The wages of labour, therefore, are likely to be higher in manufactures of the former, than in those of the latter kind. Birmingham deals chiefly in manufactures of the former kind; Sheffield in those of the latter; and the wages of labour in those two different places, are said to be suitable to this difference in the nature of their manufactures. . . .

Secondly, this equality in the whole of the advantages and disadvantages of the different employments of labour and stock, can take place only in the ordinary, or what may be called the natural, state of those employments.

The demand for almost every different species of labour is sometimes greater and sometimes less than usual. In the one case the advantages of the employment rise above, in the other they fall below the common level. The demand for country labour is greater at hay time and harvest than during the greater part of the year; and wages rise with the demand. In time of war, when forty or fifty thousand sailors are forced from the merchant service into that of the king, the demand for sailors to merchant ships necessarily rises with their scarcity; and their wages upon such occasions commonly rise from a guinea and seven-and twenty shillings, to forty shillings and three pounds a month. In a decaying manufacture, on the contrary, many workmen, rather than quit their old trade, are contented with smaller wages than would otherwise be suitable to the nature of their employment. . . .

Thirdly, this equality in the whole of the advantages and disadvantages of the different employments of labour and stock, can take place only in such as are the sole or principal employments of those who occupy them.

When a person derives his subsistence from one employment, which does not occupy the greater part of his time, in the intervals of his leisure he is often willing to work at another for less wages than would otherwise suit the nature of the employment. . . .

PART II

Inequalities Occasioned by the Policy of Europe

Such are the inequalities in the whole of the advantages and disadvantages of the different employments of labour and stock, which the defect of any of the three requisites above mentioned must occasion even where there is the most perfect liberty. But the policy of Europe, by not leaving things at perfect liberty, occasions other inequalities of much greater importance.

It does this chiefly in the three following ways. First, by restraining the competition in some employments to a smaller number than would otherwise be disposed to enter into them; secondly, by increasing it in others beyond what it naturally would be; and, thirdly, by obstructing the free circulation of labour and stock, both from employment to employment, and from place to place.

First, the policy of Europe occasions a very important inequality in the whole of the advantages and disadvantages of the different employments of labour and stock, by restraining the competition in some employments to a smaller number than might otherwise be disposed to enter into them.

The exclusive privileges of corporations are the principal means it makes use of for this purpose.

The exclusive privilege of an incorporated trade necessarily restrains the competition, in the town where it is established, to those who are free of the trade. To have served an apprenticeship in the town, under a master properly qualified, is commonly the necessary requisite for obtaining this freedom. The bylaws of the corporation regulate sometimes the number of apprentices which any master is allowed to have, and almost always the number of years which each apprentice is obliged to serve. The intention of both regulations is to restrain the competition to a much smaller number than might otherwise be disposed to enter into the trade. The limitation of the number of apprentices restrains it directly. A long term of apprenticeship restrains it more indirectly, but as effectually, by increasing the expense of education. . . .

Secondly, the policy of Europe, by increasing the competition in some employments beyond what it naturally would be, occasions another inequality of an opposite kind in the whole of the advantages and disadvantages of the different employments of labour and stock.

It has been considered as of so much importance that a proper number of young people should be educated for certain professions, that sometimes the public and sometimes the piety of private founders have established many pensions, scholarships, exhibitions, bursaries, etc.

for this purpose, which draw many more people into those trades than could otherwise pretend to follow them. In all Christian countries, I believe, the education of the greater part of churchmen is paid for in this manner. Very few of them are educated altogether at their own expense. The long, tedious, and expensive education, therefore, of those who are, will not always procure them a suitable reward, the church being crowded with people who, in order to get employment, are willing to accept of a much smaller recompence than what such an education would otherwise have entitled them to; and in this manner the competition of the poor takes away the reward of the rich. It would be indecent, no doubt, to compare either a curate or a chaplain with a journeyman in any common trade. The pay of a curate or chaplain, however, may very properly be considered as of the same nature with the wages of a journeyman. They are, all three, paid for their work according to the contract which they may happen to make with their respective superiors. . . .

In professions in which there are no benefices, such as law and physic, if an equal proportion of people were educated at the public expense, the competition would soon be so great, as to sink very much their pecuniary reward. It might then not be worth any man's while to educate his son to either of those professions at his own expense. They would be entirely abandoned to such as had been educated by those public charities, whose numbers and necessities would oblige them in general to content themselves with a very miserable recompence, to the entire degradation of the now respectable professions of law and physic.

That unprosperous race of men, commonly called men of letters, are pretty much in the situation which lawyers and physicians probably would be in upon the foregoing supposition. In every part of Europe the greater part of them have been educated for the church, but have been hindered by different reasons from en-

tering into holy orders. They have generally, therefore, been educated at the public expense, and their numbers are everywhere so great, as commonly to reduce the price of their labour to a very paltry recompence. . . .

Thirdly, the policy of Europe, by obstructing the free circulation of labour and stock both from employment to employment, and from place to place, occasions in some cases a very inconvenient inequality in the whole of the advantages and disadvantages of their different employments.

The statute of apprenticeship obstructs the free circulation of labour from one employment to another, even in the same place. The exclusive privileges of corporations obstruct it from one place to another, even in the same employment.

It frequently happens that while high wages are given to the workmen in one manufacture, those in another are obliged to content themselves with bare subsistence. The one is in an advancing state, and has, therefore, a continual demand for new hands: the other is in a declining state, and the superabundance of hands is continually increasing. Those two manufactures may sometimes be in the same town, and sometimes in the same neighbourhood, without being able to lend the least assistance to one another. The statute of apprenticeship may oppose it in the one case, and both that and an exclusive corporation in the other. In many different manufactures, however, the operations are so much alike, that the workmen could easily change trades with one another, if those absurd laws did not hinder them. The arts of weaving plain linen and plain silk, for example, are almost entirely the same. That of weaving plain woollen is somewhat different; but the difference is so insignificant, that either a linen or a silk weaver might become a tolerable workman in a very few days. If any of those three capital manufactures, therefore, were decaying, the workmen might find a resource in one of the other two which was in a more prosperous condition, and their wages would neither rise too high in the thriving, nor sink too low in the decaying manufacture. . . .

The obstruction which corporation laws give to the free circulation of labour is common, I believe, to every part of Europe. That which is given to it by the poor laws is, so far as I know, peculiar to England. It consists in the difficulty which a poor man finds in obtaining a settlement, or even in being allowed to exercise his industry in any parish but that to which he belongs. It is the labour of artificers and manufacturers only of which the free circulation is obstructed by corporation laws. The difficulty of obtaining settlements obstructs even that of common labor. . . .

To remove a man who has committed no misdemeanour from the parish where he chooses to reside is an evident violation of natural liberty and justice. The common people of England, however, so jealous of their liberty, but like the common people of most other countries, never rightly understanding wherein it consists, have now for more than a century together suffered themselves to be exposed to this oppression without a remedy. Though men of reflection, too, have sometimes complained of the law of settlements as a public grievance, yet it has never been the object of any general popular clamour, such as that against general warrants, an abusive practice undoubtedly, but such a one as was not likely to occasion any general oppression. There is scarce a poor man in England of forty years of age, I will venture to say, who has not in some part of his life felt himself most cruelly oppressed by this ill-contrived law of settlements.

2

Principles of Economics

Alfred Marshall

Alfred Marshall, *Principles of Economics,* 8th ed. (New York: The Macmillan Company, 1936), Book VI, Chaps. 3-5.

It is commonly said that the tendency of competition is to equalize the earnings of people engaged in the same trade or in trades of equal difficulty; but this statement requires to be interpreted carefully. For competition tends to make the earnings got by two individuals of unequal efficiency in any given time, say, a day or a year, not equal, but unequal; and, in like manner, it tends not to equalize, but to render unequal the average weekly wages in two districts in which the average standards of efficiency are unequal. Given that the average strength and energy of the working-classes are higher in the North of England than in the South, it then follows that the more completely "competition makes things find their own level," the more certain is it that average weekly wages will be higher in the North than in the South.[1]

Cliffe Leslie and some other writers have

[1] About fifty years ago correspondence between farmers in the North and the South of England led to an agreement that putting roots into a cart was an excellent measure of physical efficiency: and careful comparison showed that wages bore about the same proportion to the weights which the labourers commonly loaded in a day's work in the two districts. The standards of wages and of efficiency in the South are perhaps now more nearly on a level with those in the North than they were then. But the standard trade union wages are generally higher in the North than in the South; and many men, who go North to reach the higher rate, find that they cannot do what is required, and return.

naively laid stress on local variations of wages as tending to prove that there is very little mobility among the working-classes, and that the competition among them for employment is ineffective. But most of the facts which they quote relate only to wages reckoned by the day or week: they are only half-facts, and when the missing halves are supplied, they generally support the opposite inference to that on behalf of which they are quoted. For it is found that local variations of weekly wages and of efficiency generally correspond: and thus the facts tend to prove the effectiveness of competition, so far as they bear on the question at all. We shall however presently find that the full interpretation of such facts as these is a task of great difficulty and complexity.

The earnings, or wages, which a person gets in any given time, such as a day, a week, or a year, may be called his *time-earnings,* or *time-wages:* and we may then say that Cliffe Leslie's instances of unequal time-wages tend on the whole to support, and not to weaken, the presumption that competition adjusts earnings in occupations of equal difficulty and in neighbouring places to the efficiency of the workers.

But the ambiguity of the phrase, "the efficiency of the workers," has not yet been completely cleared away. When the payment for work of any kind is apportioned to the quantity and quality of the work turned out, it is said that uniform rates of *piece-work* wages are being paid; and if two persons work under the same conditions and with equally good appliances, they are paid in proportion to their efficiencies when they receive piece-work wages calculated by the same lists of prices for each several kind of work. If however the appliances are not equally good, a uniform rate of piece-work wages gives results disproportionate to the efficiency of the workers. If, for instance, the same lists of piece-work wages were used in cotton mills supplied with old-fashioned

machinery, as in those which have the latest improvements, the apparent equality would represent a real inequality. The more effective competition is, and the more perfectly economic freedom and enterprise are developed, the more surely will the lists be higher in the mills that have old-fashioned machinery than in the others.

In order therefore to give its right meaning to the statement that economic freedom and enterprise tend to equalize wages in occupations of the same difficulty and in the same neighbourhood, we require the use of a new term. We may find it in *efficiency-wages,* or more broadly *efficiency-earnings;* that is, earnings measured, not as time-earnings are with reference to the time spent in earning them; and not as piece-work earnings are with reference to the amount of output resulting from the work by which they are earned; but with reference to the exertion of ability and *efficiency* required of the worker.

The tendency then of economic freedom and enterprise (or, in more common phrase, of competition), to cause every one's earnings to find their own level, is a tendency to equality of efficiency-earnings in the same district. This tendency will be the stronger, the greater is the mobility of labour, the less strictly specialized it is, the more keenly parents are on the lookout for the most advantageous occupations for their children, the more rapidly they are able to adapt themselves to changes in economic conditions, and lastly the slower and the less violent these changes are. . . .

1. The action of demand and supply with regard to labour was discussed in the last chapter. . . . But some peculiarities in this action remain to be studied. We shall find that the influence of many of them is not at all to be measured by their first and most obvious effects: and that those effects which are cumulative are generally far more important in the

long run than those which are not, however prominent the latter may appear.

The problem has thus much in common with that of tracing the economic influence of custom. For it has already been noticed, and it will become more clear as we go on, that the direct effects of custom in causing a thing to be sold for a price sometimes a little higher and sometimes a little lower than it would otherwise fetch, are not really of very great importance, because any such divergence does not, as a rule, tend to perpetuate and increase itself; but on the contrary, if it becomes considerable, it tends itself to call into action forces that counteract it. Sometimes these forces break down the custom altogether; but more often they evade it by gradual and imperceptible changes in the character of the thing sold, so that the purchaser really gets a new thing at the old price under the old name. These direct effects then are obvious, but they are not cumulative. On the other hand, the indirect effects of custom in hindering the methods of production and the character of producers from developing themselves freely are not obvious; but they generally are cumulative, and therefore exert a deep and controlling influence over the history of the world. If custom checks the progress of one generation, then the next generation starts from a lower level than it otherwise would have done; and any retardation which it suffers itself is accumulated and added to that of its predecessor, and so on from generation to generation.[2]

And so it is with regard to the action of demand and supply on the earnings of labour.

[2] It ought, however, to be remarked that some of the beneficial effects of custom are cumulative. For among the many different things that are included under the wide term "custom" are crystallized forms of high ethical principles, rules of honourable and courteous behaviour, and of the avoidance of troublesome strife about paltry gains; and much of the good influence which these exert on race character is cumulative.

If at any time it presses hardly on any individuals or class, the direct effects of the evils are obvious. But the sufferings that result are of different kinds: those, the effects of which end with the evil by which they were caused, are not generally to be compared in importance with those that have the indirect effect of lowering the character of the workers or of hindering it from becoming stronger. For these last cause further weakness and further suffering, which again in their turn cause yet further weakness and further suffering, and so on cumulatively. On the other hand, high earnings, and a strong character, lead to greater strength and higher earnings, which again lead to still greater strength and still higher earnings, and so on cumulatively.

2. The first point to which we have to direct our attention is the fact that human agents of production are not bought and sold as machinery and other material agents of production are. The worker sells his work, but he himself remains his own property: those who bear the expenses of rearing and educating him receive but very little of the price that is paid for his services in later years.

Whatever deficiencies the modern methods of business may have, they have at least this virtue, that he who bears the expenses of production of material goods, receives the price that is paid for them. He who builds factories or steam-engines or houses, or rears slaves, reaps the benefit of all net services which they render so long as he keeps them for himself; and when he sells them he gets a price which is the estimated net value of their future services; and therefore he extends his outlay until there seems to him no good reason for thinking that the gains resulting from any further investment would compensate him. He must do this prudently and boldly, under the penalty of finding himself worsted in competition with others who follow a broader and more far-sighted policy, and of ultimately disappearing from the ranks of those who direct the course of the world's business. The action of competition, and the survival in the struggle for existence of those who know best how to extract the greatest benefits for themselves from the environment, tend in the long run to put the building of factories and steam-engines into the hands of those who will be ready and able to incur every expense which will add more than it costs to their value as productive agents. But the investment of capital in the rearing and early training of the workers of England is limited by the resources of parents in the various grades of society, by their power of forecasting the future, and by their willingness to sacrifice themselves for the sake of their children.

This evil is indeed of comparatively small importance with regard to the higher industrial grades. For in those grades most people distinctly realize the future, and "discount it at a low rate of interest." They exert themselves much to select the best careers for their sons, and the best trainings for those careers; and they are generally willing and able to incur a considerable expense for the purpose. The professional classes especially, while generally eager to save some capital *for* their children, are even more on the alert for opportunities of investing it *in* them. And whenever there occurs in the upper grades of industry a new opening for which an extra and special education is required, the future gains need not be very high relatively to the present outlay, in order to secure a keen competition for the post.

But in the lower ranks of society the evil is great. For the slender means and education of the parents, and the comparative weakness of their power of distinctly realizing the future, prevent them from investing capital in the education and training of their children with the same free and bold enterprise with which capital is applied to improving the machinery of any well-managed factory. Many of the children of the working-classes are imperfectly fed and

clothed; they are housed in a way that promotes neither physical nor moral health; they receive a school education which, though in modern England it may not be very bad so far as it goes, yet goes only a little way; they have few opportunities of getting a broader view of life or an insight into the nature of the higher work of business, of science or of art; they meet hard and exhausting toil early on the way, and for the greater part keep to it all their lives. At least they go to the grave carrying with them undeveloped abilities and faculties; which, if they could have borne full fruit, would have added to the material wealth of the country— to say nothing of higher considerations—many times as much as would have covered the expense of providing adequate opportunities for their development.

But the point on which we have specially to insist now is that this evil is cumulative. The worse fed are the children of one generation, the less will they earn when they grow up, and the less will be their power of providing adequately for the material wants of their children; and so on to following generations. And again, the less fully their own faculties are developed, the less will they realize the importance of developing the best faculties of their children, and the less will be their power of doing so. And conversely any change that awards to the workers of one generation better earnings, together with better opportunities of developing their best qualities, will increase the material and moral advantages which they have the power to offer to their children: while by increasing their own intelligence, wisdom and forethought, such a change will also to some extent increase their willingness to sacrifice their own pleasures for the well-being of their children; though there is much of that willingness now even among the poorest classes, so far as their means and the limits of their knowledge will allow. . . .

3. The next of those characteristics of

the action of demand and supply peculiar to labour, which we have to study, lies in the fact that when a person sells his services, he has to present himself where they are delivered. It matters nothing to the seller of bricks whether they are to be used in building a palace or a sewer; but it matters a great deal to the seller of labour, who undertakes to perform a task of given difficulty, whether or not the place in which it is to be done is a wholesome and a pleasant one, and whether or not his associates will be such as he cares to have. In those yearly hirings which still remain in some parts of England, the labourer inquires what sort of a temper his new employer has, quite as carefully as what rate of wages he pays.

This peculiarity of labour is of great importance in many individual cases, but it does not often exert a broad and deep influence of the same nature as that last discussed. The more disagreeable the incidents of an occupation, the higher of course are the wages required to attract people into it: but whether these incidents do lasting and widespreading harm depends on whether they are such as to undermine men's physical health and strength or to lower their character. When they are not of this sort, they are indeed evils in themselves, but they do not generally cause other evils beyond themselves; their effects are seldom cumulative.

Since however no one can deliver his labour in a market in which he is not himself present, it follows that the mobility of labour and the mobility of the labourer are convertible terms: and the unwillingness to quit home, and to leave old associations, including perhaps some loved cottage and burial-ground, will often turn the scale against a proposal to seek better wages in a new place. And when the different members of a family are engaged in different trades, and a migration, which would be advantageous to one member would be injurious to others, the inseparability of the worker from his work considerably hinders the adjustment of the supply of labour to the demand for it. But of this more hereafter.

4. Again, labour is often sold under special disadvantages, arising from the closely connected group of facts that labour power is "perishable," that the sellers of it are commonly poor and have no reserve fund, and that they cannot easily withhold it from the market.

Perishableness is an attribute common to the labour of all grades; the time lost when a worker is thrown out of employment cannot be recovered, though in some cases his energies may be refreshed by rest. It must however be remembered that much of the working power of material agents of production is perishable in the same sense; for a great part of the income, which they also are prevented from earning by being thrown out of work, is completely lost. There is indeed some saving of wear-and-tear on a factory, or a steam-ship, when it is lying idle: but this is often small compared with the income which its owners have to forego: they get no compensation for their loss of interest on the capital invested, or for the depreciation which it undergoes from the action of the elements or from its tendency to be rendered obsolete by new inventions.

Again, many vendible commodities are perishable. In the strike of dock labourers in London in 1889, the perishableness of the fruit, meat, etc., on many of the ships told strongly on the side of the strikers.

The want of reserve funds and of the power of long withholding their labour from the market is common to nearly all grades of those whose work is chiefly with their hands. But it is especially true of unskilled labourers, partly because their wages leave very little margin for saving, partly because when any group of them suspends work, there are large numbers who are capable of filling their places. . . .

But these statements do not apply to all kinds of labour. . . .

It is ... certain that manual labourers as a class are at a disadvantage in bargaining; and that the disadvantage wherever it exists is likely to be cumulative in its effects. For though, so long as there is any competition among employers at all, they are likely to bid for labour something not very much less than its real value to them, that is, something not very much less than the highest price they would pay rather than go on without it; yet anything that lowers wages tends to lower the efficiency of the labourer's work, and therefore to lower the price which the employer would rather pay than go without that work. The effects of the labourer's disadvantage in bargaining are therefore cumulative in two ways. It lowers his wages; and as we have seen, this lowers his efficiency as a worker, and thereby lowers the normal value of his labour. And in addition it diminishes his efficiency as a bargainer, and thus increases the chance that he will sell his labour for less than its normal value.

5. The next peculiarity in the action of demand and supply with regard to labour, which we have to consider, is closely connected with some of those we have already discussed. It consists in the length of time that is required to prepare and train labour for its work, and in the slowness of the returns which result from this training.

This discounting of the future, this deliberate adjustment of supply of expensively trained labour to the demand for it, is most clearly seen in the choice made by parents of occupations for their children, and in their efforts to raise their children into a higher grade than their own. . . .

. . . Not much less than a generation elapses between the choice by parents of a skilled trade for one of their children, and his reaping the full results of their choice. And meanwhile the character of the trade may have been almost revolutionized by changes, of which some probably threw long shadows before

them, but others were such as could not have been foreseen even by the shrewdest persons and those best acquainted with the circumstances of the trade.

The working classes in nearly all parts of England are constantly on the look-out for advantageous openings for the labour of themselves and their children; and they question friends and relations, who have settled in other districts, as to the wages that are to be got in various trades, and as to their incidental advantages and disadvantages. But it is very difficult to ascertain the causes that are likely to determine the distant future of the trades which they are selecting for their children; and there are not many who enter on this abstruse inquiry. The majority assume without a further thought that the condition of each trade in their own time sufficiently indicates what it will be in the future; and, so far as the influence of this habit extends, the supply of labour in a trade in any one generation tends to conform to its earnings not in that but in the preceding generation. . . .

. . . Let us now revert to the principle that the income derived from the appliances for the production of a commodity exerts a controlling influence in the long run over their own supply and price, and therefore over the supply and the price of the commodity itself; but that within short periods there is not time for the exercise of any considerable influence of this kind. And let us inquire how this principle needs to be modified when it is applied not to the material agents or production, which are only a means towards an end, and which may be the private property of the capitalist, but to human beings who are ends as well as means of production and who remain their own property.

To begin with we must notice that, since labour is slowly produced and slowly worn out, we must take the term "long period" more strictly, and regard it as generally implying a greater duration, when we are considering the relations of normal demand and supply for labour, than when we are considering them for ordinary commodities. There are many problems, the period of which is long enough to enable the supply of ordinary commodities, and even of most of the material appliances required for making them, to be adjusted to the demand; and long enough therefore to justify us in regarding the average prices of those commodities during the period as "normal," and as equal to their normal expenses of production in a fairly broad use of the term; while yet the period would not be long enough to allow the supply of labour to be adjusted at all well to the demand for it. The average earnings of labour during this period therefore would not be at all certain to give about a normal return to those who provided the labour; but they would rather have to be regarded as determined by the available stock of labour on the one hand, and the demand for it on the other. . . .

To conclude this part of our argument, the market price of everything, *i.e.,* its price for short periods, is determined mainly by the relations in which the demand for it stands to the available stocks of it; and in the case of any agent of production, whether it be a human or a material agent, this demand is "derived" from the demand for those things which it is used in making. In these relatively short periods fluctuations in wages follow, and do not precede, fluctuations in the selling prices of the goods produced.

But the incomes which are being earned by all agents of production, human as well as material, and those which appear likely to be earned by them in the future, exercise a ceaseless influence on those persons by whose action the future supplies of these agents are determined. There is a constant tendency towards a position of normal equilibrium, in which the supply of each of these agents shall stand in such a relation to the demand for its services, as to give to those who have provided the supply a sufficient reward for their efforts and sacrifices. If the economic conditions of the country remained stationary sufficiently long, this tendency would realize itself in such an adjustment of supply to demand, that both machines and human beings would earn generally an amount that corresponded fairly with their cost of rearing and training, conventional necessaries as well as those things which are strictly necessary being reckoned for. But conventional necessaries might change under the influence of non-economic causes, even while economic conditions themselves were stationary: and this change would affect the supply of labour, and would lessen the national dividend and slightly alter its distribution. As it is, the economic conditions of the country are constantly changing, and the point of adjustment of normal demand and supply in relation to labour is constantly being shifted.

3

Human Capital — A Theoretical and Empirical Analysis

Gary S. Becker

Gary S. Becker, *Human Capital—A Theoretical and Empirical Analysis, with Special Reference to Education,* Chap. 2. Copyright 1964 by National Bureau of Economic Research. Reprinted with permission of the National Bureau of Economic Research.

INTRODUCTION

Some activities primarily affect future well-being; the main impact of others is in the present. Some affect money income and others psychic income, that is, consumption. Sailing primarily affects consumption, on-the-job training primarily affects money income, and a college education could affect both. These affects may operate either through physical resources or through human resources. This study is concerned with activities that influence future monetary and psychic income by increasing the resources in people. These activities are called investments in human capital.

The many forms of such investments include schooling, on-the-job training, medical care, migration, and searching for information about prices and incomes. They differ in their effects on earnings and consumption, in the amounts typically invested, in the size of returns, and in the extent to which the connection between investment and return is perceived. But all these investments improve skills, knowledge, or health, and thereby raise money or psychic incomes.

Recent years have witnessed intensive concern with and research on investment in human capital, much of it contributed or stimulated by T. W. Schultz. The main motivating factor has probably been a realization that the growth of physical capital, at least as conventionally measured, explains a relatively small part of the growth of income in most countries. The search for better explanations has led to improved measures of physical capital and to an interest in less tangible entities, such as technological change and human capital. Also behind this concern is the strong dependence of modern military technology on education and skills, the rapid growth in expenditures on education and health, the age-old quest for an understanding of the personal distribution of income, the recent growth in unemployment in the United States, the Leontief scarce-factor paradox, and several other important economic problems.

The result has been the accumulation of a tremendous amount of circumstantial evidence testifying to the economic importance of human capital, especially of education. Probably the most impressive piece of evidence is that more highly educated and skilled persons almost always tend to earn more than others. This is true of developed countries as different as the United States and the Soviet Union, of underdeveloped countries as different as India and Cuba, and of the United States one hundred years ago as well as today. Moreover, few, if any, countries have achieved a sustained period of economic development without having invested substantial amounts in their labor force, and most studies that have attempted quantitative assessments of contributions to growth have assigned an important role to investment in human capital. Again, inequality in the distribution of earnings and income is generally positively related to inequality in education and other training. To take a final example, unemployment tends to be strongly related, usually inversely, to education.

Passions are easily aroused on this subject and even people who are generally in favor of education, medical care, and the like often dislike the phrase "human capital" and still more any emphasis on its economic effects. They are often the people who launch the most bitter attacks on research on human capital, partly because they fear that emphasis on the "material" effects of human capital detracts from its "cultural" effects, which to them are more important. Those denying the economic importance of education and other investments in human capital have attacked the circumstantial evidence in its favor. They argue that the correlation between earnings and investment in human capital is due to a correlation between ability and investment in human capital, or to the singling out of the most favorable groups, such as white male college graduates, and to the consequent neglect of women, drop-outs, non-whites, or high-school graduates. They consider the true correlation to be very weak, and, therefore, a poor guide and of little help to people investing in human capital. The association between education and economic development or between inequality in education and income is attributed to the effect of income on education, considering education as a consumption good, and hence of no greater causal significance than the association between automobile ownership and economic development or between the inequality in ownership and incomes.

This study hopes to contribute to knowledge in this area by going far beyond circumstantial evidence and analysis. . . .

. . . [T]he attention paid to the economic effects of education and other human capital in this study is not in any way meant to imply that other effects are unimportant, or less important then the economic ones. . . . I would like to urge simply that the economic effects are important and they have been relatively neglected, at least until recently. . . .

EFFECTS ON EARNINGS

On-the-Job Training

Theories of firm behavior, no matter how they differ in other respects, almost invariably ignore the effect of the productive process itself on worker productivity. This is not to say that no one recognizes that productivity is affected by the job itself; but the recognition has not been formalized, incorporated into economic analysis, and its implications worked out. I now intend to do just that, placing special emphasis on the broader economic implications.

Many workers increase their productivity by learning new skills and perfecting old ones while on the job. Presumably, future productivity can be improved only at a cost, for otherwise there would be an unlimited demand for training. Included in cost are the value placed on the time and effort of trainees, the "teaching" provided by others, and the equipment and materials used. These are costs in the sense that they could have been used in producing current output if they had not been used in raising future output. The amount spent and the duration of the training period depend partly on the type of training since more is spent for a longer time on, say, an intern than a machine operator. . . .

. . . In the following sections two types of on-the-job training are discussed in turn: general and specific.

General training. General training is useful in many firms besides those providing it; for example, a machinist trained in the army finds his skills of value in steel and aircraft firms, and a doctor trained (interned) at one hospital finds his skills useful at other hospitals. Most on-the-job training presumably increases the future marginal productivity of workers in the firms providing it; general training, however, also increases their marginal product in many other firms as well. Since in a competitive labor market the wage rates paid by any firm are determined by marginal productivities in other firms, future wage rates as well as marginal products would increase in firms providing general training. These firms could capture some of the return from training only

if their marginal product rose by more than their wages. "Perfectly general" training would be equally useful in many firms and marginal products would rise by the same extent in all of them. Consequently, wage rates would rise by exactly the same amount as the marginal product and the firms providing such training could not capture any of the return.

Why, then, would rational firms in competitive labor markets provide general training if it did not bring any return? The answer is that firms would provide general training only if they did not have to pay any of the costs. Persons receiving general training would be willing to pay these costs since training raises their future wages. Hence it is the trainees, not the firms, who would bear the cost of general training and profit from the return.[1] . . .

Income-maximizing firms in competitive labor markets would not pay the cost of general training and would pay trained persons the market wage. If, however, training costs were paid, many persons would seek training, few would quit during the training period, and labor costs would be relatively high. Firms that did not pay trained persons the market wage would have difficulty satisfying their skill requirements and would also tend to be less profitable than other firms. Firms that paid both for training and less than the market wage for trained persons would have the worst of both worlds, for they would attract too many trainees and too few trained persons.

These principles have been clearly demonstrated during the last few years in discussions of problems in recruiting military personnel. The military offers training in a wide variety of skills and many are very useful in the civilian

[1] Some persons have asked why any general training is provided if firms do not collect any of the returns. The answer is simply that they have an incentive to do so wherever the demand price for training is at least as great as the supply price or cost of providing the training. Workers in turn would prefer to be trained on the job rather than in specialized firms (schools) if the training and work complemented each other.

sector. Training is provided during part or all of the first enlistment period and used during the remainder of the first period and hopefully during subsequent periods. This hope, however, is thwarted by the fact that re-enlistment rates tend to be inversely related to the amount of civilian-type skills provided by the military.[2] Persons with these skills leave the military more readily because they can receive much higher wages in the civilian sector. Net military wages for those receiving training are higher relative to civilian wages during the first than during subsequent enlistment periods because training costs are largely paid by the military. Not surprisingly, therefore, first-term enlistments for skilled jobs are obtained much more easily than are re-enlistments.

The military is a conspicuous example of an organization that both pays at least part of training costs and does not pay market wages to skilled personnel. It has had, in consequence, relatively easy access to "students" and heavy losses of "graduates." Indeed, its graduates make up the predominant part of the supply in several civilian occupations. For example, well over 90 per cent of United States commercial airline pilots received much of their training in the armed forces. The military, of course, is not a commercial organization judged by profits and losses and has had no difficulty surviving and even thriving.

What about the old argument that firms in competitive labor markets have no incentive to provide on-the-job training because trained workers would be bid away by other firms? Firms that train workers are supposed to im-

part external economies to other firms because the latter can use these workers free of any training charge. An analogy with research and development is often drawn since a firm developing a process that cannot be patented or kept secret would impart external economies to competitors. This argument and analogy would apply if firms were to pay training costs, for they would suffer a "capital loss" whenever trained workers were bid away by other firms. Firms can, however, shift training costs to trainees and have an incentive to do so when faced with competition for their services.[3]

The difference between investment in training and in research and development can be put very simply. Without patents or secrecy, firms in competitive industries cannot establish property rights in innovations, and these innovations become fair game for all comers. Patent systems try to establish these rights so that incentives can be provided to invest in research. Property rights in skills, on the other hand, are automatically vested, for a skill cannot be used without permission of the person possessing it. The property right of the worker in his skills is the source of his incentive to invest in training by accepting a reduced wage during the training period and explains why an analogy with un-owned innovations is misleading.

---

[2] See *Manpower Management and Compensation,* report of the Cordiner Committee, Washington, 1957, Vol. I, Chart 3, and the accompanying discussion. The military not only wants to eliminate the inversion relation but apparently would like to create a positive relation because they have such a large investment in heavily trained personnel. For an excellent study, see Gorman C. Smith, "Differential Pay of Military Technicians," unpublished Ph.D. dissertation, Columbia University, 1964.

[3] Sometimes the alleged external economies from on-the-job training have been considered part of the "infant industry" argument for protection (see J. Black "Arguments for Tariffs," *Oxford Economic Papers,* June 1959, pp. 205-206). Our analysis suggests, however, that the trouble tariffs are supposed to overcome must be traced back to difficulties that workers have in financing investment in themselves—in other words, to ignorance or capital market limitations that apply to expenditures on education, health, as well as on-the-job training. Protection would serve the same purpose as the creation of monopsonies domestically, namely, to convert general into specific capital so that firms can be given an incentive to pay for training (see the remarks on specific training below). Presumably a much more efficient solution would be to improve the capital market directly through insurance of loans, subsidies, information, etc.

Specific training. Completely general training increases the marginal productivity of trainees by exactly the same amount in the firms providing the training as in other firms. Clearly some kinds of training increase productivity by different amounts in the firms providing the training and in other firms. Training that increases productivity more in firms providing it will be called specific training. Completely specific training can be defined as training that has no effect on the productivity of trainees that would be useful in other firms. Much on-the-job training is neither completely specific nor completely general but increases productivity more in the firms providing it and falls within the definition of specific training. The rest increases productivity by at least as much in other firms and falls within a definition of general training. A few illustrations of the scope of specific training are presented before a formal analysis is developed.

The military offers some forms of training that are extremely useful in the civilian sector, as already noted, and others that are only of minor use to civilians, i.e., astronauts, fighter pilots, and missile men. Such training falls within the scope of specific training because productivity is raised in the military but not (much) elsewhere.

Resources are usually spent by firms in familiarizing new employees with their organization,[4] and the knowledge thus acquired is a form of specific training because productivity is raised more in the firms acquiring the knowledge than in other firms. Other kinds of hiring costs, such as employment agency fees, the expenses incurred by new employees in finding jobs, or the time employed in interviewing, testing, checking references, and in bookkeeping do not so obviously increase the knowledge of new employees, but they too are a form of specific investment in human capital, although not training. They are an investment because outlays over a short period create distributed effects on productivity; they are specific because productivity is raised primarily in the firms making the outlays; they are in human capital because they lose their value whenever employees leave. In the rest of this section reference is mostly to on-the-job specific training even though the analysis applies to all on-the-job specific investment.

Even after hiring costs are incurred, firms usually know only a limited amount about the ability and potential of new employees. They try to increase their knowledge in various ways—testing, rotation among departments, trial and error, etc.—for greater knowledge permits a more efficient utilization of manpower. Expenditures on acquiring knowledge of employee talents would be a specific investment if the knowledge could be kept from other firms, for then productivity would be raised more in the firms making the expenditures than elsewhere.

The effect of investment in employees on their productivity elsewhere depends on market conditions as well as on the nature of the investment. Very strong monopsonists might be completely insulated from competition by other firms, and practically all investments in their labor force would be specific. On the other hand, firms in extremely competitive labor markets would face a constant threat of raiding and would have fewer specific investments available.

These examples convey some of the surprisingly large variety of situations that come under the rubric of specific investment. This set is now treated abstractly in order to develop a general formal analysis. Empirical situations are brought in again after several major implications of the formal analysis have been developed.

---

[4] To judge from a sample of firms recently analyzed, formal orientation courses are quite common, at least in large firms. (See H. F. Clark and H. S. Sloan, *Classrooms in the Factories* (Rutherford, N.J.: Institute for Research, Fairleigh Dickinson University, 1958), Chap. IV.

If all training were completely specific, the wage that an employee could get elsewhere would be independent of the amount of training he had received. One might plausibly argue, then, that the wage paid by firms would also be independent of training. If so, firms would have to pay training costs, for no rational employee would pay for training that did not benefit him. Firms would collect the return from such training in the form of larger profits resulting from higher productivity, and training would be provided whenever the return—discounted at an appropriate rate—was at least as large as the cost. Long-run competitive equilibrium requires that the present value of the return exactly equal costs. . . .

. . . But could not one equally well argue that workers pay all specific training costs by receiving appropriately lower wages initially and collect all returns by receiving wages equal to marginal product later? . . . Is it more plausible that firms rather than workers pay for and collect the return from training?

An answer can be found by reasoning along the following lines. If a firm had paid for the specific training of a worker who quit to take another job, its capital expenditure would be partly wasted, for no further return could be collected. Likewise, a worker fired after he had paid for specific training would be unable to collect any further return and would also suffer a capital loss. The willingness of workers or firms to pay for specific training should, therefore, closely depend on the likelihood of labor turnover.

To bring in turnover at this point may seem like a *deus ex machina* since it is almost always ignored in traditional theory. In the usual analysis of competitive firms, wages equal marginal product, and since wages and marginal product are assumed to be the same in many firms, no one suffers from turnover. It would not matter whether a firm's labor force always contained the same persons or a rapidly changing group. Any person leaving one firm could do equally well in other firms, and his employer could replace him without any change in profits. In other words, turnover is ignored in traditional theory because it plays no important role within the framework of the theory.

Turnover becomes important when costs are imposed on workers or firms, which are precisely the effects of specific training. Suppose a firm paid all the specific training costs of a worker who quit after completing it. According to our earlier analysis, he would have been receiving the market wage and a new employee could be hired at the same wage. If the new employee were not given training, his marginal product would be less than that of the one who quit since presumably training raised the latter's productivity. Training could raise the new employee's productivity but would require additional expenditures by the firm. In other words, a firm is hurt by the departure of a trained employee because an equally profitable new employee could not be obtained. In the same way an employee who pays for specific training would suffer a loss from being laid off because he could not find an equally good job elsewhere. To bring turnover into the analysis of specific training is not, therefore, a *deus ex machina* but is made necessary by the important link between them.

Firms paying for specific training might take account of turnover merely by obtaining a sufficiently large return from those remaining to counterbalance the loss from those leaving. (The return on "successes"—those remaining—would, of course, overestimate the average return on all training expenditures.) Firms could do even better, however, by recognizing that the likelihood of a quit is not fixed but depends on wages. Instead of merely recouping on successes what is lost on failures, they might reduce the likelihood of failure itself by offering higher wages after training than could be received elsewhere. In effect, they would offer employees some of the return from training. Matters would be improved in some respects but worsened in others, for the higher wage would make the supply of trainees greater than the demand, and rationing would be required. The final step would be to shift some training costs as well as returns to employees, thereby bringing supply more in line with demand. When the final step is completed, firms no longer pay all training costs nor do they collect all the return but they share both with employees.[5] The shares of each depend on the relations between quit rates and wages, layoff rates and profits, and on other factors not discussed here, such as the cost of funds, attitudes toward risk, and desires for liquidity.[6]

If training were not completely specific, productivity would increase in other firms as well, and the wage that could be received elsewhere would also increase. Such training can be looked upon as the sum of two components, one completely general, the other completely specific; the former would be relatively larger, the greater the effect on wages in other firms relative to the firms providing the training. Since firms do not pay any of the completely

general costs and only part of the completely specific costs, the fraction of costs paid by firms would be inversely related to the importance of the general component, or positively related to the specificity of the training. . . .

Employees with specific training have less incentive to quit, and firms have less incentive to fire them, than employees with no training or general training, which implies that quit and layoff rates are inversely related to the amount of specific training. Turnover should be least for employees with extremely specific training and most for those receiving such general training that productivity is raised less in the firms providing the training than elsewhere (as, say, in schools). These propositions are as applicable to the large number of irregular quits and layoffs that continually occur as to the more regular cyclical and secular movements in turnover; in this section, however, only the more regular movements are discussed.

Consider a firm that experiences an unexpected decline in demand for its output, the rest of the economy being unaffected. The marginal product of employees without specific training—such as untrained or generally trained employees—presumably equaled wages initially, and their employment would now be reduced to prevent their marginal productivity from falling below wages. The marginal product of specifically trained employees initially would have been greater than wages. A decline in demand would reduce these marginal products too, but as long as they were reduced by less than the initial difference with wages, firms would have no incentive to lay off such employees. For sunk costs are sunk, and there is no incentive to lay off employees whose marginal product is greater than wages, no matter how unwise it was, in retrospect, to invest in their training. Thus workers with specific training seem less likely to be laid off as a consequence of a decline in demand than

---

[5] A. Marshall, *Principles of Economics*, 8th ed. (New York: Macmillan, Inc., 1949), p. 626. Marshall was clearly aware of specific talents and their effect on wages and productivity: "Thus the head clerk in a business has an acquaintance with men and things, the use of which he could in some cases sell at a high price to rival firms. But in other cases it is of a kind to be of no value save to the business in which he already is; and *then his departure would perhaps injure it by several times the value of his salary,* while probably he could not get half that *salary elsewhere."* (My italics) However, he overstressed the element of indeterminacy in these wages ("their earnings are determined . . . by a bargain between them and their employers, the terms of which are theoretically arbitrary") because he ignored the effect of wages on turnover.

[6] The rate used to discount costs and returns is the sum of a (positive) rate measuring the cost of funds, a (positive or negative) risk premium, and a liquidity premium that is presumably positive since capital invested in specific training is very illiquid.

untrained or even generally trained workers.[7]

If the decline in demand were sufficiently great so that even the marginal product of specifically trained workers was pushed below wages, would the firm just proceed to lay them off until the marginal product was brought into equality with wages? To show the danger here, assume that all the cost of and return from specific training was paid and collected by the firm. Any worker laid off would try to find a new job, since nothing would bind him to the old one.[8] The firm might be hurt if he did find a new job, for the firm's investment in his training might be lost forever. If specifically trained workers were not laid off, the firm would lose now because marginal product would be less than wages but would gain in the future if the decline in demand proved temporary. There is an incentive, therefore, not to lay off workers with specific training when their marginal product is only temporarily below wages, and the larger a firm's investment the greater the incentive not to lay them off.

A worker collecting some of the return from specific training would have less incentive to find a new job when temporarily laid off than others would: he does not want to lose his investment. His behavior while laid off in turn affects his future chances of being laid off, for if it were known that he would not readily take another job, the firm could lay him off without much fear of losing its investment. . . .

The analysis can easily be extended to cover general declines in demand; suppose, for example, a general cyclical decline occurred. Assume that wages were sticky and remained at the initial level. If the decline in business actively were not sufficient to reduce the marginal product below the wage, workers with specific training would not be laid off even though others would be, just as before. If the decline reduced marginal product below wages, only one modification in the previous analysis is required. A firm would have a greater incentive to lay off specifically trained workers than when it alone experienced a decline because laid-off workers would be less likely to find other jobs when unemployment was widespread. In other respects, the implications of a general decline with wage rigidity are the same as those of a decline in one firm alone.

The discussion has concentrated on layoff rates, but the same kind of reasoning shows that a rise in wages elsewhere would cause fewer quits among specifically trained workers than among others. For specifically trained workers initially receive higher wages than are available elsewhere and the wage rise elsewhere would have to be greater than the initial difference before they would consider quitting. Thus both the quit and layoff rate of specifically trained workers would be relatively low and fluctuate relatively less during business cycles. These are important implications that can be tested with the data available.

Although quits and layoffs are influenced by considerations other than investment costs, some of these, such as pension plans, are more strongly related to investments than may appear at first blush. A pension plan with incomplete vesting privileges[9] penalizes employees who quit before retirement and thus provides an incentive—often an extremely powerful one—not to quit. At the same time pension plans "insure" firms against quits for they are given a lump sum—the nonvested portion of payments—whenever a worker quits. Insurance is needed for specifically trained

[7] A very similar argument is developed by Walter Oi in "Labor as a Quasi-fixed Factor of Production," unpublished Ph.D. dissertation, University of Chicago, 1961. Also, see his article with almost the same title in *Journal of Political Economy,* December 1962.

[8] Actually one need only assume that the quit rate of laid-off workers tends to be significantly greater than that of employed workers, if only because the opportunity searching for another job is less for laid-off workers.

[9] According to the National Bureau of Economic Research (NBER) study of pensions, most plans have incomplete vesting.

employees because their turnover would impose capital losses on firms. Firms can discourage such quits by sharing training costs and the return with employees, but they would have less need to discourage them and would be more willing to pay for training costs if insurance were provided. The effects on the incentive to invest in one's employees may have been a major stimulus to the development of pension plans with incomplete vesting.[10]

An effective long-term contract would insure firms against quits, just as pensions do and also insure employees against layoffs. Firms would be more willing to pay for all kinds of training—assuming future wages were set at an appropriate level—since a contract, in effect, converts all training into completely specific training. A casual reading of history suggests that long-term contracts have, indeed, been primarily a means of inducing firms to undertake large investments in employees. These contracts are seldom used today in the United States,[11] and while they have declined in importance over time, they were probably always the exception here largely because courts have considered them a form of involuntary servitude. Moreover, any enforcible contract could at best specify the hours required on a job, not the quality of performance. Since performance can vary widely, unhappy workers could usually "sabotage" operations to induce employers to release them from contracts.

Some training may be useful not in most firms nor in a single firm, but in a set of firms defined by product, type of work, or geographical location. For example, carpentry training would raise productivity primarily in the construction industry, and French legal training would not be very useful in the United States. Such training would tend to be paid by trainees, since a single firm could not readily collect the return,[12] and in this respect would be the same as general training. In one respect, however, it is similar to specific training. Workers with training "specific" to an industry, occupation, or country are less likely to leave that industry, occupation, or country than other workers, so their industrial, occupational, or country "turnover" would be less than average. The same result is obtained for specific training, except that a firm rather than an industry, occupation, or country is used as the unit of observation in measuring turnover. An analysis of specific training, therefore, is helpful also in understanding the effects of certain types of "general" training. . . .

Earnings might differ greatly among firms, industries, and countries and yet there might be relatively little worker mobility. The usual explanation would be that workers were either irrational or faced with formidable obstacles in moving. However, if specific training were important, differences in earnings would be a misleading estimate of what "migrants" could receive, and it might be perfectly rational not to move. For example, although French lawyers earn less than American lawyers, the average French lawyer could not earn the average American legal income simply by migrating to the United States, for he would have to invest in learning English and American law and procedures.[13]

---

[10] This economic function of incomplete vesting should caution one against conceding to the agitation for more liberal vesting privileges. Of course, in recent years pensions have also been an important tax-saving device, which certainly has been a crucial factor in their mushrooming growth.

[11] The military and the entertainment industry are the major exceptions.

[12] Sometimes firms cooperate in paying training costs, especially when training apprentices (see *A Look at Industrial Training in Mercer County, N.J.,* Washington, 1959, p. 3).

[13] Of course, persons who have not yet invested in themselves would have an incentive to migrate, and this partly explains why young persons migrate more than older ones. For a further explanation, see the paper by L. Sjaastad, "The Costs and Returns of Human Migration," *Journal of Political Economy,* 70 (1962 supplement *Investment in Human Beings*), pp. 80–93.

In extreme types of monopsony, exemplified by an isolated company town, job alternatives for both trained and untrained workers are nil, and all training, no matter what its nature, would be specific to the firm. Monopsony combined with control of a product or an occupation (due, say, to antipirating agreements) converts training specific to that product or occupation into firm-specific training. These kinds of monopsony increase the importance of specific training and thus the incentive to invest in employees.[14] . . .

Schooling

A school can be defined as an institution specializing in the production of training, as distinct from a firm that offers training in conjunction with the production of goods. Some schools, like those for barbers, specialize in one skill, while others, like universities, offer a large and diverse set. Schools and firms are often substitute sources of particular skills. This substitution is evidenced by the shift over time, for instance, in law from apprenticeships in law firms to law schools and in engineering from on-the-job experience to engineering schools.[15] . . .

Other Knowledge

On-the-job and school training are not the only activities that raise real income primarily by increasing the knowledge at a person's command. Information about the prices charged by different sellers would enable a person to buy from the cheapest, thereby raising his command over resources; information about the wages offered by different firms would enable him to work for the firm paying the highest. In both examples, information about the economic system and about consumption and production possibilities is increased, as distinct from knowledge of a particular skill. Information about the political or social system—the effect of different parties or social arrangements—could also significantly raise real incomes.[16]

Let us consider in more detail investment in information about employment opportunities. A better job might be found by spending money on employment agencies and situation wanted ads, by using one's time to examine want ads, by talking to friends and visiting firms, or in Stigler's language by "search."[17] When the new job requires geographical movement, additional time and resources would be spent in moving.[18] These expenditures constitute an investment in information about job opportunities that would yield a return in the form of higher earnings than would otherwise have been received. . . .

Productive Wage Increases

One way to invest in human capital is to improve emotional and physical health. In

---

[14] A relatively large difference between marginal product and wages in monopsonies might measure, therefore, the combined effect of economic power and a relatively large investment in employees.

[15] State occupational licensing requirements often permit on-the-job training to be substituted for school training. (See S. Rottenberg, "The Economics of Occupational Licensing," *Aspects of Labor Economics, A Conference of the Universities,* National Bureau of Economic Research (Princeton, N.J.: Princeton University Press, 1962), pp. 3–20.

[16] The role of political knowledge is systematically discussed in A. Downs, *An Economic Theory of Democracy* (New York: Harper & Row Publishers, Inc., 1957) and more briefly in my "Competition and Democracy," *Journal of Law and Economics,* October 1958.

[17] See G. J. Stigler, "Information in the Labor Market," *Investment in Human Beings,* pp. 91-105.

[18] Studies of large geographical moves—those requiring both a change in employment and consumption—have tended to emphasize the job change more than the consumption change. Presumably money wages are considered to be more dispersed geographically than prices.

Western countries today, earnings are much more closely geared to knowledge than to strength, but in an earlier day, and elsewhere still today, strength had a significant influence on earnings. Moreover, emotional health increasingly is considered an important determinant of earnings in all parts of the world. Health, like knowledge, can be improved in many ways. A decline in the death rate at working ages may improve earning prospects by extending the period during which earnings are received; a better diet adds strength and stamina, and thus earning capacity; or an improvement in working conditions—higher wages, coffee breaks, and so on—may affect morale and productivity.

Firms can invest in the health of employees through medical examinations, lunches, or avoidance of activities with high accident and death rates. An investment in health that increased productivity to the same extent in many firms would be a general investment and would have the same effect as general training, while an investment in health that increased productivity more in the firms making it would be a specific investment and would have the same effect as specific training. Of course, most investments in health in the United States are made outside firms, in households, hospitals, and medical offices. A full analysis of the effect on earnings of such "outside" investment in health is beyond the scope of this study, but I would like to discuss a relation between on-the-job and "outside" human investments that has received much attention in recent years.

When on-the-job investments are paid by reducing earnings during the investment period, less is available for investments outside the job in health, better diet, schooling, and other factors. If these "outside" investments were more productive, some on-the-job investments would not be undertaken even though they were very productive by "absolute" standards.

Before proceeding further, one point

needs to be made. The amount invested outside the job would be related to current earnings only if the capital market was very imperfect, for otherwise any amount of "outside" investment could be financed with borrowed funds. The analysis assumes, therefore, that the capital market is extremely imperfect, earnings and other income being a major source of funds.

A firm would be willing to pay for investment in human capital made by employees outside the firm if it could benefit from the resulting increase in productivity. The only way to pay, however, would be to offer higher wages during the investment period than would have been offered since direct loans to employees are prohibited by assumption. When a firm gives a productive wage increase—that is, an increase that raises productivity—"outside" investments are, as it were, converted into on-the-job investments. Indeed, such a conversion is a natural way to circumvent imperfections in the capital market and the resultant dependence of the amount invested in human capital on the level of wages. . . .

The effect of a wage increase on productivity depends on the way it is spent, which in turn depends on tastes, knowledge, and opportunities. Firms might exert an influence on spending by exhorting employees to obtain good food, housing, and medical care, or even by requiring purchases of specified items in company stores. Indeed, the company store or truck system in nineteenth century Great Britain has been interpreted as partly designed to prevent an excessive consumption of liquor and other debilitating commodities.[19] The prevalence of employer paternalism in underdeveloped countries has frequently been accepted as evidence of a difference in tempera-

---

[19] See C. W. Hilton, "The British Truck System in the Nineteenth Century," *Journal of Political Economy,* April 1957, pp. 246–47.

ment between East and West. An alternative interpretation suggested by our study is that an increase in consumption has a greater effect on productivity in underdeveloped countries, and that a productivity advance raises profits more there either because firms have more monopsony power or because the advance is less delayed. In other words "paternalism" may simply be a way of investing in the health and welfare of employees in underdeveloped countries.

4

The Theory of Wage Determination

John T. Dunlop

John T. Dunlop, *The Theory of Wage Determination* (London: The Macmillan Company, 1957), pp. 14-27 with deletions.

PRELIMINARY OBSERVATIONS

All wage theory is in a sense demand and supply analysis. A wage is a price, and the wage structure is a sub-system of prices. Prices and price systems are fruitfully to be interpreted in terms of demand and supply. There is no special or peculiar "demand and supply" theory of wages.

The notion of a "political" theory of wages involves confusion. In the absence of unions, firms or groups of managements make wage decisions, and under conditions of collective bargaining the parties reach agreement on wage scales. It is indeed appropriate to study the processes, procedures, and influences which determine decisions in these organizations and their agreement making processes. But it does not advance understanding of decision-making in organizations to label the process as either "political" or "economic." The decisional process internal to a management organization or a union is an appropriate area of research, but this subject does not pre-empt the theory of wages. Moreover, a large part of the institutional study of decisions should seek to show the impact of external, including market developments, on internal decisions.

It has been a problem in wage discussions from the earliest years to define and to indicate the independent effect of a strike, or power, or political action upon wage determination.[1] It is not a new issue. It is this old question which is revived under the guise of a "political" theory of wages.[2] The appropriate question is still what differences, if any, do unions make on wage determination? Are the net effects large or small? Are the effects different for various components of compensation and on different types of wage rates in the total wage structure?[3]

Wage theory has tended historically to disintegrate on the supply side. The amount of labour supplied and the wage rate came to be determined by social custom or institutional considerations. The wage rate came to be given for purposes of economic analysis. In a sense, the pivotal task of wage theory is to formulate an acceptable theory on the supply side.

It is not satisfactory to treat wage determination in terms of a single rate. In the past there have been various devices to reduce wage setting to the problem of a single rate. A single unskilled or common labour rate is envisaged into which all skilled labour may be translated as consisting of so many "units" of unskilled labour. This classical convention was followed by both Marx and Keynes. A single wage rate, out of the whole structure, is regarded as an index or barometer for all other rates. But all wage rates do not move together either in the short run nor in the long period. The wage structure is not completely rigid over time.

Moreover, the determination of the wage level and the wage structure are closely interrelated.

Wage theory must operate with the concept of wage structure—the complex of rates within firms differentiated by occupation and employee and the complex of interfirm rate structures. The concept of wage structure for the purpose of the present analysis is a central concept; the analysis of wage determination will be approached through the wage structure. Indeed, instead of reducing wage setting to the problem of a single rate, the task of analysing wage determination is rather the problem of the setting and variation in the whole structure or complex of rates. While the general level of wage rates can be thought of changing apart from variations in structure, in fact they are not dissociated. Changes in the wage level, associated with changes in output levels in the system, are necessarily associated with changes in wage structure. The interrelations between the wage level and the wage structure is itself a major area of inquiry.

A distinction is to be made between the wage structure within a plant, firm, or other grouping in which wage differentials are set by the same authority and the complex of interfirm or group structures set by a number of different agencies. From the point of view of the individual decision makers, the first wage structure is internal while the second is external. One of the central problems of wage analysis is to indicate the interrelations between the internal and external wage structure.

The analysis that follows utilizes two concepts which require explanation: job clusters and wage contours.

JOB CLUSTERS AND WAGE CONTOURS

A job cluster is defined as a stable group of job classifications or work assignments within a firm (wage determining unit) which are so

[1] See, for instance, Eugen von Böhm-Bawerk, *Zeitschrift für Volkswirtschaft*, "Nor could any sensible person deny that the existence of labour organizations with their weapon of strikes has been of pronounced influence on the fixation of wages of labour. . . . The great problem, not adequately settled so far, is to determine the exact extent and nature of the influence of both factors. . . ." ("purely economic" and "social" categories).

[2] See Arthur M. Ross, *Trade Union Wage Policy* (Berkeley, Calif.: University of California Press, 1948).

[3] See Clark Kerr, "Wage Relationships—The Comparative Impact of Market and Power Forces."

linked together by (a) technology, (b) by the administrative organization of the production process, including policies of transfer and promotion, or (c) by social custom that they have common wage-making characteristics. In an industrial plant which may literally have thousands of jobs, each wage rate is not equally related and dependent upon all other wage rates. The internal wage structure, the complex of differentials, is not rigidly fixed for all time. Neither do relative rates change in random relation to each other. The internal wage rate structure is to be envisaged as divided into groups of jobs or job clusters. The wage rates for the operations and jobs within a cluster are more closely related in their wage movements than are rates outside the cluster.

Thus a tool-room in a plant would ordinarily constitute a job cluster. The training and skill of the machinists are similar who operate the various specialized machines—lathes, shapers, cutters, and so on. Their work is closely interrelated in the productive process. They may work apart from others. They may have a common promotion and transfer pattern. The wage rates within the tool-room are more closely related with each other than they may be with the rates for other employees in the power plant, on production lines, in the maintenance crew, in the office, or in the sales force. The wage structure of a plant is to be envisaged as comprised of a limited number of such job clusters, each with a number of rates.

From the analytical point of view these job clusters are given in the short period by the technology, the managerial and administrative organization of the wage determining unit, and by the social customs of the work community. Thus, the employees on a furnace or mill may constitute a job cluster (technology); so may employees in a department (administrative organization) or the women in an office (social custom). Wage theory, for the short period, does not seek to explain these job clusters. For the longer period, it is essential to show that the scope of a job cluster within a rate structure may be expanded, restricted, or divided as a consequence of changes in the technology, administrative organization, or social customs in the plant.

The job cluster can be examined in more detail. Ordinarily, a job cluster will contain one, or in some cases several, key rates. The cluster consists of the key rate(s) and a group of associated rates. The key rate may be the highest paid, or the top step in a promotion ladder, or the job at which a large number of workers are employed. Typically, these key rates show relatively less change in job content over time. They are often relatively more standardized as between firms than other jobs. These key rates are those which managements and unions typically have in mind and explicitly discuss in considering the internal wage structure.

The smallest building block in the wage structure is thus the job cluster comprised of a key rate, or several such rates in some cases, and a group of associated rates. The internal wage structure of the plant (wage-determining unit) consists of a number of job clusters. Such is the anatomy of the internal wage structure.

It is not to be presumed that the forces which determine the wage rate for a group of jobs in a cluster are confined within a firm. The "exterior" plays a very important role. The "exterior," including the "market," cannot operate directly on a thousand slightly differentiated jobs. The key rates play a decisive role in relating the exterior to the internal rate structure. Indeed, the key rates are affected by the exterior, and adjustments in these rates are transmitted to other rates within the plant, cluster by cluster.

A wage contour is defined as a stable group of firms (wage determining units) which are so linked together by (a) similarity of product markets, (b) by resort to similar sources for a labour force, or (c) by common labour market organization (custom) that they have common wage-making characteristics. The wage rates of a particular firm are not ordinarily independent of all other wage rates; they are more closely related to the wage rates of some firms than to others. A contour for particular occupations is to be defined both in terms of the product market and the labour market. A contour thus has three dimensions: (a) particular occupations or job clusters, (b) a sector of industry, and (c) a geographical location. The firms which comprise a contour constitute a particular product market; they also may be located in one labour market or scattered throughout a region or the country as a whole.

Thus, in the United States, the basic steel contour for production jobs consists of the producers of basic steel products scattered in various communities throughout the country. The wage rates of the jobs in these firms, in their blast furnace, steel works, and rolling mill operations move together. Some other operations and occupations of the same companies, such as cement mills or shipping, are typically excluded from the basic steel contour. While there are a variety of submarkets, and each basic steel producer may have some specialized features to its product market or locality in which it hires labour, none the less the basic steel wage contour is sharply defined and distinguishable from others.

A contour may be confined to a locality in its labour market dimension. Thus, newspapers in New York City constitute a contour for wage-setting purposes. The rates for various occupations in one newspaper are closely related to those in other newspapers in that city. Specialized product markets, for other types of printing or publishing, are a part of still other wage contours.

A contour refers to particular ranges of skill, occupations, or job clusters. Not all types of labour hired by a firm will have wage rates determined in the same contour. Thus, a firm employing a professional chemist, a pattern-maker, and a clerk may be expected to be part of three quite different contours. A construction firm hiring boilermakers, operating engineers, and labourers will be a part of the construction product market in each instance, but three separate wage contours are involved. The boilermaker's rate is set over the largest geographical area while the labourer's rate is likely to be confined to a single locality.

A wage contour can be explored in further detail. In the ordinary case a wage contour contains one, or in some instances several key bargains. The contour is comprised of the rates for the key firm(s) and a group of associated firms. The key bargain may be set by the largest firm, the price leader, or the firm with labour relations leadership. Thus, in the basic steel contour, the wages determined by the U.S. Steel Company generally have been followed by all other firms in the contour. In this case the other basic steel producers have customarily followed the "pattern" almost immediately. In other cases more time may elapse before a change by the followers. Some firms may follow only at a distance, altering even the terms of the key settlement in some minor respects.

A wage contour then can be envisaged as a grouping of firms, for a given range of occupations, in which some firms are very closely related to the leaders. Other firms are less directly associated. At the exterior of the contour, furthest from the key rates, the firms may only remotely follow the leadership.

A variety of devices have been developed which relate wages determined by the key bargain to those of other firms in the contour. The existence of a common expiration date or the sequence of anniversary dates is reflective of the relations within a wage contour. Some firms commit themselves in advance to pay the wages of others; many commit themselves to consider a change when a "wage movement" has developed in the industry (contour). Specialized product markets or sources of labour supply or skill requirements may mean that a particular firm, remote from the "centre" of the contour, will modify the "pattern" established at the key bargain in some respects.

The firms which comprise a wage contour may be organized into a formal employers' association rather than appear to make wage decisions without a common organization. In an association not all firms actually have equal weight in making decisions; wage leaders exercise their same functions, although an association may mean that all wages are changed at the same time. In many instances an association constitutes only a formal difference from wage leadership conditions that would be evident without an employer's organization.[4]

Wage-making forces are envisaged as concentrated on the key rates in the job clusters. These rates "extend" out from the internal structure of the firm to the "exterior" and constitute the focal points for wage-setting forces among firms within the contour. The key rates in the job clusters constitute the channels of impact between the exterior developments in the contour and the interior rate structure of the firm. Moreover, in an analogous way, the key bargains constitute the focal point of wage-setting forces within the contour and constitute the points where wage-making forces converge that are exterior to the contour.

A theory of wages is not required to treat each wage rate in the system as of equal importance. The view of the wage structure outlined above singles out a limited number of key rates and key bargains for analysis. These particular rates are selected, at least in the short run, by the anatomy of the wage structure which is

given by (a) the technology and administrative arrangements of firms; (b) competitive patterns in product markets; and (c) the sources of labour supply.

The concepts of job cluster and wage contour are analogous. In each case a group of rates surrounds a key rate. The concepts seek to relate the internal and the external wage structure; they focus attention on the mechanics by which the internal structure through job clusters are influenced by external developments in the wage contour. Wage theory cannot reduce all structure to a single rate; the limited number of strategic rates depicted by the job clusters and wage contours are to be the focus of wage theory.[5]

WAGE STRUCTURE IN THE SHORT RUN

The concepts developed in the preceding section can be applied to a particular case. The attached table shows the union scale for motor-truck drivers in Boston for July 1951. Each rate shows the wage scale established between the union and an association or group of employers engaging in selling transportation services. Some small part of the differences in wages may be attributed to variations in the skill or work performed; some small differences may be related to differences in the length of the work week and the timing of contract expiration during a year. But the teamsters who work at these various rates are essentially similar and substitutable. Essentially the same disparity in rates is found in most other cities, with a high

---

[4] While the impact of labour organization upon wage rates is frequently discussed in current literature, the question of the effect of employer organization upon wage rates is seldom explored. Frequently, a formal employer organization only sharpens relations already apparent. The wage contour is more sharply defined at the "edges."

[5] For an imaginative discussion on the concept of labour market, see Clark Kerr, "The Balkanization of Labor Markets," *Labor Mobility and Economic Opportunity* (Cambridge, Mass.: The Technology Press of Massachusetts Institute of Technology and John Wiley & Sons, Inc., 1954), pp. 92–110. The present discussion would add to that of Professor Kerr the emphasis that the scope of product markets is reflected back into the labour market defining the scope of wage setting.

TABLE 1

Union Scale for Motor-Truck Drivers*
(Boston, July 1, 1951)

Magazine	$2.25
Newspaper, day	2.16
Oil	1.985
Building construction	1.85
Paper handlers, newspaper	1.832
Beer, bottle and keg	1.775
Grocery, chain store	1.679
Meat-packing house, 3-5 tons	1.64
Bakery, Hebrew	1.595
Wholesale	1.57
Rendering	1.55
Coal	1.518
Garbage disposal	1.50
General hauling	1.50
Food service, retail	1.475
Ice	1.45
Armored car	1.405
Carbonated beverage	1.38
Waste paper	1.38
Linen supply	1.342
Movers, piano and household	1.30
Scrap, iron and metal	1.20
Laundry, wholesale	1.20

*Bureau of Labor Statistics, *Union Wages and Hours: Motortruck Drivers and Helpers* (July 1, 1951), Bulletin 1052, pp. 9–10.

similarity in the relative ranking of rates for various branches of the trade.

In a significant sense, the case constitutes a kind of critical experiment. One type of labour performing almost identical work, organized by the same union, is paid markedly different rates by different associations of employers in the truck transportation industry. Why the wide range in wage rates? Are the disparities temporary? Do they arise from "friction" or "immobilities" in the labour market? Are they primarily the consequence of a monopolistic seller of labour discriminating among types of employers? I believe the answer to these several questions is in the negative.

Basically each rate reflects a wage contour. Each is a reflection of the product market. Within any one contour the wage rates will tend to be equal. As among beer distributors, construction firms, ice deliverers, or scrap iron and metal haulers, there will tend to be few differences in rates. But there are sharp differences in rates as among contours. Fundamentally the differences in the product market are reflected back into the labour market.

But what are the mechanics? Why do not teamsters all move to the higher paying contours? Or, why do not the employers in the higher paying contours set a lower wage rate since similar labour seems to be available to other contours at lower rates? In a perfect labour market (a bourse) such changes toward uniformity would tend to take place.

Part of the explanation is to be found in the historical sequence of growth of the trucker's wage scale as indicated in the preceding section. Newer and expanding industries or contours, such as oil, have had to pay higher wages to attract labour in the evolution of wage scales. Part of the explanation is derived from the fact that this historical structure of wages has conditioned the labour supply so that the relative rates among contours are regarded as proper. A minor part of the explanation lies in the fact that these wage rates are influenced by the wages of the group of workers these employees tend to be associated with in work operations. Teamsters hauling oil and building materials come in contact with high-paid employees in their work operations, while laundry and scrap drivers have more direct contact with lower-paid employees. A larger emphasis is to be placed on the fact that competitive conditions permit higher pay at the top end of the list. Demand is more inelastic and wages tend to be a lower proportion of the sales revenue. But why do the firms pay more, simply because they can afford to do so? If the union is brought into the explanation as a decisive factor, then an explanation can simply be made in terms of the union acting as a discriminating seller as among different industries. While this factor may be significant in some cases, the type of wage spread is so general, apart from the union, that the principal explanation should lie else-where.

In periods of tightness in the labour market the various contours are able to bid for labour, and a differentiated structure of rates reflecting the product market contours and competitive conditions tends to be established. For a variety of reasons these differentials are not readily altered in a looser labour market. There are costs involved in making a wage change or changing a differential among sectors. Newer and expanding employers using the same type of labour have to pay more to attract a labour force, and a differential once established by a contour is not easily abolished.

For these various reasons the structure of the product market tends to be mirrored in the labour market. The differentials are not transitory; they are not to be dismissed as imperfections. The differentials are not basically to be interpreted as a range of indefinite or random rates, although a community with a wide variety of firms in different product markets may present the impression of random rates. The wage contours and their relative rates reflect the basic nature of product and labour markets.

The arguments developed above can be applied to most of the cases of interfirm wage differentials that have been reported. There are some differences in wage rates which reflect differences in job content; there are differences in costs and earnings in the way firms administer the same wage structure, and there are differences in methods of compensation (incentive and time rates). These factors account for some of the statistically observed variations in wage rates. The theoretically significant differences for similar grades of labour are those which reflect different product market competitive conditions.

THE LONG-TERM DEVELOPMENT OF WAGE STRUCTURE

The structure of wage rates of a country can be conceived as reflecting the course of its industrialization and economic development. The supply of labour and the rate and pattern of industrialization are the crucial factors. A country with a scarcity of labour will likely require and establish larger wage differentials for skill than one with an abundant labour supply. A rapid rate of industrialization will produce larger skill differentials than a slow rate. The sequence in the development of industries in the industrialization process will affect to some degree the structure of wage rates as differentials are used to attract labour force to these industries from agriculture or from other industrial activity. A comparative study of the wage structures of various countries today reflects these imprints of the path of economic development.[6]

A study of the sequence in the development of the wage structure is instructive. Starting with an agrarian society, relatively small differentials are required to attract a labour force away from agrarian pursuits. The first industries historically required simpler skills, and the levels of rates over agriculture were slight. As successive industries develop, higher rates are required to draw a work force, not primarily directly from agriculture, but from lower-paid industries. Successive industries appear to require more specialized skills and higher wages result. The structure of wages thus reflects the pattern of industrialization.

Some of the same phenomena can be seen in a particular community today with the introduction of new plants. There are a variety of circumstances which may result in new employers setting higher rates. These factors will be stronger, the higher the general level of employment. The new industries may require higher standards of skill. They may be employed in plants with a minimum number of employees of several thousands. A higher rate is

[6] See John T. Dunlop and Melvin Rothbaum, "International Comparisons of Wage Structures," *International Labour Review* (April 1955).

needed to attract that number than if the plant were to grow gradually from a small figure. The labour costs are frequently a small fraction of total costs, and the product markets are often oligopolistic. These factors permit or encourage the enterprise to set a higher rate for the key jobs in comparison to others in the community. The oil, chemical, atomic, and television industries would be current examples. The discussion suggests that for comparable levels of skill there is a tendency for new industries to give the wage level a drift upwards.

The wage structure is to be approached as a reflex of the larger pattern of industrialization. The wage structure of an agricultural economy is largely undifferentiated by skill or product market divisions. Increasing industrialization creates increasing differentiation by skill, thereby creating many new occupations and job operations. Some of these occupations or jobs are key jobs and provide the basis for interfirm comparisons. Increasing industrialization also creates new groupings of products within which are unique types of competition. These product market characteristics, combined with some features of the labour market, create wage contours within which wages tend to move under common forces, relatively to wages outside the contour.

When a wage structure has been established, the labour supply tends to adapt itself to the relative structure of rates, as reflected in key rates, in a variety of ways. Preferences and relative ratings given to jobs by workers are not autonomous; they reflect the broad outlines of the established wage structure. The long established relative rate structure created as envisaged above itself influences the choice of workers and may even take on normative elements. The labour force in general, for most occupations, would appear to be highly pliable over a generation. The established wage structure comes to shape labour supply over the long run. This is not to deny that supply may not adapt readily in the short period to changes in relative demand. Nor does it deny that relative wage rates may affect long-run supply for some occupations within some limits. But the point is that the labour supply over a generation is clearly highly adaptable to the great variety of jobs created by modern industrialization, and the work force tends in important respects to adapt itself to a long-established rate structure of key jobs.

The questions which are posed for contemporary wage theory are quite different from those which challenged the wages fund and marginal productivity periods. The analysis of wage determination was in each doctrine at the very centre of economics. As these doctrines declined in popularity, a tendency developed to treat wage rates as determined outside the system and given for economic problems. Wage theory has shown a tendency to break down, particularly on the supply side.

A few suggestions have been made for future wage discussions. A single wage rate or average concept is inadequate. The structure of wages, the whole complex of differentials, needs to be explained. Moreover, the determination of the level and structure of wage rates are interrelated. In the analysis of wage structure the concepts of job clusters and wage contours define the points at which wage-making forces are concentrated. The anatomy of the wage structure is to be understood if one is to explain changes in response to demand and supply factors. These concepts help to focus attention upon the operation of demand and supply. They suggest that product market competition and conditions decisively influence the structure of wage rates. In the longer run, the wage structure is to be depicted as a reflex of the pattern and speed of industrialization.

5

Information Networks in Labor Markets

Albert Rees

Albert Rees, "Information Networks in Labor Markets," *American Economic Review,* Vol. 56, No. 2 (May 1966). Reprinted by permission of the *American Economic Review.*

This paper is not concerned with the information about the labor market provided by labor statistics. Rather it deals with the information that participants in the market have about one another—with the ways in which job seekers find jobs and employers find employees. I shall draw heavily on a study of the Chicago labor market now in progress in which my associates are George P. Shultz, Joseph C. Ullman, David P. Taylor, and Mary Hamilton.[1] The focus of

[1] I am indebted to these associates and to George J. Stigler and Arnold R. Weber for helpful comments on a draft of this paper. I am also indebted to the Ford Foundation for its generous support of this study.

the paper is accordingly on local . . . markets.

We may divide information networks in the labor market into two groups: formal and informal. The formal networks include the state employment services, private fee-charging employment agencies, newspaper advertisements, union hiring halls, and school or college placement bureaus. The informal sources include referrals from employees, other employers, and miscellaneous sources, and walk-ins or hiring at the gate.

The literature stresses the great importance of the informal channels, and our study of the Chicago labor market offers additional support for this emphasis. In the four white-collar occupations under study, informal sources account for about half of all hires; in the eight blue-collar occupations, informal sources account for more than four-fifths of all hires.

Economists have traditionally taken a dim view of informal networks of labor market information. The typical discussion of channels of employment begins with an analogy between the public employment service and stock or commodity exchanges. To be sure, various reasons are given why the analogy is imperfect and a "grain exchange for labor" cannot be established. But in the end, the disorganization of the labor market is deplored and suggestions are made for the improvement of the employment service.

For example, a recent textbook in labor economics starts a discussion of the effectiveness of the labor market by using the New York Stock Exchange as a model of efficiency. It notes that formal intermediaries in the labor market are not widely used, and concludes that "the worker who sets out to find employment very likely goes through a process of chasing down vague rumors or leads." "All too frequently," it adds, "the buyers and sellers, blindfolded by a lack of knowledge, simply grope about until they bump into each other."[2] I shall argue here that the analogies with commodity and security markets, even when qualified, are mischievous and misleading and that the effectiveness and advantages of informal networks of information have been too little appreciated.

The search for information in any market has both an extensive and an intensive margin. A buyer can search at the extensive margin by getting a quotation from one more seller. He can search at the intensive margin by getting additional information concerning an offer already received. Where the goods and services

sold are highly standardized, the extensive margin is the more important; when there is great variation in quality, the intensive margin moves to the forefront. This point can be illustrated by considering the markets for new and used cars. Since there is relatively little variation in the quality of new cars of the same make and model and since the costs of variation are reduced by factory guarantees, the extensive margin of search is the important one. A rational buyer will get quotations from additional dealers until the probable reduction in price from one additional quotation is less than the cost of obtaining it.[3]

In used cars of the same make, model, and year much of the variation in asking prices reflects differences in the condition of the cars, and this calls for a substantial change in the strategy of the rational buyer. He will invest less in obtaining large numbers of offers and much more in examining each car. For example, he may have each car he seriously considers inspected by a mechanic. He may want information on the history of the car as a substitute for the direct assessment of condition and will pass up a used taxi in favor of the car owned by the proverbial little old lady who drives only to church. It will not be irrational for him to pay a relatively high price for a car owned by a friend if he has favorable information about his friend's habits as a car owner.

Organized commodity and security exchanges deal in highly standardized or perfectly uniform contracts, where the intensive margin of search is effectively eliminated. One is entirely indifferent as to whether one buys 100 shares of General Motors from a taxi company, a little old lady, or Alfred P. Sloan, though much search may enter into the decision to buy General Motors rather than some other security. Organized exchanges perform a highly

[2] Sanford Cohen, *Labor in the United States* (Columbus, Ohio: Charles E. Merrill, 1960), p. 351.

[3] See George J. Stigler, "The Economics of Information," *Journal of Political Economy* (June 1961).

effective job of widening the extensive margin of search and need to transmit only a few bits of information (the name of the contract, the quantity, and the price) to conclude a transaction. Labor markets lie as far from this pole as used car markets, and a grain exchange for labor is about as possible as a contract on the Chicago Board of Trade for 1960 Chevrolet sedans.

The large variance of wages within narrowly defined occupations in particular local markets affords some evidence of the variance in the quality of labor and in the attractiveness of jobs, though it has other sources as well. For example, in our sample of maintenance electricians in the Chicago area we found a range of hourly earnings in June, 1963, of from $1.75 to $4.75 an hour. Their formal educations ranged from less than four years of schooling to some college. They worked in places ranging from spotless modern plants in pleasant suburbs to old loft buildings in central city slums.

Variation in the quality of applicants in many dimensions is one reason why employers invest so much in the selection of new employees. A second is that present seniority arrangements, both contractual and traditional, mean that in a large number of occupations an employee who survives the probationary period is likely to be with the firm for many years. The total of his wages over this period will run to tens of thousands of dollars. The hiring of an employee is a transaction analogous in size to the purchase of a car or even a house by a consumer and justifies substantial costs of search.

It is therefore not surprising to find employers using many different selection devices. An applicant for employment may be examined in several or in extreme cases all of the following ways: a written application for employment, an interview, paper and pencil tests, work sample tests, a medical examination, a check of credit standing, a check of school and employ-ment references, and even police record checks. The problem facing the employer is not to get in touch with the largest possible number of potential applicants; rather it is to find a few applicants promising enough to be worth the investment of thorough investigations. This is particularly true since in general the buyer and not the seller in labor markets quotes the starting wage. The employer usually has little interest in discovering applicants willing to work at less than the prevailing rate; if he is covered by a union contract, he has none at all.

Many employer hiring standards can be viewed as devices to narrow the intensive field of search by reducing the number of applicants to manageable proportions. Within the narrowed field defined by hiring standards, extensive search can be conducted through the most appropriate channels. Thus we encounter such rules as the following: clerical workers must be high school graduates; material handlers must weigh at least 150 pounds; janitors must have lived a year in the metropolitan area; employees who use public transportation must not need to make more than two transfers. Each of these rules has some relevance to job performance, but lack of the qualities specified could be compensated for by the presence of others. Such rules are often relaxed if there is a shortage of applicants who can meet them. This flexibility is illustrated by a large Chicago area manufacturing establishment whose newspaper ads for blue-collar workers when the market is loose specify, "Must be high school graduate"; when the market tightens, this is replaced by, "Average piece rate earnings $3.19 an hour." In addition to formal hiring standards, employers have a still more flexible set of preferences among job applicants, such as the preference for married men for unskilled work because they are thought to have lower quit rates.

Most employers have a strong preference for using informal information networks, for a variety of reasons. Employee referrals—the most important informal channel—usually provide good screening for employers who are satisfied with their present work force. Present employees tend to refer people like themselves, and they may feel that their own reputation is affected by the quality of the referrals. Informal sources also tend to provide applicants from the neighborhood in which the establishment is located; this is particularly important for female employees in reducing turnover, absenteeism, and tardiness resulting from transportation difficulties. Moreover, informal channels are usually costless to the employer, though we have found a few cases in which bonuses are paid for employee referrals that result in hires. Of course, some formal channels such as the state employment service are also costless. The few employers who deliberately avoid informal sources are either those who are seeking to upgrade their work force or those who have had bad experience with nepotism or cliques.

The informal sources also have important benefits to the applicant. He can obtain much more information from a friend who does the kind of work in which he is interested than from an ad in the paper or a counselor at an employment agency, and he places more trust in it. He can ask the counselor about the fairness of supervision in a factory, but he cannot often get an informed or reliable answer. If informal sources result in a placement in the applicant's home neighborhood, he minimizes transportation costs, both in time and in direct outlay. Finally, the presence of a friend in the plant may be an important "fringe benefit," making the job more attractive to the worker at no cost to the employer.

The fact that employers generally prefer informal sources does not mean they are always able to use them. As George Stigler has pointed out, high wages and high search costs are substitutes for an employer; low-wage employers are therefore forced to use high-cost information channels, such as newspaper advertising and private employment agencies.[4] This hypothesis receives strong support from the findings of Joseph C. Ullman, who has analyzed the Chicago market for two female clerical occupations: typists and keypunch operators. Ullman reports significant negative relationships between wages and the proportion of clerical workers hired through newspaper advertising and private agencies.[5]

The literature on formal information networks is uniformly hostile to private employment agencies. One of the leading scholars in the field, E. Wight Bakke, speaks of unemployed workers "falling into the clutches of exploiting fee-charging agencies, who took from ignorant people in desperate need of jobs a big toll from their pay for providing a very poor labor broker service."[6] Many employers also have little use for private agencies, or "flesh peddlers." Some complain of pirating—attempts by agencies to hire away people they have previously placed in order to earn another fee—and many complain of being pestered by phone calls from agency counselors. Some agencies do a poor screening job because of the high turnover of counselors. Since there are many agencies and there is vigorous competition among them, employers who complain about the practices of a particular agency often shift their business to a competing agency rather than turning to an alternative type of hiring channel.

Despite complaints from professors and employers, private agencies have been growing

[4] See George J. Stigler, "Information in the Labor Market," *Journal of Political Economy* (October 1962 supplement).

[5] Joseph C. Ullman, "Inter-firm Differences in the Cost of Search for White Collar Workers" (unpublished doctoral dissertation, Graduate School of Business, Univ. of Chicago, 1965).

[6] E. Wight Bakke, *A Positive Labor Market Policy* (Columbus, Ohio: Charles E. Merrill, 1960), p. 15.

rapidly. Between 1943 and 1958 the number of private employment agencies in the United States increased from 2,200 to 3,900, their receipts tripled, and their payrolls quadrupled.[7] One is forced to at least grudging admiration of an industry that can thrive on selling at substantial fees a service that the government provides gratis.

In fact, our employer interviews reveal that many employers are well satisfied with private agencies. This is especially true in the clerical market, where Chicago employers typically pay agency fees of 60 or 72 percent of a month's salary. There is some tendency for the firms that use agencies extensively to be smaller than average, with fewer facilities in their own personnel departments, which suggests the presence within limits of economies of scale in hiring. The most satisfactory relationships are often with agencies that are specialized in terms of occupation, industry, or location, and involve dealings over a prolonged period with a particular counselor who knows the employer's needs.

The number of employers in our sample who make frequent use of the Illinois or Indiana Employment Services and are well satisfied with them is considerably smaller than the number who report good results from private agencies. Private agencies placed from 10 to 32 percent of the workers in the four white-collar occupations we studied; the state employment services placed only from 1 to 3 percent. In the eight blue-collar occupations, private agencies were more important than the employment services in three and less important in three others; in no case were hires through the state employment services more than 4 percent of the total.

[7] See Eaton Conant, "An Evaluation of Private Employment Agencies as Sources of Job Vacancy Data," in *The Measurement and Interpretation of Job Vacancies* (National Bureau of Economic Research, 1966).

The highest level of satisfaction with the state employment services was reported by employers who deal with suburban offices rather than central city offices. In these cases they often mentioned regular contact with the same counselor as the key factor in good service.

We encountered some employers who object on principle to the government running an employment service, and several who avoid the employment service because, despite Fair Employment Practices Acts, they do not hire Negroes. However, such cases were clearly not the main source of dissatisfaction or nonuse in our sample. The most frequent complaints against the employment service are slowness and poor screening. Some respondents gave specific examples, such as this one from a branch store of a large department store chain: "A year or so ago we placed an order with the Employment Service for a couple of high school graduates for openings in the credit department. We didn't care too much about experience, and would take trainees. They sent over forty applicants and about half weren't high school graduates. Most of the rest were overqualified and wouldn't accept the jobs. I finally hired a couple of people, but it just wasn't worth the effort to talk to them." Stories such as this suggest that the number of referrals is a very poor yardstick for evaluating an employment service—the number of placements is a better one, and the ratio of placements to referrals may be better still.

A manufacturing firm that has employed Negro blue-collar workers for many years stated that it does not use the employment service because "instead of trying to meet our qualifications, they just send over people who have trouble finding jobs, and they aren't the best people." Such employer reactions suggest the strong tension between the employer objective of getting the best for his money and the objectives of agencies that seek to promote social welfare by referring the workers whose needs are greatest. Unfortunately, referrals alone do not alleviate need—only placements do.

Chicago area employers use newspaper advertising extensively in recruiting white-collar workers (from 14 to 23 percent of all hires in four occupations) and to a smaller but still significant extent for blue-collar workers (1 to 13 percent of hires in eight occupations). In no occupation was the employment service more important then newspaper advertising. Many employers prefer neighborhood to metropolitan papers. In some cases this is again a device for racial screening, but more often it is intended to minimize transportation costs and thus to cut turnover and encourage attendance. Trade papers and foreign language papers are important in some industries, such as men's clothing.

The preceding discussion fails to suggest the rich variety of hiring channels in a metropolitan labor market. Referrals from unions are important in trucking and in the printing trades, as well as in construction, which was excluded from our sample. Referrals from one employer to another occur in cases of layoffs and plant shutdowns. Public utilities recruit clerical workers extensively from high schools; private vocational schools are important in the data processing occupations; and college recruiting is important for professional and managerial jobs. Some of the hiring channels we discovered do not fit any of the usual categories. One manufacturer hires truck drivers through a large trucking firm located across the street; another employer hires accountants through the public accounting firm that audits its books. A large distributor of furniture and home appliances hires warehousemen from moving and storage companies, whose slack season coincides with this employer's peak season. Such arrangements seem untidy in terms of the design of an orderly information network; yet they may nonetheless be highly effective.

In some cases matching an opening with an applicant requires search over a wide geographical area. Such cases arise largely for a few highly skilled crafts and for specialized managerial and professional jobs. The employer with a sudden need for a bassoon player, a deep sea diver, or a specialist in the chemistry of fluorine compounds might be willing to recruit from across the country or around the world. Such needs are served in part by the professional office network of the United States Employment Service and in part by the private executive recruiting or "head hunting" agencies. Search at long distances is also indicated when there are serious local imbalances between supply and demand. The employer will engage in long-distance search in cases of excess demand and the employee in cases of excess supply.

It is in such cases that direct communications networks connecting widely separated locations make the most sense. A highly sophisticated network would enable the university in New England with a vacancy for a mathematical economist to call the nearest professional office of the employment service, which through its link to a computer in Washington would discover in microseconds a well-trained mathematical economist on the Pacific Coast dissatisfied because he had been passed over for promotion. Yet even a system with such capabilities would have to struggle for users against the network of personal contacts built up within industries and professions. It is quite possible that the department chairman in New England would prefer, even in making his initial list of prospects, to phone or write to one or two senior mathematical economists whose judgment he has learned to trust.

For the major portion of the market, the crucial characteristic of an effective formal information system is not the length or the number of interconnections between geographical locations or the number of applications and openings that can be brought together at one place. Rather, it is the richness and reliability of the information carried over each link. The crucial component of such a system will not in our life-times be built by IBM or Western Electric. It is the experienced employment service counselor who is a good judge of appli- cants and of their records and who knows thoroughly and respects the requirements of a small number of employers he has served for a long time. This in turn implies a compensation system in which such skill and experience are well rewarded.

6

The Balkanization
of Labor Markets

Clark Kerr

Clark Kerr, "The Balkanization of Labor Markets," in *Labor Mobility and Economic Opportunity*, ed.
E. Wight Bakke. Reprinted by permission of the Technology Press of Massachusetts Institute of
Technology and John Wiley & Sons, Inc.

Labor markets are more talked about than
seen, for their dimensions most frequently are
set by the unknown and, perhaps, mystic ideas
in people's minds. A worker wishes to be
employed in a certain area and at a certain type
of job, and an employer wants employees
drawn from certain groups and possessing
certain characteristics. Unless it is said that each
worker always has his own market area and
each employer his,[1] there must be some adding
of worker and employer preferences to get
designated "markets."

These preferences vary from person to
person and from time to time for the same
person, and when they are totaled the "market" that they constitute has vague and varying

[1] If this is said, then the term "market," with all
it implies, might better be dropped. Instead, attention
should be directed to the scales of preference of individual workers and individual employers. This approach might very well constitute a gain for realism
and for precision but a loss for comprehension. It
probably is true that no two people are alike, and for
some purposes this is the relevant generalization; but it
is also probably true that all people need to eat, and
for other purposes this is the relevant generalization.
The use of the term "labor market" implies that there
is enough uniformity of behavior among certain
workers and among certain employers to warrant
generalizations about the actions of each as a group.
Thus it might be said that the labor market for waitresses in Oakland is characterized (among other things)
by sellers who want part-time employment and buyers
who prefer married women, or by high turnover, or by
a lack of formal structure.

contours but no ultimate limits short of those for American society itself. For example, there is said to be a market for waitresses in Oakland with certain women normally attached to it and certain employers hiring from it. Since, however, a woman need not always be a waitress once having been one and a woman never having been one can become one and since a restaurant employer can hire a girl from San Francisco as well as from Oakland, the market is by no means a self-contained one with precise limits. Preferences of workers and employers are also relative to time. In a depression, a "waitress" may consider herself also available for work in a laundry, and a restaurant employer in wartime may be willing to hire former laundry workers to serve as waitresses.

Most labor markets are similarly indefinite in their specification of the sellers and the buyers. Such a labor market is merely an area, with indistinct geographical and occupational limits within which certain workers customarily seek to offer their services and certain employers to purchase them. But any single worker or any single employer may decide to go elsewhere. This might be identified as the "free choice" market or the "natural market,"[2] for which the individual and changing preferences of workers and employers set the hazy limits.

THE INSTITUTIONAL MARKET

An increasing number of labor markets, however, are more specifically defined at any moment of time and have their dimensions less constantly changed over time. These are the "institutional markets." Their dimensions are set not by the whims of workers and employers but by rules, both formal and informal. These rules state which workers are preferred in the market or even which ones may operate in it at all, and which employers may or must buy in this market if they are to buy at all. Institutional rules take the place of individual preferences in setting the boundaries. Such institutional rules are established by employers' associations, by the informal understandings of employers among each other (the "gentlemen's agreement"), by companies when they set up their personnel policies, by trade unions, by collective agreements, and by actions of government. They contrast with the independent preferences of the individuals who are directly involved.

Economists once spoke of *the* labor market. Each worker competed with all other workers for jobs, and each employer with all other employers for workers. Cairnes, however, early saw there were noncompeting groups:[3]

> No doubt the various ranks and classes fade into each other by imperceptible gradations, and individuals from all classes are constantly passing up or down; but while this is so, it is nevertheless true that the average workman, from whatever rank he be taken, finds his power of competition limited for practical purposes to a certain range of occupations, so that, however high the rates of remuneration in those which lie beyond may rise, he is excluded from sharing them. We are thus compelled to recognize the existence of noncompeting industrial groups as a feature of our economy.

Cairnes used the word "compelled" advisedly. For the existence of "noncompeting" groups adds both complications to economic analysis and impediments to the maximization of welfare. Economic society would be both simpler to understand and closer to the economist's prescription if there were only one labor market.

In the long run, perhaps over several gen-

[2] See Clark Kerr, "Labor Markets: Their Character and Consequences," *Papers and Proceedings*, American Economic Association, May 1950.

[3] J. E. Cairnes, *Political Economy* (New York: Harper, 1874), pp. 67–68.

erations, it may be correct to talk about *the* labor market. Unless society has a hereditary class system, social mobility over time will permit, if not all, at least many individuals or their descendants to prepare themselves for any specific line of work. But a medical practitioner of today can hardly be said to be competing in the market with the unborn son of a pipe fitter. Yet in the long run, defined as the time it takes for the greatest occupational shift to work itself out, *the* labor market may be said to exist.

In the long run all families may compete with all other families, but in the short run most individuals are not in competition with each other. In fact, at any instant of time the standard case is one man faced by one job—this one job is available to only this one man, and this man has only this one job available to him. We are more concerned, however, with labor markets in the short run when several men and several jobs, rather than all men and all jobs or one man and one job, may face each other. In the short run a worker can make himself available for several jobs, according to his preferences, and an employer can make a job available to several workers, according to his preferences.

The noncompeting groups of Cairnes were the several socioeconomic classes (manual, white-collar, professional workers, and so forth). We have found, however, that each of these classes is composed in turn of many largely noncompeting groups. Painters do not compete with bricklayers, or typists with accountants, or doctors with lawyers; nor individuals in Portland, Maine, with those in Portland, Oregon (except perhaps in certain professions). Barriers to movement are set up by the skill gaps between occupations and the distance gaps between locations. Beyond the specificity of skills and the money costs of physical transfer, lie such various but no less important impediments to competition as lack of knowledge, the job tastes of workers, their

inertia and their desire for security, and the personal predilections of employers. The competitive market areas within which somewhat similar men look for somewhat similar jobs, and within which somewhat similar employers try to fill somewhat similar jobs, are normally quite restricted. It has even been suggested that the only meaningful definition of a labor market is one which calls each place of employment a separate market[4] and, perhaps, beyond that, each separate class of work at each such place. More commonly, it is said that a labor market covers the several employers in the same industry in the same area. Thus there are markets and submarkets, all more or less interrelated with each other. The introduction of institutional rules, as we shall see presently, generally creates a larger number of such markets and universally makes them less interrelated.

Institutional rules put added structure into labor markets. Lloyd Fisher has lucidly described the "structureless market" for harvest labor in California.[5] The characteristics of this market serve as a point of contrast for the market types to be described later. The structureless market, according to Fisher, has five conditions: (1) there are no unions with seniority and other rules, (2) the relation between the employee and the employer is a transitory, impersonal one, (3) the workers are unskilled, (4) payment is by unit of product, and (5) little capital or machinery is employed. The employer prefers one worker to another only if he

---

[4] "There are as many labor markets as there are employers of labor." (Gordon F. Bloom and Herbert R. Northrup, *Economics of Labor and Industrial Relations,* Philadelphia: Blakiston, 1950, p. 265.) Lloyd G. Reynolds states: "The firm is the hiring unit and . . . each company employment office is really a distinct market for labor." (*The Structure of Labor Markets,* New York: Harper, 1951, p. 42.)

[5] Lloyd H. Fisher, "The Harvest Labor Market in California," *Quarterly Journal of Economics,* Nov. 1951.

accepts a lower piece rate and the worker one employer over another only if he will pay a higher piece rate. Rates vary greatly over time, but at any moment of time are uniform over space. There are no structural barriers to the mobility of workers and to the fluidity of rates. The only nexus is cash.

Structure is introduced into labor markets even without institutional rules. Many workers have skills which restrict the occupational area in which they seek work, and the number of these skills limits the supply to the employer. Moreover, workers and employers form attachments for each other which neither like to break lightly—"You must realize that the labor market is like the marriage market"[6]—and separation is for cause only. Thus most jobs, even without institutional rules, belong to single workers or to small groups of workers. The craft exists without the craft union, and informal job ties exist without formal seniority rules. Institutional rules, however, add new rights and new preferences and strengthen the old ties.

Institutional labor markets create truly noncompeting groups. Markets are more specifically delimited, and entrance into them, movement within them, and exit from them more precisely defined. Such labor markets find their definition not in the composite of individual preferences but in precise rules. "Natural" frictions are replaced by institutional ones; the free and ignorant man by the exclusive and knowledgeable group. Market forces, seemingly impersonal in the aggregate but exceedingly personal in individual situations, give way to personnel rules which may seem exceedingly impersonal when applied to specific workers. Fraternity triumphs over liberty as "no tres-

passing" signs are posted in more and more job markets.

The sources of this enclosure movement are not far to seek. Employing units are larger, and bureaucratic rules take the place of individual judgments. These rules accept or reject classes of people, instead of the single individuals who met or failed to meet the tests of judgment or the prejudices of the small employer or the foreman. Workers have organized into unions which seek to establish sovereignty over a "job territory." Within this job territory work the citizens who belong to this private government; outside are the noncitizens without rights. The demands of all citizens will be met before the petitions of the aliens are considered. The institutionalization of labor markets is one aspect of the general trend from the atomistic to the pluralistic, and from the largely open to the partially closed society.

TYPES OF INSTITUTIONAL MARKETS

Many barriers divide the totality of employment relationships into more or less distinct compartments. These barriers have five sources: (1) the preferences of individual workers, (2) the preferences of individual employers, (3) the actions of the community of workers, (4) the actions of the community of employers, and (5) the actions of government. The controls on movement flowing from the last three are defined as institutional rules, whether they are written or merely understood, as compared with the "free choices" flowing from the first two.

The institutional rules of employers, workers, and government are enormously varied, reflecting as they do a diversity of environments and desires, and consequently it is difficult to generalize about them. There are, however, two general systems of rules, each with important subtypes. We shall discuss here only the two

[6] Kenneth Boulding, "Wages as a Slave in the National Income," in *The Impact of the Union*, ed. David McCord Wright (New York: Harcourt, Brace and Co., 1951), p. 254.

broad systems and not all the variations of each, significant as they are. The two systems are the communal-ownership approach of craft groups and the private-property method of industrial workers.

Communal ownership. The craft union asserts proprietorship on behalf of its members over the jobs falling within a carefully defined occupational and geographical area. Employers needing the specified occupational skill in that area must hire union members or take the consequences. The building, printing, maritime, and teamster trades illustrate this type of arrangement.

Workers enter the market through the unions; and the unions have preferences just as do employers. They may be in favor of or against Negroes, or women, or students, or Communist party members, and these preferences will show up in the labor supply made available.[7] Entrance is sometimes through closely supervised apprenticeship systems[8] which require the worker to choose his specific occupation early in life and make initial sacrifices in order to gain admittance. These apprenticeship programs are usually pursued with government aid. Admission may also be by transfer card from another local. Occasionally, as in the case of the typographical workers, the man with a transfer card has equal rights with some local members. More frequently, however, he must go to the end of the list and wait until all local members are employed. The transfer card gives him preference only over new appli-

cants for membership. When work is abnormally plentiful, some unions issue work permits, analogous to visas, which entitle outsiders to temporary employment. When employment returns to normal, they lose their privileges. They are renters, not owners.

Once fully in the market, the craft worker can move anywhere within it. Sometimes, when there is a hiring hall with rotation of work, as for longshoremen on the Pacific Coast, he may move throughout the market. Inside the market, wages, working conditions, and job requirements are equalized, and the worker has an unusual knowledge of conditions and job opportunities. Sometimes worker performance is standardized also,[9] so that no employer need prefer any worker any more than any worker need prefer any employer. Though the men within the market are equal with each other, they are unequal with others outside the market. A little equalitarian island has been created in the midst of a sea of inequality.

Movement of workers is vitally affected. Occupational identification is unchanging and, largely because of this, other types of movement are encouraged—from one plant to another and even one industry or one locality to another. Since some fluidity is necessary in a progressive society, a tight tie to occupation forces a looser tie to employer, industry, and locality. Movement is primarily horizontal in the craft market. The worker gets his security not from the individual employer but from his skill, the competitive supply of which is controlled by his union; and he is known as a carpenter and not as an employee of a certain company. Just as the worker is free to move from employer to employer, so also are employers free to encourage such movement. "Gentlemen's agreements" against "pirating" are not the mark of the craft trades.

---

[7] Thus the "membership function" of the union, because of its restrictive preferences, may lie to the left of the "market-supply function." (See John T. Dunlop, *Wage Determination under Trade Unions,* New York: Macmillan, 1944, p. 33.) The employer may also, however, because of his preferences, draw from less than the total supply of efficient workers potentially available to him.

[8] The classic discussion of apprenticeship, as of other union rules, is by Sumner H. Slichter, *Union Policies and Industrial Management* (Washington, D.C.: Brookings Institution, 1941).

[9] When it is not standardized, competition among workers is by degree of skill. The more skilled workers are in greater demand.

Ejection from the market is controlled by the union. An employer can discharge a man from a specific job but not from the market. Few discharge grievances are filed in craft markets because the man gets his security from union control of the market and not from the employer. The union, however, may eject a man, but its reasons are not normally the same as those actuating employers. Political sins are given a higher order of value as compared with the economic sins which an employer is more apt to punish. Union ejections, which are infrequent, are not so subject to appeal to third parties as are employer discharges. . . .

Private property. In the industrial enterprise, the central rule is to each man one job and to each job one man. The typical market consists of one job for which one man is available. This is an exaggerated description of the average situation, for ability usually counts as well as seniority, but since the trend is toward strict seniority provisions it may stand as a statement of the central tendency. The man on the job (given good behavior) is the only man eligible for it, and when he leaves the next man on the seniority list (given minimum ability to perform the task) is the only eligible candidate. The market has been reduced to the irreducible minimum.

The production contract does not define the occupation. It sets forth the plant or company or industry. The plant or company or industry is the market. New workers are hired by the company,[10] not the union, but the union may impose its scale of preferences on the employer. It may, for example, refuse to accept Negroes or it may, alternatively, prohibit the employer from discriminating against Negroes. Bargained rules, however, usually first become operative once the employee is hired. The union

then seeks to set a rising scale of jobs and a rising hierarchy of workers. As jobs open up, the workers move up in order; and as they close they move down in order. The worker temporarily laid off still holds his place on the seniority roster. For each job there is a worker and thus a whole series of submarkets where one job and one man are paired.

Two important qualifications must be entered here. First, many contracts do not provide for straight seniority but for some combination of seniority and ability. Jobs are posted and all men who claim the necessary qualifications may compete. But this is still an internal submarket to which persons outside the plant have little or no access. Second, usually there are several families of jobs—production, maintenance, sales, white-collar—each with a contact point with the outside world and with an internal hierarchy of men and jobs related to each other. These families of jobs constitute noncompeting classes within the plant.

The employer, and occasionally the union (for nonpayment of dues or some other offense against the union), can separate the man from the market, usually subject to appeal to a third party. Institutional rules, set forth in a contract, often specify the proper causes for discharge—inefficiency, insubordination, and so forth.

The worker is held within this marketing apparatus not alone by prospects of advancement within the plant. He may be tied to it by a pension plan as well. More important, perhaps, is what would happen to him if he wished to leave. First of all, he would need to quit his job before finding another one since other employers, under the customary gentlemen's agreement against pirating, would be reluctant to hire him away from his firm,[11] and, second,

---

[10] For a study of employer hiring preferences, see E. William Noland and E. Wight Bakke, *Workers Wanted* (New York: Harper, 1949).

[11] For a discussion of the importance of "gentlemen's agreements," see Charles A. Myers and W. Rupert Maclaurin, *The Movement of Factory Workers* (New York: The Technology Press and John Wiley & Sons, 1943), p. 39.

in most cases, he would need to start again at the bottom of the seniority ladder in some other plant with lower status and income.

Movement, as in the craft case, is affected, but in a reverse fashion. Movement to another employer is greatly discouraged but change of occupation is almost automatic.[12] The important market for the worker is the internal plant market with its many submarkets spelled out in great detail. Movement is vertical in the plant instead of horizontal as in the craft market; and workers fight over seniority rights instead of unions over craft jurisdictions. The "haves" are separated from the "have-nots" not by a union card, but by a place on the seniority roster. When the "haves" compete among themselves, it is more in relation to the accumulation of seniority than in relation to the possession of skill.

Governmental policy supports both the communal-ownership and the private-property systems. Apprenticeship programs bolster the former; unemployment compensation rules, since they do not require an employee to leave his accustomed occupation or place of residence to accept work as a condition for the receipt of benefits, help hold workers available for openings in the same craft[13] or the same plant. These rules accept worker attachment to craft and to employer,[14] and support a pool of workers in slack times into which the union or employer can dip.

[12] Most labor market studies find the worker's chief attachment is to his occupation, yet the essence of the seniority approach is to create an employee largely devoid of narrow occupational attachment.

[13] In some states, unemployed workers report to the union hiring hall to demonstrate their availability for work rather than to the employment service.

[14] A study in Nashua, New Hampshire, found, however, that many workers took lower-paid jobs in preference to staying on unemployment compensation. But this was a situation where a large plant had ceased operation and would not reopen. (Charles A. Myers and George P. Shultz, *Dynamics of a Labor Market*, New York: Prentice-Hall, 1951, p. 100.)

Neither the craft nor the industrial institutional rules are completely new departures. Even without formal contracts, the craft worker holds to his craft, and the industrial worker to his plant. Employers hired craft workers for craft jobs and promoted from within before closed shops and seniority clauses tightened the rules. The institutional rules, however, do match men and jobs more precisely in the craft case, and the man and the job in the industrial case, than was done informally before their introduction.[15]

INSTITUTIONAL LABOR MARKETS IN OPERATION

Ports of entry. Not all jobs are open at all times to all bidders except in the structureless market. Even in the absence of institutional rules, most employers consider a job not open for bid so long as the incumbent fills it satisfactorily; and employers generally prefer to promote from within to canvassing the outside market. Institutional rules, however, set sharper boundaries between the "internal" and "external" markets and define more precisely the points of entrance.[16] In the craft case, the

[15] The case of the operating crafts in the railroad system is an interesting one, for it has elements of both the craft and industrial patterns. Normally, craft workers can obtain transfer cards, but production workers cannot transfer seniority from one plant to another. On the railroads, seniority rights are rigidly defined but employees do have the right to take their seniority to another location and "bump" less senior men there.

[16] Labor markets are of two broad types: (1) the structureless and (2) the structured. In the structureless market, there is no attachment except the wage between the worker and the employer. No worker has any claim on any job and no employer has any hold on any man. Structure enters the market when different treatment is accorded to the "ins" and to the "outs." In the structured market there always exists (1) the internal market and (2) the external market. The internal market may be the

internal market is the area covered by the jurisdiction of the local union, and in the industrial case it is the individual plant. The port of entry in the former instance is the union office, and union membership (achieved through apprenticeship, transfer, or application) provides access to all the jobs on the inside. In the latter case, there are usually several ports of entry (each reached through the company personnel office)—common labor for production workers, lower clerical occupations for the white-collar workers, and junior posts for sales and executive personnel, among others—although if qualified candidates are not available almost any job on an *ad hoc* basis may be opened to outsiders.[17] The external market is the totality of the labor force outside this one market or submarket, or at least that part of it which potentially might like to gain entry.

Thus the internal market has points of contact with the external market rather than interconnections all along the line-up of jobs. Workers inside the market, though they may compete with each other in a limited way, are not in direct competition with persons outside. Outside workers compete directly with each other, not with the inside workers, to gain admittance.

At these ports of entry, the individuals are selected who may enter. Employers have their hiring preferences which are usually dominant when it comes to hiring into the plant, although unions can and do affect these preferences; and the unions have theirs[18] which determine who gains access to the craft, although employers can and do affect them also.

The process of selection is also the process of rejection. Decisions are made in favor of certain individuals but at the same time against others. The individuals and groups which control these ports of entry greatly affect the distribution of opportunities in economic society. The rules that they follow determine how equitably opportunity is spread and the characteristics for which men are rewarded and for which they are penalized. The controlling individuals and groups may and do choose between prospective efficiency and prospective social acceptability. Since labor resources are being distributed, as well as individual opportunities, the comparative emphasis on efficiency and on acceptability affects the productivity of the economic system. When men fail to find jobs, it may be because there are not enough jobs to go around, or because they do not know about the jobs which do exist or do not think such jobs fit their expectations, or because they do not meet the specifications set by employers and unions. In the last case, as the specifications become more formal and cover more jobs, determination of the specifications becomes of

---

plant or the craft group, and preferment within it may be based on prejudice or merit or equality of opportunity or seniority or some combination of these. The external market consists of clusters of workers actively or passively available for new jobs lying within some meaningful geographical and occupational boundaries, and of the port or ports of entry which are open or are potentially open to them. It may happen that some such markets have only one port of entry, but this can hardly be the standard case as Northrup and Reynolds state (Northrup, *Economics of Labor and Industrial Relations*, p. 265, and Reynolds, *The Structure of Labor Markets*, p. 42). They may be right where certain large manufacturing plants are involved, but more commonly such a cluster of workers will face several ports of entry. The extreme cases would be (*a*) one worker facing one port of entry and (*b*) large numbers of workers facing a large number of ports of entry. The more structured the market, the more precise will be the rules on allocation of opportunity within the internal market and the fewer will be the ports of entry and the more rigid will be the requirements for admission. Institutional rules do not usually introduce structure into a market—it often arises from the individual preferences of workers and employers—but they uniformly add to it.

[17]Thus there are more ports of entry in a period of prosperity than in a period of depression.

[18]For a discussion of union preferences, see Clyde Summers, "Admission Policies of Labor Unions," *Quarterly Journal of Economics*, Nov. 1946.

increasing concern to persons in the external market who are universally unrepresented in the councils which set the specifications. For society to remain free and open, many ports of entry should exist and the immigration barriers should not hold outside the able and the willing. . . .

All societies are stratified to a degree, although the degrees vary enormously, and a key element in any society is the character and the intensity of stratification. For our purposes here we shall designate three systems of organization: the "open," the "guild," and the "manorial." The pre-Cairnes classical version of the labor market was of the truly open type—all workers competed for all jobs all of the time. The guild system stratifies the labor force horizontally. Walter Galenson has described such a "closed labor market" under the control of craft unions as it operates in Denmark.[19] The manorial system places its emphasis not on skill but on attachment to the place of work and thus on vertical stratification. The industrial worker may demonstrate (albeit for somewhat different reasons) the same perpetual adherence to the plant as the serf did to the soil of the estate, although he does have opportunities for upward movement unknown to the serf.

The institutional rules we have been discussing move the labor force farther away from the open system of the classical economists which never, however, was as open as they thought it was or hoped it might be. But as it moves toward the guild and manorial systems, which will predominate? For they follow quite different principles of societal organization. The conflict in the United States evidences itself in the conflict between craft and industrial unions over the representation of skilled workers in industrial plants, in the effort of skilled workers in such plants to have their own job families and seniority lists, in the insistence of craft workers that their wages follow the market rather than the dictates of a job evaluation plan dedicated to internal consistency. In Denmark, the guild system is dominant; in Germany, with all the paternalistic devices of large employers and the life-long attachment of the worker to his plant, the manorial system, and this is one source of the union insistence on codirection at the plant level.

The stratification of the labor force affects the worker as citizen. Is he a free-roving mobile person ranging widely horizontally and vertically and probably having a middle-class outlook,[20] is he a carpenter, or is he a UAW-GM man? How he is located economically will affect his view of society and his personal identification with society and its constituent groups, and thus his political behavior.

Institutional rules and wage setting. "Potential mobility," Hicks noted, " is the ultimate sanction for the interrelations of wage rates."[21] Other sanctions do exist and many times are the more important, but the less the potential mobility of workers the less the economic pressures that relate wage rates to each other. Institutional rules, to the extent that they reduce mobility, also lessen the economic pressures. As we have seen, some internal markets are quite isolated from their external markets by the working of these rules, and the interrelatedness of wage rates may be traced more to political, ethical, or operational than to labor market considerations. How do

---

[19] Walter Galenson, *The Danish System of Labor Relations* (Cambridge, Mass.: Harvard University Press, 1952), pp. 195–200. See also remarks by Gladys Palmer on European labor markets in a paper presented to the Industrial Relations Research Association, May 1952.

[20] S. M. Lipset and Joan Gordon, "Mobility and Trade Union Membership," in *Class, Status and Power*, ed. R. Bendix and S. M. Lipset (Glencoe, Ill.: The Free Press, 1953), p. 498.

[21] J. R. Hicks, *The Theory of Wages* (New York: The Macmillan Co., 1935), p. 79.

the rules we have been discussing impinge on the wage-setting process?

Extensive discussions with craft union leaders and the employers dealing with them in the San Francisco Bay area indicate that these unions do not generally use their control over the supply of labor to force up wage rates. They employ it rather to adjust supply to demand once the wage has been fixed.[22] If the supply falls too far short of demand, the employers are encouraged to introduce machinery or look to another craft for workers or even to non-union men. If the supply is too great, some union members are unemployed. This is politically uncomfortable for the union leaders and may require the members to undertake some work-sharing device. Further, employers may point to this unemployed group at the next wage negotiations and the members may be less willing to support wage demands with an effective strike threat. All in all, it is better to adjust supply to demand as closely as possible. This is done by controlling the flow of new members and by issuing work permits.

In neo-classical wage theory, supply (which is assumed to be relatively fixed in the short run) and demand are the independent variables which simultaneously determine the wage and the volume of employment. The standard craft market process runs instead along these lines: (1) the wage is set by collective bargaining in response to many considerations (including economic ones) and usually for a one-year duration; (2) demand which changes constantly determines the amount of employment at the fixed rate; and (3) supply is constantly adjusted by the union to keep close

contact with the changing volume of jobs offered by the employers.[23] Control over supply is used more to preserve the integrity of the wage rate rather than to create it.[24] The wage rate determines supply more than supply the wage rate. Demand itself is subject to some control (foremen are limited in the work they may perform; one man may handle only so many machines; certain work must be reserved for a certain craft, and so forth). Demand, the wage rate, and supply all respond to more or less control by the bargaining institutions.

The production case is a different one. Industrial unions cannot control the supply of workers. Their attention is turned rather to stabilizing the demand for labor so that all workers with seniority rights may have assured employment, for example, by introducing the guaranteed wage or heavy dismissal bonuses.[25] These devices have no appeal to the craft unions. But, for the industrial union, the supply of workers with seniority rights is fixed, and this makes it more conscious of the impact of fluctuating demand. Institutional rules have two further wage results. Since seniority ties workers to the plant, the industrial union must be more concerned with the effect of a negotiated wage rate on employment. Were it not for seniority rules, wage rates probably could not have deteriorated comparatively so greatly for telegraph and railroad employees during the

---

[22] "The jobs must be rationed among the seekers for jobs. And this is the important economic function which so-called restrictive practices play." Milton Friedman, "Some Comments on the Significance of Labor Unions for Economic Policy," in *The Impact of the Union*, ed. David McCord Wright (New York: Harcourt, Brace and Co., 1951), p. 213.

[23] The supply curve may be shown as a straight line which stops at or shortly before the volume of jobs normally expected at the fixed wage rate. If demand moves to the right temporarily, the supply line can be temporarily extended by the issuance of work permits, which can be cancelled if it moves again back toward the left.

[24] This sets the craft groups apart from certain professional groups. These professional groups do not control the wage (the fee) and so they influence it by control of supply.

[25] Once the wage has been set, the craft union tries to adjust supply to demand; the industrial union, demand to supply.

past quarter of a century. The seniority tie to the industry has reduced the minimum price which would hold the workers in the industry. Industrial unions, also, are more willing than are craft unions to make exceptions to the common rate to meet the necessities of the individual company and its employees. Further, institutional rules by reducing the contact points with the external markets encourage formal or informal job evaluation plans as a means of setting rates acceptable in the internal market.

Under both systems of rules, wage rates are less effective in allocating labor (just as the movement of labor is less potent in setting wage rates) than they are in less structured labor markets.

The locus of control. This reconstitution of labor markets reflects the shift in locus of control from the individual entrepreneur to the bureaucratic manager and to the work group. And with this shift goes a change in values. The entrepreneur felt personally the pressure for efficiency and expressed personally his prejudices, sometimes quite violent, about men. The hired manager and the work group both respond more to considerations of security, of order, and of certainty—and, in the case of the craft group, of preservation of the all-around skilled worker. By making men alike and jobs alike and placing each in a certain order, decisions are more or less automatically made by the rules rather than by individual men;[26] but these rules can reflect prejudice just as men in their actions can evidence it. These prejudices may be the same (racial) or different (seniority, instead of merit), but prejudices, or perhaps

better, value judgments, they remain. The rule of law is still the rule of men—once removed.

A further shift in locus of control may lie in the future. If the laws of the private governments of industry and labor fail by too great a margin to meet the definition of welfare as conceived by the public at large, then government may enter the labor market and try to impose its set of values. For example, in Denmark there is agitation against the closed labor market; and in the United States against discriminatory practices.* The "planned labor market" may succeed the institutional market.[27]

CONCLUSION

Institutional rules in the labor market, as we have seen, establish more boundaries between labor markets and make them more specific and harder to cross. They define the points of competition, the groups which may compete, and the grounds on which they compete. The study of the import of these rules,[28] though less exciting than the examination of wage policies, is more needed. It is debatable whether wage policies of unions and employers have much impact on wage determination. It is not debatable that institutional rules in the labor market do have substantial effects on the performance of our economic system. These rules increasingly affect both the opportunities held open to workers and the contributions which they can make to the national product.

When private functional governments es-

---

[26] The rules are a method of settling the intense disputes between men over job preferment. While the rules settle the individual disputes, they are themselves subject to dispute. See, for example, Leonard R. Sayles, "Seniority: An Internal Union Problem," *Harvard Business Review*, Jan.–Feb. 1952.

Editor's note: Ten years after this was written, the Civil Rights Act of 1964 outlawed labor market discrimination on the basis of race, color, religion, sex, or national origin.

[27] See C. Kerr, "Labor Markets: Their Character and Consequences."

[28] For a list of research suggestions see Gladys L. Palmer, *Research Planning Memorandum on Labor Mobility*, Social Science Research Council, 1947.

tablish rules which so affect the unrepresented worker and the unrepresented consumer, the cry for public intervention is not long in being sounded even though it may not be very loud. Sir William Beveridge has called for "organized mobility" in the labor market,[29] as have others. This cannot be accomplished mainly as a consequence of guaranteeing full employment, as he claims, although full employment does reduce some barriers; for craft unions will want to control entrance to the craft, and industrial unions to provide for seniority rights,

regardless of how full employment may be. Nor may the market be made much more fluid by other governmental actions. Seniority rules probably restrict the freedom of the worker and retard his efficiency more than the craft rules which are the customary target of criticism, yet government is not going to do much about them. At most, governmental policy can make more equitable the rules affecting entrance at those points of entry left open by the private agencies. Security will not be taken away from those who own the jobs, but non-owners can be placed on a more equal footing one against another in contesting for the vacancies.

[29] William H. Beveridge, *Full Employment in a Free Society* (New York: W. W. Norton, 1944), p. 172.

7

Theories of the Low–Wage Labor Market

Peter B. Doeringer and Michael J. Piore

Reprinted by permission of publisher from *Internal Labor Markets and Manpower Analysis* by Peter B. Doeringer and Michael J. Piore (Lexington, Mass.: Lexington Books, D.C. Heath and Company, Copyright 1971, D.C. Heath and Company).

THEORIES OF THE LOW-INCOME LABOR MARKET

There are several conceptual approaches which can be adopted for analyzing the behavior of low-income labor markets. Although the policy implications of these theories have much in common, the *emphasis* and the range of the policies are somewhat distinct. Two concepts—the *queue theory* and the *dual labor market theory*—are presented.

The Queue Theory

Stated in its simplest form, the queue theory asserts that workers are ranked according to the relationship between their potential pro-

ductivity and their wage rates. Given wage and job structures which are rigid, at least in the short run, this theory holds that employers ration the available jobs among workers according to their hiring preferences. The most preferred workers are selected from the queue first, leaving the less preferred to find work in the least desirable jobs on the fringes of the economy or to remain unemployed. Thus the number and the characteristics of the employed are determined by total labor demand, the wage structure of the economy, and relative worker productivities. By definition, therefore, the disadvantaged are located at the rear of the labor queue and have limited access to the most preferred employment opportunities.

According to the postulates of the theory,

expanding employment should encourage employers to reduce their hiring standards, to recruit from the disadvantaged labor force, and to provide additional training to raise the productivity of the disadvantaged. . . . Evidence is provided by aggregate studies of the ability of the economy to absorb and upgrade nonwhite workers during the 1960s.[1]

The Dual Labor Market Theory

This theory argues that the labor market is divided into a *primary* and a *secondary* market. Jobs in the primary market possess several of the following characteristics: high wages, good working conditions, employment stability, chances of advancement, equity, and due process in the administration of work rules. Jobs in the secondary market, in contrast, tend to have low wages and fringe benefits, poor working conditions, high labor turnover, little chance of advancement, and often arbitrary and capricious supervision. There are distinctions between workers in the two sectors which parallel those between jobs: workers in the secondary sector, relative to those in the primary sector, exhibit greater turnover, higher rates of lateness and absenteeism, more insubordination, and engage more freely in petty theft and pilferage.

Disadvantaged workers, the theory asserts, are confined to the secondary market by residence, inadequate skills, poor work histories, and discrimination. Although the interconnections between primary and secondary labor markets are seen as either weak or nonexistent on the supply side, primary employers, through devices like subcontracting and temporary employment, can convert primary employment into secondary employment. The central goal of public policy is to overcome the barriers which confine the disadvantaged to this market.

The high rates of unemployment found in poor neighborhoods and upon which the queue theory focuses are viewed in the dual market theory as frictional, reflective of the relatively high rates of labor turnover in the secondary market. Comments of both employers and workers are indicative of this instability. Employers complain of lateness, absenteeism, and turnover. Workers are especially bitter about arbitrary management, low wages, and job insecurity. As these complaints suggest, the instability appears to be a characteristic of both jobs and workers. Certain of the jobs available to the disadvantaged—jobs in hospitals and hotels, for example—although menial and low-paying, are stable, but turnover among the employees who hold them is relatively high. Other jobs—in nonunion construction, seasonal manufacturing and the like—are very unstable and are not organized to provide continuous employment. Whatever its cause, however, the amount of job changing means that any given level of employment in the secondary sector is associated with a much higher level of frictional unemployment than in the primary sector. In a sense, therefore, high levels of turnover and frictional unemployment may be taken as the salient characteristic of the secondary market.

To a certain extent, the terms *primary* and *secondary* are poorly chosen. They are conventionally associated with the literature on labor force participation in which the term "secondary" is applied to workers such as women and teenagers, who are thought to have a relatively weak attachment to the labor market. But the association with labor force participation which the terms carry is not altogether misleading. "Secondary" workers in the labor force participation literature, because their labor force attachment is low, exhibit high turnover as is characteristic of the secondary labor market. Moreover, because their job attachment is low, they are not interested in chances of advancement and are more tolerant of an unattractive work environment. Thus they tend to be employed in jobs which

[1] See Lester Thurow, *Poverty and Discrimination* (Washington, D.C.: Brookings Institution, 1969).

share many of the characteristics of those available to disadvantaged workers. This parallel is instructive. It suggests that it is not the existence of secondary employment per se that constitutes the policy problem. It may be quite appropriate for workers for whom the job itself is a secondary aspect of their lives, whose income requirements are limited (as in the case of teenagers without families), or who foresee eventual access to primary employment. It is the permanent and involuntary confinement in the secondary market of workers with major family responsibilities that poses the problem for public policy.

To the extent that the problems of the disadvantaged are characterized by a dual labor market, policy must concern itself not only with the number of jobs relative to the number of workers, but with their distribution between the primary and secondary sectors as well.

Primary Markets and Internal Labor Markets

The queue theory and the dual market theory may be reconciled by emphasizing the association between the primary sector and internal labor markets. ... The process of entry into "primary" internal markets appears to operate like an employment queue. Prospective employees are ranked in some order related to their productivity, and employers hire along the queue until they have filled their requirements.

In contrast, the secondary labor market consists of three kinds of employment situations. First, some secondary employment is completely unstructured, not belonging to any internal market. Such jobs are the polar opposite of those in internal labor markets and resemble the jobs postulated in competitive theory. Examples are casual laboring jobs in construction, domestic work, and dishwashing

in restaurants. Second, other jobs lie in what might be called "secondary" internal labor markets. These markets do possess formal internal structures, but they tend to have many entry ports, short mobility clusters, and the work is generally low paying, unpleasant, or both. Typical of such markets are blue-collar jobs in foundries, stitching and pressing jobs in apparel plants, and menial jobs in hospitals.

Finally, secondary jobs having few, if any, steps of promotion or transfer rights are occasionally found attached to internal labor markets in which the remainder of the jobs are primary. In manufacturing establishments there may be one seniority district composed of such secondary jobs, and entry standards for these jobs are considerably less stringent than for other districts in the plant. In pulp and paper mills, for example, there is the wood yard; in some machine tool companies there are foundry and laboring districts; in light manufacturing there are often temporary packaging lines. Secondary jobs in internal labor markets closely resemble the other two types of secondary jobs described above. Similar enterprises may man these same jobs on a casual basis, without providing incumbent employees any of the privileges of the internal labor market. Other enterprises may subcontract the same work to "secondary" internal labor markets. To the extent that secondary jobs in "primary" internal labor markets are governed by seniority, formal grievance procedures, job evaluation plans, and so forth, this appears to be more the product of the need for consistent internal administrative practices than the result of compelling economic and social forces.

It is characteristic of all three types of secondary employment that the forces promoting internal labor markets appear to be weaker than is the case for primary employment. Entry into secondary employment is less characterized by a queueing process than it is in primary employment. Many employers do not appear to draw distinctions between one secondary worker and another other than on the basis of sex or physical strength, and almost seem to be hiring from an undifferentiated labor pool. Since turnover is high and the right to discharge relatively unrestricted, more careful pre-employment screening is not generally warranted.

For some disadvantaged workers, movement between the secondary and the primary sectors may be described as a queue phenomenon comparable to that through which workers enter internal labor markets in the primary sector. When the labor market is loose, many workers in the secondary sector stand at the end of the queue for employment in primary internal labor markets. As the market tightens, primary employers are forced to move down this queue and eventually reach those at the back. However, other workers in the secondary sector, the most seriously disadvantaged, may not be included in the queue for entry to primary employment at all. If primary employees reach the end of the queue and refuse to expand employment further by hiring the most seriously disadvantaged, other instruments of adjustment to market conditions such as subcontracting, technological change and the like may be utilized instead. Some of these instruments, such as subcontracting and the use of "temporary" workers, may then serve to shift the expanding employment opportunities from the primary to the secondary sector.

This view which associates primary employment with internal labor markets, and secondary labor markets with a mixture of internal markets and jobs not belonging to internal markets suggests that the distinction between primary and secondary markets need not imply the strict separation of the two embodied in the concept of a dual labor market. Whether a dichotomous or a continuous model

of the labor market is appropriate is a matter of both emphasis and empirical judgment. . . .

THE DETERMINANTS OF THE SECONDARY LABOR MARKET

A number of factors operate to distinguish the secondary labor market from the primary market. These are interrelated and interact with each other in complex ways, making it difficult to analyze each factor separately without doing violence to the simultaneous nature of the processes at work. For example, the characteristics of the secondary labor market most closely related to each other are the relative instability of employment, the comparative instability and the high unemployment rates of the work force, low wages and poor chances of advancement, the paucity of training opportunities, and the arbitrariness in the administration of work rules. It is possible, however, to understand these interactions by starting with any one characteristic of the secondary market and demonstrating how the other market characteristics can be derived from it.

Employment in the secondary labor market fails to provide the kinds of job security, wages, and working conditions required to stabilize the work relationship. This may occur because employers in the secondary sector cannot economically establish internal labor market conditions which are conducive to reducing turnover or because the technical aspects of the jobs are such that the reduction of turnover has little value to the employer. Second, the attitudes and demographic traits of the secondary labor force may be such that workers place little value upon job security in particular enterprises. These two explanations, while examined separately, are not independent. Unstable and undesirable jobs may encourage workers to place low value upon job security, while a work force prone to turn-over may make the costs of its reduction prohibitively high. In this section, the implications of the forces determining internal labor markets for the analysis of the secondary labor market are examined.

The Value of the Internal Labor Market to Secondary Employees

There are groups of workers in the labor force whose economic position or phase in their life cycle leads them to place little value upon permanent employment and chances of advancement. Such is the case with certain working mothers who are preoccupied with their families. ... Another group of workers seeking similar employment are students, whose major activity is school attendance and who seek part-time work to supplement family allow-ances or school stipends. Some of these youths, in fact, may only be looking for short-duration work during summers, holidays, or simply for a couple of weeks during the term to finance a "heavy weekend." Still another group of work-ers with slight interest in security or advance-ment are moonlighters whose major concern is with the characteristics of their main job and who expect only short tenure in this secondary employment. Finally, whenever one job can be readily replaced with another yielding similar rewards, workers generally place less value on job security in particular internal markets and derive job security from the external labor market. While a portion of the instability which characterizes the secondary labor force can be understood on the basis of demographic charac-teristics, other factors—the instability of jobs, the influence of "street life," discrimination, and the like—operate on both the supply and demand sides of the market to weaken internal labor markets and to foster the secondary labor market.

The Value of Internal Labor Markets to Secondary Employers

The effect of an unstable work force. If it is assumed initially that the secondary labor market is attributable to worker characteristics, that is that workers can be divided into two groups, a group of stable workers and an un-stable group who tend to have high rates of absenteeism and frequently arrive late for work, employers can respond to that labor supply in a variety of ways. Those lucky enough to have the stable workers can simply hire a number of workers equal to the number of work stations. If employers do not differ in their needs for a stable labor force and if the employers must compete with each other in the product market, then enterprises which hire unstable workers will have to make a series of adjustments to operate effectively. Two kinds of adjustment are possible. The company can institute a "shapeup," hiring each day from a gang of workers appearing at the gate a num-ber equal to the number of its work stations. Under this arrangement, productivity per employee will be the same as that in the stable market, and the firm can afford to pay the same daily wage, *provided that the gang is al-ways large enough to fill all available jobs.* Because workers are unstable, however, the gang is likely to vary in size from day to day. The guarantee against job vacancies provided elsewhere by worker stability can only be obtained, therefore, if even on the worst day the shapeup gang is at least as large as the num-ber of jobs. This, in turn, implies that on most days the gang must be larger than the number of jobs, and unemployment among unstable workers will exceed that among stable workers.

The alternative to a "shapeup" policy is "overmanning," insuring that all work stations are covered, despite absenteeism and turnover, by maintaining a labor force substantially larger than the number of work stations. Complete insurance, however, requires that, on the average, there will be idle employees present. Thus, while productivity *per work station* is equivalent to that in firms hiring stable workers, productivity *per employee* is lower, and to induce firms to hire unstable workers the lower productivity must be compensated by lower wages.

In practice, firms hiring unstable workers will probably tend to pursue a combination of the "shapeup" and "overmanning" policies. Thus, the market with unstable workers will tend to be accompanied by both low wages and higher levels of unemployment.

The other characteristics of the secondary market can also be explained by employee instability. Because the labor force is unstable, the employer has no incentive to invest in training on the job. Indeed, he could not recoup the returns to such investment. Lacking an interest in on-the-job training, the employer is also less interested in building lines of progression which might facilitate such training or capture the training which occurs automatically. The absence of lines of progression reduces promotion opportunities within the enterprise. Indeed, given high turnover and the consequent difficulty of internal training, the employer has an incentive to minimize the skill involved in the work, utilizing as "unskilled" a technology as he can, and this further reduces training opportunities. Finally, to the extent that the labor force is unstable and turnover is high, cohesive work groups do not develop: custom is, therefore, weak, the work rules tend to be ambiguous, and there is little pressure from the labor force for their fair and equitable administration.

The effect of unstable jobs. The preceding has been developed on the assumption that it is workers who are more or less unstable, but that jobs all possess the same degree of sta-

bility. Clearly, that is not the case. Removing this assumption, and attributing all or part of the instability in the secondary labor market to the nature of jobs does not basically change the characteristics associated with it. Unstable work will continue to be found among jobs which, relative to stable employment, involve little training, small chance of advancement, and less equitable work-rule administration. Among the secondary employers who can be understood in this way are those in highly seasonal industries with short employment periods (like the construction business, or industries where demand is generally temporary). In other industries, the job itself may be stable, but the nature of the industry may make turnover relatively inexpensive. Thus it may be possible to understand the secondary character of menial jobs in hospitals by the fact that these jobs are themselves unskilled, and the industry is prevented by licensing requirements and professional attitudes from utilizing any learning that occurs on the job to upgrade low-skilled employees. Thus, either inherently unstable employment or lack of training costs will discourage employers from instituting internal labor structures which will serve to reduce turnover.

The impact of collective bargaining and trade union organization. While, to a certain extent, the development of internal labor markets may be understood as a free response of employers to the advantages which the internal market provides them, they have in many cases been forced by union pressure to provide greater job security than is otherwise to their advantage. For example, in industries where the labor force has traditionally borne heavy costs of cyclical and seasonal variability in product demand or of labor-saving technological change, rules have been introduced which considerably limit these costs. Some of them—seniority provisions, limitations on layoffs, emphasis upon promotion from within, and union control over jobs—directly created the internal labor market. Others—guaranteed annual wages, formalized work sharing arrangements, grievance procedures to limit arbitrary discharges, supplemental unemployment benefits and termination pay, pension plans, and so forth—have substantially increased the attractiveness of jobs within internal markets.

A side effect of this trend, however, has been the encouragement of some types of secondary employment, such as temporary employment, as a means of providing manning flexibility in the primary enterprise. The costs of economic instability in primary labor markets are therefore transferred to temporary jobs and to smaller nonunion internal labor markets such as job shops, which produce for the residual product market left by the larger enterprises.

Numerous examples of this process can be found. In the cyclical industries, such as steel and automobiles, strong seniority systems have reinforced natural training ladders, and income guarantees have stabilized both income and employment. Small job and specialty shops bear the brunt of the cyclical instability in these industries. In longshoring, employment guarantees, decasualization of work, and automation funds have been the culmination of this process. In some East Coast ports, decasualization has been associated with the formal recognition of a permanent pool of casual workers with little or no attachment to the industry and only residual employment rights. In major nonunion companies such as IBM and Polaroid, employer initiative has carried this logic further by providing virtual guarantees of

employment to all incumbent workers.

Grievance procedures and fringe benefits have a similar influence. Any limitation on the employer's use of layoffs or discharges to achieve efficient manning levels creates incentives to stabilize employment and a preference for stable employees. Fringe benefits such as paid vacations and holidays, severance pay, and health and retirement plans that link employer contributions to the size of the labor force, as well as to hours worked or wages paid, all discourage primary employers from adapting to absenteeism and turnover by overmanning. The replacement of piece rates by day rates has also operated to raise the costs of turnover, while increasing the incentives which encourage worker stability.

The extent of labor organization, and the concomitant influence of unions on unorganized internal labor markets, is largely determined by the size and stability of the internal labor market. Where markets are small or employment unstable, the costs of labor organization, and of maintaining organizational strength, are high relative to the membership obtained. Rather than attempting to organize the entire product market, unions frequently tolerate a small segment of enterprises paying below union standards. An illustration of this is the residential housing sector which is typically nonunion. These are often secondary employers whose output is too small, or whose efficiency is too low, to jeopardize the union rate. Thus the distinction between primary and secondary employment is similar to the distinction between employment directly or indirectly influenced by union activity, and that which is not. . . .

8

Toward a Theory of Discrimination

Kenneth Boulding

Kenneth Boulding, "Toward a Theory of Discrimination," in *Equal Employment Opportunity and the AT&T Case*, Phyllis Wallace, ed. (Cambridge, Mass.: The MIT Press, 1976).

Discrimination is a phenomenon which is so pervasive in all human societies that there is no doubt at all that it exists. It is not, however, a unitary phenomenon but a complex of a number of related forms of human behavior, and this makes it not only hard to define but frequently difficult to comprehend fully.

The history of the word itself is a strange one as it has two almost entirely opposite meanings, one very good and one very bad. On the good side, it means a correct appraisal of complex issues and valuations, as in the expression "a discriminating taste." A person who has a discriminating taste is supposed to be able to reject what is meretricious and to discount what is only superficially either attractive or repellant, and is thus able to exercise true judgment not only in matters of aesthetics but presumably in all other fields in which judgment applies. To say that a person has discriminating taste is indeed a high compliment, but like most high compliments it has a slightly ironic edge to it, implying perhaps that a person is a little too much above the common run of mankind.

At the other end of the scale the word discrimination in a bad sense means precisely the opposite of the discriminating taste, that is, a failure to make correct judgments, especially of other people. The consequence of discrimination in the bad sense, then, is illegitimate differences, that is, differences in the treatment or rewards of different individuals which are not in accord with some standard of equity. We can distinguish at least three sources of discrimination in the bad sense in which it will be used in the rest of this essay. One is the desire for monopoly power; this has been particularly stressed by Lester Thurow.[1] The second is personal prejudice, the theory of which is particularly associated with the name of Gary Becker.[2] The third is role prejudice, which is particularly significant when it comes to sex discrimination.

Any form of exercise of monopoly power implies some capacity to exclude persons from some occupation or activity. The excluded persons may be defined as those who would prefer to be in this occupation with the existing structure of rewards if they were not prevented by some essentially artificial means, usually supported or created by the people who are enjoying the benefits of the monopolized occupation. Monopoly power may be exercised in a great many ways. There may, for instance, be legal restrictions on entering into some occupation, created, for instance, by licensing or immigration restrictions, often obtained as a result of the political power and political pressures of those who are already in the occupation. There may be contractual restrictions—usually depending, of course, on a legal basis for the contract, such as trade union restrictions on entry through closed shops, restrictive hiring practices, and so on. There may also be quite informal and customary restrictions of which prejudice in terms of culture, race, class, sex, religion, or any other distinguishing feature is the most striking example. Unfortunately, any occupational group which develops prejudice is likely to be rewarded

by some rise of income as a result of monopoly power. From this point of view it does not matter in the slightest who is kept out as long as somebody is kept out. The excluded may be females, males, blacks, whites, Catholics, Jews, Protestants, tall people, short people, red-haired people, black-haired people, people with strange accents or peculiar customs. The more kinds of people excluded, indeed, the easier it is to keep people out of the occupation and the easier it is to obtain some sort of monopoly power. Often the most effective form of discrimination is familistic. In some cities I understand it is virtually impossible to become a plumber unless one has at least an uncle in the trade. At the extreme this becomes a caste system in which everyone is excluded from an occupation who cannot claim descent from somebody in it.

Monopoly discrimination need have no particular effect. It is not necessary at all to hate or even to dislike the people who are excluded. They may indeed be liked very much as long as they do not try to enter the occupation. In practice, however, exclusion frequently goes along with dislike simply because this is the easiest way to justify it. Excuses are nearly always more important than reasons, especially when the reasons, like the desire for monopoly power, are a little shady and hard to justify in strictly ethical terms. Under these circumstances, excuses are multiplied, and the simplest excuse is that the excluded party is in some way inferior, undesirable, immoral, dirty, uncouth, or in general someone with whom one would not wish to associate. Monopoly discrimination, therefore, frequently has a tendency to be reinforced by personal prejudice, but the two sources of discrimination should be kept intellectually distinct.

Personal prejudice, which is the second principal source of discrimination, may arise, as we have seen, out of the attempt to excuse monopoly power. Nevertheless, it has other sources and it has a certain independence of

[1] Lester C. Thurow, *Poverty and Discrimination* (Washington, D.C.: Brookings Institution, 1969).

[2] Gary S. Becker, *The Economics of Discrimination,* 2nd ed. (Chicago: University of Chicago Press, 1971).

its own as a source of discrimination related to "taste." The taste for discrimination may, as Gary Becker has pointed out, actually result in a diminution of the income of those who practice the discrimination. In this sense it may have quite opposite effects from the exercise of monopoly power. The taste for discrimination, however, has a number of different origins and may take several forms. Its most defensible form is a simple taste for homogeneity in surroundings and associates. There may be quite real costs of heterogeneity in terms of information and learning costs in dealing with widely different varieties of persons and circumstances. Homogeneous environments are easier to adapt to and to behave in than heterogeneous environments. The taste for homogeneity, therefore, cannot be wholly condemned as irrational, although like many other tastes it often becomes addictive, and then it can be damaging to all parties.

There are difficult questions of social ethics involved here. If people of the same race have a taste for being together, at what point does this become illegitimate? We have a similar problem in the case of sex. The taste for sexual segregation may be quite strong, as is often observed at parties, where the men gather at one end of the room and women at the other. Similarly, there may be tastes for men's colleges and women's colleges, men's drinking clubs and women's sewing circles. At what point these become illegitimate is also hard to say. It seems clear that the extremes are worse than the middle. Something would be lost if no gathering were ever allowed to take place which did not contain both sexes, and even more would be lost if there were no gatherings at which the sexes mingled on equal terms. In the middle, however, is the famous Aristotelian mean—though where it lies is a matter of judgment which is hard to decide.

We have similar problems in educational prejudice. Educated people and professional people tend to gather together; so do the uneducated. Homosexuals segregate themselves and one would certainly hesitate to argue that every homosexual gathering should have an appropriate quota of heterosexuals. It is clear that this is an area where there are no simple rules. It is easy to postulate that there are optimum structures of heterogeneity and homogeneity. The principle of self-determination in the international system, for instance, suggests that within political units a certain amount of homogeneity is a positive good. On the other hand too much homogeneity leads to dullness and stagnation and a lack of human development and learning. Where the optimum in this case lies, however, is clearly beyond the powers of operations research or even of the present state of human wisdom.

Just as the exercise of monopoly power does not necessarily involve any distaste for the excluded, so the exercise of taste for homogeneity does not necessarily imply a distaste for the "other." We see this, indeed, in the ideology of toleration, which indeed can easily put a positive value on variety so that we can actually rejoice in the contemplation of suitably separated differences. We see this especially in the United States in the ideology of religious toleration: "You go to your church and I'll go to my church and we'll walk along the road together." This treats religion as a taste rather than as a burning conviction of the truth, though this raises problems of religious identity. Nevertheless, when, as in the past, burning convictions have often led to the burning of people, the philosophy of mutual toleration seems to have much to recommend it, even if it leads to some loss in intensity. A similar toleration for cultural and linguistic separation is even easier to justify. One may contemplate the rich variety of human languages and cultures with great satisfaction, especially as long as one does not have to go outside one's own language and cultural group. The concern for richness and variety of species which leads us to seek to protect the whooping crane and the whale from extinction should also apply to the Amish, the Hari Krishnas, the Fijians, and the Hungarians, without any of which the whole world would surely be poorer.

However the record of history is all too grim: differences often lead not to toleration and joy in the contemplation of variety but to mutual distrust and hatred, and situations in which everybody becomes worse off. The separation of the human race into different nations, classes, cultures, linguistic groups, races, and so on has had a strong tendency to lead to disruptive conflict which has been strongly adverse to human welfare and development. The control of these conflict processes is indeed one of the high priorities of the human race. Indeed, they threaten to destroy the human race altogether if they are not controlled. The study of these processes would carry us far beyond the scope of this book. One can suggest, however, that a good deal depends on the nature of the identity of the persons and communities involved. Where the basic identity is a "positive identity" built around certain positive values in the culture and the person, it is much less likely to result in destructive conflict. When we have a "negative identity" built around "not being" the enemy, conflict easily becomes pathological. One sees this, for instance, in the extraordinary contrast in regard to religious conflict between Northern Ireland and the Republic of Ireland. In the north of Ireland Protestants organize their identity about not being Catholic and Catholics about not being Protestant, no doubt as a result of a long, unfortunate history of conquest, displacement, and settlement. By contrast, in the south of Ireland with a somewhat different, though no less unhappy history, Protestants and Catholics have a more positive identity and hence do not feel the acute need for conflict. There is something indeed in the "I'm OK, you're OK" doctrine. An accepting attitude toward differences certainly leads to the diminution of pathological conflicts.

A third source of personal prejudice is false generalizations which lead to a failure to discriminate in the good sense of the word. Generalizations of the form "all A are B" are very dangerous, because usually only some A are B. If we dislike B, perhaps for legitimate reasons, then if we make the false generalization that all A are B we would dislike all A, whereas we should only dislike some. This might be described as a "cue problem." Our impressions and judgments about the world are inevitably derived from cues, all of which are more or less misleading. There may indeed be some rational grounds for believing false generalizations and forming images with imperfect cues if the cost of improving the generalizations is too great. This may be so in the case of highly complex realities, where ignorance, if not bliss, is at least kept cheap. This problem emerges very clearly in the assessment of persons, each of whom is an extremely complex reality. It becomes particularly acute in hiring practices. Judgments as to whether individuals are suited for particular jobs are often made on the seemingly most irrelevant cues such as a facial expression, body posture, trace of accent, and, for all we know, even unconscious perceptions of body odor, simply because the reality about any individual is so complex that it is almost impossible to discover. Not even psychological tests and measurements have done much to alleviate this problem. It may be indeed that job and career discrimination against people with funny faces is more severe and harder to deal with than discrimination against people of different races.

One has an uncomfortable feeling sometimes that the really important categories of humankind are quite unidentifiable, and that the most intractable discrimination is against those people who have the bad luck to fall into one or other of these unidentifiable categories.

A corollary of this proposition, however, is that the obvious categories of race, sex, class, and culture are often not the significant ones from the point of view of real abilities. In trying to eliminate these false forms of discrimination, then, what we are really trying to do is to improve the "cue process" by which images of people, especially, are derived from fragmentary and imperfect cues. By eliminating some of the false cues, at least we have some hope of improving judgment in regard to the really significant cues.

A third source of discrimination may be called role prejudice. This is similar in some respects to personal prejudice, but it is sufficiently different to deserve being placed in a separate category. Role prejudice involves processes in the upbringing of children, and even the training of adults, which predispose them to certain skills and roles and exclude them from others, even though these predispositions have no foundation in genetic differences. Thus, the adult brought up under a system of role prejudice may be actually unfitted for certain roles because of the processes of nurture, education, and training, so that denying access to such roles would not involve simple personal prejudice but would be a mere recognition of the facts of the distribution of skill and ability as they exist at the moment. Personal prejudice involves denying people opportunities for roles for which they are in fact fitted at the present time. Role prejudice involves the unfitting of persons for certain roles because of their life experience and not because of any genetic differences.

Role prejudice may be present in all forms of discrimination. In class discrimination, for instance, even though the genetic differences between the upper and the lower class may be very small, the rearing practices of the lower class are designed to produce individuals who will fit into it and who will not, therefore, have the skills of the upper class. A caste society is

perhaps the extreme form of role prejudice. All the educational influences on individuals compel them to conform to the practices and occupations of the caste. Class differs from caste only in the degree of mobility; the difference may not be very great. Thus, we see role prejudice as one of the aspects of inheritance through the family. Children are much more likely to be culturally similar to their parents than they are to anybody else.

When some very obvious characteristic of the person such as skin color or sex becomes the basis of what is essentially a class structure, then the role prejudice which is characteristic of class structures likewise becomes identified with these other distinguishing characteristics. What we call "race" is mainly a combination of varying degrees of caste and class, for the genetic differences between the races are really much smaller, for instance, than the genetic differences between the sexes. Men are genetically far more different from women in general than blacks in general are from whites. Both race and sex, however, are strongly associated with role prejudice. Sex discrimination is undoubtedly the most flagrant case of it. All societies tend to form stereotyped roles for men and women. Men are supposed to be "masculine" and women are supposed to be "feminine," although the content of these roles differs very widely from society to society, suggesting that they are determined in large part at any rate by cultural rather than by genetic inheritance.

Some genetic differences between men and women are, of course, important in determining role structures and the comparative advantages of the two sexes in different roles. Men tend to have more muscular strength than women, though there is a very wide overlap between the weakest man and the strongest woman. Women have an overwhelming comparative advantage in having babies and providing them with milk, and this no doubt is the origin of the primitive division of labor between men and women. In a developed society, however, women do not have to spend very much time on child rearing by comparison with what they have to do in primitive societies with high infant mortality. And the combination of the virtual abolition of infant mortality together with the technical revolution in the household, largely as a result of electrical appliances, has enormously diminished the need for relative difference in role structures between men and women.

Role prejudice in regard to sex may be compared with role prejudice between the left- and right-handed.[3] Genetic factors produce populations in which a certain percentage of the people are strongly left-handed, physiologically, and perhaps a somewhat larger percentage are strongly right-handed, but in which most of us occupy the middle ground so that we could easily learn to be ambidextrous. Social pressures, however, force most people in most societies into being right-handed and indeed actually discriminate against the left-handed. The emancipation of the left-handed is a phenomenon by no means dissimilar to the emancipation of women in that it represents the correction of fallacies of social learning. There has been strong tendency in many societies, indeed in almost all societies, to overgeneralize the genetic predominance of right-handedness into the false generalization that right-handedness is "right" (how significant the language is at this point!) and that left-

handedness is "wrong." Truer appreciation of reality can undo the damage caused by this false generalization and release resources for human betterment.

Prejudice in all forms can be regarded as a kind of "mine," a natural resource which can be mined or used up by suitable activity in the production of better states of the world. Alternatively it can be thought of as a burden which prevents the human race from achieving levels of satisfaction which are feasible for it. Like any other mine, however, it has to be discovered and identified before it can be utilized through its diminution. Just what the optimum degree of role differentiation is we cannot easily determine. There is certainly a case for some role differentiation between the sexes, a very much poorer case or no case at all for role differentiation between the races and classes. Where indeed there is a waste of human resources, this is clear evidence of prejudice that could be "mined," that is, diminished to the benefit of all. Furthermore, there is a strong case for having prejudice against prejudice. The dynamics of human learning almost ensures that we will have too much prejudice rather than too little, just as we tend to learn to have too much hostility and malevolence. Techniques, however, by which prejudice can be diminished have to be learned, just as the techniques of mining have to be learned, and it is clear that we still have a great deal of learning to do. Research in prejudice reduction indeed is likely to be one of the most profitable of intellectual activities, parallel in many ways to the research in the discovery and utilization of natural resources.

[3] See Rodney Needham, ed., *Right and Left: Essays on Dual Symbolic Classification* (Chicago: University of Chicago Press, 1973).

9

The Overeducated American

Richard B. Freeman

Richard B. Freeman, *The Overeducated American* (New York: Academic Press, Inc., 1976).

... I have stressed the economic aspects of college education—the return to college in the form of salaries and jobs, and the behavioral response of individuals to this return. If the analysis and forecasts are reasonably on target, the decade of the 1970s will prove to be a significant turning point in the job market for the highly educated. The relation between education and the economy will be different in the future than in the past, with ramifications for the overall functioning of the society.... [T]he major findings ... are briefly summarized [here] and the potential broad societal implications of the changing economic value of higher education are considered, albeit speculatively.

SUMMARY OF FINDINGS

[My] purpose ... has been threefold: to analyze the dimensions of the new depression in the college job market; to explain the reasons for the collapse of the market and the differential experience of various professions and groups; and to peer, cautiously, into the future. [The] major findings can be summarized briefly:

1. The college job market underwent an unprecedented downturn at the outset of the 1970s, with young graduates just beginning their careers most severely affected. Real and relative earnings of graduates dropped, employment prospects and occupational attainment deter-

iorated, and large numbers were forced into occupations normally viewed as being below the college level. For the first time in recent history, the economic value of an investment in college education fell, though with considerable variation among professions and groups.

2. In response to the depressed market, the proportion of young men enrolling in college dropped substantially, reversing the long-term upward trend in educational attainment. The decline in enrollments relative to the population of eligibles occurred in all social strata but was most marked among the lower middle class. However, the enrollment of black youngsters, whose relative position in the college job market improved and the enrollment of women, whose position improved in some respects and worsened in others, did not decline but rather leveled off. At the graduate level, there was also a fall in the proportion of the relevant group enrolled, particularly for degrees in the sciences.

3. Student career decisions were substantially altered by the changing economic fortunes of the various high-level occupations. Where the market was extraordinarily depressed, as in physics, enrollments dropped precipitously; while, in occupations that fared relatively well, applications (as in medicine) or enrollments (as in law through the early 1970s, engineering in the early 1970s, and business administration) rose. Overall, the shift was from the academic and scientific to the traditional professional and business-oriented specialties.

4. Despite the market downturn, black college graduates fared reasonably well—the result of affirmative action and related antidiscriminatory activity. Corporations, which first began to recruit on black college campuses in the mid-1960s, continued seeking out and hiring black graduates, particularly in engineering, accounting, and the technical fields. Starting black graduates obtained roughly the same salaries as whites and, in response to new opportunities, moved increasingly out of traditional professional services into management and business-oriented majors.

The rate of return for blacks investing in undergraduate and graduate education rose to exceed those for whites.

5. The job market for women graduates did not deteriorate significantly, save in the case of teachers. The salaries of female graduates in business and the employment of women in traditionally male occupations increased in the late 1960s and early 1970s, while the overall premium for female college graduates fell only slightly. As a result, the proportion of college students and graduates who were women rose, and an increasing number of them elected to enter fields dominated by men. Sizable differences between male and female college earnings and occupational attainment remain, however. The future economic position of college women will depend on the net effect of declines in demand for schoolteachers and increases in demand for women in traditionally male areas. Which of these forces will dominate is not clear.

6. Four major factors determine the dynamic functioning of the college job market: the responsive supply behavior of the young; the long working life of graduates, which makes total supply relatively fixed in the short run; the concentration of graduates in certain sectors of the economy and moderate substitutability between college-trained and other workers; and the cobweb feedback system, which leads to recurrent market oscillations, as high salaries and good job opportunities induce many students into fields, producing a flood of graduates 2 to 5 years later, and, all else the same, a relative surplus that in turn reduces salaries and employment opportunities, depressing enrollments, and so on.

7. The downturn of the 1970s was caused by slackened growth of demand, due to reduced expansion of industries that employ many college-trained workers, and continued increases in supply. In education, a critical employment sector, the number of schoolchildren began to fall, lessening the demand for teachers. In many high-technology industries, the reduction of federal R&D and defense

spending and of the space program led to a contraction of employment relative to total employment in the economy. On the supply side, there was a sizable increase in the number of graduates seeking work, as the large cohorts of the post-World War II baby boom reached the labor market, their entry having been delayed by the tendency to invest in postgraduate training. Because the number of young persons in college far exceeds the number of persons of retirement ages with college training, relative supply will continue to increase in the 1980s, despite the fall in the fraction enrolled.

8. The decline in the college market was most severe in the teaching and research professions, and least in business-oriented specialties, reversing the pattern of the 1960s. Elementary and high school teaching was one of the hardest hit professions, and it is likely to continue to suffer from a weak job market through the mid-1980s. Specialists with doctoral degrees also experienced an extreme market downturn, substantially cutting the pecuniary value of the degree. Within the research and teaching areas, however, the market experiences of different professions varied greatly: the economic position of physicists plummeted, that of biologists did not; new high school teachers in English and in foreign languages had smaller chances of obtaining jobs than those in mathematics. In response to the job market, proportionally fewer students elected academic fields in the mid-1970s. As for the future, the depressed market is likely to be maintained in most academic areas, with some of the fields that still had strong markets in the mid-1970s experiencing declines at the turn of the decade. In others, however, such as physics, market equilibrium may be overshot, generating reversals of current relative surpluses.

9. By contrast, graduates with degrees in business specialties, including those in accounting and business administration especially at the master's level, in medicine, and in engineering fared reasonably well in the falling job market. These fields had not expanded so rapidly in the boom-

ing sixties, nor were they heavily dependent on education and research spending (save for engineering). In some, cyclical "cobweb" adjustments caused distinct market conditions. Engineering, for example, enjoyed a cobweb upsurge in the mid-1970s, which strengthened the economic position of new engineers relative to other graduates. Law, on the other hand, underwent a similar boom at the turn of the decade and began a downswing in the mid-1970s. As more students switch to business and engineering, however, the decline in the market will be diffused more evenly among college fields.

10. Federal policies exacerbated rather than ameliorated both cobweb and longer-run adjustment problems. Federal R&D spending, which increased greatly in the early and middle 1960s and fell relative to GNP thereafter, was a major contributor to the sixties boom and seventies bust. Fellowships and scholarships encouraged "overproduction" of master's and doctoral graduates in the 1960s and discouraged enrollment in the 1970s. The high variability of federal spending and the demand for high-level manpower, often responding to short-term crises, was the "squeaky wheel" in the market, inducing cyclical ups and downs and the uneven production of graduates.

11. While the income and occupational attainment of college graduates began falling in the 1970s, college-trained workers continued to have higher earnings and better prospects than their high school peers. Indeed, in some white-collar jobs, as in the sales, managerial, and clerical areas, the relative surplus of college-trained workers appears to have made it more difficult for high school workers to obtain positions. Moreover, there is no indiction that less value is being placed on the other, less tangible, rewards of a college education. The continued, though diminished, value of the degree in the job market and the continued nonpecuniary rewards suggest that, for many, college remains a good investment.

12. Forecasts of the state of the college labor

market using the recursive adjustment model indicate that the economic position of new bachelor's men is likely to remain depressed through the end of the 1970s, will improve moderately in the early 1980s and rapidly in the late 1980s, though not to the boom conditions of the 1960s. The major force improving the market will be a reduced supply of new baccalaureates. The proportion of young men choosing college will stabilize in the mid-1970s, after having fallen from the peak of the late 1960s, and rise in the 1980s in response to the market upturn. Because the population of college age will be small in the 1980s, however, total enrollments will still drop, which will act to depress the market for Ph.D. and master's graduates until the late 1980s.

While the position of new graduates will improve, that of older graduates, including the classes of the 1970s, may not. The supply of all graduates will grow relative to the working age population until the end of the 1990s, so that supply pressures for reduced economic rewards to the college trained will remain, despite smaller numbers of new graduates. Throughout the period, however, various professions and social groups are likely, as in the past, to fare very differently in the job market, with some graduates doing relatively well and others relatively poorly. Overall, the period of severe "overeducation" is likely to last for about a decade, to be followed by a period of market balance at a lower plateau. In contrast to the past, higher education will be a "marginal" investment, and not a sure "guarantee" to relatively high salaries and occupational standing.

SPECULATIONS ABOUT SOCIAL IMPLICATIONS

What are the likely impacts of the ongoing and forecasted changes in the economic value of college education on a society in which college has traditionally been a major route to economic progress and social mobility? How will a society in which higher education has a smaller economic payoff, in which further expansion of college training reduces economic rewards, and in which colleges and universities are no longer a leading growth sector function in comparison to societies where education is a much scarcer resource? What actions may improve the position of the overeducated American?

The declining economic value of education can be expected to have direct and indirect impacts on the functioning of the economy and the social system. It is likely to alter the degree and form of social mobility, the distribution of income, the rate of economic growth, and the link between schooling and work. In addition, the spirit or ethos of the "overeducated society" may differ significantly from that of the recent past.

Social Mobility and Income Distribution

Paradoxically, perhaps, the fall in the economic value of college training is likely to have opposite effects on the extent of social mobility and the distribution of incomes. With respect to mobility, the drop in the material rewards to education and stabilization in the fraction of persons choosing the investment implies the end of education as a means of upward mobility in society as a whole, though some groups, such as blacks, many continue to advance via schooling. However, the decline in mobility via education does not mean that the social structure will become more rigidly stratified. Assuming that financial access to colleges and universities remains open to those from poorer backgrounds, there will continue to be movement up the socioeconomic ladder by the school route, accompanied, however, by some intergenerational downward mobility. For the first time in American history non-negligible numbers of young persons will obtain less education than their parents.

In response to the decline in the value of education, individuals and society are likely to search for alternative routes of economic advancement. Training and promotion policies within firms may attain greater importance than in the past. Competition for income and status may come to center more on place of employment and the job market than on the school system.

The reduced role of schooling in social mobility could, depending on the type and efficacy of alternative routes of upward movement, lead to greater class consciousness and conflict. With the potentiality of exiting from one social stratum to another by formal education reduced, individuals may accord greater "loyalty" to their social group. The importance of college as a social melting pot, yielding contacts and friendships across groups, will be diminished. More importantly, if, as some believe, education has served as a "safety valve," helping to maintain social stability in the same manner as was alleged of the frontier years ago, the narrowing of the valve may diminish an important force for stability. The discontent of individuals and families experiencing downward generational mobility and of those from the lower strata who looked upon schooling as their "ticket to the middle class" could have destabilizing political consequences.[1]

At the same time, however, income distribution is likely to become more egalitarian as a result of the relative surplus of the educated. With the number of persons having various levels of education fixed, reductions in the economic value of higher education necessarily creates more equality in labor incomes. With the number going to college falling, relative to current levels, while the total number of graduates continues to increase, the situation

is more complex, because income distribution depends not only on wage differentials but on the number of persons in various categories. While detailed calculations are needed to measure the impact, inequality in incomes among workers is likely to diminish. This could ameliorate or counterbalance the deleterious effects of the reduction in mobility.

Economic Growth

Unless new areas of investment are found to replace education, the growth rate of the economy will slacken in the period of over-education. In the context of standard growth accounting, which makes the effect on growth of a factor depend on its share of income and rate of change, the lower education premium and diminished flow of new college graduates implies a smaller increase in the share of the educated, both in income and in the work force, than in the recent past. As a result, the once sizable contribution of schooling to increases in income per head—estimated to be from one-quarter to one-third of total growth—will drop greatly.[2]

Schooling and Work

The deterioration in job opportunities and occupational attainment for over a decade will create a sizable group of dissatisfied educated workers whose position will be incommensurate with their training and aspirations.

---

[1] The "exit-loyalty" terminology is taken from A. Hirschman, *Exit, Voice, and Loyalty* (Cambridge, Mass.: Harvard University Press, 1970).

[2] Denison's calculations provide a variety of possible estimates, depending on time period and treatment of various factors. The increase in national income per person with economies of scale isolated and allocated among other sources was 1.54% in 1929-1969 and 1.18% in 1929-1948. Education improved labor inputs by 0.41% in the former and 0.40% in the latter, giving relative contributions of 27% and 34% in the two periods, providing the bounds given in the text. See E. Denison, *Accounting for United States Economics Growth 1929-1969* (Washington, D.C.: The Brookings Institution), Table 9-7, p. 136.

The way in which they adjust to the new status of the educated and the way in which society, particularly employers, adjust to their position will be important factors in the social fabric of society. Lacking, in a weak market, the "exit" option of quitting for better jobs, some of the highly educated in non-college-level jobs may resort to political protest and related modes of expressing discontent. Many, however, may come to accept a sharp break between schooling and work, viewing their education more as a consumption than as an investment activity. They will relinquish the belief that college has clearcut vocational consequences and seek satisfaction from its nonoccupational benefits. The extent to which those with dashed aspirations accept the new reality or seek to change it may turn out to be an important element in the political future.

On the job side, employers can be expected to alter the organization of work to use the newly available educated workers most efficiently. Changes in the nature of work could reduce the division between blue-collar and white-collar workers, permitting greater upward mobility at work places and greater autonomy and responsibility in nonprofessional, nonmanagerial jobs. It could also, however, lead many to concentrate on nonwork leisure activities, with jobs reorganized to reduce their "disutility" by requiring less time, rather than to reduce undesirable features. Traditional promotion patterns and supervisory responsibilities are likely to come under attack and possibly be changed. With declining numbers of young college workers in some fields, the normal transition from professional to administrative or managerial work over the life cycle may be difficult. There will, after all, be fewer young graduates to supervise. More importantly, the young whose promotion and career paths are blocked by older persons in a declining market are likely to be discontented, creating potential intergenerational conflicts at the work place.

A major burden is going to be placed on employers to adjust to the new availability of college graduates for jobs that have traditionally been held by the less educated and to the distorted age structure of the college work force.

HIGHER EDUCATION

Colleges and universities will face especially severe pressures and problems in the era of overeducation, as they switch from a growing to a declining economic setting. While my analysis foresees a smoother, more gradual decline in enrollment than standard forecasts, as a result of responsive supply behavior, the situation will still be difficult. Some institutions will close or be absorbed by stronger schools. New sources of students will be sought and offerings changed to increase demand. Some institutions are likely to seek additional older persons by focusing on retraining and vocational programs, possibly mimicking for-profit proprietary schools, which have long sought to attract part-time older students by tailoring programs to their needs. Others may concentrate on nonvocational cultural programs similar to those in many adult education centers. Overall, two divergent patterns are likely to be found on campuses: among students who continue to use schooling as a route for economic advancement, greater seriousness, greater specialization in occupation-oriented fields, greater vocationalism; among those who see little chance of their interests yielding salable skills, a concern solely with the consumption aspects of education, possibly on a part-time basis.

The demographic composition of the student population is also likely to differ from that of the past, with more woman and black students and, depending on policies of financing, possibly fewer from the lower middle class.

In addition, because some specialties will be more affected by the falling job market than others, students are likely to choose different majors. More students can be expected to enter business-oriented fields and independent professions, at the expense of academic and research occupations, changing the areas of study of the nation's future leaders, with possible consequences for decision making. Departments faced with declining enrollment are likely to stress the vocational value of their training and offer more job-oriented courses. Because demand will be especially limited in the education sector itself, many graduate programs will undergo a major reorientation, from the preparation of teachers to the preparation of business and government employees, which will require changes in the content and subjects taught.

Changes in educational offerings are unlikely to come smoothly. The traditional mode of adjusting the distribution of faculty to new educational needs—by new hires—will be seriously hampered by no-growth or declining-growth conditions. Substantial attacks on the major element of rigidity in the educational system, tenure, are to be expected, though with uncertain prospects for success. Because there will be a sizable supply of highly qualified young Ph.D.'s seeking work at relatively low salaries in the 1970s, schools that have not locked themselves in by giving tenure to many in the past or by union contracts could significantly raise their standing in academia. Several new centers of excellence are likely to be created as a result. If other institutions can find ways of reducing older tenured staff, the relative surplus of Ph.D.'s could lead to a widespread improvement in the academic qualifications of university personnel.

If academia is unable to find adequate positions for bright young Ph.D.'s and other researchers and scholars, there could be a major shift in the locus of intellectual effort. Research centers and government and business research groups can be expected to upgrade the quality of their staff, thus becoming intellectually more competitive with higher education.

The weakness of the academic market will alter the relative power of faculty, administrators and students. For better or worse, administrators are likely to attain greater power relative to faculty in the next decade. Teaching and contributions to the institution may, accordingly, become important criteria for academic success, relative to publications and related professional activities. For better or worse, competition for students will give students greater power within colleges. Such competition may reduce the relative cost of higher education for the more able, with scholarships once again given widely for ability as well as need. These changes in power will undoubtedly be resisted and lead to conflicts on campuses, though of a very different nature than those experienced in the riots of the late 1960s.

OPTIONS FOR INSTITUTIONS AND INDIVIDUALS

There are several alternative strategies or changes in modes of behavior that institutions of higher education and individuals may find beneficial in the era of overeducation.

Colleges and universities might ameliorate some of the problems of declining enrollments by linking liberal arts to vocational nonacademic training, such as for union crafts, possibly through new degree offerings and operating procedures. By bringing together vocational nonacademic and liberal arts programs, the opportunity for blue-collar workers to undertake artistic and intellectual pursuits unrelated to their careers could be enhanced.

It may also be desirable to alter tuition charges to better reflect costs of different educational programs. For example, graduate programs are often subsidized by undergraduate tuitions, suggesting that graduate tuitions are too low. Such changes will tend to limit graduate enrollments, an effect that is not inconsistent with the anticipated lower demand for Ph.D.'s in many areas. If such price changes are not possible, it may be desirable to limit certain graduate programs even beyond the size determined by student choice. University policies should be such that educational prices or allocation decisions reflect true social costs, no matter who pays.

A third possibility is to reduce the amount of time required for studies, by operating full-time during summer and vacation periods. The present 4 years needed for the bachelor's degree could be reduced, with considerable saving of forgone income to students and at no serious loss of educational quality. All else the same, the reduction in the time needed to obtain a degree, from 4 to 3 years, would cost a student four summers of work at low pay and gain him or her 1 year of work as a graduate at higher pay, raising the economic value of a college training. While in the past the desire for summer leisure may have made a concentrated course of studies attractive to only a few, in the changed market more students are likely to find this option desirable. At the least, experiments in altering the time period of courses and the operations of academia should be made to learn the best ways to deal with the new market reality.

Because the American higher educational system is, despite its flaws, generally superior to that in the rest of the world, attention should be given to the possible expansion of foreign student enrollments, particularly from the newly rich oil countries and such developing countries as Brazil, Mexico, and others, whose human resource demands are likely to outstrip the capacity of domestic universities. Already, Venezuela has initiated a major program to "export" thousands of students to the United States for higher education. We have a comparative advantage in producing college training, it could be "sold" overseas, taking up some of the slack in domestic student enrollment.

As for individuals, while there are no panaceas to a declining market, students can improve their employment prospects in several ways. First, they can undertake earlier and more careful career planning than in the past, giving close attention to the different opportunities within broad fields; to the greater likelihood of obtaining a teaching job by specializing, say, in mathematics, rather than in foreign languages; to the better opportunities for civil, rather than aeronautical, engineers; to the greater demand for applied, rather than pure, mathematics; and so forth. Second, lemminglike rushes into particular areas, such as into law in the late 1960s, and doctoral science studies in the early 1960s, should be avoided. When more and more students are flocking into an area, that is a good indication of possible cobweb surpluses in the future. Third, for those concerned with long-term careers, job searching should not be concentrated in the East Coast and West Coast areas, where the demand-supply imbalance is most severe. Teaching jobs are scarce all over, but they are far more difficult to find in New York and San Francisco than in small towns in the interior of the country. Architecture positions are hard to come by in Boston but not so hard to find in Houston, and so forth. College graduates need not, like the unemployed coal miners of the 1960s, worsen their chances for good careers by being geographically immobile. Fourth, women and blacks—who have good chances for positions in some nontraditional fields—should not be deterred from these careers even when, as in, say, physics, overall job prospects look bad. While the market for academic faculty will be weak in the future, unless affirmative action disappears the relative paucity of qualified blacks and women means that there are good chances for these groups in academia. Fifth, those with arcane interests may find they have an advantage when competing for specific kinds of jobs, for example, a specialist in Slavic literature is likely to have a better chance for a job with a firm likely to do business in Eastern Europe. It is probably better to follow specific "odd" courses of study, rather than standard majors that fail to distinguish a student from his peers. Finally, even students with strong liberal arts interests should take some vocationally oriented courses, such as computer programming, which will help obtain jobs.

As for the graduates of the early and mid-1970s, who have already experienced weakened labor market prospects, the forecasted upturn of the 1980s holds some promise. To take advantage of the potentially improved market, these graduates should seek to maintain college-level skills, preserve career options, and prepare to move into better jobs in the 1980s. Some may find it fruitful to undertake retraining in colleges to restore atrophied skills when the market begins to improve.

RESPONSE OF THE GOVERNMENT AND BODY POLITIC

How will the political system respond to the period of overeducation? There are several possible government reactions to a continued depression in the college market. Governments could "let nature take its course" by permitting the natural market adjustment processes to operate. Such a laissez-faire policy does not mean that the government will not influence the market but that any effects will be the by-product of other policies and not of specific actions to aid the depressed college graduate. Alternatively, the national government could

seek to lessen cyclical fluctuations in the college market just as it currently seeks (unsuccessfully) to ameliorate the fluctuations in the business cycle. Dampening cobweb ups and downs might involve "countercobweb" scholarships and aid to education—leaning against the wind in order to maintain programs and yield more steady supplies in the future. Specialists in such technical areas as physics, where possible increased manpower demands and the long period of training make shortages conceivable in the next decade, might be "stockpiled" by awarding longer postdoctoral grants or by other forms of nonpermanent employment that would maintain research skills, in much the same way as we have stockpiled certain natural resources, including agricultural commodities. Policies designed to reduce the shortage-surplus cycles will require additional manpower analyses and planning, possibly as part of overall national economic planning of the type that some have recommended to Congress.

Under pressure from college-trained workers and their families, governments might also try to increase the demand for graduates directly. One reaction to a surplus of teachers would, for example, involve expansion of early childhood education, as the AFT and NEA would like. Through the political system we could opt for a society that is overeducated in relation to the labor market, rather than one that is undereducated in relation to human potential. Because the college trained continue to have better incomes and job prospects than the less educated, however, I do not believe that special "aid to the educated" programs are desirable.

Moreover, on the basis of past governmental behavior and responses in the early 1970s, ranging from federal fellowship cutbacks to state educational policies, these prospects seem unrealistic. Despite the political power of higher education and its clients, the government is more likely, if anything, to overreact to the market depression by reducing the support for the college and university systems as part of the general rejection of higher education as having "failed" to live up to the promises of the 1960s.

ETHOS OF THE OVEREDUCATED SOCIETY

A society in which higher education has a reduced economic value and is marginally rather than highly desirable is likely to have a very different spirit than traditional societies, where education is a scarcer resource. On the positive side, there may be a substantial decline in the formalistic use of schooling as a credential or screening device. New roles will be filled by educated persons, and the structure of economic achievement and progress will be less closely tied to classroom performance than in the past. Some of the social distinctions between college graduates and other persons and the national obsession with degrees are likely to decline, especially if relatively many persons from better family backgrounds choose alternative career patterns. Individuals are likely to seek out new routes for socioeconimic progress, with potentially fruitful outcomes, depending on the form of institutions created.

On the negative side, because the value and prestige attached to education and high-level jobs is at least partly due to high salaries, the overall social evaluation of schooling is likely to fall in the period of overeducation. Contrary to the hopes of Galbraith, the "scientific-education estate" will face hard times, in terms of prestige, income, and power, due to its skills no longer being very scarce. Knowledge is power only if most people do not have it. More dangerous, perhaps, the failure of relatively many educated persons to achieve their career goals and the possible failure of others to find ways of improving their position outside of the educational sector could lead some to political extremism.

THE REST OF THE WORLD

There is some evidence that other developed "Western" countries, ranging from Japan to Sweden, are also on the verge of an era of overeducation. In Japan, the relative income of college graduates appears to have fallen sharply, though rapid economic growth maintained significant real absolute differences in income through the 1970s. Ulrich Teichler and Yoko Teichler-Urata of the Max Planck Institute of Germany have found, for example, that the ratio of university to high school graduates incomes in Japan dropped from almost 2.5 to just 1.5 to 1.0 between 1955 and 1971.[3] OECD reports suggest some waning of the job market for graduates in Western Europe. In Great Britain it was reported that "the 15% margin of difference enjoyed by the degree-holding graduate in 1967 (was) cut by about half" through 1975.[4] At the same time, however, there remain enormous premiums to the educated in less-developed countries with, in some cases (Venezuela, the Arab oil states, Iran, Ecuador, and Brazil, among others) college workers having potentially higher salaries than in the West. If political circumstances permit, this could lead to the migration of college-trained Americans overseas to obtain the graduate-level jobs and salaries they cannot find in the United States—a reverse braindrain. The outflow of highly educated workers from Great Britain could be a harbinger of the future.

[3] See U. Teichler and Y. Teichler-Urata, *Die Entwicklung der Beschäftigungsmöglichkeiten für akademisch ausgebildete Arbeitsdräfte in Japan* (Göttingen: Schwartz, 1975).

[4] *N.Y. Times* (18 Feb., 1976).

FINAL PROVISO

An economist is not trained either to analyze or to forecast the broad social consequences of such far-reaching developments as long-run declines in the economic value of college training and of slackened growth in higher education. Even for those elements of reality for which his training is suitable—namely, the quantitative dimensions of change in supply, demand, employment, and salaries—the history of forecasts is replete with failure. Accordingly, the preceding discussion of the period of over-education and its possible characteristics must be viewed as speculative guesswork that merely points the way for more detailed analysis and thought by other social scientists.

Labor Supply, Women, and Family Economics

In an article written especially for this volume, Glen Cain demonstrates the continuing increase over time in the percentage of married women who desire market work. In contrast, the labor force participation of men has been decreasing. Cain then develops the economic theory of labor supply, with particular attention to the "income" and "substitution" effects of higher wage rates. Since, in general, home work is a closer substitute for market work for wives than for husbands, the substitution effect is larger for wives, both absolutely and relative to the corresponding income effect. Thus, the changes in labor force participation over time are consistent with the hypothesis that, as real wage rates have risen, the income effect has predominated for men but the substitution effect has predominated for women.

Although the female labor force has been growing rapidly with an increasing number of women aspiring to careers in high-paying occupations, the earnings of women remain low relative to those of men. Among full-time workers, the average woman continues to earn only about 60 percent as much as the average man. Nancy Barrett discusses the earnings differences between the sexes and how these differences relate to discrimination, sex roles, and occupational segregation. She also reviews the laws prohibiting discrimination in employment.

Partly as a result of the increase in the number of families where both parents work, including families with young children, there has been some increase in nontraditional work schedules, including part-time and flex-time work arrangements. The advantages and disadvantages of these alternative workweek arrangements are analyzed in the selection on the workweek from the Employment and Training Report of the President.

During the past decade or two, labor economics has expanded its scope to be much more concerned with the economics of the family and the time allocation of family members. Isabel Sawhill discusses both the strengths and weaknesses of economists' analysis of such topics as marriage, divorce, fertility, and child raising.

10

Married Women in the Labor Force

Glen G. Cain

Glen G. Cain, "Married Women in the Labor Force," written especially for this volume.

HISTORICAL TRENDS

During this century two trends have changed the composition of the labor force with far-reaching economic and social consequences. One trend is the decline in the amount of time that men spend in market work during their lifetime. This decline is a result of a later age of entrance into the labor force by young men, a shorter workweek for working men, and an earlier age of retirement. The second trend is the increase in market work by women. Compared to earlier periods, a larger proportion of women work in the labor market at some time in their adult life, and, more importantly, the women who work spend a larger fraction of their lifetime at work. The increase in employment by women is the main subject of this article, although, as explained below, the essential fact is the increase in work by married women.

These trends for men and women are sharply revealed in Table 1, which gives labor force participation rates (LFPRs) for selected demographic groups from 1900-1980. A LFPR for a group may be roughly defined as the number in the group who are either employed or unemployed (actively seeking work) divided by the total population of the group. The statistics in Table 1 refer to groups who are age 14 or over, although in 1967 the official definition of the labor force was changed to exclude 14- and 15-year-olds.

The first row shows the relative stability from 1900-1980 in the fraction of all adults who are in the labor force. The rows that follow show dramatic contrasts in the LFPRs for the two sexes and for various subgroups. The sharpest decline is for men age 65 and over. The rates of young men also decreased substantially from 1900-1940 but have been fairly stable since then. The overall LFPR for men decreased from 86 percent in 1900, when the average workweek was around 60 hours, to 74 percent in 1980, when the average workweek was less than 40 hours.

The LFPR of women more than doubled from 1900-1980, increasing quite steadily from 20 percent to 50 percent. The increase occurred

TABLE 1

Labor Force Participation Rates (LFPR) from Decennial Censuses for Selected Demographic Groups, 1900, 1920, 1940-1970

Group	1900[a]	1920[a]	1940[b]	1950[b]	1960[b]	1970[b]	1980[c]
Total	54	54	52	55	57	58	62
Males	86	85	79	82	80	77	74
14-19	62	52	35	40	38	35	38[c]
20-24	91	90	88	82	86	81	82[c]
25-64	93	94	93	91	93	91	90
65+	63	56	42	41	30	25	19
Females	20	23	26	30	36	41	50
14-19	27	28	19	23	24	25	29[c]
20-24	32	38	46	43	45	56	67[c]
25-64	16	20	28	32	40	48	59
65+	8	7	6	8	10	10	8
Females, by Marital Status							
Single	44	51	46	46	43	41	46[d]
Married, husband present	6	9	14	22	31	40	50
Widowed, divorced	33	34	30	33	36	37	44

[a]*Historical Statistics*, U.S. Bureau of the Census.

[b]*U.S. Census 1970. Characteristics of the Population. U.S. Summary, Vol. I, Part 1*, p. 372, U.S. Bureau of the Census.

[c]*Employment and Earnings*, May 1980. U.S. Bureau of Labor Statistics. (See Tables A-3 and A-31.) Note: The Current Population Survey for April, 1980 is the basis for these statistics. April is the month of the decennial censuses, but the CPS LFPRs are usually somewhat larger than those for the census for the younger age groups. The ratio of the CPS/Census LFPRs for April 1970 is used to adjust the CPS LFPRs for April 1980 to make them more comparable to the earlier census years. (See *Employment and Earnings*, May 1970, U.S. Bureau of Labor Statistics, Tables A-3 and A-27.)

[d]In addition to the statistical adjustment of CPS to Census LFPRs to achieve comparability, noted in footnote c, a second adjustment is made to allow for the elimination of 14- and 15-year-olds from the labor force population in 1967. The only marital status group that requires adjustment is "never married," and the ratio of the LFPRs: 14-19/16-19 for 1967 is used to adjust the 1970 and 1980 LFPRs.

despite the impediments of two trends that affected younger and older women. One is the rise in school enrollment rates of women between the ages of 14 and 24. The other is the increase in the life span of women who are at the age when retirement is customary, which adds to the number of nonworking women. In fact, as shown in the bottom part of Table 1, it is the increase in LFPRs of wives, who constitute most of the 25-64 age group, that is singularly responsible for the large increase in women's LFPRs over the long run.

The LFPRs of the other marital status groups have been held back for special reasons. Never-married women tend to be young, and school attendance has tended to replace employment (and early marriages). Among divorced, separated, and widowed women, many have been able to maintain themselves without working because of aid from various programs of public assistance. Three programs have been especially important: (1) Aid to Families with Dependent Children (AFDC); (2) Old Age, Survivors, and Disability Insurance (often called the Social Security program); and (3) Supplementary Security Income (SSI).

Women made up 43 percent of the labor force in 1980, an increase from 30 percent in 1950. The fraction of the labor force that is made up of wives shows an interesting comparison with that for husbands. In 1950, 53 percent of the labor force were husbands, spouse present, and only 14 percent were wives, spouse present. By 1980, husbands were 37 percent of the labor force, and wives made up 24 percent of the labor force.[1]

Another perspective on the rise in work rates of wives and on the social importance of this trend is provided in Table 2, showing the LFPRs of wives by presence and age of children

[1] The sources for these statistics are the same as those in Table 1, but keep in mind the distinction between the percent a group is of the labor force and the percent of that group that is in the labor force. LFPRs refer to the latter percent.

for selected years from 1948-1980. (These statistics are from the Current Population Survey, which is the official source for the Bureau of Labor Statistics, and 1948 is the first year of their availability. Females under age 16 are excluded.) We see that mothers with one or more children under six have experienced the sharpest rise in work rates—a four-fold increase, from 11 percent in 1948 to 45 percent in 1980. The rates for mothers whose youngest child is between 6 and 17 rose by a factor of 2.3. Although the table shows that the LFPRs for this group of mothers are higher than the rates for wives with no children under 18 years of age from 1960 on, this would not be true if age were held constant. Wives with no children under 18 have an average age that is much higher than wives with a youngest child between 6 and 17.

In summary, the outstanding change in the composition of the labor force during this century is the increased proportion of working wives. Women are now less dependent on males for their economic well-being, and the trends point to even greater independence. This development has brought about dramatic changes in family life and in the relation between the sexes in public life and school, as well as in the work place. Our laws and political institutions have adapted in ways that reflect and generally reinforce the economic gains women have achieved. Thus, the historical data describing the employment trends of women provide the backdrop and sometimes the central interest for all economists who engage in research on women in the labor force.

THE APPROACH AND MODEL FOR STUDYING LABOR SUPPLY BEHAVIOR

The economic study of women in the labor force mainly consists of labor supply, rather than demand, analysis. The economist's theory

TABLE 2

Labor Force Participation Rates of Married Women, Husband Present, by Presence and Age of Children 1948-1980 (Selected Years)*

Year	Total	With No Child Under 18	Child 6-17 Only	Children Under 6
1948	22	28	26	11
1950	24	30	28	12
1960	30	35	39	19
1970	41	42	49	30
1978	48	45	57	42
1980	50	46	62	45

*The population on which these statistics are based is the civilian, noninstitutionalized population, aged 16 and over. The sample is that of the Current Population Survey.
Sources: 1948–1978: Employment and Training Report of the President, 1979, p. 295.
    1980: "Marital and Family Characteristics of Workers, March 1980," News Release of the Bureau of Labor Statistics, U.S. Dept. of Labor, Dec. 9, 1980.

of labor supply takes the household or family as the basic unit of analysis. The family is assumed to allocate the time of its members among four activities: market work, home work, leisure, and subsistence. The allocation is constrained by the given resources (or wealth) of the household, the market prices for these resources, and, of course, the natural limits of time. Income and prices are the main economic explanatory variables, which does not mean that economists necessarily believe these variables are the most important ones in all contexts.

Two related features of the wife's time-allocation decisions differ importantly from those of a male family member. First, the wife is traditionally the main producer of home services, of which bearing and raising children are usually the most important. Second, the wife has more discretion about working in the market. Indeed, it is usually assumed that husbands (or adult men generally) have discretion only between market work and leisure in their time-allocation decisions. Subsistence time is considered fixed (nondiscretionary) for both sexes, and home work is assumed to be negligible for males. This latter assumption is becoming increasingly unrealistic as a consequence of

the shorter workweek, the two-earner family, and the women's equal rights movement. But it is still reasonable to view the wife's decision about market employment to be much more discretionary than that of the husband. This point is a key to understanding the economist's explanation for the divergent trends in labor supply of men and women.

In the economic model of labor supply for an adult man, his market wage rate measures the opportunity cost of not working, and it represents the price of leisure (per time unit). The supply of labor may be analyzed as the demand for leisure. The demand function for leisure contains the following explanatory variables: (1) the income (or wealth) of the person, wherein more income permits more leisure to be "purchased" at a price measured by the forgone goods and services that could be obtained from the alternative of market work; (2) the price of leisure—the market wage; (3) the prices of goods and services complementary to leisure (such as theatre tickets) or, alternatively, complementary to work (such as work clothes); (4) the person's preferences or tastes for leisure (or against work), where it is understood that the source of preference changes are noneconomic, or, more precisely, are exogenous—that is, not affected by the other variables in the model; (5) the legal or institutional constraints that limit one's hours of work, such as laws and labor union regulations.

Economists give particular attention to wage rates because they not only define the price of leisure but have been the dominant source of changes in the average worker's income over time. The long-run increase in wage rates has carried an "income effect" (item 1 preceding) that retards work and promotes leisure, given the usual assumption that leisure is a normal good whose consumption increases as income increases. At the same time, the increase in wages (item 2) carries a "substitution effect" that promotes work and retards leisure consumption, since leisure has become more expensive relative to its alternative of market goods. An axiom of rational economic behavior is that a consumer will shift away from goods and services that have risen in relative price and towards those goods and services that have fallen in price—other things being equal, including income.

The long-run decrease in time devoted to market work by males, along with the long-run increase in wages, implies that the income effects have outweighed the substitution effects, given small (or offsetting) changes in items 3-5 above—other relevant prices, tastes, and institutions. The "backward bending," or, more accurately, "negatively sloped," supply curve of labor expresses this dominance of the income effect over the substitution effect for men.[2]

We should view the time series of male LFPRs (or hours-worked-per-year) as being *described* by a negative relation to (or coefficient of) wages. Economists have then tested this hypothesized relation with a variety of studies using cross-section data. These studies have generally verified the hypothesis of a negative effect of wages on labor supply. A more stringent test involves the separate measurement of an income effect—using variations in nonlabor income—and the demonstration that it is negative and large enough in absolute value to be consistent with a positive substitution component of the total (negative) wage effect. This test has not always been successful, but the gross (total) negative wage effect found in cross-section studies of male labor supply functions agrees with the time series.[3]

Now consider women. We have noted that market work is not the only important alternative to leisure—that cultural and biological factors make home work the most important type of work for the wife over most of her married life. The list of factors in the economic model used for men must be modified for women to include a special price in item 3: the price of home-produced goods and services, for which the most important component is the value of the wife's time—her "home wage."

There are two possible versions of the home wage as it affects the lifetime decision that the wife makes about her time allocation. First, when the wife engages in market work during her married life, we assume that she has a "margin" of choice between home and market work. Her home wage can be evaluated by her market wage, or, to be more precise, the market wage measures the home wage associated with the marginal (or "last") hour of home work. In fact, the wife's marginal hours in market work, home work, and leisure should be equal in value for an optimal and

---

[2] Typically, the graphical illustration shows the quantity of labor plotted on the horizontal axis and the wage rate on the vertical axis. According to the above interpretation, however, the wage rate is the explanatory variable, and the quantity of labor is the dependent variable, so the axes would be reversed.

[3] A number of studies in which labor supply functions of males were estimated, with special reference to the estimation of income and wage effects, are reported and reviewed in *Income Maintenance and Labor Supply,* edited by G. G. Cain and H. W. Watts, a Markham book from Rand-McNally Co., Chicago, 1973. See especially Chapter 9 and pp. 332-35.

equilibrium allocation of time. Second, if the wife never works in the market, then we have no direct measure of her home wage, except that its lowest (marginal) value is assumed to exceed the market wage she can earn. The case where the wife never works is increasingly uncommon, however. Probably 90 percent of married women do or will work at some time in their married life.

There are several important and practical consequences of our attention to home work and its value to the wife and her family. One is the intrinsic interest we have in the "outputs" of home production; especially, children, child care, and household management generally. Secondly, the estimation of labor supply functions is made more complicated. The reason is that the average (not the marginal) home wage of the wife is defined to be a determinant of her total allocation of time, and this variable is unmeasured. Therefore, the average home wage is an omitted variable from the wife's labor supply model, and as a consequence we may misestimate the true effects of other variables, such as the market wage.[4]

Finally, the presence of home work as an important alternative to market work for wives will affect the substitution effect of market wage changes. In general, the substitution effect will be small and the supply of labor inelastic if good substitutes for one's

working time are lacking. The substitute of leisure time is available to husbands, single men and women, and wives, but the home work alternative should induce a greater responsiveness of wives to variation in the market wage; in other words, the wife's substitution effect should be relatively large and her labor supply curve should be relatively elastic.

This generalization is meant to apply to work choices in the context of a lifetime. At a particular moment the generalization may not hold. When young children are present, for example, the wife's time may be perceived as not being easily substitutable for market work. At other times the presence of older children or other adults besides the husband and wife, who may be productive as either home or market workers, will influence the work decisions of the wife. An even more temporary event is unemployment of the husband. This will tend to make home work a relevant alternative use for his time. But if we summarize the lifetime experience of the family and suppress the life-cycle and transitional events, the generally greater area of choice between work alternatives (home and market) for wives than for husbands does imply a larger substitution effect for wives.

Herein lies the foundation of Jacob Mincer's reconciliation on theoretical grounds of the time series differences in market labor supplied by wives and other adults.[5] For the latter group the income effect exceeds the substitution effect, but for wives the reverse is eminently reasonable. In the face of rising incomes and wages, market work declines for males and single women and their leisure increases, while home work declines for wives and their leisure and their market work both increase.

---

[4] A variable (or variables) measuring the average value of nonmarket time in the labor supply function of any person is worth more attention by economists. It should be noted that the justification for ignoring such a variable in the case of adult men requires special assumptions; for example, that: (a) home work by men is negligible; (b) if home work is significant for men, then their home wage is either constant or independent of other relevant variables in the labor supply function, such as the market wage and family income; (c) preferences for leisure, which may be assumed to determine the value of leisure time, are similar among all men; or (d) if leisure preferences are varying, then the value of leisure is independent of other relevant variables in the labor supply model.

[5] Jacob Mincer, "Labor Force Participation of Married Women," in *Aspects of Labor Economics,* A Conference of the Universities, National Bureau of Economic Research (Princeton: Princeton University Press, 1962).

RESULTS OF EMPIRICAL ESTIMATION OF LABOR SUPPLY FUNCTIONS FOR WIVES

Although the central fact that has motivated our discussion of wives' labor force behavior is the long-run increase in their work rates, the time series has relatively few observations to permit reliable estimates of the effects of wages, incomes, and so on. The time-series behavior is consistent with the hypothesis that the wage elasticity of wives' labor supply is positive and larger than the presumed negative income effect, but we require testing these hypotheses with independent data. The standard approach by economists has been to use cross-section data to estimate wage and income effects (or elasticities) and the effects of other variables of interest.

The cross-section estimates of the parameters of the wife's labor supply function have been found to be reasonably consistent with the time series, but some qualifications and interesting points may be mentioned. In the contexts of both cross-section and time-series data, the assumptions that various explanatory variables are exogenous are usually open to question. The wage rate facing the wife is commonly assumed to be exogenous, for example. In the time series this is justified in part by accepting the long-run rise in wage rates (and the evolution toward lighter work that is more accommodating of female employment) as inevitable outcomes of preordained technological change and capital accumulation. In the cross sections it is usually assumed that geographic variation in female wage rates for a given quality (productivity) of labor is exogenously determined by such factors as the industrial structure of the area.

Another variable that affects the wives' labor supply and that may be endogenous (that is, affected by labor supply) is the presence of children. In the earlier estimations (and much that occurs today) children were assumed to be an independent (exogenous) variable that represented the value of home work for wives.[6] Later models specified children as endogenous, and multiple equation systems of fertility and labor supply were estimated.[7] Not surprisingly, cross-section models consistently reveal negative effects of children on the wife's labor supply. It is interesting to point out, however, that the LFPRs of wives in the period from 1940-1960 rose rapidly at a time when birth rates were rising. And, as we have seen above, the rise in work rates of mothers with young children has been more pronounced than those for other groups of wives. The correspondence between time-series and cross-section relationships in economics is often at odds, and this presents a challenge to economic research.

The labor supply models that have been estimated for cross sections deal with two types of data. The first type consists of aggregative (or grouped) data and uses market variables, such as LFPRs, average income, and average wage rates. These variables correspond to the time-series, which also consists of grouped data. An advantage of the data in this form is the suppression (via the averaging process) of the wide variations in preferences (or tastes) among individual wives regarding market work, home work, and leisure. Transitory wage and income variation is also suppressed, and this is beneficial because our theory of the long-run labor supply behavior of wives deals with normal wages and incomes. The principal disadvantage is that the assumption of single-direction causation, *from* wages *to* labor supply, may be false, and satisfactory simultaneous equation models with these data have not been estimated.

[6] Glen G. Cain, *Married Women in the Labor Force* (Chicago: University of Chicago Press, 1966).

[7] Glen G. Cain and Martin D. Dooley, "Estimation of a Model of Labor Supply, Fertility, and Wages of Married Women," *Journal of Political Economy,* August 1976, pp. S179-S201.

The second type of cross-section data is disaggregated, with individual wives as units of observation. Information about market variables is limited, and in their place are measures of personal characteristics of the subject. The troublesome problems are: (a) errors in variables (which encompasses the problem of transitory variation in income and wages); and (b) distinguishing between the effects of variables that impinge upon the wife's decisions from those that merely reflect her decisions—perhaps via some factor like tastes that is common (causal?) to both the decision and to the variable in question.

Estimates of wage and income elasticities from both types of data, covering specific years between 1940 and 1970 are reported in Cain (1966), Cain and Watts (1973), and Dooley (1980).[8] Labor supply of wives is measured by their hours worked per year as well as by labor force participation status for individuals or the LFPR for aggregates. The market wage for wives (or for women) has a positive effect—+0.62 is the average wage elasticity for regression estimates from the four census years (1940-1970). The husband's income, or that of the family, (not including the wife's earnings) has a negative effect, and -0.61 is its corresponding average elasticity.[9]

The combination of cross-section wage and income effects do not fully explain the time-series increase for wives, however, and we have noted that fertility changes have not been uniform during the last 80 years. Additional explanation for the time-series increase in work is provided by the cross-section estimated positive labor supply effect of the wife's educational attainment, which has risen over time. Indeed, education partly represents a wage effect, because it captures such non-pecuniary returns to working as fringe benefits, pleasant working conditions, and so forth. Further explanation of the time-series requires more information about changes in work in the home, about noneconomic aspects of market work, and about changes in attitudes (or tastes).

Cain (1966) also examined the labor supply of black wives.[10] At a point in time the LFPRs of black wives are higher than those for white wives. Over time, however, work rates of white wives have increased more rapidly, so the differential is narrowing. Part of the slower growth in work rates of black wives is probably related to the decline in the occupation of domestic service, where a large proportion of black women were employed prior to recent years. In addition, regression analyses showed larger income effects relative to wage effects for black wives in comparison to white wives. This is consistent with the time-series difference for the two color groups, but why the income and wage effects differ is not evident.

The relatively higher LFPR of black wives is related to the fact that the presence of children appear to have a less inhibiting effect on labor supply for black wives. Four explanations of the higher work rates of black wives and black mothers are suggested:

1. The simplest point is that labor force participation rates overstate the amount of labor supplied by nonwhite wives compared with white wives, since the latter are likely to be working more hours per week or more weeks per year if working at all. Nonwhite females are disproportionately represented in service occupations, particularly domestic service, that involve part-time work. Their occupational characteristics in turn reflect relatively low educational attainments, lesser training, and market discrimination.

---

[8] Cain, *op. cit.;* Cain and Watts, *op. cit.;* Martin D. Dooley, "Labor Supply and Fertility of Married Women: An Analysis With Grouped and Individual Data from the 1970 Census." Oct. 1980 (unpublished).

[9] These estimates are nicely summarized in Dooley, 1980, p. 12.

[10] The next three paragraphs are taken from Cain, 1966, pp. 119-20. The term "nonwhite" is used instead of "black" when referring to census data, because separate statistics for blacks were often not available. Blacks constitute about 90 percent of the nonwhite group.

2. Discrimination in the housing market is a source of poorer housing conditions, smaller dwelling units, and more doubling up of families among nonwhites, and these conditions are all generally conducive to more market work and less home work by wives.

3. Relative instability of nonwhite families leads the wife to maintain closer ties to the labor market. This tendency is reinforced by her typically low income status and limited chances of obtaining alimony or adequate financial support for her children.

4. Finally, the nonwhite husband may face greater discrimination in the labor market than the wife, leading to some substitution in market work between them. It is unlikely that this disadvantage to the male would be entirely captured in the measures of his earnings and unemployment experience that are included in the standard analyses.

These explanations are interrelated and reinforcing. They contribute to explaining both the higher levels of participation among black wives and the lesser importance of children as a deterrent to work.

SOME IMPLICATIONS

I will conclude by pointing to a few implications of this analysis for some current theoretical and policy issues. Married women have become so important a segment of the labor force that attention to their work patterns is necessary for a full understanding of many important economic problems: economic growth and the cyclical behavior of national income, the personal distribution of income, the effects of income taxes on labor supply, the impact of income maintenance laws on labor supply, and birth rates.

Consider first the effect of unemployment conditions on labor force participation. Decreases in the availability of jobs are likely to result in relatively large decreases in the quantity of labor supplied by wives and, prob-

ably, for other secondary earners who similarly possess good alternatives to leisure and market work. This prediction is consistent with the result in cross-sections of a reduction in labor supplied for areas of depressed business conditions and high unemployment. The time-series evidence is not clear. From 1950 to the late 1960s the LFPRs of wives were procyclical and inversely related to unemployment (after controlling for the time-trend), but in recent years the effect of unemployment has not been found to be negative in time-series analysis.[11]

We should keep in mind that, while declines in LFPRs decrease the Gross National Product, a decline in GNP is not necessarily a decline of the same magnitude in the well-being of the population, particularly when unmeasured home work (or school work) is increasing. Nevertheless, the withdrawal from the labor force of secondary workers in the face of high unemployment can be a source of hardship, particularly in depressed areas.

The distribution of income and poverty are both related to the role of secondary earners in a family. At the upper end of the income distribution, 64 percent of families in 1960 earning $10,000 or more had two or more earners.[12] By 1978 inflation made the equivalent high income figure $22,000, and about 78 percent of the families with incomes this high or higher were multiple-earner families.[13] The wife is by far the most common second earner in families with a male primary earner.

[11] See Olivia S. Mitchell, "The Cyclical Responsiveness of Married Females' Labor Supply: Added and Discouraged Worker Effects," *"Proceedings of the Thirty-Second Annual Meeting of the Industrial Relations Research Association,* University of Wisconsin, Madison, 1980, pp. 251-57.

[12] U.S. Census of Population, 1960. Subject Reports, "Sources and Structure of Family Income," Table 1, p. 1.

[13] U.S. Bureau of the Census, Current Population Reports, Series P-60, No. 123. *Money Income of Families and Persons in the United States: 1978.*

At the other end of the income spectrum where unemployment is an important cause of low income, secondary earners often provide the means for economic solvency. The Bureau of Labor Statistics reported that in 1977 the husband was unemployed at some time during the year in 7.5 percent of all husband-wife families. In 50 percent of the families where the husband was unemployed the wife was the only other earner; in another 13 percent of the families there was another family member employed; and in 37 percent of the families no other family member worked to supplement the losses from the unemployment of the husband.[14]

Another important issue concerns the effect of the personal income tax on the household's work decisions. The economist's analysis of this problem calls for determining whether the substitution effect of the tax on work reduces the supply of labor more or less than the income effect of the tax increases the supply of labor. The impression obtained from prior research is that the income tax does not reduce the quantity of labor supplied, but the evidence pertains mainly to primary earners.[15] Wage or substitution effects are expected to be small among primary earners, but not for secondary earners, so the effects of taxation may be different for the latter. Indeed, on the basis of the evidence at hand, the substitution effect appears to outweigh the income effect of the tax, and a net deterrence to work is implied. One qualification, however, is that the suggested special importance of nonpecuniary aspects of employment for wives and, perhaps, other secondary workers provides a means of avoiding the incidence of the tax, since payment for work in this form is not taxed.

Currently and for the past fifteen years, one of the most widely debated "taxes" on work effort has been that associated with public assistance (welfare) and other forms of income transfer payments, such as social security retirement benefits. These programs typically provide an income guarantee and income payments to participants, and the programs impose high implicit taxes on earnings by reducing the transfer payments when earnings are received. The income payments are predicted to have a negative effect on the labor supply. The implicit tax on the earnings effectively reduces the wage rate of the recipient and is also a disincentive to work. Therefore, unlike the situation for positive taxes, the reduced wage rate is associated with positive income transfers, and both income and substitution effects imply reduced work effort.

Proposals to reform the welfare system by providing benefits to low-income husband-wife families raise the issue of the relatively large responsiveness of wives to changes in wage rates, which suggests a larger work disincentive effect in husband-wife families than in one-adult families. This issue has received considerable research, including several controlled experiments.[16]

Finally, the labor supply of women and wives has some obvious and perhaps not-so-obvious cause and effect relationships with several aspects of demographic behavior: decisions about schooling, marriage, fertility, the type of child care provided, and—receiving increasing attention in recent years—decisions

[14] Howard Hayge, "The Effect of Unemployment on Family Income in 1977," *Monthly Labor Review,* December 1979, pp. 42-44.

[15] See Marvin Kosters, "Effects of an Income Tax on Labor Supply," in *The Taxation of Income Capital,* ed. A. C. Harberger and M. J. Bailey (Washington D.C.: The Brookings Institution, 1969), pp. 301-24, for a brief review of the literature and for his estimates of wage effects on the labor supply of males aged 50-64, which support the conclusion that the substitution effect for males is small.

[16] Two issues of the *Journal of Human Resources,* Spring, 1974 and Fall, 1980, are devoted to these experiments.

about marital stability. The interdependence of these decisions—the fact that they are both causes of changes in labor supply behavior of women and effects of such labor supply behavior—are particularly challenging to contemporary research in the social sciences.

11

Women in the Job Market: Occupations, Earnings, and Career Opportunities

Nancy S. Barrett

Nancy S. Barrett, "Women in the Job Market: Occupations, Earnings, and Career Opportunities," from *The Subtle Revolution,* Ralph E. Smith, ed. (Washington: The Urban Institute, 1979).

The rapid growth and changing character of the female labor force together with new attitudes and conceptions about women's role in society pose new opportunities and challenges for the American labor market in the years ahead. Indeed, the past decade has witnessed many changes in the stereotypical views of women's work and in the career expectations of young women. The growing propensity of women to remain continuously in the labor force while their children are young and the recognition that women are quite likely to depend on their jobs for financial support and status have already had an effect on people's attitudes about women workers.

Despite the widespread view that a rev-olution in societal sex roles is taking place, most economists agree that women's progress in the job market—as measured by their earnings and employment opportunities—has not matched the pace of expectations. Although the increased emphasis on paid employment and careers for women and a lessening of sex-role stereotypes point in the direction of an upgrading of women's labor market status, women workers have made relatively little progress toward equality, at least according to the official statistics. In 1977, for instance, the median income of female college graduates (including those with advanced degrees) who worked full time, year round, was below the median income of male high school dropouts.[1] And there has been remarkably little increase in women's relative earnings over the past decade, despite the upsurge in female labor force participation, an increase in the average number of years spent in the labor force, and the enactment of legislation outlawing sex discrimination in pay and employment.

Although it would be naive to expect that historical and institutional practices that have relegated women to second-class status in the past will miraculously disappear as women exhibit a strengthened commitment to the labor force, it is clear that new responses by employers, government policy makers, and women themselves are needed if society is to take full advantage of the opportunities presented by the growing female labor force. This chapter analyzes recent employment and income patterns of women workers with a view to identifying the barriers to progress to date, and assessing the likelihood that changing aspirations and attitudes will erode the inequalities that currently exist between women and men in the labor market.

THE MALE-FEMALE EARNINGS GAP

Although women have increased their labor force participation, demonstrated a growing stability in their commitment to paid employment, and sought more responsible job opportunities, their average earnings have remained far below those of men. In 1977, less than 20 percent of men working full-time, year round, earned less than $10,000, compared with more than half the full-time, year-round women workers (Figure 1). The ratio of median earnings of full-time, year-round women workers to male workers actually dropped from about

[1] U.S. Department of Commerce, Bureau of the Census, *Current Population Reports,* series P-60, no. 116, 1978.

63 percent in the mid-1950s to below 60 percent in the mid-1960s and 1970s. (See Table 1.)

Regardless of the criterion chosen—age, education, or prior work experience—women in each category earn far less than men with the same characteristics, even when they work the same number of hours.

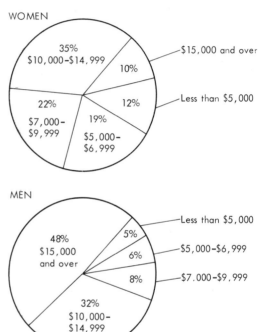

FIGURE 1

Earnings Distributions of Men and Women, 1977

Note: Median earnings of full-time, year-round workers 14 years of age and older. Numbers have been rounded, so percentages do not total 100 exactly. *Source:* U.S. Department of Commerce, Bureau of the Census.

As Table 1 shows, women's earnings are far below men's earnings within all the major occupational groups. And for many occupations, women's relative position has deteriorated over the past decade. What accounts for the stubborn persistence of the pay gap between men and women?

TABLE 1

Women's Relative Earnings by Occupation, 1956-1975

(Median Earnings of Full-Time, Year-Round Women Workers as a
Percentage of Men's Median Earnings)

Occupational Group	1956	1960	1965	1970	1975
All Workers	63.3	60.7	59.9	59.4	58.8
Professional and technical workers	62.4	61.3	65.2	64.1	65.9
Teachers, primary and secondary	NA	75.6	79.9	79.5	83.0
Managers and administrators	59.1	52.9	53.2	54.6	56.7
Clerical workers	71.7	67.6	67.2	64.0	62.2
Sales workers	41.8	40.9	40.5	42.7	38.9
Operatives	62.1	59.4	56.6	58.4	56.1
Service workers (nondomestic)	55.4	57.2	55.4	55.6	57.1

Source: U.S. Department of Commerce, Bureau of the Census, *Current Population Reports,* series P-60, various issues.

Historical Antecedents

The existence of a sizable gap between the earnings of women and men is as old as recorded history. There is even a biblical reference to sex-segregated pay scales. Leviticus (27:1–4) describes a conversation between the Lord and Moses in which adult males are valued at fifty shekels of silver and adult females at thirty shekels—a ratio strikingly like that encountered today. Possibly the different pay rates for men and women in primitive society were linked to their relative ability to perform hard manual labor—a rationale that today's advanced technology has made obsolete.

During the Industrial Revolution in nineteenth-century England, workers had practically no bargaining power and employers based wages on the perceived subsistence requirements of the workers. Contemporary records show that women's wages were set at around 60 percent of men's, purportedly because of women's lower subsistence requirements. Because single women workers' subsistence needs were presumed to be less than the needs of men with families to support, and married women were assumed to be merely supplementing husbands' income, employers felt justified in paying women less. Moreover, equal pay would have been inconsistent with the established order of male dominance.[2] As labor market rewards increasingly determined an individual's status, lower pay scales for women were at once a cause and effect of women's inferior social position.[3]

Although these events are now history, the fact remains that the average wage for full-time, year-round women workers still stands today at around 60 percent of the male wage. Although many changes in women's social and political status have occurred since the Industrial Revolution, the relative economic position of women workers has not advanced greatly in modern times.

[2] For a revealing account of the employment and pay practices and attitudes toward women workers during this period see Ivy Pinchbeck, *Women Workers and the Industrial Revolution* (London: G. Routledge, 1930).

[3] The tendency of the industrial wage structure to reproduce preindustrial status hierarchies rather than reflect the relative skill or productivity of classes of workers was noted by John Stuart Mill in 1848. See J. S. Mill, *Principles of Political Economy,* vol. 2.

Equal Pay But Different Work

Equal pay for equal work became the law with the passage of the Equal Pay Act of 1963. (The details of this and subsequent legislation affecting women's earnings will be discussed later in this chapter.) Yet the statistics show that women's earnings have remained far below those of men since equal pay was mandated.

How is the equal pay principle consistent with the persistent gap between men's and women's earnings? Quite simply, the law does not mandate equal pay for individuals doing different work. And much of the discrepancy between women's and men's earnings is accounted for by differences in their job assignments.[4]

Sex differences in job assignments can take the form of allotting men and women different qualitative tasks. In business concerns, for instance, personnel officers may routinely seek women for secretarial positions and men as management trainees. Some professions, such as nursing or teaching young children, are socially stereotyped as "women's work," while other jobs like airline pilot and police officer are considered "men's work." In most cases, jobs that are perceived as "women's work" pay less than do "men's" jobs requiring comparable levels of skill and effort.

A related mechanism that perpetuates a wage gap between men and women is the assignment of men to jobs needing specialized skills and training that can only be learned on the job, or to supervisory positions with extra responsibility. In practice, differences in upward mobility for men and women interact with the practice of giving men and women qualitatively different job assignments. Career-ladder jobs are often restricted to male turf,

[4] Occupational segregation that is done with the clear intent of paying women less than men for work of equal value is illegal. But it is difficult to demonstrate intent and to determine what constitutes work of equal value.

while women's jobs afford fewer opportunities for advancement. The male management trainee, for instance, will receive specialized training and will be assigned to positions of ever-increasing responsibility with, of course, higher pay. The secretary, meanwhile, often finds herself in a dead-end job, with much smaller increases in pay than those the male executive receives, even if she spends years in the company.

LIFE-CYCLE EARNINGS OF MEN AND WOMEN

Examination of the pattern of earnings over the life cycles of men and women reveals a marked contrast between the sexes. The earnings profile for males rises sharply from the postschool years through their twenties and thirties, peaks in their mid-forties, and declines somewhat thereafter. (See Figure 2.) In marked contrast, women's earnings rise hardly at all, and, on average, they peak at about age thirty.

Table 2 shows the same pattern. The youngest women who worked full-time, year-

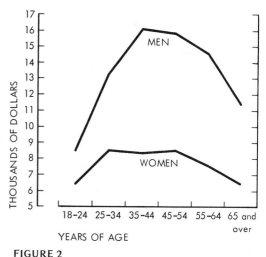

FIGURE 2

Life-Cycle Earnings Profiles of Men and Women, 1975

Note: Mean earnings of full-time, year-round workers. *Source:* U.S. Department of Commerce, Bureau of the Census.

TABLE 2

The Sex Differential in Earnings, by Age, 1975

(Mean* Earnings of Full-Time, Year-Round Workers)

Age Group	Female Earnings (Mean)	Male Earnings (Mean)	Ratio
All Ages	$7,940	$14,047	56.5
18-24	6,345	8,360	75.9
25-34	8,462	13,071	64.7
35-44	8,320	16,030	51.9
45-54	8,358	15,919	52.5
55-64	7,916	14,405	55.0
65+	6,309	11,286	55.9

*The Census Bureau does not tabulate median earnings broken down by sex and age.

Source: U.S. Department of Commerce, Bureau of the Census, *Current Population Reports*, series P-60, no. 105, 1977.

round, in 1975 earned 75 percent as much as men of the same age, in contrast to women aged forty-five to fifty-four, whose earnings averaged 52 percent of earnings for men in their age group.

Adjusting for such factors as education and occupation does not affect the general picture portrayed by these statistics. Alan Blinder, in a study that corrected age-earnings data for women and men by education and occupation, concluded that "the failure of women *in the same education-occupation category* [as men] to rise in the economic ladder over their working lives is seen to be the single largest cause of the male-female difference [in earnings] among whites."[5]

One factor frequently alleged to depress older women's wages is their relative lack of work experience. Certainly, women who drop out of the labor force to raise families cannot expect to earn as much when they return as persons with uninterrupted careers are earning. If women work only intermittently, they can-

not expect much upward mobility over their life cycle. Yet Isabel Sawhill has found that single (never-married) women had age-earnings profiles that were almost identical to those of married women despite the fact that single women's average job tenure was about the same as tenure for men in the same age bracket. Her study found that continuous work experience raised the earnings ratio of females by only one percentage point.[6] Even after adjusting for differences in age, education, hours worked, and other factors, she found that, compared with married women who earned, on average, 56 percent of the average earnings of men, women who never married averaged 57 percent of men's earnings.

Dead-End Jobs

If the failure of women's earnings to rise over the life cycle cannot be accounted for by a lack of stability in their attachment to the

[5] Alan S. Blinder, "Wage Discrimination: Reduced Form and Structural Estimates," *Journal of Human Resources*, 8 (Fall 1973), p. 448.

[6] Isabel V. Sawhill, "The Economics of Discrimination Against Women: Some New Findings," *Journal of Human Resources*, 8 (Fall 1973), pp. 383-96.

TABLE 3

Earnings of Women and Men in the Federal Government Civil Service System

(Full-Time, White-Collar Employees of Federal Government Agencies as of November 30, 1977)

General Schedule (GS) Grade	Salary	Number of Women Employed	Women as a Percentage of Total Employed
Total GS Employees	–	615,342	43.1
1	$ 6,561	1,277	65.7
2	7,422	15,818	74.1
3	8,366	73,187	77.5
4	9,391	134,602	77.5
5	10,507	126,060	68.1
6	11,712	60,560	69.6
7	13,014	64,631	49.4
8	14,414	16,374	50.3
9	15,920	54,455	35.1
10	17,532	8,547	32.4
11	19,263	30,621	19.4
12	23,087	16,997	11.1
13	27,453	7,670	6.8
14	32,442	2,878	4.9
15	38,160	1,435	4.5
16	44,756	159	3.4
17	47,500	55	3.2
18	47,500	16	3.7

Note: The salary rate shown is basic pay for employees in step 1 of the grade as of October 1978.

Source: U.S. Civil Service Commission, *Equal Employment Opportunity Statistics* (Washington, D.C.: U.S. Government Printing Office, 1978), p. 2.

labor market, how can we account for the flat age-earnings profiles for women that we observe in the official statistics? One possibility is that women find it more difficult than men to move up the ladder to high-status jobs.

A case in point is the distribution of women among the classification grades of the Federal Government Civil Service system. Although the government professes to be an equal opportunity employer, it is clear from Table 3 that women are disproportionately employed at the bottom end of the scale. More than three-fourths of the jobs in classifications 1 through 3 (paying $6,561 to $8,366) are held by women. In contrast, women hold only around 4 percent of jobs in classifications

14 through 18 (paying more than $32,000).[7]

Similar patterns are characteristic of the distribution of women in the job hierarchies of large private corporations. Barbara Bergmann notes the case of an insurance company that achieved notoriety as a result of a sex-discrimination lawsuit brought by some of its employees under Title VII of the Civil Rights Act of 1964.[8] Between 1965 and 1970, the

[7] For a more detailed breakdown, see U.S. Civil Service Commission, *Equal Employment Opportunity Statistics* (Washington, D.C.: U.S. Government Printing Office, 1978).

[8] Barbara R. Bergmann, "Reducing the Pervasiveness of Discrimination," in Eli Ginzberg, ed., *Jobs for Americans,* by the American Assembly (Englewood Cliffs, N.J.: Prentice-Hall, Inc., 1976).

company recruited 2,000 individuals from outside the company for professional positions designated "claims adjuster" and "claims representative." For each category, the only formal requirement was a college degree. Yet, only men were designated claims adjusters, while claims representatives were almost exclusively women. New claims adjusters were paid $2,500 more than claims representatives, but what is more important, only adjusters could obtain promotions beyond a low supervisory level. While the men who stayed with the firm advanced into higher-paying jobs as they gained experience and were given increased responsibility, women were stuck in jobs paying little more than their starting salary. Thus, although the designation of women as claims representatives resulted in a starting wage $2,500 lower than the wage for male claims adjusters, this gap was small compared with the later discrepancy associated with the fact that claims adjusters were promoted to higher-paying jobs while claims representatives were not.[9]

Are Women Committed Workers?

The perception that women are temporary participants in the work force is often cited as a rationale for paying women low wages and offering them limited opportunities for advancement. How committed are women to work outside the home, and what effect does their commitment or lack of it have on their working lives?

Labor force participation and continuity of experience obviously help shape the life-cycle earnings profiles of women. One explanation for why men's age-earnings profiles rise while women's are relatively flat is that men are more likely to invest early in education and training that pay off later in higher earnings. Because men view their careers in long-term perspective, they are allegedly willing to forgo short-term earnings opportunities and to undertake costly education and training with a view toward a later payoff. Women, conversely, are said to invest less in education and training because they expect to have fewer years of labor force activity in which to benefit from education and training.[10]

Another explanation for the differences in men's and women's age-earnings profiles is that employers provide superior training opportunities for men in the expectation that men will stay with the firm longer than will most women. Training decisions are usually made early in a worker's career, before he or she has had the opportunity to establish a work history. To the extent that employers hold traditional attitudes regarding the intermittency or unreliability of women employees, even women who never leave the firm will have received fewer training opportunities than will similarly qualified men. Hence, on average, women have flatter life-cycle earnings profiles.[11]

There seems to be some truth in each of these explanations. Both women and employers

---

[9] A growing body of academic literature has addressed itself to this phenomenon. One approach conceptualizes two distinct labor markets. One set of jobs, generally the low-paying, dead-end positions, is filled by recruits of new workers from outside the firm. The other set of higher-paying jobs is filled internally, through the promotion and upgrading of currently employed workers. For a complete discussion, see Peter B. Doeringer and Michael J. Piore, *Internal Labor Markets and Manpower Analysis* (Lexington, Mass.: D.C. Heath and Company, 1971).

[10] See, for instance, Gary S. Becker, *Human Capital: A Theoretical and Empirical Analysis* (New York: Columbia University Press, 1964); Jacob Mincer, "Investment in Human Capital," *Journal of Political Economy,* 66 (August 1958); and Jacob Mincer and Solomon W. Polachek, "Family Investments in Human Capital: Earnings of Women," *Journal of Political Economy,* 82 (March/April 1974), pp. S76-S108.

[11] See Barbara R. Bergmann, "Sex Discrimination in Wages: Comment," in Orley Ashenfelter and Albert Rees, eds., *Discrimination in Labor Markets* (Princeton: Princeton University Press, 1973), pp. 152-54.

underestimate how long the average woman will remain in the labor force. A national survey that followed the labor market experiences of two groups of women for five years revealed that younger women (ages fourteen to twenty-four in 1968) grossly underestimated their future labor market participation when their predictions were compared with the actual work experience of older women.[12] Young white women predicted a participation rate of 29 percent at age thirty-five, compared with an actual rate of 48 percent for the older women at age thirty-five. Black women predicted a rate of 51 percent compared with an actual rate of 67 percent. And the gap between the responses of the younger women and the actual participation rate they will experience at age thirty-five is likely to be even greater than these numbers show, given the national trend to higher female labor force participation.

When women underestimate their future labor market participation, they will invest in less education and training than their prospects warrant. Moreover, they may be less concerned about the quality of their education and may be careless about career planning. Women in college still tend to specialize in the arts and humanities, while men predominate in science and business. Part of this difference is, no doubt, the result of an educational system that encourages boys to excel in science and competitive sports and girls to pursue artistic and literary studies. Further, our society does not emphasize career planning for girls. Marriage has been seen as the primary mechanism through which a woman achieves status; hence many women's efforts have been concentrated on securing desirable husbands, rather than on achieving through their own merits. In

the past, a woman's college education has sometimes been viewed more as a way to improve social acceptability than as a vehicle for acquiring the skills requisite to a career.

But myopia about future work experience is only one factor in explaining women's relatively flat life-cycle earnings profiles. Studies indicate that women get less payoff from education and training than men do in terms of earnings.[13] Figure 3 shows the life-cycle income profiles of men and women by years of education. For men in their mid-forties, the income of the average college graduate is about $9,000 a year more than for high school graduates. For women, the difference between high school and college graduates' earnings is only about $4,000. Furthermore, women who have finished college have lower incomes than do male high school graduates of all ages; in fact, as already noted, their median incomes are about on a par with those of male high school dropouts.

Not all the differential between male and female college graduates can be explained by differences in their choice of major or in the quality of the institution attended. One study paired female college graduates with male counterparts with the same academic degree from the same institution. The outcome showed a substantial wage gap between the sexes, even when quality of output and work experience were taken into account.[14]

It appears, then, that a combination of factors adversely affects the upward mobility of women. To the extent that women discount their probable future labor market participation, they will invest in less education and training, but because of externally imposed

---

[12] Reported in U.S. Department of Labor, Employment and Training Administration, *Women and Work,* Manpower Research Monograph No. 46 (Washington, D.C.: U.S. Government Printing Office, 1977), p. 15.

[13] See, for instance, Gary D. Brown, "How Type of Employment Affects Earnings Differences by Sex," *Monthly Labor Review,* 99 (July 1976), pp. 25-30.

[14] Nancy M. Gordon and Thomas E. Morton, "The Staff Salary Structure of A Large University," *Journal of Human Resources,* 11 (Summer 1976), pp. 374-82.

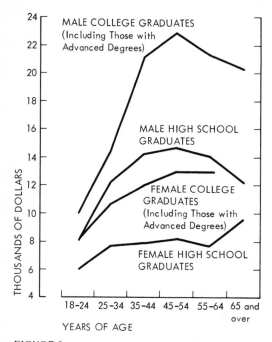

THOUSANDS OF DOLLARS

MALE COLLEGE GRADUATES (Including Those with Advanced Degrees)

MALE HIGH SCHOOL GRADUATES

FEMALE COLLEGE GRADUATES (Including Those with Advanced Degrees)

FEMALE HIGH SCHOOL GRADUATES

18-24 25-34 35-44 45-54 55-64 65 and over

YEARS OF AGE

FIGURE 3

The Effects of Education on the Life-Cycle Incomes of Men and Women, 1975

Note: Median incomes of full-time, year-round workers, 1975.
Source: U.S. Department of Commerce, Bureau of the Census.

barriers to their upward mobility, women also get less payoff for education and training than do men. Thus there is a vicious circle in which women have less incentive to undertake costly education and training than men do, not only because they expect to spend less time in the labor market, but also because education and training do not pay off in higher earnings for women to the same degree that they do for men.

Women's Labor Force Commitment and Upward Mobility

Although years of experience in the job market enhance earnings, women's progress in the labor market may ultimately depend on whether they strengthen their job attachment. In low-

income families, for instance, a large percentage of the women work, but they work intermittently and change jobs often. These practices mean loss of seniority, a principal avenue of advancement. In more affluent families, women often drop out of the labor force during their childbearing years, just when their male counterparts are aggressively moving up the career ladder. When women return to work, they have to compete for jobs with younger men who are preferred because presumably they have more working years ahead during which the firm can benefit from its investment in them.

Of course childbearing and child rearing are not the only reasons women leave their jobs. If women's employment is viewed as secondary within the family, the wife may be expected to relocate as her husband's career may require. Studies show that among couples who migrate, the husband's wage generally increases while the wife's wage declines.[15] This fact suggests that the average couple moves because of a better opportunity for the husband, at the cost of a drop in earnings for the wife. The longer-range consequences of the move may be even more adverse, if the woman forgoes a job that would have provided upward mobility in later years.

Employers may expect that if they invest in training a man and he receives a better offer, they can retain him by paying a higher wage. By the same token, they may feel they have less prospect of retaining a woman's services if a family's moves are determined by the husband's needs.

As in the case of education and training investments, many factors contribute to women's relatively weak job commitment. High rates of job turnover are common among low-

[15] See Solomon W. Polachek and Francis W. Horvath, "A Life Cycle Approach to Migration: Analysis of the Perspicacious Peregrinator," in Ronald G. Ehrenberg, ed., *Research in Labor Economics*, Vol. 1 (Greenwich, Conn.: Jai Press, 1977).

paid workers of both sexes who correctly perceive little advantage to job continuity. From the employer's perspective, job continuity rather than labor force commitment is the principal concern; yet it is often assumed that the two are synonymous. Actually, the concentration of women in low-paying, dead-end jobs weakens their *job* attachment, regardless of whether their *labor market* commitment is continuous. This reduced job attachment results in another vicious circle in which women are perceived to be less stable workers than men, and hence are not given responsible positions. But studies document that when account is taken of job status, men and women show very little difference in job attachment.[16] Further, although workers in the lowest-ranked jobs have relatively high absentee rates, absenteeism in equivalent job categories is no higher for women than for men.[17]

Women have begun to realize that dropping out of the labor force in the early years can adversely affect their job prospects should they eventually want to return to work. One reason the overall female labor force participation rate has risen so fast is that women who enter the labor force are remaining longer than before. The Bureau of Labor Statistics reports that although the average number of years men spend in the labor force has been declining

since 1950, the average number of years women work has been sharply rising, especially among married women with children. After 1950, work-life expectancy among women rose at a faster rate than did overall life expectancy, and the time women spent out of the labor force began to decline.[18]

Many young women are postponing childbearing until they have established careers and demonstrated a commitment to continuous participation in the labor force. Provided they drop out for only a short period, it is often possible for them to return to similar positions. The prospect of good, well-paying jobs is likely to entice them to return to the labor force more quickly than would be the case if less desirable options are available. Hence working women who have delayed childbearing until they have established careers or seniority are expected to have higher labor force participation rates when they have children than do those women who dropped out earlier and have less attractive reentry prospects.

OCCUPATIONAL SEGREGATION BY SEX

An important factor that keeps the equal pay principle from closing the male-female earnings gap is so-called *occupational segregation.* Traditional conceptions of women's work, derived from societal sex roles and sex-based division of labor at home, characterize the jobs women do in the paid labor force. As Figure 4 shows, more than two-thirds of employed women hold jobs in stereotypically female occupations as nurses, librarians, teachers, social workers, clerical workers, and service workers.

[16] See, for instance, John B. Parrish, "Employment of Women Chemists in Industrial Laboratories," *Science,* April 30, 1965; and U.S. Department of Labor, Women's Bureau, *Facts About Women's Absenteeism and Labor Turnover* (Washington, D.C.: U.S. Government Printing Office, 1969).

[17] Ibid. According to the Women's Bureau report, among federal government workers in 1961, sick leave averaged 9.6 days for women and 7.9 days for men. However, among those earning $9,000 to $10,000 per year, sick leave averaged 6.9 days for women versus 6.3 days for men. Further, a Public Health Service study showed an average of 5.6 days lost by women as compared with 5.3 by men in all employment in 1967. "Current Estimates from the Health Interview Survey," *Vital and Health Statistics* (Washington, D.C.: U.S. Government Printing Office, 1967).

[18] Howard N. Fullerton, Jr., and James J. Byrne, *Length of Working Life for Men and Women, 1970,* U.S. Department of Labor, Bureau of Labor Statistics, Special Labor Force Report No. 187 (Washington, D.C.: U.S. Government Printing Office, 1977).

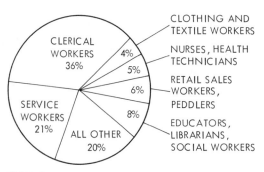

FIGURE 4

Occupational Profile of the Female Labor
Force, 1977

Percentage of These Groups That Are Female

Clerical workers	79%	Sales clerks, etc.	67%
Service workers	62%	Nurses, etc.	83%
Educators, etc.	64%	Textile workers, etc.	76%

Source: U.S. Department of Labor, Bureau of Labor Statistics, 1977.

Several traits characterize jobs typically held by women. First, women are rarely put in positions of authority. The assignment of male supervisors to a predominantly female work force limits women's upward mobility even in female-dominated occupations. In elementary and secondary schools, for example, two-thirds of the teachers are women, but only a third of the principals and other school administrators are women.

Both white-collar and blue-collar jobs that women hold are stereotyped according to certain attributes commonly perceived as feminine. Jobs that require caring for others and nurturing small children are viewed as appropriately feminine, since these are tasks to which females are exposed from childhood.

Another characteristic of women's work assignments is that women are allowed only vicarious rather than direct achievements. The secretary who prepares her boss for business dealings, the nurse who assists the doctor in the operating room, and even the school teacher whose success lies in the achievements of her students exemplify indirect achievers. Society has long encouraged women to accept vicar-

ious satisfactions. Girls have been taught to enjoy competitive sports as spectators or cheerleaders. Women have learned home economics with a view to pleasing husbands and raising healthy children.

Among blue-collar workers, too, sex-role attitudes affect job assignments. Women allegedly are better than men at tedious, repetitive tasks and at jobs requiring manual dexterity. Further, women are supposed to be more sensitive than men to loud noises and dirty places, and are presumed less able than men to work with heavy equipment (even though modern technology is such that most heavy equipment operates mechanically and physical strength often is not particularly important). As in the white-collar world, traditional sex roles dictate that blue-collar women should be supervised by men.

Social and Psychological Pressures

Although occupational segregation of women may be a rather obvious way for employers to circumvent the Equal Pay Act, the mechanisms that perpetuate segregation are extremely powerful. When women attempt to move out of vicarious roles, they are often seen as unfeminine and in many cases they are ridiculed. Women who try to achieve directly are said to "threaten" men and may be subjected to ostracism by fellow workers. The psychological impact of male disapproval can be devastating for many women, particularly because society has taught them the importance of pleasing men as a way to obtain status.

Overt sex harassment is common when blue-collar women try to do traditionally masculine work. Pornographic material is sometimes displayed to embarrass women and show them "their place." Work areas are sometimes arranged so as to make it difficult for anyone of short stature to have access to the equipment used. In many cases, rearrangement of the work place would not inhibit production, but male workers resist changes and ridicule women who try to work under the adverse conditions.[19]

The male buddy system also operates. In many factory environments, teamwork is essential for effective completion of jobs, and men often refuse to cooperate with a woman who dares to invade male territory, particularly if she refuses to exchange sexual favors.[20]

Among blue-collar workers a genuine conflict exists between union solidarity and the question of women's rights. The problem becomes acute when equal employment opportunity for women comes into conflict with union seniority systems.

Many of the work rules that make it difficult for women to perform traditionally male jobs are set by the male-dominated trade unions. Union meetings are often held in bars and male lodge halls where working-class women do not go. Women workers report that their husbands will not allow them to go to union meetings, even if they could find the time when the housework is completed.

As long as sex roles within the family presuppose male dominance and female submission, occupational segregation in the marketplace will be hard to overcome. Women and men have trouble adjusting to different sex-role patterns at home and in the office. A man who is accustomed to a submissive wife has trouble taking orders from a woman at work, while a female executive with a position of authority in the office may find it hard to accept a dominant husband at home.

Wages in Female-Dominated Occupations

Female occupations are noted for their low wages; hence occupational segregation of wo-

men has contributed to the persistence of the male-female wage gap. If women are disproportionately concentrated in the low-wage sectors of the economy, a redistribution more in line with male employment patterns would result in an increase in relative earnings for women.

One study of men's and women's wages in more than 400 detailed occupations concluded that about 28 percent of the male-female wage rate differential among whites and about 22 percent among blacks is attributable to sex differences in the occupational distribution of employment.[21] (The rest of the wage gap is accounted for by sex differences in earnings *within* occupational categories.) The study revealed that the relative contribution of occupational segregation in explaining wage differentials varied considerably by age, marital status, and education. Occupational segregation had the largest effect on married, white college graduates; among them, it accounted for nearly 70 percent of the differential.[22]

Estimates of this kind understate the losses to women from occupational segregation to the extent that segregation itself causes lower wages in predominantly female occupations. Unless the number of jobs in the female job sector keeps pace with the number of women seeking employment, or unless job segregation by sex is alleviated, the rapid growth of the female labor force will drive down wages in female-oriented occupations.

---

[19] For a discussion of some of these factors in the construction trade, see Sandra Hofferth, Katharine Fisher, and Donna Heins, "Occupational Segregation in Construction: A Case Study in Washington, D.C.," (mimeographed), The Urban Institute, Washington, D.C., 1977.

[20] Ibid.

[21] The amount of the wage gap attributable to occupational segregation depends on how detailed the occupational definition is. The greater the detail, the more the wage gap appears to be affected by occupational differences. For instance, in the extreme case in which each job is treated as a separate occupation, all wage differences would be attributed to occupational differences.

[22] Barry Chiswick, J. Fackler, June O'Neill, and Solomon Polachek, "The Effect of Occupation on Race and Sex Differences in Hourly Earnings," *Proceedings of the American Statistical Association*, 1974, pp. 219-28.

TABLE 4

Employment of Women in Clerical and Service Occupations, 1960-1977

Year	Total Female Labor Force (thousands)	Clerical		Nondomestic Service	
		Number (thousands)	Percentage of Total	Number (thousands)	Percentage of Total
1960	21,374	6,617	30.3	3,236	14.8
1965	24,748	7,862	31.8	3,826	15.5
1970	29,667	10,233	34.5	4,909	16.5
1971	29,875	10,132	33.9	5,192	17.4
1972	31,072	10,777	34.7	5,435	17.5
1973	32,446	11,140	34.3	5,678	17.5
1974	33,417	11,676	34.9	5,955	17.8
1975	33,553	11,773	35.1	6,116	18.2
1976	35,095	12,248	34.9	6,282	17.9
1977	36,685	12,730	34.7	6,567	17.9

Source: U.S. Department of Labor, Employment and Training Administration, *Employment and Training Report of the President, 1978,* p. 205.

Occupational Crowding

Many observers attributed the rapid growth of the female labor force during the 1960s to the increase in job opportunities in the traditionally female sector—particularly in clerical work, teaching, and health services. More recently, however, the growth in job opportunities in the female sector does not appear to have kept pace with the large number of female job seekers.

Trends in the clerical field have particular significance for the female work force as a whole because one in three women workers is employed in clerical work and 80 percent of all clerical workers are women. Between 1968 and 1977, female jobholders increased by 8.9 million, and 3.3 million of these were in clerical occupations. As Table 4 shows, clerical employment as a percentage of total female employment has risen from less than 32 percent in the mid-1960s to about 35 percent in the mid-1970s.

Although clerical employment has been increasing at a faster rate than the overall labor force has grown, clerical wages have not kept pace with the earnings of other female workers. Median earnings of female full-time, year-round clerical workers rose only 4.9 percent in real terms between 1965 and 1975 (less than 0.5 percent a year), compared with a 25.4 percent increase in real median earnings for all other female full-time workers over the same period.[23] At the same time, unemployment among clerical workers increased substantially. In 1965, clerical workers represented 11 percent of all unemployed workers, compared with nearly 15 percent in 1977.

These figures suggest that the demand for clerical workers since 1968 simply has not kept

[23] In 1975, median earnings for male clerical workers were $12,152, compared with $7,562 for women clericals working full time, year round. This suggests considerable segmentation on the basis of sex within the clerical category. Most male clerical workers are post office mail carriers, shipping and receiving clerks, and stock clerks and storekeepers, all categories with a minority of women. Secretaries, typists, telephone operators, bank tellers, and bookkeepers are almost exclusively female.

up with the supply of women seeking clerical work. Occupational crowding in this field makes it a poor career choice, yet the number of people in clerical jobs continues to increase at a rapid pace. Similar trends are evident among service workers and in some female-dominated occupations within the professional and technical categories.

Trends Among Younger Workers

Why are women continuing to enter the clerical field when job opportunities there seem less attractive than in the past? One factor in the growth of clerical employment is the change in the age composition of the female labor force— a much higher proportion of younger women now participate—that has accompanied its rapid growth. In 1977, 45 percent of the members of the adult female labor force were twenty to thirty-four years old, up from 35 percent in 1968. (The comparable figures for men are 40 percent versus 33 percent.)

Younger women are much more likely to be in clerical occupations than are older women. According to the Bureau of Labor Statistics, more than 42 percent of women age twenty to twenty-four were in clerical jobs in 1977, compared with 29 percent of women over fifty-four. But in 1968 more than 48 percent of younger women compared with about 24 percent of older women were in clerical jobs. For many women, clerical employment seems to have become a way station to other jobs. A higher proportion of older women are employed in the professional, technical, and managerial categories than are younger women.

That the rise in clerical employment is associated with the greater representation of younger workers in the female labor force is apparent from Table 5. Between 1968 and 1977, the occupational distribution of younger women age twenty to thirty-four shifted

TABLE 5

Occupation Distribution of Young Women Workers (Ages 20-34) in 1977 Compared with 1968

Occupation	Distribution (percent)	
	1977	1968
Professional, technical, and managerial	24.5	20.0
(of which, teachers*)	(7.1)	(7.1)
Clerical	38.0	41.7
Services	17.4	16.7
(of which, private household)	(1.4)	(3.0)
Operatives	10.4	14.5
Craftsmen	1.8	0.6
Sales	5.6	4.4
Other	2.3	2.1

*Excludes college and university teachers.
Source: Unpublished tabulations provided by the U.S. Department of Labor, Bureau of Labor Statistics.

slightly away from clerical work toward the professional, technical, and managerial occupations. Because of the higher proportion of younger women in the work force, who are still more likely than older women to be employed as clerical workers, however, the absolute proportion of clerical workers among all employed women has risen. But if the trend among younger workers away from clerical jobs continues, the proportion of women in clerical employment should decline in the future, thereby easing the crowding. The simultaneous trend toward the professional and managerial categories is encouraging. It suggests that the male-female wage gap might be expected to narrow somewhat in the future.

Other occupational trends among young women workers are less significant, but suggest a generally positive outlook. For example, although the proportion of young female workers in the service category has increased, fewer are in private household employment. The decline in blue-collar employment reflects a general shift in the economy toward service-producing industries; hence some of the increase in service employment is directly associated with a decline in manufacturing employment. But it is notable that the younger women have increased their representation among craft workers, although they are still grossly under-represented in the skilled blue-collar trades.

Although these trends among younger workers are important and encouraging as indicators of potential improvement, occupational segregation of women remains widespread and most women coming into the labor force are taking jobs in traditionally female occupations. A recent survey of 5,000 young women aged twenty-one to thirty-one revealed that of those who expected to be working outside the home by age thirty-five, the overwhelming majority aspired to traditionally female occupations. Of the noncollege females, 81 percent of the whites and 87 percent of the blacks said they would prefer to be in a typically female job by age thirty-five; among college females, the numbers aspiring to traditional careers were 75 percent for whites and 78 percent for blacks.[24]

Thus, although there are a few encouraging signs in the occupational statistics, there is also evidence that attitudes about job options for women are changing very slowly. Even though barriers to women in previously male sectors are eroding as a result of affirmative action plans and enforcement of equal opportunity guidelines, these changes have not occurred rapidly enough to keep pace with the growth of the female labor force. And although the struggle for equal rights and the egalitarian ideology accompanying it have produced a philosophical environment that encourages women to seek new opportunities, many still opt for traditionally female labor market activities even as they reject the role of full-time homemaker.

Sex-based division of labor has taken many forms as our society has evolved. In primitive times, men were the hunters, women the gatherers. During industrialization, men worked primarily outside the home; women in domestic activities and cottage industry. The rapid growth of the female labor force over the past decade has signaled the emergence of a new era in which the major distinction between men's work and women's work will no longer be associated with market versus nonmarket labor. This development could portend greater economic and social equality between the sexes. But another possibility is that traditional views about "women's place" will simply be translated into more rigid sexual stereotypes in the labor market, and crowding in traditionally female jobs will continue to depress women's wages relative to those of male workers.

Sex Discrimination

If so much of the male-female earnings gap is to be explained by differences in opportunities for advancement and occupational segregation, is the root of the problem then not pure discrimination?

The most blatant forms of discrimination —separate pay schedules for men and women and rules prohibiting women from taking certain jobs—are illegal. But occupational segregation of the sexes makes it fairly easy to circumvent the Equal Pay Act in many cases and the pervasive gap in male-female earnings suggests that much remains to be accomplished.[25] The female administrative assistant may do the

---

[24] Patricia K. Brito and Carol L. Jusenius, "Occupational Expectations for Age 35," in U.S. Department of Labor, *Years for Decision*, Vol. 4, R&D Monograph No. 24, 1978.

[25] For an excellent discussion and specific documentation of the practice of reclassifying jobs solely to sanction separate pay scales for women and men, see Winn Newman, "Combatting Occupational Segregation: Policy Issues," in Martha Blaxall and Barbara Reagan, eds., *Women and the Workplace* (Chicago: University of Chicago Press, 1976), pp. 265-72.

same work as a male executive, but usually she does it for far less pay. The female operative may aspire to learn a skill that would increase her earnings, but often is unable to pass the test without the cooperation of male coworkers, who routinely provide assistance to male trainees. To the extent that such behavior derives from traditional attitudes about women's place rather than deliberate attempts to shut women out of better-paying jobs, it may be difficult to agree on whether it constitutes discrimination in a legal sense. But the effect is the same.

LAWS AND REGULATIONS GOVERNING WOMEN'S EMPLOYMENT

While outdated stereotypes regarding women's long-range commitment to work and traditional views about "women's place" in the job market are changing rather slowly, legislation governing women's employment has changed radically since the early 1960s. Over the years prior to that time, the so-called protective labor laws (which limited women's total hours of work and prohibited women from lifting heavy objects, working during pregnancy, and working at night) had become mechanisms through which firms could legally refuse to hire women for certain jobs. In many cases, appeals to these laws were the basis on which women were denied equal employment opportunity.[26] But beginning with the Equal Pay Act of 1963, which amended the 1938 Fair Labor Standards Act, a new policy evolved. With it came a set of laws and regulations that not only overturned

the protective labor laws of individual states, but also provided a legislative and psychological climate in which overt discrimination on the basis of sex is more difficult to achieve.

The Equal Pay Act outlaws separate pay scales for men and women for work requiring similar skills and performed under the same working conditions. Inasmuch as it did not require nondiscrimination in hiring, promotion, or work assignments, however, the Equal Pay Act did not mandate equal employment opportunity. Some say the motivation of the Equal Pay Act was actually to increase employment security for men who feared competition from women who would do their jobs for lower wages.[27] Nonetheless, this piece of legislation represented a watershed, a turning away from a legal system that facilitated and sanctioned discrimination against women to a legal environment that prohibits sex discrimination in employment.

The Civil Rights Act was passed in 1964 on a wave of public concern over the injustices of racial discrimination. Legislative historians note that inclusion of the word "sex" in Title VII of the bill that sought to prohibit discrimination in employment was an attempt by the bill's opponents to engineer its defeat.[28] Yet, with the strong support of Congresswoman Martha Griffiths, the bill became law, closing the major loophole of the Equal Pay Act. Title VII prohibits all forms of discrimination in employment, including hiring, firing, promotion, training, and fringe benefits.

Title VII also established an enforcement agency, the Equal Employment Opportunity Commission (EEOC). Although initially the EEOC concentrated its efforts on prohibiting racial discrimination, more recently it has increased its efforts to monitor discrimination

---

[26] Two excellent discussions of the adverse effects on women of the protective labor laws are Jo Freeman, "The Legal Basis of the Sexual Caste System," *Valparaiso Law Review,* 5 (1971), pp. 213-30; and Mary Eastwood, "Legal Protection Against Sex Discrimination," in Ann H. Stromberg and Shirley Harkess, eds., *Women Working* (Palo Alto, Calif.: Mayfield Publishing Company, 1978), pp. 111-13.

[27] Freeman, "The Legal Basis of the Sexual Caste System," pp. 226-27.

[28] Jo Freeman, *The Politics of Women's Liberation* (New York: Longman, 1975), pp. 53-54.

on the basis of sex.[29] The EEOC still lacks effective enforcement powers and is over-burdened with a heavy caseload, but its guidelines have clarified important legal issues. For instance, the guidelines have made it illegal for firms to attribute characteristics to individuals based on the attributes of a group. Further, since 1972, EEOC has been empowered to bring civil action suits against private firms engaged in discriminatory practices.

In 1967 Executive Order 11375 extended an earlier prohibition against racial discrimination in employment under federal contracts and subcontracts to sex discrimination. This action was followed in 1969 by Executive Order 11478 prohibiting sex discrimination by the federal government as an employer. In 1978 President Carter announced a reorganization plan to consolidate federal equal employment activities. He also took action to strengthen EEOC as an enforcement agency.[30]

Because the Equal Pay Act does not cover professional employees, and because Title VII of the Civil Rights Act excludes educational institutions, additional legislation was needed to satisfy the grievances of women teachers who were denied promotional activities. The Educational Amendments Act of 1972 and the Women's Educational Equity Act of 1974 enabled women teachers to seek legal redress. At the same time, [they] nullified school board practices requiring pregnant teachers to take [unpaid] leave and opened the door to elimination of sex biases in school curricula and academic programs.[31]

The legislative and judicial record of the post-1963 period has clearly established the principle of equal employment opportunity for women. Various class-action suits charging sex discrimination have won sizable back pay settlements, including an out-of-court agreement in 1973 under which the American Telephone and Telegraph Company agreed to pay $38 million to women employees in back pay and salary adjustments.[32]

By the beginning of the 1970s, policy gradually shifted, without congressional action, away from simple prohibition of discrimination to affirmative action to remedy the effects of past discrimination and to eliminate more subtle institutional barriers to equal employment opportunities. This policy shift meant that firms were required to seek out women for jobs in which they were underrepresented, and to give preference to qualified women (and minorities) even if male candidates appeared to have better credentials.

Various rulings have prohibited the denial of employment to mothers of preschool children and have upheld the rights of husbands of women employees to receive the same dependents' benefits as dependents of male employees.[33] In a reversal of these trends, however, the Supreme Court in 1976 upheld the constitutionality of disability insurance systems that deny benefits to women unable to work because of pregnancy or childbirth.[34]

The rapid evolution of the law from sanctioning sex discrimination in the guise of protecting the weaker sex, to establishing the principle of equal employment opportunity, and finally to mandating the eradication of

---

[29] See Phyllis A. Wallace, "Employment Discrimination: Some Policy Implications," in Orley Ashenfelter and Albert Rees, eds., *Discrimination in Labor Markets* (Princeton: Princeton University Press, 1973), pp. 163-64.

[30] Office of the White House Press Secretary, February 23, 1978.

[31] Terry Tinson Saario, "Title IX: Now What?" in Allan C. Ornstein and Steven I. Miller, eds., *Policy Issues in Education* (Lexington, Mass.: Lexington Books, D.C. Heath and Company, 1976).

[32] Freeman, *The Politics of Women's Liberation,* p. 190. Also see Phyllis A. Wallace, ed., *Equal Employment Opportunity and the AT&T Case* (Cambridge, Mass.: The MIT Press, 1976).

[33] Mary Eastwood, "Legal Protection Against Sex Discrimination," pp. 117-21.

[34] Ibid., p. 118.

discrimination through affirmative action is one of the most significant legislative developments of the post-World War II era. However, affirmative action as policy is extremely difficult to enforce. In an attempt to facilitate the enforcement effort, the federal courts have, since around 1971, shifted the burden of proof to employers. Where women workers as a group are paid less than men, employers must demonstrate that the discrepancy is not the result of discrimination. Further, employers must show that the lower earnings of women result from less education, less prior experience, or other relevant factors. In addition, where women are underrepresented in high-paying jobs and in management, employers must establish an acceptable affirmative action plan and demonstrate a "good faith" attempt to recruit and hire more women (and minorities) for these posts.[35]

The effectiveness of these laws and judicial rulings for improving the labor market prospects of women will depend to a large extent on whether women and employers take advantage of the opportunities they offer. Women must seek wider horizons, move out of traditional occupations, and plan for long-term careers. Equal employment legislation may open new doors for women, but women themselves must be prepared to walk through them.

Then too, employers must recognize that it will be unproductive, in the long run, to relegate women to traditionally female roles. Employment opportunities in female occupations are limited and the growing female labor force needs to enter other areas where there is a scarcity of workers. Of course, moving women into "men's turf" means a breaching of the age-old practice of paying women less than men, and will be met with

considerable opposition from male workers who will view integration of the work place as a threat to their jobs and self-esteem.

Equal employment for women will not be an easy road, as prejudices against women are strongest in traditionally male strongholds. But the law that mandates affirmative action to increase the representation of women in these fields will be a powerful ally.

Legislative support for equal employment opportunity for women has never been stronger, and the requirement that firms take affirmative action to promote women and move them into formerly male occupations is a major achievement in the struggle for women's rights in the labor market. But it must be emphasized that the effective application of these laws is facilitated by a strong and growing economy. In a prosperous economy, mobility barriers and prejudicial attitudes about women workers will erode much faster than under the slack economic conditions that have typified the recent past.

CONCLUSIONS AND RECOMMENDATIONS

Today the average married woman with children will spend about twenty-five years in the labor force.[36] Some women will never marry, others will be divorced or widowed, and will—at some point in their lives—be dependent on their own earnings for financial support and status.

This chapter has examined some of the factors behind the persistent gap in men's and women's earnings, a gap that has not narrowed appreciably as women have increased their labor force participation and long-term career commitment. Segregating the labor market by sex

---

[35] Freeman, *The Politics of Women's Liberation,* pp. 191-93.

[36] U.S. Department of Labor, Bureau of Labor Statistics, *Length of Working Life for Men and Women, 1970,* Special Labor Force Report No. 187 (Washington, D.C.: U.S. Government Printing Office, 1977).

has been a mechanism that has perpetuated the practice of paying women less than men. Moreover, the belief that women are intermittent workers affects both their job content and opportunities for advancement. Women continue to underestimate their future work life, and hence fail to consider careers that will lead to higher earnings over the life cycle. Employers continue to view women as less stable workers than men and hence resist placing women in training or management positions that will lead to higher pay.

Assignment to low-status jobs, in turn, has reinforced the view of women within their own families as secondary earners. This subordinate status has meant that women are expected to do a disproportionate share of the housework, and to relocate or perform unpaid services (like entertaining) to further their husbands' careers. These demands, in turn, make it more difficult for women to compete on an equal basis with men in the most challenging and demanding jobs.

Many factors contribute to the vicious circle that prevents women's earnings from achieving parity with men's. But this diversity means that there are also many potential points of intervention to break the self-reinforcing process. From a policy perspective, intervention at several points simultaneously is likely to pay off most effectively. Affirmative action laws must be accompanied by more realistic career counseling of young women to encourage them to plan for a lifetime of labor market activity and to consider nontraditional career options. Employers, too, need up-to-date information about the probable job tenure of women workers. And married couples need to become more sensitive to the likelihood that the wife's long-term job prospects must be taken into account when planning the division of household responsibilities and deciding where to live.

Maintaining job continuity is important if women are to expect equal access to training

and career-ladder spots. Unfortunately, the time for women and men to begin building a career coincides with the peak of domestic responsibilities associated with child rearing. Marital strains arise when the peak effort associated with moving up the career ladder occurs simultaneously for both partners. Working women and the firms that train them need to consider ways to relieve some of the tensions of two-earner couples so as to make the individuals more effective employees. Many young couples have postponed childbearing until both careers are solidly grounded. Some couples alternate moves in response to the job requirements of each; others move only when better opportunities can be found for both. In a few cases, couples live apart when job requirements so dictate.

Employers can help by providing parental furloughs to men and women with guaranteed restoration of seniority within certain limitations. A worker is more likely to return to a firm in which he or she had acquired job-specific skills and a responsible position than to go to a new firm and begin at the bottom.

Provision of improved child care facilities and arrangements for more flexible work schedules are some other steps companies can take to reduce the strains on two-earner families in the crucial years when young children are present. All these programs increase the probability that women will remain on the job after children are born, enhancing the payoff to their training. Just as life-cycle wage increases are the most logical way to ensure retention of male workers, good wages will shorten periods of labor force inactivity for women and attract them to their old jobs.

Job restructuring is needed not only in traditionally female-dominated occupations but also in male strongholds. Historically, as occupations have become "feminized" they have been adapted to the needs of an intermittent work force. But as female commitment to work continues to strengthen, more on-the-job training and increased responsibility are likely to pay off.

Some job restructuring may be needed for male employees, too. Married men with working wives—about half the population of married men—need more flexibility than they did in the past to relocate, to work shorter hours, and in some cases to interrupt market work to participate in housework and child care. The trend for couples to locate only where both can find suitable jobs greatly reduces the flexibility of employers to transfer male employees and increases the financial risks associated with training them. Outdated nepotism rules must surely go by the board when two valuable executives marry, or when the firm cannot secure an attractive prospective employee unless a job can be found for the spouse.

Restructuring jobs in male-dominated occupations to allow more flexibility, and increasing possibilities for career advancement in female-dominated occupations, should reduce some of the built-in incentives for men and women to pursue traditional careers. Men who seek flexible and less demanding work arrangements will begin to find attractive career options in formerly "female" areas, while women will be able to take advantage of the more attractive career opportunities and new flexibility to be found in the "male" labor market.

As women gain economic independence they will be less susceptible to psychological pressures to pursue feminine careers. The threat of ostracism by men is less important to a woman with an independent source of income and status. Also, as women move into responsible jobs with good pay, their economic power will be reflected in increased leverage in the home. And they will learn ways of taking an active role in many areas of life in which women's activity traditionally has been vicarious.

Affirmative action plans must stress the importance of increasing female representation in male-dominated fields, regardless of the inevitable resistance from employers, coworkers, and sometimes women themselves. The reasons that this approach is essential have been outlined above. First, there simply is not room in traditionally female occupations for the growing female labor force; the crowding phenomenon is depressing women's wages. Second, sex segregation of jobs permits employers to circumvent both the Equal Pay Act and Title VII of the Civil Rights Act, allowing firms to pay women less than men for comparable work and denying women equal access to training and promotional opportunities. Finally, unless women increase their representation in jobs formerly dominated by men, a status differential based on sex will be perpetuated in the labor market, with women workers clearly second-class citizens. Until they achieve status parity with male workers, women cannot expect to exercise their rights on an equal basis with men in the broader range of economic, social, and political activities.

12

Worktime: The Traditional Workweek and Its Alternatives

"Worktime: The Traditional Workweek and its Alternatives," from the *1979 Employment and Training Report of the President of the United States.*

Is there a standard workweek? According to data compiled by the Bureau of Labor Statistics, about half of all nonagricultural employees work between 35 and 40 hours a week, including more than two-fifths who work 40 hours. (See Figure 1.) In addition, a marked concentration appears at particular starting and stopping times, with most workers beginning work somewhere between 6:30 and 9:30 a.m. and ending between 3:30 and 6:30 p.m. In a recent survey, almost two-thirds of nonfarm wage and salary workers who usually work full time reported that they work a 40-hour, 5-day schedule during a typical week.

Despite the prevalence of this schedule, however, some individuals—employers as well as employees—do manage to develop other schedules that are more compatible with their needs or preferences. We see evidence of this in the systematic variations among labor force groups—by sex, age, and marital status—in the average number of hours worked. On average, men work about 7 hours a week longer than women do, and married men living with their wives work over 8 hours longer in a typical week than do single men. (See Table 1.) Table 1 also reveals important variations over the life cycle in weekly hours of work. There is a clear upsurge for both men and women in the prime working years between the ages of 25 and 44, with the average working hours declining slightly for men—but not for women—aged 45 to 64 years.

Group differences also appear in the time of day at which work is performed. For instance, women are underrepresented in

118

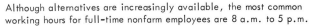

Although alternatives are increasingly available, the most common working hours for full-time nonfarm employees are 8 a.m. to 5 p.m.

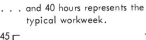

. . . and 40 hours represents the typical workweek.

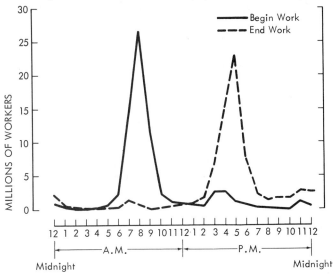

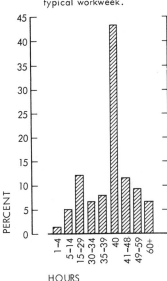

FIGURE 1

Source: U.S. Department of Labor.

evening and night shift work. Moreover, among part-time workers, women with small children are less likely to be employed in the late afternoon, when school is out, while young men (many of whom are students) are overrepresented in that time interval.

Thus, although the 5-day workweek of around 40 hours is clearly the norm for American workers, the data also show that many employees work on atypical schedules. To what extent do these work schedules reflect employer preferences, employee choices, or both? What are the relative economic and social impacts of innovative schedules (flexitime and compressed workweeks), which appear to be of growing interest, and more traditional ones, including part-time employment and overtime?

These questions are addressed in the following pages, along with descriptions of nontraditional work schedules designed to offer employees more control over their own work schedules.[1]

[1] This chapter focuses on worktime and, in particular, the alternative schedules that break the

HOURS OF WORK: A BRIEF HISTORY

Evolution of the 40-Hour Workweek

Weekly hours of work have changed gradually since the 1930s and 1940s. The average workweek declined by about 10 percent, or some 1-1/3 hours per decade, over the last 30 years. (See Table 2.)

However, beyond the average, the different industrial sectors vary widely. For example, weekly hours of work in manufacturing have

usual pattern of a 5-day workweek of around 40 hours followed by most U.S. wage earners. However, another, even broader issue now being addressed by social scientists involves the standard "linear life plan," in which education, work, and leisure follow one another in rigid sequence. Some have begun to question this pattern and to suggest that viable and preferable alternatives may exist, and, in fact, may even now be emerging—just as more flexible work schedules such as flexitime and job sharing (discussed in this chapter) are becoming more common. For more on the issue of worklife trends, see Fred Best and Barry Stern, "Education, Work, and Leisure: Must They Come In That Order?" *Monthly Labor Review*, July 1977, pp. 3-10.

TABLE 1

Weekly Hours of Work for Persons in Nonagricultural Industries, by Sex, Selected Age Groups, and Marital Status, May 1978

(Numbers in Thousands)

Sex, Age, and Marital Status	Total Persons At Work	Percentage Working—			Average Hours
		1 to 34 Hours	35 to 40 Hours	41 or more Hours	
Age					
Men:					
16 years and over	50,630	15.7	48.5	35.8	41.7
16 to 24 years	10,501	35.4	42.1	22.5	35.1
25 to 44 years	23,570	8.9	49.7	41.4	44.2
45 to 64 years	15,169	9.2	52.9	37.9	43.5
65 years and over	1,390	54.2	28.2	17.6	29.6
Women:					
16 years and over	36,281	34.9	51.2	13.9	34.3
16 to 24 years	9,096	44.1	45.4	10.5	31.2
25 to 44 years	16,205	30.2	54.7	15.1	35.7
45 to 64 years	9,971	31.4	53.5	15.1	35.7
65 years and over	1,008	62.2	25.6	12.3	27.2
Marital Status					
Men:					
Married, spouse present	35,415	9.9	49.5	40.6	43.7
Widowed, divorced, or separated .	3,803	13.9	51.5	34.6	42.4
Single (never married)	11,413	34.6	44.4	21.1	35.4
Women:					
Married, spouse present	20,297	35.1	51.5	13.4	34.5
Widowed, divorced, or separated .	6,916	26.7	55.5	17.8	36.8
Single (never married)	9,068	40.8	47.4	11.9	32.0

Source: U.S. Department of Labor, Bureau of Labor Statistics.

changed very little since 1948, but hours in retail trade dropped by over 20 percent, to less than 32 hours per week in May 1978. One factor responsible for that sharper decline was the rapid expansion of part-time employment, which brought down the overall average workweek.

Figure 2 sketches, for the period 1948-1977, average hours worked by men (not including students) employed in nonagricultural industries. Unlike the results reported in Table 2, the curve shows no net decline in weekly hours over the past 30 years. There are several reasons for this different finding. First, these data were collected from workers or their families and thus include some hours of work in "moonlighting" jobs not reported by employers. Second, because the data are restricted to nonstudent men, they are controlled for changes in the composition of the labor force since 1948.[2] Third, they include workers in all

[2] In the past 37 years, the proportion of the work force that is female has risen from 26 to 48 percent. Since women, on average, work fewer hours a week than do men, the result has been a reduction in the average workweek. The proportion of students in

TABLE 2

Weekly Hours of Workers* on Private Payrolls, by Industry Divison, Selected Years, 1948 – 1978

Industry	Annual Averages									
	1948	1953	1956	1966	1969	1971	1973	1975	1977	May 1978**
Total, private industry	40.0	39.6	39.3	38.6	37.7	37.0	37.1	36.1	36.1	36.0
Mining	39.4	38.8	40.8	42.7	43.0	42.4	42.5	42.3	44.1	43.7
Contract construction	38.1	37.9	37.5	37.6	37.9	37.2	37.0	36.6	36.9	36.5
Manufacturing	40.0	40.5	40.4	41.3	40.6	39.9	40.7	39.4	40.3	40.3
Transportation and public utilities				41.2	40.7	40.2	40.6	39.6	40.1	40.2
Wholesale trade	41.0	40.6	40.5	40.7	40.2	39.8	39.5	38.6	38.9	38.8
Retail trade	40.2	39.1	38.6	35.9	34.2	33.7	33.3	32.4	31.7	31.4
Finance insurance, real estate† .	37.9	37.7	36.9	37.3	37.1	36.9	36.9	36.5	36.6	36.6
Services				35.5	34.7	34.2	34.0	33.8	33.4	33.2

*Gross average hours. Mining and manufacturing data refer to production and related workers; contract construction, to construction workers; all other divisions, to nonsupervisory workers.
**Preliminary and seasonally adjusted.
†Excludes data for nonoffice salespersons.
Sources: *1978 Employment and Training Report*, p. 265, and *Monthly Labor Review*, July 1978, pp. 66-67.

occupations whereas the hours in Table 2 refer only to those of production or nonsupervisory workers on private payrolls.

While weekly hours leveled off for non-student males, vacation and holiday time has increased in the past 30 years. The adjusted curve for hours of work, reflecting the effect of vacations and holidays, is shown as a dotted line in Figure 2.

The leveling off in weekly hours of work since World War II contrasts sharply with earlier history. (See Figure 3.) In the late 19th century, workers spent about 60 hours a week at their jobs. The workweek declined by 10 hours between 1900 and 1929. As unemployment rose during the depression, the 40-hour work-week was widely adopted in industry, often as a means of sharing the available work among more employees.

the work force has also risen from an insignificant level in 1940 to about 6 percent today. Male students average about 23 hours of work per week, so that their inclusion also reduces the statistical average of weekly hours. Hence, Figure 3, which excludes women and students, would appear to offer a more consistent index of the long-term stability in work schedules than does Table 2.

Economists attribute these early reductions in working hours to rising real hourly wage rates. Higher pay permitted workers simultaneously to enjoy a higher material living standard and more leisure. It has been estimated that workers took as much as one-fifth to one-quarter of their wage gains in the form of more leisure, rather than more goods and services, in the late 19th and early 20th centuries. But while real hourly wage rates rose at a more rapid pace from 1948 to 1978 than they had in the preceding half century, no comparable reduction in weekly hours took place.

Among the explanations offered by economists for the leveling off in weekly hours during the past 30 years are:

1. The postwar baby boom, combined with a remarkable increase in the average number of years young Americans spend in school, burdened mature worker-parents with enormous expenditures. Since parents could meet these costs only by much higher take-home pay, they preferred more pay to more leisure.

2. Many firms now make more extensive investments in recruiting, screening, and

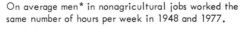

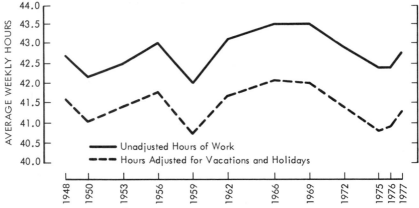

FIGURE 2

*Data do not include students.

Source: John D. Owen, *Working Hours: An Economic Analysis* (Lexington, Mass.: Lexington Books, 1979).

especially training new employees than was the case a generation ago. Hence, employers would rather increase the hours and pay overtime to their skilled employees than hire less experienced or part-time workers at standard hourly wages.

3. The steady lowering of the average retirement age, together with population growth in the older age groups, has increased the proportion of the population that must be supported in retirement by the work force. Some have argued that the social security and other retirement savings systems have diverted the interest of employees from further reductions in hours during their prime working years.

Pressures for Change

Employees who need or prefer more flexible work schedules have been a major source of pressure for change in the traditional workweek. It has been argued, for example, that, since the multiworker family has become the solution to both inflation and rising economic expectations for about half of all U.S. families, working hours must become more flexible to adjust to their needs. In addition, parents of young children, students, older workers, handicapped persons, and couples desiring to share work and home responsibilities, as well as persons who wish to upgrade skills or switch careers through a return to school—all have found that the rigid scheduling of the 8 a.m. to 5 p.m., Monday through Friday workweek hampers their efforts to combine work with personal needs. Other workers simply prefer more leisure—a shorter workweek, longer vacations, or a block of time such as a 6-month sabbatical leave, to pursue nonwork interests. Still others are less concerned with flexibility in scheduling but see in the shortened workweek the opportunity for the creation of more jobs.

Some systematic research has been done on employee attitudes concerning the balance between work and leisure hours. A recent survey of this research indicates that "... the idea of trading income for more time was found to be more popular among women, younger and pre-retirement workers, white-collar employees, and respondents with few or no de-

The workweek declined by nearly 20 hours from 1901
to 1948 and then leveled off at around 40 hours.

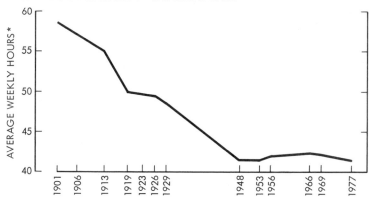

FIGURE 3

*Adjusted for vacations and holidays beginning with 1948. Data are for male
nonstudents in nonagricultural industries.
Source: John D. Owen, *Working Hours: An Economic Analysis* (Lexington,
Mass.: Lexington Books, 1979.)

pendent children." The review also concluded
that the idea of reduced hours was more popular among workers who could choose the
time at which they took their leisure. According to a national survey completed in 1978, a
third of the American workers employed 20 or
more hours per week reported problems related
to inconvenient or excessive hours, with more
than a fourth of these problems involving
interference with family life. Also 12 percent
of the respondents would prefer to work different days and 19 percent different hours.

Modification of the traditional 40-hour,
5-day week has also been urged by some employers, who have become convinced that
revised work schedules raise the morale of their
workers, help attract new employees, and in
other ways benefit their organizations. In some
cases, the benefits of overtime and shiftwork
schedules—especially where they permit a firm
to utilize its capital more intensively—are
obvious and readily measurable. Many retail
trade and service industries, as well as government agencies, require a labor force to be on
duty during evening and weekend hours to

serve the public. These considerations have
become more significant in recent years—partly
because of rising capital costs and more rapid
obsolescence of equipment and partly because
a growing share of consumer activity takes
place outside normal business hours. Other
employers may introduce more innovative work
schedules, such as job sharing or flexitime, as
a means of retaining valuable employees or
benefiting from the reduced absenteeism and
tardiness that, in many cases, has been shown
to accompany the introduction of flexitime
schedules.

A third impetus for change is government, acting in the public interest. Traditionally, the role of government has been primarily
that of controlling excessive hours of work,
where such scheduling might have an adverse
effect on workers' health and safety. Lately,
this interest has broadened to encompass
wider social and economic concerns. For
example, while a standardized workweek has
obvious advantages in promoting efficient
production and business communications, the
effects on the wider community are often neg-

ative. Rush-hour traffic congestion is the most dramatic example. Others include peak-hour drains on electrical power and the increasing need to provide access to government facilities and services outside of the standard workweek hours.

Another social objective, now that the working-age population is growing at a much slower rate, is to provide nontraditional schedules that permit women with child-care responsibilities to enter the labor force. This concern is also relevant to employers whose affirmative action goals include expanded employment of women.

NEW PATTERNS OF WORKTIME

The Compressed Workweek

A harbinger of change in work scheduling practices in the 1970s was the 4-day workweek, with no reduction in the traditional 35 or 40 weekly hours. Other compressed workweeks, including a 3-day, 12-hour schedule, have also been tried, and indeed are still in use, but the most popular version remains the 4-day workweek. One of the perceived advantages of this arrangement is the fact that some compressed workweek schedules can be arranged to provide a weekly holiday of 3 consecutive days. Apart from the obvious recreational opportunities provided by a 3-day weekly holiday, a reduction in weekly workdays also reduces the number of commuting trips workers must make.

However, unlike earlier worktime reforms, the compression concept has not been widely embraced by employees. Trade unions, especially, regard a 10-hour day, without payment for overtime, as a major step backward in the struggle to improve labor standards and protect workers from undue fatigue. Their opposition also stems from the view of overtime as a factor that reduces job creation. Premium pay for

overtime hours originated as one means of discouraging employers from requiring work beyond regular hours, rather than as a means of increasing take-home pay. Consequently, most union representatives are proceeding with caution before embracing any alternative work schedule that involves an increase in hours.

Another possible drawback of the compressed workweek involves child-care considerations and parent-child relations—although the evidence is mixed. When schools are in session, the longer workday may result in parents spending less time with their children than they did under the standard workweek. On the other hand, a recent study of the adjustment of male blue-collar workers to 4-day workweeks found that almost twice as many 4-day as 5-day workers were actively involved with their children on their days off, and a 1970 study of 13 firms employing the 4-day workweek showed that 75 percent of the workers studied reported spending more time with their families.

Furthermore, this change in work schedules may have profound social and psychological effects on some individuals. For example, the study of male blue-collar workers on the 4-day schedule found that, while some workers liked the new schedule, they were at the same time less satisfied with their jobs. The investigator speculated that the 3 days off per week raised workers' interests in leisure-time activities, a change that generally detracted from the appeal of their worklives. Subtle effects of the new schedule on marital relationships were also found. Some marriages were strengthened by the increased time for recreation and communication between spouses available if the wife was not employed; other marriages suffered stress when these expanded opportunities to pursue mutual interests underlined the lack of such interests. Protracted workdays may also lead to such physical effects as increased fatigue and stress.

Just as many employees view the compressed workweek with mixed feelings, so do many employers. For example, where daily setup costs are important (especially in large factories), a compressed schedule that eliminates one daily setup each week can save the employer significant sums. In other job situations, rotating a 4-day schedule over a 5- or 6-day week can permit a plant or retail store to operate many more hours a week, thereby improving capital utilization without using part-time or shift workers or paying overtime.

On the other hand, compressed workweeks are not suitable in many enterprises. When it is important for employees to interact with each other and with workers in other firms who are likely to be on a 5-day week, the 4-day schedule can impose serious problems. Finally, for jobs in which fatigue would reduce productivity substantially over a 10-hour day, the compressed workweek could prove costly indeed to both employers and employees.

These mixed reactions help to explain why only 1.8 percent of the full-time nonfarm work force (about 1.1 million workers) now follow a compressed 3- or 4-day workweek schedule. Furthermore, the adoption of this nontraditional work schedule has been confined, for the most part, to nonunion employees.

Flexitime

A major disadvantage to employees of a companywide compressed workweek plan is that it allows the individual worker no choice. Even if many are satisfied with the change, some may still prefer the original schedule. However, other alternatives to the standard workweek do permit employees some choice in devising their own work schedules. The most important of these innovations is the flexitime concept.

There are three basic types of flexitime systems, distinguished by the degree of choice

given to the individual. The first type is the least elastic: an employer simply gives employees a range of starting times; for example, a worker can begin at any quarter hour between 7:30 and 9 a.m.; the 8-hour workday for that employee ends at the corresponding quarter hour between 4:30 and 6 p.m. In the second variant, employees design their own schedules, but once chosen and approved, these schedules must be adhered to for a specified period of time. In the most liberal flexitime programs, employees may vary their schedules from day to day without advance supervisory approval.

Employers typically place limits on employee choice in both the second and third variants. There is a bandwidth period during which everyone's working hours must fall and a core period when all workers must be on the job. Figure 4 illustrates these concepts. Other common restrictions—for the health of employees—include at least minimum meal periods and a maximum workday.

In many instances, when introducing a flexible system, managers find it prudent to add an important proviso: departures from the standard schedule will be permitted only so long as they do not interfere with production efficiency. It is then left up to the supervisor and occasionally the work group to determine ways of offering more flexibility to the employees without sacrificing efficiency.

Flexitime was developed in 1967 in West Germany, in the Messerschmidt research and development facility outside Munich. The plan was originally introduced with the modest goal of alleviating rush-hour traffic congestion on the access road leading to the plant. The plan become immensely popular with employees, and efficiency in the establishment improved markedly. Once these results were publicized, the new system of *gleitzeit* (or "gliding time") spread rapidly. It is estimated to account for 5 to 10 percent of white-collar employment in Germany and as much as 40

Even under flexitime, employees must work in certain
core periods and during an overall bandwidth of hours.

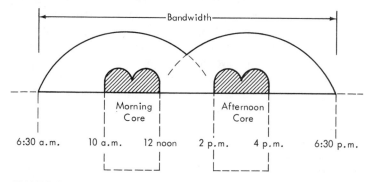

FIGURE 4

Source: John D. Owen, *Working Hours: An Economic Analysis* (Lexington,
Mass.: Lexington Books, 1979).

percent in parts of German-speaking Switzerland. Flexitime has been widely adopted in England, France, and other Western European nations.

In the past 5 years, flexitime has become more popular in the United States, although it is difficult to obtain reliable statistical estimates of its current use. A survey published in 1975 estimated that 1 million workers were on flexitime schedules. A more recent survey by the American Management Association estimates flexitime usage at 6 percent of the work force (2.5 to 3.5 million persons). Over 200,000 Federal workers participate in flexitime variants—about 10 percent of general schedule employees (excluding postal workers and the military). Several major life insurance and computer firms in the private sector have also adopted flexible schedules for employees.

The published case studies about flexitime probably contain a built-in positive bias, because unsuccessful experiments are often either canceled before an outside evaluation can be made or are not reported for public relations reasons. The most common pitfalls of these failed experiments seem to be: (1) Inadequate planning by managers; (2) lack of consultation with employees before the system is introduced, (3) employee dislike of time clocks or other methods of monitoring the individual's hours, and (4) failure to provide a satisfactory schedule for supervisors. (A common error is to continue to hold supervisors responsible for a given work group for the entire "bandwidth" period, say 6 a.m. to 6 p.m., with no provision for their spelling each other.) However, a sufficient number of successful experiments have been observed over the past decade to prove that a well-designed flexitime system can be compatible with improved productivity, as well as worker interests, in a wide variety of job situations.

Optimistic advocates believe that flexitime will one day become the standard scheduling system in this country. Certainly, technical job design considerations would not prevent its use by many more employees than now enjoy the system—perhaps even a majority of the work force. But there are a number of institutional or nontechnical obstacles to the widespread adoption of flexitime arrangements.

One such barrier is trade union opposition to the more ambitious variants of flexitime. The union position has been that any hours worked in excess of 8 per day should be paid at time and a half or better. This objection would not apply to a flexitime system in which employees compensate for their early or late arrival during the same 8-hour day (unless the "comp time" occurs during a period when a shift differential is called for by the union contract). However, union opposition would interfere with a system in which workers vary their total hours from day to day, *averaging* 8 per day over a week or month. The AFL-CIO position is that time and one half should be paid on long days, even if the schedule has been chosen by the employee in order to work fewer hours on another day.[3]

Some problems with flexitime schedules may also originate in government regulations. For example, under the Walsh-Healey Public Contracts Act, workers employed by firms holding Federal Government supply contracts in excess of $10,000 must be paid time and one-half their basic rates of pay for all hours worked over 8 in a day or 40 in a workweek. A similar provision is contained in the Contract Work Hours and Safety Standards Act, which generally applies to federally financed construction contracts and Federal service contracts. Furthermore, the Fair Labor Standards Act requires the payment of time and a half beyond 40 hours in a workweek. Such overtime pay requirements impede any attempts to develop flexitime schedules that involve longer workdays than usual and will need to be dealt with in the development of flexitime standards.

[3] The concept of work modules has been advocated as a means of providing some schedule choices to those blue-collar workers for whom flexitime is impractical. Under the work module system, employees would state their schedule preferences at the beginning of the year, and schedules would be assigned on that basis—with all ties broken by seniority. Presumably, employees who favored summer recreational activities would work longer hours in the winter, while hunting or skiing enthusiasts would elect the opposite seasonal pattern.

In the Federal Government itself, however, the Federal Employees Flexible and Compressed Work Schedules Act of 1978 (Public Law 95-390) authorizes widespread experimentation with employee-chosen hours of work. Some 2 million Federal Government employees are now eligible to participate in a variety of alternative work schedules, including flexitime and, in some cases, 4-day compressed workweeks. Whether these schedules will actually be introduced depends upon the mutual interest and agreement of managers and employees within each department. This major innovation will be closely studied by those concerned with the development of alternative working patterns. . . .

TRADITIONAL ALTERNATIVES TO THE STANDARD WORKWEEK

Part-Time Employment

While the standard workweek has changed very little for most full-time workers in recent decades, the proportion of part-time employees (defined as those working less than 35 hours a week) has grown rapidly, from about 1 in 12 to 1 in 7 workers over the past 20 years. About 15 million Americans now work exclusively on part-time schedules, with another 4 million moonlighting at part-time jobs in addition to their regular full-time employment. Part-time workers constitute the largest single group on nonstandard work schedules at present.

Not all part-time workers are pleased with their situation. According to data from the Bureau of Labor Statistics, about one-fifth of them would prefer full-time jobs. These people are called involuntary part-time workers—those who have accepted less than full-time employment for economic reasons, the clearest alternative being unemployment. When jobs are scarce, involuntary part-time employment goes up. In fact, the involuntary part-time rate mirrors the conventional unemployment rate rather strikingly.

Still, 4 out of 5 part-time workers are satisfied with their status. Reasons given for working less than full-time schedules include school attendance, family responsibilities, physical limitations, and a preference for leisure time. Part-time jobs (unlike flexitime or 4-day compressed workweeks) often permit employees to determine (and in most cases shorten) the number of hours they work in a week—18 hours being the average workweek for voluntary part-time workers. On the other hand, about 4 million moonlighters, who use part-time employment as a second source of income, actually extend their weekly hours of work through this means.

Certain segments of the labor force are more likely to work part time than the others. Students and other young people who are not ready to or cannot make a full-time commitment to employment provide one large group of users of the part-time labor market. In May 1977, teenagers accounted for almost half of the male and one-fifth of the female voluntary part-time workers.

Parents and other householders who must reconcile paid employment with their home and child-care obligations constitute a second large group of part-time workers. Women, particularly adult women, are more than twice as likely as men to be working part time. To a great extent, this difference can be attributed to the traditional roles of husbands and wives. However, for reasons not as easily understood, since 1948, the proportion of single women working part time voluntarily has risen, while the reverse is true of single men.

A third group holding part-time jobs is made up of older workers who seek a semi-retirement option. Of all employed persons aged 65 years and older in May 1977, over half of the women and two-fifths of the men were

working part time voluntarily. Part-time work can also be helpful in assisting workers near retirement age to gradually adjust to the new stage of their life. In Sweden, pension laws were changed in 1976 to permit persons near retirement age to work part time and collect a partial pension (equivalent to 65 percent of the employment income lost by changing to part-time work).

Lastly, part-time workers include many moonlighters—typically men in the prime years of 22 to 45—who supplement earnings from their primary jobs with wages from part-time employment.

Data from the Bureau of Labor Statistics (BLS) indicate that voluntary part-time workers are most likely to be employed in the trade or service sectors of the economy. (See Figure 5.) The rapid growth of the service-producing industries may have been one of the most important factors in expanding part-time employment opportunities. Both the retail trade and service sectors are especially receptive to part-time scheduling—first, because of the uneven flow of demands over an extended workday in these industries and, second, because services must often be provided on weekends. The standard 5-day, 40-hour week cannot

The trade and service sectors attract most voluntary part-time workers.

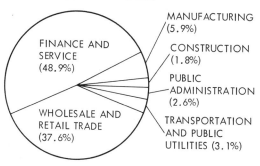

FIGURE 5

Source: U.S. Department of Labor, *Employment and Earnings,* June 1978, p. 42.

be easily manipulated to cover peak activity periods, when working people are forced to do their shopping, patronize restaurants, use recreation facilities, and the like. Thus, owners and managers have come to depend heavily on part-time workers to supplement, or even replace, full-time employees on standard work schedules.

Outside the retail trade and service sectors, there are many jobs in which part-time and full-time workers can (and do) substitute for each other. Routine clerical jobs fall into this category.

Despite the usefulness of part-timers in many such jobs, they often do not fare as well in the labor market as do their full-time counterparts. For example, part-time workers are sometimes denied fringe benefits, although a survey by the American Management Association indicates that employers have started extending such benefits to part-time workers in recent years.

Another significant finding is that part-time workers are often paid less than full-time employees. When adjustment is made for personal characteristics (including sex, race, education, and years out of school), part-time workers earn about 29 percent less per hour than do full-time employees. Statistical analysis shows that most of the wage gap is due to the fact that part-time workers are frequently confined to low-wage jobs. Workers who choose part-time schedules may often settle for relatively low-wage and low-prestige jobs, because full-time employment at their education, experience, and skill levels is simply not available or because (as already indicated) they are willing to accept low wages in exchange for more flexible work schedules.

The typically low pay of part-time workers stems, in part, from some managers' unwillingness to modify company practices; e.g., by dividing one high-level, full-time job into two equally high-level part-time positions

and prorating fringe benefits for the part-timers.

However, more serious obstacles than management inertia block the employment of part-time workers in better paid jobs. Higher level positions typically require a considerable initial outlay by the company in recruiting, screening, and training the new employee. These initial costs can be recovered only from the productive labor of the employee over many working hours. Although turnover rates of the two groups are similar, part-timers average about half as many hours per month as full-time workers. Hence, the period required for an employer to recoup initial expenses is twice as long for part-time employees . . . and hiring them is twice as risky from the employer's standpoint.

The line supervisor's task may also be complicated by divided full-time positions into many more part-time jobs. This larger group of workers must be coordinated and monitored and lines of communication established among them. The more complex and high level the job, the more difficult, time consuming, and therefore expensive are the supervisor's problems.

A bar to part-time jobs in well-paid blue-collar work, especially in mining, manufacturing, and rail transportation, is employer concern about high capital costs. Most employers insist that their expensive plants and equipment can be fully and smoothly operated only by full-time workers. Employers in this country have generally been unwilling to establish morning and afternoon shifts for part-time workers—or even to set up "mini-shifts" following a full-time day shift, which would actually increase capital utilization.

While a number of objective factors may militate against using part-time workers in high-level jobs, there still is considerable room for improving their position. To tap the market of skilled and experienced people who cannot accept full-time positions, the Federal Government has attempted to expand permanent part-time employment in civil service positions; while the number of employees in this category has grown by about 33 percent in the past 2 years, they still make up less than 3 percent of all Federal employees.

New legislation, the Federal Employees Part-Time Career Employment Act of 1978 (Public Law 95-437), eliminates two important obstacles to increased employment of part-timers. Hiring by Federal Government agencies has long been limited by assigned employment levels or ceilings. Under the new law, part-time permanent positions will be counted as the appropriate fraction of a full-time position in the agency's personnel ceiling, as of October 1, 1980. The law also permits the Federal Government to prorate its health insurance contribution for part-time employees—long a standard practice in many private firms. These reforms are expected to result in a higher level of part-time opportunities with the Nation's largest employer. . . .

Overtime

Employers often find it worthwhile to pay overtime wages to employees as a means of extending the standard workweek, despite the risk that fatigue will affect workers' output and the fact that Federal and State statutes or collective-bargaining agreements usually require time and a half or larger wage premiums for extra work hours. One advantage of overtime to employers is that fringe benefit costs do not increase with longer workdays; another is that the costs of recruiting and training extra workers are avoided. Finally, overtime, like shift work, permits fuller use of capital stock. But unlike shift work, overtime can readily be cut back when demand slackens.

Not surprisingly, employer use of overtime fluctuates in tandem with the state of the economy. Production workers on manufacturing payrolls averaged 3.4 hours of weekly overtime in May 1978, whereas the average was

only 2.6 hours per week during the recession year of 1975. (See Table 3.)

In part because of premium pay, some workers may prefer overtime schedules. In fact, overtime assignments are often rationed among willing workers by seniority, rotation, or some other equitable principle. However, sometimes the employer's demand for extra work hours exceeds acceptable levels. For example, in the automobile industry, where industrial conditions periodically dictate many hours of overtime per week per worker, the United Auto Workers insisted upon and obtained modest controls over involuntary overtime.

SUMMARY AND CONCLUSION

While a majority of nonagricultural employees work a standard 5-day, Monday through Friday week of around 40 hours, a large and growing minority work on nontraditional schedules, which serve the special needs of the workers and/or their employers. For those who have home or other responsibilities, flexitime or part-time work, is becoming increasingly popular. The growing interest in more usable leisure time expressed by many workers is also reflected in flexitime and the 4-day compressed workweek. . . .

Taking all potential changes into account, one researcher has noted that "it is conceivable and likely that rearranged work schedules may herald the introduction of important social change with regard to family life, life styles, quality-of-life perceptions, and the division of labor along traditional sex-role lines." Whether the changes prove to be as far reaching as this remains to be seen. Yet even the most cautious experts seem to agree on at least the following prospect: Whatever the future demand for scheduling freedom, workers who want or need to escape the 5-day, 40-hour standard workweek may look forward to an expanding array of alternatives.

TABLE 3

Average Weekly Overtime Hours of Production Workers, on Manufacturing Payrolls for Selected Industries, Selected Years, 1956-1978

Industry	1956*	1966*	1969*	1974	1975	1977	May 1978
All manufacturing	2.8	3.9	3.6	3.2	2.6	3.4	3.4
Machinery excluding electrical	3.9	5.5	4.5	4.3	3.0	3.8	3.8
Paper and allied products	4.5	5.5	5.5	4.6	4.0	4.7	4.8
Transportation equipment	3.1	4.7	3.8	3.2	2.6	4.8	4.7
Stone, clay, and glass products	3.3	4.5	4.8	4.4	3.7	4.6	5.1
Fabricated metal products	3.1	4.5	4.2	3.5	2.6	3.6	3.7
Textile mill products	2.6	4.4	3.9	3.3	3.0	3.5	3.6
Rubber and plastics products	2.1	4.4	4.2	3.4	2.7	3.6	3.4
Lumber and wood products	2.6	4.0	3.8	3.6	3.0	3.8	3.7
Primary metals	2.8	4.0	4.1	4.0	2.6	3.7	4.0
Food and kindred products	3.1	4.0	4.2	4.1	3.8	3.9	3.7

*Full-employment peak years.

Source: U.S. Department of Labor, Bureau of Labor Statistics, *Handbook of Labor Statistics, 1975,* table 80, and *Employment and Earnings,* various issues.

13

Economic Perspectives on the Family

Isabel V. Sawhill

Isabel V. Sawhill, "Economic Perspectives on the Family," *Daedalus*, Vol. 106, No. 2 (Spring, 1977).

INTRODUCTION

Back in the fifties, a colleague of mine in the economics department of a small college was sitting in his office preparing a class in "money and banking." He was interrupted by a call from an anxious housewife who thought she had been referred to the department of home economics. She wanted to bake bread and was seeking advice on the amount of yeast to use. Partly in amusement and partly in irritation at having been interrupted, he responded: "Madam, I know something about how one raises money but nothing about how one raises

dough."[1] Today, even though economists have not gone so far as to study the art of bread-making, there is a whole new literature within the discipline labeled the "new home economics" and devoted to examining such topics as marriage, fertility, and decisions about the use of both time and goods within the household or family.[2] These interests are quite new—

[1] An incident reported by Professor Frederick Reuss, now retired from the department of economics at Goucher College in Baltimore, Maryland.

[2] See *Economics of the Family: Marriage, Children, and Human Capital,* ed. Theodore W. Schultz (Chicago, 1974); see also *Sex, Discrimination, and the Division of Labor,* ed. Cynthia B. Lloyd (New York, 1975).

dating perhaps from the early or mid sixties and heavily influenced by the development of human capital theory and the theory of the allocation of time.[3] Before their appearance, economists had concentrated almost exclusively on markets and exchange; in such a context, the household or family was only relevant as a final consumer of market-produced goods and services or as a supplier of productive inputs, chiefly labor. What went on *within* the household was largely ignored.

There are several reasons for the economist's newly discovered interest in the family. One stems from the common views of most economists and their own definition of the scope of their discipline, the core of which is that an economic problem exists whenever resources that have multiple and competing uses are scarce. Scarcity requires *choice,* and choices are best guided by comparing the costs and benefits of all the possible alternatives. Once one had defined "resources" and "costs and benefits" broadly enough, there is almost no area of human behavior to which the economic paradigm cannot be applied.

—Resources include not only the physical environment (land, other natural resources) and the finiteness of earthly space, but also human resources and the finiteness of human time. Increases in the quantity or quality of either natural or human resources are called "investments" and lead to an accumulation of either physical or human "capital." A major activity which takes place within the family is investment in human capital—e.g., the rearing of children—while the ultimate scarcity for this purpose is parental time.

—It is assumed in economic theory that individuals are rational, that they attempt to maximize their own welfare, and that they have information with which to evaluate and choose among alternative courses of action.

—Individuals begin by deciding whether to marry, and when, and whom to pick from among all possible mates. Once formed, households face a number of additional decisions about how much work to do, by whom (husband or wife), and where (in the home or in the market). They must also choose which set of market goods and home-produced goods to consume, and whether to have children (one type of home-produced good).

All the above decisions are influenced by the costs and benefits associated with the various alternatives. Costs are measured in both time and money and include psychic elements as well as opportunities forgone (e.g., one of the costs of marrying individual A is not marrying individual B). Similarly, benefits may be monetary or nonmonetary (e.g., if a woman quits her job to keep house, it is because her time at home is valued more than the income she would have earned). Thus, the broad applicability of economic theory to a wide range of nonmarket phenomena is one reason for the economist's emerging interest in the family.

A second reason is the realization that differences in earnings and in family economic well-being cannot be explained solely in terms of the operation of labor markets. Two of the critical determinants of individual earnings are education and experience, but a great deal of that education either goes on within the home or else is successful because of its interaction with family influences. As for experience, the problem is that those (for example, married women) who devote a great deal of their time to family activities will be handicapped in the labor market as a result of an insufficient investment in marketable skills.[4] Finally,

[3] Gary Becker, "A Theory of the Allocation of Time," *Economic Journal,* 75 (September 1965), p. 512, and *Human Capital: A Theoretical and Empirical Analysis with Special Reference to Education* (New York, 1964).

[4] Jacob Mincer, *Schooling, Experience, and Earnings* (New York, 1974).

family economic well-being may depend as much on the ratio of earners to non-earners within the household as it does on individual earnings, but this ratio is determined by decisions about marriage, childbearing, and labor force participation (especially by wives).[5]

SPECIFIC CONTRIBUTIONS

To date, what has the economist's foray into these new areas produced? Most of the literature has been devoted to analyses of (1) fertility, (2) marriage and divorce, and (3) the division of labor within the home and its concomitant effects on labor-force participation and the earnings of men and women. What follows is a brief review of the findings of, and the insights emerging from, this literature. Throughout this review, I shall attempt to reproduce the flavor of the economic writing on these subjects as accurately as possible without commenting on its merits. Later, I shall try to provide an evaluation of the economist's contribution.

Fertility, Childbearing, and Child Rearing

In the "old" economics, the size of the population was occasionally viewed as either a cause or a consequence of the rate of economic growth, but at a microeconomic level, no attempt was made to explain why people had children and why some people had more than others. Children either arrived with the stork (i.e., exogenously) or as the unintended outcome of sexual activity (i.e., almost randomly). In the new home economics all of this has changed.[6] Children are viewed as either "pro-

ducer durables" (i.e., producing a stream of future income for their parents—perhaps when the latter are old and retired, if not sooner) or as "consumer durables" (i.e., producing a stream of future satisfactions for their parents in the same fashion as does an automobile or a house).[7] In a modern, industrialized country with a well-developed system of social insurance and little or no child labor, children are most clearly analogous to consumer goods. In the rural areas of industrialized nations or in the less developed parts of the world, their value as workers is greater, and this is undoubtedly one explanation for the higher fertility in these areas.

Because of children's value—whether as producer or as consumer goods—parents are willing to invest both time and money in childbearing and child rearing. They make decisions not only about how many children to have, but also about how much time and money to devote to each child. In other words, the demand for, and supply of, children has both a quantity and quality component, with various trade-offs between the two being possible. In either case, children tend to be extremely time-consuming. Not only is the basic care of children demanding of adult (especially the mother's) time, but the enjoyment that parents are presumed to derive from their companionship, growth, and development also takes many hours, and it must compete with alternative uses of such time, including other leisure-time activities. In a past era, spending time with one's children did not so often have to compete with trips to Europe, Sunday golf games, or evenings at the theater. Nor were women's wages high enough or their employment opportunities sufficient to cause many families to consider a mother's forgone income as an important cost of having children.

---

[5] *Five Thousand American Families: Patterns of Economic Progress,* I–IV, ed. Greg J. Duncan and James N. Morgan (Ann Arbor, 1973–76).

[6] See Part Two, "Economics of Family Fertility," in T. W. Schultz (cited in footnote 2).

[7] For a critique, see Judith Blake, "Are Babies Consumer Durables?," *Population Studies,* 22 (March 1968), pp. 5–25.

In poor societies, alternative uses of time are neither as attractive nor as available. In fact, as Steffan Linder has noted, there may even be "idle time," that is, time which is truly a surplus in that it is not devoted to productive work, to the active enjoyment of leisure pursuits, or to personal maintenance (sleep, etc.).[8] In any case, the time costs of children are low and the (producer) benefits are high relative to what they become in a more affluent and industrialized society. Thus, it is not surprising that fertility declines with economic growth.

In an industrialized economy, the much greater productivity of human resources increases the value of time relative to the value of goods, and it changes people's behavior in subtle but important ways. Rather than bake our own bread, we buy it in the store. Even if valued at the minimum wage, the "time cost" of baking bread is about four dollars while the same product is available for less than one dollar in a commercial bakery or a local supermarket. It will be protested that the quality of the latter is inferior, but it may not be inferior to the tune of the other three dollars or so. Most people, then, bake bread only because they regard it as an enjoyable activity. Even at this level, however, it must still compete with riding a bicycle and playing the piano. In the past, more people baked their own bread not only because the store-bought variety was relatively more expensive, but also because they could less easily afford bicycles, pianos, television sets, and cameras to fill their leisure hours.

In a somewhat similar fashion, the amount of time needed to raise and enjoy one's children has led to a reduction in the size of families. Where possible, there has also been a substitution of market goods and services (analogous to the store-bought bread) for parental time, as when we send children to a day-care center or sit them in front of the television set or buy them records and books instead of talking, singing, or reading to them.[9] The point is that what some have labeled the "dehumanization" of family life or the neglect of children may simply be a matter of the economics of time. As the price of time increases, those commodities the production or consumption of which are time-intensive (e.g., children) will be less in demand than those which are more goods-intensive. Thus, as the parent's (usually the mother's) actual or expected wage rate rises, the demand for children tends to decline. On the other hand, holding the price of time constant, we would expect the demand for children to increase with family income, as is the case with other consumer goods.

Turning to the empirical evidence,[10] the economic literature on fertility has established quite unequivocally that childbearing is negatively related to the price of the mother's time. The effects of income on fertility are much weaker once the possible confounding influences of education and of the price of time have been removed. One likely possibility is that there is a substitution of quality for quantity at higher income levels—that is, more affluent families may devote more time and money *per child* than their less affluent counterparts in the same way that they buy higher quality food or more expensive clothes. These investments in children, in turn, have important implications for the transmission of inequality to succeeding generations. To date, we have had little success in using extra-family institutions or programs to compensate for these inequalities in family investment.

[8] Steffan B. Linder, *The Harried Leisure Class* (New York, 1970).

[9] Some young couples I know view their household pets as partial and inexpensive substitutes for children.

[10] The empirical literature for the United States is summarized in an appendix to an article by T. Paul Schultz which appears in T. W. Schultz (cited in footnote 2).

Finally, it has been found that better-educated parents have fewer children, even after controlling for income. This could be because they have a different set of preferences, because they are relatively more adept at producing high-quality children and thus inclined to make still further substitutions of quality for quantity, or because they are better contraceptors. There is growing empirical support for the last-mentioned possibility. The better educated use more effective contraceptive techniques and also use a given set of techniques with a higher degree of success.[11]

If further improvements in contraceptive efficiency and additional increases in the cost of children contribute to a continuing decline in fertility, what are the implications for marriage?

Marriage and Divorce

The economic theory of marriage has been developed by Gary Becker.[12] In his view, a major motivation for marriage is the desire to have one's own children. In addition, the frequent contact and sharing of resources which people who love one another find desirable can occur more efficiently if the individuals share the same household on a relatively permanent basis. Still a third motivation stems from the efficiency associated with the specialization of male and female time within marriage. If women's market productivity and wages are lower than men's, but women are at least as productive within the household as men, then marriage permits a substitution of the wife's less expensive time for the husband's more expensive time in household activities and a corresponding substitution of the husband's time for the wife's time in the labor market.

[11] See Robert T. Michael, "Education and the Derived Demand for Children," *ibid.*

[12] See Gary Becker, "A Theory of Marriage," *ibid.*

As Becker puts it, "Each marriage can be considered a two-person firm with either member being the 'entrepreneur' who 'hires' the other at... [a] salary... and receives residual 'profits'...."[13] Men "hire" women to bear and rear children and to do housework because they are physically incapable of the first and because their time is too valuable to devote to the second and third. Women "hire" men to be breadwinners and to earn the wages which they are generally not able to command. Thus, each marriage partner gains by teaming up with the other.[14] On most traits, other than wage rates, husbands' and wives' activities are seen as complementing, rather than substituting for, one another, and in these cases positive assortive mating is predicted to occur, i.e., likes marrying likes. Finally, if spouses love one another sufficiently—if there is what Becker calls "full caring" within the marriage—then each individual will take pleasure in the "consumption" or well-being of the other, effectively doubling the potential gains from the marriage.[15]

The gains from marriage have to be compared with the costs, which include not only such things as wedding ceremonies or license fees, but, more importantly, the costs of searching further for an appropriate mate (or learning more about the present candidate). The net

[13] *Ibid.*, p. 310.

[14] However, as I have suggested elsewhere, it seems clear that the monetary gain generally accrues to the wife and all the compensating nonmonetary gains—including greater power and authority within the marriage—generally accrue to the husband. See Heather L. Ross and Isabel V. Sawhill, *Time of Transition: The Growth of Families Headed by Women* (Washington, D.C., 1975), chapter 3.

[15] Another potential gain would come from "economics of scale" which occur when two can live together more cheaply than either can live alone. However, economics of scale also exist in nonmarried communal households. Both male and female time are viewed as necessary to married living in Becker's model, since it takes both to produce a child and since love and sexual attraction are more common between members of the opposite sex.

gain, then, will be positively related to a potential spouse's unearned income, to relative *differences* in the earnings (and household productivity) of the two partners, to the desire for children, and to the degree of caring. A general increase (equal for both men and women) in real wages will have uncertain effects, because the cost of time-intensive activities may or may not loom larger in the lives of married than of single individuals.

What kinds of empirically testable implications emerge from this analysis, and where does the evidence support the theory?

Love and caring are not readily observable, and the (ex ante) desire for children is also difficult to measure. Hypotheses about the effects of income on marriage should be a good deal easier to test, although past studies of marriage and divorce have not distinguished earned from unearned income or the wife's earnings from the husband's.[16] However, as a result of the theoretical developments described here and the availability of new data, some evidence is beginning to appear which suggests that the level of earned income within the family is not as important a determinant of marital stability as differences in the earnings of husbands and wives and the level of unearned income. It is also fairly well established that husbands and wives tend to be similar with respect to age, race, IQ, education, and religion and that homogeny along most of these dimensions increases marital stability.[17] All these findings are consistent with the predictions of the theory.[18]

[16] For a review of this literature, see Isabel Sawhill, Gerald Peabody, Carol Jones, and Steven Caldwell, *Income Transfers and Family Structure* (Washington, D.C., 1975).

[17] See, for example, Larry L. Bumpass and James A. Sweet, "Differentials in Marital Instability: 1970," *American Sociological Review,* 37 (December 1972), p. 754.

[18] See Sawhill et al. (cited in note 16); Mary Jo Bane, "Economic Influences on Divorce and Remarriage" (Wellesley College, unpublished paper);

One of the most dramatic and consistent findings has been the greater prevalence of marriage and the lower probability of divorce where women's wages or labor-market participation are relatively low. To understand marital behavior, then, we must pursue these topics further and inquire why women's wages are lower than men's. This exercise will reveal a certain circularity of reasoning, which is an important element in understanding and evaluating the new home economics.

Sex Roles

As we have seen, in the economic theory of marriage, differences in the wages of men and women determine the gains from marriage along with love, the desire for children, and some other factors. And if we refer back to our earlier discussion of fertility, it will be recalled that one of the more important determinants of the demand for children is the price of time which is largely captured by the mother's wage rate. In both cases, female earnings are a key explanatory variable, but one which is treated as essentially "given" for the purpose of these analyses. What happens if we now ask why women earn so little relative to men? The answer, which is derived from human capital theory, is that *because* women marry and bear and rear children, they fail to participate in the labor force as continuously or at the same level as men. As a result they fail to acquire valuable on-the-job experience (a type of human capital) and this lowers their market productivity and their earnings.[19] In this case,

Andrew Cherlin, "Social and Economic Determinants of Marital Separation" (dissertation in progress, University of California at Los Angeles), Thomas Kneiser, "On the Economics of Marital Instability" (unpublished paper, University of North Carolina at Chapel Hill).

[19] Jacob Mincer and Solomon Polacheck, "Family Investments in Human Capital; Earnings of Women," in T. W. Schultz (cited above, note 2).

it is marriage, fertility, and the division of labor within the household that are treated as the "givens" in the analysis. So we have come full circle. We have seen that women earn less than men because of their special role within the family, but that their special role within the family—and indeed the desirability of marriage and children—are importantly related to the economic status of women.

One place, then, to begin an assessment of what economists have contributed to the study of the family is to ask whether they have done anything more than describe the status quo in a society where sex roles are "givens"— defined by culture, biology, or other factors not specified in the economic model. But this would be only one of many observations which one might wish to make in the broader assessment to which I now turn.

AN ASSESSMENT

The secret to understanding the family, and particularly variations in family life over time and across cultures, may not be within the grasp of the economist, but then it is not clear that other disciplines have done much better. The difference between economists and other social scientists is that the latter are much more modest. Paul Samuelson has called economics "the queen of the social sciences,"[20] while Gary Becker has argued that "economic theory may well be on its way to providing a unified framework for *all* behavior involving scarce resources, nonmarket as well as market, non-monetary as well as monetary, small group as well as competitive."[21] Certainly his own work has been extraordinarily influential in moving economics in that direction. The question is,

Would some other line of inquiry have been more fruitful?

To anyone who has been trained as an economist, the charms of economic analysis are nearly irresistible. It is intellectually clean, challenging, and rigorously deductive. In addition, the methodological sophistication of most economists, although not essential to good theory, gives them a competitive edge in empirical work. Most importantly, the economic paradigm does have a certain "unifying power" because it is highly general and highly abstract. This power, however, has been purchased at the price of obliterating most of the trees from the forest. Many of the variables found in sociological literature, for example, are included in the economist's household-production function in a normal sense, but they are only occasionally illuminated by being viewed in this context. It might be argued that the trees can easily enough be put back into the forest as extensions of the basic analysis, but the danger is that the forest will turn into a Procrustean bed—the variables and observed relationships from empirical work being forced to fit the received microeconomic doctrine.

Second, many of the assumptions underlying the economic theory of the household could be questioned. Are scarce resources the only constraint on people's freedom to choose from among alternative courses of action? As Duesenberry has put it, economics is all about why people make choices, while sociology is all about why they don't have any choice to make.[22] Preferences are shaped by social norms and by individual psychology, and we must look at both. It is not particularly instructive simply to assume that people do what they want to do. Kenneth Boulding's statement

[20] Paul A. Samuelson, *Economics,* 9th ed. (New York, 1973), p. 6.

[21] Gary Becker, "A Theory of Marriage" (cited in note 12), p. 299.

[22] James Duesenberry, "Comment on 'An Economic Analysis of Fertility,' by Gary S. Becker," in *Demographic and Economic Change in Developed Countries (Universities-National Bureau Conference Series,* 11 [Princeton, 1960]).

that the economist's indifference curve (representing individual preferences) was "immaculately conceived" gets at the heart of the matter.[23] Finally, the people marching through the economist's household are an enviable group: they are motivated by love and caring and rarely by hate or fear. Very little attention is given to the nature of conflict or to the use of power within the family. In fact, everyone's preferences are swept into one household utility function because different family members are assumed to care enough about one another to weigh each other's preferences in arriving at family decisions. Under these circumstances, it is surprising that divorce ever occurs. Stories of abused children and battered wives together with the statistics that show a large proportion of murders being perpetrated by one family member on another need to be explained. Why is it that marriage sometimes leads to positive and sometimes to negative caring among family members? The economist has no answers.

A third problem with the economist's view of the family is that it is not particularly dynamic. Divorce, for example, is probably best viewed as reflecting a disequilibrium in a relationship, a point at which costs and benefits are out of line and recontracting occurs. In general, many changes in family relationships and behavior occur over the life cycle, and these changes are difficult to explain with existing models.

On the other hand, theory, by its very nature, can never illuminate all reality, so perhaps what has been said thus far should be given less weight than some additional considerations. There will always be (in the social sciences at least) more than one theory or conceptual framework consistent with observed behavior, and there will always be facts that

even the best of theories cannot explain. There are, then, other criteria by which we can judge the usefulness of abstract ideas. One of these criteria is the extent to which the ideas, or the additional questions or empirical work they generate, are ultimately a force for positive change. Has the development of an economic theory of the family provided us with new information or insights that give us greater control over our own destinies and the wisdom to make enlightened individual or collective decisions? Much of science, especially the policy sciences, is devoted to this end. The policy analyst begins with the normatively based question, "What do we need to know in order to control and thus improve our lives?," while the more academically oriented social scientist asks, "What are our lives like?" Although the latter may draw out the policy implications of the analysis, these are a by-product rather than a stimulus to work. Let me, then, try to suggest some of the research issues in the area of family life which the more policy-oriented scientist might wish to address.

First, there are questions about the various consequences of individual decisions which often have implications for both personal and social well-being. In economic theory, it is generally assumed that people have sufficient information about alternatives to make reasonably intelligent choices. In some areas, it is easy to obtain such information either before one acts or through experience, and mistakes are not very costly. For example, if one chooses a restaurant and it serves a poor meal, one need not go there again. On the other hand, if one marries or has a child and either decision turns out badly, the situation is not so easily corrected. Furthermore, one's own reactions to it have serious ramifications for the lives of others. Unfrequented restaurants will, and should, go out of business; unloved spouses and children are not so easily written off. Moreover, the costs of these mistakes are

---

[23] Kenneth E. Boulding, *Economics as a Science* (New York, 1970), p. 118.

often shifted onto the state, as when a mother and children are deserted and forced to seek public assistance, or when an abused child must be institutionalized or a neglected child grows up to be a delinquent.

The mistakes occur, first, because some alternatives are never considered or because current benefits tend to loom large in people's thinking relative to future costs of which they may be only dimly aware. They also occur because, even where the future costs are known, individuals can conveniently ignore the social, as opposed to the private, consequences of their own behavior and will usually act accordingly. Finally, they occur through imitating the behavior of a previous generation which is often codified in a set of social norms. These may once have served as a reasonable inexpensive surrogate for the accumulation of individual wisdom, but they may be inappropriate in a more modern context. Thus, there are essentially three reasons for poor choices: insufficient knowledge of private consequences, failure to consider social consequences, and the obsolescence of social guidelines and mores in a rapidly changing world. Each of these reasons for what I shall call "the failure of individual choice" gives rise to a new set of research issues.

The first is to scrutinize the consequences of individual decisions in the areas of marriage, childbearing, and child-rearing. For example, does having a first child at age 17 rather than at age 21 reduce the probability that one or both parents will finish school and embark on a successful career? What is the "cost" of such early childbearing (if any) in terms of foregone income at, say, age 35? Or, to take another example, does the amount of time one's children spend watching television affect their school achievement or the likelihood that they will enter a life of crime? The number of examples could be greatly expanded, but the point is that decisions are continually being made in the face of great uncertainty about the probable outcomes. Ironically, the objective of research on such questions is to make all human beings more like "economic man"—that is, possessing sufficient knowledge about the consequences of alternative behavior patterns to be able to act rationally and wisely.

The second need is for more information about *social* consequences. Early childbearing, for example, may have no long-term impact on the well-being of parents, but it may impose costs on the child, on the child's grandparents, or on society generally—all of whom may have to compensate in one way or another for the relative immaturity or lack of financial resources of the parents. Such costs (or benefits) need to be estimated in each instance. Then, if the findings suggest an overwhelming public interest in encouraging or discouraging various types of behavior, the appropriateness of providing incentives or disincentives to promote the public good might be considered. This idea will not be popular because the privacy of family life has traditionally been viewed as inviolable. But the time has come at least to examine the implications of a laissez-faire family policy and to consider where decisions not to intervene may be doing more harm than good. Nor should we be lulled into believing that existing policies fail to influence family behavior, even though the effects they elicit may not have been those foreseen or intended. Some effort has recently been made to analyze these effects. For example, the feasibility of developing "family impact statements" is being investigated by Sidney Johnson,[24] while the Urban Institute has given some attention to the effects of existing and proposed welfare programs on family composition, and it has studied the impact of liberalized abortion laws on out-of-wedlock fertility and

[24] A grant has recently been made to the Institute for Education Leadership at George Washington University for this purpose.

subsequent public dependency.[25] Still another example is the extent to which rigidities in the work schedules of most employees affect the ability of parents to combine job and family life. These rigidities stem, in part, from government policies that require extra compensation for hours worked in excess of 8 per day or 40 per week, making flexible schedules more costly for employers. They are also related to the structure of social security and unemployment compensation laws, which increase the costs of hiring part-time workers.[26]

A third area of research growing out of "the failure of individual choice" centers on the need to know how the future will differ from the past. In stable societies, the wisdom of prior generations guides the choices of the young and the rules by which they live. In an unstable one, changing attitudes and new technology may quickly make such wisdom obsolete. Perhaps nowhere are public policies and individual decisions as much in danger of being guided by obsolete norms as they are in the area of sex roles. Yet changing sex roles have profound implications for home and family life.[27] These changes need to be understood, so that we can begin to plan for a set of policies that can replace those appropriate only to some earlier time.

This overview of policy-oriented research on the family contrasts quite sharply with the new home economics and suggests that the latter has not yet moved directly into the policy arena. However, as John Maynard Keynes once noted:

> ... the ideas of economists and political philosophers, both when they are right and when they are wrong, are more powerful than is commonly understood. Indeed the world is ruled by little else. Practical men, who believe themselves to be quite exempt from any intellectual influences, are usually the slaves of some defunct economist. Madmen in authority, who hear voices in the air, are distilling their frenzy from some academic scribbler of a few years back. I am sure that the power of vested interests is vastly exaggerated compared with the gradual encroachment of ideas.[28]

Similarly, the intellectual influence of this new school of home economists is likely to be considerable. Their ideas will find their way into the more practically and empirically oriented work of the policy analyst and eventually into the political domain. Of all of the ideas that have emerged from this body of work perhaps the most central and potentially the most influential is the emphasis on the value of human time. In the past, economists believed that the ultimate scarcity was the finiteness of nature. As the population increased relative to land and other natural resources, standards of living would eventually fall to a subsistence level (although the decline might temporarily be offset by the benefits of technology). Thus, economics was labeled "the dismal science." The popularity of such books as *The Limits to Growth* and *Small Is Beautiful* attest to the modern-day appeal of the Malthusian view.[29] But T. W. Schultz has now given us a more optimistic future to ponder.[30] The ultimate

[25] Sawhill et al. (cited in note 16); and Kristin A. Moore and Steven B. Caldwell, *Out-of-Wedlock Pregnancy and Childbearing* (Washington, D.C., 1976).

[26] Testimony of Isabel V. Sawhill and Ralph E. Smith before the Subcommittee on Employment, Poverty, and Migratory Labor, April 8, 1976.

[27] Implications that I have discussed elsewhere; See Kristin A. Moore and Isabel V. Sawhill, "Implications of Women's Employment for Home and Family Life," August, 1975.

[28] John Maynard Keynes, *The General Theory of Employment, Interest and Money* (New York, 1960), p. 383.

[29] Donella H. Meadow, Dennis L. Meadows, Jørgen Randers, and William B. Behrens, III, *The Limts to Growth* (New York, 1972); and E. F. Schumacher, *Small Is Beautiful* (New York, 1973).

[30] T. W. Schultz, "Fertility and Economics Values," in *Economics of the Family* (cited in note 2).

scarcity in his vision of the future is not natural resources but human time. Investment in human capital (e.g., education, health) keeps occurring so that each generation is more productive, and the value of what they can accomplish in an hour or a year increases.[31] But as the value of human time rises, fertility will fall and standards of living will continuously improve. The process will come to a halt when there is no time left to consume the products of an affluent society and thus no reason to seek further increase in per-capita income. There will, in short, be a sufficiency of goods, given the time people will have to enjoy them. It is an interesting, if not entirely credible, view.

For the nearer term, the likely prospect

is an increase in the labor-market participation of women as the higher value of their time makes home-based activities, including the rearing of children, more expensive. There will not only be fewer children but also fewer marriages as the wage differential between the sexes narrows. Does this mean that the nuclear family will wither away? I suspect that in a quantitative sense it will diminish in importance, but that the quality of life for children and the relationships between husbands and wives can only improve. In the past, marriage was too often an economic necessity for women, and childbearing either the unintended outcome of sex or an insurance policy against the insecurities of old age. In the future, economics and technology are likely to ensure that the act of having a child and the decision to share life with another adult are freely and consciously chosen for the personal satisfactions they entail rather than as a means to some other end. Personal values and psychological needs met by marriage, children, and family life will be the final arbiters of choice.

---

[31] These investments continue to be "profitable" because new knowledge improves the *quality* as well as the *quantity* of education, health care, early childhood experiences, and so forth, thus preventing any diminishing returns (e.g., a declining return to higher education) from setting in over the long run.

Unemployment

Unemployment is officially defined to include those who are not employed, but have been actively seeking work in the last four weeks. The widely cited unemployment rate represents the unemployed as a percentage of all those in the labor force—either employed or unemployed. This unemployment rate is used for many purposes. In addition to indicating how many are actually experiencing the economic and psychological hardship of unemployment, the unemployment rate also serves as an indicator of the underutilization of all resources in the economy.

Although the unemployment rate is generally regarded as a reasonably good measure of short-term changes in underutilization, there has been considerable controversy concerning the implications of the long-term increase in unemployment. Many economists emphasize changes in aggregate demand for goods and services as the primary explanation for both short- and long-term changes in unemployment. In contrast, Charles Killingsworth argues that much of the long-term increase in the unemployment rate since the 1950s has been due to structural factors, including changes in technology and in the characteristics of the labor force.

Robert Solow presents an alternative viewpoint on the importance of structural changes in explaining increases in unemployment over the past two decades. He discusses how, in the early 1960s, many people adhered to the structuralist view that unemployment was concentrated among a rather small group of hard-core unemployables, who spent much of their time unsuccessfully seeking work. Now the emphasis is on the frequent, relatively short spells of unemployment experienced by certain groups of workers, especially young people. Although Solow considers some policy responses to this problem, he emphasizes that there are no easy solutions apparent.

Unemployment rates for youths, especially black youths, have been much higher than adult unemployment rates. Richard Freeman and David Wise discuss the causes and consequences of the high unemployment among young people.

Many different employment and training programs have been established by the government in an effort to reduce unemployment and improve the labor market opportunities of the disadvantaged. Garth Mangum traces the history of such programs from the 1930s to the 1970s.

During the 1970s, job creation programs received particular attention. Irwin Garfinkel and John Palmer discuss the case for public employment programs, including subsidies to private employers as well as direct job creation in the public sector.

In addition to reducing unemployment by increasing the demand for disadvantaged workers, another approach is to reduce the competition for available jobs. During the past decade or so, illegal immigration has increased dramatically, especially across the Mexican border. Since most such immigrants have limited education and job skills, but are willing to work hard, they may be reducing the job opportunities available to unskilled nonimmigrants. Walter Fogel discusses the causes and consequences of this illegal immigration and some of the policy alternatives that have been proposed.

14

The Fall and Rise of the Idea of Structural Unemployment

Charles C. Killingsworth

Charles C. Killingsworth, "The Fall and Rise of the Idea of Structural Unemployment," Presidential Address, *Proceedings of the Annual Meeting of the Industrial Relations Research Association*, 1978.

The task that I have set for myself is to review and evaluate, in the light of experience, the clash of ideas about structural unemployment in the 1960s and early 1970s; then to indicate very briefly some of the main events that have led to the recent turn-around of views; and finally to draw some conclusions. I believe that the natural history of the idea of structural unemployment during the past two decades can teach us something worthwhile about the nature of modern economic analysis and some of its leading practitioners. In short, this is a cautionary tale.

The Issue

When John Kennedy became President in 1961, the national unemployment rate was 6.6 percent. In those innocent days, that figure was almost universally considered to be alarming and even intolerable. What was becoming equally alarming was a kind of stair-step progression of unemployment rates during successive prosperity periods. We had less than 3 percent unemployment during the early 1950s; 4 percent in the mid-1950s; 5 percent in the late 1950s; and in 1963, after two full years of

Kennedy and recovery, unemployment was still 5½ to 6 percent.

During the 1950s, there had been increasing discussion of rising structural unemployment as a cause for this upward creep of prosperity unemployment rates. Structural unemployment to put the matter as briefly as possible, is joblessness—usually long-term—which results from basic changes in the economic structure: new technology, the decline of some industries and the growth of new ones, geographic relocation of industries, permanent changes in consumer tastes, changes in labor force characteristics, and so on. There was abundant evidence of such structural changes in the United States since World War II, and unemployment rates did vary greatly as between various labor force groups and various localities.

In its first public utterances, the new Kennedy Council of Economic Advisers had rejected the idea that structural changes were responsible for the upward creep of prosperity unemployment rates. The Council elaborated this view in later statements, with its fullest statement in Senate hearings in the fall of 1963. The essence of the Council's view can be stated as follows: Structural change does create unemployment and other human problems, but there is no evidence that structural unemployment has increased at all since the end of World War II; it is certainly not the cause of higher and higher levels of prosperity unemployment. The real cause is the growth of "fiscal drag," which is the tendency of the progressive tax system to increase revenues more rapidly than government spending increases during a recovery period. This fiscal drag, the Council argued, had repeatedly choked off recovery before full employment was reached. The remedy, the Council argued, was a large tax cut for individuals and businesses. (The amount was originally set at $10 billion, but the ultimate value was about $13 billion.) The tax cut would stimulate aggregate demand

sufficiently to reduce unemployment to 4 percent, and everybody would benefit. But, the Council said again and again, the benefits would not be equal—the greatest benefits would go to the labor force groups and geographic areas where unemployment was the highest. The unemployed worker would not get a tax cut, but he would get a job that would be worth a lot more than any conceivable tax refund.

The Council did not oppose the so-called "structural programs"—manpower training, worker mobility assistance, area redevelopment, and the like—but they warned that these programs could not have any significant effect on the unemployment problem as long as there was an inadequacy of aggregate demand. Only after the tax cut reduced the unemployment rate to the 4 percent level would the structural programs have any chance of success. When the Council was advocating a $13 billion tax cut, the appropriation for activities under the Manpower Development and Training Act was about $130 million. This was a ratio of about 100 to 1. The Council expressed no dissatisfaction with that ratio.

The Council's insistence that structural problems had not contributed to recent increases in prosperity unemployment rates rested squarely on the view of the labor market which was most frequently stated in economic theory textbooks. Thus, in its 1963 Senate Committee presentation, the Council said the following:

> [The structural analysis fails] to make any allowance for the proven capacity of a free labor market . . . to reconcile discrepancies between particular labor supplies and particular labor demands. If relative shortages of particular skills develop, the price system and the market will moderate them, as they have always done in the past. Employers will be prompted to step up their in-service training programs, as more jobs become

available, poorly skilled and poorly educated workers will be more strongly motivated to avail themselves of training, retraining, and adult education opportunities.

Many similar statements were made by the Council and others as the discussion of this issue developed. One more example will suggest the general flavor. The *Report* of the Automation Commission included the following statements:

> It is the proper function of a market to allocate resources, and in this respect the labor market does not function differently from any others. If the available resources are of high quality, the market will adjust to the use of high quality resources; if the quality is low, methods will be developed to use such resources. . . . The total number of employed and unemployed depends primarily on the general state of economic activity. The employed tend to be those near the beginning and the unemployed those near the end of the [hiring] line. Only as demand rises will employers reach further down the line in their search for employees.

In earlier days, it was conventional for economic theorists to assume that labor is homogeneous. The economists of the early 1960s modified that assumption. They argued, in effect, that although labor was not really homogeneous, the labor market acted as a powerful automatic homogenizer. When demand rose, employers redesigned jobs in order to make use of less-skilled workers, and they increased their on-the-job training: the workers themselves sought out ways to improve their skills, and they migrated to where the jobs were. These economists conceded that there might be some time lags in this process. But they insisted that the automatic homogenizing function of the labor market had held the structural component of unemployment to a low, constant level throughout the years since World War II.

Those who came to be called "structuralists" offered an abundance of statistics to support their view that the Council of Economic Advisers and others of like mind had misdiagnosed the unemployment problem. This audience will be relieved to learn that it will not hear today a rehashing of all of the statistics that were flung back and forth in those days. Neither will you hear a restatement of all of the structuralist arguments. You will hear simply the bare bones of the particular line of argument with which I happen to be most familiar—my own.

There was general agreement, as I have hinted, that there had been a substantial amount of structural change in the economy since World War II. My basic contention was that technology and other kinds of economic change had developed some new characteristics in the post-war world. Such developments as the dramatic decline of agricultural employment and the equally dramatic rise of employment in such fields as education, health care, and research and development had combined to "twist" the demand for labor—pushing down the demand for low-skilled, poorly-educated workers, and pushing up the demand for highly-skilled, well-educated workers. The labor force had partially adapted to this great shift. The numbers of workers at the lower end of the scale had decreased and the numbers at the upper end had increased. And the labor market had guided most of those displaced in declining industries (like agriculture) to new jobs. But there had been a growing lag in adaptation. The growth of the lag was shown, in my opinion, by rising unemployment rates among less-educated workers at the same time that unemployment rates for better-educated workers were falling. I granted that there was some validity to the fiscal drag argument. But it seemed quite unlikely that a sharp rise in aggregate demand would create many more jobs for less-skilled workers than for high-skilled workers. It seemed much more likely that excessive reliance on stimulation of aggregate demand would create inflationary bottlenecks in labor supply before an unemployment rate as low as 4 percent was achieved. On a more general level, I argued that the Council's depiction of the labor market as a powerful and efficient homogenizer of labor was contradicted by the conclusions of a number of empirical investigators of labor markets. One of them had summed up the consensus of the empirical investigators in these words: "Labor markets are less adequate than any other type of factor or product market in the economy." . . .

The Grand Fallacy

. . . As early as 1966, some of the participants in the debate of a few years before were pointing to the reduction in the unemployment rate as the final and unanswerable proof that the structuralist position had been completely mistaken. As the rate continued downward, other voices joined the chorus, and the theme was heard well into the 1970s. On other occasions I have presented a lengthy collection of quotations from eminent economists proclaiming the doctrine that the dramatic decline in the unemployment rate (and the rise in employment) in the late 1960s refuted once and for all the arguments of the structuralists. There is inadequate time today to read the entire collection of quotations. I will read only one, which is typical of many: "The history of the 1960s demonstrated that the American economy can reach unemployment rates of close to 3 percent through the use of simple fiscal and monetary policy." It should be noted that among the authors who expounded this view were four recent presidents of the American Economic Association and—no doubt—some future presidents of that organization. Econo-

mists are noted for their disagreements; but here, at least, was a verity about which there could be no rational disagreement. The official figures were there for everybody to see, and the reasoning was simple and easy to understand.

The trouble was that this generally accepted proposition rested on a grand fallacy. The implicit assumption is that nothing but the tax cut had a substantial effect on the employment rate between 1964 and 1969. This is a classic example of the *post hoc ergo propter hoc* fallacy. It is not hard to demonstrate that in fact there were other factors which, in combination, had a much greater effect on the unemployment rate than the tax cut did. These other factors included the Vietnam War, two changes in the definitions of employment and unemployment, and large increases in manpower and poverty programs.

By 1969, the Vietnam War had removed a large number of young men from the civilian labor force and had induced a substantial number of others to enroll as full-time students in colleges. By conservative estimating methods, it can be shown that these effects had reduced the reported unemployment rate by 0.9 percent by 1969. The two sets of changes in the definitions of unemployment took place in 1965 and in 1967. The 1965 change was to count as "employed" the enrollees in certain manpower and government-subsidized employment programs (such as College Work-Study and Neighborhood Youth Corps), although historically the enrollees in comparable programs (such as WPA in the 1930s) had been counted as "unemployed." This change, plus the expansion of the relevant programs, contributed 0.5 percent to the lowering of the unemployment rate by 1969. The 1967 definition changes were estimated by the Bureau of Labor Statistics to reduce the reported unemployment rate by 0.2 percent by 1969. There is no "double counting" involved in these estimates. The combined effect is 1.6 percentage points.

There were other significant effects not yet discussed. I will simply note two of them without elaboration. First, between 1965 and 1968, approximately 50 percent of the *new* blue-collar jobs that were created in the U.S. economy were in defense industries. Second, the employment of less-educated men *declined* despite the war boom from 1965 to 1969. The labor market twist operated almost as strongly in the period of rapid expansion as it had during the period of stagnation.

The reduction in the unemployment rate from 5.4 percent in early 1964 to the lowest monthly rate reported for 1969 (3.3 percent) is 2.1 percent. Factors *other* than pure and simple fiscal policy, or tax cuts, accounted for about three-fourths of that decrease. Thus, one may reasonably conclude that, in the absence of these other factors, the unemployment rate would not have fallen below about 4.9 percent. The actual decline below that level was caused by factors that are antithetical to the idea of a free labor market: a military draft and governmental programs of direct job creation. There is particular irony in the fact that many of our leading economists interpreted the effects of the draft and government job creation as proof of the power and efficiency of the free labor market.

The About-Face

Through the late 1960s and into the 1970s, there were a few of us who continued to argue that the Vietnam War and the changes in the definitions of unemployment had only temporarily masked the problems of structural unemployment, and that these problems would reappear. But I strongly doubt that this continuing insistence on our part was a factor of any real significance in the about-face that has now taken place in Washington and in the hinterland. Galbraith was right. It was the march of events, not ideas, that overthrew the conventional wisdom about the basic causes of excessive unemployment in the United States.

When the Vietnam War began to taper off, unemployment started to rise. The then Chairman of the Council of Economic Advisers advised the nation that this rise—to about 4 percent—was purely a "transitional" problem. But the rise continued. In 1969, the average number of persons unemployed was 2.8 million. The average number unemployed in the 1970s thus far has been 5.7 million, or more than double the 1969 average. In the past three years, the average has been more than 7 million unemployed. If we applied the pre-1965 definitions of unemployment, the three-year average would exceed 8 million.

Now I am not suggesting that these totals by themselves prove the validity of the structural viewpoint. What they do prove is that we have a severe problem of chronic and excessive unemployment. And the patterns which are indicative of structural problems have reappeared, some even more clearly than in the early 1960s. So the official diagnosis has changed. . . . Let me give you a more detailed statement of the present Administration viewpoint, from testimony presented to the Joint Economic Committee a couple of months ago.

> While our overall performance record has been remarkable, there are segments of our society who have not shared equally in this recovery and who have historically suffered disproportionately during the cyclical swings. During the past year, the unemployment rate for nonwhites has remained about the same at 12.3%, while the rate for whites dropped from 6.7% to 5.2%. Teenagers of all races are experiencing unemployments of 16.5%, with the nonwhite teenage rate at a totally unacceptable level of 38.4%. Unemployment is particularly high in central cities and remote rural communities. For these localities, lack of adequate job opportunities has a permanent structural character which persists in both good times

and bad. . . . It is clear . . . that macro-economic policies, by themselves, are not sufficiently precise to solve specific structural labor market problems without causing unacceptable side effects. Selective labor market policies, on the other hand, are more flexible . . . [and] more cost effective than macroeconomic policies in solving structural problems. . . .

If it occurs to you that talk is cheap, consider one more fact: In 1976 while Congress debates a possible tax cut of the magnitude of $15-20 billion, the expenditures on manpower programs are running at an annual rate of about $12 billion.

The recent discussion of structural unemployment emphasizes some kinds of changes, such as more teenagers and women in the labor force, that were not present 15 years ago. I think that some of the recent converts to the structural viewpoint may have reached the right conclusions for the wrong reasons. There have been important offsetting changes in labor force composition and there have also been further changes in demand for labor that have been neglected. But these are subjects for another paper.

Lessons

It is hardly noteworthy any longer when the march of events proves that the majority of professional economists have been wrong. But, unless we are ready to give up completely on economics and economists, we should continue to try to figure out (if we can) what went wrong in particular cases. I have some observations along those lines which grow out of my involvement in the aggregate demand-structural controversy. I do not intend to generalize beyond my data base. Not only economists were involved in that controversy, and my observations are certainly not intended to apply to all economists generally, nor to those

who emphasize mathematical analysis of economic problems.

What led the aggregate demand school astray?

Probably the most important factor was one which the CEA, early in the day, called "the nub of the issue." The aggregate demand group, as *general* economists, has a quasi-religious faith in "the market" as an extremely powerful, highly efficient regulator of the economy, and a corollary belief that labor markets were like all others. That faith affected their perceptions. They quickly and uncritically embraced "evidence" which seemed to support their preconceptions, and they almost automatically rejected as "implausible" and "insufficient" any evidence which was inconsistent with these preconceptions, such as my statistical demonstrations of the labor market twist.

Second, some of them misunderstood the data on which they relied. This country generates an enormous volume of numbers relating to employment, unemployment, and the labor market. There is no substitute for a painstaking and often tedious investigation of the characteristics and meanings of the numbers that you want to use. To cite one example, the occupational classification system—especially the highly aggregated version used in monthly labor force data—is of questionable utility for any purpose, and unemployment rates by occupation are probably the most questionable of all. Again, changes in the national average unemployment rate are produced by a multitude of factors, including such artifacts as definition changes. It should be obvious that a single factor, such as a tax cut, is not likely to be an adequate or accurate explanation for a large change in reported unemployment over several years. But what one aggregate demand supporter once wryly referred to as "the enthusiasm of advocacy" can dull the caution with which sweeping generalizations might otherwise be approached. One lesson which should be emphasized is that reliance on inappropriate statistics can be as misleading as reliance on unrealistic assumptions.

In a broad sense, the aggregate demand-structural controversy carried into the public arena a conflict among economists that previously had been confined mainly to the groves of academe. Some economists preferred to draw conclusions about the economy and economic policy from the assumptions of perfect competition (and all that this implies); other economists preferred to draw conclusions from direct observation of economic behavior in the real world. Most of the aggregate demand supporters came from the former group, and most of the structuralists came from the latter group. The aggregate demand school relied primarily on the theoretical model of the labor market, which makes little or no distinction between labor markets and other types of markets. The structuralists relied primarily on the large number of empirical studies of labor markets that were available in the early 1960s.

The common theme of the empirical studies is that the gritty reality of labor markets departs widely from the simplistic assumptions of economic theory. Knowledge is imperfect, mobility is limited, wage competition among employers is unusual, workers often behave differently from the theoretical "economic man," jobs are almost never redesigned (in peacetime) to adapt them to changes in the quality of labor available, and so on. The point is certainly not that labor markets are completely ineffective, or that the forces of competition and self-interest are nonexistent. Rather, the point is that labor markets and the forces that operate within them are often inadequate to overcome the imbalances that grow out of structural changes in the economy.

Since the structuralist view of labor markets now seems to have achieved rather general acceptance, some of you may ask, why rake over the dead coals of an old controversy? My answer is in two parts. First, the misdiagnosis of the causes of unemployment in the 1960s probably retarded the development of adequate employment policies for about ten years. During that time, some aspects of the unemployment problem became even more intractable. And we still do not know nearly as much as we should about how to remedy the weaknesses and imperfections of the labor market. After we are sure what works best, we will still have the task of building institutions to apply the remedies. We tried the easy, palatable answer, and it was inadequate. Now we must work on a slow, laborious answer.

Second, the past errors of analysis have not been generally recognized and corrected. Some of the current forecasting models still incorporate the simplistic view that the decline in unemployment in the late 1960s was due entirely to fiscal and monetary policy, and this misreading of the past undoubtedly contributes to the impressive record of error in efforts to predict the future. The great overstatement of the effects of the tax cut of 1964 has recently led to proposals from the radical right to cut taxes by roughly $120 billion over the next three years. One somewhat unexpected result of this proposal is that some of the tax cut enthusiasts of the 1960s are becoming the nay-sayers of the 1970s. The 1964 tax cut was not really as effective as today's tax cutters claim, some old tax cutters are now saying—and besides, they suggest, there were other things happening that contributed to economic expansion in the 1960s. I conclude with the observation that it is better to discover the truth late than never to discover it at all.

15

What Happened to Full Employment?

Robert M. Solow

Robert M. Solow, "What Happened to Full Employment?," *Quarterly Review of Economics and Business*, Vol. 13, No. 2 (Summer 1973). Reprinted by permission of the Bureau of Economic and Business Research, College of Commerce and Business Administration, University of Illinois.

THE STRUCTURAL UNEMPLOYMENT CONTROVERSY

I want to begin with some history.

When I went to work for the Council of Economic Advisers (CEA) at the very beginning of the Kennedy administration, my first assignment was one for which I was absolutely unprepared. It had to do with the correct interpretation of the unemployment figures. Early in 1961 we were, as it turned out, at the bottom of a recession. The unemployment rate was something like 6.9 percent, having increased precipitously in the second half of 1960. The recession itself may very well have provided John Kennedy's narrow margin of victory. It

began in May 1960, just in time to be blamed unmistakably on the Republican administration. At the May 1960 peak, the unemployment rate was about 5.1 percent. At the previous peak, just before the recession of 1957–58, the lowest unemployment rate that was achieved was about 4 percent. If you go back before that, before the recession of 1954–55, you come to the Korean War and that may well have been a special situation, not to be compared with peacetime periods. Nevertheless it was hard not to notice that in 1953 we had achieved unemployment rates slightly below 3 percent.

To the economists at the CEA, it seemed obvious and urgent that the first priority of economic policy was to get the country back on the track to full employment. Wherever full employment was, we were sure it was nowhere near an unemployment rate of 6 percent or 7 percent. A sequence of unemployment rates of 3 percent, 4 percent, and 5 percent at successive business cycle *peaks* was certainly an ominous sign, but we took it as a sign that macroeconomic policy had been excessively restrictive on the average, at least since the recession of 1958. Some such view had been written into candidate Kennedy's speeches, and he had promised to "get the country moving again."

I think that we—innocent academics freshly arrived in Washington—were astonished to discover that there was a contradictory view. We learned that some people in Congress, in the agencies, and in the universities believed that it would be wrong and dangerous and fruitless to launch any massive effort of fiscal and monetary policy to lift the economy to a substantially higher macroeconomic plane and to lower the unemployment rate greatly.

Their reasoning went like this. Obviously we were in a recession, and obviously the "normal" forces of cyclical recovery would soon take hold and turn the economy around. It might be harmless if the federal government took some gentle and conventional counter-cyclical actions, such as temporarily extending the duration of unemployment compensation benefits or speeding up outpayments to the states from the highway trust fund. These policies would be automatically self-liquidating anyway. But it would not pay to be too ambitious. Those successive, 3 percent, 4 percent, and 5 percent unemployment rates at the tops of the booms really were trying to tell us something. Their message was that more and more of the unemployment experienced in the postwar period was "structural." That meant that it was not merely the reflection of an inadequate aggregate demand for goods and services. If it were that kind of unemployment,

then indeed fiscal and monetary policy would be the answer: by adding to the total demand for goods and services they would add to the demand for labor and the unemployed could and would fill the jobs opened up by expanding markets for the things they could produce.

But the theory I am describing denied that very much of the unemployment was of that sort. Instead, most of it, and an increasing proportion of it, was said to arise because a growing fraction of those looking for work lacked something indispensable for the employment in the modern world. The missing ingredient might be formal education, or native skills, or learned skills, or perhaps just the right location; but in any case there was a serious and worsening mismatch of the kinds and qualities of labor needed by industry and commerce and the kinds and qualities of labor offered by the unemployed. Technological progress, automation, the replacement of manual labor by complicated machines and by the skilled people to run them, the predominance of white-collar over blue-collar work and the increasing complexity of white-collar work—these were the causes of worsening unemployment.

The structuralists argued that it would do no good, in fact it would do harm, to pump up demand for goods and services by easy money, or government spending, or tax reduction. If that were attempted on a large scale, the economy would run out of employable labor long before the unemployment rate had fallen to 4 percent of the labor force, let alone 3 percent. Employers would have to scramble for the limited supply of eligible workers. Wages and prices would be bid up and, most important of all, the unemployment rate still would not fall below 5 percent, say, because it could not. Some 5 percent of the labor force was essentially unemployable except under extreme forced-draft conditions.

I was given the task of looking into this

argument, though I had no closer acquaintance with the unemployment statistics than I had with the rings of Saturn. I studied them up, however. And I convinced myself that although there undoubtedly was a significant amount of "structural unemployment" there was no evidence to suggest that it had become substantially worse since 1957, say, and quite a bit of evidence to suggest that it had not got substantially worse since then. We concluded that the structuralist argument was false and that it was quite reasonable to aim at the 4 percent unemployment rate that had been achieved during the boom—and creeping inflation—of 1955–57.

I do not want to rehearse all the arguments and counterarguments that went into this controversy. But I do want to emphasize that it was not a matter of disagreement about the raw facts but about the interpretation of the facts. For instance, part of the structuralist case was the fact that the proportion of all the unemployed who had been unemployed for a long time, say six months or more, was extraordinarily high in 1961. In fact, over a sixth of all the unemployed fell into this category. This was interpreted to mean that the unemployment was becoming increasingly concentrated in a group of unemployables. The fact was certainly a fact; but I thought it could more accurately be interpreted to mean something different. The proportion of long-term unemployed should naturally depend not only on the current degree of softness of the labor market but on the length of time during which the labor market had been soft. After all, to be unemployed a long time, you must have become unemployed a long time ago and failed to find work in the meanwhile. If the data were allowed to look at the matter that way, they seemed to say that the long-term unemployment of 1961 was adequately explained by the long period of economic slack that preceded 1961 with very little upward drift beyond that. There was no

need for the hypothesis of a special class of long termers who had increased drastically in numbers since the early postwar period. . . .

A NEW VERSION

The old structural-unemployment theory is pretty clearly even less tenable now than it was in 1961. It was, as I have mentioned, primarily an assertion about a large and growing discrepancy between the mix of skills demanded by employers and the skills available among the "hard-core" unemployed. It drew attention to the decline of manufacturing employment, the disappearance of the manual worker, especially the unskilled manual worker, and the hopeless position of the uneducated in a world of delicate instruments, computers, and automated factories. Whatever was true in 1961, the situation is certainly better now in those particular respects. The labor force is certainly more educated now than it was a dozen years ago. I shall quote just one measure. In 1957, 45.6 percent of the civilian labor force 18 years or older had at least finished four years of high school. In 1962 it was 53.8 percent. By 1971 two-thirds of the labor force had at least finished high school. It is conceivable that the fraction of all jobs that require a high school education had increased that fast, but it is hardly believable.

The new structural theory appears to be much less concerned with the educational qualifications of the unemployed. It does, however, rest on the considerable, and probably increasing, extent to which the existing volume of unemployment is concentrated in certain subgroups of the labor force. The subgroups we talk about now are usually demographically defined—classified by age, sex, and race—because that is the way the figures come; it is hard to know whether there would be more significant ways of cross-classifying people in the labor market, because the data do not exist for a systematic study of, say, simultaneous classification by age, sex, race, and education. The crude facts are too well known to need much documentation. . . .

So, with demographic characteristics substituted for skills and education, the 1961 story repeats itself. Then it was thought that the economy would run out of skilled workers able to participate effectively in modern industry before the unemployment rate could be reduced to 4 percent of the labor force. That turned out not to be so. Now it is thought that the economy would run out of what? Out of mature white males, before the unemployment rate could be reduced to 4 percent of the labor force. This newer argument is based on rather more sophisticated statistical and economic analysis than the older one; but it raises some real puzzles of its own, which have to be pursued further.

UNEMPLOYMENT AND TURNOVER

The old structural-unemployment theory at least would have made sense if it had been true. One can understand that a severe shortage of skilled and trainable labor might arise while there remain a lot of unskilled, untrained, and perhaps untrainable people still unemployed. It need not happen, either because the likelihood of a shortage of skilled workers is exaggerated, or because industry is better able to substitute unskilled for skilled workers than the structuralists had thought. But what does it mean to say that the economy will run out of mature male workers while there are still a lot of teen-agers and women unemployed? A factory may need so and so many skilled machinists but hardly so and so many adult white males. The explanation could be simple discrimination by race, sex, or age, which has been known to happen. But greed is also a pretty powerful motive and it is hard to imagine that very

many employers would let production and profit go by rather than hire a 19-year-old worker, even a hairy one. Is there anything else that could generate those high unemployment rates for the young, the female, and the black?

Recent research has begun to give some possible answers, though only tentative ones because they are based on skimpy evidence. And, as you will see, there is room for alternative interpretations of what little evidence there is.

The key point appears to be this. If you think about it for a minute, you will see that there are two ways in which a single person or class of persons could pile up a lot of unemployment in a year. One way is to become unemployed once and to stay unemployed for a long time. The other way is to experience a larger number of spells 'of unemployment, each one of them relatively short. For example, I have already said that male teen-agers had an unemployment rate of 16.7 percent in 1971. That means, of course, that on the average one-sixth of all the male teen-agers in the labor force were unemployed in any given week. (In fact, there may have been more of them unemployed early in the year than toward the end; but that is not the point, so we might as well assume that there was a constant unemployment rate throughout the year.) You should also keep in mind that in any given week, most of the teen-aged males in the US are neither employed nor unemployed; they are not in the labor force, neither employed nor looking actively for work. Individuals may move from being employed to being unemployed to being out of the labor force, and back again. This is one of the factors that make the analysis difficult, but I shall be concentrating on other aspects of the problem. Another way to say that one-sixth of male teen-agers are unemployed in any week is to say that the average male teen-ager was unemployed for 8.5 weeks in the year. That is the average male teen-ager; not all of them will have the same experience, and some may never become unemployed at all. Still, consider the average member of the group: he can do his eight weeks of unemployment in one spell of eight weeks duration or two spells of four weeks each or even, in principle, eight one-week spells. It does not matter, so far as the aggregate count of teen-age unemployment is concerned. But it does matter when it comes to understanding what actually goes on in the labor market for the different age-sex-race groups. If the unemployment suffered by any group comes in a few long spells, it means that members of the group have a hard time finding jobs when they are unemployed, but not so much in keeping a job once they have it. The opposite pattern, many short spells of unemployment, means something quite different: that those people do not have much trouble finding jobs when they are unemployed, but do not keep the jobs they find for very long.

The evidence, as I have said, is scattered. Nevertheless it appears to point to a rather surprising conclusion. Typically, the reason teenagers suffer more unemployment than, say, 25- to 44-year old men is that they have many more spells of unemployment, not because they are unemployed for a longer time during each spell of unemployment. In fact one set of statistical results shows that males 16 to 19 have shorter spells of unemployment than 25- to 44-year-olds. To give a precise illustration, the estimate is that when the overall unemployment rate is 6 percent the average teen-aged male in the labor force suffers two spells of unemployment in a year, each lasting about 4.3 weeks. Thus the average teen-aged male is unemployed for 8.6 weeks, which corresponds to an unemployment rate of almost 17 percent. The 25- to 44-year-old males have an unemployment rate between a quarter and a fifth as great, 3.7 percent. That

is to say, they are unemployed for about two weeks in the year on average. That comes about from three-tenths of a spell of unemployment lasting six and a half weeks. Or, to put it more sensibly, on the average a 25- to 44-year-old man suffers a spell of unemployment only three times in 10 years (when the overall unemployment rate is 6 percent) but, when he does, he is unemployed for some six and a half weeks before finding another job (or, just possibly, leaving the labor force).

The differences in unemployment experience between men and women in any given age group are rather smaller than those between age groups. Women over 25 have more unemployment than men over 25; under the age of 25, there is not much difference. Generally speaking, women have more spells of unemployment than men and those spells are shorter.

My colleague Robert Hall has made some estimates of race differences in the frequency and duration of unemployment controlling for age and some other characteristics. His conclusion should not be surprising in view of what I have already said.

> For men, the results show that most of the very substantial differences between the unemployment rates of blacks and whites is associated with higher frequency rather than longer duration of unemployment. Blacks are 73% more likely to become unemployed than whites and, if unemployed, are 21% less likely to find work each week.

In other words, black men have more spells of unemployment than white men, *and* longer spells on the average, but they have almost twice as many spells, and those are only a fifth again as long. So most of the difference in unemployment is accounted for by the larger number of spells.

IMPLICATIONS FOR EMPLOYMENT POLICY

What emerges from this sort of research is a rather unexpected picture of the labor market. It is as different as can be from the old structuralist picture. The emphasis is not on a small (though perhaps growing) group of hard-core long-term unemployables who spend most of their time vainly looking for work. On the contrary, it appears that the groups with the highest risk of unemployment—women, blacks, and young people—move back and forth between employment and unemployment rather frequently, and perhaps equally frequently into and out of the labor force. It is actually easy for them to find jobs. Of course, it is incorrect to describe the situation as if everyone within any demographic group lives out an identical labor-force history. Within any demographic group there will be some people who are almost never unemployed and others who are almost never employed. But that is true within any demographic group. We can still make meaningful statements about the average differences among demographic groups. They are tentative statements, as I have stressed, because the statistical material is fragmentary and incomplete. Nevertheless, the simplest summary statement one can make is the one I have made: groups with relatively high unemployment rates have them because they have relatively many short spells of unemployment, not so much because they become unemployed and stay unemployed for long periods of time. Among the young, this pattern of rapid turnover is reinforced by movements between the labor force and school or other activities. Reentry to the labor force is often accompanied by a spell of unemployment, so this is quite consistent with the general picture.

This discovery raises still further questions about the nature of unemployment. And since the statistical evidence peters out pretty rapidly as one goes further down this path, there is more and more room for impressionism and prejudice.

If, in fact, disadvantaged workers are able to find jobs—because after all they do find jobs, and frequently—then one has to wonder whether their unemployment is not voluntary. If it is voluntary, then perhaps it becomes debatable whether public policy ought to try very hard to eliminate it. At the very least, it might appear that general expansion of the economy, with the accompanying risk of inflation, is not an appropriate way to reduce residual unemployment that exists mainly because those who bear it choose to be unemployed.

Let me put this more starkly. We are concerned with a definition of full employment, or with the specification of a social target for policy. I think that the realization that a disproportionate fraction of that last 5 percent of unemployment consists of women and young people already disposes some officials and politicians to relax a little. They do not fit the traditional picture of the hardworking, breadwinning, full-time family man. For him a job is an economic and emotional necessity and when he is out of a job something is wrong. But women and the young are somehow less real members of the labor force. Work is for them a luxury, not a necessity. Why take chances to create it for them? Mind you, this is not the way it appears to me, but I think one can practically hear that thought going around in the backs of Washington minds. Now how much more plausible that line becomes if you discover that not only the female and the young, but also the black unemployed suffer not so much from a shortage of jobs but from a failure—maybe even an unwillingness—to hang on to jobs when they have them. It is not hard to see that this view of the labor market provides an excellent excuse for the five-percenters to argue that a slack economy is not so bad as we used to think.

Unfortunately, at this crucial stage of the analysis there is a vacuum. How much of this high turnover that characterizes the work experience of the young and the black is voluntary and how much involuntary? How much is quit and how much is layoff? How much represents the instability of the *people* concerned, and how much the instability of the *job* or the *employer*? No one can know with any confidence at all, because there is almost no hard information, and what exists is ambiguous. The result is that this question becomes something like a Rorschach test and many people think what they would like to think.

There is some evidence that some employers, generally those offering unpleasant work at low wages, hire workers for specifically short-run jobs. In this part of the labor market there is no job security, no seniority provisions, and no seniority. The employers survive only because they can thrust the burden of unstable business on a casual labor force. One piece of research indicates that men who have been employed in a given job only for a week or two are fairly likely to be laid off in any given week and that this likelihood diminishes very steeply as the period of employment lengthens. (The probability of quitting is also fairly high in the early weeks of tenure of a job and also tails off, but more slowly than the probability of being fired.) It is entirely plausible that a substantial part of the turnover in this secondary labor market (as my colleague Michael Piore calls it) is employer-determined. Nonunion construction, seasonal manufacturing, some warehousing and restaurants, carwashes, and the like are simply sources of unstable employment. They are not organized for steady employment. Those who, for one reason or another, are confined to this part of the labor market will necessarily find themselves involved in a series of short and not so sweet jobs.

On the other hand, there is also evidence that much of the turnover of young and black workers is voluntary, initiated by the worker himself. The people are engaged in a deliberate rapid movement from job to job, from employment to unemployment, to being out of the labor force to employment and out again. Even employers such as hotels and hospitals, offering unattractive but potentially stable jobs, find themselves beset by rapid turnover. One must face the fact that in many large cities the street offers semilegal and illegal activities that are both more interesting and more lucrative than these casual dead-end jobs.

As I have read descriptions of this secondary labor market it has seemed to me that the distinction between quit and layoff almost evaporates. There are some jobs so unpleasant and meaningless that no one would hold them for a long time willingly and no employer would expect anyone to do so. Maybe it is best just to think of the problem of high-turnover unemployment—and high-turnover employment—as a problem endemic to the secondary labor market itself, with workers and jobs each contributing to the instability of employment.

CONCLUSION

Where does this leave the problem of full employment? I said at the beginning that I would end with uncertainty, and I shall. Let me summarize. Full employment seems to elude us because unemployment is so unequally distributed among social groups. When white adult male unemployment is brought down to very low levels, workers who are young or black or female are still unemployed in large numbers. Most people, I hope, would find it easier to tolerate somewhat higher unemployment—if that were necessary to control inflation, say— provided these disparities were much reduced. Besides, if most of us suffered more frequently from unemployment we would find ways to make it more pleasant to be unemployed. On closer inspection it appears that the high-unemployment pool does not suffer from any lack of available jobs; ghetto employers usually report that labor is scarce and jobs unfilled. The high-unemployment pool can get jobs but it does not keep them. They are not, in fact, the sort of job it would be anyone's ambition to keep. How, then, can we proceed? I shall offer two suggestions.

First, I find it hard to believe that a slack economy makes this problem any better. It is argued that a tight, booming, even inflationary economy can do very little for those trapped in the secondary labor market. It is said that when employers who offer good, stable jobs that lead somewhere run out of white adult males, they will not hire youths or women or blacks; they will at best subcontract some of their extra work to the secondary labor market. Perhaps so, though I would count on the profit motive to promote some breaking down of the barriers to steady work. So I am not happy with holding back the economy. But I must confess that I am an expansionist from way back, so I would say this anyway.

Second, most direct attacks on the problem of the high-unemployment pool—in the form of manpower development and training programs—are an attempt to change the workers in the secondary labor market. Perhaps some ingenuity should be spent on ways to change the jobs. Dock work and longshoring used to be an important part of the casual labor market but that has now changed. Maybe "decasualization" can be made to occur elsewhere, though I confess I do not see how to go about it within the framework of present institutions. There may be some industries that could not survive decasualization: the 35-cent hamburger might have to go, and the jiffy carwash, and even the cheap bellbottoms and plastic toys. Perhaps that should be taken as an unexpected bonus. In any case, I would like to see a tight, prosperous economy combined with some clever attempt to force all those fringe jobs into a more normal pattern. A voluntary army is a poor substitute.

I think I will have to stop there because, as I said, I do not have a really good answer. Everyone or nearly everyone in this room has already made it out of the secondary labor market. But the next time you hear the argument that we have to be content with 5 percent unemployment, I hope you will realize that what it means is that not everybody has made it out of the secondary labor market and that what is proposed is that we do very little to change that.

16

Youth Unemployment

Richard B. Freeman and David A. Wise

Richard B. Freeman and David A. Wise, "Youth Unemployment," *NBER Conference Papers* (Cambridge, Mass.: National Bureau of Economic Research, 1980).

INTRODUCTION

Teenagers and young adults have traditionally worked less than older persons. While some youths work less than adults because they are devoting a major portion of their time to schooling or to leisure activities, others work less because they have great difficulty obtaining jobs or because they are in the midst of switching their primary activity from schooling to employment, a process that involves considerable searching and job changing before settling into more or less permanent employment. In recent years, large numbers of youths have entered the job market. Because some groups of young persons have lower employment

rates than comparable youths of the past, there has been rising concern about the operation of the youth labor market. Youth unemployment has become a major issue, as evidenced by Congressional legislation such as the Youth Employment and Demonstration Projects Act of 1977.

Under the auspices of the National Bureau of Economic Research (NBER), for the past year, economists from several universities have been engaged in extensive investigation of the nature of youth employment: the causes of changes in youth employment rates over time, the causes of individual differences in employment experiences, and the consequences of youth unemployment. This paper represents a distillation of the findings of that work.

TABLE 1

Employment and Unemployment Rates, 1954-1977

	Whites				Blacks and Others			
	1954	*1964*	*1969*	*1977*	*1954*	*1964*	*1969*	*1977*
Men								
Percent Employed by Age								
16-17	40.6	36.5	42.7	44.3	40.4	27.6	28.4	18.9
18-19	61.3	57.7	61.8	65.2	66.5	51.8	51.1	36.9
20-24	77.9	79.3	78.8	80.5	75.9	78.1	77.3	61.2
25-54	93.8	94.4	95.1	91.3	86.4	87.8	89.7	81.7
Percent of Labor Force Unemployed by Age								
16-17	14.0	16.1	12.5	17.6	13.4	25.9	24.7	38.7
18-19	13.0	13.4	7.9	13.0	14.7	23.1	19.0	36.1
20-24	9.8	7.4	4.6	9.3	16.9	12.6	8.4	21.7
25-54	3.9	2.8	1.5	3.9	9.5	6.6	2.8	7.8
Women								
Percent Employed by Age								
16-17	25.8	25.3	30.3	37.5	19.8	12.5	16.9	12.5
18-19	47.2	43.0	49.2	54.3	29.9	32.9	33.9	28.0
20-24	41.6	45.3	53.3	61.4	43.1	43.7	51.5	45.4
25-54	40.1	41.0	46.2	54.1	49.0	52.7	56.3	57.4
Percent of Labor Force Unemployed by Age								
16-17	12.0	17.1	13.8	18.2	19.1	36.5	31.2	44.7
18-19	9.4	13.2	10.0	14.2	21.6	29.2	25.7	37.4
20-24	6.4	7.1	5.5	9.3	13.2	18.3	12.0	23.6
25-54	5.0	4.3	3.2	5.8	8.3	8.4	5.0	9.8

THE NATURE OF THE YOUTH EMPLOYMENT PROBLEM

A few basic statistics will motivate thinking and provide a background for our subsequent discussion. Employment and unemployment rates for selected years by race, sex, and age are shown in Table 1.

These data show divergent levels and trends in the percentages of youths who have jobs and the percentages of youths who are unemployed; they describe the primary characteristics of the youth labor market.

Although youth unemployment is sometimes perceived and portrayed as a crisis of youths in general, these data do not support this interpretation. The employment rate of white male youths has changed only modestly in the past two decades; indeed, the trend has been upward since the mid-1960s. The percent of white females employed has also risen substantially, even in the 1970s.

On the other hand, since 1954, the percent of black youths with jobs has fallen dramatically and there has been a correspondingly large increase in the black unemployment rate. This disturbing trend is even more troublesome in light of the fact that it is a relatively recent one. In 1954, approximately equal percentages of black and white youths were employed. Since that time, unemployment rates for black youths have risen and their employment position has deteriorated greatly. As can be seen in the preceding figures, the unemployed proportion of black youths has increased relative to black adults as well as relative to white youths. (In 1954, the unemployment rate of black youths was about one and a half times the rate for black adults; by 1977, the youth rate was almost four times the adult rate.)

Thus, to the extent that trends in the data signify a deterioration in the employment of youths, that deterioration is concentrated among blacks. Nonetheless, because a much greater proportion of the population is white, the vast majority of unemployed youths are white.

What the numbers in Table 1 do not reveal is that almost half of the teenagers classified as unemployed are also in school. The unemployment of a young person in school, most would agree, represents less loss to society than that of an adult seeking full-time work.

The Bureau of Labor Statistics (BLS) defines unemployment as the ratio of persons looking for work to the number employed plus the number looking. According to this (BLS) definition, 18 percent of male teenagers aged 16 to 19 were unemployed in October 1976. Since most full-time students are not included in the youth labor force, this figure overstates the fraction of young persons who are ready to work but have no productive way to spend their time. Just 4.9 percent of teenagers are both unemployed and not in school. On the other hand, the unemployment data ignore youths who are not in the labor force. In October 1976, 9 percent of male teenagers 16 to 19 years old were either unemployed or out of the labor force and not in school. Moreover, only 70 percent of the out-of-school teenagers (many of whom were high school dropouts) held jobs, according to the Current Population Survey data.

Whichever groups are considered, unemployment is concentrated among those with the lowest levels of education. Among out-of-school teenagers, persons with less than twelve years of school account for 58 percent of the unemployed. Unemployment rates are much higher among high school dropouts than among high school graduates. Moreover, unemployment is also concentrated among relatively few persons—those unemployed for very long periods. If we add up all periods of unemployment for male teenagers, for example, we find that 54 percent of the total is composed of persons who are unemployed for more than six months of the year. Even more striking, 10 percent of all teenagers account for more than half of total teenage unemployment. The majority of young persons move in and out of the labor force and obtain jobs with ease; many youths either experience no unemployment at all between transitions or are unemployed only for very short spells. However, the concentration of unemployment among a small fraction of youths has presumably higher social costs than the even distribution of unemployment among all young persons might have.

In short, the data suggest that most teenagers do not have substantial employment difficulties, but that for a minority of youths, there are long periods without work that constitute severe problems. This group is composed, in large part, of high school dropouts and

includes black youths in numbers disproportionate to their representation in the population.

It is commonly believed that young
persons have much more difficulty finding
jobs than their adult counterparts. Measured
by the lengths of spells of unemployment,
the evidence does not support this view. The
average duration of periods of unemployment
for teenagers is in fact less than the average
for adults. However, many spells of teenage
unemployment end not when a job is found but
when the young person drops out of the labor
force. Still, out-of-school male teenagers average
only three months between the loss of one job
and attainment of a new job; the comparable
figure for adult males is over four months.
(The volatility of the youth labor force, with
persons frequently entering and leaving the
officially measured labor force, suggests that
the data do not adequately distinguish between
active labor force participation and being out
of the labor force.)

Unemployment can be decomposed into
three components: (1) the rate at which persons
change jobs or switch from out of the labor
force into the labor force, multiplied by (2)
the rate at which those who change or switch
are unemployed, times (3) the average duration
of unemployment. Analysis of these three
components of unemployment shows that
young persons are unemployed more than
adults because they change jobs or situations
more often than adults, not because they have
a greater chance of unemployment given a
change in status nor because they are unemployed longer than adults.

About one fourth of young men aged 18
to 24 change jobs in a year, compared to less
than one tenth of adult men aged 35 to 54.
The differential proportion of those who
change jobs by age can itself be largely attributed, according to Leighton and Mincer's

calculations, to differences in seniority by age.
Low-seniority workers, of necessity primarily
young workers, change jobs frequently, while
high-seniority workers, of necessity primarily
older workers, change jobs less frequently and
are as a result less likely to be unemployed.
One of the key factors behind the high rate
of youth joblessness is the high mobility and
short job tenure of the young.

Finally, we emphasize that the interpretation of all these data is complicated by un-
certainly about the accuracy of their magnitudes. Recent large-scale surveys that interview
young persons themselves (rather than resident
adults in a household as is common in the widely
used Current Population Survey) reveal higher
rates of employment and different rates of
unemployment than the official government
statistics.

For example, for October 1972, employment rates for out-of-school male high school
graduates, based on the National Center for
Educational Statistics study of the high school
class of 1972, were 88 percent for whites and
78 percent for blacks. The comparable Current
Population Survey data (the basis for official
Bureau of Labor Statistics) implied substantially lower employment rates of 82 percent
and 68 percent respectively. Similar differences
arise when comparing the Current Population
Survey rates with those based on the National
Longitudinal Survey of Young Men. A large
portion of the difference among the various
rates can be attributed to who the survey
questions. Youths report more employment
activity for themselves than is reported by the
household members most likely to respond to
government population surveys, the youths'
mothers. The differences in reports are larger
for in-school youths with full-time jobs. It is
important to remember that until the discrepancy in survey results is completely resolved
and the "correct" rate of youth employment

determined, there will be ambiguity about the causes and consequences of the problem.

THE CAUSES: MARKET DETERMINANTS OF YOUTH EMPLOYMENT

Whether or not a youth is employed depends partly on the strength of the economy and on broad demographic conditions and partly on individual characteristics of the youth himself. The aggregate determinants are those that influence the average level of youth employment at a given time; the individual influences are those that determine differences among individuals at a given time. The broader influences on the average youth employment rate are discussed in this section, and individual differences are presented in the next section.

The most important aggregate determinant of differences in youth unemployment among geographic areas and of year-to-year fluctuations in countrywide youth unemployment rates is the level of economic activity. There is strong evidence that when the economy is strong, youth and adult workers are better off, relative to the average long-term trend. A widely used indicator of the level of aggregate economic activity is the unemployment rate for adult males.

Young persons living in areas where the local unemployment rate is high have more spells of unemployment than comparable youths in areas with strong economies. Analysis of differences among metropolitan areas, based on 1970 Census data, indicates that an increase in the adult male unemployment rate is associated with disproportionately large decreases in the proportion of youths who are employed. When the adult unemployment rate rises by one percentage point, the proportion of youths who are employed drops by the percentage amounts in Table 2.

TABLE 2

Drop in the Proportion of Youths Employed Associated with a One Percentage Point Rise in Adult Unemployment

All Young Men		Out-of-School Young Men	
Age	*Percent*	*Age*	*Percent*
16-17	5	16-17	5
18-19	2	18-19	3
20-24	3	20-24	3

Evidence based on changes in adult unemployment over time confirms these findings. The time-series data show that a one percentage point increase in the adult male unemployment rate is associated with a 5 percent decrease in the proportion of young men aged 16 to 19 who are employed. Thus, youth employment is highly sensitive to cyclical movements in the economy.

A second indicator of aggregate economic activity, the growth rate of personal income, also shows a substantial positive relationship to youth employment, according to our comparative analysis of metropolitan areas. If these indicators reflect aggregate demand, then demand forces have a substantial effect on youth employment.

Two other measures of aggregate economic conditions are also strongly related to youth employment. One is the "industrial mix" in the area where the young person lives, and the other is the average income level in the area. Based on comparisons across metropolitan areas, youth employment is higher in those areas with a large number of industries that traditionally employ many young workers. Some of these industries have large numbers of jobs that do not require extensive training; other industries may simply have developed production processes, and organized their work forces, in such a way that large numbers of young persons are accommodated. Among youth aged 16 to 19, the industrial mix and the level of aggregate economic activity (as measured by the adult unemployment rate) are of approximately equal importance in explaining differences in employment across areas. Among those aged 20 to 24, aggregate economic activity is the more important of the two factors. . . .

Another frequently mentioned aggregate determinant of the percent of youths who are employed is the proportion of the total population who are young. Over the past decade and a half, this proportion has increased dramatically. It is argued that production technologies and institutional arrangements may make the economy slow to adapt to large changes in the relative numbers of younger versus older workers, thereby increasing unemployment and reducing the fraction of youths who work.

Our evidence suggests that while there may be some such effects, especially for teenage youths, the large increase in the number of youths relative to adults in the labor force has affected wage rates more than employment. The fact that during the period of rapid increase in the proportion of youths in the population the fraction of white youths employed did *not* fall (see Table 1) casts doubt on the importance of the number of young persons as a major determinant of their employment.

The large increases in the youth labor force that occur in the summer months without a corresponding increase in youth unemployment also bring into question the effect of the proportion of youths in the population on their employment rate. During the summer months, the labor market absorbs large numbers of teenagers. Although teenage labor force participation has been almost 40 percent higher in July than the annual average, in July the teenage unemployment rate has been somewhat lower than the annual average.

Evidence from geographic areas with different fractions of young persons, however,

suggests that a one percentage point increase in the proportion of the population who are young may lead to a noticeable reduction in the employment rate of teenagers. Additional evidence based on movements over time in the employment of youths suggests that increases in the relative number of youths are, in general, associated with declines in the employment ratio of most youth groups, though not by enough to dominate the other factors contributing to youth employment.

Perhaps the greatest effect of the increasing proportions of youths in the population has been a decrease in youth wages relative to adult wages, rather than a decrease in youth employment. The earnings of black and white male youths, as a percent of earnings of adult males, are shown in Table 3 for 1967 and 1977 and for selected age groups.

TABLE 3

Earnings of Black and White Male Youths by Age,*
1967 and 1977

Age	White		Black and Other	
	1967	*1977*	*1967*	*1977*
18	54	49	44	44
20	66	58	63	52
22	79	63	59	54
24	87	75	60	63

*As a percent of the earnings of adult males.

The earnings of young white men in all age groups declined rather dramatically relative to adult wages between 1967 and 1977. On the other hand, the earnings of black youths have changed less, on average, relative to adult earnings. Thus, the market adjustment to larger numbers of youths has been reflected to some extent in a relative decline in youth wages. Indeed, for white youths, wages may have been the primary equilibrating mechanism, allowing the employment rate to be maintained in the face of large increases in the relative number of youths in the population. Traditional supply and demand analysis suggests that whenever the supply of any group of workers increases relative to the demand for them, the larger numbers will be employed, only at a lower wage rate. In contrast to the decline in the white youth wage rates relative to adult wages, the wages of black youths—both male and female—rose relative to the wages of adults. At the same time, black youths were finding it increasingly difficult to find jobs. It is likely that the change in the relative wages of the two groups contributed to the deterioration in black versus white employment.

It is also possible that the employment of both white and black youths is handicapped by the minimum wage. Some results suggest larger effects on employment for 16 to 17 year olds, and for black youths in general, than for other groups, although it is difficult to disentangle the effects of the minimum wage from the effects of other social programs. Both the evidence on the relationship between youth employment and youth wage rates and the evidence on the effect of the minimum wage are consistent with evidence from the United Kingdom where youth employment appears to be quite sensitive to the level of youth wages. The downward trend in youth wages relative to adult wages in the United States may, however, have been a more important determinant of youth employment in the 1970s than changes in the legal minimum wage. In addition, although most discussions of the minimum wage focus on its likely effects on youth employment and wages, it is also possible, in theory, for the minimum wage to shorten the duration of teenage jobs and thus increase the frequency with which youths change jobs.

Although some headway has been made in determining the causes of changes in youth employment experiences, it is important to stress that major questions remain unanswered. In particular, the differential pattern of change between white and black youths remains unexplained.

THE CAUSES: INDIVIDUAL DETERMINANTS OF YOUTH EMPLOYMENT AND WAGES

There also are individual characteristics that contribute to differences in employment experience among youths. These are attributes that influence the experience of one youngster relative to another at a given point in time. It is important to realize from the start that most of the variations in employment and wages among individuals cannot be explained by differences among them that we can observe and measure, such as education or family income. Most of the variations are due to factors, such as individual tastes, opportunities, or chance, that we are unable to explain. Nonetheless, the effect of some characteristics is very substantial. Among the most important determinants of youth employment and wages are education, family background and race.

Education

As already emphasized, high school dropouts are employed fewer weeks per year on average than high school graduates. More generally, out-of-school youths of any age with below average education for their age group are employed noticeably less than other out-of-school youths in that age group.

Particular educational experiences may also affect employment and wages. Many past and current employment programs have been motivated by the potential influence of job training on later ability to find and do jobs. Yet, vocational training in high school appears virtually unrelated to subsequent employment and wage rates, even for persons who obtain no further education after leaving high school.

Academic performance, on the other hand, is positively related both to the number of weeks per year that youths are employed and to their wage rates after entering the labor force full time.

But most important, and possibly surprising, there is a very strong relationship between hours worked while in high school and later employment and wage rates. Youths who work in high school are employed many more weeks per year and have higher wage rates when they enter the labor force full time than those who do not work in high school. There are two possible explanations for these relationships: that working in high school reflects an underlying commitment and ability to perform well in the market or that the work experience itself enhances these characteristics. Actually both of these possibilities may interact. The relationship suggests, however, that high school work experience may hold significant potential for enhancement of later work experience. At the same time, high school work experience raises the possibility that unemployment among in-school youths, while different from that of out-of-school youths, may result in lost preparation for future work.

Family Background

It is widely accepted that early family experiences are likely to affect later employment and educational attainment of youths. Data on the early family experiences of youth that can be used to predict current labor market performance are scarce, but measures of some family characteristics are available. Such measures are related to both school and labor force experiences, but the relationships are not entirely what might be expected. For all youths, family background, as measured by parents' income, shows little relationship to employment. Thus, family income apparently has little to do with the inclination of youths to seek employment or with their ability to find jobs, although it may affect inclination *and* ability to find work in an offsetting way. However, youths whose brothers and sisters have jobs are more likely to have jobs themselves. This finding is subject to several interpretations. It may reflect local labor market conditions or characteristics common to all family members, or it could mean that employed siblings help other youths in the family to secure jobs.

Although children from wealthier families seem to be no more successful in finding jobs than those from poorer families, youngsters from wealthier families obtain jobs that pay more per hour. The reasons for this pattern have yet to be determined. . . .

Race

As noted earlier, black youths have noticeably lower chances of working than white youths, although the magnitude of black-white differences in employment differ by survey. In some surveys, the differences are modest for high school graduates. In contrast, black and white youth wages tend to be quite similar for all educational levels, so that employed young blacks earn about as much as employed young whites. One possible reason for the downward trend in black youth employment has been a marked increase in the school attendance of young blacks. The increase in black schooling, however, explains only a small proportion of the black-white differences in employment that have arisen since 1954.

We find it implausible to explain the decreased employment of blacks in terms of increased discrimination by employers, particularly in view of increased legal and other pressures placed on discriminators. Perhaps other factors having to do with the social conditions of inner city slums have contributed to the weakened employment experiences of blacks. It is possible that other social conditions and youth unemployment have mutually interacted to the detriment of young blacks. No empirically verified explanation presently exists.

THE CONSEQUENCES

Many persons have expressed the fear that periods of unemployment early in one's working career could have substantial adverse effects on employment in future years. We have found that these fears are largely unfounded, and that the evidence has often been misinterpreted to imply that there were large effects. In fact, there is little evidence that time spent out of work early in a youngster's career leads to recurring unemployment. Rather, the cost of not working is the reduction in wages persons suffer later because they failed to accumulate work experience that employers reward. That early unemployment has little effect on later unemployment does not mean that young men and women who have unusually low levels of employment early in their working lives are unlikely to work less in later years. Young men who do not enroll in college and spend some time unemployed their first year out of school, for example, are twice as likely to experience unemployment again than are their peers who escaped early unemployment. This effect is due almost entirely to the persistence of individual differences like education, academic ability, and motivation. The existence of such characteristics creates a positive correlation between time worked in one year and that worked in the next and subsequent years. To isolate the effect of unemployment itself on future unemployment, it is necessary to control for these individual differences. Once individual differences are controlled for, so that persons can be compared only on the basis of early work experiences, there is little relationship between employment experience after high school and employment four years later.

This conclusion holds for widely differing groups of young men and probably for young women as well. It is supported by evidence on young men who do not enroll in college, including high school dropouts, who were followed in the National Longitudinal Survey of Young Men. It is also supported by evidence from a large national sample of high school graduates surveyed as part of the National Longitudinal Study of the High School Class of 1972. Comparable evidence on the relationships between employment in one year and subsequent years based on young women surveyed in the National Longitudinal Survey of Young Women shows a pattern similar to that for young men. This does not mean, of course, that we should be unconcerned that some persons will always tend to have poorer labor force experience than others. But it does mean that initial employment in itself does not increase or decrease employment over the long run. Thus, for example, simply creating jobs for persons right after high school should not be expected to increase the number of weeks that they will be employed four years hence.

Not only does early employment have little effect on subsequent employment, but initial wage rates in themselves have little effect on subsequent wage rates. Once persistent individual differences are controlled for, there is virtually no relationship between wage rates early in a person's labor force experience and wages earned several years later. After allowing for individual characteristics, a low-paying job one year will not by itself lead to a low-paying job three or four years later, according to our findings. Thus, the fear that a low-level job one year—as indicated by a low wage rate—will harm one's chances of obtaining a better job in later years appears to be unfounded.

Since wage rates increase with experience, there is, however, a cost of not working today. Individuals who are unemployed in their youth obtain lower wages in subsequent years because they have accrued fewer years of experience. The effect for high school graduates three or four years later appears to be modest, and it is somewhat less for women than for men. Evidence for young men with less than twelve years of education showed considerably higher estimates of the effects of early experience on wage rates three or four years later, upwards of 15 percent per year of unemployment. All of this evidence is consistent with previous research findings on the relationship between earnings and experience. In short, unemployment does not by itself foster later unemployment, but the effect of unemployment is felt in lower future wages, and this effect may be quite substantial.

These findings are distinct from the observation that unemployment varies according to occupational characteristics. Young persons working in occupations with high initial wages but slow wage growth, and in occupations whose work force is highly mobile across industries, also have higher rates of unemployment. Although occupational characteristics appear to explain some of the employment advantage of the more educated, they don't explain the large differences between the employment experiences of blacks and whites.

CONCLUSIONS

We have found that severe employment problems are concentrated among a small proportion of youths with distinctive characteristics but that for the vast majority of youths, lack of employment is not a severe problem. Thus, the youth unemployment crisis should be thought of as one specific to only a small proportion of youths, not as a general problem. Black youths are less likely than white youth to be employed, but once employed the two groups have similar wage rates. This rough equality is a recent development. While work experience and academic performance in school have been found to be related to employment and wages, vocational training in school has not. Aggregate economic activity has been found to be a major determinant of the level of youth employment.

Early employment experience has virtually no effect on later employment, after controlling for persistent characteristics of individuals, like education. Similarly, wages earned upon entry into the labor force have no effect themselves on wage rates earned a few years later. But not working in earlier years has a negative effect on subsequent wages because wage increases are related to experience.

Finally, we have found large differences between employment and unemployment rates based on Current Population Survey data—the traditional source for such information—and evidence based on two other recent large-scale surveys. These differences not only lead to questions about the magnitude of youth employment and unemployment but also complicate the analysis of youth employment experiences.

17

Federal Policies and Worker Status since the 1930s

Garth L. Mangum

Garth L. Mangum, "Federal Policies and Worker Status since the 1930s" in *Federal Policies and Worker Status since the Thirties,* Joseph P. Goldberg et al., eds. Reprinted by permission of the Industrial Relations Research Association.

... Comparative manpower policies over time are best understood if visualized within the broad historical sweep of industrialization. That is the approach of this paper: What were the historical social and economic forces that led to the manpower policies of the 1930s? What were the responses to those policies? What were the social and economic forces emerging to produce the explosion of manpower-related policies and programs of the 1960s? What are the particular responses, and how did they work out? What are the social and economic forces extant and forseeable today that will underlie the policies of the years ahead? But first, what is this stuff we call "manpower policy" anyway?

WHAT IS MANPOWER POLICY?

Policy is defined by a standard dictionary as "a definite course of action, selected from alternatives, and in light of given conditions, to guide and determine present and future decisions." Upon reading that definition, one is inclined to respond to public policy, "We've never had any." The political world simply does not work that way. Be that as it may, there are always governmental decisions in any important area of activity related to the public welfare that can be dignified by the term "policy."

Manpower (a notably sexist term for which no one has yet found a satisfactory substitute—"personpower?")* has come by usage and logic to refer to the efforts of human beings in employed activities. It is a subset of human resources which, though even more vague, seems to encompass human beings in all of their productive activities, whether or not in paid employment. Thus, manpower policy refers to all of those policies directly concerned with the participation of human beings in paid employment at any or all occupational levels. Its concerns are employability, employment, and productivity as they occur in labor markets. It recognizes that people are the most essential factor in any form of production and that employment is the primary source of family income in an industrial society. It acknowledges that employment policy is related to but is not coextensive with manpower policy. Since the demand for labor is a derived demand, jobs are created only by the spending of money for the purchase of goods and services. Generation of purchasing power . . . is the key to employment at the aggregate level.

However, manpower policy involves itself only in the labor market. It has few tools to affect that vital product-market generation of derived demand. In general, manpower policy is recognized as dealing with all labor-supply concerns—foreseeing need, motivating people to seek employment, preparing them to perform jobs, and helping them to find jobs. On the demand side, it is particularistic—how to assure

Editor's note: Recently, the term "manpower policy" has been changed to "employment and training policy," by the U.S. Department of Labor which has also changed the name of its Manpower Administration to the Employment and Training Administration.

that there are specific employment opportunities for particular groups and that the structure of employment opportunities is compatible with the labor-supply structure.

Essentially, manpower policy has two overriding concerns: (1) the development of human resources and their allocation within labor markets to those activities upon which society has placed the highest priority, and (2) satisfactory working careers (involving income, status, and job satisfaction) for all individuals who can be prepared and motivated to prefer paid employment as their primary source of income. . . .

THE 1930s

The 1930s are best understood as the period when the political power of America's industrial workers first became sufficient to enable them to do something about the consequences of industrialization. It was not that the consequences had not been felt during the previous 60 years, but not until then had sufficient time passed for the number of industrial workers to increase as a proportion of the body politic as well as of the labor force to have an impact in a pluralistic society governable only by coalition among social and economic interests. Also, events occurred that were sufficiently dramatic to diminish adulation for the industrialist-hero of American progress and to develop sympathy for the plight of the worker. The need was already recognized at the intellectual level, and now conditions were ripe. Unemployment, which never for a dozen years dropped below 15 percent and peaked at 25 percent of the labor force, provided the immediate setting for long-range reform.

The permanent reforms were the National Labor Relations Act, the Social Security Act, the Fair Labor Standards Act, the banking and securities reforms, and, though it came a decade later, the Employment Act of 1946. The latter legislation required a spread of Keynesian thought and the wartime demonstration that a country could spend itself into prosperity.

The work-relief programs that more generally characterize the New Deal in the public mind were emergency, short-run, and disorganized as compared to the more unique and carefully developed permanent reforms. They had been used before, though never on such massive scale, and they emerged without planning from the necessity to do something immediately, which the long-term reforms could not do.... If similar tools were in use today proportionate to the labor force and the GNP, the combination of public-service and youth employment programs would enroll 5.8 million persons at a budgetary cost of $39 billion.

THE SECOND WORLD WAR AND ITS AFTERMATH

Manpower policy in the 1950s and 1960s can be analyzed in the contexts of both the long-term advance of industrialization and the more immediate forces of the times. The second world war was the bridge between the two, accelerating long-run trends to the critical levels necessary for political action. Beginning in the late thirties, with the necessity to supply material support to allies already at war and later, at the end of 1941, for all-out war, the dozen years of labor market slack ended suddenly in the strongest demand for labor the nation had ever experienced. The 10 or 11 million people who, on the average, made up the armed forces of 1941-1945 ... were drawn from a prewar labor force of 45 million (1940: 34 million males). At the same time, the nation had not only to feed, arm, and transport this fighting

force, but also to do the same for its allies while continuing to support the civilian population. The production challenge was unprecedented, requiring draconic measures and producing irreversible changes in the U.S. manpower system. These interacting war-motivated developments were the social and economic forces to which the manpower policies of three decades later are still responding. The most important were:

1. A speed-up of rural-to-urban migration. Output per manhour in agriculture, which had been following a long-term rising trend of 1 percent per year, leaped to an annual average increase of 6 percent and has not yet dropped below 5 percent as a continuing trend.

2. A faster pace of technological change, overall. A sharp shift in output per manhour from an average annual rise of 2 percent per year before the war to around 3 percent per year during and after it is the simplest representation.

3. Rising labor-force participation of women. The 19 percent of adult women in the labor force before the war became 27 percent by 1947 and 44 percent by 1975. Meanwhile, the age-pattern of that participation changed from "enter the labor force in the teens and leave at marriage" to "enter, leave at the birth of first child, and return when the last child enters school," to "have fewer children and put them in day-care situations so as to pursue a continuous working career."

4. The increased sophistication of military technology. Civilian spinoffs and continuing cold-war developments made new demands on the structure and preparation of the labor force.

5. The post-war baby boom. The high birth rates of the 1947-1957 period, falling off in the next decade to a new low plateau after 1967, predetermined youth employment problems from 1963 to sometime in the 1970s.

6. The World War II G.I. Bill. Whether by cause or effect, educated people became

available, engineers designed technology assuming an educated labor force, employers expected it, and labor-market competition demanded it.

Item 4 (above) had the first notable impact on postwar manpower policy. The others were time-bombs ticking away inexorably toward the 1960s. For the 1950s, the perceived need was for scientific, engineering, and technical manpower, not so much for the sake of economic development as for national defense. Since our international competitors were obviously not as smart as we, it must have been spies who enabled them to crack our nuclear monopoly. But executing spies did not prevent them from beating us into space, where no one could have stolen the secret since we were not there yet. We had to increase our flow of high-talent manpower or our technological superiority would wither away—hence, the National Defense Education Act and related developments.

Meanwhile, everything was related to everything else. The old rural-urban migration had seen European peasants migrating to America's new industrial cities. Their first requirement was housing and, since the immigrants were poor, this meant cheap housing, which, of couse, was in the oldest or central parts of cities from which previous residents had progressed outward. The next pressing need was for unskilled and semiskilled jobs which, by happy coincidence, were contiguous with the cheap housing. With those needs met, their children could be educated to sound and look American and join the trek to suburbia, leaving a vacuum for the next wave.

But the post-World War II wave was a domestic migration from the rural South and Southwest and Puerto Rico. The war-time wave, which had not been heavily shared by minorities, had ensconced its participants on seniority rosters in plentiful semiskilled jobs.

But in the postwar era, that happy contiguity of housing and job for the immigrant was shattered. The new technology now required continuous process industry and technically skilled workers. The open space and favorable property tax rates for the former and the location of the latter subsized by housing programs, was now suburban. Yet the economies of housing and racial discrimination in its distribution trapped the new migrants in the central city where there were mainly two kinds of jobs: (1) the white-collar office jobs held by commuting suburbanites because the central city residents lacked the required education skills, and cosmetic attributes, and (2) low-skilled, lowly paid jobs servicing those commuters and the central city. . . .

Pent-up shortages from war-time and the demands of the cold war reduced interest in the Full Employment bill of 1945 and resulted in the largely rhetorical Employment Act of 1946. Following the close of the Korean conflict, unemployment trended persistently upward through a series of short, mild recessions and recoveries. With each recession, unemployment rose higher and, with each recovery, left behind a higher residual. Every elementary economics text had the proper prescription: A most modest stimulus to purchasing power would have prevented the accumulation of unemployment and the persistent deficits in the federal budget. But notions of budget balance and fear of balance-of-payments consequences tied fiscal and monetary policies to past orthodoxies.

Meanwhile, off in another corner, some black youth in North Carolina could not understand why they could not sit down and drink their cokes like the white kids did, and a black woman could not understand why she should sit in the back seats of a bus, behind a curtain, when she paid the same fare as the white folks. And in the 1960 presidential campaign, a rich man's son from Boston . . . saw poverty face-to-face in West Virginia. All the forces—long-, medium-, and short-run—were in place for the manpower policy developments of the 1960s.

MANPOWER POLICY RESPONSES DURING THE 1960s

Three essential differences distinguish the manpower-related policies of the 1960s from those of the 1930s: (1) Those of the 1960s were based on less careful analysis and forethought. (2) Those of the 1960s were far smaller in magnitude, relative to the size of the economy and labor force. (3) Training and other preparation for employment played a major role in the 1960s, but none in the 1930s. These three points will be easier to demonstrate after a brief review of the policy responses that occurred during the 1960s.

Despite having narrowly won an election on the slogan, "Get America moving again," the Kennedy Administration was remarkably ill-prepared to get into motion. There were many hypotheses but no concensus on what was wrong and what needed to be done. General economists in and around the Council of Economic Advisers were convinced that all that was needed was a healthy fiscal stimulus to raise the rate of economic growth. Labor economists in and around the Labor Department had discovered "structural unemployment"—concentration by age, sex, race, education, and location. Swirling around were kibitzers convinced that automation was the source of all ills, with the extreme suggesting that the nation give up full employment and prepare for the coming world of full unemployment.

Since the Administration was not prepared to move, the initiative lay by default with Congress. Senators and congressmen tended to see the world from the vantage points of their own constituencies and to be influenced by the popular press rather than the professional journals. Structural unemployment best represented the level of detail at which they were prepared to operate: Who is unemployed from what past job in my district? Not, how many are unemployed nationwide related to what aggregate purchasing power?

The depressed-areas bill of Paul Douglas had been thoroughly aired by twice passage in the Senate and once in the House, followed by veto by President Eisenhower. It needed only reintroduction as the Area Redevelopment Act for passage. Never mind that aiding limited spots of persistent depression in a generally buoyant economy is something quite different from trying to attract industry to such locations when the entire economy is operating below its capacity.

The unemployed the legislators knew best in 1961 were white male family heads of long labor-force attachment. Who now stood at the work stations where they were formerly employed? Often, a machine. Apparently, those whose substantial skills had suffered technological obsolescence now needed retraining. After all, witnesses as prestigious as the chairman of the Federal Reserve Board and the former chairman of the Council of Economic Advisers had testified before congressional committees that there was no lack of jobs. Anyone who could read the newspaper help-wanted ads could see that. The problem was one of square pegs in round holes. The people did not fit the jobs.

Designed in 1961 and passed in March 1962, the Manpower Development and Training Act was not funded until the autumn, and the first enrollments were during the winter of 1962-1963. But by the spring of 1963, unemployment of married men had fallen from the 4.5 percent of 1961 to 3.2 percent. With the first products of the postwar baby boom now turning 16 years of age, youth unemployment jumped to 17 percent. With the experienced male adult workers being recalled, the characteristics of those enrolling in the new MDTA program soon demonstrated that what was needed was not a retraining program, but a training program for those who had never had substantial skills or stable work experience. But this was not going to be like training high school seniors and graduates in vocational schools. Remedial adult basic education, orientation to the world of work, guidance in occupational choice for those of limited work exposure, personal counseling, and other supportive services would be needed and could be best provided within the training institution. Since the techniques never had been developed, there was no base in experience, nor any institutions capable of supplying the needed services. Years of trial-and-error development were necessary before the MDTA institutional training program became viable. Even then, it became viable only for those locations where jobs existed and housing, transportation, race and sex discrimination, and other social pathologies were not overwhelming. Where they were, training too often provided a "hunting license" to search for jobs that did not exist or were out of reach.

Meanwhile, trial-and-error experimentation continued with a 1963 emphasis on youth and a 1964 addition of poverty and race. The Vocational Education Act of 1963 represented the first serious reconsideration of federal vocational education legislation since its inauguration in 1917. The influence of industrialization's progress was obvious. The Morrill Act of 1862, recognizing the need for engineering skills in agriculture and in the infant industry, established the agricultural and mechanical land-grant colleges. By the time of the first world war, industrialization was entering adolescence, and the need for a limited number of skilled tradesmen was recognized. The Smith-Hughes Act of 1917 offered matching grants to the states for vocational training in the

specific occupational categories designated by the Congress. Education and training still was not a prerequisite for employment for most people. The Vocational Education Act of 1963 [updated the Smith-Hughes Act and reflected the changing needs of the labor market] . . . .

The New Deal had not involved education or training. Among the long-run reforms, formal preparation for jobs was not yet that important. Why train for jobs that do not exist? The total short-run concentration was on temporary job-creation. Whether or not there were enough jobs to go around, it was clear that youths were not getting them. And had not the Civilian Conservation Corps and the National Youth Administration been the least criticized of the work-relief programs of the 1930s? Senator Hubert H. Humphrey had introduced and guided through the Senate in 1957 a bill to reestablish these programs, but it had died in the House. A Youth Employment Act of 1963, with the same two provisions, had the same experience. All that could be done for youth in 1963, beyond the longer range reforms of vocational education, was to increase the youth component of MDTA training. But the stage was partially set for 1964.

There were other pieces of staging. The civil rights movement had progressed beyond lunch-counter sit-ins, bus boycotts, and freedom rides to demands for equal access to jobs. Continuing interest in Appalachia and the gradual discovery of the central city generated a flow of popular literature on poverty. Staff analysts within government began to search income data to explore the incidence and extent of poverty. These pressing problems and a proposed massive tax cut, representing the Administration's conversion to Keynesian economics . . . [was the situation at the time of President Kennedy's assassination].

. . . A southern President with civil-rights sympathies and "arm-twisting" abilities was better situated than his predecessor to win the Civil Rights Act of 1964 with its Title VII prohibition on racial and ethnic (and sex) discrimination in employment. . . .

Under pressure to devise strategy for the already declared antipoverty war and to do so at a cost no greater than $1 billion the first year (part of the deal to get the tax cut), the interagency task force designing the new Economic Opportunity Act was limited largely to bits and pieces of programs, legislation, and experience scattered about the landscape. The New Deal precedents were large among the contributions.

The Neighborhood Youth Corps was the reincarnation of the National Youth Administration. The Job Corps conservation centers were direct descendents of the Civilian Conservation Corps. The Job Corps urban centers were new. The Defense Department was then under pressure to close obsolete defense facilities and proposed using them as residential vocational schools. The Labor Department suggested a full-scale reinauguration of the Works Progress Administration (WPA) work-relief program financed by a cigarette tax. Its proposal was rejected as too expensive and was folded into the Title V Work Experience and Training program to allow welfare recipients and other poor to earn the equivalent of public-assistance benefits. Its vindication came year by year as EOA was amended to add Operation Mainstream (a miniscule rural WPA for older workers) and the New Careers program (to provide jobs as sub-professional aides), and as the Emergency Employment Act of 1971 (first vetoed in 1970 as a "WPA") and subsequent "public service employment" provisions made special job-creation targeted by socioeconomic group and locality an apparently permanent part of the manpower tool kit.

Such was the manpower-policy development through 1968. Only the Vocational Education Act of 1963 and its 1968 amend-

ments evidenced the careful study and preparation which went into the National Labor Relations Act and the Social Security Act. All other legislation and administratively created programs of the 1960s were more comparable to the emergency New Deal work-relief programs. They were trial-and-error efforts forced by crisis and designed by intuition.

The legislation of the 1930s went to the heart of worker status. It guaranteed the right of workers to be represented by collective bargaining agents of their own choosing and required employers to bargain with those agents. It insured the worker in a major way against the insecurities of the business cycle and dependent status during old age. It created emergency jobs for 6.6 percent of the labor force and persisted in doing so for a total of nine years. It chose for those jobs a series of activities—construction, art, writing projects—which made a permanent contribution to the infrastructure of communities and the quality of life. All of these programs, long and short term, were designed for the mainstream industrial labor force and their children. There were other provisions for rural recovery (which inadvertently had the effect of driving marginal farmers off the land). No one seems to have worried much about non-European minorities and others at the margins of society.

Manpower programs of the 1960s never achieved enrollments of the equivalent of 1 percent of the labor force nor 1 percent of the federal budget. There were no basic reforms in worker security and worker status and only one significant intervention in the way labor markets work—the equal-employment-opportunity legislation and machinery. There was trial-and-error experimentation and significant, though small-scale, success at bringing the "outs" in to share whatever was available at the lower margins of the labor market. The almost total emphasis was on the problems of minorities and other groups facing competitive disadvantages in central-city labor markets. There was no consensus on the basic cause of the problems: Was it behavioral characteristics that caused individuals to be disadvantaged, or was it the institutional structure of society and the labor market? However, there was relatively more emphasis on changing people (primarily through skill-training) than on changing institutions.

MANPOWER POLICY AND WORKER STATUS, 1968–1975

... Prior to 1965, there had been a notable correlation between unemployment and public assistance. AFDC rolls rose as unemployment increased, and as unemployment declined, the welfare load would diminish. But when unemployment decreased sharply after the 1964 tax cuts and the escalation of the Vietnam war in 1965, AFDC did not decline; instead, it accelerated.

By the end of 1967, Congress was aroused. Something had to be done to make "taxpayers out of those taxeaters." Still not having recognized the new phenomenon of the female-headed family, Congress thought it would be a simple task to solve the problem by purging the welfare rolls of all but mothers of preschool children. They should all be placed in jobs or trained for jobs, or jobs should be created for them in a Work Incentive Program. The normal initial-letter approach to an acronym, WIP, was modified as sounding too coercive, but, as originally conceived, WIP would have been more descriptive than WIN, the acronym chosen. Because funding was not sufficient to finance the day-care and job-creation load that would have been required, WIN became primarily a training and placement program for welfare mothers. ...

At the same time the WIN program was introduced, Congress also amended the Economic Opportunity Act to decentralize much of the decision-making in its manpower programs to the community level. It followed up this trend in 1968 by also enlarging the state role in MDTA decisions. The concern was that nationally uniform programs were not sufficiently adaptable to local situations. "Decentralize and decategorize" was the new slogan. Fold all of the several categorical programs into one, with authority to provide any or all of the services formerly under the various agencies. Then give decision-makers at the local labor-market level authority to decide within limits whom to serve, what services to provide, and whom to use as deliverers of the services. Congress gave the Department of Labor and the Office of Economic Opportunity clear instructions to do just that. Both agreed philosophically with the directive, but they never complied with it because they could not agree upon which local agencies should be assigned the decision-making functions. It was exactly four years later, in December 1973, that decentralization and decategorization became a fact with the passage of the Comprehensive Employment and Training Act (CETA). By that time Congress had answered the difficult question: Decentralize to the governors, mayors, and county officials who face voter retribution if they do not perform satisfactorily.

The impact of the first of these significant manpower-policy developments from 1968 to 1975 was on a group that was either outside of or only marginally in the labor force. The second was an administrative change that may or may not noticeably affect worker status. The third was that often-advocated reinauguration of work-relief programs, but in a form very different from the 1930s model.

The public-job-creation proposals of the 1960s had focused, as had most other manpower policies of the period, on those unable to compete successfully in the normal labor markets. The philosophy was "government as employer of last resort," but first to use fiscal and monetary policy aggressively to create high levels of employment and then to abolish discrimination and use training programs and relocation allowances to enable workers to compete more successfully for the available jobs. For those still left out, useful jobs providing needed public services would be created, and sheltered workshops for the severely handicapped would be added. Finally, there would be income-maintenance programs for those not employable under any conditions. That proved to be an unsalable recipe.

Public-service employment came into being because of reluctance to use the job-creating tools of fiscal and monetary policy. Having little control over general economic policy, Congress could mandate a contracyclical, direct job-creation program by offering local governments and public agencies additional funds to expand their work forces. Title II of CETA was conceived as a permanent program of public job-creation in those areas suffering above-average unemployment. But the Emergency Employment Act of 1971 and Title VI added to CETA in 1975 were everybody's second-best solution to the job-creation problem. They echoed the thirties, but only dimly. Unemployment, though high (peaking at 8.9 percent), did not approach 1933's 25 percent. The construction industry was now a high-technology and well-organized sector, no longer an outlet for masses of unskilled labor. ... [Thus the thrust of these programs was not on construction.] Adding members here and there to already large government staffs was more appropriate in the current occupational structure, but it was not massive job creation.

Perhaps most significant in the 1968-1975 period was the perception of one Administration that lower middle- and middle-class workers felt that their status was threatened by policies favoring the disadvantaged, and the perception of another that it did not matter what anyone below the middle thought. . . .

MANPOWER POLICY, WORKER STATUS, AND LABOR MARKETS

It must be said for most of the manpower programs from 1960 to 1975 that, in general, they worked. That is, from the best information available, most of the people who went through such programs came out sufficiently better off in employment stability and income to justify the expenditure. But usually the average gain was from well down in the poverty ranks to its upper levels. The improvements were significant, but less than the rhetorical promises.

It must also be said that only the civil rights and equal-opportunity-employment policies had a significant impact on the way labor markets work and on the status of the body of working men and women. Everything else was designed to make those on the margins of the labor market less marginal or to provide income alternatives for those unable to "make it" in the job market.

In retrospect, it is quite clear that little could be expected of a manpower policy under which programs were designed without full recognition of the realities of functioning labor markets. Not that labor markets are sacred and beyond intervention. People can be aided to participate in labor markets only if those aids are consistent with the workings of labor markets. To intervene in labor markets to make their results more consistent with policy objectives requires a sensitive understanding of labor-market functions and what is possible without undesirable effects.

A few examples should make the point: Accept as three of the "first principles" of labor economics the truisms that (1) the demand for labor is a derived demand, (2) jobs are created only by the spending of money for creation of goods and services, and (3) the primary function of a labor market is to allocate labor supplies among alternative uses according to social priorities. A nation concludes that it must take anti-inflation actions which, by cutting purchasing power, destroy four million jobs in the private sector of the economy, and then it uses as its main lines of defense $18 billion of unemployment insurance and some 300,000 temporary public-sector jobs purchased at a cost of some $2.5 billion. Are the policy decisions consistent with the labor-market premises?

Manpower-training activities for women were concentrated in clerical and health occupations, but for men the training occupations were automotive repair, machine operation, welding, building service, food service, and upholstery—mostly occupations where formal skill-training is not the normal entry route. That many of the disadvantaged were at a subentry level was a justification, but lack of skill was the major barrier to job entry for few. Inadequate attention was given to the concept of ports of entry through which program graduates could find attractive employment; thus, most ended up employed in marginal firms.

Despite a great deal of empirical research over the years, practical theory capable of describing and predicting labor-market behavior and suggesting ways it could be improved is remarkably limited. Take as another example the major conceptual hypotheses concerning labor-market functioning that have been the basis for major policy prescriptions over the past 15 years: The staffs of the Council of Economic Advisers and the Joint Economic Committee viewed the supply side of the labor market as a simple queue, with the entire labor force ranked in order of individual productivity. Employers usually started at the front and went down the line until they had met the demands of their customers. Reducing unemployment was a simple process of increasing aggregate demand until the desired point in the queue was reached. My own contribution was the substitution of a shape-up for the queue, with workers ranked by whatever criteria employers chose to use—objective ones related to skill and productivity perhaps, but also subjective ones related to age, race, sex, education, etc. Increasing aggregate demand could increase the demand for labor, but might motivate employers to compete more vigorously for the most desired workers rather than simply to pick up the next best. High aggregate demand was a necessary but not a sufficient condition. Training programs, remedial education, anti-discrimination laws, relocation allowances, subsidized private employment, etc., could at the same time reduce employer reluctance and change relative rankings by making the disadvantaged more competitive. Government as the employer of last resort for those at the back of the line after all else was done, with income maintenance for those who could not even get into the line-up, was the logical completion of the formulation.

Piore and Doeringer added further sophistication in their dual labor market theory. To them, both of the previous formulations were faulty in that (1) they did not account for the fact that jobs had desirability rankings also and some might be rejected by workers, and (2) they failed to recognize that there was a primary and a secondary labor market with an almost impervious wall between. That is, in the labor market there are good jobs and bad jobs, the former typically secure, steady, well paid, and accompanied by a variety of fringe benefits; the latter, the opposite. There are employers who restrict themselves to one or the other of these markets, and there are workers who, by choice or lack of opportunity, are restricted to them. For those restricted to the secondary labor market, there is no advantage in being steady and productive since jobs available have no future and other jobs, no better and no worse, are readily at hand. The policy implication of that concept is that programs concentrating on the supply side, to change people, are useless. Only efforts on the demand side, to open access to primary jobs, can change economic opportunity.

Few refute the usefulness of the dual labor market concept, but the imperviousness of the wall is challenged. Most youth, it is argued, go through something like a secondary labor market on the way to the primary one. Workers can be assisted to vault the wall into the primary market.

Others have carried the dual labor market concept further into a theory of labor-market segmentation. A variety of protected enclaves of attractive employment is posited, each shielded from the competition of outsiders. Some find the source of the segmentation in a conspiracy of "capitalists" to keep the workers in subjection, apparently unaware that the secondary labor market encompasses generally the competitive sector of the economy. Others attribute it to the natural desire of the "ins" to protect themselves from competition from the "outs."

It may be more useful to conceive of the labor market as a stacked pinochle deck, one half a stack of jobs ranked by their desirability and the other half a stack of labor-force participants ranked by socioeconomic status. The shuffle, by and large, matches the best jobs with the most advantaged workers, but occasionally a job-seeker from the bottom of the deck does manage to make it to the top.

All of these conceptualizations are useful to the extent they aid simplified understanding of complex reality, predict results, and prescribe solutions. The critical issue is that there are only so many good jobs, even in the best of times and in the country with the most widespread opportunity. Policy alternatives can range over expansion of opportunity and sharing of that which exists. The enhancement of worker status was pursued in the 1930s by strengthening the hand of workers vis-á-vis their own employers and protecting them against times when no employment opportunities existed. The Employment Act of 1946 represented an emphasis on the total supply of jobs, but it has never been fully implemented for fear of inflationary consequences. The emphasis of the 1960s was on equal access to whatever opportunity existed, whether enforced by anti-discrimination rules or promoted by adding to the competitive abilities of those not enjoying their share of opportunity.

That is where manpower policy stands stymied in the mid-1970s. The traditional solution of enlarging a pie by economic growth so that each slice gets bigger without redistributing the relative shares seems blocked by fears of inflation, environmental concerns, resource constraints, and a possible long-term decline in the rate of productivity growth. Yet growth offers no real solution as long as each expansion of opportunity further raises expectations. No matter what the total supply of opportunity may be, jobs still vary in relative attractiveness. There may be more jobs, but there are still good ones and bad ones. The sharing approach is blocked by the perpetual reluctance of the "haves" to share with the "have nots" and by the desire of the former "have nots" to protect their gains against new insurgents.

Yet there are no other than the three alternatives: (1) convert the whole social philosophy from a competitive struggle to a cooperative sharing; (2) move the whole structure upward through economic growth, maintaining the "stacked deck" structure of good and bad jobs, in the hope that those on the bottom will compare their progress with their own past status rather than with the relative distance between themselves and those who are ahead; or (3) continue to plug away at the dual piecemeal task of opening access to segmented markets and preparing the "outs" to slip in one by one. The first is such a sharp departure from tradition to be unrealistic, and who would know how to do it if it were possible? The second appears to have lost much of its charm, but it is a prerequisite to the third:

Maintaining a rapid rate of economic growth and job-creation while compromising as little as possible with environmental quality and finding means other than unemployment for restraining inflation, tinkering with the job structure while chipping away at obstacles to equal access, and preparing individuals to compete for what is available is a messy formula but the only one available. It offers little departure from the policies of the 1930s and 1960s, but where is the realistic alternative?

THE SOCIOECONOMIC BASE OF FUTURE POLICIES

The long sweep of industrialization and the more immediate consequences of depression and war were identified as the major determinants of worker status and manpower policies in the 1930s and the 1960s. What will be the major social and economic forces that will determine worker status and to which manpower policy will respond in the years ahead? Undoubtedly there will be many surprises, but some of those forces are already apparent.

The rural-to-urban migration so critical to the postwar scene could not continue at its old pace. In fact, a mild reverse trend seems to be beginning—not enough to drain the cities but enough to generate significant economic development and jobs in rural settings. It is always dangerous to declare an end to technological change, but it does seem unlikely that anything as dramatic as the electronics, computer, television, nuclear power, wonder drugs, etc., of 1945-1975 will be equalled in 1975-2000. Maintaining the current average pace of productivity increases is likely to be a tough challenge in the years ahead. Demographers have been caught by surprise before, but it does not seem likely that the nation will rediscover how to make babies at the 1947-1957 rate. Only the labor-force participation of

women, generated by the second world war, appears likely to continue unabated.

Demographically, a slower rate of labor-force growth and an aging labor force already seem foreordained. Implied also is a rising ratio of the retired to the economically active population, unless trends toward earlier retirement reverse. Perhaps an increase in the second-career trend will be the resolution. Immigration is already an important component of labor-force growth after a 50-year gap, and it may become the most important source of new manpower.

Productivity gains will depend increasingly on what happens in the service and government sectors. Opportunities for greater efficiency are present but unlikely to be as pervasive as those in manufacturing, communications, transportation, etc., have been in the past. It seems doubtful that the near 3-percent pace of productivity increase to which we have become accustomed in the postwar period can continue. The labor force and productivity outlet together forecast slower economic growth, a reduced rate of improvement in standards of living, and persistent inflationary pressures as various claimants attempt to maintain their customary rises in living standards. . . .

Other critical forces can undoubtedly be identified and forecast by more knowledgeable minds. The point of this review is that, after the experiences of the period 1930-1975, manpower policies for the years ahead should be carefully planned in full recognition of (1) demographic, social, and economic trends, and (2) labor-market realities.

WHITHER MANPOWER POLICY OR WORKER STATUS?

The manpower policies of the 1930s and 1960s were responses to both the long sweep

of industrialization and its immediate consequences. Those of the 1930s, which were designed for permanence, were more fundamental,
better thought through, and more significant
for worker status. Those of the 1960s were
primarily responses to changing demographic,
social, and economic trends accelerated by
the second world war and its immediate after-
math. They were generally successful, but
only marginal in their impact. Their major
shortcoming was failure to take labor-market
reality into account in their formulation.

Now a new set of demographic, social,
and economic forces has emerged, and policies
of the next 25 years must be responsive to
them. Everyone who will enter the labor force
in the early 1990s is now born. Technological
surprises do not overwhelm an economy in a
few short years, though we now know that
international relations may. There will be
surprises, but a great many of both the supply
and the demand developments can be foreseen
a quarter-century ahead.

Manpower policy now seems stalled
dead center. It has not progressed far beyond
the 1930s, and few of the innovations of the
1960s were fundamental. Only the equal-employment-opportunity emphasis deserves that
title. Now is not a time for new legislation. We
would not know which way to move if we were
compelled to do so. It is a time for basic and
thorough reexamination. Any lasting improvement in worker status that is produced by
manpower policy must rest on realistic understanding of labor markets and the practicality
of various interventions into their workings.
What is now needed is the same kind of fundamental thinking that went into the Social
Security Act and the National Labor Relations
Act, but extended 25 years out from 1975.

18

Creating Jobs

Irwin Garfinkel and John L. Palmer

During the mid- 1970s both unemployment and inflation in the United States set post-World War II record highs. Even after several years of vigorous recovery from the 1974–75 recession both are well in excess of comfortable rates. And many economists maintain that the persistence of high levels of structural unemployment may make it difficult to lower unemployment much below 6 percent through conventional macroeconomic policies without reaccelerating inflation. (Although unemployment rates are generally lower in Western Europe, a similar problem exists there.) For these reasons, selective federal policies to promote directly the creation of jobs are increasingly seen as desirable means of promoting two related objectives–reaching and sustaining low levels of unemployment without excessive inflationary pressure and insuring minimally adequate incomes for families with workers. These approaches have two distinctive characteristics: federal funds are granted to public or private employers conditioned on their performance in providing employment; and restrictions are placed on eligibility and, possibly, other aspects of employment.[1]

[1] These features differentiate direct creation of jobs both from ordinary government expenditure activities and from government actions such as income tax cuts that affect the job market only indirectly.

183

Such job creation programs can take many forms. Until recently they had been used intensively in the United States only during the Great Depression. At that time, a large portion of the labor force was at one time or another in federally subsidized and administered public employment programs, generally in outdoor work performing tasks ranging from construction to sanitary maintenance. On the other hand, many Western European countries have made use of public employment programs or employment-related subsidies to private employers for structural purposes since the 1950s. With the high unemployment rates of the 1970s, job creation programs once again have been heavily used in the United States. The two predominant types are state and locally administered public service employment programs and employment tax credits for private employers.[2]

Public service employment in the United States has evolved from very limited use in the late 1960s for particular groups of disadvantaged workers into several major programs with a mix of countercyclical and structural objectives. The federal budget for 1978 provides for 725,000 public service jobs for previously unemployed workers under titles 2 and 6 of the Comprehensive Employment and Training Act (CETA) at a cost of about $6 billion. The

[2] The term *public employment* is intended in this paper to be broader than public service employment. It also can include specially created, subsidized jobs in the public sector that involve labor-intensive activities other than the delivery of public services. This use of the term is approximately consistent with Kesselman's use of the term *work relief.* Public works, on the other hand, are generally considered skill- and capital-intensive construction projects that are contracted out to the private sector; such policies are not considered in this volume. However, public works that involve direct hiring onto public payrolls for relatively labor-intensive construction (as was done in the Great Depression) fall under our use of the term *public employment.*

programs are administered by designated agents (local prime sponsors) of state and local governments. Almost $1 billion more is being spent on public employment projects for unemployed youth, and smaller amounts on other special groups. Other large expenditures on public employment are being considered by Congress in conjunction with welfare reform, and passage of the Humphrey-Hawkins full employment and balanced growth bill would increase the likelihood of large-scale, long-term use of public employment for broader purposes.

Employment tax credits have only recently come into use in the United States. They are simply employer wage subsidies administered through the federal income tax system. The work incentive (WIN) tax credit, first passed in 1971 and then expanded in 1975, reimburses private employers for a flat percentage of the first year's wages they pay to any recipient of aid to families with dependent children (AFDC). It has operated only on a very small scale. A second, temporary measure, passed as part of the economic stimulus package in 1977 and estimated to cost $2.5 billion in 1978, provides a tax credit to private employers for wages paid in excess of a base related to their prior year's wage bill. The credit applies only to wages that are less than half the median annual level; thus it favors low-wage workers. Many other forms of employer wage subsidies have been proposed recently that could cost several billions of dollars per year. In many instances they are targeted on specific groups of workers—such as youth and the long-term unemployed—with particularly difficult employment problems.[*]

Despite the recent expansion of the use

[*] *Editors' Note*: A Targeted Job Tax Credit (TJTC) for seven groups of disadvantaged workers was established as part of the Federal Revenue Act of 1978.

of and interest in federal programs to create jobs, their efficacy is in considerable dispute. This is in part due to a dearth of contemporary analysis on this subject. (The voluminous literature concerned with the Great Depression experience has not been well integrated into current thought.) Not surprisingly, views differ widely on the degree of reliance that should be placed on jobs programs of various types. For each of the policies of interest the following questions need to be answered. How many jobs can be created for a given expenditure or budgetary impact? How fast will employment be increased and with what degree of inflationary pressure? Who will get the jobs and what effect will this have on the overall composition of employment and unemployment? What net additional output will be provided and what will be its value to society? What will be the effect on the employment and earnings of target groups? How do answers to these questions vary between the short term and long term and with specific aspects of the program design?

The conference reported on in this volume was an attempt to shed light on several of these questions and the issues underlying them. Both wage subsidies to private employers and public employment programs were considered, although the emphasis was on the latter.[3] This paper draws on the conference papers, formal and informal discussion at the conference, and other analyses to present an overview of the current state of knowledge of direct job creating policies. . . .

[3] In fact, public employment programs can be viewed as a special case of employer wage subsidies—one that approaches 100 percent and is limited to the non-profit sector. (Under CETA, local prime sponsors may contract with private non-profit organizations to provide public service jobs. Also, the federal subsidy may be supplemented by other monies to achieve higher wage rates.) . . .

POLICY IMPLICATIONS

What uses ought to be made of policies for creating jobs in the future and how should they be designed? . . . Since value judgments often are crucial in determining the desirability of job creating relative to alternative policies, conclusions ought to be approached cautiously. Nevertheless, the already extensive use of public employment and wage subsidies, and the strong and immediate interest among policymakers in improving and possibly expanding their use, make it imperative that these questions be addressed. . . . .

Countercyclical Policy

During periods of high unemployment, any expansionary fiscal policy is likely to yield strong economic benefits on balance. However, although they have some merits, the case for the use of public employment programs or wage subsidies for countercyclical purposes in preference to other macroeconomic policies is not strong.

The primary advantage of public employment programs is the potential for targeting the jobs directly created by the additional stimulus. This, in turn, could help disadvantaged workers or regions to participate more fully in the economic recovery and may exert less inflationary pressure than alternative fiscal stimuli of comparable magnitude. Public employment programs may also have a greater employment impact per temporary dollar increase in the federal deficit. But both effects are likely to be quite modest if state and local governments are the administering agents because there are strong incentives for such governments to choose the most qualified applicants from among the eligible population and to use the federal funds to underwrite activities they otherwise would have undertaken with unrestricted funds.[4]

On the negative side, the timing and efficiency of public employment programs intended for countercyclical purposes appear to be less favorable than alternative fiscal stimuli that emphasize expansion of the private and regular public sectors. Rapid implementation is possible, but may come at some expense to targeting on the disadvantaged and avoiding fiscal substitution. (It is more difficult to design and implement special projects than to expand employment already being performed.) And the timely phasing down of countercyclical public employment programs is politically difficult. Similarly, such programs appear unlikely to provide additional output that would be valued as highly by society as the output that would result from an expansion of the regular public and private sectors of the economy, since the former is subjected to neither regular market or political tests. And while in theory public employment might have a training effect that could raise the postprogram productivity of the working population beyond what an equivalent expansion of the regular sectors of the economy would, there is no evidence that this would happen—nor should it be expected of temporary programs that must be rapidly implemented and subsequently phased out.

It has been argued that the very large public service employment grants made in the mid-1970s have been a critical source of revenue and employment support for many cities during the recent economic recession and recovery. However, given the relative size, cyclical stability, and skill distribution of public-sector

employment, it is not clear that it should receive a higher priority than the expansion of employment in the private sector during a recession. And to the extent that it is desired to provide a federal subsidy for state and local activities, general revenue sharing grants or employer wage subsidies may have more desirable characteristics than public service employment programs.

It is also difficult to make a strong a priori case for preferring employer wage subsidies for countercyclical purposes to more conventional macroeconomic policies. . . .

Structural Policy

The usefulness of direct job creating policies for structural rather than countercyclical purposes appears more promising. This is largely due to the lack of sufficiently effective alternative structural policies, whereas other countercyclical macroeconomic policies than jobs programs have proven quite effective. However, considerable modesty about both the current state of knowledge and expertise regarding their use and their likely ultimate potential is in order.

If certain conditions are met, direct job creating policies can permit continued expansion of employment at relatively full employment levels with less long-run inflationary pressure than conventional fiscal policies. Appropriate targeting is necessary but not sufficient. In addition, the disproportionately high unemployment rates among certain groups of workers must be due to particular kinds of rigidities in wage determination and wage adjustment processes. Since these are currently issues of considerable uncertainty and dispute, the extent to which the inflationary consequences of direct job creating policies are superior to those of other expansionary policies is a speculative matter. However, their potential is clearly greatest if they are narrowly targeted

---

[4] There are indications that the restrictive targeting criteria for the expansion of CETA title 6 during the latter part of 1977 increased somewhat the participation of disadvantaged workers in the program. Representation of AFDC recipients, blacks, and members of low-income families increased. The average level of education of participants, however, remained above that of all those unemployed.

and carefully designed. The more they are restricted to workers with the poorest regular employment opportunities, and the lower the wage paid in public employment programs, the better their prospects for minimizing inflationary pressures. Even so, higher employment among workers in the target group may be partially at the expense of higher unemployment among other workers.

Public employment and employer subsidy programs also can help to insure minimally adequate incomes to families with workers. The targeting requirements for this purpose are likely to overlap considerably with those for the objective of increasing employment with minimal inflationary pressure. When the primary objective is distributional, a jobs program that has the disadvantage of reducing gross national product over the long run may nevertheless be desirable, if its economic efficiency compares favorably with direct cash assistance programs or if a high premium is placed on providing assistance through jobs rather than cash. . . .

Although structurally oriented job creating programs do not have to promote economic efficiency to be desirable, the degree to which they do should influence the extent of their use, and the maximization of their economic efficiency should be a principal policy objective. Little is known about the economic efficiency of narrowly targeted public employment and wage subsidy programs, largely because the experience with them has been extremely limited and not subject to rigorous scrutiny. What is known suggests that they have potential, but that it is difficult for them to be efficient.

In the case of wage subsidies the main problem is to induce employers to hire and train workers with characteristics other than those of their usual employees. Once this is successfully accomplished, one can be reasonably hopeful about the outcome since the output will be meeting the market test and the workers will have learned a salable skill while in the regular labor market. In the case of public employment programs, it should be easier to provide jobs for the desired target groups. However, deciding what to produce and how to produce and market the output is difficult, as is helping workers make the transition to regular employment. Furthermore, the incentive structure faced by managers of public employment programs is unlikely to lead them to place much weight on achieving economic efficiency.

For these reasons, policymakers should proceed cautiously. The inherent limitations of job creating programs probably will preclude their ever becoming a panacea for structural unemployment, but they may be able to play a sizable constructive role for particular groups of workers. (Given the severity of structural unemployment among many groups in the population, considerable experimentation with policies with any promise is worthwhile.) Wage subsidies might be more advantageously focused on the more employable members of disadvantaged target groups, with public employment programs reserved for those who are most difficult to employ. In the latter case, though, considerable thought has to be given to the design of regulations and funding procedures to provide an appropriate incentive structure for program operators.

Program Design

The design and operational requirements of countercyclically and structurally oriented job creating policies are quite different and, ideally, ought to be pursued through different program structures. Trying to accomplish both types of objectives within a common framework will compromise both.

Table 1 lists the desirable design features of public employment programs. If such pro-

TABLE 1

Major Desirable Design Features of Public Employment Programs with Countercyclical and Structural Objectives

Countercyclical Criteria	*Structural Criteria*
Temporary funding with level varying inversely and rapidly with aggregate unemployment rate	Permanent funding [a]
Funds allocated primarily to those local areas suffering from higher unemployment	Funds allocated to all local areas[b]
Broad targeting on the unemployed	Narrow targeting on those with poor employment prospects even in a high employment economy
Emphasis on highly valued output	Emphasis on relevance of work experience to regular employment opportunities and transitional assistance
Employment of a type that can be promptly and effectively phased in and out	Employment in carefully designed, long-term projects[c]
Wage rates that can be as high as prevailing rates	Wage rates close to minimum wage

[a]Structural unemployment will be a problem even at relatively low rates of aggregate unemployment. The amount of money expended for this purpose might vary somewhat with the overall rate of unemployment.

[b]Even in relatively low-unemployment areas there is likely to be some structural unemployment. The allocation formula could be weighted in favor of areas with high unemployment rates (adjusted for size of labor force).

[c]Although length of tenure of participants in programs should be restricted, considerable time will be needed to design and implement projects; they should not be forced to terminate if they prove effective.

grams are going to be administered through state and local governments for countercyclical purposes, their eligibility criteria ought to be fairly broad, and state and local governments should not be restricted to special projects.[5] Even though these conditions encourage fiscal substitution, they are important to facilitate rapid implementation and the

provision of highly valued output. (Since the program is to be temporary, the degree of fiscal substitution will be limited.) The wage rate is not crucial from the point of view of displacing regular employment because of the assumed widespread cyclical unemployment.

In contrast, for structural programs, quite restrictive eligibility criteria are appropriate, as are low wage rates, in order to insure participation of workers with lower opportunity costs. These also may be favored on distributional grounds since they reserve the jobs for the most needy and, within a fixed appropriation level, reach the greatest number of workers. Emphasis on special projects will be necessary since the nature of the work generally will have to

[5] This does not mean there should be no attempt to restrict eligibility to the program, only that the restrictions should not interfere with the desired implementation schedule or jeopardize the ability of state and local governments to provide highly valued additional services. In fact it would be desirable for state and local governments to have a set of well-designed projects that can be rapidly implemented sitting on the shelf awaiting the next recession.

be tailored to meet the characteristics and needs of particular target groups and because the relatively permanent funding and assumed high employment rate make fiscal substitution and other forms of displacement more severe problems.

Although wages at or very near the minimum are desirable on some grounds in structural public employment programs, they can present difficulties. In many locales such wages are well below those of the lowest paid jobs in the regular public sector. Consequently, the program jobs could either become dead-end with no relevance to regular employment or undermine standards in the public sector. In any event, the creation of a very large number of public employment jobs at a subsidized minimum wage raises the spectre of a stigmatized second-class work force being permanently "warehoused" in the public sector. Thus, the setting of the wage rate structure for public employment programs presents a severe dilemma. It can be sidestepped partially if structural programs are not very large, even though they pay prevailing wage rates. Eligibility criteria could be relied on heavily to insure narrow targeting on those with the lowest opportunity costs and tenure in the program could be limited to force participants to search for regular employment.[6]

The distinction between countercyclical and structural policies also has implications

for the design of employer wage subsidies or of employment tax credits. In both cases it is important to minimize (consistent with other objectives) the reporting requirements and other red tape associated with the subsidy. A subsidy with countercyclical objectives should be temporary, also varying in size inversely with the aggregate unemployment rate. . . .

On the other hand, eligibility for structurally oriented employer subsidies should be restricted to workers being hired from appropriate target groups. The availability of the subsidy to employers should be relatively permanent, but its applicability to given employees should be gradually phased out. . . .

CONCLUSION

More research is needed on most of the issues raised in this paper. However, a great deal of the necessary understanding of the consequences of job creating policies—particularly ones with structural objectives—can best be obtained through a learning-by-doing process with careful monitoring and analysis of a host of planned and natural variations. Several useful experimental public employment efforts are under way but there is little relating to employer subsidies.

Both public employment programs and wage subsidies have significant advantages and disadvantages for dealing with structural unemployment. Until more is learned about them, the scale on which they eventually might operate effectively is highly uncertain. There appears to be no general reason to greatly prefer one approach over the other (although one may have more potential effectiveness than the other for particular target groups). . . .

[6] This resolution obviously would not be available if public employment programs were ever used to establish a job guarantee as envisioned under early versions of the Humphrey-Hawkins bill. In such a case either minimum (or even subminimum) wages would have to be paid in the program or the long-run effects on inflation would be no different than if conventional macroeconomic policies were used to push the unemployment rate down.

19

Illegal Alien Workers
in the United States

Walter Fogel

Walter Fogel, "Illegal Alien Workers in the United States," *Industrial Relations*, Vol. 16, No. 3 (October 1977).

This paper is a synthesis of knowledge about illegal alien workers in the U.S., regardless of the country of origin of the "illegals."[1] Within this general scope, Mexico receives the greatest emphasis because it is by far the greatest supplier of illegal aliens to the U.S. and most of the information on this subject refers to Mexican illegals.

The overriding theme of the paper can be stated rather briefly. Because of its *de facto* past policy of expedient use of foreign labor supplies, especially Mexican, and because of the rising urgency of international population and economic differences, the U.S. now faces a flow of illegal immigration which it cannot control. This fact, together with the domestic and international contexts of the flow, is certain to produce changes in U.S. *de jure* immigration policy and may also produce

[1] I shall use the term "illegal alien" rather than "undocumented workers," the designation preferred by some. The latter is intentionally less pejorative than the former and, as used by some writers, implies that the Mexican-U.S. border is simply an artifact, established rather recently in the history of the area. The former term, however, more accurately conveys the fact that these aliens are violating U.S. immigration laws.

fundamental changes in U.S.-Mexican relations as well.

HISTORICAL BACKGROUND

Illegal immigration to the U.S., especially that of Mexicans, is not a new phenomenon—but it is not an old one either, its history being confined largely to the twentieth century. Until legislation excluded Asian immigrants in the late nineteenth century, restrictions on the migration of people to the U.S. had only been qualitative, banning criminals, persons with various diseases, and those who were thought unlikely to be able to earn a living in the U.S. The last qualification was interpreted loosely, because immigration policy until World War I was dominated by the desire to provide unskilled labor for America's farms and industries. Able bodied workers were admitted when national unemployment was high as well as when it was low.

When the Immigration Act of 1924 established country of origin quotas, it also established the possibility of large-scale illegal entry to the U.S. Interestingly, however, illegal immigration became significant only from Mexico—a country whose people, at least according to the immigration statute, continued to enjoy the right of unrestricted entry to the U.S., a right held by the citizens of all Western Hemisphere nations until 1968 when a hemisphere limit of 120,000 was imposed. During the twenties, several hundred thousand Mexican workers and their families simply walked or swam across their northern border to join the nearly half a million of their countrymen who bothered to obtain visas for legal immigration in that decade. The fact of the matter is that U.S. government officials and employers alike made almost no distinctions

in World War I and the twenties between Mexicans who were legally here (had obtained visas) and those who were not. Workers were needed for the war effort, and later for the business boom, and there seemed to be little point to taking a hard line toward the illegals, especially since most were eligible for visas anyway.

The story had changed completely by the Great Depression. Racial prejudice and fear of job competition produced Congressional bills to bring Mexico under the quota system. The bills were not passed, but legal immigration from Mexico was reduced to less than 30,000 in the decade of the thirties simply by administrative means involving rigorous enforcement by U.S. State Department consuls of provisions in immigration law, which banned persons likely to become public charges and required the submission of various documents by visa applicants. Illegal immigration also dropped sharply in the decade, quelled by high unemployment in the U.S. and the massive deportation of Mexican Nationals to Mexico.

Illegal entry to the U.S. did not again reach large numbers until after World War II when Mexicans were once more predominant. This "wetback" era, oriented largely to agricultural employment, was set off by a wartime Mexican-U.S. contract labor agreement and reached its peak in 1954 when over one million illegals were apprehended. The Mexican border was fairly well sealed against illegal entry for the next ten years, but this was accomplished only with the assistance of an expanded program of contract labor which supplied Mexican Nationals to U.S. agriculture, primarily in California and Texas. This so-called *bracero* program, initiated during World War II labor shortages, was attacked by organized labor and other groups and finally ended in December 1964. Predictably, illegal immigration immediately began to increase and the *bracero* was fully replaced by "greencarders" and illegals within one year.[2] Our current problem of illegal entry began with the end of the *bracero*; however, other more fundamental causes brought it to today's massive level.

The recent development of illegal entry can be observed by studying the figures on the apprehension of illegals, with the caveat that these figures suggest only the approximate rate of growth of the phenomenon rather than its absolute magnitude. Ninety thousand illegal aliens were apprehended in 1964, just prior to the end of the *bracero* program. Apprehensions rose to 285,000 in 1969, 500,000 in 1972, and to a 1976 level of over 850,000. . . .

Before proceeding to the issues of the current illegal phenomenon, I wish to draw several conclusions from this limited though essential historical overview. First, illegal entry has been and continues to be largely from Mexico, although a significant volume now appears to be coming from other nations (especially the Western Hemisphere). Second, illegal immigration from Mexico has been an integral part of a *de facto* U.S. policy with respect to use of Mexican labor. Bluntly stated, the *de facto* policy has been—bring them in when they are needed, send them back when they aren't. But this policy is no longer working.

[2] This term, named for the, then, color of the Alien Registration Receipt Card provided by the Immigration and Naturalization Service, refers to persons who have been admitted as permanent resident immigrants to the U.S. A number of Mexican "greencarders" prefer to live in Mexico and commute on a seasonal or more frequent basis to jobs in the U.S. The legality of this practice has been challenged, but was affirmed by the U.S. Supreme Court. See Vernon M. Briggs, Jr., *Chicanos and Rural Poverty* (Baltimore, Md.: Johns Hopkins University Press, 1973), pp. 33-42. On the replacement of the *bracero*, see William E. Martin, "Alien Workers in the United States Agriculture: Impacts of Production," *American Journal of Farm Economics*, XLVIII(1966), 1143; and Phyllis Groom, "Today's Farm Jobs and Farmworkers," *Monthly Labor Review*, XC (April 1967), 1.

Present statistics and expert opinion suggest that the flow of illegal immigration cannot now be shut off, even with increased enforcement efforts and high levels of unemployment in the U.S.

CAUSES OF INCREASED ILLEGAL ENTRY

The *bracero* program during its peak years annually employed over 400,000 Mexican workers who had to be replaced when the program ended in 1965. Western growers had been able to obtain cheap foreign labor throughout the twentieth century; consequently, it was predictable that they would employ illegal Mexican workers to replace their *braceros*. Indeed, after 1965, many former *braceros* entered the U.S. illegally and regained their old jobs. The end of the contract labor program initiated our current flow of illegal immigration, but several other influences brought it to its present massive level.

One of these influences has been the population growth of Mexican border cities—especially Tijuana, Mexicali, Ciudad Juarez, and Nuevo Laredo, which had population increases of almost ten fold between 1940 and 1970, bringing the four city total to 1,300,000. Tremendous growth in these border cities occurred because: (1) they became places of embarkation for *braceros*, illegal entrants, and "greencard" commuters; (2) they experienced increased commerce with U.S. border cities (the local economies of the U.S.-Mexican border areas are very much intertwined in spite of the artifact of a mutual border); and, ironically, (3) as a result of Mexico's Border Industrialization Program, which was designed to provide border city jobs for unemployed *braceros* and to offer wage incentives and favorable import tax treatment to U.S. firms establishing plants in Mexican border areas. In spite of the fact that most of the jobs created went to women, the accompanying expansion of local economies has greatly increased population within Mexico to the border areas. More generally, the population of Mexico has been growing rapidly and will continue to do so, from 62,000,000 in 1976 to an estimated 134,000,000 by the year 2000.

This tremendous population growth (produced by an annual rate of increase of 3.5 per cent) must be placed in the context of standard of living differences between the U.S. and Mexico in order to glimpse the true potential for illegal U.S. immigration. Per capita income in Mexico is roughly one-seventh of that in the U.S., but more pertinent differences in welfare are suggested by the $2.00–2.80 average daily earnings of employed landless workers in rural Mexican communities in comparison to the U.S. statutory minimum hourly wage of $2.30 in manufacturing. The 1976 devaluation of the peso, which temporarily raised the purchasing power in Mexico of the U.S. dollar, added to the substantial wage incentives already existing for migrating to the U.S.

Perhaps the most important proximate cause of the present level of illegal immigration was the tight job market which prevailed in the U.S. in the late sixties, with annual unemployment rates from 1966-1969 all below 4 per cent of the labor force. Many industrial employers began to hire illegal immigrants in this period, not so much because they couldn't find native workers, but because the illegals were usually more reliable and productive. A cumulative effect then began to operate, bringing more and more illegals and employers together as a result of their mutually satisfactory experiences.

Another factor thought by some observers to have provided great impetus to illegal immigration was the 1965 Immigration Act. This law established a Western Hemisphere ceiling for immigration to the U.S. of 120,000 persons a year (effective in 1968), on a first come, first served basis. The ceiling itself, however, has not caused illegal immigration to the U.S. to increase, since most Western Hemisphere nations supplying illegal entrants have experienced *increases* in legal U.S. immigration under the Act. Mexico, for example, had about 40,000 people a year immigrate to the U.S. prior to 1968 (when only qualitative rules governed), but the figure is now running over 70,000 a year.

The 1965 Act probably has had a small effect on illegal entry through making immigration by a Western Hemisphere person who is not a relative of a U.S. citizen or legal resident alien exceedingly difficult. Almost all adults who do not enjoy such a relative status are eligible for immigration only after they have received a job offer from a U.S. employer who has obtained for that job a "labor certification" (a Department of Labor determination that there are no resident workers available for the job and that employment of an immigrant in it will not have an adverse impact on local labor market wages and working conditions). Both job offers and labor certifications are hard to obtain; the former because employers do not want to wait the two and a half years for the immigrant to show up (the current waiting period for a visa in the Western Hemisphere), and the latter because there are many unemployed resident workers looking for jobs. No doubt, some Western Hemisphere citizens who have little if any chance of legally immigrating to the U.S. under current immigration law do enter illegally, or, alternatively, enter on a tourist visa with the intention of violating its conditions by taking a job. Ludicrously, once they are working in violation of immigration law, they stand a good chance of receiving a labor certification and, ultimately, a permanent immigrant status. The labor certification requirement should be removed from our immigration law. It does not protect the labor market, since more than four-fifths of all immigrants enter without it, and it does encourage unlawful behavior. But its removal will not end illegal entry by any stretch of the imagination. The fact is that the demand for entry to the U.S. is now well in excess of the immigration places available under law (290,000 a year plus another 100,000 or so which are exempt from hemisphere ceilings) and immigration outside of the law is not very difficult or hazardous.

THE ENFORCEMENT PROBLEM

Why can't illegal immigration be stopped or at least controlled through better law enforcement? The two answers to that question are first that it is easy to break immigration law and escape detection, and second that there is apathy and reluctance on the part of the U.S. institutions for enforcement of immigration law.

The most widely known method of illegal entry is simply to walk or swim across one of the U.S. borders, principally the border with Mexico. This kind of entry simply cannot be controlled by the Border Patrol with any methods now considered feasible. Probably the most widely used method of entry currently is with a border crossing card which permits entry to the U.S. for 72 hours for purposes of business or pleasure, but prohibits employment. Mexican nationals who enter in this fashion and wish to work simply mail the card back to Mexico, to avoid the risk of its seizure by Immigration and Naturalization Service (INS) personnel, and then look for a job. Other illegals are smuggled into the U.S. or use false documents to get through entry stations. Some tightening of port-of-entry procedures against these methods of entry are possible but the magnitude of that task is great—in part because each year there are almost 200,000,000 border crossings (of both Mexican and U.S. citizens)

from Mexico to the U.S. The San Ysidro entry station south of San Diego admits a daily average of 100,000 persons. The flow across the several El Paso entry points is even greater.

One other increasingly used method of becoming an illegal immigrant is that of entering legally as a tourist or student and then violating the entry visa (thus, the term "visa abuser") by accepting employment or overstaying the length of stay permitted. It is not now possible to trace down the people who do not report a departure from the U.S. under a nonimmigrant visa (many tourists leave without notifying U.S. officials); but, INS officials believe that 10 to 20 per cent of those who enter each year under nonimmigrant visas (about 7,000,000) may overstay their period of admission (often to accept jobs).

Because of the ease of illegal entry, enforcement of immigration law under any circumstances would be exceedingly difficult. Under existing circumstances, a legal and institutional aura of apathy and even opposition to stopping illegal immigration limits effective law enforcement.

First of all, the penalties for being caught as an illegal alien are weak or nonexistent. The law specifies punishment by fine and imprisonment for illegal immigration, but it is rarely applied because prosecution of hundreds of thousands of cases a year is impractical, and punishment of people whose only crime is crossing an international border to improve their poor livelihoods has little public support. Consequently, most illegals who are apprehended suffer nothing more than a free bus ride (voluntary deportation) out of the country. This can be painful, of course, depending on individual circumstances, but for many it is anticipated and for some, welcomed. Even smuggling of aliens, when convictions are obtained, is punished lightly—a couple of months in prison and fines of a few hundred dollars.

Secondly, U.S. courts have increasingly restrained the interrogation and search activities of the INS in the last few years, adversely affecting the agency's enforcement efforts in the opinion of agency officials. The judicial rulings have applied due process constitutional rights to either limit or halt massive "surveys" and arrests in "barrios," interrogation of individuals in public places, "surveys" of employers, and the use of checkpoints and patrols on highways. These decisions may have lessened intervention of INS officers into the lives of law abiding Hispanic citizens and resident aliens (who must necessarily bear the brunt of INS inquiry and search so long as most illegal aliens are Hispanic), but they have also improved the illegal alien's chances of avoiding detection once he has made it through the border area.

Finally, the INS has little support from other institutions in its enforcement effort, and a number of institutions indirectly assist alien violation of immigration law. Local police departments provide the most help by notifying the agency when they arrest illegals for criminal offenses, but this practice is not uniform. Employers provide by far the most important institutional aid to illegal aliens by hiring them. Other institutions such as welfare agencies, schools, and hospitals provide services to illegals, albeit to a small proportion, which facilitate their stay in this country. Certainly the ideal of community shared responsibility for upholding the law is not approached in the area of illegal immigration. This cannot be explained by unpopularity of the laws which restrict immigration: a recent Gallup poll disclosed that 89 per cent of those polled were in favor of either keeping immigration (legal) at its current level or reducing it.

It is evident that illegal immigration cannot now be controlled with existing law and enforcement efforts; the incentive structure is stacked against it. The potential income benefits for breaking the law are great, the chances of getting caught are slight, and the penalties if one is caught are practically nonexistent. . . .

CHARACTERISTICS OF ILLEGAL ALIENS

Although everyone agrees that Mexico sends far more illegal immigrants to the U.S. than any other nation, there is some disagreement about the relative size of the Mexican share. Disagreement can exist because there are now a large but unknown number of illegals in this country from other countries of the world, particularly Canada, the West Indies, Haiti, the Dominican Republic, Greece, China, and nations of Central and South America. Presumably, most illegals from these countries enter the U.S. legally on tourist or student visas and then simply overstay their time limits. But Mexico sends far more people to the U.S. under tourist and student visas than any other country, so it seems likely that Mexicans still probably comprise at least two-thirds of all illegal aliens in the U.S. This is below their 90 per cent share of all apprehensions because the latter figure results from the concentration of INS officers on the U.S.-Mexican border.

Because Mexicans predominate in illegal entry, most illegal aliens are concentrated in California and Texas, near the border. But the southwestern labor markets which are open to the illegals have become rather saturated, causing many to go farther north to Denver, Portland, Seattle, Kansas City, Milwaukee, Detroit, and especially Chicago. (Chicago already ranks behind only Los Angeles, San Antonio, and, possibly, El Paso in the size of its Mexican origin population.) In the East, the New York and Washington metropolitan areas are the most frequent destinations of illegal aliens, though practically all of them originate from countries other than Mexico.

There have been several surveys of illegal aliens themselves (most of whom were under arrest when questioned). Consequently, we have a fair amount of information about the characteristics of this population. Most are young, male, and support several dependents in their home country. As would be expected from these characteristics, the dominant reason for illegal entry is to obtain employment, and few fail to do so. Few illegals are accompanied by their families. Mexicans have very little schooling, are unskilled, and have little facility with the English language. They tend to stay in the U.S. for less than a year, but frequently re-enter this country illegally several times. Non-Mexican illegals have more schooling and usually settle in the U.S. more or less permanently.

Probably not more than 20 per cent of all illegals are now employed in farm work. Their predominant employment is in all types of low wage nonfarm firms, with concentrations in apparel and textile manufacturing, food processing and preparation, and other services. A small minority are able to get fairly good jobs in construction and durable goods manufacturing. Average 1975 earnings of the illegals surveyed by North and Houston were $2.34 an hour for Mexicans, $3.05 for those from other Western Hemisphere countries, and $4.08 for those from the Eastern Hemisphere. Even in the Southwest, where almost all illegals are Mexican, considerable variation in wage rates was found: $1.74 an hour in the border counties, $1.98 in the total Southwest, and $2.60 in California.

EFFECTS OF ILLEGAL ALIENS

Much controversy surrounds the question of illegal alien impacts on the U.S. Disagreement is possible, in part, because the number of illegals in this country is impossible to estimate accurately. Beyond the numbers, there is dispute over fact—for example, do illegals displace legal resident workers—and values—if there is displacement, does that justify legislation aimed at illegal entry.

The impact least subject to factual dispute is that on population. U.S. annual population growth is now running at about 1,600,000. Thus, legal immigration at an annual rate of nearly 400,000 accounts for one-quarter of the total, while illegal immigration accounts for another one-quarter or so, depending on one's estimates. However, if "zero population growth" is achieved through equalization of births and deaths (and this appears likely at some future date) then immigration, legal and illegal, will account for all of the growth in the U.S. population. The resulting growth rate will be very small, most likely less than 0.5 per cent a year; nevertheless, adherents of tight population control are already zeroing in on illegal immigration as the major potential factor in population growth of the U.S.

The impact of illegals on direct social welfare costs is subject to greater factual dispute, although most people who have studied the matter tend to agree that this cost is slight. Several studies have found that very few illegals collect unemployment compensation, go on welfare, receive food stamps, or use medicaid. Some do use free public hospitals and send their children to public schools, but the incremental costs involved are probably small. On the tax revenue side, it is clear that most illegals do have social security and federal income taxes withheld from their pay, although a sizeable proportion apparently pay less than their legal obligation of the latter.

The very low incidence of social welfare payments to illegals is not a mystery. These payments are usually made only to the unemployed and most illegals are working. When they are not, fear of detection and deportation keeps them from applying to benefit programs. Thus, the direct social welfare costs of illegals are low. But this says nothing about the indirect costs which they may produce by displacing domestic workers from employment to various social welfare programs. . . .

LABOR MARKET IMPACT

The economic impact of illegals clearly depends upon the state of the economy. During periods of full employment, immigrant workers, legal or illegal, are largely complements of resident workers and produce mainly economic benefits. By increasing the amount of labor available, immigrants provide lower production costs and prices, higher profits, and greater general economic growth. The wages of most native workers will increase as the presence of illegals employed in low skilled jobs permits the occupational upgrading of natives. These consequences are ascribed to much of the historical immigration to the U.S. and are also the rationale for the use of "guest" workers in northern Europe.

But it is evident that even in the best of times, those native workers who have no better alternative than competition with immigrants will suffer lower incomes because of their availability. Historically, in the U.S. the major groups hurt by immigration have been blacks, browns, and low skilled whites living away from urban areas.

In the polar case of high unemployment, immigrants are simply substitutes for domestic workers and, consequently, produce only economic costs. These costs fall principally on the resident workers whom they displace, but are also borne by all citizens to the extent that they contribute to the social welfare programs which support the displaced resident workers.

The above analysis does not differentiate between legal and illegal immigrant workers. Both will have a similar labor market impact, depending on the degree to which they are complements or substitutes for native workers. In actuality, illegal immigrants tend to be more productive and docile than do lawful workers, in order to offset their insecure status. These characteristics appeal to many employers and provide a competitive advantage to illegals in labor markets where long tenure of employment is not important. The exploitable status of illegals also produces an effect on labor standards.

The economy of the U.S. since World War II has been characterized by something between full employment and massive unemployment; therefore, it is not surprising that much public discussion of the impact of illegals involves the empirical question—do illegal aliens really displace domestic workers? More sophisticated discussions examine wage as well as displacement effects.

Unfortunately, an empirically based answer to these questions cannot be given because the necessary research has not been done and probably won't be done given the nature of the problem. There are a couple of pieces of evidence that illegals do lower wages in labor markets where they are concentrated, but the nature of this evidence is not strong. The author found that within California, wage rates increased from the south (the border) to north for unskilled manual occupations (where illegals tend to be employed), but not for most skilled ones. Another study, after controlling for individual differences in human capital, found incomes of resident workers (especially Mexican American) lower in Texas border cities than in Houston 150 miles away from the border. The problem with both findings is that influences other than illegal aliens are also plausible explanations.

It is also very difficult to get evidence on the displacement of resident workers by illegals.

The presence of illegals in labor markets which employ them in large numbers presumably has lowered relative wages and working conditions in these markets to the point where few resident workers are interested in these jobs, given some alternative income possibilities. Those resident workers who might seek employment in the jobs held by illegals—youth and others well down in employment queues—tend to be discouraged from doing so because they are seen by employers as less productive than the illegals. Thus, it is often true that resident workers do not appear to be available for the jobs held by illegals.

That fact, however, says nothing about the availability of resident workers if illegals became unavailable. In the latter event, certain wages would rise and the employment of residents increase. No doubt some firms would switch to labor saving technologies and some would go out of business. Cost and price increases would occur in affected industries.

The displacement debate tends to be carried out in "either-or" terms which are not enlightening. A complete removal of illegals tomorrow would certainly not result in their one-for-one replacement by resident workers; the amount of replacement would be governed by the wage elasticities of labor supply and demand. Not knowing these elasticities, it still seems safe to say that removal of illegals would result in some re-employment of the nearly seven million people who are now unemployed in the U.S.

Why do some people disagree with this conclusion? One reason is that they accept at face value statements by employers of illegal aliens, especially growers, that domestic workers are unavailable. But it is always in the self interest of employers to increase the supply of labor available to them. This is especially true when the workers in question are productive and relatively powerless to oppose the working conditions which are offered. Growers in the fifties and sixties exaggerated the unavailability of domestic workers because they preferred to employ *braceros*. Similar preferences often lie behind the current employment of illegal aliens.

Many people also believe that illegal aliens earn only the statutory minimum wage and that domestic workers will not work at that wage level, in part because of the availability of unemployment compensation and welfare. While it is true that Mexican illegals usually earn from $1.80 to $2.80 an hour, most others earn substantially more, as cited earlier. But it is likely that domestic workers *are* available, even for the jobs held by Mexican illegals, or would be if the wages for them were to increase.

If illegals were no longer available to growers and apparel manufacturers, for example, these employers would be forced to recruit resident workers. It is hard for me to believe that they would not find some, if not at currently prevailing wage rates, then at somewhat higher wages. And it would not obviously be a "bad" thing for farm and apparel wages to increase, even if there were corresponding increases in prices.

In sum, there is no precise knowledge of the market effects of illegals, nor even certain knowledge of the direction of the effect. My own view is that in the slack economy which has prevailed in the U.S. over the last few years, many illegals have been substitutes for resident workers and, consequently, have produced significant displacement of the latter while their cost and price benefits have been limited.

The final impact of illegals that I will mention is on labor standards. Because they are reluctant to support collective bargaining or seek enforcement of labor statutes, they help to maintain substandard labor conditions in some labor markets. These markets are frequently referred to as "secondary" and are characterized, among the other well known attributes of such markets, by frequent violation of wage and hour statutes and weak employee power relative to that of employers.

POLICY

It will not be easy to develop widely accepted policy on the illegal immigration phenomenon. First, as indicated in these pages, important factual information on the number and effect of illegals is missing. Secondly, difficult "value" questions are involved. These include our society's relative emphasis on economic growth, full employment, population control, equality of income distribution, elimination of poverty, and international relations, especially with Mexico. Ethical questions are also involved concerning our obligation, if any, to (especially poor) people outside of the U.S., relative to our internal obligations. If one believes, as I do, that illegals are substitutes for a good deal of resident labor, then the ethical question becomes a liberal dilemma, where a choice must be made for one of two poor populations— the inside poor or the outside poor.

The experience of northern European countries toward their "guest" workers (12,000,000 of them in 1973), who are rather analogous in economic terms, at least, to illegal aliens in the U.S., might be instructive for policy making purposes except that no settled policy has been arrived at by these countries. Until rather recently, the northern European policy has been one of controlled recruiting and encouragement of foreign workers in order to perpetuate robust economic growth in the face of very low rates of domestic unemployment. The receiving European countries have also attempted to control the immigrant workers by registering them with their governments, restricting their employment, discouraging their relatives from coming, and preventing their permanent settlement in the host country. These policies have not been entirely effective, which accounts for some of the disillusionment with the use of "guest" workers which now prevails in Europe.

The ultimate solution to our problem of illegal immigration—namely, an equalization of living standards in the Western Hemisphere and eventually the world— is easily agreed upon, but this is a very long-run solution which provides little immediate help. Even a long-run policy of encouraging economic growth must face some thorny issues. With respect to Mexico, for example, is there a way for the U.S. to aid that country's development within its prevailing political rhetoric which stresses the "revolution" and independence from the U.S.? Mexico already has achieved rapid economic growth— 7 per cent a year from 1960 to 1970. Its greater economic problems are the distribution of income and population increases. Could the U.S. couple aid to Mexico with pressure for distributional equity and birth control programs? The single answer, which must suffice here because of space limitations, is no, the Mexicans would not allow it. Yet, economic aid without population control as a minimum response, would not reduce the Mexican emigration potential. Another solution, an open border for capital and labor is not now feasible, but this idea will begin to receive serious attention if alternative policies for dealing with illegal immigration are unsuccessful.

Possibilities for Immediate Solutions

Proposals for more immediate policies can be divided into two groups by the criterion of whether they favor or oppose legislation which would assess criminal or civil penalties against employers who hire illegal aliens. Legislation of this type (the Rodino Bill) has twice passed the U.S. House of Representatives, but has not come before the Senate—purportedly because of the opposition of Senator James Eastland, Chairman of the Senate Judiciary Committee, to employer penalties unless a *bracero* type program is re-established.

The major institutional support for employer penalties comes from the AFL-CIO, because illegal aliens undercut the efforts of some of its affiliates, especially those in apparel, textiles, and food manufacturing. Opposition to employer penalties comes principally from growers' organizations and other employer groups, civil rights organizations, most notably the American Civil Liberties Union, and some Chicano groups. The latter argue that a Rodino Bill would increase the employer discrimination which already exists against Hispanic workers in the U.S.

The Carter Administration very quickly announced its support for employer penalties, apparently based on the judgment that displacement efforts of illegals greatly exacerbate U.S. unemployment and hinder policies aimed at reducing it. This position appears to be also politically sound. A recent Gallup poll found 86 per cent of its respondents in favor of outlawing the employment of illegal aliens, and 12 states have now passed legislation to this effect. Some students of the problem say that employer penalties won't work, but this is an assertion which should be tested before it is accepted.

A work card has been proposed as a means of both simplifying enforcement of an employer penalty law and preventing job discrimination against Hispanics. Employers could then easily meet their responsibility for not knowingly hiring illegal aliens by asking to see this card. Since all job applicants would have to show it, there could be no discrimination against Hispanics on the grounds that they might be illegal aliens. Their possession of the card would immediately establish their legal right to employment. The attractiveness of a required work card is enhanced by the fact that it would add

little to existing requirements under the OASDI system. Almost all workers are now required to have a social security number and almost all employers are required to record that number on payroll records. The use of a counterfeit-proof, nontransferable social security card, which would not be issued to illegal aliens, would merely tighten existing regulations somewhat.

One objection to a work card is the cost and inconvenience which would be involved in developing and issuing 100,000,000 cards. This could be lessened by limiting the card requirements to those who apply for new jobs or to employees of those industries known to employ large numbers of illegal aliens. The major objection to a required work card is on the grounds that it could become a kind of national passport, required for identification purposes, and consequently used to restrict civil liberties. This objection will probably prevail because it seems to strike a sensitive nerve among many Americans, in spite of the legislative prohibitions which could be placed on use of a work card for identification purposes, our existing requirements for the possession of driver's licenses and Selective Service cards, and the common use of identification documents in European countries.

Another thorny policy question is that of "amnesty"—the legalizing of illegal entry which occurred prior to some cut-off date. My own position is for a liberal amnesty, up to a quite recent date, in order to make the illegal alien problem prospective rather then retrospective. Few illegals who have been in the U.S. for any length of time are apprehended anyway, and I can see no reason to maintain a fugitive status for the illegals already here in order to deport a relatively small number. This policy would also avoid the administrative burden of adjudicating the "equity" status of illegals on a case-by-case basis if amnesty were granted only up to an earlier date—1970 for example. Liberal amnesty would also be well received by Chicanos and might help reduce their opposition to tighter control of illegal entry.

In the last regard, I believe that any policy on illegal immigration should recognize that Mexico requires special treatment. The need for special treatment exists because of history, the forceful acquisition of much of the southwestern U.S. from Mexico, because of the 2,000 mile border which joins the two countries, and because of the greater differences in standards of living between the two countries. The appropriate special treatment is not a new *bracero* program which would make Mexicans welcome only part of each year while they perform the lowest paid jobs in our society, but, rather, an increase in the numbers permitted to immigrate permanently to the U.S. The number of permanent immigrants annually permitted to enter from Mexico should vary with the level of unemployment in the U.S. In years of low unemployment, 100,000-125,000 seems to me to be a reasonable number.

Appallingly, our most recent policy move was in the opposite direction. In October 1976, the Congress passed and the President signed an Amendment to the Immigration Act which adopts the Eastern Hemisphere immigration provisions for all countries of the Western Hemisphere. Among other provisions this means that a 20,000 annual immigration limit now applies to all Western Hemisphere countries. Most affected by far is Mexico, whose immigration to the U.S. under the total Western Hemisphere numerical limitation of 120,000 had been running at an annual rate of about 45,000 in the seventies.

Thus, there has been a very rapid shift in immigration policy toward our southern neighbor—from the complete absence of quantitative restrictions which existed before 1968 to a 20,000 limit in 1977. This change is insensitive to the widespread poverty of the Mexican people, and it also insures the continued existence of an illegal alien problem for the U.S.

The illegal flow, in a broad perspective, is simply one manifestation of the instability which is inherent in a world of great wealth disparities among and within its nations. Despite the hopes of national policy makers for the last 10 years, the problem will not go away; it will simply get worse if it continues to be neglected. Policy changes will come, but it is not clear whether they will occur in a reasoned, timely fashion or will be put off until catalyzed by some kind of visceral reaction, possibly in a period of national crisis. . . .

Inflation

Probably the most visible economic problem over the past decade has been the rate of inflation. Robert Solow discusses the nature of inflation and some of its causes. He also suggests that the costs of inflation may not be as great as the costs of policies, such as sustained high unemployment, that may be necessary to eliminate inflation.

A more pessimistic view of inflation and its costs is presented by Arthur Okun. He develops the theory of implicit contracts (the invisible handshake) and shows how such understandings are undermined by inflation.

In an effort to guard against the effects of future price increases, many union contracts include cost-of-living-adjustment (COLA) clauses. As Victor Sheifer indicates, however, these clauses only provide limited protection.

After adjusting for inflation the purchasing power of labor earnings was virtually unchanged over the 1970s. The primary reason why "real" incomes did not increase, as they have during most of our history, was that productivity did not increase. In other words, there was no increase in the amount of output that could be produced for a given level of inputs, including labor. The more difficult question is why, as of about 1974, productivity stopped increasing. Edward Denison considers a number of alternative hypotheses and concludes that it is not possible to single out which factors are most responsible.

There are many causes for inflation as well as for productivity changes. From the perspective of labor economics, most of the research related to inflation has focused on wage determination and the effect of unions. Daniel Mitchell summarizes his own work and the work of other labor economists on this topic. Based on the evidence of the early 1960s, he concludes that collective bargaining is compatible with price stability. On the other hand, wage inflation is very difficult to stop once it has begun, in part because of the development of inflationary expectations. In this context, he also discusses some of the arguments for and against wage-price controls and guidelines.

In contrast to Mitchell, most economists are very unenthusiastic about controls. This negative view is expressed by William Poole, who argues that any benefits from controls will be far exceeded by their costs. These costs include the loss of individual freedom; a likely misallocation of resources; and the administrative costs of enforcing controls, especially when firms respond by changing product specifications and hiring and promotion standards in lieu of directly increasing prices and wage rates. Instead of establishing controls, Poole prefers to combat inflation through a set of structural reforms to increase competition in both product and labor markets.

20

The Intelligent Citizen's Guide to Inflation

Robert M. Solow

Robert M. Solow, "The Intelligent Citizen's Guide to Inflation," *The Public Interest,* No. 41 (Fall 1975).

... Inflation is *a substantial, sustained increase in the general level of prices.* The intrinsic vagueness of "substantial" is harmless. One would not want to use a heavyweight word to describe a trivial rise in the price level; granted, it will never be perfectly clear where to draw the line, but neither can it be important since only a word is at stake. "Sustained" is a little trickier. One would not want to label as inflationary a momentary (six-month? one-year?) upward twitch of the price level, especially if it is soon reversed. There is no point in being forced to describe mere short-term fluctuations in prices as alternating bouts of inflation and deflation. "Sustained" also carries some connotation of "self-perpetuating" and that raises broader questions. It is obviously important to know whether each step in an inflationary process tends to generate further inflation unless some "outside" force intervenes, or whether the inflationary process is eventually self-limiting. The answer need not be the same for all inflations, and it certainly depends on what you mean by "outside." So it is probably best not to incorporate this aspect as a part of the definition.

It is the notion of the "general price level" that will lead us somewhere. Economists make a sharp and important distinction between the system of relative prices and the general price level. Relative prices describe the terms on which different goods and services exchange for *one another;* the general price level describes the terms on which some representative bundle of goods and services exchanges for *money.* Imagine an economy in which the only goods produced are meat and vegetables, and first suppose that all exchange is barter; some people trade meat for vegetables with other people who want to trade vegetables for meat. If one pound of meat exchanges for three pounds of vegetables, then the relative price is established. But since there is no money, there is no such thing as the general price level. Notice that inflation is inconceivable in a barter economy. It would be logically contradictory for "all prices" to rise at the same time. Suppose that, because of a change in tastes or a natural catastrophe, one pound of meat should come to exchange for six pounds of vegetables. One could say that the price of meat (in terms of vegetables!) had doubled. But that is exactly the same thing as saying that the price of vegetables (in terms of meat!) had halved. A carnivorous farmer would find himself worse off; but a vegetarian rancher would be sitting pretty. . . .

MEASURING INFLATION

In the real world there are thousands of goods and services, whose relative prices are changing all the time in complicated ways. The measurement of the general price level thus becomes a major statistical enterprise. But it is done, and generally according to the principles just described. . . .

The Consumer Price Index (CPI—what is sometimes called the cost-of-living index) is produced and published monthly. . . . At intervals of a decade or more, the Bureau of Labor Statistics (BLS) conducts an expensive survey of the spending habits of families of different size, income, and other characteristics. From this survey it calculates the typical budget of a middle-income, urban wage-earner or clerical

worker with a family of four. Then each month it actually prices out that budget in a number of cities around the country. If the cost of that bundle goes up or down by one per cent, the CPI goes up or down by one per cent.

That is certainly a reasonable and meaningful price index, but it does have some drawbacks. (Of course, any method of reducing all those thousands of price changes to a single number will have drawbacks.) It relates only to consumers; the prices of industrial machinery and raw materials could go sky-high, and the CPI would register that fact only later, when cost increases filtered down to retail prices. Moreover, the CPI relates only to some consumers—those middle-income, urban, wage-earning families of four. Old people, or poor people, or oil millionaires, who buy different bundles, may have different experiences. . . .

All price indexes suffer from a common difficulty. Commodities change in character and quality. . . . If the price of an ordinary shirt rises 10 per cent in the course of a year, but simultaneously the wrinkle-resisting properties of the shirt are improved, how is one to decide how much of the 10 per cent represents the greater value of an improved product and how much represents pure price increase? The agencies do the best they can, but it is hardly a job that can ever be done perfectly. It used to be thought that there was systematic underallowance for quality improvements to such an extent that an annual rise of one or two per cent in the measured price level could be ignored as not being a true price increase; but no one knows for sure. Perhaps the best conclusion is that one ought not to attach great significance to small changes in price indexes. . . .

WHAT ARE THE CAUSES?

There is a vast and subtle literature on the causes of inflation and the mechanism of the inflationary process. I cannot hope to survey it fairly, especially since it contains contradictory strands. My sketch of the state of play may be idiosyncratic.

One of the central issues in the theory of the subject—with roots going back hundreds of years in economics—concerns the nature of the connection between monetary goings-on and the real economy of production, consumption, and relative prices. The very concept of inflation presupposes a monetary economy, as we noted earlier. Moveover, our discussion of the simplified meat-and-vegetables economy seemed to lead to a proposition like this: You could imagine two identical islands, one of them (A) with unchanging prices and the other (B) experiencing perfectly anticipated pure inflation at X per cent per year, but with exactly the same *real* events taking place on both of them. The main preconditions for this conclusion are (1) that the money supply should be increasing X percent a year faster on island B than on A, so that the amount of purchasing power represented by the money supply could be the same in both places, and (2) that it be possible to pay interest on whatever is used for money, say bank deposits, so that the nominal interest rate could be X per cent per annum higher on island B, to keep the real rates of interest equal.

Now that is pretty abstract; but the further development of such reasoning leads one school of economists to conclude that the real and monetary spheres are in principle separate, and that the true and only cause of inflation is excessively fast expansion of the money supply. It follows that the only way to reduce or stop inflation is to slow down the growth of the money supply. Moreover, if the real and monetary spheres really are separate, then doing so will not have real effects, and will thus be quite harmless. (Of course, one can argue that if inflation has no real effects, or negligible ones, there is hardly any point in stopping it.)

I hasten to say that this is a caricature. This school of thought recognizes perfectly well—and the recognition goes back to David Hume—that real-life inflations are not pure and perfectly anticipated. Any attempt to slow or stop an inflation by tightening money will certainly have redistributional effects and may well cause recession, diminished production, unemployment, and excess capacity. All the "new Quantity theorists" claim is that these real consequences will not last forever. Eventually, as the new state of affairs comes to be embedded in expectations and business decisions, the real effects will disappear. Island B will get to be like Island A. The intervening period of bad times has to be regarded as an investment whose payoff is the reduction of inflation, whatever that is worth.

A practical man would want to know how long that period of bad times is likely to last. The new Quantity theorists are not really able to say, and it is hard to blame them. It is a difficult question, and the experiment has never been tried. The sterner protagonists of this view have occasionally hazarded the guess that the period of purification might conceivably last a long time, to be measured more nearly in decades than in quarters. . . .

This question of timing is an analytical question as well as a practical one. The opposing school of thought holds—to caricature once again—that there is a permanent connection between the monetary sphere and the real economy. But what does "permanent" mean? Presumably it does not mean literally forever; nothing is forever. If it means "a long time"—as, for instance, decades—then the distinction between the two schools seems to be more a matter of emphasis or taste than of principle, more a matter of applied economics than of pure theory. But those questions of application are terribly important, as we will see.

THE "TRADE-OFF" VIEW

I shall give a grossly oversimplified sketch of one version of the alternative doctrine. It is based on the famous "Phillips curve," named after A. W. Phillips, who started the whole thing with a purely statistical study of British figures. Let us take it for granted that for extended periods of time in many countries there is a reliable inverse relationship between the unemployment rate (to be thought of as a measure of the degree of prosperity) and the contemporaneous percentage rate at which the level of wages rises. That is to say, in a year in which the economy is strong and the labor market is tight, workers—individually or through their organizations—will be inclined to hold out for relatively large wage increases, and employers will be inclined to offer them; in a depressed year, when the unemployment rate is high, workers will be less pushful and employers will feel more hard-pressed and hard-boiled. Naturally, there are other forces affecting the behavior of wage rates, but this is the one we are concentrating on. Observe carefully: The Phillips curve is a relation between the rate of increase of wage rates (a *monetary* magnitude) and the unemployment rate or level of production (a *real* phenomenon). I have given a plausible but casual rationalization of such a relation; I must warn you that this apparently simple proposition has been the object of whole volumes of the most subtle theoretical and empirical research, which is only beginning to converge. There are still wide differences of opinion within the profession.

So much for wages. If there were no improvements in productivity, labor costs per unit of *output* would move along in step with wage rates (i.e., labor costs per *hour*). . . . Subtleties aside, unit labor costs rise when wages rise more rapidly than productivity in percentage terms, decline when the opposite

holds true, and remain constant when wage rates and productivity both rise at the same percentage rate.

But we are interested in prices, not only wages. The simplest acceptable preliminary explanation of the behavior of the price level in the private non-farm economy is that it is cost-determined. Market conditions are clearly part of the story too—think of oil!—but for simplicity let us just keep that in the background. Suppose that the general price index simply comes out as a mark-up on unit cost of production. That is practically the same thing as a mark-up on unit labor cost, since labor costs amount to more than three quarters of all costs in the economy as a whole. If the price level is roughly proportional to unit labor costs, then the price level will rise when unit labor costs rise, fall when they fall, and stay the same when unit labor costs are stable. So the price level will rise, fall, or remain unchanged according to whether wage rates are rising faster than, slower than, or at the same pace as productivity.

But the wage level—apart from the other market forces we are now ignoring—rises faster when the unemployment rate is low, and slower when it is high. And so the price level—again ignoring other market forces—rises when unemployment is low and the economy prospers, and falls when unemployment is high and the economy is depressed. This is the famous "trade-off between inflation and unemployment" that has found its way into everyday talk. A stable price level can be achieved only at that unemployment rate that allows wages to rise about as fast as productivity is increasing.

According to this line of argument, the real and the monetary are intimately connected. The rate of inflation is governed by the real condition of the economy, in particular by its "tightness" or prosperousness. Moreover, the options for policy are clear but limited. Society can have a slower rate of inflation or no inflation at all, if and only if it is prepared to generate and maintain enough unemployment and excess capacity to hold prices and wages in check. . . .

The reply of the trade-off school to the monetary school is: Yes, tight money and balanced budgets can stop inflation, but only by depressing the economy for a long time, perhaps a very long time. . . .

The actual behavior of the American economy from the end of the Korean War price controls to the middle 1960s seemed generally to confirm the trade-off view. That is to say, there seemed to be a reasonably reliable relation between the tautness of the economy and the behavior of wages and the price level, after the various other market forces had been taken into account. Beginning about 1966 there was a perfectly classical inflation associated with the deliberate malfinancing of the Vietnam War. (Can it be that wars get the economic policy they deserve?) But thereafter something seemed to go haywire. There has been, more or less ever since, a tendency for wages and prices to rise faster than those old, previously reliable relationships would have predicted. . . .

Modern mixed-capitalist economies seem to have an inflationary bias near full employment. That is a description, not an explanation, but it seems to summarize the situation. An economy that is running along moderately prosperously, but hardly straining its capacity to produce, will see its price level drift upward. In the good old days, the demands of war or the stimulus of excessively expansionary policy might bring an economy to flat-out operation and consequent inflation, but a return to more normal levels of demand would stabilize prices, and a touch of recession might bring on actual deflation. The trouble is that nowadays economies begin to inflate while they are showing no signs of excess pressure, and to reverse the price rise would appear to require longer and deeper recessions than seems reasonable or natural. The question is: Why should that be? Why, for instance, do so few prices ever actually fall?

Let me answer a question with a question. Is it possible that the price level was *more* stable on the average in the good old days because the economy was *less* stable on the average? More particularly, until very recently it was reasonable to fear that any momentary weakness in the economy might be the prelude to substantial and prolonged recession. Under those circumstances, businesses might see the wisdom of cutting prices early and often, to protect markets and market shares against competitors in their own and neighboring industries who would also be feeling the pinch of widespread market softness. The same fear might be expected to stiffen the resistance of employers to wage demands; a longish period of reduced sales and lowered prices is no time to bear the burden of higher wage costs, and discontent in the workplace is easier to handle when production has to be cut back anyway. To complete the circle, the danger of prolonged unemployment would induce workers to accept wage reductions. . . . It is not hard to believe that the reality of major recessions and depressions would account for greater flexibility of prices and wages in the downward direction.

If the threat of prolonged recession is absent, the situation is quite otherwise. There is less pressure to reduce prices when markets soften, if it is expected that they will soon improve. Similarly, there is less incentive to resist wage increases if prices are being maintained or even raised themselves; and if production will soon need to be increased, one is less likely to tempt strikes, ill will, and the reputation of being a lousy employer. Finally, when mass unemployment is unlikely, workers are able more confidently to keep up the pressure for higher wages.

THE INFLATIONARY BIAS

Here, then, we have the beginnings of an explanation of the inflationary bias of modern economics near full employment. Workers and employers nowadays fear prolonged recession and mass unemployment less than they used to, *and they are right.* Those things are very unlikely to happen. Modern governments know how to prevent major depressions, they have the legislative and administrative tools they need in order to apply their knowledge, and they have the motivation: No government could survive in an advanced democracy if it permitted a major depression and serious unemployment on a scale that occurred more or less regularly in the good old days. So 1932 will not come around again, and there is not much reason to look for those forms of behavior that were conditioned by the ever-present possibility that it might.

If this is a reasonable explanation of the fact that prices hardly ever fall, then it is not hard to suggest why they should seem always to be rising. In any developing and changing economy, there will always be good reasons why *relative* prices have to change. Technological progress proceeds at different speeds in different industries, so relative costs of production are changing. Consumer demands shift, from grains to meat, from wool to synthetics, from hats to jeans, from restaurants to home freezers and back to restaurants. As in the meat-and-vegetables economy, it is possible for relative prices to change while the general price level remains constant: All that is necessary is that some prices rise and some prices fall. But if most prices have got out of the habit of falling, the only way that relative prices can change is for all prices to rise, but some more than others. If prices are inflexible downward, then normal market forces will set up a more or less perpetual tendency for the price level to float upward. . . .

. . . Labor-market experts agree that the pattern of relative wages—of differentials by skill level, by occupation, by industry—has an extraordinarily persistent life of its own. No doubt it corresponds in part to economic reality, and in part to strong feelings of equity and propriety in the workplace. Once disturbed, the traditional structure reasserts itself. But then consider a large and decentralized economy like our own, operating reasonably prosperously but not necessarily at very high pressure. There is bound to be a stream of occasions when some group in the labor force, somewhere, will succeed in getting a substantial wage increase. It may come about because a successful trade union is able to bargain its way to a notable victory, or because piece-workers are able to capitalize on a major increase in productivity, or because an expanding industry bids up wages in an effort to acquire labor. Such a local gain inevitably disrupts the traditional relativities, and sets in motion an attempt to restore them. Piecemeal, with timing depending on the expiration of contracts and other more or less extraneous factors, other wages will rise, and the traditional pattern may be further disturbed. Eventually, something like the old structure will be restored, but inevitably at a higher level of wages and, therefore, prices. It's the same story: The system of wages and prices accommodates to relative changes by floating upward.

WHAT IS TO BE DONE ABOUT IT?

. . . This analysis of contemporary inflation does not lend itself to a sweeping Solution. In fact, it suggests that there has been altogether too much leaping to Solutions without any clear understanding of the nature of the Problem. On close inspection, the social costs of ordinary inflation turn out to be mostly a matter of socially useless or harmful redistributions of purchasing power. Since there are straightforward ways of repairing that kind of damage if we seriously want to do so, it appears that most of the sweeping solutions that have been proposed—such as a prolonged dose of unemployment and underproduction, or universal and rigid price controls—are likely to be at least as costly to economic efficiency as the problem they are intended to solve. . . .

21

The Invisible Handshake
and the Inflationary Process

Arthur M. Okun

Arthur M. Okun, "The Invisible Handshake and the Inflationary Process," *Challenge,* Vol. 22, No. 6 (January-February 1980). © 1980 by the Brookings Institution, Washington, D.C.

Inflation has plagued the American economy and the economics profession throughout the decade of the seventies. Although the prospects for the economy over the near term are grim, I believe that developments within the profession are encouraging, and that they provide significant new insights into the inflationary process.

THE NEW EXPERIENCE
OF CHRONIC INFLATION

The economy's problems with persistent inflation date back to the mid sixties. But economists had no trouble explaining the inflation of the Vietnam period, which was clearly associated with excess demand. That experience fitted all our models, whether we were Keynesian, monetarist, eclectic, or erratic. We explained simply and succinctly that the price level rose because demand in the aggregate exceeded overall supply, just as the price of apples rose when the demand for apples exceeded the supply. The problems for economists emerged in 1970–71 when inflation persisted in the face of excess supply and survived a recession for the first time in the annals of U.S. business-cycle history. And they intensified with a vengeance in 1975–77, when after a severe recession, prices rose at a rate of nearly 6 percent a year while supply in the aggregate exceeded demand by all recognized criteria.

Chronic inflation that persisted in the

face of excess supply confronted economists with many problems of interpretation and explanation. Let me focus on one particular puzzle, which I regard as the critical observation of behavior in the inflationary era of the seventies. In millions of instances, we have observed nonunion employers with no contractual obligations granting general pay increases when they had abundant applicants, no vacancies, and negligible quit rates. Profit-seeking employers presumably try to minimize the payroll costs of obtaining the quantity and quality of workers they wish to hire. Why would those employers *raise* pay when their wage and salary scales were already evoking an excess supply of labor? How can that action at such a time make sense—regardless of how employers perceived monetary and fiscal policy or what rates of unemployment or inflation they expected for the future?

I submit that their behavior is sensible. The employers are in fact striving to minimize payroll costs, *reckoned over a substantial time-horizon.* They know that experienced workers deciding whether to stick with or quit their jobs in periods of prosperity evaluate those jobs in terms of the way the employer has treated them during periods of both tight and weak labor markets. Any management that holds down the wages it pays when most wages are rising must expect to be penalized when opportunities for good jobs become abundant. And so the calculations of firms are sensibly focused on quit rates and hiring requirements, not merely for today or tomorrow, but over a longer period, including intervals of prosperity and boom.

The firm finds it worthwhile to make an investment in personnel relationships; it seeks a reputation as a good employer to maintain an experienced and reliable work force for the long run. Thus the employer opts to treat the worker "fairly," invoking standards of relative wages (how other employers are adjusting pay) and real wages (how the cost of living is affecting the purchasing power of workers' incomes). And once the employer adopts and announces such a personnel policy, the workers are led to expect that their pay will reflect those criteria.

IMPLICIT CONTRACTS

This line of reasoning is called the theory of "implicit contracts": firms with no explicit contractual obligations nonetheless act, in the pursuit of long-term profitability, to fulfill certain general commitments to their employees. They are guided by an invisible handshake, as well as by Adam Smith's invisible hand.

This theory, which provides important insights that I will discuss, has had many fathers within the economics profession during the seventies. Had I been asked a decade ago to account for general wage increases in recession, I am not certain exactly how I would have responded. But I am quite certain that my answer would have deserved a failing grade. Of course, all economists recognized that overall pay increases in a very weak economy had occurred in the United States in the mid-thirties and in Brazil on many occasions. But such episodes were explained by special factors rather than by an appeal to sensible strategies of employers and workers.

In retrospect, I can see the theory of implicit contracts foreshadowed in some earlier writings—mainly by labor economists but also by some macroeconomists. But I must confess that I first became impressed with the phenomenon in 1970–71 as a result of some informal conversations with a number of owners and executives of small businesses. I remember one who had experienced declines in sales and profits, had cut back employment, and yet had raised the pay of his workers by 7 percent. He faced no union, saw no threat of unionization, had no need to recruit employees, and was not concerned about current quits. In response to my probing, he explained articulately that, as a conscious policy, he did not "take advantage" of his workers while he had the "upper hand" in the labor market and that he could count on their remembering his actions when the job market tightened. Others echoed the same theme. Some managers mentioned current morale and productivity as well as future labor supply. Whenever I have discussed these issues with business executives, I have been struck by their straightforward, matter-of-fact emphasis on their reputations as employers. Economic theorists have taken a little longer to recognize these considerations. But, after all, we have never met a payroll.

The implicit contract view embraces as a special case the Keynesian assumption of a floor under money wages. Clearly the firm that hires a worker with a career job in mind must lead him to believe that his position will gradually improve, not worsen. Once the firm paints a bright future in order to recruit the worker, any subsequent cut in wages would be a disappointment and a source of antagonism. Hence the firm is inhibited from reducing wages, as Keynes posited. In fact, in any economy where wages normally rise over time, the same inhibitions can also apply to hold-downs or even slowdowns in wages for employees who had been led to expect fairly steady raises.

The same insights also help to resolve puzzles about behavior in many product markets. In periods of boom, many firms that experience excess demand lengthen their backlogs of unfilled orders and some even place their customers on allocation quotas, clearly eschewing price increases that would enhance their current profitability. Their decisions not to exploit fully the potential short-term benefits of tight markets are the understandable result of a longer-run view of their relationships with customers. By forgoing king-size markups in tight markets, the sellers build a clientele

and establish a reputation that helps to retain customers when markets ease.

In many industries, firms feel obliged to justify price increases to their customers in terms of cost increases; they want to convince their customers that they are not exploiting a tight market to capture a larger share of the benefits from continuing relationships. And as the mirror image of that behavior in tight markets, these firms adjust prices in line with costs during periods of recession and slack, allowing percentage markups over standard costs to narrow only slightly. During recent recessions, prices in customer markets have not fallen; nor have they even been rigid or sticky. Rather they have kept rising, responding to the push of higher costs but resisting the pull of lower demands.

The cost-oriented pricing in product markets geared to customer relationships offers a dramatic contrast with the behavior of prices for products traded on auction markets. For the latter group, the traditional supply-demand model is confirmed beautifully. The prices of industrial raw materials, which are generally traded in organized commodity markets, fall in periods of recession. For example, they declined on average by 15 percent from a peak in May 1974 to a trough in March 1975. During that same ten-month interval, producers' prices of finished consumer goods other than food and fuel *rose* by 10 percent. Sellers in nonauction and auction markets alike experienced weak demand; they had essentially the same information about their costs and markets; the two groups presumably had similar expectations about the future course of the general price level and economic activity. Their prices behaved differently because they are set differently—one by an impersonal mechanism that equates supply and demand continuously and the other by a managerial strategy oriented strongly toward long-term customer relationships.

THE MICROECONOMIC ASPECTS

The theory of implicit contracts was developed by macroeconomists investigating various aspects of unemployment and inflation in the overall economy. But the theory has important microeconomic aspects, amending many traditional concepts of market efficiency. To be an effective mechanism, an auction market must have a large number of buyers and sellers competing for a standardized product that can be readily defined in terms of quantity and quality. Those requirements are met by products like soybeans, cotton, hides, and lumber, as well as by many financial instruments ranging from common stocks to foreign exchange. And those items are indeed traded through brokers or auctioneers who find the price that equates demand and supply. But that mechanism for making transactions would be abysmally inefficient for neckties, restaurant meals, haircuts, machine tools to produce bicycles, or blue Chevrolets with standard transmission and stereo but without air conditioning. Most important, the labor market cannot rely on an impersonal auction system, because jobs are specialized and the quality of workers cannot be objectively graded. The isolated cases in which hiring decisions are, in effect, made through brokers—for example, for office temporaries and snow shovelers—underline the nearly universal preference for the face-to-face, personalized transaction.

In the absence of the auctioneer, buyers and sellers must make transactions by search and shopping, which are costly activities. Pursuing rational strategies, they will not play at do-it-yourself auctioneering, but will aim to hold down those costs. Because of the high costs of finding a job and of obtaining a productive worker, continuing relationships in career jobs become worthwhile to both workers and employers in most industries. Because sellers in many product markets depend on sales efforts by employees or on shopping by buyers, the firms promote patterns of recurrent purchases, seeking to convert buyers into regular customers by establishing the reliability, predictability, and generally satisfactory character of pricing and services. Even when purchases are not recurrent, sellers strive to build a reputation whereby the satisfied buyer of the past passes a good word along to the potential buyer of the future. While the sellers are serving their own interests with such a strategy, they also improve the efficiency of the economy by reducing transactions costs. These customer and career relationships are efficient adaptations to the realities of a complex, interdependent economy; they should not be interpreted as evidence of some evil monopoly power.

In some cases, the relationships between buyers and sellers are expressed in written formal contracts that specify the obligations of the two participants to each other. But such explicit contracts have a limited scope because of the expenses of negotiating, formulating, and enforcing them, and because of the rigidity that they can impose on the parties. And thus, in many areas, the efficient way to do business is through understandings and conventions involving fair play and good faith. The participants act to facilitate recurrent transactions, but they do not assume legal contractual obligations. Each has an incentive to satisfy the other in order to maintain the relationship that is mutually beneficial.

The arrangements that people make for such continuing relationships take diverse and sometimes contrasting forms, which cannot be precisely predicted or, at this point, fully explained. For example, under the widely recognized implicit contract between large Japanese firms and their employees, the firm is expected to provide a steady job throughout the careers of the workers, regardless of the state of the business cycle. The employers thereby assume the risk of excessive payrolls during recessions but may obtain compensating benefits through greater loyalty or more moderate wage demands by their workers. In contrast, implicit and explicit contracts in the United States give the employer substantially more discretion over the amount of employment, with the result that mass layoffs are a standard feature of our recessions. Much research lies ahead to explain the rationale and the consequences of different types of implicit contracts.

Another challenging area of investigation concerns the issues of equity that implicit contracts bring into the workings of the private marketplace. Implicit contracts can be effective only in a social atmosphere that incorporates a sense of mutual respect and a consensus on principles of fair play and good faith. Equity is thus not an extraneous irritant imposed upon the market by political institutions, but rather a vital lubricant of market processes.

IMPLICIT CONTRACTS AND INFLATION

The implicit contracts governing wages and prices in many areas are a key reason why any sudden change in total spending has only a small initial impact on inflation and a correspondingly large initial impact on output and employment. Thus an overheated economy initially has a rosy glow from low unemployment rates, ebullient capital formation, and strong productivity growth. For example, during the boom of the late sixties, workers and firms in many sectors gladly supplied more labor input and more output with only moderate deviations of wages and markups above the path regarded as customary and satisfactory. The implicit contracts were in effect shaded, but they were not scrapped. And thus inflation was slow-starting in that prolonged period of excess demand. But for the same reasons, inflation was slow-stopping when demand weakened. In the recession as well as in the boom, output and employment were affected a great deal, but wages and prices only a little.

The slow-starting, slow-stopping nature of inflation has been evident to some degree throughout the era since World War II. Wages and industrial prices responded less sensitively to the business cycle than was the case earlier in our history, reflecting in part the growing role of implicit and explicit contracts. Indeed, the mildness of the postwar business cycle encouraged a longer-run emphasis in wage and markup decisions. During the fifties and sixties, most private behavior was adapted to a modest upward creep in the price level that yielded a secular average inflation rate of 1 or 2 percent, with recurrent cyclical bumps and dents around the trend.

In the seventies, that underlying belief in the long-term stability of the price trend was severely shaken by prolonged experience with rapid inflation. The notion of par-for-the-course on wage increases shifted upward. Thus a pay raise of 4 percent, which seemed decent and fair to a career worker in 1965, was inadequate and insulting in 1970 and has remained so ever since. Similarly, prices in customer markets became depressed relative to prices in auction markets, and have been subject to recurrent upward pressures. Business and labor practices were altered to depend less heavily on the stability of the dollar. Those changes have sped the transmission of cost increases into price increases through the system—with the institution of cost-of-living escalators; the abandonment or shortening of fixed periods for price-setting like the model-year pricing of automobiles; and the erosion of the willingness of sellers to accept orders with guaranteed prices at delivery.

In general, as people adapt to an inflationary world, they make inflation more rapid and more persistent. Any prolonged experience with an inflation rate well above the secular average to which the system has become adapted alters implicit and explicit contracts in ways that make the inflation feed upon itself. And that has been the continuing experience of the seventies in periods of weak demand as well as of strong demand.

Yet even today, Americans continue to depend heavily on the dollar as a yardstick and a standard. Our economy is not adapted to double-digit, or even to 6 percent, rates of increase in prices. If inflation is not brought under control in the near future, the eighties will be marked by even more indexing, further shortening of the lags in transmission of cost increases, and a continuing shift away from dependence on money in implicit and explicit contracts. And such adaptations would further intensify our inflationary woes.

THE COSTS OF INFLATION

Implicit contracts introduce new dimensions in the reckoning of the costs of inflation to society. First, even when added inflation stems from a general, economy-wide cause like an excessively stimulative monetary policy and even when it is reasonably predictable, various types of wages and prices respond differently. Auction prices outrun customer prices; escalated wages outpace other wages in career jobs; wages of workers in casual jobs are likely to rise more rapidly than most wages and salaries in career jobs. These changes in relative prices and wages serve no useful function as rewards or market signals; yet they reshuffle income among families. The redistribution is not primarily from rich to poor or from poor to rich; rather it takes the form of a lottery that renders prizes and penalties arbitrarily and inequitably.

Second, because inflation can feed on itself, an acceleration of inflation must increase uncertainty about the future course of inflation.

The record over time and across nations makes clear that, when and where the average rate of inflation is higher, the rate for any year is more variable and more volatile. And uncertain inflation generates a crawl away from money. In asset markets, deposits, bonds, and other fixed-dollar assets become less attractive relative to the time-honored inflation hedges like real estate, precious metals, and art objects. Yet these investments are inherently less liquid than monetary assets and subject to large transactions costs for buyers and sellers.

Finally, in job and product markets, the crawl away from money impairs the most important yardstick and means of communication in the economy. A nation that has learned to keep score in dollars on the fairness of implicit contracts, on balance-sheets and income-statements, and in planning for the future, gradually finds that its training has become obsolete. These developments impair significantly the sense of security and well-being of a society, even when they do not show up as a subtraction from real GNP.

THE FISCAL-MONETARY ARENA

This view of the inflationary process highlights the dangers of excessively stimulative fiscal and monetary policies that permit inflation to become established in the system and feed upon itself. Moreover, it suggests the need for a consistent and determined strategy to slow the growth of aggregate spending—that is, the dollar total of GNP. But it also underlines the high cost of a cure for inflation based solely on monetary and budgetary restraint. Unquestionably, such a cure is available: inflation can be halted by a policy of tight money and tight budgets maintained intensively enough and long enough. But the costs are extremely high. Because of implicit (and explicit) contracts, a restrictive policy will, for a considerable period, push down output and employment drastically in an effort to slow prices and wages. According to past experience, the current recession, or a deepening of that recession engineered by restrictive monetary and fiscal policies, will sacrifice roughly $200 billion of production for each point that it reduces the basic inflation rate.

A $1 trillion cure for chronic inflation is unthinkable. It would resurrect the dark days of the thirties and jeopardize the political and social viability of our market institutions. To be sure, some economists argue persuasively that a credible and consistent policy of demand restraint would reduce that cost. But it is impossible to predict with any confidence whether the resulting "discount" from the trillion-dollar figure would be 20 percent or 80 percent. If an anti-inflationary strategy relying solely on demand restraint is adopted on the basis of exceedingly optimistic estimates of its costs, subsequent disappointments could readily discredit and reverse the effort. An undiversified anti-inflationary program is an inefficient, high-risk strategy. Fortunately, there are ample opportunities for diversification.

PRICES AND THE PRICE LEVEL

In an economy with a significant network of implicit contracts, a jump in the price of any major product raises the price level, and indeed the inflation rate. That connection between particular prices and the price level does not exist in a world of universal auction markets, and that may be the most fundamental difference between the two worlds.

The jump in petroleum prices imposed by the Organization of Petroleum Exporting Countries this year offers a timely example of this distinction. Suppose that the budgetary and monetary dials are controlled in such a way that the dollar total of GNP is not altered by the OPEC action. In an auction world, the consequence of higher fuel prices would then be lower prices for most other things. In particular, the auctioneer in the labor market would ensure that money wages fell enough to keep supply and demand in balance, thus preventing the emergence of unemployment.

It can be true as well in the real world that, if more dollars are spent on petroleum, fewer will be spent on most other items. But the reduced spending on those other items, and particularly on labor, will reduce output and employment—not merely hold down wages and prices. At a given unemployment rate, there is no mechanism to slow wages. Indeed, they will speed up via the chain reaction from fuel prices to the consumer price index to cost-of-living escalators. Given a jump in fuel prices, a policy strategy of stabilizing dollar GNP must put people out of work, waste productive capacity, and discourage investment—including even investment in energy-saving projects and alternative energy sources. It pushes the economy in an inflationary and a recessionary direction at the same time.

The recessionary effects can be avoided if total spending is stimulated by monetary and fiscal policies. But then the inflationary consequences are exacerbated. In addition to the rise in the price level from higher oil prices, the nation is subjected to a prolonged increase in inflation operating through cost-of-living escalation of wages and higher import costs from a likely devaluation of the dollar. The dilemma is genuine. And, incidentally, the more that wages (and other contracts) are indexed to the cost of living, the worse that dilemma is.

The adverse effects of OPEC actions can teach us how to take actions for ourselves with favorable effects. The OPEC price increase is the equivalent of an excise tax imposed on the American consumer, and that quasi-tax can be neutralized by reductions in actual excise taxes—by cuts in state sales taxes or in federal payroll taxes on employers, which act in part as hidden sales taxes on consumers. Although it cannot repeal the higher real costs of oil, that neutralizing strategy can avoid the grim alternatives of accepting a recession or adding to inflation.

The lowering of indirect taxes can also help to counter the inflationary inertia that is now built into our implicit contracts. It can push down on consumer prices and have favorable secondary effects on wages. Various other cost-reducing measures can be used similarly to counter inflation without courting recession. For example, subsidies for low-income workers could substitute for the minimum wage; and acreage controls on farm products could be eliminated. In fact, in recent years, the nation has suffered self-inflicted wounds in the form of higher payroll taxes, much higher minimum wages, and renewed acreage controls. These have inflationary consequences in the real world of the American economy, although not in the hypothetical world of universal auction markets.

The linkage of prices and the price level applies even more broadly. Indeed, the discretionary price and wage decisions made by major American firms (and unions) affect the entire economy. By opting for the top of the relevant range in setting prices or wages, the private decision-maker acts as a mini-OPEC with the same inflationary-recessionary consequence. On the other hand, a decision on the low end of the range bestows upon society the benefit of less inflation and the opportunity for more growth. And so the whole nation is an affected third party when such private decisions are made.

These are macroeconomic examples of what economists have traditionally identified as "externalities"—effects on other parties stemming from a transaction between a buyer and a seller. Wherever important externalities exist, the market can generate an efficient outcome only if the costs or benefits of the bystanders are somehow incorporated into the reckonings of the decision-makers. To reflect the social benefits of certain private actions, we grant tax credits for the purchase of productive machinery and the employment of unskilled workers. The same reasoning establishes the social desirability in principle of tax-based income policies, which apply tax penalties or rewards to encourage restraint in wage and price decisions by reflecting the social benefits of such restraint.

Circumstances in the months ahead may provide a neat opportunity to institute a tax-based incentive for price and wage moderation. As one part of a tax reduction, which will probably be appropriate in 1980, investors in plant and equipment are likely to be granted the opportunity to depreciate their assets more rapidly for tax purposes. Such a stimulus to investment would brighten the outlook for productivity growth. But any anti-inflationary benefits it can provide are clearly limited and long delayed. Prompt and substantial anti-inflationary benefits could be obtained by linking major tax benefits of accelerated depreciation to compliance with the price and wage guidelines. Large firms should be required to exercise price and wage restraint as a condition for obtaining the full benefits of the faster writeoffs. The task of enforcing such a provision could be kept simple by imposing the requirement only on firms obtaining a tax reduction in excess of, say, $100,000. These large firms would file certificates of compliance with the Council on Wage and Price Stability, and that agency would be authorized to deny the validity of any certificate, subject to appeal in the courts. Such a measure would test in practice the ability of a tax incentive to help curb inflation, and it would couple the nation's urgent short-term need for price and wage restraint with its longer-term need for strengthened capital formation and improved productivity performance.

THE INVISIBLE HANDSHAKE

The recognition of the invisible handshake and of its role in the inflationary process highlights the many sources of inflation that go beyond excess demand and the many costs of inflation that go beyond short-term surprises. It reveals the inflationary consequences of value-added and sales taxes, and the dangers of the emerging general trend toward cost-of-living escalators and indexing. It corrects the fundamental errors of economic policy and economic analysis that stem from the assumption of universal auction markets. The hawks and the doves on inflation policy make the same mistake of modeling the American economy as a giant soybean market. The hawks then prove that price stability can be achieved readily by monetary policy alone; and, based on the same "soybean illusion," the doves proclaim that inflation, once it becomes anticipated, is not costly.

Implicit contracts help to explain why inflation is costly and why it is difficult to eliminate once it has become entrenched. But those institutions also create the opportunity for cost-reducing measures and tax-based incomes policies to help curb inflation, along with a consistent fiscal-monetary strategy to slow the growth of total dollar spending. Fundamentally, our economy is more efficient because it is guided by the invisible handshake as well as the invisible hand. And it will work even better when policy-makers and theorists recognize the implications for the cure of chronic inflation—in short, when they choose to act as wise owls rather than fierce hawks or passive doves.

22

Cost-of-Living Adjustment: Keeping up with Inflation?

Victor J. Sheifer

Victor J. Sheifer, "Cost-of-Living Adjustment: Keeping up with Inflation?" *Monthly Labor Review* (June 1979).

Escalator clauses gained prominence in 1948, when General Motors and the United Auto Workers negotiated what was then a long-term contract (2 years) calling for quarterly wage adjustments to offset price changes and stipulating annual pay increases to improve living standards. Since then, escalator provisions have been adopted in a number of industries, their popularity fluctuating over the years with the pace of inflation. This article examines the prevalence of escalator clauses and the extent to which they afford protection against inflation and compares the experience under contracts with and without escalator clauses.

Escalators provide for periodic automatic adjustments of wage rates based on movements in a specified price index.[1] Despite the interest cost-of-living adjustment (COLA) provisions have aroused, their overall coverage is relatively limited. A rough estimate is that 9 million workers currently have escalator protection, about 10 percent of nonagricultural civilian employment. The overwhelming majority of covered workers are unionized and, typically, are in large bargaining units. At the beginning of 1978, escalators covered 5.8 million (60 percent) of the 9.6 million workers under private nonfarm major collective bar-

[1] Escalator increases reported in this article exclude guaranteed minimum adjustments, which are treated as deferred increases.

TABLE 1

Wage Adjustment Provisions of Agreements Covering at Least 1,000 Workers

	Agreements	Workers Covered
All agreements	1,570	6,741,750
Escalator only	41	275,150
Deferred increase only . .	592	1,695,100
Reopening only	72	333,350
Escalator and deferred increase	518	2,742,000
Escalator and reopening	4	47,600
Deferred increase and reopening	139	497,500
Escalator, deferred increase, and reopening	131	956,300
No reference to wage adjustments . . .	73	194,750

gaining units (those covering 1,000 workers or more).

Of course, escalator clauses are not the only hedge workers have against rising prices. Under collective bargaining, anticipated and past changes in the cost of living can be considered when negotiating immediate wage adjustments. Furthermore, escalators rarely provide the sole wage adjustment mechanism during long-term agreements. In such agreements, price changes also can be treated through negotiating scheduled deferred increases and providing wage reopenings. Typically, COLA's are combined with deferred wage increases, as shown in the above tabulation of wage adjustment provisions based on the Bureau of Labor Statistics (BLS) analysis of 1,570 private sector agreements covering at least 1,000 workers and in effect on or after July 1, 1976 (Table 1).[2]

Although COLA coverage is limited, escalator increases are significant. In 1977, the average escalator increase in major bargaining units where clauses actually produced increases

[2] As would be expected, the relative frequency of the provisions varies by contract duration.

was 3.9 percent.[3] COLA yields accounted for 21 percent of all increases going into effect in 1977 in major bargaining units. Of course, no method of wage adjustment should be evaluated solely by its pay impact. Such aspects as relationship to contract duration and industrial relations stability also should be considered.[4]

Detailed knowledge of escalator clauses and their yields is largely limited to the major bargaining units. Discussion in the balance of this article is restricted to this group.[5]

COLA CONCENTRATION

At the beginning of 1978, the average major bargaining unit covered about 4,600 employees; those with COLA provisions covered about 6,800, and those without such clauses about 3,000.[6] Looked at in a different light, COLA provisions were in only 38 percent of the agreements for 1,000 to 4,999 workers, but in 78 percent of the agreements for 50,000 to 99,999 workers and in all contracts affecting 100,000 workers or more.

COLA provisions are concentrated in certain industries. Agreements in only four

[3] See Joan Borum, "Wage increases of 1978 absorbed by inflation," *Monthly Labor Review* (June 1979), pp. 10–13.

[4] See Joseph W. Garbarino, *Wage Policy and Long-Term Contracts* (Washington: Brookings Institution, 1962) and Jack Stieber, "Evaluation of Long-Term Contracts," in Harold W. Davey et al. eds., *New Dimensions in Collective Bargaining* (New York: Harper, 1959), pp. 137–53. In some contracts, cost-of-living changes trigger wage-reopening negotiations. Regarding the role of price changes in the arbitration of wage-reopening disputes, see Irving Bernstein, *Arbitration of Wages* (Berkeley and Los Angeles: University of California Press, 1954), pp. 35–39.

[5] A more detailed analysis, containing updated statistical material, is forthcoming from the BLS.

[6] Escalator adjustments apply to social security benefits and to Federal civil service and military pensions. To a limited degree, private pensions have been tied to the cost of living. This analysis, however, is limited to wage-rate escalation.

industries—transportation equipment, communications, motor freight transportation, and primary metals—accounted for 49 percent of all workers in the major bargaining units with escalator coverage on January 1, 1978. Similarly, only four unions—the Auto Workers, Communications Workers, Teamsters, and Steelworkers—accounted for 48 percent of the covered workers. Escalator coverage was relatively more common in manufacturing industries, where it covered 70 percent of the workers in major units, as against 53 percent in nonmanufacturing.

Significantly, coverage tends to be in pattern-setting industries—economic sectors that can better afford the uncertainty in labor costs introduced by escalator arrangements.[7] However, COLA provisions are relatively infrequent in construction—affecting only 9 percent of the workers in major bargaining units on January 1, 1978—where pricing patterns typically are more dependent on future pay rates.

Data for the major bargaining units show a higher incidence of escalators among long-term agreements. As of January 1, 1978, COLA clauses covered only 3 percent of the workers under 1-year contracts and 17 percent of those under 2-year agreements but 71 percent of those under 3-year pacts.[8]

Escalator clauses almost universally relate wage rates to changes in the BLS Consumer Price Index (CPI). About 90 percent of the workers are under clauses geared to the U.S. city average index, while the remainder—typically in smaller, local units—are affected by individual city indexes. Because both U.S. and Canadian workers are involved, the major automobile company contracts use an index derived by combining U.S. and Canadian national indexes.

At the beginning of 1978, only 208,000 workers—4 percent of those under major bargaining agreements with COLA—were covered by clauses specifying percentage wage adjustments. The bulk of the escalator clauses provided for uniform cents-per-hour adjustments, thereby tending to compress relative occupational pay differentials. However, hourly deferred adjustments increasing with wage levels countered this tendency in many of the contracts. For nearly 800,000 workers in units of the American Telephone and Telegraph Co., COLA clauses called for adjustments containing *both* percentage and absolute amounts.

ESCALATOR YIELDS TRAIL INFLATION

A basic question raised by the foregoing discussion is the degree to which escalator clauses afford protection against inflation. The 1948 GM-UAW escalator provided wage increases of 1 cent for each 1.14-index-point rise in the CPI. At then existing levels of wages and the CPI, this formula yielded pay adjustments proportionate to price changes. In 1959, Joseph Garbarino concluded that most of the COLA provisions of contracts then in effect "fully compensate for price changes."[9]

One could not reach this conclusion today. In the 10-year period 1968–77, the average annual escalator increase—for workers in major bargaining units where clauses resulted in pay increases—ranged from 1.6 percent in 1968 and 1969 to 5.8 percent in 1974. In no year did the increase match the CPI rise. The closest correspondence was in 1971, when

---

[7] Jules Backman, "Wage Escalation and Inflation," *Industrial and Labor Relations Review* (April 1960), p. 400.

[8] "Duration" is the time span from a contract's effective date to its expiration or reopening date, if any.

[9] J. W. Garbarino, "The Economic Significance of Automatic Wage Adjustments," in Davey et al., *New Dimensions in Collective Bargaining*, p. 162.

escalator increases were 91 percent of price changes; the lowest, 26 percent in 1969. A simple average of the annual escalator yields for the period is 57 percent.

In 1977, when the CPI rose 6.8 percent, escalator increases averaged 3.9 percent, ranging from less than 1 percent for 2 percent of the workers under clauses effective throughout the year to 7 percent or more for less than 1 percent of the workers. Significantly, 27 percent of the workers under these COLA clauses received no increase, primarily because no reviews took place during the year.[10]

Several factors contribute to the average COLA's less-than-full compensation for inflation:

1. *Formulas are insufficient to produce full compensation.* The most common formula—1 cent increase for each 0.3-point CPI rise—is relatively liberal.[11] (Among covered employees are those in the auto, steel, trucking, and railroad industries.) At the April 1978 level of the revised CPI for urban wage earners and clerical workers (191.4), such a formula would produce full compensation with a wage rate of $6.38 or less. However, in each of the 10 largest bargaining units with this formula, average straight-time earnings were greater, averaging $8.44. (Together, the 10 units covered 1,538,000 workers, about half of all workers covered under the 1-cent for 0.3-point formula.)
2. *Limits may be placed on the maximum COLA increase.* At the beginning of 1978, one-fourth of the workers in major bargaining units with escalation were affected by "caps" or ceilings on escalator increases. Average annual caps on wage increases over the contract term ranged from less than 1 percent to 6.1 percent, averaging 2.7 percent. The largest concen-

[10] Data in this paragraph are limited to COLA clauses effective throughout 1977.

[11] Other common formulas are 1 cent for each 0.4-index-point rise and 1 cent for each 0.3-percent rise.

tration of caps was in the railroad industry, affecting 469,000 workers. . . .

3. *Escalator adjustments lag behind price changes.* The significance of a lag, of course, is related to the pace of inflation. In the 1968–77 period, escalator yields were more than 60 percent only in the 4 years with diminished rates of price increase. While the lag effect on wage rates may be important in an individual year, the long-run impact is on aggregate purchasing power. The degree of lag depends largely on frequency of escalator review. As of January 1, 1978, 43 percent of covered workers had annual reviews (including those in trucking, communications, and electrical equipment); 39 percent had quarterly reviews (mainly metalworking); 15 percent had semiannual; and the balance had monthly, CPI triggered, or other periodicty. Of all workers covered, 51 percent were *not* covered by a review in the first contract year; only 1 percent were not covered in the second and 2 percent in the third. Primarily in Auto Workers contracts, a minor lag is introduced by using a 3-month average CPI rather than a single reference month.
4. *Escalator yields may be diverted.* Often, escalator yields are withheld, either permanently or temporarily, to finance supplementary benefits. About 1 million workers are so affected, most covered under Auto Workers' contracts.
5. *Escalators may not operate until a significant CPI rise occurs.* For example, contracts covering 100,000 Clothing and Textile Workers yield gains only for CPI advances of more than 7.5 percent in the second contract year and 6 percent in the third.

In addition, overall costs of escalator clauses are commonly curbed by not immediately including such payments in base rates, thereby possibly isolating benefit obligations from current COLA impacts. Conversely, periodically incorporating all or part of the COLA float into base rates curbs the downward flexibility of escalators, for wage reductions commonly are limited to the size of the float.[12]

One conclusion is inescapable: COLA provisions vary considerably, as the degree of protection afforded by a particular clause depends on the outcome of collective bargaining. Liberality of escalation is part of a settlement package—including other wage and benefit items—that reflects attitudes, skills, and power of the negotiators.

ESCALATOR VERSUS NEGOTIATED INCREASES

Anticipated and past price changes usually are considered in negotiating immediate and deferred wage adjustments. Hence, total wage-rate changes over the contract term could be the same with or without escalation. Remembering that escalator reviews are less frequent in the first contract year, it is notable that 1977 major settlements for longer than 30 months, with and without COLA, showed little difference in first-year negotiated adjustments, but second- and third-year gains were substantially larger without escalator clauses.

Other things being equal, bargained changes that anticipate price increases produce greater take-home pay; catch-up increases have the opposite effect, due to the lag involved. To compensate for wages eroded by inflation, negotiators frequently front-load settlements, which provide greater increases in the first contract year. The larger deferred increases in contracts without COLA's are more typical of the anticipation of *future* rises in the cost of

living.[13] However, negotiators may be conservative in estimating future price changes; between 1972 and 1977, major settlements of units without escalation coverage showed greater year-to-year variability in average first-year than in deferred increases.

The key issue, of course, is how overall wage gains compare, in timing and amount, between units with and units without COLA's. In major units concluding bargaining in 1977, prior negotiated wage adjustments averaged 5.9 percent annually over the contract term in units with COLA provisions in the expiring and renewed agreements and 8.3 percent in units without COLA in either contract. Adding COLA yields subsequently received, the total gain in the former group averaged 10.1 percent a year under the expiring contract.

One might have expected the unions without COLA coverage to seek to compensate in 1977 bargaining for this shortfall. However, the new average negotiated adjustments—4.9 percent annually in units with COLA's and 7.0 percent in units without—were in almost the same proportion as in the prior bargaining. Whether this result testifies to the wage impact of COLA clauses, is a reflection of conditions peculiar to the period studied, or stems from differing environments in the two sectors—which could in fact determine the incidence of escalation—is still an open question.[14] Findings of existing studies do not appear conclusive.

[12] The float is that part of the cost-of-living allowance not incorporated into base wage rates.

[13] See H. M. Douty, *Cost-of-Living Escalator Clauses and Inflation* (Washington: U.S. Council on Wage and Price Stability, 1975), pp. 33–38.

[14] It would be desirable to extend this analysis back over a series of contracts. The computer data base used for the tabulation is limited to information for 1974 and subsequent years.

23

The Puzzling Setback to Productivity Growth

Edward F. Denison

Edward F. Denison, "The Puzzling Setback to Productivity Growth," *Challenge* (November-December 1980) M.E. Sharpe, Inc., Armonk, N.Y.

The growth of American productivity was rapid by historical standards during most of the period following World War II. But in the latter half of the 1960s the rate began to slacken. Until 1974 this slackening was not particularly disturbing from the standpoint of long-term growth. It was partly the consequence of short-term fluctuations in determinants of output that typically display irregular movements, chiefly a drop in the intensity of use of employed labor and capital from a peak reached in 1965-66. The remainder resulted from developments that were inevitable or even welcome. The transfer of surplus workers from farming to nonfarm jobs, in which they produce output of greater value, diminished as the pool of such labor approached exhaustion. The proportion of inexperienced workers among the employed was boosted by great increases in the working-age population under 25 years of age, a rising ratio of employment to population in the young age groups, and the entry of many adult women into the labor force. Costs of regulations that the government presumably felt had benefits in excess of their costs began to impinge upon productivity.

This comfortable characterization of the productivity slowdown is not applicable to more recent years. Beginning in 1974 the situation became disturbing and also puzzling. The productivity trend turned far more adverse, and the influences responsible for the slowdown

226

prior to 1974 were no longer sufficient to explain the shortfall from the earlier trend. All the major productivity series—output per person employed, output per hour, and output per unit of input—show the same pattern of retardation.

My discussion will be organized by reference to output per person employed. The estimates I shall cite refer to the nonresidential business sector, which makes up more than three-fourths of the whole economy. I measure output by national income in constant (1972) prices.

In nonresidential business, national income per person employed, which I shall shorten to the rather wintry acronym NIPPE, increased by an average of 2.4 percent a year during the quarter century from 1948 to 1973—a total of 82 percent over the period. It then dropped for two years. Even after a recovery in 1976, NIPPE remained lower than it had been three years earlier; its 1973-76 growth rate was—0.5 percent a year. The detailed analysis of growth sources upon which I shall draw has been carried only to 1976, but it is evident that slow productivity growth has characterized the entire period after 1973, continuing to the present time. In 1977 and 1978, NIPPE increased barely more than enough to regain its 1973 level. 1979 was below 1978—or 1973. So over the whole six-year period from 1973 to 1979, NIPPE did not grow at all. I don't expect 1980 to be any better.

There seem to be three phases of productivity slowdown—a slackening before 1973; slow growth since 1973; and a sudden drop in 1979. Of the three, it is slow growth since 1973 that should concern us most. Slackening before then was not disturbing. The much publicized drop in 1979 probably resulted from a cyclical movement superimposed on a continuation or intensification of the bad performance of the preceding five years. Its main significance is that it further confirms the fact that we are

in an extended period of poor productivity performance that as yet shows no sign of abating.

Growth analysis is of limited use unless it is quantitative. For some time I have studied economic growth in advanced countries quantitatively by techniques that have become known as "growth accounting" or "sources of growth" analysis. The contributions, positive or negative, that were made to the growth rate by changes in a large number of output determinants are estimated. This is done for as many determinants as is feasible. The combined contribution of the remaining determinants is obtained as a residual.

The directly estimated determinants of nonresidential business output accounted for almost all of the *variation* in the rate of growth of NIPPE within the period from 1948 to 1973. But they explain only part of the subsequent decline in this growth rate.

One can think of the growth of national income per person employed as resulting from changes in the composition of labor, changes in working hours, changes in capital and land per person employed, and changes in output per unit of input, that is, in the output that is obtained from a given quantity of labor, capital, and land.

PRODUCTIVITY CHANGES, 1948–73

Before one can consider recent changes effectively, it is necessary to know what various determinants of output contributed to the growth of NIPPE in the past. From 1948 to 1973 the growth rate of NIPPE was 2.4 percent a year. Table 1 shows how that figure is divided.

There were changes in the composition of labor of two types. The first has to do with education. A person's education decisively affects both the kinds of work he is able to perform and his proficiency in any particular

TABLE 1

Sources of Growth of National Income per Person Employed,
Nonresidential Business Sector, 1948-1973 and 1973-1976

Item	1948-1973	1973-1976
	in percentage points	
Growth rate[a]	2.4	-0.5
Irregular factors	-0.2	0.1
Adjusted growth rate	2.6	-0.6
Changes in labor characteristics		
Education	0.5	0.9
Age-sex composition	-0.2	-0.3
Hours at work	-0.2	-0.5
Changes in capital and land per person employed		
Nonresidential structures and equipment	0.3	0.2
Inventories	0.1	0.0
Land	0.0	0.0
Improved allocation of resources	0.4	0.0
Legal and human environment	0.0	-0.4
Economies of scale from larger markets	0.4	0.2
Advances in knowledge and n.e.c.[b]	1.4	-0.7

[a] The growth rate from 1973 to 1979 was a small negative. Sources of growth are not available for this period.

[b] n.e.c.—Not elsewhere classified.

Source: Edward F. Denison, *Accounting for Slower Economic Growth: The United States in the 1970s* (Washington, D.C.: The Brookings Institution, 1979).

occupation. The educational distribution of employed persons moved steadily and strongly upward, and contributed an estimated 0.5 percentage points to the growth rate—over one-fifth of the total.

The other compositional change was demographic. Changes in the age-sex composition of the labor force subtracted 0.2 percentage points because the proportion of total hours worked by the most productive groups, particularly males 35 to 64 years of age, declined.

Changes in average hours at work also subtracted an estimated 0.2 percentage points from the growth rate in 1948-73. This is not an estimate of the growth rate of average hours, which was—0.5 percent, but an estimate of the net effect of changes in average working hours upon the growth rate of output, a different matter.

The contributions of capital and land result from changes in the amounts of inventories, nonresidential structures and equipment, and land that are used in nonresidential business, per person employed. The main points to note are that dwellings and governmental assets, which are not in the nonresidential business sector, are excluded, and that capital input is so defined and measured that changes in output resulting from advances in the design of capital goods are classified as contributions made to growth by advances in knowledge, not by capital.

From 1948 to 1973, inventories and fixed capital both increased more than employment, so that capital input per person employed rose. The contribution of capital to the growth rate of NIPPE was 0.4 percentage points. If this seems low, remember that part of the increase in the stock of capital was required just to keep capital per worker constant. The land available per worker declined as employment increased. This subtracted *less* than 0.1 percentage points from the 1948-73 growth rate, however.

Other growth sources affected output per unit of total labor, capital, and land input. First, improved allocation of resources contributed an estimated 0.4 points to the growth rate. Two types of changes in resource allocation are covered by this estimate. One is the reduction in the percentage of the labor used in non-residential business that consists of surplus labor in farming. The other is the reduction in the percentage of labor that is misallocated to nonfarm self-employment and unpaid family labor in enterprises too small for efficiency.

Second, the institutional and human environment within which business must operate has changed in several ways that adversely affect output per unit of input. The effect of three such changes has been estimated. New or strengthened governmental controls require business to divert from ordinary production to pollution abatement a growing share of the labor and capital that it employs, so that these resources are no longer available to produce measured output. Other controls have similarly diverted labor and capital to the protection of worker safety and health. In addition, rising crime has forced business to divert resources to crime prevention, and thefts of merchandise have directly reduced measured output. Important changes in these conditions began only toward the end of the 1948-73 period, and they are estimated to have subtracted less than 0.1 percentage points from the growth rate over that period as a whole.

Gains from economies of scale refer to the rise in output per unit of input that is made possible by changes in the size of the markets that business serves. Economies of scale are not limited to those internal to firms; specialization of all sorts, including production runs and larger transactions, is covered by my use of the term. Economies of scale are estimated to have contributed 0.4 percentage points to the 1948-73 growth rate, and thus they are an important source of growth.

Irregular fluctuations also affect output per unit of input. My estimates cover three types. Two—the effect of weather upon farm output, and the effect of work stoppages—are rather minor, but the third is often important. This is the effect of changes in the intensity with which employed labor, capital, and land are used as a result of fluctuations in demand. These changes are related to the business cycle, but swings in productivity usually run substantially ahead of those in total output or unemployment. The position was much less favorable to high output per unit of input in 1973 than in 1948, and irregular factors subtracted 0.2 percentage points from the 1948-73 growth rate.

The last source is the contribution of advances in knowledge and miscellaneous determinants. It is obtained, statistically, as a residual. As its title indicates, it has two main parts.

The contribution of advances in knowledge is, conceptually, a comprehensive measure of the gains in measured output that result from the incorporation into production of new knowledge of any type—managerial and organizational as well as technological—regardless of the source of that knowledge, the way it is transmitted to those who can make use of it, or the way it is incorporated into production.

The term "miscellaneous determinants" refers to a large number of determinants that can be specified but whose effects have either been estimated at zero or not quantified. The effects of the determinants included are believed to be small, and as a group they are as likely to be favorable as unfavorable, *in the 1948-73 period.*

The advance in knowledge was the largest source of increase in NIPPE from 1948 to 1973 unless I am altogether wrong in my judgment that miscellaneous determinants were not important in that period. The contribution of advances in knowledge and miscellaneous determinants is estimated at 1.4 percentage points in 1948-73.

In summary, important contributions to the growth of NIPPE in 1948-73 were made by advances in knowledge (1.4 percentage points), increased education of employed persons (0.5 points), increased capital per worker (0.4 points), improved resource allocation (0.4 points), and economies of scale (0.4 points). Reductions in average hours of work, shifts in age-sex composition, and irregular factors were the main negative sources, each subtracting 0.2 points from the growth rate.

THE RECENT PRODUCTIVITY SLOWDOWN

The growth rate of NIPPE fell from 2.4 percent in 1948-73 to –0.5 percent in 1973-76. This decline of nearly 3.0 percentage points occurred even though changes in three determinants were more favorable than in 1948-73. First, the contribution of education increased as the educational level of persons employed by business moved upward at an accelerated rate. Second, the drag of a fixed quantity of land was a trifle less than it had been in 1948-73 because employment increased less. Third, irregular factors made a positive contribution to the 1973-76 growth rate, whereas they reduced the 1948-73 rate. Together, these determinants would, in themselves, have *raised* the growth rate by more than 0.6 percentage points.

Other sources for which specific estimates are made would, in themselves, have taken nearly 1.5 percentage points off the previous growth rate of NIPPE, an amount that is equal to three-fifths of the earlier rate. Six groups of sources contributed to this amount. An accelerated reduction in average hours was responsible for 0.3 percentage points, a faster shift in age-sex composition for 0.1 points, and a slower increase in capital per worker for 0.1 points. Gains from the reallocation out of farming and nonfarm self-employment both disappeared, and this reduced the growth rate by 0.4 points. The three specified types of changes in the legal and human environment in which business operates—environmental regulation, worker safety and health regulation, and crime against business—cut the earlier growth rate of NIPPE by 0.4 points. Finally, gains from economies of scale were down by 0.2 points as growth of the economy slackened; this is a very crude estimate but there is no doubt that there was an appreciable reduction.

A drop of almost 2.2 percentage points from 1948-73 to 1973-76 appears in the residual series for advances in knowledge and miscellaneous determinants. After rising steadily until 1973, the series dropped sharply in 1974 and 1975, then in 1976 made only a normal gain from the lower level. The series has not been carried beyond 1976, but it is evident from other data that the behavior of the residual was little or no better for the whole period from 1973 through 1979 than it had been from 1973 to 1976.

Why the sudden change? It must be evident that I do not know why the residual collapsed; otherwise, I would have provided specific estimates for them and their effects would not remain in the residual. But the last chapter of my recent book for Brookings [*Accounting for Slower Economic Growth: The United States in the 1970s* (Washington, D.C.: The Brookings Institution, 1979).] evaluates, or perhaps I should say speculates about, 17 possible factors that others assert are the cause. Most of them could not reasonably be alleged to have come into play suddenly only after 1973 but I have included them anyway. I can do little more here than list the headings under which the suggestions are discussed. I cannot stress too strongly that the fact I list them does not necessarily mean that I believe they affected output per unit at all, much less that they were important.

It would be absurd to blame advances in knowledge, as distinguished from miscellaneous determinants, for the entire change in the path of the residual, but they could have contributed to it. Four of the seventeen suggestions would affect these advances. They are:

1. Curtailment of expenditures on research and development.
2. A decline in the opportunity for major new advances.
3. A decline in Yankee ingenuity and deterioration of American technology.
4. An increased lag in the application of knowledge due to the aging of capital.

Seven of the suggestions refer to alleged effects of government regulation and taxation. They include:

5. Diversion of input to comply with government regulation. Pollution abatement and worker safety and health are excluded here because I estimated their effects separately.
6. Government-imposed paperwork.
7. As the importance of regulation and taxation increased, the efforts of business executives were diverted from ordinary business affairs, including cost reduction, to dealing with government.
8. The delay of new projects by government regulation.
9. Misallocation of resources resulting from regulation and taxation.
10. The effects of high tax rates on incentives and efficiency.
11. The capital gains provisions of the Revenue Act of 1969. *The Wall Street Journal* editorialists took me to task for suggesting that this could hardly have been significant, but they did not convince me.

The five remaining suggestions fall into no general grouping.

12. "People don't want to work any more" and its variant, "Young people don't work like we did at their age." This is without any doubt the most popular suggestion for the recent poor productivity performance. But one must ask, is this something new?
13. Impairment of efficiency by inflation.
14. The lessening of the pressure of competition within business, and resulting deterioration in the quality of management. That there actually has been a decline in competition, I must note, is not well-established.
15. The rise in energy prices. This suggestion is appealing because the timing is right, and some analysts think higher energy prices affected output per unit of input importantly. However, most analysts suggest, I think correctly, that the effect on the growth rate did not exceed one-tenth of a percentage point.
16. The shift to services and other structural changes. This one, I believe, was not a factor at all.
17. Possible errors in the data. It would be comforting to be able to believe, as some do, that the whole productivity setback is a mirage caused by bad data, but in my opinion it unfortunately just isn't so.

None of these suggestions individually seems to me able to explain more than a small part of the decline. Perhaps we have been experiencing a situation where everything went wrong at once.

Two facts should be borne in mind as one seeks to explain the productivity slowdown since 1973. One is that the slowdown is very general among industries; it is by no means confined to special parts of the business economy. The other is that almost all industrial countries have experienced a sharp reduction in the growth rate of productivity since 1973. Rates abroad have remained positive, and in most cases appreciably above that in the United States, but in most foreign, industrial countries the reduction from the earlier rate has been even larger than in the United States.

What of the future? With such uncertainty concerning the cause of a large part of past productivity retardation, I am clearly not in a position to project the future. I might add that no one else is either. But each year that slow productivity growth continues makes it seem more probable that, whatever the causes, they are not transient developments but fundamental changes likely to last for some time. There may be only slight productivity growth in the next decade and we may have to face the implications of such a performance for living standards, inflation, and conflict over the division of a no-longer-growing pie.

24

Unions, Wages, and Inflation

Daniel J. B. Mitchell

From Daniel J. B. Mitchell, *Unions, Wages, and Inflation* (Washington, D.C.: The Brookings Institution, 1980). ©1980 by the Brookings Institution.

HIGHLIGHTS OF THE STUDY

The Extent of Unionization

. . . Unionization covers a distinct minority of the work force. Even with the well-publicized expansion into the public sector, the union share of employment has declined since the mid-1950s. The big growth period for unionization came in the 1930s and 1940s and was associated with a change in workers' attitudes and in public policy, galvanized by the Great Depression. Shifts in the composition of the labor force toward a service economy and toward the greater participation of women have been reflected in shifts in union membership patterns. But unions have not kept up with these trends. Unless there is another abrupt revolution in social attitudes, the relative decline in the unionization of the work force can be expected to continue.

Union representatives have stated that increased management resistance and the use of sophisticated legal and human relations techniques are major obstacles to increased unionization. Since the Wagner Act was passed in 1935, nonunion employers have unquestionably become more adept at using available legal channels to fend off union organization drives. But such explanations cannot be the whole story. There was strong employer resistance during the period of rapid union growth. And in recent years unions themselves have come up with some innovative tactics involving the exertion of financial leverage. However, with a given set of social background conditions, unionization efforts seem to realize diminishing returns. . . .

The Union Wage Premium

Measurement of unions' effect on pay levels has fascinated labor economists for many years. Most observers would agree that unions provide their members with services in the form of industrial jurisprudence. However, it hardly seems plausible that industrial jurisprudence is the only service rendered. Workers expect unions to provide them with higher wages and fringe benefits than they would otherwise receive. They are willing to bear the costs of strikes to back up their unions' demands. The gains might be illusory and wages might end up at the market level, but it seems unlikely that there would be no union wage effect.

The most widely cited estimate of the union-nonunion wage differential is the 10-15 percent reported for the 1950s in H. Gregg Lewis's celebrated study.[1] Economists were comfortable with this estimate because 10-15 percent does not seem large. It allows the observer both to acknowledge that unions have some effect on wages and to believe that classical influences set wages. However, the widening of the union-nonunion differential since the period observed by Lewis requires some boosting of this estimate. By the mid-1970s, 20-30 percent seemed a more likely range, especially for production and nonsupervisory workers.

Estimates of the type just described are usually made on the assumption that the union is an exogenous wage-raising influence. Of

[1] H. G. Lewis, *Unionism and Relative Wages in the United States: An Empirical Inquiry* (Chicago: University of Chicago Press, 1963), p. 193.

course, few economic institutions are truly exogenous, that is, totally uninfluenced by the economy they influence. While there is always the possibility that high-wage workers simply purchase more union services, creating the illusion of a union wage premium, this possibility is more beguiling than probable.

The interindustry pattern of unionization was established by the late 1940s. It grew from worker unrest in the depression, the resultant public policies that promoted collective bargaining, and World War II wage controls. For most workers, the choice is not whether to purchase union services but where to work. A blue-collar worker who finds himself in the automobile industry will almost certainly work under a union contract. A worker who takes a job in banking almost certainly will not.

There has been ample opportunity for union-nonunion wage premiums to change since the 1940s, but little opportunity for a change in the inter-industry pattern of unionization. Wages and unionization are not really simultaneously determined today. And models that assume simultaneous and continuous determination must be viewed with suspicion. They are sensitive to the precise specification of the simultaneous structure and can yield confusing and contradictory results. The simple exogenous models are more believable.

Wage Imitation

The observation that wages are often evaluated in terms of other wage rates has long been incorporated in industrial relations texts. This can be viewed as simply a peculiar feature of the labor market or as a rational response to decisionmaking under uncertain conditions. Where there are long-term employer-employee relationships, for example, neither party is likely to be in a position to define exactly what the relationship implies for the indefinite future or in all possible contingencies. A long-term commitment for fair treatment by employers—especially if a union is to police the commitment—requires some agreement on what is fair. Certainly, following what others are doing could be one definition of fairness. In the judicial setting, after all, the concepts of precedents and equal treatment are entrenched.

However, acceptance of the principle of wage imitation by labor-market analysis does not require acceptance of any particular model of how that imitation is accomplished. There are two main versions of wage-imitation models. In one version, units look at each other's wages and attempt to achieve target wage differentials. A world of mutual interaction in which everyone is watching everyone is potentially unstable; there may be no consensus on what the long-term wage differentials should be. This version suggests that an external spark such as a sudden increase in labor demand could set off a wage explosion like that in the construction industry in the late 1960s and early 1970s. Certainly, explaining the behavior of construction wages during that period would require reference to that type of wage imitation.

A second version involves one-way causal flows. In this version there are "key" wage determination units that set patterns for other units. The model can be based either on adaptive attempts to maintain wage differentials by follower units or solely on the wage increment. Either view suggests that the course of wage determination can be easily affected throughout the economy by manipulating a few wage-setting units.

Unfortunately, beyond the observation that wage changes across industries are highly correlated, it is difficult to distinguish one version of wage imitation from another. In fact, it is difficult to distinguish wage imitation from the tendency of wages throughout the economy to be influenced by common causes such as the rate of price inflation. For this reason, the wage-imitation concept is of greater use to practitioners of industrial relations than to those making economic policy. Policymakers should be cautious about building their strategies on the elusive wage-imitation concept.

The limited empirical evidence available suggests that there are spheres of wage imitation, which emanate from certain major-union contracts, and that deviations from the pattern are likely as the perimeter of the sphere is approached. Clearly, a multiplier effect should be attributed to certain union agreements: for instance, the contracts with the big three automobile companies affect workers outside those companies. But what is not known is the ultimate extent of the multiplier. Nor is it certain that key contracts significantly influence each other. Casual evidence suggests that they do under some circumstances but not under others. Imitation may take the form of making components of the compensation package similar to some other contract rather than following the other contract's absolute value.

Essential to wage imitation is a mechanism for spreading information about wages. Within a plant or other place of work, such information is likely to be readily available, especially where wages are set by union contract so that occupational wage rates are known to all members of the unit. Once industry lines are crossed, information is more difficult to obtain. Even here, however, there are potential channels of information. Some of the large unions cross industry lines, and large firms often have operations in several industries.

While cross-industry channels of information are available, the complexity of the information has increased. Fringe benefits are particularly hard to compare. There are many ways in which seemingly similar wage *rates* can hide differences in actual compensation. Units may appear to follow patterns while actually deviating from them. Even in the earliest studies of pattern bargaining, such deviations were reported.

Finally, it must be recalled that structures of wage imitation have been reinforced—and possibly created in some instances—during periods of wage control. This reinforcement was especially apparent during the controls of World War II and the Korean War. Any comprehensive program of controls will soon have a substantial caseload of requests for wage increases. It is administratively convenient for the authorities to group requests together according to some type of tandem-relationship criterion so that many cases can be handled with a single decision. Units seeking wage hikes have an incentive to produce evidence of links with units that have already received above-standard increases.

INFLATION AND WAGE DETERMINATION

Theories of inflation fall along a spectrum ranging from pure excess-demand models to structural explanations. The pure excess-demand view attributes price inflation to monetary and fiscal policies that raise the level of aggregate demand above the capacity of the economy to produce. Under such circumstances, prices are bid up as markets attempt to clear. Many variations of this view are possible. For example, some monetarists would deny that fiscal policy creates excess demand, except to the extent that budget deficits lead to monetary expansion. It is not necessary to assume that all product markets are perfectly competitive to believe in the excess-demand view. Even monopolies will raise prices continually if government policy keeps expanding demand.

In contrast, the structural view of inflation pictures general price increases as symptoms of a struggle between various interest groups over the distribution of income. If the sum of the claims on income made by all groups exceeds the actual income being generated at current prices, prices will rise. Such theories are more common among European than American economists and sometimes have a Marxist tinge.[2] They probably account for the fact that Americans refer to "wage and price control" and Europeans prefer the phrase "incomes policy." Incomes policy in Europe is frequently seen as a way of attempting to reconcile competing claims for income by persuading the major interest groups to accept a common agreement. Sometimes the structural view is supplemented by the idea that workers do not save enough so that wage increases lead to excess consumption and insufficient saving. When intended saving falls short of intended investment in the Keynesian model, the economy is stimulated. If the economy is operating near full capacity, such stimulation is inflationary.

The excess-demand view, with its emphasis on governmental monetary and fiscal policy, includes neither collective bargaining nor wage determination as a cause of inflation. Economic stimulation by government policy initially expands the demand for goods and services. A by-product of this first-round effect is the expansion of the derived demand for labor as employers seek to produce those goods and services. A combination of rising prices and growing excess demand for labor leads to wage increases. But the wage increases are seen as a result of inflation, not as a cause.

The structural view, in contrast, is compatible with a wage-push mechanism of inflation. Organized labor is seen as one of the aggressive interest groups, perhaps the most aggressive. European observers on the right and on the left have been able to agree on a wage-push mechanism, though with different moral

[2] See Daniel J. B. Mitchell, "Incomes Policy and the Labor Market in France," *Industrial and Labor Relations Review*, 25 (April 1972), p. 315.

interpretations. Those on the left interpret inflation as one of the perversities of capitalism; that is, when workers struggle to increase their wages to a "just" level, inflation is engendered, robbing them of their well-deserved gains. Those on the right may view wage demands as the work of left-wing union militants who do not understand the importance of an adequate profit level to finance investment and future growth.

The structural and excess-demand views can be reconciled by making monetary and fiscal policies endogenous rather than exogenous—if for political reasons these policies accommodate or rationalize wage demands, inflation will be unchecked.[3] In effect, the individual decisions of micro-level wage setters, when summed up, become the basis of monetary and fiscal policy. Those who make monetary and fiscal policy know that if they attempt to restrict demand to restrain inflation, increased unemployment and economic slack will result. According to this accommodating view, since recessions are not popular, the authorities resist causing them.

Applied to the United States, however, the reconciliation of structural and excess-demand views of inflation through a model of accommodation is not wholly satisfying. Monetary and fiscal policies have not always avoided creating recessions. Despite resistance to slamming on the aggregate-demand brakes, it is sometimes done. For example, in the recession of 1974-75 the unemployment rate was allowed to rise as high as 9 percent while industrial production dropped by 17 percent from its peak-to-trough value.[4]

Moreover, a look at the early 1960s, when prices were rising by well under 2 percent a year, suggests that collective bargaining is not incompatible with price stability. Thus theories suggesting that collective bargaining or wage determination or pressure from interest groups spontaneously generates inflation must be approached with caution. The politicization of income distribution found in some European countries is less of a factor in the United States. Inflation is usually the cause of such politicization rather than the result.

To explain the initiating cause of inflation in the United States, an excess-demand theory is crucial. The buildup of inflation in the late 1960s was certainly a demand phenomenon. In fact, collective bargainers at first failed to appreciate the trend in price inflation and permitted their wage decisions to lag behind the more responsive nonunion sector, making it difficult to construct a wages-were-the-villain model for that period. But the excess-demand view alone is not entirely satisfactory. Experience in the mid-1970s showed that exogenous pricing elements—crop shortages, oil cartels, and dollar devaluation—could substantially affect overall price changes. Those who relied on a demand approach alone greatly underestimated the acceleration of inflation that began in 1973, when exogenous pricing elements began to play a major role.[5]

If the initiating causes of American inflation are mainly monetary and fiscal policies and occasional exogenous price shocks, wages

---

[3] John R. Hicks, "Economic Foundations of Wage Policy," *Economic Journal*, 65 (September 1955), p. 391, described the shift toward accommodative monetary policy as a move from the gold standard to the "labour standard."

[4] The unemployment rate (seasonally adjusted) peaked at 9 percent in May 1975. Industrial produc-

tion fell 17 percent between September 1974 and January 1975 despite the resumption of work after a coal strike ended in December. Bureau of Economic Analysis, *Business Statistics, 1977* (Government Printing Office, 1978), pp. 19, 69.

[5] Commodity inflation was estimated to account for 45 percent of the rise in the consumer price index in 1973. Joel Popkin, "Commodity Prices and the U.S. Price Level," *Brookings Papers on Economic Activity, 1:1974*, p. 256.

might appear to play little part in the process. This is because the analysis so far, like much of the literature on inflation, has been concerned only with finding initiating causes, and wage determination is not one of them. But it is an important element in explaining the perpetuation of inflation. The wage-price spiral is not a figment of some editorial writer's imagination; it is very real and flourishing in the modern American economy.

It is difficult to stop inflation once it has started. On the basis of past experience, wage setters have every reason to suspect that inflation will continue. In writing long-term contracts, they will therefore extrapolate from the past for the future. Even in the nonunion sector—where annual wage determination is common—current price changes will play a role in determining current wage changes. If inflation has been accelerating so fast that past estimates of inflation turn out to have been too low, wage decisions will include catch-up elements as well as trend extrapolations. In short, ongoing inflation tends to go on, and accelerating inflation tends to accelerate. Monetary and fiscal restraints can be applied to slow the process, but wage determination as a whole is not very sensitive to economic slack and in the major-union sector is even less sensitive. Monetary and fiscal restraints will help inflation only over an extended period; at first they will affect only some wages and prices. As these first-round effects filter through into general reductions of the rate of price inflation, they will have a wider effect on wage determination. As the wider effect filters through into price determination, further wage restraint will follow. But the time needed to attain some anti-inflation goal may stretch into years.

The monetary and fiscal authorities may be willing to resist political pressure to avoid recession for a time, but the longer the time required to attain a given goal, the greater these counterpressures will be. If the restraints work only gradually and if their effect can be easily masked by exogenous price shocks, the time available for monetary and fiscal restraint to achieve the goal may be shorter than is necessary.

DIRECT INTERVENTION IN WAGE SETTING

Beginning with World War II, there have been three episodes of formal wage and price controls and two episodes of "voluntary" wage-price guidelines. Between these episodes were periodic vague calls for restraint or ad hoc interventions in particular wage or price decisions. All of the formal episodes have certain common elements such as administrative problems and public relations. All were instituted because it was believed that monetary and fiscal policy alone would not achieve economic objectives in an efficient (least-cost) manner. But there were significant differences between the direct intervention programs as well.

The General Issue

The wage-price controls of World War II were part of a general effort to allocate resources to military needs. In principle, a system composed only of monetary and fiscal restraint and taxes on nonessential products can be imagined, but in a wartime emergency it is difficult to find the correct combination of general and specific taxes and monetary policy to carry out the required allocation of resources. So a system of quantitative allocation, rationing, and direct wage-price controls was used. The policy worked in that the war was won and inflation was checked during the war. But it did not result in stable prices in the immediate postwar period.[6]

---

[6] Consumer prices rose 8.5 percent in 1945-46 and 14.4 percent in 1946-47. Bureau of Labor Statistics, *Handbook of Labor Statistics, 1975–Reference Edition* bulletin 1965 (GPO, 1975), p. 316.

The controls in effect during the Korean conflict were more modest because the economic resources devoted to the military effort were smaller in proportion to overall economic activity. Inflation restraint rather than resource allocation was the major emphasis. Although the Korean War program is often viewed as ineffective,[7] once controls were fully in effect, consumer prices were quite stable, and when the controls were lifted, prices did not leap upward. The period immediately after the controls ended was one of stable, even falling, prices, which contradicts the conventional wisdom that bubbles of repressed inflation explode when controls are lifted.[8] From an anti-inflation viewpoint, therefore, the economic policy that accompanied the Korean conflict was "successful."

Wage-price guideposts during the early 1960s operated in a period of economic expansion after a period of economic slack. The surge in aggregate demand that accompanied the Vietnam military buildup led to the program's demise in early 1966. However, an interesting "what if" question remains. Had excess-demand pressure been checked, so that the economy continued to operate at about the 1964 level, would the guideposts have contributed to restraining inflation and prolonging the expansion? The fact that union wage adjustments did not fully anticipate the rate of inflation in the mid-1960s suggests that inflationary expectations had not been allowed to develop.

Much the same question could be asked about the 1971-74 controls. Like the earlier guideposts, they were established in anticipation of a recovery from a period of economic slack. In part it was hoped that the controls would persuade wage and price setters to reflect the slack more fully in their behavior. The inevitable catch-up wage increases left over from the late 1960s could be labeled special cases so that they would not contribute further to inflationary expectations. And the controls of Phase II (November 1971-January 1973) did seem to have a calming effect.[9] However, in retrospect demand policy seems to have been excessively expansionary in 1972. More important, exogenous food, oil, and devaluation price shocks destroyed the program as the authorities vainly sought to hold back an engulfing tide of inflation. Again the "what if" question arises. Suppose that demand policy had been less expansionary in 1972 and that there had not been crop shortages and the 1973 war in the Mideast. If under these circumstances the administration had gradually removed the Phase II controls,[10] would expectations about inflation have remained sanguine?

[7] Mills states that the Wage Stabilization Board "had little if any discernible effect in controlling wages" and that "price increases were generally allowed ... to offset the wage increases." Daniel Quinn Mills, *Government, Labor, and Inflation: Wage Stabilization in the United States* (Chicago: University of Chicago Press, 1975), p. 36.

[8] Consumer prices rose 0.5 percent from 1953 to 1954 and fell 0.4 percent from 1954 to 1955. Bureau of Economic Analysis, *Business Statistics, 1977*, p. 229.

[9] For example, the use of escalator clauses did not increase during Phase II despite regulations encouraging them. Nor was there a wage bulge when Phase III began despite the virtual decontrol of most smaller wage-setting units. See Arnold R. Weber and Daniel J. B. Mitchell, *The Pay Board's Progress: Wage Controls in Phase II* (Washington: Brookings Institution, 1978), pp. 368-72; and Arnold R. Weber and Daniel J. B. Mitchell, "Further Reflections on Wage Controls: Comment," *Industrial and Labor Relations Review*, 31 (January 1978), p. 157.

[10] The actual shift to Phase III was abrupt, apparently because administration officials feared that the Pay Board and the Price Commission of Phase II were becoming entrenched. In view of the general public suspicion of both agencies, this fear is difficult to understand. However, the abrupt shift led to confusion about the degree to which controls were still in effect, aroused apprehension that the authorities were no longer trying to stop inflation, and probably hastened the dollar devaluation. Thus the shift from Phase II was itself inflationary. On the administration's motives, see George P. Shultz and Kenneth W. Dam, "Reflections on Wage and Price Controls," *Industrial and Labor Relations Review*, 30 (January 1977), pp. 143-44.

In general, economists oppose wage-price controls and guidelines because they "create distortions" and because they "don't work." Seldom are these verdicts based on detailed analyses or even on the right questions. Controls and guidelines do create distortions, although these are usually concentrated on the price side of the program rather than the wage side. It is clear that these distortions mount up in time, however, so that the controls, or intervention, option can only be considered on a temporary basis.

The important question about controls or guidelines is whether they can dampen inflationary expectations quickly enough to avoid heavy costs of distortion. In any event, the distortions argument cuts both ways. Monetary and fiscal restraint also creates distortions. The distortions of controls and guidelines tend to be in the form of shortages, those produced by monetary and fiscal restraint to be excess supplies and under-utilized resources (including labor). Most monetarists will attribute the depression of the 1930s to the improper use of monetary policy, but they do not draw from that monumental distortion the conclusion that monetary policy should not be used,[11] or that monetary policy inevitably entails mistakes that cause depressions. Rather they conclude that monetary policy must be used correctly. Surely the controls and guidelines options should be afforded the same benefit of the doubt. If applied, direct intervention should be used correctly—that is, briefly and with the specific aim of checking the wage-price spiral during periods of moderate or slackening demand.

A permanent system of wage-price controls would ultimately turn the economic system into a bureaucratic, centralized regime

[11] Milton Friedman and Anna Jacobson Schwartz, *A Monetary History of the United States, 1867-1960* (Princeton University Press for the National Bureau of Economic Research, 1963), chap. 7.

in which commodity rationing, with all the inconveniences and costs entailed, would become the normal state of affairs. Most people would find this highly undesirable. Even voluntary guidelines operated over an extended period could produce extreme economic rigidities. If controls or guidelines are used for transitional purposes, they must be administered flexibly. They should not be expected to hold back the consequences of excessive aggregate demand stimulation or to prevent exogenous price shocks from affecting consumer purchasing power.

Past programs of controls or guidelines make it clear that the implicit emphasis in direct intervention programs is on the wage side. The point of effective control is a wage standard expressed in absolute terms: 3.2 percent, 5.5 percent, 7.0 percent. Prices are generally subject to cost-pass-through rules of varying stringency. But since labor is a large element in total aggregate costs and since most prices are simply costs to producers at later stages of production, restraint of prices is primarily conditioned on restraint of wages. This is not because wages are the villain and prices the victim, but because wages are easier to define administratively and the labor market is less subject to distortion. A rule that prices should increase by no more than 3.2 percent would have quickly resulted in product shortages, even in the early 1960s. The same type of rule applied to wages did not have that effect on the labor market.

Numerical Guidelines

When interventions in the labor market are undertaken, various approaches can be used. As noted above, a general numerical standard for wage increases has been the practice in recent programs. Although the number chosen may be rationalized in various ways, such standards perform several common functions.[12] Increases below the standard are permitted with little or no review. Unless the standard is set far below the going rate of wage increase, many increases will be automatically allowed, reducing the difficulty of administration. A numerical standard—although it may be encrusted with exceptions . . .—is a simple concept. Because it is easily understood, it facilitates compliance. Finally, a numerical standard can be viewed as a suggested norm. It suggests to the parties that they should look beyond last year's price increase (or average wage increase) for a guide to their behavior. It gives them a new number to think about. If the wage standard is not too far from what the parties might otherwise have chosen and if they are convinced that the program will slow inflation, the guideline can calm inflationary fears.

A wage guideline has the virtue of applying to every unit. It does not single out—as some informal jawboning efforts have done—a few wage determination units as pattern setters for everyone else. A deliberate focus on a few units alleged to be key contracts is presumably based on a theory of pattern bargaining. But not enough is known about wage imitation to justify this type of approach. There is no guar-

[12] For a discussion of the rationales (productivity, cost-of-living increases, and so forth), see D. Quinn Mills, "The Problem of Setting General Pay Standards: An Historical Review," Industrial Relations Research Association, *Proceedings of the Twenty-sixth Annual Winter Meeting* (Madison, Wis.: IRRA, 1974), pp. 9-16.

antee that a domino theory of the labor market (affect one unit, affect them all) would work in actual application. In contrast, a broadly applied numerical guideline does not depend on any particular theory of wage imitation.

Another form of intervention could be case-by-case reviews of requests for wage increases without the application of a specific numerical standard. The authorities might have a numerical target in mind for the average settlement but would not seek to apply it in any particular instance. This approach, which was tried during the 1971-74 controls program in selected sectors, rests on the theory that distortions in wage relationships must be removed before wage inflation can be slowed, and it assumes that the authorites intuitively know what stable wage relativities should be. Beyond this, the case-by-case approach presents severe administrative problems. A theory of distorted wage relationships suggests that all wage setters, even the very small ones, should be included. This would make the potential caseload in such a program enormous if it were applied at the economywide level. World War II controls resembled this type of intervention but involved a complex network of industry and regional wage review boards and a large accompanying bureaucracy. Except in national emergencies on the scale of World War II, public support for such economywide efforts would be doubtful. If economywide programs of controls or guidelines are considered, the choice is likely to be a numerical standard or no program at all.

25

The Costs of Controls

William Poole

William Poole, "Thoughts on the Wage–Price Freeze," *Brookings Papers on Economic Activity*, 1971-72, Arthur M. Okun and George L. Perry, eds. © 1971 by the Brookings Institution.

. . . The economists who favor controls generally do so with the idea that they are a lesser evil than inflation accompanied by unemployment. The controls issue is more one of differing empirical judgments about benefits and costs than of differing doctrinal viewpoints. While economists give different weights to various aspects of their ideals of "the good life," most cherish the maximum possible freedom for economic decisions, a reduction of which is one of the costs of controls. But individual decisions, of course, ought to be taken within the context of the full employment economy necessary to provide genuine choices among job opportunities and among investment opportunities, as well as the stable incomes and goods required for a widely shared prosperity. . . .

. . . Controls incur three different types of costs. The first is the loss of individual freedom resulting from central control over individual wage and price decisions. The second is the misallocation of resources resulting from controls. And the third is the administrative cost. All these costs are interrelated. For example, if administrative cost is kept low, enforcement of the controls will be weak and will have relatively little effect after a time. Also, it is obvious that the costs of controls are a function of their duration.

The resource allocation and administrative costs of controls are not likely to prove great if the controls last for at most several years, especially if they are of the mild variety and really "buy" lower unemployment and greater price stability. In any event, a rich society can bear these costs. The important issue concerns the costs in individual freedom and the way in which they affect the nature of controls that are politically acceptable. The question is whether temporary mild controls will make any lasting contribution to the goals of full employment and price stability. . . .

Several examples may serve to amplify the hitherto vague references to "individual freedom." These examples should not be taken to concern "mere details," for one of the major arguments against controls is that there is no satisfactory way of handling these details. To consider the problems of enforcing wage controls, suppose that a firm wants to increase the pay of an employee to a level above the controlled level, perhaps because he is threatening to take a job with a competitor. An obvious technique is to promote him—indeed, so obvious that one of the first clarifications issued during the current freeze was that wages could be increased only in the event of a "bona fide" promotion.

What is a "bona fide" promotion? One approach is not to allow promotions into newly created positions. A firm is not permitted to create new vice presidents, or new foremen, or new senior accountants just to have more higher paying slots to put employees in. But clearly this approach to wage control cannot last very long since many firms have valid reasons for creating new positions.

What criteria can the controllers then use to distinguish between bona fide and control-avoidance promotions? Beyond the cases where the issues are clear-cut, many problems will arise, for example, in connection with corporate mergers and reorganizations. To offer another example, how does a government official know how many foremen are needed in a new plant producing a new product?

Comprehensive wage control is no easy matter. Many arbitrary decisions must be made. Wage control will be relatively easy and most complete over standardized types of jobs, including most blue collar and clerical jobs. Managerial and professional jobs, on the other hand, are more varied and more subject to change. The inequities will multiply, and so will the pressure for a more and more elaborate control machinery to limit the inequities by adjusting wages and salaries.

To obtain wage increases some individuals will be forced to change jobs because one firm, though willing, is not permitted to grant an increase in pay, while another obtains permission for a new position, or has a vacancy in an existing position. Excessive job changing is not only inefficient but also tends to break down wage control. To combat this tendency, controls may be imposed on job moves, or directly on the pay of individuals rather than of jobs.

Price control presents problems that are just as serious. How is the price on a new product to be determined? To set the price on the basis of the firm's cost requires the perhaps expensive attempt to understand its cost accounting methods. To set it equal to that of the closest competitive product is unsatisfactory if the new product costs more to produce but has superior characteristics that are not permitted to bring a higher price, or if it has roughly the same performance characteristics but costs less to produce. In the latter case the cost savings are not passed on to the purchasers of the new product.

Another problem arises when firms face cost increases, some of which in practice will prove unavoidable. Is a firm to be permitted to pass these increases on in the form of higher prices? If not, what happens if the firm simply stops production of an unprofitable item? Will a firm be forced to continue production of an item "vital to the national interest"? If cost increases on "vital" products, however defined, are considered a valid reason for price increases, how many officials will be required to administer the price controls?

Product specifications are constantly changing, sometimes reflecting improvement, sometimes deterioration. In comprehensive price control firms have an obvious incentive to reduce the quality of their goods and services. If the inflationary pressures to be suppressed by controls are powerful, control over product specifications will be required.

Although economists disagree as to the severity of these problems, they acknowledge their existence and believe that they will become more apparent with time. As problems appear, some economists will call for an escalation of controls, while others, like me, will argue that there is no natural end to the escalation of controls. How can these administrative problems be handled without a large bureaucracy? Only administrative guidelines that permit individuals, firms, and control administrators to know what changes in wages and prices, and in job and product specifications, are and are not permitted could make a small bureaucracy feasible. I do not believe such guidelines can be constructed, and, if these matters must be handled on a case-by-case basis, will not the sheer volume of cases overwhelm the control bureaucracy? Will the decisions by controllers be subject to legal appeal, and if so what is the case load likely to be? . . .

STRUCTURAL REFORMS AS AN ALTERNATIVE TO CONTROLS

. . . A strong case can be made for attacking some of the structural causes of high prices and excessive unemployment. It should be emphasized that the word used here is "high" and not "rising." Structural deficiencies in the economy raise the level of unemployment consistent with stability in the rate of inflation, but do not by themselves cause the inflation. But while structural reforms were being put into effect the result would be downward pressure on some wages and prices. This transitional effect would be most welcome, given the present public concern over inflation, and would help to generate support for the reforms.

Steps could have been taken—through executive action where possible and submission of new legislation where necessary—in at least the following areas: (1) modification or elimination of minimum wage laws; (2) modification of the tax laws to provide for the inclusion of all corporate profits rather than dividends alone in the definition of personal taxable income of common stock shareholders, in order to encourage increased dividend payouts and discourage corporate agglomerations, (3) antitrust action leading to dissolution of large firms in excessively concentrated industries; (4) elimination of farm price supports to reduce the cost of food; (5) elimination of regulation of transportation fares and rates; (6) elimination of tariffs and quotas on imported goods and services; (7) strengthening of retraining programs and employment services, perhaps including subsidies to encourage migration out of labor surplus areas. This list could no doubt be extended, but it is long enough to give the flavor of the reforms I would favor.

At the same time, to ease the burdens of unemployment, unemployment benefits should be extended and the welfare reform program enacted. In addition, temporary adjustment assistance should be provided to cushion the impact on individuals and firms unduly affected by the structural reforms proposed above. . . .

These structural reforms discussed above would generate much political opposition. For this reason many will dismiss them as the equivalent of a "do nothing" program on the grounds that they could never be enacted. I am not optimistic about the chances for large-scale structural reforms, but I believe that some of them might be enacted, given the mood of the nation.

It is a mistake, I believe, to think that controls will be politically viable for very long. Most people seem to believe that controls will be more effective on what they buy than on what they sell. My prediction is that the problems with controls will become more and more apparent as time goes on, that mild controls will prove ineffective, and that comprehensive controls will have less long-run political viability than structural reform. . . .

Protective Legislation

In an effort to protect workers, labor markets are subject to several kinds of governmental regulations. Prior to the 1930s, state governments played the largest role, with much of the regulation designed to protect women and children. During the depression of the 1930s, the federal government expanded its responsibilities, especially with regard to union-management relations and the regulation of wages and hours. The Social Security system was also established in this period. In the last two decades, the major developments have been new federal efforts to reduce labor market discrimination and to improve occupational safety and health.

In this section we focus on four aspects of protective legislation: occupational health and safety, equal employment opportunity, minimum wage rates, and income security. Other topics, covered elsewhere in this volume, include wage-price controls and government regulation of unions.

One of the more controversial government programs of the past decade has been the Occupational Safety and Health Act (OSHA) of 1970. The selection by Murray Weidenbaum discusses some of the difficulties that have arisen in the government's effort to reduce health and safety hazards on the job.

Another controversial area has been the equal employment opportunity policies of the federal government. The selection by Barrett, presented in Section II, outlines the legislation and executive orders in this area, especially as they apply to women. Ever since the Civil Rights Act of 1964 outlawed discrimination by employers on the basis of sex, race, or national origin, the courts have become heavily involved in determining when such discrimination exists. Harriet Zellner and Beth Niemi discuss the role of the economist in such litigation.

Much protective legislation has attempted to reduce poverty and economic insecurity among workers. To the noneconomist, one obvious way to reduce the poverty resulting from low wage rates is through minimum wage legislation. Economists have generally been critical of this approach on the grounds that low-skilled people would find fewer jobs available. Finis Welch reviews the theory and empirical evidence available on the employment effects of minimum wage legislation. He also discusses some of the current policy questions, including the issue of a lower minimum wage for youths than for adults.

While minimum wage legislation is designed to improve the earnings of low-wage workers, much protective legislation is designed to cushion income losses suffered by workers. The Social Security Act of 1935 provides many forms of such protection, including unemployment insurance and retirement income. Daniel Hamermesh discusses our present unemployment insurance program and presents suggestions for making the program both more equitable and more efficient.

The social insurance program with the largest expenditures—and probably the greatest political support—is the retirement component of Social Security. Despite the general success of this program in protecting workers and their families from poverty in their old age, Social Security is facing some important issues. Robert Lampman discusses the evolution of this program, with emphasis on the financing problems that are expected as the elderly become an increasing percentage of the total population.

The overall income support system in this country is discussed in the selection by Irwin Garfinkel and Stanley Masters. These authors show how our income maintenance programs—and recent efforts to reform them—have been influenced by concern for effects on the labor supply of beneficiaries. In this context, they discuss estimates of the labor supply effects of income transfer programs, giving special emphasis to the evidence from recent income maintenance experiments.

26

Four Questions for OSHA

Murray L. Weidenbaum

In examining the role of the U. S. Occupational Safety and Health Administration, it may be helpful to focus on four key questions. (1) Has OSHA carefully examined the basic causes of job-related illnesses and accidents? (2) Has OSHA carefully examined the alternative ways of reducing job-related illnesses and accidents? (3) Has OSHA carefully chosen the most effective ways of reducing job-related illnesses and accidents? (4) Has OSHA had a significant impact in reducing job-related illnesses and accidents?

. . . The answer to all four of the questions, in my judgment, is a simple and straightforward "no." We must acknowledge that, despite the importance of the task and the magnitude of the resources devoted to it, the OSHA approach has not worked.

According to the Bureau of Labor Statistics, days lost due to work-related injuries have been rising since OSHA started. Days lost rose from 51 per 100 workers in 1973 to 60 in 1977, a rise of 17 percent. More recent statistics are far from reassuring. Fatalities rose 20 percent, from 3,940 in 1976 to 4,760 in 1977. The number of reported occupational injuries and illnesses rose from 5.0 million in 1975 to 5.2 million in 1976 to 5.5 million in 1977. The rate of job-related illnesses and accidents rose slightly, from 9.2 per 100 workers in 1974 to 9.3 in 1977. It is these sad statistics, rather than green eyeshade analysis of dollar amounts, that are the heart of the economist's dissatisfaction with OSHA.

What OSHA has done is to provide cartoonists, columnists, and comic strip writers with a seemingly endless supply of raw material for poking fun at bureaucratic nonsense. Unwittingly, to be sure, the performance of OSHA has not only inhibited its effectiveness in achieving its mission, it also has badly hurt the image of regulatory agencies as a whole. You or I may or may not think that is fair, but it is the truth.

We hear so much about Kepone. That truly was a sad case. But where was OSHA? I do not recall that it was OSHA that blew the whistle on that horrible situation. Were they too busy checking on the size of toilet seats and the cleaning of spittoons?

Likewise, the grain elevator explosions are another awful case. So far, the regulators seemed to have ignored the obvious. Those explosions have taken place *since* the Environmental Protection Agency issued regulations that ignored the need for workplace safety—a sad and classic case of the conflict among and the stupidity of regulators.

What can be done to improve the situation? Personally, I have refused to join the effort to eliminate OSHA. Although I sympathize with the complaints of the agency's opponents, I do believe strongly in its end purpose—to provide safer and healthier working conditions.

THE CAUSES OF ON-THE-JOB HAZARDS

For starters, I would go back to my four questions. First of all, let us examine what we know about the causes of job injuries and illnesses. From the studies I have seen, it seems clear that inexperienced workers have high accident rates. The same applies to tired workers on long or varying shifts. Some of the statistics are

noteworthy. Over the period 1942–1970, a one-percent decline in the unemployment rate tended to generate a one-quarter of one-percent rise in the work-injury rate. On reflection, those results should not be surprising.

At slower rates of output, there is more time for maintenance and repair of equipment. During expansions, in contrast, there is more pressure on workers to produce and less time for maintenance of machinery. Moreover, new hires tend to be less experienced, or their skills may be rusty if they have been out of work for some time.

Under the circumstances, there would seem to be an important role for training. And here OSHA may have been counterproductive. We should not forget that many companies have had professional safety departments long before the Occupational Safety and Health Act was enacted in 1970. In practice, OSHA may have diverted much of the focus of these safety units from their traditional task of training workers in safer procedures to following bureaucratic procedures—studying the regulations, filling out the forms, meeting with the inspectors, responding to their charges, and so forth.

ALTERNATIVES

Let us now turn to the second question, to examining the alternative ways of dealing with the job safety and health problem. Standards, we must realize, are only one approach. Moreover, a number of state-level studies show that most accidents on the job do not involve violating standards. Even if full compliance was achieved, large numbers of job-related accidents would still occur.

It is naive to expect that any group of mortal men and women sitting in Washington, or anywhere else, can develop standards that will apply sensibly all over the country. The present OSHA approach of relying on standards, inspections, and sole sanctions on employers just is not working. The sensible answer is not to redouble an ineffective approach. Instead, the emphasis in OSHA regulation should be shifted to performance, to the achievement of the desired end results.

That is the general conclusion that flows from the analyses that have been made by a variety of analysts. Albert L. Nichols and Richard Zeckhauser of the Kennedy School of Government at Harvard concluded that "OSHA . . . has become a prominent symbol of misguided Federal regulation. It accomplishes little for occupational safety and health yet imposes significant economic costs."[1] President Carter's Interagency Task Force on Workplace Safety and Health reported that "OSHA knows little more about what works to prevent injury today than it did in 1971."[2]

Exactly how a safe and healthy work environment is achieved is a managerial matter. Some companies might reduce job hazards by buying new equipment. Others might install new work procedures. Still others might provide financial incentives to their employees— paying them to wear the earmuffs instead of spending much larger sums on so-called engineering noise containment.

In this vein, a recent U.S. District Court barred OSHA from preventing Continental Can Company's use of "personal protection devices" instead of the more expensive engineering controls. The judge noted that the company's current program of earplugs and earmuffs was more effective than OSHA's preferred alternative.

Another example of the kind of thinking that results from this "managerial" concept

in contrast to the standards approach is the findings of Donald L. Tasto, a clinical psychologist who was director of the Center for Research on Stress and Health at SRI. According to Dr. Tasto, "the data are very clear that people who rotate shifts have significantly more accidents than those who work permanent shifts."[3] They reported more stomach problems, cramps, colds, chest pains, fatigue, menstrual problems, nervousness, alcohol consumption, and use of sleeping pills and stimulants. Standards, we must acknowledge, just do not deal with this type of work-environment problem.

CHOOSING THE MOST EFFECTIVE ALTERNATIVES

In evaluating performance, we need to turn attention to the third question, which deals with economics. OSHA's new general carcinogenic proposal is a fine example of the wrong approach. Ironically, OSHA seems to be embracing a variant of the zero-risk concept just as that outmoded notion is becoming so widely discredited in the area in which it has traditionally been used. I am referring to the FDA's experience with the Delaney Amendment on food additives. As we have seen in the case of nitrites, a simple-minded application of the lowest possible risk would indeed eliminate the carcinogenic threat posed by nitrites—but the ban also would likely result in losing far more lives because of the greater danger of botulism.

Voltaire may have said it all: "The best is the enemy of the good." The emphasis surely should be on the serious, lethal health hazards and not on the minute trace quantities that present the most hypothetical and remote risks to worker health. Such a commonsense

[1] Albert L. Nichols and Richard Zeckhauser, "Government Comes to the Workplace: An Assessment of OSHA," *Public Interest* (Fall 1977), p. 39.

[2] Philip Shabecoff, "Job Safety Changes Are Sought," *The New York Times* (December 19, 1978), p. D3.

[3] Donald L. Tasto, "Shift Workers' Health Suffers," *Investments in Tomorrow*, 8, *3* (1978), p. 7.

statement would seem to be superfluous. But OSHA's performance to date, under several different administrations, just does not inspire much confidence about the abundance of good judgment at that agency. As has been documented so well, OSHA shows all of the shortcomings of the bureaucratic mentality at its very worst. As an ex-bureaucrat, I feel obliged to make note of that, hopefully to evoke some badly needed change.

CONCLUSION

The basic reason for criticizing OSHA's current approaches is not economic. It is to get a more positive answer to my fourth question—to reform OSHA so that it can indeed have a significant impact in reducing job-related illnesses and accidents. Surely that will take a fundamental overhaul of the basic OSHA statute—such as shifting the focus from standards to performance, extending sanctions to employees as well as employers, etc. That difficult task is worthy of very considerable attention—on the part of labor, management, government, and academic researchers alike. The drafters of new job safety and health legislation should learn from the sad OSHA experience. The problem is not to punish employers for not meeting standards. Rather, the need is to identify those approaches that will provide maximum incentives to workers and employers alike to achieve and maintain a safer and healthier work environment.

27

Discrimination and Affirmative Action: The Nature of Economic Evidence

Harriet Zellner and Beth Niemi

Harriet Zellner and Beth Niemi, "Discrimination and Affirmative Action: The Nature of Economic Evidence, " a paper presented at the Annual Meeting of the American Economic Association, Denver, Colorado, September 1980.

In Equal Employment Opportunity (EEO) litigation, we are engaged in a legal process which differs in several respects from that generally followed in criminal cases. In both situations, we must determine whether an observed outcome—in one case a wage differential, in the other a missing wallet or a dead body—is attributable to a particular cause. However, the nature of the evidence brought to bear and the standards by which we judge whether guilt has been proven beyond a reasonable doubt differ radically. Generally, in the case of employment discrimination, we use statistical techniques to help determine whether a violation of the law has occurred. If, for example, a woman accuses her employer of failing to promote her because of her sex, we try to determine whether in this firm women *in general* are promoted less often than similarly qualified males. That is, we estimate the magnitude and statistical significance of the relationship between sex and promotion rates. This is consistent with the notion that discrimination is, in essence, a crime against a group; it involves differential treatment of individuals solely because they are members of that particular group.

Since the courts have not required a demonstration of intent to discriminate, but have focused instead on the outcomes of a firm's personnel practices, a statistical finding of systematic differentials—*all else constant*—has become central to proving violation of EEO law. Statistical evidence, which can be

253

usefully viewed as one particularly telling type of circumstantial evidence, is often the crucial indicator of whether or not disparate treatment or impact has occurred. Thus, lawyers and judges who have never had a statistics course are put in the position of having to evaluate quite sophisticated statistical evidence. However, it has been our experience that they are impressively quick in picking up the uses and interpretation of such evidence. EEO litigation has been described as a "battle between experts" and we can expect this battle to rage on.

Since a statistical finding of a systematic and significant race or sex differential—all else constant—has become central to proving a violation of EEO law, the phrase "all else constant" is a crucial one. What factors are to be controlled for in estimating the existence and size of a discriminatory differential? As the voluminous economic literature on this subject indicates, an observed differential in earnings or promotion rates by race or sex within a given firm may be attributable to a number of factors other than discrimination, and the size of the estimated residual differential will depend upon the characteristics which are included in the analysis.

The central factor dictating the choice of control variables in such an analysis is its judicial context. We are asked to determine the portion of the female/male (or minority/nonminority) differential in earnings or promotion rates for which a *particular* employer can be held legally responsible. Controlling for schooling and experience obtained prior to joining the firm is thus entirely appropriate. On the one hand, both influence productivity. On the other hand, the current employer ought not to be held responsible for the amounts of each obtained. These decisions were made before his or her behavior could influence the outcome. Some of the issues which must be resolved when the *total* effects of labor market discrimination are to be estimated are not, therefore,

relevant in this context. It may well be the case, for example, that the amount and type of prior work experience acquired by different groups are in part representative of different opportunities rather than different preferences or qualifications and, thus, that some of the difference in measured productivity is itself the result of labor market discrimination. However, to the extent that this is true, it reflects the behavior of all employers and is thus clearly exogenous in a model of earnings determination within a single firm.

However, controlling for post-hire schooling, on-the-job training, tenure, occupation and job history with the firm, in estimating the size of discriminatory differentials, is legitimate only if we can assume that none of the male/female or white/black differences with respect to these characteristics are themselves attributable to discriminatory behavior on the part of the current employer. But this is a hypothesis to be tested rather than an assumption to make, since all these job history variables are endogenous to the firm. Discriminatory preferences could cause or enlarge differences by race or sex with respect to each of these characteristics. And these differences, particularly in occupational distribution, do explain significant portions of the male/female and white/black earnings gaps.

A fairly typical example of the type of pattern observed can be seen in the results obtained in a recent sex discrimination case on which we were retained. We found positive and consistently significant male/female earnings differentials with broad occupational category accounting for approximately 40–50 percent of these differentials. At hire, men earned, on average, $4416 more than women who were similarly qualified in terms of education, vocational training, and estimated years of experience. Controlling for broad occupational category reduced this net differential to $2226. After several years with the firm, the earnings gap had widened to $6685, of which $2849 was "explained" by current occupational category. (All these earnings differences were statistically significant at the 1 percent confidence level.) Clearly, occupational category is a significant determinant of earnings. It is essential, therefore, that we control for this factor only to the extent that it is independent of discriminatory behavior within the firm under consideration.

There is an obvious analogy here to the way in which labor pool analysis is often performed. The purpose of such analysis is to determine whether the representation of minority or female workers in firm hires differs significantly from their relative supply to the firm. Relative supply is estimated as the portion of black or female workers represent of those "qualified and available" for particular jobs in the relevant labor market. The relevant labor market is defined by the geographic boundaries within which the employer may be reasonably expected to recruit and the labor pool is defined as those workers within these geographic boundaries that have the specified qualifications. Let us abstract from the question of how to correctly define the relevant labor market in order to focus on those worker characteristics that constitute qualification and availability.

The labor pool can be most unambiguously defined in the case of entry level jobs requiring specific qualifications with respect to formal education. It is clear, for example, that law firms require their new associates to have a law degree and to have been admitted to the bar. Thus, the relevant labor pool for these positions is easily identified as *recent* law school graduates admitted to the bar.

However, in many cases we must determine the relevant labor pool for jobs that are not necessarily entry level, have rather flexible educational requirements and for which experience and on-the-job training are, in any case, at least as important as formal schooling. Estima-

ting relative supply to these occupations is considerably more difficult than in the simple case described above. Reliable data on who possesses the necessary qualifications (which are themselves not clearly defined) do not exist. Precision gives way to pragmatism. We know that those employed in an occupation are by definition qualified and available for that occupation. Thus we test the hypothesis that a firm is discriminatory in its hiring of, for example, women managers or black clerical workers by comparing the proportion women represent of its managerial hires to the proportion women represent of *managers*, or the proportion blacks represent of its clerical hires to the proportion blacks represent of *clerical workers* in the relevant labor market. However, although the courts have accepted the standard of labor pool representation, this is clearly a conservative or lower limit estimate of relative supply since it already reflects the level of discrimination practiced by other employers in that labor market. That is, if other employers have preferred and currently prefer to hire men as managers and whites as clerical workers, the representation of women among managers and of blacks among clerical workers in the relevant labor market underestimates the actual relative supply of women managers and black clerical workers to the firm.

An alternative estimate of the relative supply of women managers to the firm, one which does not "control" for current occupation, would be the proportion women represent (in the relevant labor market) of college educated workers with a given number of years of work experience. Of course, this proportion probably overestimates the relative supply of women managers to the firm. The ideal estimate probably lies between these two extremes. However, unless we have sufficient data to estimate the relative supply curve of women to a particular occupation, and the point on it that would represent market equilibrium in the absence of discrimination, we must resort to such approximations.

The crucial point to note here is that the within-occupation comparison of the firm to the labor market will yield no evidence of discrimination if the firm under consideration is no more discriminatory in its hiring and promotion practices than all other firms in the labor market have, on average, been over the past several decades. When we control for occupation, by looking only at female representation in the experienced managerial work force or black representation in the experienced clerical work force, we reduce the probability of discovering significant underutilization, just as we reduce the probability of discovering significant pay differentials when we control for occupation.

Obviously, the two examples of female managers and black clerical workers were not chosen at random to illustrate this issue, but rather because there is considerable evidence that blacks continue to be underrepresented in white-collar jobs in many areas, as women continue to be underrepresented in positions of authority. For example, we recently analyzed the case of a firm 16 percent of whose managerial hires during the 1972–1976 period were female. Although this figure may appear low, managers in the relevant labor market for this firm were 15.9 percent female in 1970 and 20 percent female in 1976. Thus, the managerial hiring practices of this firm did not differ significantly from the average in that labor market. We found, therefore, no statistical evidence of discrimination. It was left to the lawyers to develop the qualitative evidence that strongly implied discrimination, i.e., that the relative supply of women to this occupational category in fact exceeded 16 percent.

Another recent case involved a firm in the South that, among other things, hired almost no black clerical workers. However, although the labor force in the local labor market was approximately one-quarter black, only about 6 percent of clerical workers were black. Once again, the hiring practices of a firm with respect to a particular occupational category were no worse than average. Did the firms in these two examples discriminate against women as managers and blacks as clerical workers respectively? If so, evidence other than that from conventional labor pool analysis would be required to show it. Fortunately, hiring in these particular occupations did not emerge as the crucial issue in either of these cases.

Conventional labor pool analysis is even less suitable to the requirements of affirmative action, which make even greater demands on the economist's powers of estimation. In this case, the firm is required to go beyond merely ceasing to discriminate and to actively recruit women and minorities—through, for example, advertisements, on-campus interviews and training programs—for occupations in which past discrimination has reduced current relative supply. In economic terms, an effort should be made to shift the relative supply curve outward, presumably to the position it would have occupied had discrimination never occurred. In this case, estimating the current relative supply curve of women or minorities to a particular occupation, and then determining the point on it that would prevail in the absence of discrimination, will yield an estimate of the equilibrium relative supply of women or minorities that underestimates the goal or target representation for which the firm is to aim.

The question raised here is an increasingly important one. Against what availability criteria can we reasonably judge whether a firm is making good faith efforts to open up so-called "non-traditional" jobs to women and minorities? For example, the occupation "welders and flamecutters" was 5.8 percent female in 1970. (See 1970 Census of Population, PC(1)-D1, *Detailed Characteristics United States*

Summary, Table 223, p. 743.) In assessing a firm's recruitment of women for welding jobs, the use of 5.8 percent female as a standard of comparison would simply institutionalize the *status quo*. This is inconsistent with the goal of breaking down traditional barriers—on both the supply and demand side—to occupational entry. On the other hand, the assumption that the underrepresentation of women in welding is *completely* due to these barriers, rather than to any supply-side differences that are independent of market discrimination, is too extreme. The standard to which we ideally would wish to compare a firm's hiring practices is, as we have indicated, the percentage of welders who would be female in the absence of any discriminatory barriers, a statistic that, unfortunately, does not exist. However, it is clear that we must, in the very near future, agree upon a reasonable way to determine what figure, between the extremes of 6 percent and 40 percent (the proportion women represent of the labor force as a whole), should be used in such a case.

Having devoted the major portion of this article to a consideration of some statistical issues involved in the analysis of discrimination, we might also consider a subtler phenomenon which is not readily accessible to statistical analysis but which does influence the results we obtain in such analysis.

We refer to this phenomenon as the unencouraged worker effect. It is obviously a variant of the discouraged worker effect. Discouraged workers, as you know, are by definition those who desire employment but have ceased (or have not begun) to actively seek it because they believe no jobs are available. Unencouraged workers are defined as workers who fail to seek *better* jobs because they believe these are not available to them. Unencouraged workers are produced by a discriminatory environment. Just as we underestimate the importance of unemployment when we fail to count discouraged workers, so we underestimate the social significance of discrimination when we fail to take its deeply unencouraging effects into account. To the extent that women and minority workers fail to invest in certain types of education and training, to apply for certain positions or to press for certain promotions because they believe they would be unwelcome, and thus uncomfortable and even unsuccessful, fewer *direct* acts of discrimination need occur to produce an employment situation characterized by significant sex and race differentials. An act of discrimination against one person may serve to deter many more.

However, looking at the same situation from another, more optimistic viewpoint, each *reduction* in discriminatory behavior is likely, for analogous reasons, to have a disproportionate impact in reducing observed differentials by race and sex. . . .

28

Minimum-Wage Legislation in the United States

Finis Welch

Finis Welch, "Minimum-Wage Legislation in the United States," in *Evaluating the Labor Market Effects of Social Programs,* Orley Ashenfelter and James Blum, eds. (Princeton: Industrial Relations Section, 1976).

A legislated wage floor has existed for some sectors of the economy since the Fair Labor Standards Act of 1938. Aside from one major deviation in 1945, the legislation has been updated about every five years, bringing the minimum wage to one-half the average manufacturing wage. In the interims, the minimum is eroded by inflation and rising labor productivity. Table 1 lists nominal minima and relative minima before and after legislative changes.

Coverage is incomplete and depends on industry and product line and, in some cases, gross sales of the firm. For twenty-three years after the initial legislation, coverage was un-changed. The industries included were the more "industrial" or machine-intensive: slightly over half of total employment was in firms subject to the federal legislation. Extensions in 1961 and again in 1966 raised the proportion of covered workers to 60 and then to 80 percent. Table 2 summarizes these coverage rates for 1947 and for years following the extensions in 1961 and 1966. Agriculture (where coverage was extended to some large farms in 1966) and government are excluded from these data. Among the industries shown, the extension of coverage in retail trade and services is the most notable....

The Fair Labor Standards Act does not

TABLE 1

Changes in Federal Minimum Wages, 1938–1974

Year	Nominal	Minimum Wage Relative to Manufacturing Wage Before Legislated Increase	After Legislated Increase
1938 (FLSA)	$0.25	. . .	0.403
1939[a]	0.30	0.398	0.478
1945[a]	0.40	0.295	0.394
1950[b]	0.75	0.278	0.521
1956[b]	1.00	0.385	0.512
1961[b]	1.15	0.431	0.495
1963[a]	1.25	0.467	0.508
1967[b]	1.40	0.441	0.494
1968[a]	1.60	0.465	0.531
1974[b]	2.00	0.374	0.467

[a]Programmed increment contained in prior legislation.
[b]Legislated amendment to FLSA of 1938.
Source: Manufacturing Wage is average annual hourly wage published in U.S. Department of Labor (1970).

encompass all minimum-wage legislation. For example, the U.S. Department of Agriculture has administered a minimum wage for sugar workers since 1934, and many states have their own wage regulations. In 1958, thirty-two states had some form of minimum-wage legislation (U.S. Dept. of Labor, 1963). Legislation in twenty-one of these was restricted to women and minors, and in only three states (Alaska, Connecticut, and New York) did minima exceed the federal level. As is to be expected, coverage by state legislation usually extends only to those industries (retail trade, laundry and dry cleaning, personal services, etc.) not covered by federal legislation. As federal coverage is extended, state minima that fall short of the federal level are becoming unimportant.

The objective of this paper is to summarize evidence of the employment effects of minimum wages. . . .

TABLE 2

Percentage of Employed Persons in Firms Covered by Minimum-Wage Legislation by Industry and for the Aggregate, Selected Years

Industry	Year 1947	1962	1968
Mining	99	99	99
Construction	44	80	99
Manufacturing	95	95	97
Transportation and communication	88	95	98
Wholesale trade	67	69	76
Retail trade	3	33	58
Finance, insurance, and real estate	74	74	74
Services	19	22	67
Aggregate	56	61	79

Source: Unpublished data obtained from the U.S. Department of Labor, Bureau of Labor Statistics.

THE ISSUES

The purpose of this section is to state as simply as possible some a priori implications of minimum-wage legislation and to summarize that part of the empirical literature which, in my opinion, has increased our knowledge of minimum-wage effects on employment and which has not been supplanted by more recent studies using either superior techniques or data. Many very good studies are omitted in this summary, either because they have been supplanted by more recent evidence or because their scope is limited to effects on particular industries or to smaller areas of the country. The emphasis here is upon employment effects for particular demographic groups for the country as a whole. A more complete survey is contained in the study of the U.S. Department of Labor, *Youth Unemployment and Minimum Wages* (1970). The empirical literature is largely restricted to effects on youth employment, not because older workers—especially the aged—or lower-wage workers of intermediate age are less affected, but because the data are less complete for these workers.

It is my view that knowledge of the direction, i.e., the qualitative dimensions, of effects is quite good but that empirical estimates lack precision. The distinction between our knowledge of direction and of magnitude of effects is a distinction between the state of the theory and the state of the data. While the theoretical implications are quite simple, the data are not very good. First, there have been only four legislative amendments, with an additional four adjustments or step-increments prescribed by preceding legislation, and the data forming the basis of any reasonable analysis of distributional effects among demographic subgroups of the population are available only since 1954, originating with the household data of the Current Population Surveys (CPS). Since 1954, there have been

only five legislative modifications, of which three increased the nominal minimum and another two extended coverage and increased the minimum. (The 1974 amendment is excluded because data indicating effects are not yet available.) Further, the CPS data are only for employment and labor-force participation. Wage rates and wage distributions are not generally available. Finally, the amendment passed in September 1966 is empirically confounded by the federally sponsored youth-employment programs that began a year earlier. Virtually all our evidence of minimum-wage effects has been gleaned from implications of erosion of the nominal minimum as labor productivity has grown between the steplike increases in the minimum.

In principle, much information can be gained by focusing on the implications of uneven industrial coverage, but few studies have acknowledged incomplete coverage and, among those that have, attention has been restricted to aggregate effects; effects on the industrial distribution of employment have not been considered. Nonetheless, four studies of aggregate effects that I know of have explicitly introduced coverage in the empirical analysis, and all have found statistically significant evidence of the effect predicted by the straightforward theory, that minimum wages have reduced employment. In each of these studies, incomplete coverage is introduced only as an empirical correction of the minimum-wage variable, not as a distinct analytical phenomenon. Yet . . . the analytical mode for determining effects on, say, total employment is completely different in a world with universal coverage than in one with partial coverage. The reasons are obvious. With full coverage, employment effects of wage floors are demand-determined in a competitive market. Supply is irrelevant, because there is excess supply at above-equilibrium wages. With partial coverage, employment is demand-determined only in the covered sector. As wages in that sector are constrained to above-equilibrium levels, jobs in that sector are rationed and supply increases in the uncovered sector. Employment in sectors not covered is then determined jointly by demand and supply.

What Does Theory Predict?

For persons who would have earned less than the minimum, legislated wage floors are at best a mixed blessing. There is the obvious potential to increase earnings, but there is the burden that these workers must find an employer who perceives their labor to be at least worth the legal minimum, find jobs in uncovered sectors where—owing to the legislation—wages will be depressed, or be unemployed. It is always true that workers have incentives to find jobs offering the greatest satisfaction. The fact that, without legislation, some earn less than the minimum is proof that either these workers are unable to find jobs paying as much as the minimum or, even if they are offered such jobs, they prefer others on consideration of chances for advancement, fringe benefits, or convenience. The rub is that, although wage laws can be established, productivity cannot be directly increased by legislative fiat.

In this section I consider implications of minimum-wage legislation as predicted by fairly conventional theory, under the assumption of full coverage only. The distinction between full and partial coverage is important for analyses of total employment, unemployment, and, of course, industrial distribution of employment. It is not important for analyses of cyclic stability of employment or for the classroom example of wage determination under monopsony.

We are concerned only with effective wage constraints, so that if a minimum wage exists the presumption is that in the absence

of the minimum at least one worker would have earned a lower wage. In a competitive labor market, the implications of a minimum wage for at least some workers who would have earned less than the minimum are straightforward: Labor demand, i.e., hours of work, will fall. This requires only the assumption that demand functions for productive inputs are negatively inclined, and they must be, for there are no Giffen producer goods.

The standard classroom example is depicted by the Marshallian cross in Figure 1, where the equilibrium wage and employment levels that would otherwise exist are denoted as w_0 and E_0. The legislated wage floor is w_m; under this constraint, employment falls to E_1. This rarefied example tells us only two things: (1) If there is an effect, employment will fall, and (2) if the supply is positively inclined (as drawn), the number of workers who would choose to work at w_m, if jobs were available, would exceed employment. This simple description glosses over questions of fringe benefits, nonpecuniary attributes of jobs, and chances for on-the-job training. The latter are all substitutes for current wages and are restricted by legislated wage minima. More

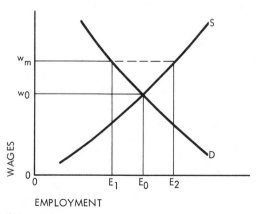

FIGURE 1

An Illustration of Employment Effect for Wages Constrained to Exceed Equilibrium Level

important, this simple model makes no prediction of the effects of minimum wages on unemployment.

Note that available statistical measures of unemployment include only those persons who do not have a job and are actively searching for one. The assumption underlying labor-supply functions like the one depicted in Figure 1 is that at a specified wage all choosing to work can find a job. When legislated minima exceed equilibrium wages, jobs are rationed: Not all who choose to work at the minimum wage will find jobs. In this situation, the extent of job search can be determined only by reference to probabilistic models which take into account chances of successful search. It is not the purpose of this paper to derive a model of job search under rationing. The purpose is only to point out that there is no simple relationship between excess supply at above-equilibrium wages as read from the Marshallian cross of Figure 1 and available measures of unemployment.

Because of the ambiguity of the standard model concerning effects of minimum wages on unemployment, it is surprising that the majority of empirical analyses of minimum-wage effects have focused on unemployment rather than on employment, where, at least for competitive labor markets, predictions are unambiguous. Empirical studies of effects of minimum wages on unemployment rates are not discussed here. In several cases, the specified model is inadequate for probabilistic inference. In others (especially Hashimoto and Mincer, 1970), specifications are adequate but results are often inconclusive.

The result that employment will fall if wage minima exceed equilibrium wages does not extend to all who would have earned less than the minimum. With a single legislated wage floor, it is clear that the greatest proportionate increase in wages is imposed on those who, in the absence of legislation, would have earned the least. Barring correlations between demand elasticities and fractional wage increases, it follows that effects on employment will be most adverse for those whose proportionate wage increase is greatest. For those who would have earned less, but not much less, than the minimum, effects on employment are uncertain. If all who would earn less than the minimum are substitutes, employers will substitute in favor of the workers whose relative costs have increased least, and these (indirect) effects may dominate. This is the assumption underlying the "ripple effect," which holds that labor demand increases for workers above the minimum, and the effect declines with distance from the minimum. For workers who would have been below the minimum, the converse holds and adverse-employment effects increase with distance from the minimum.

The necessary assumption for this monotone effect to hold is that all workers are substitutes and that the smaller the wage discrepancy that would have existed in the absence of legislation, the larger the degree of substitutability. In this case, it is possible that employment of some who would have earned less than the minimum will rise simply because, with the legislation, costs of employing them have fallen relative to others with lower wage potential. . . .

EVIDENCE AND UNSETTLED ISSUES

The available empirical evidence refers almost exclusively to teenagers and can be summarized as follows:

1. Minimum-wage legislation has reduced employment. The extent of this reduction remains conjectural because a variety of estimates are available. In the period since teen-age employment data became

available in 1954, minimum wages probably had their least effect just prior to the 1956 increase from $0.75 to $1.00 per hour, when the minimum was 38.5 percent of the manufacturing wage, and only 38 percent of teenagers worked in covered establishments. The greatest cumulative effect would have accompanied the 1968 increase to $1.60 per hour, by which time coverage had been raised to 72 percent of the teen-age work force.

2. Minimum-wage legislation has heightened the vulnerability of teen-age employment to the vagaries of the business cycle. On balance, over the 1954-68 period, teenagers accounted for 6 percent of employment, but, as employment varied about its trend, teenagers accounted for 22 percent of this variation. The evidence is that a substantial part of the discrepancy between 22 and 6 percent is attributable to minimum wages.

3. Minimum wages have had very large effects on the industrial distribution of teen-age employment. The change between 1930 and 1940, when teen-age employment shifted to uncovered sectors, held through the 1945 and 1950 legislated adjustments, when—under constant coverage—the minimum was first raised to 39 and then to 52 percent of the manufacturing wage. Throughout the 1954–68 period, the industrial distribution of employment remained sensitive to uneven industrial coverage.

In addition to these effects on the level of teen-age employment and its pattern of change over the business cycle and between industries, Hashimoto and Mincer (1970) report significant disemployment effects for nonwhite workers 20 to 24 years old and for workers above 65 years of age. Other empirical accounts of minimum-wage effects have not addressed these groups but have focused on teenagers, for whom the data are more easily obtained. For teenagers, the evidence of substantial employment effects is convincing, yet many questions

of equity and efficiency remain unanswered. What is the effect of minimum-wage legislation on school attendance? Should legislated minima vary by industry and by demographic group? Can wage and income policy be integrated to mitigate adverse effects?

One argument favoring minimum-wage legislation is that, although a major share of the adverse employment effect falls upon teenagers, they have a good alternative use for their time. School attendance has offered and apparently continues to offer an attractive substitute to employment for the young. I know of no empirical study of the effect of minimum-wage legislation on school enrollment, however. Such a study, focusing especially upon traditionally economically disadvantaged demographic groups, would be an important addition to our arsenal of knowledge of these effects.

Unlike employment, the a priori effects are not unambiguous, because of the role of part-time work in financing education. The traditionally disadvantaged are precisely the groups whose employment is most threatened by minimum-wage legislation, and they may well be the groups most dependent on part-time work for support while in school.

In a recently completed paper, Parsons (1973) offers important new evidence on this score. Reporting estimates based on the National Longitudinal Surveys, Parsons notes that students working part-time earn sharply lower wages (about 25 percent lower) than their contemporaries who have dropped out of school for full-time employment. The $1.60 minimum wage became effective in February 1968. Using earnings data for 1967 with Parson's estimates, my calculations are that an enrolled student working part-time would be in his fourteenth year of school (the second year of college) before his hourly wage would average $1.60. But a dropout would need only eleven years of schooling to earn $1.60 in his first year of employment. When employment of persons whose part-time wages fall short of the minimum is prevented, the student is confronted with a choice. He can continue in school if support from alternative sources is forthcoming, or he can leave school to work full time. The dependence between this choice and family income is obvious. It may be that minimum wages increase school enrollment, but the same legislation may force some to opt for full-time work; those who do so are likey to be those whose families can afford the least support for their children's education. This is an empirical question that can be addressed with available data.

Among policies designed to "improve the condition" of those who would otherwise receive low incomes, minimum wages are amazingly perverse. So long as demand curves are negatively inclined, those who gain by securing legislated wage increments do so at the expense of others who, in the absence of the legislation, would have earned the lowest wages. With partial coverage, those who lose either work in uncovered sectors at depressed wages or withdraw from the work force. . . .

The Thorny Question of Differentials

Youth differentials are currently much discussed. The idea is that, since the most adverse employment effects are realized by persons who have the lowest productive capacity and that these persons are disproportionately young, these effects can be mitigated by introducing a differential minimum that is lower for young workers.

There are a number of problems associated with a simple differential of this sort. What of adults who would otherwise earn less than the minimum? To date, we have insufficiently reliable estimates of substitution possibilities to make even remotely accurate estimates.

This issue of cross-effects with a differ-

ential is further confounded by the possibility that the level of the minimum set for adults may depend upon the existence of a youth differential. Historically, the minimum following legislative adjustments has been one-half the average manufacturing wage. Would the minimum set for adults be raised if a youth differential existed?

Nonmarket alternatives probably are superior for teenagers than for adults. These alternatives are expressed in labor-supply elasticities; the more elastic the supply, the greater the buffer offered by nonmarket activities to employment adversities generated by minimum wages. A youth differential has the potential of shifting the brunt of the adverse-employment (and, with incomplete coverage, wage) effects from youths whose alternatives outside the labor market offer insurance against market adversities to older workers with inferior alternatives.

Should the minimum wage vary among industries and, if so, how? Aside from distributional issues, the answer seems obvious: Yes. So long as wage minima exist, on the basis of efficiency in use of resources the objective should be to minimize distortions in patterns of resource allocation. As in the case of taxation when not all activities are taxable, the objective should be to impose the greatest marginal price distortions where response is most sluggish. This would correspond to imposing the highest wage minima on sectors with the least elastic demand for low-wage labor. Unfortunately, we have scanty evidence of industrial patterns of labor demand.

Incomes Policies

It is probably safe to assume that minimum-wage legislation in some form will always be with us and the trend to complete coverage will continue. Interaction between wage legislation and incomes policies is relevant. For example, negative-income-tax proposals operating through reinforcement of income and substitution effects on labor supply have the effect of raising reservation wages, of increasing the wage level at which workers withdraw from the work force rather than accept lower wages. Wage-subsidy programs differ, since the substitution effect is toward increased labor supply. With incomplete coverage, minimum-wage legislation exacerbates labor-force withdrawal associated with negative income taxes, but if the wage subsidy is counted as part of the minimum, a program of this kind reduces the adverse employment effects associated with minimum-wage legislation. Whatever the relative merits of the two alternative incomes policies, the position of wage-subsidy programs is improved with the existence of minimum-wage legislation.

29

Jobless Pay and the Economy

Daniel Hamermesh

Daniel Hamermesh, *Jobless Pay and the Economy* (Baltimore, Md.: The John Hopkins University Press, 1972).

Our knowledge of the economic effects of unemployment insurance has been severely limited by two interacting factors. First, the legal and administrative provisions of the systems are so complex and the interstate differences so varied that many economists have been discouraged from working in the area in the past twenty-five years. Second, even when interest has been present, the data needed to provide answers have in most cases been lacking. For these reasons, until recently we have known very little about the economic effects of the system, and that lack of knowledge has guaranteed that economic considerations have had a minimal impact on the policy debate.

... We have calculated the magnitudes of each of a number of effects of the current system of regular UI benefits on the civilian unemployment rate. For some of these the direct evidence is fairly strong, while for others the best available evidence has been pieced together from diverse sources. To gauge the overall effect on unemployment, these separate effects can be combined. Our bases for comparison are a low unemployment rate of 4 percent and a recession unemployment rate of 7.3 percent, each assumed to occur in the absence of the regular unemployment-insurance programs. To make the comparisons, we combine the percentage increase in the number of spells of unemployment induced by the increased seasonal variation in employment; the percentage increase in duration of unemployment; the induced increase in the labor force at full employment; and the effect on macroeconomic activity during a recession induced by increased UI benefits.

Table 1 lists these effects as percentage-point increases in the unemployment rate. Our best estimates are that the civilian unemployment rate is 0.7 percentage points higher at low unemployment and 0.45 percentage points higher during a deep recession than it would be in the program's absence. Expressed differently, if low unemployment in the late 1970s is 4.7 percent, it could be as low as 4 percent if regular UI benefits are not paid. The 0.7 figure implies that nearly one third of the insured unemployed during low-unemployment periods would be at work (0.7 divided by 2.2, the hypothetical insured-unemployment rate based on the assumption that insured unemployment as a fraction of civilian unemployment would be 0.47, as in 1969). This estimate may appear high, but most of the induced unemployment is based on the well-documented effect of UI benefits on the duration of unemployment when labor markets are tight.

These estimated total effects mask several important considerations. First, if we believe that individuals would save sufficiently to provide for their periods of unemployment

TABLE 1

Estimated Total Effects of Regular State UI Programs on the Civilian Unemployment Rate (in percentage points)

Change	At Low Unemployment	At High Unemployment
Real	+0.61	+0.27
Measured	+0.10	+0.51
Macroeconomic effect		-0.33
Total	+0.71	+0.45

or that the macroeconomic effects of UI benefits operate through monetary channels alone, there is no net effect of UI on the magnitude of cyclical fluctuations in unemployment. If so, induced unemployment in a recession is 0.78 percentage points, not the 0.45 estimate listed in Table 1.

A second consideration, however, is that the estimates of the amount of induced unemployment include some measured unemployment, reflecting shifts into unemployment by people who otherwise would have been out of the labor force. These shifts do not represent wasted human resources. If we are concerned only with real effects of the program, we can conclude that it induces only 0.61 and 0.27 percentage points of unemployment at low and high unemployment, respectively (assuming for the moment that the true macroeconomic effect is zero).

Third, the induced real increase in unemployment may be overstated because of behavioral and institutional effects. In the absence of publicly provided UI benefits, some private scheme of unemployment insurance would probably arise. (The existence of privately financed Supplementary Unemployment Benefits above regular UI benefits suggests that people wish to reduce the variability of their incomes and that removing UI benefits would produce a sharp growth in private benefit plans.) Any such plan, no matter how it is financed or how the benefits are structured, would provide greater incentive for unemployment than would occur in its absence. The institutional factor is that workers forced off UI would find their incomes partly maintained by other transfer programs. These often contain schedules that reduce payments as earnings increase, and thus they too contain disincentives to work that increase unemployment. Abolishing UI would lower unemployment only to the extent that potential private substitutes and current welfare programs are more successful in avoiding disincentives. Public programs can perhaps be altered or cut, but any cut in UI would certainly spur the growth of private substitutes.

These effects represent only what would occur if the U.S. economy did not contain a regular UI program structured as ours was in 1975. They do not allow us to make any statements about the true severity of recessions in the 1970s as compared with the recessions of 1948, 1954, 1958, or 1961, except to the slight extent that permanent extensions of coverage in 1970 broadened the impact of the program. They merely imply that part of the unemployment we observe is induced by the current structure of unemployment insurance. They do suggest, however, that further extensions of the program—of coverage, benefit amounts, or potential duration of benefits—will produce increases in the unemployment rate. Thus the permanent program of triggered Extended Benefits and the temporary programs enacted in 1974 and 1975 produce some (probably small) addition to the amount of unemployment induced by UI. Our best estimate is that the temporary programs added between 0.3 and 4 percentage points to the unemployment rate of 1975.

The induced unemployment should be construed partly as an investment made by society to subsidize job search, which can result in a more efficient labor market. In part, however, it is a needless diversion of human resources away from their best uses, produced by the combined effects of legislated accretions to the program and changes in the labor market and the tax system. Whether the real and measured effects are too large or too small depends on one's beliefs about the importance of efficiency in the labor market. Observers who believe that any inefficiency in the labor market must be removed, regardless of its other beneficial effects, will regard these effects as too large to justify the program;

those who feel that society should be willing to pay a high price to aid the unemployed or that UI offsets the effects of other inefficiency in the economy will consider these effects small. The appropriate question for this second group is, can the same improvement in the stabilization of incomes of the experienced unemployed be achieved without the likely loss in efficiency?

SUGGESTIONS FOR CHANGE

Without altering the fundamental structure of the program, much of the inefficiency and inequity it now produces can be removed. Our suggested changes do not tamper with the essential diversity of the program that Becker has called "competitive socialism." They do not alter its reliance on experience-rated taxes and its attempt to replace the income losses of out-of-work individuals who are attached to the labor force. Instead, they streamline the program and steer it to meet the goals that it was designed to meet, and they abandon secondary aims that have to some extent interfered with its primary endeavors and caused much resentment.

Our program for UI reform, summarized below, entails changes in a number of areas. Each program change affects the budget for UI. Because UI is just one of several income-maintenance programs, if adopted each would eventually have an impact on these others as well.

FINANCING

1. The tax base should gradually be increased until it equals the base for Social Security ($15,300 in 1976). This would remove some of the tax burden that now falls on low-skilled employees and would somewhat ease their chances of finding employment.

2. Employers tax rates should be based more heavily on the amount of unemployment for which they are responsible. The experience rating of taxes should be strengthened by the elimination of minimum and maximum rates.

COVERAGE

Coverage should encompass all sectors of the economy. If most employment in a sector is highly seasonal, the seasonal employees can be excluded by tightened eligibility requirements. Year-round employees should not be denied coverage because many of their co-workers are seasonal employees.

BENEFITS–MISCELLANEOUS RECOMMENDATIONS

1. Eligibility should be based on weeks of work during the base period, and some minimum-earnings requirement should also be applied. At least twenty weeks of work, each at a minimum weekly earnings, should be required. This would eliminate mainly those recipients whose demonstrated attachment to the labor force is usually quite weak.

2. The ceiling on maximum benefits should be removed, partly because individuals whose earnings are above average should not be denied the same percentage replacement of income lost as lower-wage individuals, partly because this is only fair if the tax base is raised substantially.

3. Dependents' allowances should be discontinued. They make the extent of benefits under UI, a work-related program, conditional on family size, which is not related to work. Furthermore, in the few states where they are offered, they can raise the net replacement rate so sharply that the incentive to seek work may be weakened.

4. Benefits for partial unemployment can provide an incentive for the fully unemployed to seek some work. The incentive exists, however, only when the loss of benefits is less than the extra earnings received. Partial-benefit schedules must be revised to guarantee that this incentive is maintained over the entire range of the schedule.

5. Potential duration should vary with the claimant's base-period earnings up to the maximum potential duration.

BENEFITS–AMOUNT

Because UI benefits are not taxed, replacement rates, based on lost earnings only, seem to exceed the 50-percent gross replacement rate facing most beneficiaries. Our findings imply, however, that when all factors are counted, net replacement rates for the average beneficiary are generally around 50 percent, which is not greatly different from gross replacement rates. If our recommendation is adopted and eligibility is based on weeks worked, most of the beneficiaries who are least closely attached to the labor force will be screened out. The incentive to seek work will thus be very strong, as will the degree of attachment to the labor force among the remaining low-wage beneficiaries. Only among one group (the high-wage unemployed eligible for increased benefits if the benefit ceiling is removed) will net replacement rates approach 100 percent, for only for them is the tax rate on earnings fairly high.

These considerations suggest, first, that gross benefits should be raised to two thirds of weekly earnings during the base period for all beneficiaries; second, that UI benefits should be taxed exactly as are earnings; and third, to effect these changes, benefit standards should be legislated at the federal level, and the tax code should be changed to permit the taxation of transfer income.

These recommendations and those on eligibility, maximum benefits, and dependents' allowances made above would (1) increase net replacement rates for the low-wage unemployed who have a demonstrated attachment to the labor force; (2) leave the average beneficiary essentially unaffected; (3) reduce net replacement slightly for workers barely at the current benefit maximum; and (4) increase net replacement slightly for those few unemployed workers whose current benefits replace much less than 50 percent of their wage loss because their base-period earnings are so high. These alterations are similar to recent changes made in Canada except that they include provisions for tightened eligibility requirements, whereas Canada eased these. They would probably lower the program's effect on unemployment by screening out those persons most likely to enter the labor force because of the inducements of future UI benefits and those others for whom the effect on duration of unemployment is probably greatest.

BENEFITS—MAXIMUM POTENTIAL DURATION

During the recession year 1975 approximately $4.6 billion in extended UI benefits (Extended and Federal Supplemental Benefits) was disbursed. These payments were authorized partly by the 1970 UI amendments and partly by the emergency legislation of 1974 and 1975. If we wish to extend benefits for up to sixty-five weeks in a recession, the extension should be triggered automatically to avoid possible legislative inertia. But the basic question is, Should such benefits be paid out at all? Would the $4.6 billion not have been more useful in some other income-maintenance or job-creation scheme?

Consider two alternatives: paying $4.6 billion a year in extended benefits or spending the same amount on a public-service employment program (either federal or shared). The employment program would have an advantage to the extent that (1) society values the output produced by its enrollees; (2) it does not displace spending by lower units of government; (3) enrollees maintain their skills better than they would if they were not working and were drawing extended UI benefits; (4) enrollees, especially the unskilled, develop both specific and general job skills as a result of the program; and (5) enrollment in the program does not hinder a participant's job search as labor demand rises at the end of the recession.

The value society places on the output of an emergency public jobs program is not known. Was the WPA "leaf-raking," or was it a major investment in the infrastructure of the U.S. economy? While the question cannot be given a conclusive answer, it should remind us to look carefully at the projects proposed under any emergency jobs program. If only a small part of spending by lower governments is displaced, the stimulatory effect of the allowances paid to enrollees will not be lost. While some displacement is likely, it can be minimized if the program is operated on a federal basis rather than through shared revenue.

Comparing the alternatives of enrolling in a jobs program or continuing to draw UI benefits beyond twenty-six weeks, it is fairly easy to conclude that during a recession there is little successful job searching in any case. If so, there is little fear that putting an individual into a public jobs program instead of paying him extended benefits will greatly reduce his chances of finding private-sector employment or increase the rate at which his skills deteriorate.

Taking these considerations together, we recommend that all extended-benefit programs be phased out and that a federally-run work-project program be created. Enrollment in this program should be limited to individuals who have exhausted their regular UI entitlement.

Allowances should equal the weekly benefits the enrollee would have received had he still been drawing unemployment compensation. (The hourly wage should be the minimum wage, and weekly hours should then equal the ratio of the person's weekly UI benefits to the minimum wage.) This ensures that an incentive to seek private-sector employment is maintained for most enrollees. Participants should be allowed to remain enrolled so long as they wish, provided they perform the tasks required of them. Funding, on a federal basis, should cover the allowances of all exhaustees of regular UI benefits who wish to enroll in the public employment program.

These recommendations are made in full awareness that they represent a sharp departure from the recent trend toward an ever-greater maximum potential duration of UI benefits. (Late in 1975 Senator Jacob Javits proposed extending benefits through seventy-eight weeks of unemployment.) Nonetheless, this trend is dangerous, for the UI system assumes more and more welfare-program aspects. The evidence suggests that if a person has not found work in a recession after twenty-six weeks of unemployment, he is not likely to do so thereafter unless demand conditions improve. Offering him the opportunity for dignified work in the public sector enables him to support himself, maintains the incentive to seek reemployment, and gives the rest of society some output in return for the resources transferred from taxpayers to UI recipients. At low unemployment the program would be very small. Few people exhaust benefits, and it is likely that many of those who do would prefer to seek higher paying, private-sector employment or drop out of the labor force.

CONCLUSIONS

A major conclusion of most studies of government programs is that more research is needed. If that recommendation is valid for other employment and welfare programs, it is even more valid for UI. The importance of the economic issues for fashioning appropriate policies and the current lack of a satisfactory resolution of most of them make the need for increased, more careful research crucial.

The UI program has operated for nearly forty years as a "first line of defense" against income losses produced by individual and mass unemployment. With the implementation of the changes we have suggested it can continue to do so. However, it cannot function simultaneously as a second, third, and fourth line of defense without limiting its ability to succeed in its primary mission. It should not be used as a vehicle for maintaining the incomes of individuals whose labor-force attachment is slight, nor should it be the vehicle by which the incomes of the long-term unemployed are maintained. It is now successful in meeting its basic goal, and with the modifications suggested here its success can be maintained and its small, negative effects on economic performance removed.

30

The Future
of Social Security

Robert J. Lampman

Robert J. Lampman, "The Future of Social Security," *Proceedings of the Annual Meetings of the Industrial Relations Research Association*, 1976.

The retirement class of 1980 will be the first to include a substantial number who will have spent all their working years in employment covered by the Social Security Act of 1935. In that sense the "old age" part of Old Age, Survivors, Disability, and Health Insurance (OASDHI) is approaching "maturity." The system is also maturing in the sense that successive Congresses have extended coverage and improved benefits so that virtually all workers are now covered, and the risks of income loss associated with old age, survivorship, and disability are confronted in a reasonably effective manner. The existing system stands as a monument to the political strategy of incrementalism and cautious reform. With regard to the risk of health-care cost, however, the system may be said to be in a state of arrested development. After President Roosevelt postponed action on that area in 1935, it was not until 1965, with medicare and medicaid, that the federal government took a major step toward a national health insurance plan.

CONTRACT OF PRESENT
AND ORIGINAL SCHEMES

The existing system of providing old-age benefits is different in several regards from that envisaged by its original planners. They seemed to believe or to hope that the need for old-age assistance would gradually wither away. However, the recent (1972) adoption of a national minimum in the form of Supplementary Security Income (SSI)—financed out of general revenue but administered by the Social Security Administration—signaled acceptance of the idea that the antipoverty goal, as opposed to the purpose of offsetting income loss, could not be fully reconciled with contributory social insurance.

Private pensions were originally viewed as beyond the appropriate reach of governmental policy. In response to complaints that many workers weren't receiving pensions that they had anticipated, Congress passed the Employee Retirement Income Security Act of 1974 (ERISA) in an effort to regulate and reinsure private pensions. It is important to note that, although about half of all workers are covered by pensions from private or state and local government employers, many of those covered will not receive such a pension since benefits are normally conditional on length of service with a single employer. The adequacy of private pensions is highly variable from one employer to another but tends to be more prevalent among high-wage, unionized firms. While SSI and private pensions are important for many families, only a minority of retired workers will receive benefits from any source other than Old Age Insurance (OAI).

Old Age Insurance's pay-as-you-go financing is quite unlike the original plan to accumulate a reserve until 1980, at which time the earnings of the reserve were to pay one-third of the cost of benefits. That plan was set aside in 1939 and finally dropped from consideration in the 1950s. However, OAI has made only a few exceptions to the principle of funding OAI benefits by employer and employee contributions. No doubt the original sponsors of the strategy of ear marked, closed funding would attribute to that strategy success in avoiding the two great hazards of (1) run-away promises of

future benefits that could not be funded, and (2) "raids" for other government purposes of monies needed for, but not "locked in" to, social security.

Also, OAI has observed the social insurance principle of paying most classes of workers (married women workers are an exception) a positive rate of return on their contributions. That principle has been relatively easy to observe during the time of an expanding labor force, a slow growth in the ratio of retirees to covered workers, and stable growth in the real wage rate. We will return to that topic later.

APPRAISAL OF EXISTING REPLACEMENT RATES

In 1975 replacement rates of OAI benefits now stand near what may be considered maturity levels. A single person now retiring at age 65, whose earnings have been at median levels, can draw a benefit equal to 44 percent of his last year's earnings. If his spouse is also 65, his replacement rate is 67 percent. These rates are about 30 percent higher than they were twenty years ago, and they are now, since 1972, protected against future increases in the Consumer Price Index (CPI).

Replacement rates well above 44 percent are in effect for below-median earners. Close to a fourth of all aged persons are eligible for SSI, and replacement rates under SSI may exceed 100 percent. Earners above the median have lower replacement rates, but many of them, particularly among the top 25 percent, have additional retirement benefits available from another public program or from one of the flourishing private pensions plans. So it may be argued that OAI benefit levels are adequate for the great mass of the workers who will be retiring in the near future.

This argument is strengthened by the point that the new aged, in comparison with the preceding generation, are an affluent group.

Not only do many of them have access to private pensions, which are certified and reinsured by the federal government, but they have a median net worth three times as high in constant dollars as did early OAI beneficiaries. Not only do they have the SSI money-income floor, which is set at poverty-income levels, but they also have access to medicare and medicaid and food stamps and a number of social services. It used to be that the incidence of poverty among the aged was far above the national average. That is no longer the case, and with the advent of SSI, the poverty rate among the aged should approach zero, even while the national average rate stands near 12 percent. A good number of the new aged have incomes high enough to benefit from tax favoritism in the form of the double personal exemption, the exclusion of social security benefits, and the retirement income credit. The aged, who make up 10 percent of the population may now do more than 10 percent of all consumption.

The new aged as a group are also affluent in the sense that they have plenty of children to pay the freight for social security. These people are, after all, the parents of the post-World War II record crop of babies. They are the people who made the two-earner family the standard, partly in response to unusually heavy burdens of child dependency which they carried. They may be expected to use their affluence to extend recent trends of opting for earlier retirement with or without good health (and chances for a longer life and better health after age 65 seem to be improving) and for separate living, apart from younger relatives.

Four decades of gradual change have produced an OAI system that seems suited to the political and social environment. It is comprehensive in terms of coverage, and adequate, in concert with SSI and private security arrangements, in terms of replacement rates of benefits. All this might suggest that the future of OAI will be unexciting and that no major changes

are likely to occur. But, before we can reach a conclusion on that, we need to look at the taxation side.

PROJECTIONS OF FUTURE REPLACEMENT AND TAX RATES

As recently as 1973 the Trustees of OASDI assumed that, with constant replacement rates for OAI, they would need only about a 10 percent combined payroll tax to fully fund the program until the year 2015. Subsequent to that, and until 2050, they foresaw a need for a tax rate of 12 percent. These rates sound low enough to leave some room for health insurance to make use of payroll taxes, and stable enough to let one believe that the rapid growth of "social welfare expenditures" of the last fifteen years, which had been led by social security, might be coming to an end. This calm outlook has been shattered by several recent developments. First there are a set of problems that have arisen in the 1970s. In addition, there is a demographic phenomenon that will have its primary impact in the twenty-first century.

In the 1970s there was an unexpected increase in claims for disability benefits, a move toward earlier retirement, and a chronic shortage of funds for Medicare. There also was a smaller increase in real earnings then expected, resulting partly from lower productivity increases and partly from greater unemployment. All these problems resulted in a downturn in the contingency reserve for OAI and the threat of a deficit in that fund.

This fiscal problem was heightened by the discovery that benefits for those retiring had been overindexed for inflation. This overindexing arose out of a decision made at the time of switching over to an automatic adjustment for inflation in 1972. At that time, Congress and its advisers in the Social Security Administration elected to follow ad hoc procedures that had been used in making periodic benefit adjustments since 1950. In effect, the 1972 formula adjusted benefits for price increases on top of wage increases which have occurred in response to inflation. These procedures were associated with gradual rises in replacement rates during the 1950s and 1960s, but apparently no one figured they could cause such spectacular changes in replacement rates in the future. This over-indexing procedure was corrected with the 1977 Amendments to the Social Security Act, but there remains concern over how to deal with increases in the cost of living. Annual double digit increases in inflation have led many policy makers to question whether Social Security recipients should receive full cost-of-living adjustments and even whether a special CPI more tailored to the purchasing practices of the aged should be used in making Social Security benefit adjustments.

Apart from these recent developments is the realization that the nation's birth rate has dropped to much lower levels than were forecast only a few years ago. We have been experiencing fertility rates below those required for zero population growth! This means, of course, that the labor force, and, hence, the taxable wage base will be sharply below previously predicted levels twenty years from now. While the number of future retirees is growing, the number of future workers is stabilizing. If the low birth pattern persists, those who are working after 2030, rather than paying a 12 percent tax rate, will have to pay a 17–19 percent tax rate, assuming that existing benefit replacement rates are held constant.

QUESTIONS RAISED BY THE DEMOGRAPHIC TWIST

It may help in discussing this situation to identify retirement classes in thirty-year intervals, starting in 1980. The second generation, retiring in 2010, represents the post World War II baby boom. The third generation, retiring in 2040, is made up of children born in 1975, and the fourth, retiring in 2070, will be born in 2005. All four of these generations are involved in the transition to a radically different relationship between the number of retirees and the number of tax-paying workers.

The tax rate will start to rise rapidly around 2010, when the post-war babies, in their great numbers, start to retire. This increase in tax rate will fall first on the retirement class of 2040, that is, the relatively small group born in 1975. Each worker in the class of 2010 has to pay current retirement costs of one-third of an aged person; the worker in the class of 2040 will need to pay for one-half of an aged person. The 50 percent jump in this ratio explains the 50 percent jump in the tax rate. If replacement rates are held constant, the class of 2040 will get a relatively bad deal out of OAI. They will pay more per capita than their parents did and get the same share of earnings replaced. In other words, they will get a lower rate of return on their contributions than will the class of 2010. It is unlikely that the retirement class of 2070 will get that kind of a bad deal, that is, a lower rate of return than their parents. That would happen only if population growth were to fall substantially below zero in 2005.

OAI is a treaty among generations and that treaty is likely to be quite strained as a result of this demographic twist. It is worth pointing out that the rate of return of a pay-as-you-go, fixed replacement rate OAI system is bound to fall as it matures even without any other change. The system has already registered such a fall, but it has been gradual. A decline in the rate of population growth will cause a further reduction in the system's rate of return. A zero population growth rate may mean that the only factor remaining to cause the rate of return to be positive is a positive rate of growth of the average real wage—and some people have doubts about the future of that variable.

Is it fair to plan to impose such a high tax rate as 17 to 19 percent on the retirement class of 2040, knowing that their rate of return is going to be low? Is it fair for their parents (the retirement class of 2010) to have a relatively easy time in paying the current retirement cost of the class of 1980 without helping to lighten the burden for their children in the class of 2040? This class of 2010, after all, has a lower child-dependency burden than did the class of 1980 as well as a lower old-age-dependency burden than the class of 2040.

In the pursuit of fairness, should the class of 1980 volunteer now to accept lower replacement rates than they are scheduled to enjoy? That class, it may be said, is the one that is at fault. They caused the prospective jump in the tax rate to be so extraordinarily great by departing dramatically from the historic downward trend in the fertility rate. Should this class of geriatric delinquents pay now for their youthful follies of creating such a large retirement class in 2010? Or should we honor their use of the classic defense of "No malicious intent"?

Would it be more fair for the class of 2010, who have virtuously returned the nation to its historic fertility trend, to now accept lower replacement rates, effective in 2010, and thereby hold down the taxes their children will have to pay at that time? Since the median benefit is now projected to be about $10,000 (in 1975 dollars) a year in 2010, it would not seem like a great hardship to accept a somewhat lower replacement rate. Alternatively (and this is reminiscent of a controversy "settled" over twenty years ago), should they volunteer to pay higher payroll taxes now in order to accumulate a trust fund which could be used to reduce the payroll taxes to be paid after 2010 by the class of 2040? Should that fund be drawn down by 2040, or maintained as an earning asset for the class of 2070? Who should answer these mind-boggling questions? Should they be voted on by the class of 2010 alone, or should the class of 2010 also have a say in a decision that will affect their grandchildren?

Quite aside from the issue of intergenerational fairness is the question of how to hold all earners in the system when the average rate of return falls to low levels. The redistributive tilt in the benefit formula and the relatively low replacement rate for people earning the maximum taxable wage produce a low return for high-income earners now. But this could turn into a negative rate of return for them if the average rate falls sharply. Will they want, then, to withdraw from the system and direct their contributions to private pensions? Alternatively, will they use political pressure to modify the distributional tilt in the formula and to eliminate dependents' benefits and to push more of the retirement burden onto SSI? Will more and more low-income workers try to escape from the effect of higher payroll taxes via earned income credits of the type introduced into the income tax of 1975? Is it possible that, because of such political pressure, OAI will disintegrate into SSI and private pensions?

These questions would all be easier to answer if the rate of return could be protected by maintaining a higher growth in the real wage base, which of course, equals the number of covered earners times the average real wage. One way to raise the rate of increase for a few years is to push out the typical retirement age from 65 to, say, 68. This could be encouraged by lower (or zero) penalties on earnings past the retirement age or by increasing to 68 the age at which full benefits can be collected. A way to get a higher rate of increase in real wages is to stimulate a higher rate of increase in plant and equipment per worker. A method to finance that extra investment is to raise payroll taxes to accumulate a permanent social security trust fund. Some critics see use of this method as a logical corollary of the plausible notion that our present rate of *ex ante* saving would be higher if workers did not have the promise of future retirement benefits to be paid for on a pay-as-you-go basis. The argument goes that since OAI has the side effect of holding down savings, it should do something about it. However, as Keynes taught us, a shift in *ex ante* saving does not necessarily lead to an increase in *ex post* investment. Moreover, if the demand for investment goals is strong, saving will be forced via a higher national income. This takes one off into a full inquiry into macro-economic theory and policy, out of which a social security trust fund emerges as but one of numerous devices to accommodate a change in the rate of capital formation. Whether present workers want to reduce present consumption in order to enable higher consumption by future generations is the major question; whether they want to reduce consumption now in order to defend the rate of return on social security contributions is, by comparison, a trifling question, and one internal to social security. The decision was made earlier to place responsibility for fiscal stabilization and economic growth in the hands of the Treasury and the Federal Reserve System. It is often asserted that social security has more than enough goals as it is, without assuming more.

SOCIAL SECURITY IN A BROADER CONTEXT

Between 1960 and 1975, cash income maintenance benefits for the aged, survivors, and disabled rose from an amount equal to 4 percent to an amount equal to 7 percent of gross national product (GNP). This was the leading component in the great rise of "social welfare expenditures under public programs" from an amount equal to 11 percent to 20 percent of GNP. The rise of 9 percentage points comprised the following: (1) cash benefits for the aged, survivors, 3; (2) education, 2; (3) health care, 2; and (4) public aid [cash and in-kind benefits exclusive of those in (1), (2), and (3)], 2 percentage points.

It has been assumed that the rapid rise in

cash benefits for the aged might slow down when OAI reached maturity. However, as the preceding discussion indicates, a rapid transition to zero population growth will urge a further rise in the proportion of total income going to OAI and SSI. This is likely to be the case even if Congress adopts the conservative position of preventing future increases in replacement rates and even if it stands firm against the trend toward earlier retirement.

This rise in cash benefits for the aged, survivors, and disabled will be competitive with pressures for rises in other social welfare expenditures. At present, 40 percent of the nation's health care bill is paid for out of public funds, and it seems reasonable to project demands to shift an even larger share of that cost onto public funding. Zero population growth should yield savings for some public education budgets, but they may be claimed by quality improvements and new forms of education such as pre-school, special, and continuing education. The broad set of "public aid" programs may continue to expand with housing allowances, public service employment, or a new cash benefit for intact families. All of this is to suggest that social welfare expenditures could rise to levels well above the current 20 percent of GNP.

The coming generations between now and the year 2050 may evolve quite different views than we now hold of social welfare issues. The words "social security" connote a certain way of thinking—of problems and remedies, of ways and means—that has come down to us from the 1930s. But new programs come into being in response to new perceptions of need, new social inventions, and new enthusiasms. As programs expand and overlap with one another, their side effects become more consequential. Social welfare expenditures interact with policies in taxation and labor markets and several other areas. The future of this interacting set of policies will be shaped by the relative importance our successors attach to the goals of social security.

31

Welfare Reform and Work Incentives

Irwin Garfinkel and Stanley Masters

Irwin Garfinkel and Stanley Masters, "Welfare Reform and Work Incentives," written especially for this volume.

In this article, we discuss the present income support system in the United States, how it has changed in recent years, and the major issues that have made this system a source of considerable political controversy. We emphasize how these issues relate to the work disincentive effects of such programs and discuss the empirical evidence on the magnitude of these work disincentive effects.

THE INCOME SUPPORT SYSTEM

In the United States there are more than 40 separate programs that constitute the income support system. Table 1 presents, for 1979, the expenditures for the most important ones. These expenditures amount to $211 billion, or about 9 percent of GNP and 28 percent of all government expenditures.

Several characteristics of the current system stand out in Table 1. First the system clearly differentiates among various groups of society. Most of this categorization is a response to the issue of work disincentives—an attempt to categorize those who are and are not expected to work and then to treat the latter more generously. For example, there are separate programs for veterans, single-parent families (Aid to Families with Dependent Children, AFDC) and the aged, blind, and disabled (Social Security, and Supplemental

TABLE 1

Estimated Expenditures for Major Income Support Programs, 1979 (billions of dollars)

Program	Expenditures		
	Federal	State and Local	Total
Social Insurance[a]	154	9	163
Cash benefits			
Old age, survivors and disability insurance (Social Security)	104	0	104
Unemployment compensation[b]	10	0	10
Veterans pensions and compensation[c]	11	0	11
Workers compensation	0	9	9
In-kind benefits			
Medicare	29	0	29
Welfare[d]	31	17	48
Cash benefits			
Aid to families with dependent children (AFDC)	6	5	11
Supplemental security income (SSI)	6	1	7
General assistance	0	1	1
In-kind benefits			
Food stamps	7	0	7
Medicaid	12	10	22
Totals for these programs	185	26	211
As a percent of GNP[e]			9%
As a percent of all government expenditures[e]			28%

[a]*Source:* Social Security Bulletin, January, 1981. These data are for calendar year 1979.

[b]Benefits are paid from a Federal trust fund and are financed by both federal and state taxes.

[c]About 60 percent of these expenditures are service connected compensation to veterans and their survivors. The remaining 40 percent, which is not service related, is probably more appropriately included in the welfare category.

[d]Except for General Assistance, all data are from The Budget of the United States Government, Fiscal Year 1981, Appendix. These data are for fiscal year 1979.

[e]Data for GNP and government expenditures are from the Economic Report of the President, 1981.

Security Income, SSI). Only food stamps, a relatively recent program, is available to all poor families.

Expenditures for social insurance programs are substantially larger than for welfare programs. Social insurance programs such as Social Security provide benefits to workers and their dependents who might otherwise suffer dramatic income losses because of old age, disability, or unemployment. Eligibility is not limited to the poor. Social insurance benefits are financed not out of the general revenues of government but rather from payroll taxes on employers and employees. Workers with higher earnings pay higher payroll taxes and generally obtain larger benefits. As earnings increase, taxes generally rise faster than benefits, however.[1]

In contrast, welfare programs limit eligibility to those with low income and provide benefits that are unrelated to previous employment. Payments decrease as earnings or other sources of income increase. Finally, welfare programs are financed largely out of general tax revenues. Until the last two decades, these welfare programs were designed to aid those not expected to work. Although many people identify the AFDC program with welfare, this program accounts for less than one-fourth of welfare expenditures. By far the most costly welfare program is Medicaid, which covers the medical expenses of most welfare recipients.

Cash benefits account for about two-thirds of the total expenditures for income maintenance presented in Table 1. Among the welfare programs, however, the two in-kind programs, food stamps and Medicaid, account for a majority of expenditures. Moreover there are many in-kind programs not listed in the table that provide benefits for the poor. These programs include subsidized housing; child nutrition; social services, such as day care and family counseling; employment and training programs; and a variety of educational programs. Although a great many programs have reducing poverty as one objective, some, such as many agricultural subsidies, mainly benefit those with relatively high incomes. Others, such as free public education, provide many benefits to the poor even though they are not generally considered part of our income support system.

The achievements of our income support system can be summarized in terms of the effects on the incidence of poverty in this coun-

try. Under the official definition, a family is poor if its income is below a poverty threshold that varies by family size, and changes over time in proportion to changes in the consumer price index. For a nonfarm family of four in 1981, this poverty threshold was just over $8,400 per year. If only market income is included in the income measure, then about 20 percent of all persons would be poor, a figure virtually unchanged since the start of the poverty program in 1964. In contrast, after taking account of cash transfer payments and the monetary equivalent of in-kind transfers, only 4 percent are poor, down from 13 percent in 1964. Thus the income support system contributes significantly to the reduction of poverty. In addition the income support system also cushions income losses due to old age, disability, and unemployment, thereby not only reducing poverty but also reducing the economic burden on the relatives of those who cannot support themselves. Despite these important achievements, our income support programs have been subject to numerous criticisms. In the next section we discuss very briefly the changes in the welfare system that have occurred or been seriously considered over the past 20 years.

A BRIEF HISTORY
OF WELFARE REFORM

During the past two decades, expenditures on income maintenance programs have increased dramatically. Medicare and Medicaid were established in 1965. Large increases in participation in AFDC occurred in the late 1960s and early 1970s. The food stamp program became national in scope in 1974, the same year that SSI provided a federal minimum income standard for the aged, blind, and disabled. Social Security payments also increased substantially during the 1970s. Since the mid-

---

[1] Low-wage workers are also more likely to become unemployed and disabled. On the other hand, low-wage workers are less likely to live as long as high-wage workers and therefore collect less retirement benefits.

1970s, however, there has been little change in the real value of income maintenance expenditures. No new programs have been established. Social Security was overindexed for inflation, but this was corrected in 1977. For programs like AFDC that are not indexed, during the past several years inflation has reduced the real value of benefits.

Although the social insurance programs have remained very popular, there has been much dissatisfaction with welfare. Major efforts to reform welfare were initiated by both Presidents Nixon and Carter. In contrast to the intent of the Reagan administration, the Nixon and Carter reform plans would have led to a larger federal role, especially with regard to AFDC.

Because AFDC has been the most controversial of the welfare programs and has been at the center of all recent welfare reform proposals, we shall trace its history in somewhat greater detail. This program was established under the Social Security Act of 1935 to provide income assistance to single-parent families. Initially the program was viewed as primarily for families where the father had died. By the 1960s however, Survivors Insurance coverage made recourse to welfare unnecessary for most widows. Most participating families were receiving benefits because of divorce, separation, and out-of-wedlock births, all of which were increasing.

The AFDC program has been criticized both for being too costly and providing aid to some who do not deserve it, and also for inadequate benefits and coverage. As the national commitment to reduce poverty grew in the 1960s, the program's failure to provide aid to poor two-parent families came under attack. Since such families were ineligible for aid, the program was criticized for encouraging family dissolution. In response, Congress amended the Social Security Act in 1961 to provide federal support to states that aided families

with an unemployed father. However, only about half the states provide aid to such families.

During the late 1960s AFDC was also the center of controversy because of large increases in the number of beneficiaries and the continued low employment rates of those on AFDC. In response to the criticism that 100 percent marginal tax rates eliminated any economic incentive for recipients to work, Congress amended the Social Security Act in 1967 to prohibit states from imposing marginal tax rates in excess of 67 percent (that is, benefits cannot be reduced by more than two dollars for every three additional dollars earned by the family).[2] In addition, training programs for AFDC mothers were expanded. But employment rates of AFDC recipients did not increase substantially in response to the program. Moreover the number of beneficiaries increased further, in part because the lower marginal tax rates enabled families with higher earnings to continue to receive some benefits from the program.

The Family Assistance Plan (FAP) initially proposed by President Nixon in 1969 would have radically changed our welfare system. The most important change proposed was to provide aid to all low-income families with children. This innovation was favored on equity grounds since it was considered unfair to provide little assistance to poor two-parent families, especially if they were poor despite full-time employment of the family head. Providing such aid also would have reduced the economic incentive for family breakups. A second important element of FAP was the proposal to establish national minimum benefit levels, thus reducing the large differentials in

[2] Prior to the 1967 amendment, marginal tax rates were actually greater than 100 percent, since no allowance was made for work expenses. Since that time, work expenses have been deducted before applying the 67 percent rate.

benefits across states that were widely regarded as inequitable and that could provide migration incentives.

The Family Assistance Plan did not survive the Senate Finance Committee partly because of its cost and partly because considerable opposition developed to extending cash benefits—and high marginal tax rates—to many additional two-parent families. Instead the food stamp program was established on a national basis, with a relatively low marginal tax rate of 30 percent.[3] Although its benefits, which are uniform nationally, can only be spent on food, the money saved on food expenditures by beneficiaries can be spent in any fashion.

The Program for Better Jobs and Income (PBJI) proposed by President Carter in 1971 was similar to FAP in that it would have extended aid to two-parent families and established minimum national payment levels. PBJI was designed to provide stronger work incentives than FAP for those expected to work.[4] Yet, while FAP passed the House of Representatives twice, PBJI never came close to passing either branch of Congress. Congress appeared to have little enthusiasm for reopening the political battles that FAP had generated, especially

---

[3] Although the marginal tax rate for this program is low, a problem develops when separate programs are established for different in-kind benefits such as food, housing, and medical care. If each of these programs is designed to provide benefits primarily to the poor, then benefits for each program must decrease as earnings increase. The cumulative marginal tax rate for all programs can be significantly greater than the rate for any individual program. This cumulative tax rate problem was emphasized in the criticism of FAP by the Senate Finance Committee.

[4] These incentives included: (1) low minimal payment levels for families with an able-bodied parent and no small children or with two able-bodied parents; (2) an expansion of the earned income tax credit to supplement the private sector earnings of low-income families; and (3) the creation of more than 1 million new subsidized public service jobs for those who could not find private sector employment.

since the number of AFDC beneficiaries had leveled off and there were no longer any powerful political forces arguing that something had to be done.

Recently the Reagan administration has modified the AFDC program to tighten eligibility standards and to reduce benefits for those who are employed. These changes have been made in an attempt to reduce costs without decreasing benefits for those who are most needy. For beneficiaries, however, the reward for working is substantially reduced. Once a job has been held for 4 months, benefits are reduced one dollar for every dollar earned.

ESTIMATING THE LABOR SUPPLY EFFECTS OF INCOME MAINTENANCE PROGRAMS

In this section, we begin with a brief discussion of the importance of the work incentive issue. Next we review the economic theory of how income maintenance programs affect the amount people work. Then we review the empirical evidence on the magnitude of these employment effects, focusing especially on the results of recent large-scale experiments designed specifically to investigate this issue.

Generosity, Cost, and Work Incentives

A basic issue of income maintenance policy is whether to spend more to increase generosity or less to reduce costs. This issue is closely related to that of work incentives.

Most income maintenance programs involve a guarantee, G, the amount of money a family can receive if it has no other income, and a marginal tax rate, r, the reduction in benefits for each extra dollar of earnings. Together the guarantee and tax rate determine the breakeven level, G/r, the earnings level at which the family will no longer be eligible for benefits. The larger the guarantee and the lower the tax rate, the greater the number of people who will be eligible for benefits, the greater the benefit each eligible person is entitled to and the more costly to nonbeneficiaries the program will be. A more generous plan will also provide beneficiaries with greater income, thereby enabling them to work less if they choose to do so. Any resulting decline in work effort will lead to increased program costs, thus making a generous system more expensive.

Effects on taxpayer costs, though important, are not the only reason for being concerned with work incentive effects; another major reason for concern is the work ethic. According to the Puritan work ethic, hard work is virtuous; not to work is immoral. There are also those who believe that valuing hard work is a prerequisite to a vigorous economy. Although concerns for the work ethic and for taxpayer costs obviously reinforce each other, they are not identical. For example, a reduction in overtime hours by many workers could have more effect on program costs than a few family heads stopping work entirely. Yet the latter is likely to be seen as a more serious violation of the work ethic.

Economic Theory

Economic theory assumes that an individual's choice between work and leisure (or other nonwork activities) depends on the person's net wage rate and nonwage income. Since, other things being equal, the individual is assumed to prefer leisure to work, an increase in nonwage income will lead him or her to work less and "consume" more leisure. In other words, there is a negative income effect on labor supply.

An increase in the net wage will have a similar income effect on labor supply. However, there will also be a positive substitution effect

in this case since an increase in the net wage means that each hour of leisure is now more expensive. Thus, an increase in the wage may lead to either an increase or a decrease in the supply of labor depending on whether the substitution or income effect dominates.

Income maintenance programs not only increase the beneficiary family's nonwage income, but, as a result of the marginal tax rate, there is also a reduction in the net wage of each family member. Therefore both the income effect and the substitution effect will act to reduce the family's work effort. The theory, however, makes no prediction concerning the magnitude of the reduction in labor supply.

While economic theory does not indicate the magnitude of the reduction in hours worked that income maintenance programs would induce, economic and sociological considerations suggest the effect would be different for different demographic groups. Consider, for example, prime-aged (25–60) married men compared to prime-aged married women. Traditional differences in the roles of husbands and wives would lead us to expect the effects of a transfer program on the hours worked by these two groups to differ. Husbands are expected, as breadwinners, to work full time. At least until recently, most wives were expected to raise children, to do housework, and only secondarily, if at all, to do market work. These role expectations are, of course, becoming less distinct; but the distinction is still far from unimportant. One would thus expect an income maintenance program to reduce the hours worked by wives by a greater percentage than by husbands for two closely related reasons. Working less than full time (or even not at all) is more socially acceptable for wives and the alternative uses of time by wives—raising children and doing housework—are seen as more valuable than husbands' traditional alternatives to market work.

Empirical Evidence:
Cross-Section Studies

Our brief overview of economic and socio-logical theory has suggested the following: (1) income maintenance programs will lead beneficiaries to reduce their hours worked;[5] (2) the magnitude of those reductions will be different for different demographic groups; and (3) the size of the reductions in the hours worked of any demographic group is an empirical question.

Since an income maintenance program increases the amount of nonemployment income available to beneficiaries and simultaneously decreases their net wage rates, one way of estimating the labor supply effect of such programs is to examine the differences in labor supply of individuals with differing wage rates and differing amounts of nonemployment income. For example, to estimate the effect of a program with a guarantee of $3,000 and a tax rate of 50 percent on the labor supply of a worker with a $4.00 per hour wage rate and no nonemployment income, one would compare the labor supply of individuals with $4.00 per hour wage rates and no nonemployment income to the labor supply of individuals of the same sex, age, race, years of schooling but with a wage rate of only $2.00 per hour and non-employment income of $3,000. Several researchers, including ourselves, have devoted considerable effort to use sample survey data for this purpose. These studies indicate that any reasonably generous program would lead to fairly substantial reductions in the labor supply of wives in beneficiary families. In all the carefully done studies, the estimated effects are much smaller for husbands. Still the precise magnitude of the labor supply

---

[5] Possible exceptions are wage or earnings subsidies (including the earned income tax credit) that have a zero guarantee and a negative tax rate.

effects is uncertain. The cross-section studies are based on the assumption that there are no important unmeasured differences across individuals that may affect labor supply and also be correlated with wage rates and nonemployment income. In fact, however, this assumption is probably not valid. For example, workers earning $4.00 per hour are likely to have more secure and less onerous jobs than those earning only $2.00 per hour. They may also be more economically ambitious. Similarly, the more economically ambitious an individual is, the more likely he or she is both to work long hours and to try to accumulate assets that yield nonemployment income from rents, dividends, or interest. Because of these problems, economists have focused their attention on the results of a set of income maintenance experiments.

Empirical Evidence
Experimental Studies

Because it is so difficult to determine causation when studies are based on nonexperimental data and because the labor supply issue is so important, the federal government has spent over 100 million dollars on experiments to investigate the effect of income maintenance on hours worked. These experiments offer people the opportunity to participate in an experimentally controlled set of alternative negative income tax programs. A negative income tax program differs from present income maintenance programs mainly in that payments are based only on family income and family size and not on other measures of need. The experiments were developed in the late 1960s when concern focused on the labor supply effect of extending welfare assistance to two-parent families.

Four income maintenance experiments have been conducted. The New Jersey experiment was the first, followed by the Rural

TABLE 2

Labor Supply Elasticity Estimates, Based on the Seattle-Denver Experiment*

	Elasticity		
	Total Income	*Substitution*	*Wage*
Husband	−.22	.09	−.13
Wife	−.31	.20	−.11
Female Family Head	−.22	.18	−.04

*These estimates are for the second year of the experiment and are taken from Michael C. Keeley, *Labor Supply and Public Policy: A Critical Review* (New York: Academic Press, 1981).

The substitution elasticity is the percentage change in annual hours worked due to the change in tax rates (holding income constant) divided by the percentage change in the net wage. The wage elasticity is defined similarly except that income is not held constant.

The "total-income" elasticity is the conventional income elasticity times the ratio of the individual's earnings to total family income. The conventional income elasticity is the percentage change in annual hours worked due to the increased income from the experiment (holding the net wage constant) divided by the percentage change in total family income that would have occurred in the absence of any labor supply effects. Rough estimates of these conventional income elasticities are − 0.3 for husbands, −1.2 for wives, and −0.3 for female family heads. The total-income elasticity can also be viewed as the negative of the marginal propensity to consume leisure as income increases.

Experiment in North Carolina and Iowa, the Gary Experiment, and finally the Seattle-Denver experiment. The Seattle-Denver experiment which began in 1970 had the largest sample (4,800) and the most generous treatment plans (guarantees varying from 75−125 percent of the poverty line). Therefore we shall focus our attention primarily on the results for this experiment. For most experimental families the tax rates in the Seattle-Denver experiment ranged from 50−70 percent. The experimental treatment lasted for either 3 or 5 years and was a substitute for existing income maintenance programs such as AFDC and food stamps.

In Table 2 we present estimates of income, wage, and substitution elasticities based on the Seattle-Denver experiments. The results are presented as elasticities since such estimates are easier to compare with results of other studies. The estimates in Table 2 are all consistent with the predictions of economic theory since the income elasticities are all negative and the substitution elasticities are all positive. The absolute value of these elasticity estimates is a little larger for the income effect than for the substitution effect. The income elasticity concept used in Table 2 has been defined so that it equals the difference between the wage and substitution elasticities. (See the footnote to Table 2 for discussion of the various elasticity concepts.) Therefore, *over the range of the tax rates in the experiment,* an increase in the tax rate, holding the guarantee constant, will lead to modest increases in hours worked.

The elasticity estimates in Table 2 are larger for wives than for husbands, with intermediate results for female family heads.[6] For

[6] The estimates are for the second year of the experiment. The results for later years are similar for husbands and wives but substantially larger for female family heads.

husbands, these experimentally-based estimates are not very different from the best estimates based on cross-section data. For wives and female family heads, on the other hand, the experimental estimates of the substitution effects are considerably lower than those in the nonexperimental literature and the wage effects are negative rather than positive.

Although the experimental evidence is probably the best available, it is still subject to some significant limitations.[7] First, despite the surprisingly small values of the substitution effect, at least for wives, relative to the income effect, there are some reasons to believe that the experiment underestimates the substitution effect. For example, the estimates are based on self-reported data and thus include the effect of incentives not to report earnings as well as incentives to reduce employment. Moreover, the incentive to underreport depends primarily on the experimental tax rate so that any such underreporting is expected to lead to a positive bias in the substitution and wage elasticity estimates.[8]

Another reason the estimates of the substitution effect in the experiment may be biased downward, especially relative to the estimates of the income effect, arises from the short-term nature of the experiment. Assuming no cost of adjustment, the estimate of the substitution effect will be biased upward since leisure is less costly and thus "on sale" during the experiment. On the other hand, the esti-

mate of the income effect will be biased downward, assuming that the demand for leisure depends on long-term or "permanent" income and not only on income during the experimental period. The results for those in the 5-year experiment do show somewhat smaller substitution effects and somewhat larger income effects than those for the 3-year group. Moreover, the total experimental effect is generally somewhat larger for those on the 5-year experiment.

There is also some reason to believe that the experiment may lead to an underestimate of the substitution effect. For experimentals who are only slightly below the breakeven level, any sizable reduction in hours worked due to the high experimental tax rates would lead to a reduction in total money income. Although in the absence of other commitments some of these experimentals might want to work less, many may be locked into high mortgage payments or other commitments that would make it difficult for them to adjust to reduced money income in the short run. In contrast, many experimentals well below the breakeven level may be able to reduce hours worked substantially without suffering a decline in their money income. Consequently, no previous commitments would limit their ability to work less. Such families presumably would respond to both the guarantee and tax parameters of the experiment. The experimental effect would be estimated as primarily an income effect, however, assuming, as indicated above, that the substitution effect is substantial only for those for whom there is a sizable positive experimental effect on money income. Consequently, we believe it is possible that, on balance, the experiment may overestimate the income effect relative to the substitution effect. As a result, the true wage elasticities may be positive rather than negative, especially for wives where the nonexperimental literature generally finds a positive wage effect.

---

[7] One problem is that estimates based on the same experimental data vary considerably, depending on the particular model estimated. For example, see the range of estimates, based solely on the Seattle-Denver experiment, in Michael C. Keeley, *Labor Supply and Public Policy: A Critical Review* (New York: Academic Press, 1981).

[8] The experimental results would not be biased for estimating the cost of a national program, assuming that such underreporting would be the same in the national program as in the experiment.

It is also possible that the experiment underestimates both the substitution and income effects of a permanent national program. In addition to being of short duration, none of the experiments were large enough to include a sizable proportion of those in any geographic area. Therefore, we expect that the experiments" would have had little effect on either the employment policies of employers or on community attitudes. Feldstein discusses these limitations in the following words:[9]

> First, this is a short-term experiment; there is little time for a change of individual attitudes. Second, because of the relatively small number of participants, there is no change in the supply of part-time jobs. Individuals in the experiment may prefer a 10 a.m. to 4 p.m. job and such jobs might be available with a universal program, but there is no scope for such a response in the current experiment. Finally, individual behavior is governed in part by peer group mores, the "brother-in-law effect": What would your brother-in-law say if you took a lower-paying job or were continually quitting work? Only when a program is generally available will its disincentive effects be reinforced rather than countered by social mores.

Consequently, the long-term labor supply effects of a national program might be considerably larger than those estimated on the basis of the (relatively) short-term smaller scale experiments.

Although there are limitations to both the experimental and nonexperimental studies, the qualifications are quite different in each case. Our confidence in the results is increased by the fact that both approaches give reasonably similar results, especially for husbands.

[9] See Martin Feldstein, "Seven Principles of Social Insurance," *Challenge*, 19, (8), page 8.

While the income maintenance experiments were designed primarily to provide better estimates of the effect of income maintenance programs on the amount people work, they have also provided valuable information on many other issues. Perhaps the most important nonlabor supply finding has been an apparent increase in marital breakups among experimentals. This result was not expected since one of the motivations for extending cash assistance to two-parent families was to reduce the incentive for such breakups. At least in the Seattle-Denver case, however, a more important factor may have been the easy availability of financial assistance to women in the experiment who want to terminate unsatisfactory marriages.

POLICY IMPLICATIONS

In this section, we discuss some implications of the labor supply estimates for the welfare reform debate. Then we conclude with a very brief discussion of evidence on the effects of policies to increase the employment of the poor, an alternative to providing assistance in the form of cash transfer payments.

Implications of the Empirical Evidence on Labor Supply Effects

Research results from both cross-section and experimental studies have been used to simulate the effects of welfare reform proposals on work effort and program costs. Such simulations are based on a nationally representative sample of families. For each family, first changes in income and tax rates are calculated under the assumption of no change in labor supply or other family characteristics. Then, based on the empirical estimates of income and substitution effects, changes in labor supply are determined. The final step of the simulation is to determine the effect of the labor supply changes on such outcomes as program cost and the money income of beneficiaries.

Several results from such simulations are worth noting. First, the percentage reductions in the labor supply of beneficiaries that would be induced by most welfare reform proposals do not appear to be very large, generally 10–15 percent even for a generous plan that would provide all families with children a guarantee equal to the poverty line, together with a marginal tax rate of 50 percent.[10]

Second, even though the percentage reductions in labor supply would not be especially large, such reductions do contribute notably to program costs. For example, for the plan described above with a poverty line guarantee and a 50 percent tax rate, estimates based on the Seattle-Denver experiment indicate that about 25 percent of the costs would occur because of reductions in labor supply. Moreover, these estimates imply that a dollar transfer would lead to only about a fifty cent increase in the money income of beneficiaries. How this result is viewed, of course, depends upon whether the objective of income transfer programs is solely to increase the money income of the poor. For example, if poor mothers choose to spend a large part of the increase in income from a new transfer program on staying home more and providing better care for their children, many might consider the program to be worth its costs.

Third, the results depend on the particular guarantee and tax rate. Holding the tax rate constant, an increased guarantee means a more generous, costly program. On the other hand, an increase in the tax rate, holding the guarantee constant, means a less generous program. The latest results from the Seattle-Denver experiment indicate that changes in the guarantee and tax rate do not have any dramatic effect on the percentage of the costs that is due to reductions in labor supply. On the other hand, the percentage of the program cost consumed as leisure is somewhat lower for the less generous plans.

Fourth, it is not always appropriate to look only at how beneficiaries respond to transfers and to ignore how taxpayers respond to the taxes required to finance the transfers. If the focus is on the work ethic and whether people will stop working when cash benefits are available, then the emphasis on beneficiaries is appropriate. On the other hand, if we are concerned with effects on aggregate labor supply and output in the economy, then we should also be concerned with the labor supply effects on taxpayers. When the effects of both tax and transfer payments are taken into account, it appears that increases in transfer payments might actually increase rather than decrease total output.[11]

Providing Employment Assistance

The income maintenance experiments have provided very valuable information on the labor supply effects of providing cash assistance.

---

[10] These estimates are based on the results from the Seattle-Denver experiment in Keeley et al., "The Labor-Supply Effects and Costs of Alternative Negative Income Tax Programs," *Journal of Human Resources* (Winter, 1978) and on cross-section estimates in Stanley Masters and Irwin Garfinkel, *Estimating the Labor Supply Effects of Income Maintenance Alternatives* (New York: Academic Press, 1977).

[11] See the paper, "A Simulation Analysis of the Economic Efficiency and Distributional Effects of Alternative Program Structures: The Negative Income Tax Versus The Credit Income Tax" by David Betson, David Greenberg, and Richard Kasten, in *Income-Tested Transfer Programs*, Irwin Garfinkel, ed. (New York: Academic Press, forthcoming).

This result occurs, in part, because the Seattle-Denver estimates on which this simulation are based imply large income effects of tax increases for wives in high-income families.

Concern with such effects has led to more attention to increasing employment opportunities as a way of increasing the income of the poor while simultaneously decreasing welfare payments. Employment assistance has taken many forms, including job search assistance, training in occupational skills, and the provision of subsidized jobs. In most cases, however, these programs are only available to a small percentage of welfare beneficiaries.

A number of these programs have been subject to careful evaluation studies, with the findings frequently quite positive. A recent evaluation of the WIN program indicates that providing different kinds of jobs and training generally increases the earnings of participants substantially.[12] In addition, an evaluation of a transitional work experience program called Supported Work, based on a large sample and an experimental design, finds large long-lasting post-program earnings gains for long-term AFDC recipients who volunteer to participate in the program—gains that appear to substantially exceed the program's costs.[13]

Certain job search assistance programs also appear to have substantial benefits.[14]

Given this evidence, it appears reasonable to do more to assist AFDC recipients to obtain jobs. Not all welfare recipients will be able to work, however, especially since some are on welfare mainly because of disabilities or the need to care for very small children. An emphasis on increasing employment opportunities will do little to assist such people. In addition, an emphasis on employment opportunities could easily lead to greater enforcement of work requirements, perhaps under degrading conditions. Thus, as for most welfare issues, there is no simple answer to the emphasis that should be given to employment versus cash programs. While empirical evidence is useful in illuminating many issues, political decisions remain heavily dependent on value judgments expressed through the political process. Such value judgments include both the relative importance of generosity versus cost and the emphasis to be given to cash versus employment assistance.

---

[12] See Ketron, Inc., "The Long Term Impact of WIN II," (Wayne, Pa.: Ketron, Inc., 1980).

[13] See Stanley Masters, "The Effect of Supported Work on the Earnings and Transfer Payments of its AFDC Target Group," *Journal of Human Resources* (Fall, 1981). The post-program earnings results of this program are considerably stronger for long-term AFDC recipients than for the other target groups, ex-addicts, ex-offenders, and disadvantaged youth. Although work experience programs in this country have been targeted primarily at disadvantaged youth, the Supported Work evaluation finds no evidence of

postive post-program employment effects or any crime effects for such youth.

[14] For example, see Nathan Azrin, "The Job Finding Club as a Method for Obtaining Employment for Welfare Eligible Clients," *A Report to the U.S. Department of Labor,* Grant No. 51-17-76-04 (Anna, Ill.: Mental Health and Development Center, 1978). On the other hand, the Ketron study of WIN finds that the more traditional job search assistance provided by WIN has no apparent effect on employment.

II

INDUSTRIAL RELATIONS

The Labor
Movement

Labor market analysis is concerned with the determinants and consequences of decisions made by large numbers of individuals and firms. In much of the analysis, such decisions are assumed to be made independently. Yet, in many labor markets, workers make decisions collectively through a union. Trade unions and other worker organizations have arisen for many reasons and have taken a wide variety of forms. The selection by Philip Taft discusses some of the many theories that have arisen to explain the origin and behavior of the labor movement. Among the theories discussed are those developed by the Webbs, Marx, Hoxie, and Commons.

The Webbs, writing in England at the end of the nineteenth century, defined a trade union as "a continuous association of wage earners for the purpose of maintaining or improving the condition of their working lives." In *Industrial Democracy,* they argue that the primary method of unions is the establishment of common rules, rules that apply equally to all workers in a group. If they do not act as a group, workers have little bargaining power in establishing wages and other conditions of employment. The Webbs indicate that, despite agreement on the necessity of common rules, trade unionists have different views of the principles that should determine the conditions of employment. They outline three views, which they label as the Doctrine of Vested Interests, the Doctrine of Supply and Demand, and the Doctrine of the Living Wage. These views still appear to have relevance, not only with regard to unions but also in political struggles among different economic interest groups.

Another very influential theory of the labor movement is the one developed by Selig Perlman in *A Theory of the Labor Movement*, written in 1928. In his view workers generally have had their economic attitudes "determined by consciousness of scarcity of opportunity" and thus have tended to band together to control and ration job opportunities. In attempting to achieve their objectives, workers have had to combat not only the capitalist employers, but also the anti-capitalist intelligentsia, which has tried to channel worker protest into a more fundamental revolution against capitalism. Although the intelligentsia has been a very important force in the historical development of the European labor movement, it has been much less influential in America. In this country the major protagonist of the labor movement has been the capitalist class, a class whose position has been strengthened by many of our pioneer traditions.

The differences between the labor movements in the United States and in Europe are also discussed by Everett Kassalow. European workers generally have been more concerned with transforming society and advancing the entire working class. Thus they have put much greater emphasis than their American counterparts on political activities. In the last half century, however, the differences between the American and European labor movements appear to have diminished.

George Hildebrand analyzes changes in the extent of unionization in the United States since World War II and discusses why there has been little growth in union membership since 1970. He also considers the future of the trade union movement and concludes that how it changes will be determined mainly by changes in the business community and especially in the relation between business and government.

The opinions of unions held by American workers, both union and nonunion members, are summarized by Thomas Kochan, based on data from a recent national survey. Although many workers are critical of union leaders, most consider them effective in promoting member job interests. Union members are generally satisfied with their leaders and one-third of nonmembers indicate they would vote to unionize.

32

Theories of the Origin of the Labor Movement

Philip Taft

Philip Taft, "Theories of the Labor Movement," in *Interpreting the Labor Movement*, George W. Brooks et al., eds., 1952 Reprinted by permission of the Industrial Relations Research Association.

Generalizations to explain the origin and nature of the trade union movement have been developed by a variety of writers. Even a superficial observation of the labor movement reveals a multitude of facts, some of them isolated and some contradictory. A theory is an attempt to give an ordered explanation, to account for the origin and behavior of labor unionism. . . .

BRENTANO

One of the earliest attempts by a nonsocialist writer to deal with this question was made by the German economist and historian, Lujo Brentano. Writing in the third quarter of the 19th century, Brentano was convinced that "Trade-Unions are the successors of the old Gilds."[1] Brentano, unlike the contemporary critics who see trade unions as a "gild type" of monopoly, was not opposed to organizations of workers. On the contrary, he believed they were both necessary and desirable as offsets to the power of the employer. Unions, in Brentano's opinion, arose under "the breaking up of an old system, and among the men suffering

[1] Lujo Brentano, "On the History and Development of Gilds," in *English Gilds*. Toulmin Smith, ed. (London: Early English Text Society, 1870), p. clxv.

from this disorganization, in order that they may maintain independence and order."[2] . . .

Brentano emphasized that the objectives of the trade unions as of the craft gilds "was the maintenance of an entire system of order," or of a standard of life which was being undermined by the growing factory owners. Instead of being a revolutionary mass bent on destroying the system of private property, Brentano emphasized the conservative aspects of trade unionism in its desire to return to an earlier time. In this view, the trade union arose as a result of the breakdown of the customary rights enjoyed by the worker, and it was an attempt to create a new equilibriu.n by elaborating a system of rules to govern industry. The view that the trade unions were descended from the gilds has been challenged by the Webbs. Nevertheless, the notion that the trade unions arose because of the disturbance of an established custom shows that Brentano well understood one of the essential causes for the origin of trade unionism. An attempt to change a rule or a rate has frequently led to organization. Considering that his essay was written in the 1860's, when most of the English unions were groupings of skilled men, the insistence upon their resemblance to craft gilds is perhaps better understood.

Moreover, the scarcity consciousness which is a characteristic of the skilled unions, in the United States as well as elsewhere, shown in the restrictive rules and the limitation upon admission, is certainly an attitude found in the gilds. Even where no direct connection exists, the spirit is not different. However, Brentano neglected the difference between the "mercantile" attitude of a gildsman and the wage consciousness of a worker. Yet, his emphasis upon the conservative traditional nature of unions, their insistence upon protecting their job territory by restrictions upon free entry and

technological change, caught a significant aspect of early trade unionism.

THE WEBBS

The Webbs, who followed Brentano chronologically, refused to accept the latter's interpretation of the origin of the labor movement, although they admired many of his insights. To the Webbs, the origin of trade unionism depended upon the separation of classes. The Webbs defined a trade union as "a continuous association of wage earners for the purpose of maintaining or improving the conditions of their working lives."[3] They, therefore, dated the beginning of English trade unionism in the latter part of the 17th century with the appearance of a property-less wage earner. The journeymen's revolts of earlier times were interpreted largely as movements against the authority of the gild, and the "bachelors" companies they find to have been a subordinate branch of the masters' gild. It was only when the skilled journeyman found his prospect for advancement into the ranks of the masters greatly diminished that stable combinations among the handicraftsmen arose. It was only when "the changing conditions of industry had reduced to an infinitesimal chance the journeyman's prospect of himself becoming a master, that we find the passage of ephemeral combinations into permanent trade societies."[4]

The basic cause for the origin of trade unions, according to the Webbs, was "in the separation of classes, or in the separation of the worker from the means of production. This is itself due to an economic revolution which

---

[2] *Ibid.*, p. xlvi.

[3] Sidney and Beatrice Webb, *The History of Trade Unionism* (London: Printed by the Authors for the Students of the Workers Educational Association, 1919), p. 1.

[4] *Ibid.*, p. 6.

took place in certain industries." Unions arose as soon as "the great bulk of the workers had ceased to be independent producers, themselves controlling the processes and owning the materials and product of their labour, and had passed into the conditions of lifelong wage-earners, possessing neither the instruments of production nor the commodity in its finished state."[5] This separation of classes or the separation of the worker from the means of production preceded, to some extent, the development of the factory system. The reduction of the worker to a mere wage-earner, dependent upon others for employment, may have come about as a result of one or many of several causes. In the tailoring trade, the masters came from a small segment—the journeymen who had acquired the highest level of skills. The great majority of the workers were poor, employed as sewers who prepared the material for their more skilled brethren. Increasing capital requirements accentuated the class divisions within the trade. It was possible

> to start a business in a back street as an independent master tailor with no more capital or skill than the average journeyman could command, yet the making of fine clothes worn by the Court and the gentry demanded then, as now, a capital and a skill which put the extensive and lucrative trade altogether out of the reach of the thousands of journeymen whom it employed.[6]

In the woolen industry, class differentiation with its mass of permanent wage-earners followed the rise of the "rich clothiers," who provided the raw materials, and encouraged the division of labor so that a different set of workers would be employed at each stage of manufacturing. The merchant capitalists or clothiers purchased the wool, had it carded and spun into yarn by one group of workers, had

it changed into cloth by another group, the weavers, and finally turned the product over to a new set of workers to be dressed. While the workers still retained the tools of their trade, they could acquire, as a rule, neither the capital nor the knowledge to enter business. Consequently, a class of permanent wage-earners who had scant hopes of ever becoming capitalists arose, with the result that permanent organizations of labor were devised to protect the standard of life.

The universal cause which accounts for the origin of trade unionism is the separation of the worker from the means of production with the consequent rise of a permanent class of workers dependent upon an employer. While other conditions may tend to create a permanent class of wage-earners, the rise of the factory system was the most pervasive cause of the separation of the worker from the means of production. For the Webbs, it had

> become a commonplace of modern Trade Unionism that only in those industries in which the worker has ceased to be concerned in the profits of buying and selling—that inseparable characteristic of the ownership and management of the means of production—can effective and stable trade organization be established.[7]

Yet, this explanation raises a problem, for there had always existed in English industry a large class of unskilled and low-paid workers virtually debarred from rising to independent craftsmen. The ill-paid farm laborer, and others of low skill, however, had not been the pioneers of trade unionism. On the contrary, it was the highly skilled journeyman who for years had been the object of government protection who was the first to form labor unions. It was not the worker who had the lowest bargaining

[5] *Ibid.*, p. 26.
[6] *Ibid.*, p. 31.

[7] *Ibid.*, p. 41.

power but the one with the greatest sense of independence who pioneered the trade union movement. This was inevitable, for only the worker with a great sense of independence was willing to challenge the authority of the employer in the early days of organization, and it required some threat to existing customs and standards to initiate organization. Therefore, it was not the property-less proletariat of Marx but the labor aristocrat who was the pioneer of trade unionism. The Webbs and Brentano agreed that a threat to established relations is likely to stimulate organization of labor in defense of the old conditions or in an effort to establish a new equilibrium. The Webbs, however, placed emphasis upon the class nature of a union; that it arose when the possibilities of class mobility had been reduced and when the worker felt that he had nothing but his labor to sell. The Webbs' view underlines the special character of the trade union which, despite many attitudes of the old gild, was a new type or organization. . . .

MARXISM

Marxist ideas on trade unions are intimately and inextricably related to the general Marxist assumptions and conclusions on social institutions and the directions of their development. In common with the Webbs, Marx and his followers explained the origin of trade unions by the rise of a working class bereft of control over the instruments of production. While the Webbs regarded labor unions as a means used by workers to maintain or improve their traditional standards of life, Marx regarded them as only one—and by no means the most important—weapon in labor's armory for waging the class war. . . .

At best, trade unions could only deal with short-run, day-to-day problems. They were a response to the need of labor to protect its day-to-day interests. They were spontaneous

efforts by workers to restrict the effects of competition in the labor market.[8] Unions were class organizations, which came into existence to protect the worker against the employer. It was the pressure of the employer which drove the worker to revolt. Soon, however, labor established

permanent associations in order to make provision beforehand for these occasional revolts. . . . Now and then the workers are victorious but only for a time. The real fruit of their battle lies not in the immediate result but in the expanding union of workers. The union is helped on by the improved means of communication that are created by modern industry and that place the workers of different localities in contact with one another. It was just this contact that was needed to centralize the numerous local struggles, all of the same character, into one national struggle between classes. But every class struggle is a political struggle.[9]

This statement, although it was written in 1847, expressed the essentials of the Marxist view of trade unionism, even though Marx continued to write for 35 years and Engels for almost 50 years after these words appeared. Union organizations were an attempt to support the revolts made inevitable by the exploitation by the capitalist. Labor might have been able to gain temporary concessions but not permanent relief. Therefore, the isolated revolts had to be continually enlarged until they became the living embodiment of the struggle between classes. In line with his views on the origin and nature of trade unionism, Marx inspired a resolution at the first congress of the International Workingmen's Association (First International) which advised the trade

[8] A. Lozovsky, *Marx and the Trade Unions* (New York: International Publishers, 1942), p. 16.

[9] Karl Marx and Frederick Engels, *Manifesto of the Communist Party* (Chicago: Charles H. Kerr and Company, no date), p. 26.

unions to seek actively the abolition of the wage system. The trade unions[10] were more than institutions for the daily struggle with employers. They were a means of mobilizing the strength of labor against the capitalist class. "While, however, the trade unions are absolutely indispensable in the daily struggle between labour and capital, still more important is their other aspect, as instruments *for transforming the system of wage labour and for overthrowing the dictatorship of capital.*"[11]

SELECTED CATHOLIC
WRITERS ON TRADE UNIONISM

The attitude of Catholic clergymen and writers on trade unionism was extremely important in the United States because members of the faith were heavily represented among industrial workers. The question before Catholic students was whether the unions arose to defend the worker against superior economic force or were a section of a movement challenging religion and existing governments. . . .

Catholic laymen and theologians had been watching the evolution of modern industrialism, with its accompanying evils, with growing concern. Not only was modern industry threatening to undermine established institutions, but the excesses of some businessmen and their inordinate lust for gain were encouraging the spread of radical social doctrines. The Bishop of Mainz, Wilhelm Emanual von Ketteler, insisted that the church take the lead in eradicating the industrial evils of his time. . . .

The writings and works of these reformers culminated in Pope Leo XIII's *Rerum Novarum,* a document which addressed itself to the social problems of the time. At the outset,

the Pope attacked the doctrines of materialistic socialism then making considerable headway on the continent. He, however, fully endorsed the trade unions seeking the protection of the worker in industry. Trade unions arose, according to Pope Leo, to redress the advantages held by the employer and to form voluntary associations as was the natural right of man.

ROBERT HOXIE

Robert Hoxie was impressed by the diversity in the structural arrangements and in the functioning of unions. He found "that unionism has not a single genesis, but that it has made its appearance time after time, independently, wherever in the modern industrial era a group of workers, large or small, developed a strong internal consciousness of common interests."[12] He was convinced, moreover, that unions, over time, responded to changes in conditions, needs and attitudes. He found that unionists "are prone to act and to formulate theories afterward,"[13] and that they attempted to meet whatever problems events had placed before them. Unions arose out of group needs and as they were not uniform, a single theory will not suffice. The

> union program, taking with it all its mutations and contradictions, comprehends nothing less than all the various economic, political, ethical and social viewpoints and modes of action of a vast and heterogeneous complex of working class groups, molded by diverse environments and actuated by diverse motives; it expresses nothing less than ideals, aspirations, hopes and fears, modes of thinking and action of all these working groups. In short, if we can think of

---

[10] Oscar Testut, *L'Internationale* (Paris: E. Lachaud, 1871), p. 126. Lozovsky, *op. cit.,* p. 16.

[11] G. M. Stekloff, *History of the First International* (London: Martin Lawrence, Ltd. 1928), p. 84. Italics in source.

[12] Robert Hoxie, *Trade Unionism in the United States* (New York: D. Appleton and Co., 1928), p. 34. The first edition was published by D. Appleton & Co., 1919.

[13] *Ibid.*

unionism as such, it must be as one of the most complex, heterogeneous and protean of modern social phenomena.[14] . . .

Hoxie was a shrewd and careful observer, but he overstressed the importance of the differences he noticed between unions. Significant differences in the structure and function of unions existed, but these differences may have reflected the differences in the industrial environment or in the make-up of the membership. If unions are a response to differing group psychology, it is difficult to explain why, despite differences, unions always perform certain basic functions for their members. While one may find Hoxie's explanation of the origin of unions incomplete, his stress on diverse causes did highlight the differences in the structure and the functioning of unions, both with respect to their internal affairs and with respect to collective bargaining. These differences have always existed within American trade unionism, and the attitudes of the workers composing the union have undoubtedly played some role in determining the quality of a particular labor organization. It is difficult to give weight to specific factors, but the make-up of the membership and its response to the problems of industry obviously contribute to determining a union's form and attitudes. Hoxie's emphasis upon variety of origin called attention to a facet in the origin of labor organizations unstressed by other writers.

JOHN R. COMMONS

John R. Commons was one of the pioneer investigators of labor. In explaining the origin of labor unions, Commons, similarly to the Webbs, in England, based his conclusions upon an examination of records rather than upon an *a priori* theory. Commons attributed

the rise of labor organizations to the differentiation of classes, which was in turn due to the expansion of the market. The artisan who embodied within himself the mercantile, manufacturing, and labor functions is, over a period of time, metamorphosed on one side into a capitalist merchant; on the other, into a manufacturer buying labor, and a wage-earner selling labor power. The differentiation in function was accompanied by increasing competition—both due to the widening of the market. Facing increasingly severe competition, the merchant capitalist attempted to impose the burdens upon labor by depressing wages. Labor responded by forming labor unions, which sought "the practical remedy . . . the elimination of the competitive menace through a protective organization or protective legislation."[15]

Commons maintained that unions arose to overcome the workers' inferior bargaining position. Moreover, he saw in labor organizations the culmination of an age-long process of extending freedom.

> The restraints which laborers place on free competition, in the interests of fair competition, begin to be taken over by employers and administered by their own labor managers. Even organized labor achieves participation with management in the protection of the job, just as the barons and the capitalists achieved participation with the King in the protection of property and business. A common law of labor is constructed by selecting the reasonable practices and rejecting the bad practices of labor, and by depriving both unions and management of arbitrary power over the job.[16] . . .

[14] *Ibid.*, p. 35.

[15] John R. Commons, *Labor and Administration* (New York: The Macmillan Co., 1913), p. 261.

[16] John R. Commons, *Legal Foundations of Capitalism* (New York: The Macmillan Co., 1924), pp. 311-12.

33

The Assumptions of Trade Unionism

Sidney and Beatrice Webb

Sidney and Beatrice Webb, *Industrial Democracy,* published by the authors in London, England, 1897.

... For the improvement of the conditions of employment, whether in respect to wages, hours, health, safety, or comfort, the Trade Unionists have, with all their multiplicity of Regulations, really only two expedients, which we term, respectively, the Device of the Common Rule, and the Device of Restriction of Numbers. The Regulations which we have described in our chapters on the Standard Rate, the Normal Day, and Sanitation and Safety, are but different forms of one principle—the settlement, whether by Mutual Insurance, Collective Bargaining, or Legal Enactment, of minimum conditions of employment, by Common Rules applicable to whole bodies of workers. All these Regulations are based on the assumption that when, in the absence of any Common Rule, the conditions of employment are left to "free competition," this always means, in practice, that they are arrived at by Individual Bargaining between contracting parties of very unequal economic strength. Such a settlement, it is asserted, invariably tends, for the mass of the workers, towards the worst possible conditions of labor—ultimately, indeed, to the barest subsistence level—whilst even the exceptional few do not permanently gain as much as they otherwise could. We find accordingly that the Device of the Common Rule is a universal feature of Trade Unionism, and that the assumption on which it is based is held from one end of the Trade Union world to the other. The Device of Restriction of Numbers stands in a different position.... The assumption on which they are based—that better conditions can be obtained by limiting the number of competitors—would not be denied by any Trade Unionist, but it cannot be said to form an important part in the working creed of the Trade Union World....

But these initial assumptions as to the need for Trade Unionism and the efficacy of its two devices do not, of themselves, account for the marked divergence between different Unions, alike in the general character of their policy and in the Regulations which they enforce. The universal belief in a Common Rule affords, to begin with, no guidance as to how much wages the members of a particular trade will claim or receive, or how many hours they will consider to be a proper working day. There is, in fact, no "Trade Union Rate of Wages," but many different rates—not even a "Trade Union Working Day," but hours of labor varying from occupation to occupation. This divergence of policy comes out even more strikingly in the adoption or rejection of the Device of Restriction of Numbers, a few trades still making the strict Limitation of Apprentices and the Exclusion of Illegal Men a leading feature of their policy, whilst others throw their trades absolutely open to all comers, and rely exclusively on the maintenance of the Common Rule.... The Trade Unionists, in their narrower sphere of the conditions of employment, are influenced by three divergent conceptions of the principle upon which wages, hours, and other terms of the labor contract ought to be determined. These three assumptions, which we distinguish as the Doctrine of Vested Interest, the Doctrine of Supply and Demand, and the Doctrine of a Living Wage, give us the clue to the conflicting policies of the Trade Union world.

By the Doctrine of Vested Interests

we mean the assumption that the wages and other conditions of employment hitherto enjoyed by any section of workmen ought under no circumstances to be interfered with for the worse....

When, at the beginning of this century, the Doctrine of Vested Interests was, as regards the wage-earners, definitely repudiated by the House of Commons, the Trade Unionists were driven back upon what we have termed the Doctrine of Supply and Demand. Working men were told, by friends and foes alike, that they could no longer be regarded as citizens entitled to legal protection of their established expectations; that labor was a commodity like any other; and that their real position was that of sellers in a market, entitled to do the best they could for themselves within the limits of the law of the land, but to no better terms than they could, by the ordinary arts of bargaining, extract from those with whom they dealt. It was the business of the employer to buy "labor" in the cheapest market, and that of the workman to sell it in the dearest. It followed that the only criterion of justice of any claim was ability to enforce it, and that the only way by which the workmen could secure better conditions of employment was by strengthening their strategic position against the employer....

The Doctrine of Supply and Demand is manifestly inapplicable [to some of the most vital conditions of employment]. It is impossible, for instance, to adjust the ventilation, drainage, temperature, sanitary conveniences, and safety of a cotton-mill or an engineering establishment, in proportion to the strategic position of each of the eight or ten different sections of workpeople there employed. These conditions must, in practice, be the same for the piecer and spinner, the boilermaker and his helper. If no other consideration than Supply and Demand entered into the question, it would pay the employer better to silence, by the bribe of higher wages, any minority strong enough to grumble, rather than incur the expense of improving the conditions for the whole establishment.

We reach here a point on which the community has long since become convinced that neither the Doctrine of Vested Interests, nor that of Supply and Demand affords any guide in determining the conditions of employment. In all that concerns the sanitary condition of the workplace, or the prevention of accidents, we are not content merely to protect the "established expectation" of the workmen, nor yet to leave the matter to settle itself according to the strategic position of each section. By common consent the employer is now required, in all this range of conditions, to give his workpeople, not what has been customary, nor yet what they can exact, but what, in the opinion of Parliament and its expert advisers, is necessary for their health and efficiency. . . .

When we pass from the circumstances amid which the wage-earner is to work . . . to the amount of money which he will receive as wages, we find the protest against the Doctrine of Supply and Demand much less universal, and only recently becoming conscious of itself. During the whole of this century middle-class public opinion has scouted the idea that the actual money wages of the operative could possibly be governed by any other considerations than the relative strategic positions of the parties to the bargain. And although the Trade Unionists have never thoroughly accepted this doctrine, even when that of Vested Interests had become manifestly impossible, they have, until recent years, never succeeded in intelligibly setting forth any contrary view. No reader of the working-class literature for the last two hundred years can, however, doubt the existence of an abiding faith in quite another principle. Deep down in their hearts the organised workmen, even whilst holding the Doctrine of Vested Interests,

or acquiescing in that of Supply and Demand, have always cherished a feeling that one condition is paramount over all, namely, that wages must be so fixed that the existing generation of operatives should at any rate be able to live by their trade. . . .

We can now form a definite idea of the assumption which this generation has set up against the Doctrine of Supply and Demand, and which we have termed the Doctrine of a Living Wage. There is a growing feeling, not confined to Trade Unionists, that the best interests of the community can only be attained by deliberately securing, to each section of the workers, those conditions which are necessary for the continuous and efficient fulfilment of its particular function in the social machine. From this point of view, it is immaterial to the community whether or not a workman has, by birth, servitude, or purchase, acquired a "right to a trade," or what, at any given moment, may be his strategic position towards the capitalist employer. The welfare of the community as a whole requires, it is contended, that no section of workers should be reduced to conditions which are positively inconsistent with industrial or civic efficiency. Those who adopt this assumption argue that, whilst it embodies what was good in the two older doctrines, it avoids their socially objectionable features. Unlike the Doctrine of Vested Interests, it does not involve any stereotyping of industrial processes, or the protection of any class of workers in the monopoly of a particular service. It is quite consistent with the freedom of every wage-earner to choose or change his occupation, and with the employer's freedom to take on whichever man he thinks best fitted for his work. Thus it in no way checks mobility or stops competition. Unlike the Doctrine of Supply and Demand it does not tempt the workmen to limit their numbers, or combine with the employers to fix prices, or restrict output. It avoids, too, the evil of fluctuations of wages, in which the income of the workers varies, not according to their needs as citizens or producers, nor yet to the intensity of their exertion, but solely according to the temporary and, as far as they are concerned, fortuitous position of their trade. On the other hand, the Doctrine of a Living Wage goes far in the direction of maintaining "established expectation." Whilst it includes no sort of guarantee that any particular individual will be employed at any particular trade, those who are successful in the competition may feel assured that, so long as they retain their situations, the conditions of an efficient and vigorous working life will be secured to them.[1]

The most obvious drawback of the Doctrine of a Living Wage is its difficulty of application. There is, to begin with, a loss of theoretical perfection in the fact that the indispensable minimum conditions prescribed for each occupation cannot practically be adapted to the requirements of each individual, but must be roughly gauged by needs of the normal type. It may well be that a consumptive weaver or a short-sighted engineer requires, for his continued preservation, atmospheric conditions or elaborate fencing of machinery which would be wasted on the vast majority of his colleagues. It might be found that an exceptionally delicate girl ought not to work more than five hours a day, or that a somewhat backward laborer with a sick wife and a large family could not maintain himself in physical efficiency on the standard wages of his class. But this is not a practical objection. The prescription of certain

[1] Thus, the Doctrine of a Living Wage does not profess, any more than does the Doctrine of Vested Interests or that of Supply and Demand, to solve the problem of the unemployer or the unemployable. All three doctrines are obviously consistent with any treatment of that problem, from leaving the unemployed and the unemployable to starvation or mendicancy, up to the most scientific Poor Law classification, or the most complete system of state or trade insurance.

minimum conditions does not prevent the humane employer from voluntarily granting to any exceptionally unfortunate individuals for whom the minimum is insufficient whatever better terms are physically possible. What it does prevent is the taking advantage of the strategic weakness of such individuals, and their being compelled to accept positively worse conditions of employment than their stronger colleagues. A more serious difficulty is our lack of precise knowledge as to what are the conditions of healthy life and industrial efficiency. . . .

The foregoing exposition of the assumptions of Trade Unionism will have given the reader the necessary clue, both to the historical changes in Trade Union policy from generation to generation, and also to the diversity at present existing in the Trade Union world. As soon as it is realised that Trade Unionists are inspired, not by any single doctrine as to the common weal, but more or less by three divergent and even contradictory views as to social expediency, we no longer look to them for any one consistent and uniform policy. The predominance among any particular section of workmen, or at any particular period, of one or other of the three assumptions which we have described—the Doctrine of Vested Interests, the Doctrine of Supply and Demand, and the Doctrine of a Living Wage—manifests itself in the degree of favor shown to particular Trade Union Regulations. The general faith in the Doctrine of Vested Interests explains why we find Trade Unionism, in one industry, or at one period, expressing itself in legally enforced terms of apprenticeship, customary rates of wages, the prohibition of new processes, strict maintenance of the lines of demarcation between trades, the exclusion of "illegal men," and the enforcement of "patrimony" and entrance fees. With the acceptance of the Doctrine of Supply and Demand we see coming in the policy of inclusion and its virtually compulsory Trade Unionism, Sliding Scales, the encouragement of improvements in machinery and the actual penalising of backward employers, the desire for a deliberate Regulation of Output and the establishment of alliances with employers against the consumer. Finally, in so far as the Doctrine of a Living Wage obtains, we see a new attention to the enforcement of Sanitation and Safety, general movements for the reduction of hours, attempts by the skilled trades to organise the unskilled laborers and women workers, denunciation of Sliding Scales and fluctuating incomes, the abandonment of apprenticeship in favor of universal education, and the insistence on a "Moral Minimum" wage below which no worker should be employed. . . .

These successive changes of faith explain the revolutions which have taken place in Trade Union opinion as to the relation of Labor to the State. When men believe in the Doctrine of Vested Interests, it is to the common law of the realm that they look for the protection of their rights and possessions. The law alone can secure to the individual, whether with regard to his right to a trade or his right to an office, his privilege in a new process of his title to property, the fulfillment of his "established expectation." Hence it is that we find eighteenth-century Trade Unionism confidently taking for granted that all its regulations ought properly to be enforced by the magistrate, and devoting a large part of its funds to political agitations and legal proceedings. When the Doctrine of Vested Interests was replaced by that of Supply and Demand, the Trade Unionists naturally turned to Collective Bargaining as their principal method of action. Instead of going to the State for protection, they fiercely resented any attempt to interfere with their struggle with employers, on the issue of which, they were told, their wages must depend. The Common Law, once their friend, now seemed always their most dangerous enemy, as it hampered

their freedom of combination, and by its definitions of libel and conspiracy, set arbitrary limits to their capacity of making themselves unpleasant to the employers or the non-unionists. Hence the desire of the Trade Unionists of the middle of this century, whilst sweeping away all laws against combinations, to keep Trade Unionism itself absolutely out of the reach of the law-courts. The growth of the Doctrine of a Living Wage, resting as this does on the assumption that the conditions of employment require to be deliberately fixed, naturally puts the State in the position of arbitrator between the workman who claims more, and the employer who offers less, than is consistent with the welfare of other sections. But the appeal is not to the Common Law. It is no longer a question of protecting each individual in the enjoyment of whatever could be proved to be his customary privileges, or to flow from identical "natural rights," but of prescribing, for the several sections, the conditions required, in the interest of the whole community, by their diverse actual needs. We therefore see the Common Rules for each trade embodied in particular statutes, which the Trade Unionists, far from resisting, use their money and political influence to obtain. The double change of doctrine has thus brought about a return to the attitude of the Old Unionists of the eighteenth century, but with a significant difference. To-day it is not custom or privilege which appeals to the State, but the requirements of efficient citizenship. Whenever a Trade Union honestly accepts as the sole and conclusive test of any of its aspirations what we have termed the Doctrine of a Living Wage, and believes that Parliament takes the same view, we always find it, sooner or later, attempting to embody that aspiration in the statute law.

The political student will notice that there exists in the Trade Union world much the same cleavage of opinion, upon what is socially expedient, as among other classes of society. All Trade Unionists believe that the abandonment of the conditions of employment to the chances of Individual Bargaining is disastrous, alike to the wage-earners and to the community. But when, in pursuance of this assumption, they take concerted action for the improvement of their condition, we see at once emerge among them three distinct schools of thought. In the special issues and technical controversies of Trade Unionism we may trace the same broad generalisations, as to what organisation of society is finally desirable, as lead, in the larger world of politics, to the ultimate cleavage between Conservatives, Individualists, and Collectivists. The reader will have seen that there is, among Trade Unionists, a great deal of what cannot be described otherwise than as Conservatism. The abiding faith in the sanctity of vested interests; the strong presumption in favor of the *status quo;* the distrust of innovation; the liking for distinct social classes, marked off from each other by corporate privileges and peculiar traditions; the disgust at the modern spirit of self-seeking assertiveness; and the deep-rooted conviction that the only stable organization of society is that based on each man being secured and contented in his inherited station of life—all these are characteristic of the genuine Conservative, whether in the Trade Union or the State. In sharp contrast with this character, and, as we think, less congenial to the natural bent of the English workman, we have, in the great modern unions, a full measure of Radical Individualism. The conception of society as a struggle between warring interests; the feeling that every man and every class is entitled to all that they can get, and to nothing more; the assumption that success in the fight is an adequate test of merit, and, indeed, the only one possible; and the bounding optimism which can confidently place the welfare of the community under the guardianship of self-interest—

these are typical of the "Manchester School," alike in politics and in Trade Unionism. But in Trade Unionism, as in the larger sphere of politics, the facts of modern industry have led to a reaction. As against the Conservative, the Individualist Radical asserted that "all men are born free and equal, with equal rights to life, liberty, and the pursuit of happiness." But it is now obvious that men are not born equal, either in capacity or in opportunity. There has accordingly arisen, in the Trade Union as in the political world, a school of thought which asserts that a free struggle among unequal individuals, or combinations of individuals, means the permanent oppression and degradation of those who start handicapped, and inevitably results in a tacit conspiracy among the more favored classes to maintain or improve their own positions of vantage at the cost of the community at large. The Collectivist accordingly insists on the need for a conscious and deliberate organisation of society, based, not on vested interests or the chances of the fight, but on the scientifically ascertained needs of each section of citizens. Thus, within the Trade Union movement, we find the Collectivist-minded working-man grounding his regulation of the conditions of employment upon what we have called the Doctrine of a Living Wage. In the wider world of politics we see the Collectivist statesman groping his way to the similar conception of a deliberate organisation of production, regulation of service, and apportionment of income—in a word, to such a conscious adjustment of the resources of the community to its needs as will result in its highest possible efficiency. In the Trade Union world the rival assumptions exist side by side, and the actual regulation of industry is a perpetually shifting compromise between them. The political student may infer that, in the larger organisation of society, the rival conceptions of Conservatism, Individualism, and Collectivism will long co-exist. Any further application of Collectivism, whether in the Trade Union or the political world, depends, it is clear, on an increase in our scientific knowledge, no less than on the growth of new habits of deliberate social co-operation. Progress in this direction must, therefore, be gradual, and will probably be slow. And the philosophical Collectivist will, we think, foresee that, whether in the regulation of labor, the incidence of taxation, or the administration of public services, any stable adjustment of social resources to social needs must always take into account, not only the scientifically ascertained conditions of efficiency, but also the "established expectation" and the "fighting force" of all the classes concerned.

34

A Theory of the Labor Movement

Selig Perlman

Selig Perlman, *A Theory of the Labor Movement* (New York: The Macmillan Company, 1928). Reprinted with permission of the author.

This article does not claim to give a full history of the several national labor movements, which the author has chosen as the most significant—the British, the German, the Russian, and the American. Rather it gives a survey of the historical development of these movements in order to show the grounds upon which the author, in the course of more than fifteen years of study and research, has arrived at his theory of the labor movement. . . .

    Three dominant factors are emerging from the seeming medley of contradictory turns and events in recent labor history. The first factor is the demonstrated capacity, as in Germany, Austria, and Hungary, or else incapacity, as in Russia, of the capitalist group to survive as ruling group and to withstand revolutionary attack when the protective hand of government has been withdrawn. In this sense "capitalism" is not only, nor even primarily, a material or governmental arrangement whereby one class, the capitalist class, owns the means of production, exchange, and distribution, while the other class, labor is employed for wages. Capitalism is rather a social organization presided over by a class with an "effective will to power," implying the ability to defend its power against all comers—to defend it, not necessarily by physical force, since such force, however important at a crisis, might crumble after all—but to defend it, as it has done in Germany, through having convinced the other classes that they alone, the capitalists, know how to operate the complex economic apparatus of modern society upon which the material welfare of all depends.

The second factor which stands out clearly in the world-wide social situation is the role of the so-called "intellectual," the "intelligentsia," in the labor movement and in society at large. It was from the intellectual that the anticapitalist influences in modern society emanated. It was he who impressed upon the labor movement tenets characteristic of his own mentality; the "nationalization" or "socialization" of industry, and political action, whether "constitutional" or "unconstitutional," on behalf of the "new social order." He, too, has been busily indoctrinating the middle classes with the same views, thus helping to undermine an important prop of capitalism and to some extent even the spirit of resistance of the capitalists themselves.

The third and most vital factor in the labor situation is the trade union movement. Trade unionism, which is essentially pragmatic, struggles constantly, not only against the employers for an enlarged opportunity measured in income, security, and liberty in the shop and industry, but struggles also, whether consciously or unconsciously, actively or merely passively, against the intellectual who would frame its programs and shape its policies. In this struggle by "organic" labor[1] against dominance by the intellectuals, we perceive a clash of an ideology which holds the concrete workingmen in the center of its vision with a rival ideology which envisages labor merely as an "abstract mass in the grip of an abstract force."[2]

Labor's own "home grown" ideology is disclosed only through a study of the "working rules" of labor's own "institutions." The trade unions are the institutions of labor today, but much can be learned also from labor's institutions in the past, notably the guilds.

It is the author's contention that manual groups, whether peasants in Russia, modern wage earners, or medieval master workmen, have had their economic attitudes basically determined by a consciousness of scarcity of opportunity, which is characteristic of these groups, and stands out in contrast with the business men's "abundance consciousness," or consciousness of unlimited opportunity. Starting with this consciousness of scarcity, the "manualist" groups have been led to practising solidarity, to an insistence upon an "ownership" by the group as a whole of the totality of economic opportunity extant, to a "rationing" by the group of such opportunity among the individuals constituting it, to a control by the group over its members in relation to the conditions upon which they as individuals are permitted to occupy a portion of that opportunity—in brief, to a "communism of opportunity." This differs fundamentally from socialism or communism, which would "communize" not only "opportunity," but also production and distribution—just as it is far removed from "capitalism." Capitalism started from the premise of unlimited opportunity, and arrived in its classical formulation, at "laissez faire" for the individual all along the line—in regard to the "quantity" of opportunity he may appropriate, the price or wage he may charge, and in regard

---

[1] Trade unionists and intellectuals alike use the term "labor," which has an abstract connotation. But, to the trade unionists, "labor" means nothing more abstract or mystical than the millions of concrete human beings with their concrete wants and aspirations.

[2] I frequently use the term "ideology" in imitation of the usage of socialist intellectuals taken over from Napoleon's term applied by him in con-

tempt to the idealists of his day. I find, however, that the term has quite the same meaning as that which scientists call "ideas" and "theory," philosophers call "idealism" or "ethics," and business men and working men call "philosophy." Unionists speak of "the philosophy of trade unionism." If they were "intellectuals," they would call it "theory," "ideology," "ideas," or "idealism," or "ethics," all of which I sometimes include in the term "mentality."

to the ownership of the means of production. "Communism of opportunity" in the sense here employed existed in the medieval guilds before the merchant capitalists had subverted them to the purposes of a protected business men's oligarchy; in Russian peasant land communities with their periodic redivisions, among the several families, of the collectively owned land, the embodiment of the economic opportunity of a peasant group; and exists today in trade unions enforcing a "job control" through union "working rules."

But, in this country, due to the fact that here the "manualist" had found at hand an abundance of opportunity, in unoccupied land and in a pioneer social condition, his economic thinking had therefore issued, not from the scarcity premise but from the premise of abundance. It thus resulted in a social philosophy which was more akin to the business men's than to the trade unionists' or guildsmen's. Accordingly, the American labor movement, which long remained unaware of any distinction between itself and the "producing classes" in general,— which included also farmers, small manufacturers, and small business men,—continued for many decades to worship the shrine of individualistic "anti-monopoly." "Anti-monopoly" was a program of reform, through politics and legislation, whereby the "producing classes" would apply a corrective to the American social order so that economic individualism might become "safe" for the producers rather than for land speculators, merchant capitalists, and bankers. Unionism, on the contrary, first became a stabilized movement in America only when the abundance consciousness of the pioneer days had been replaced in the mind of labor by a scarcity consciousness—the consciousness of job scarcity. Only then did the American wage earner become willing to envisage a future in which his union would go on indefinitely controlling his relation to his job rather than endeavoring to afford him, as during the anti-monopoly stage of the labor movement, an escape into free and unregulated self-employment, by willing for him a competitive equality with the "monopolist."

In America, the historical struggle waged by labor for an undivided expression of its own mentality in its own movement was directed against the ideology of "anti-monopoly." But in Europe the antithesis to the labor mentality has been the mentality of the intellectual.

Twenty-five years ago, Nicolai Lenin[3] clearly recognized the divergence which exists between the intellectual and the trade unionist, although not in terms of an inevitable mutual antagonism, when he hurled his unusual polemical powers against those in the Social-Democratic Party, his own party at the time, who would confine their own and the party's agitational activities to playing upon labor's economic grievances. He then said that if it had not been for the "bourgeois intellectuals," Marx and Engels, labor would never have got beyond mere "trifling,"—going after an increase in wage here and after a labor law there. Lenin, of course, saw labor and the trade union movement, not as an aggregation of concrete individuals sharing among themselves their collective job opportunity, as well as trying to enlarge it and improve it by joint effort and step by step, but rather as an abstract mass which history had predetermined to hurl itself against the capitalist social order and demolish it. Lenin therefore could never have seen in a nonrevolutionary unionism anything more than a blind groping after a purpose only vaguely grasped, rather than

[3] "The history of all countries attests to the fact that, left to its own forces, the working class can only attain to trade union consciousness,—that is, the conviction that it is necessary to unite in unions, wage the struggle against the bosses, obtain from the government such or such labor reforms, etc. As to the socialist doctrines, they came from philosophic, historic and economic theories elaborated by certain educated representatives of the possessing classes, the Intellectuals. In their social situation, the founders of contemporary scientific socialism, Marx and Engels, were bourgeois intellectuals." Lenin in *What Is To Be Done?*

a completely self-conscious movement with a full-blown ideology of its own. But to see "labor" solely as an abstract mass and the concrete individual reduced to a mere mathematical point, as against the trade unionists' striving for job security for the individual and concrete freedom on the job, has not been solely the prerogative of "determinist-revolutionaries" like Lenin and the Communists. The other types of intellectuals in and close to the labor movement, the "ethical" type, the heirs of Owen and the Christian Socialists, and the "social efficiency" type, best represented by the Fabians— to mention but English examples—have equally with the orthodox Marxians reduced labor to a mere abstraction, although each has done so in his own way and has pictured "labor" as an abstract mass in the grip of an abstract force, existing, however, only in his own intellectual imagination, and not in the emotional imagination of the manual worker himself.

LABOR AND CAPITALISM IN AMERICA[4]

The most distinctive characteristic of the development of the labor movement in America has not been, as in Germany, a slow but certain shedding of the philosophy originally imparted by an intellectual leadership. No intellectuals, in the true sense of the word, presided at its birth. The main feature of its development has been rather a perpetual struggle to keep the organization from going to pieces for want of inner cohesiveness. For, it has had to cope with two disruptive tendencies: First,—American labor has always been prone,—though far more in the past than now,—to identify itself in outlook, interest, and action, with the great lower middle class, the farmers, the small manufacturers and business men,—in a word, with the "producing classes" and their periodic "anti-

[4] See my *History of Trade Unionism in the United States* (The Macmillan Co., 1922).

monopoly" campaigns. Second,—and here is a tendency of a rising rather than diminishing potency,—the American employer has, in general, been able to keep his employees contented with the conditions, determined by himself, on which they individually accepted employment. Both these tendencies have seriously hindered the efforts of trade unionism towards stability and solidarity. The first tendency proved inimical because the organized wage earners would periodically be drawn into the whirlpool of politics under the banner of the "antimonopoly" parties,—so, under the American system of party politics, invariably suffering dissension, and ultimately disintegration. The second of the tendencies mentioned has balked unionism because the employer, wielding the initiative, has been able successfully to carry his own individualistic competitive spirit into the ranks of his employees. Moreover, both factors making for disintegration go back to a common cause. For whether the labor organization has succumbed to the lure of a political reform movement aiming to shield the "small man" and the "man on the make," and has broken up in political dissension; or whether it has failed to get started because the individual laborer has accepted the incentive of a bonus wage and of a better opportunity for advancement within the framework of a non-union bargain,—the ultimate explanation, at all events, lies in the basic conditions of life in the American community—economic, political, ethnic, mental, and spiritual. Some of these are a heritage from the past, others, of more recent origin, but all are closely interwoven with the present and the future of American Labor.

The Basic Characteristics of the American Community

The strength of the institution of private property. A labor movement must, from its very nature, be an organized campaign against the rights of private property, even where it stops short of embracing a radical program seeking the elimination, gradual or abrupt, "constitutional" or violent, of the private entrepreneur. When this campaign takes the political and legislative route, it leads to the denial of the employer's right to absolute control of his productive property. It demands and secures regulatory restrictions which, under American constitutional practice, are within the province of the "police power" vested in the states and granted by specific authority to Congress; only they must, in every case, square with "public purpose," as that term is interpreted in the last analysis by the United States Supreme Court. When the same campaign follows the economic route,—the route of unionism, strikes, boycotts, and union "working rules"—the restrictions on the rights of property are usually even more thoroughgoing and far-reaching, since unions are less amenable to judicial control than are legislatures and Congress. A third form of the labor movement seeks to promote cooperative production and distribution,—neither of which is practiced appreciably in this country. This cooperative movement sets out to beat private capitalism by the methods of private business: greater efficiency and superior competitive power. To the advocates of the rights of private property, this third mode of the labor movement is the least offensive.

Because the labor movement in any form is a campaign against the absolute rights of private property, the extent to which the institution of private property is entrenched in the community in which a labor movement operates is of overwhelming importance....

The enormous strength of private property in America, at once obvious to any observer,[5] goes back to the all-important fact that, by and large, this country was occupied and settled by laboring pioneers, creating property for them-

selves as they went along and holding it in small parcels. This was the way not only of agriculture but also of the mechanical trades and of the larger scale industries. Thus the harmony between the self-interest of the individual pursuing his private economic aim and the general public interest proved a real and lasting harmony in the American colonies and states. This Adam Smith saw in 1776, his eye on the frugal and industrious class of masters of workshops still on the threshold of their elevation by the industrial revolution yet to come. Every addition to the total of the privately held wealth was at the same time an addition to the productive equipment in the community, which meant a fuller satisfaction of its wants and a higher level of the general welfare. Moreover, being held in small parcels, wealth was generally accessible to whomever would pay the price in industry, frugality, and ingenuity. Furthermore, this condition has not been destroyed even with the coming in of modern "big business," combinations, mergers, and "trusts." For, too often does the grandeur of business on its modern gigantic scale, the magnitude of billion dollar corporations completely hide from one's view those other millions of small businesses. These, here and now, may be forced to struggle hard for existence, perhaps only to fail in the end. But failing, still others will take their place and continue to form a social layer firm enough to safeguard against even a possible revolutionary explosion from below. The earnestness with which judges will rush to stand between legislatures and menaced property rights; the rigor of their application of the injunction to keep unionists and strikers from interfering with those rights in their own way; the ease with which a typically American middle class

---

[5] The utter disregard of the property rights of distillers, brewers, and others engaged in the drink traffic resulted from the intensity of the moral passion evoked—the historical heritage of puritanism. Had private property been less entrenched than it is, the property owning groups would have been more hesitant to remove even one stone of the arch.

community may work itself up, or be worked up, into an anti-radical hysteria, when Soviet missionaries or syndicalist agitators are rumored to be abroad in the land; and the flocking to the election polls of millions to vote for the "safe" candidate—all are of one piece, and are to be explained by the way in which the American community originated and grew. . . .

The lack of a class consciousness in American labor. The overshadowing problem of the American labor movement has always been the problem of staying organized. No other labor movement has ever had to contend with the fragility so characteristic of American labor organizations. In the main, this fragility of the organization has come from the lack of class cohesiveness in American labor. . . .

The cause of this lack of psychological cohesiveness in American labor is the absence, by and large, of a completely "settled" wage earning class. Sons of wage earners will automatically follow their fathers' occupations in the mining districts, which, because of their isolation, are little worlds in themselves. The Negroes in industry are, of course, a hereditary wage earning group. And apparently such a class has developed also in the textile centers. To be sure, the great mass of the wage earners in American industry today, unless they have come from the farm intending to return there with a part of their wages saved, will die wage earners. However many of these do not stay in a given industry for life, but keep moving from industry to industry and from locality to locality, in search for better working conditions. Moreover, the bright son of a mechanic and factory hand, whether of native or immigrant parentage, need not despair, with the training which the public schools give him free of charge and with whatever else he may pick up, of finding his way to this or that one of the thousand and one selling "lines" which pay on the commission basis; or, if his ambition and his luck go hand in hand, of attaining to some one of the

equally numerous kinds of small businesses, or, finally, of the many minor supervisory positions in the large manufacturing establishments, which are constantly on the lookout for persons in the ranks suitable for promotion. It is, therefore, a mistake to assume that, with the exhaustion of the supply of free public land, the wage earner who is above the average in ambition and ability, or at least his children, if they are equally endowed (and the children's opportunities color the parents' attitude no less than do their own), have become cooped up for good in the class of factory operatives. For today, the alternative opportunities to being a lowly factory hand are certainly more varied and entail less hardship than the old opportunity of "homesteading" in the West and "growing up with the country.". . .

Another cause of the lack of "class-consciousness" in American labor was the free gift of the ballot which came to labor at an early date as a by-product of the Jeffersonian democratic movement. In other countries, where the labor movement started while the workingmen were still denied the franchise, there was in the last analysis no need of a theory of "surplus value" to convince them that they were a class apart and should therefore be "class conscious." There ran a line like a red thread between the laboring class and the other classes. Not so, where that line is only an economic one. Such a line becomes blurred by the constant process of "osmosis" between one economic class and another, by fluctuations in relative bargaining power of employer and employee with changes in the business cycle, and by other changing conditions.

Next to the abundant economic opportunities available to wage earners in this country, and to their children, immigration has been the factor most guilty of the incohesiveness of American labor. To workers employed in a given industry, a new wave of immigrants, generally of a new nationality, meant a competitive menace to be fought off and be kept out of that industry. For, by the worker's job consciousness, the strongest animosity was felt not for the employer who had initiated or stimulated the new immigrant wave, but for the immigrants who came and took the jobs away. When immigrants of a particular nationality acquired higher standards and began rebuilding the unions which they destroyed at their coming, then a new nationality would arrive to do unto the former what these had done unto the original membership. The restriction of immigration by the quota system has at last done away with this phenomenon, which formerly used to occur and recur with an inevitable regularity.

American labor remains the most heterogeneous laboring class in existence—ethnically, linguistically, religiously, and culturally. With a working class of such a composition, to make socialism or communism the official "ism" of the movement, would mean, even if the other conditions permitted it, deliberately driving the Catholics, who are perhaps in the majority in the American Federation of Labor, out of the labor movement, since with them an irreconcilable opposition to socialism is a matter of religious principle. Consequently the only acceptable "consciousness" for American labor as a whole is a "job consciousness," with a "limited" objective of "wage and job control"; which not at all hinders American unionism from being the most "hard hitting" unionism in any country. Individual unions may, however, adopt whatever "consciousness" they wish. Also the solidarity of American labor is a solidarity with a quickly diminishing potency as one passes from the craft group,—which looks upon the jobs in the craft as its common property for which it is ready to fight long and bitterly,—to the widening concentric circles of the related crafts, the industry, the American Federation of Labor, and the world labor movement.

35

The Development of Western Labor Movements: Some Comparative Considerations

Everett M. Kassalow

Everett M. Kassalow, "The Development of Western Labor Movements: Some Comparative Considerations," in *Labor: Readings on Major Issues*, Richard A Lester, ed. (New York: Random House, Inc., 1965).

As a means of making analysis of labor movements abroad more dramatic and vivid, let us first examine the special nature and character of the American labor movement. Needless to say, any brief survey of Western labor movements must necessarily be oversimplified at practically every stage.

SPECIAL INFLUENCES IN U.S. LABOR MOVEMENT DEVELOPMENT

A number of special forces shaped the development of the American labor movement. In the United States the capitalist enterprise system did not have to contend with a previously existing feudalism and a rigid set of class attitudes and practices. There were some traces of a feudal land system in America, but these were relatively unimportant. Indeed, the free frontier tended to encourage the emergence of new landholders.

The absence of feudalism meant, of course, that the triumph of capitalism for this and other reasons was ultimately more widespread and more successful in the United States than anywhere else. There were none of the usual aristocratic inhibitions on willingness to work, nor any excessive preoccupation with leisure pursuits that characterized the ruling classes of Europe.

The lack of a feudal tradition also served to blur class lines from an early period in American history. When an explosive, dynamic capitalism was combined with this, social mobility—though perhaps exaggerated in some of our literature—was certainly greater in American life than in that anywhere in Europe. Again, as a consequence of these factors, there was less tendency for class lines and attitudes to develop in the lifelong pattern that they had in Europe. The special form of American capitalism with its great emphasis on internal markets early resulted in a relatively high standard of living for the great mass of people, further weakening the possibility of the emergence of persistent class attitudes. The heavy flow of immigration into America also made any "unity" of the working classes more unlikely.

Full citizenship and voting rights for the male, white, urban working class existed at a relatively early date in American history. This too made the workers feel they were full partners in the growing society.

The establishment of free public education for all citizens long before the Civil War helped complete the integration of American workers into their society. Illiteracy among the masses persisted in most of Western Europe well into the latter half of the nineteenth century and was certainly a factor in alienating workers from the newly developing social orders.

The possibility of a higher standard of living and the possibility of social mobility into managerial and entrepreneurial positions tended at a relatively early point to make the American labor movement a highly economically oriented institution. By the latter part of the nineteenth century its feet were rather firmly set on the road of wages, hours, and working conditions, all of which were to become institutionally contained within the framework of collective bargaining and written agreements. (Of course, there were syndicalist and socialist exceptions, but in retrospect they were just that—exceptions to the main pattern of development.)

All these factors tended to give what Bruce Millen has called an "exclusionist" character to the American trade union movement. Its con-centration was upon benefits to members rather than any great interest in the economic fate of the working class as a whole. Finally, for a great part of its history the American movement largely confined its activities to a limited number of trades and industries. Since the rise of the mass unionism of the thirties, the horizon of American labor has broadened considerably; but even today it is a relatively narrower movement than those in other Western countries.

On the other hand, the lack of class feeling as well as powerful opposition from employers (and often from public authorities) made both the existence and the continuity of unionism difficult in the American environment. This in turn led the unions to lay great emphasis upon exclusive bargaining rights, closed and union shops, and other forms of union security. Since the limitations of space do not permit a return to this point, suffice it to note that European unions have almost never resorted to these forms. This is largely true because the cement of class attitude made this additional bond unnecessary for the permanent existence of unionism. Since, as we shall see below, the typical European union was ideologically committed, it also would have been somewhat contradictory to compel "non-believers" to join the union and pay dues to it.

EUROPEAN LABOR: A CLASS MOVEMENT

Let us now examine some broad contrasts with the labor movements which developed in Western Europe. In the first place the social and political background was considerably different in Europe. To an extent (though this is still argued among historians) some of the early unions were influenced by the medieval guild tradition. Feudalism was firmly intrenched, leaving rigid class lines and social and economic distinctions many of which still persist. By the same token, European capitalism was less successful in shattering older attitudes and practices, which also reinforced the tendency to develop or continue class distinctions and class attitudes. The idea of the "naturalness" of group activity and group recognition has deep and lasting roots in Europe.

Against this background the European labor movement emerged as part of the attempt of the European working classes to achieve broad social, economic, and political objectives. In keeping with other European class movements, it created or inherited a total ideology and *Weltanschauung*. The European working class, developed within a more rigid type of society than that of the United States, committed itself to the advancement of the entire working class. It bent to [the] task [of] radically transforming the entire society. Political democracy developed later in Western Europe than in the United States, and this too tended to consolidate a class attitude of opposition on the part of European workers toward their societies and governments. The working-class movements in most countries, in these earlier years, came to embrace Marxism and the doctrine of revolutionary change—though not necessarily by violent means. More generally, it was committed to replacing the system of capitalism and private property and production with socialism and production for use.

It is worth noting that the ideological aspects of the British Socialist Party and trade-union movement, however, differed from those of the continent. British socialism was colored by Britain's nonconformist religious tradition in much the same way that Marxism colored the continental movements. British socialist feeling was, however, no less intense because of its religious—as opposed to the continent's Marxist—background.

It should be clear immediately that all these movements were less exclusionist than the American labor movement. Basically they embarked upon a course of advancing the entire working class by transforming the total society, in contrast to the emphasis of the American

movement on the immediate specifics of wages, hours, and working conditions for its members only.

The discussion that follows presents the main forms and programs the European working class movements took. However, what is described is not entirely true of any one movement, since generalizations are necessary. Even what is described as the general model is certainly more true of the United Kingdom, Scandinavia, Holland, Switzerland—and to an important extent Germany, Austria, and probably Belgium—than it is of France and Italy.

Typically, the European labor movement developed country by country as a two- or three-pronged affair. There were first of all the trade unions; second, the labor, political, or socialist movements; and third, workers' cooperative movements—both of the consumer and producer variety. Each of these parts of the over-all working-class movement was intended to play an important role in the transformation of the society, but we shall focus upon the trade unions and the political parties. The cooperative movements have tended to become a bit less important in Europe in the post-World War II decades as central state planning and the elaboration of social welfare programs have come to be the pivot of socialist economics. The cooperatives may therefore be less important than the trade unions or the political parties in today's socialist complex, but they should be kept in mind, since they do indicate the broad front behind which the work of European labor has operated to engage its members' lives, in contrast to the almost exclusively trade union form of the American movement. . . .

PARTY-UNION RELATIONSHIPS

It is sometimes difficult for Americans, especially American trade unionists, to understand the great emphasis European workers place upon political movements and workers' political parties. In the eyes of European workers, however, the party and the trade-union movement are of equal importance in the advancement of the working class.

Since this development of parallel movements, party and union, is of critical importance in the study of labor movements anywhere in the world—especially outside the United States—this aspect should be stressed. There is no simple formula which determines which will emerge first, the political or the industrial (or union) arm of the working class. . . .

In general, it can be said that where the trade unions developed before the socialist party, they generally had a hand in organizing the party and tended to exercise great influence in it. The lack of universal suffrage in a number of countries gave the unions a priority in development.

The unions, as opposed to the parties, tended to be more pragmatic and less dogmatic or doctrinal than the parties. Inevitably, working in the day-to-day industrial sphere, the unions concentrated on more immediate gains, while the party was concentrating on a global program. This was particularly true before World War I, when the parties were remote from any day-to-day responsibilities in most countries and continued to expound a "purer" brand of socialism. However, membership and leadership in the unions and party were often intermixed, especially in the early days, and both subscribed broadly and equally to the general goal of a socialist society.

During the period from World War I to World War II a pattern tended to appear in which the union continued to be to the right and the socialist parties to the left of the combined labor movement. However, as the socialist parties began to approach and share government power . . ., the situation [changed]. Confronted with the difficult problems of actually governing and the necessity to con-ciliate other forces, such as the farmers and the new white-collar groups, if they were to remain in power, the parties moved away from the old dogmas. Since World War II this tendency has been accelerated as socialist parties have, on occasion, governed either alone or in coalition in almost every European country. Today it is often the union wing of the labor movement which is out on the left expressing irritation with the excessive "statesmanship" and conciliatory tactics of the party leadership.

These are broad generalizations; no attempt has been made to set up any rigid rules for judging union-party relations. Moreover, it might be fairer to say that the parties and the unions are arms which perform different functions for the working class. As these functions and needs vary in the course of social evolution, each arm receives changing emphasis.

Returning to historical development, the important advances of the unions, the rise in living standards, the establishment of social security systems, the obviously effective and influential roles which most of the socialist parties have come to play within existing parliamentary systems—all of these factors have tended to cool the revolutionary ardor of most of the Western labor movements with the passage of time. Their very achievements and growing power help to integrate these labor movements into their societies.

Most of the socialist parties, as already noted, started out under strong Marxist influence.[1] Today in Scandinavia, Austria, and the Netherlands (to choose some examples), Marxism has long since been overtaken by reformism, and there is only moderate interest in the nationalization of industry. The emphasis today tends to be more and more upon plan-

[1] The British Labour Party is an important exception. Differences in class relationships, civil rights traditions, and the influence of non-conformist religion helped produce a non-Marxian socialism in England.

ning for full-employment and welfare programs.

The rather recent *formal* conversion of the German Social Democratic Party from Marxism to something like welfare-statism is a good case in point (I emphasize the word formal here, for most European socialist parties long ago abandoned Marxism as a matter of practical operations). At its 1959 Congress the German SPD made its "final break . . . with the fundamental tenets of Marxism. . . . The name of Karl Marx and the concept of Marxism are missing from the declaration of principles, . . . words like 'class' and 'class struggle' are also carefully avoided. . . . The notion that the working class . . . is destined, by overthrowing capitalist class-society, to bring about the classless society, . . . has now been thrown by the German Social Democrats on the scrap heap of social utopias. . . . The transfer of the means of production to common ownership, which has hitherto represented the essence of every socialist program, has been stripped of its overriding importance. . . . The SPD has dropped the idea that socialism requires the nationalisation of the whole of industry, not only 'for the time being' but as a matter of principle."[2]

The same kind of transition, for practical purposes, has been accomplished by nearly all the socialist parties of Europe. Occasionally, however, some diehard traditionalists, as in Great Britain, have resisted formal changes in the official party program, and the theoretical commitment to extensive nationalization of industry lives on as a doctrine, if not a reality.

STRAINS OF ECONOMIC PLANNING ON PARTY-UNION RELATIONSHIPS

While each has its separate province, party and union sometimes encounter severe strains and some conflict of interest in their relationships.

[2] F. R. Allemann, "German SPD Party Abandons Marxism," *Forum-Service* (December 26, 1959).

Particularly is this the case today in the face of the central economic planning for full employment that is being undertaken by some socialist governments. The reconciliation of such economic planning with the traditional freedom of unions to bargain freely for wage increases can present some severe problems for the labor movement. . . .

An almost classic example of the tension which can develop between the twin poles of party and union can be found in a description of the activities of Ernest Bevin in Alan Bullock's brilliant biography of that great British union leader. The first Labour government in Great Britain took office at the end of 1923. This period coincided with an economic upswing, and Bevin, on behalf of the dock and tramway workers, was anxious to make an effort to restore some wage cuts suffered in earlier years. He moved swiftly, and after a successful strike these unions won an impressive economic victory. Bevin was highly satisfied with the results. Bullock notes, however:

> This satisfaction was not shared by the Labour Government, MacDonald, in particular, out of sympathy with down-to-earth trade-union demands and increasingly inclined to take a high line about national responsibilities, was greatly angered by the strikes and never forgave Bevin for the embarrassment he caused the Government. This did not worry Bevin. But there were others in the Labour Party besides MacDonald who felt that Bevin had behaved irresponsibly and shown less than the loyalty the unions owed to the first Labour Government ever to take office. This impression was strengthened by the aggressive manner in which Bevin asserted his independence and expressed his contempt for politicians as a race.

A controversy broke out in the Socialist press in which the economist J. A. Hobson accused the unions of following a "separatist" policy. Bevin had to deal with the question of whether or not it was incumbent upon the unions to wait for the government to set up some new machinery to settle the workers' wage claims or whether the unions' strike action was correct. He commented:

> We are all too aware of the Government's difficulties and desire as much as anyone to assist in the success of Britain's first Labour Government. A policy of industrial truce would, in our view, even if it were possible, not be to the best interests of the Government. There is work to do on the industrial field as well as in the political arena. While it is true that the two are to some extent part of the same effort, we must not lose sight of the fact that governments may come and governments may go, but the workers' fight for betterment of conditions must go on all the time.

Bullock further notes:

> Nor did the rank-and-file members of the Union disagree with Bevin. They had waited a long time to recover the wage cuts they had suffered and to see some practical benefit from the Union they supported. They saw no reason why, the first time they gained the advantage in a dispute, they should not press it home simply because a Labour Government was in office. If that fact made the employers more reluctant to fight it out, so much the better: what did they pay the political levy and support the Labour Party for, if not to secure such advantages? No one could say the employers were reluctant to take advantage of the Tories being in office to force wages down and use the power of the State to defeat the miners. It was too high a price to pay for office if the only way the Labour Government could retain the Parliamentary support of the Liberal Party was to take sides against the unions in the legitimate defence of their members' industrial interests.

There is, however, a postscript to this interesting interlude. When Labour came to power in 1945, it had gained a clear majority in Parliament, unlike the 1923 Labour government, which was a minority government dependent upon the votes of other groups if it was to stay in power. Then Bevin was willing to face the issue of the national responsibility of the labor movement, as opposed to the immediate sectional interests of the trade unions. During this period he came, as a member of the government, to recommend to the unions a policy of "wage restraint which placed a heavy strain on the loyalty and forbearance of the trade unions."[3]

In a sense we have here an illustration of the pressures in today's world which often tend to put the socialist party to the right of its trade union ally. From what has already been said, it is scarcely necessary to add at this point that although these movements are two- and three-pronged, the trade unions jealously guard their own independence. Americans sometimes have the feeling that these union and political movements are one and the same thing. This is simply not the case. The unions, for example, have their own independent financing, policy conventions, and officers. In terms of structure and finances, the unions are in some ways more clearly independent of the parties than are the parties from the unions. The parties frequently, as we have seen, are highly dependent upon the unions for financial support. Furthermore, it is quite common for a socialist party specifically to reserve a few seats on the party's executive committee for representatives of the trade union movement. The same is not true in the reverse.

Some American experts have tended to see this process as one in which the unions

[3] Alan Bullock, *The Life and Times of Ernest Bevin, Trade Union Leader, 1881–1940*, Vol. 1 (London: William Heinemann, Ltd., 1960), pp. 242–45.

gradually "emancipate" themselves from the parties. This is also inaccurate. Rather, as one writer describes the situation in Sweden, the relationship is essentially "one of interdependence."[4] Functions and responsibilities vary as economic and political conditions change, but both arms continue to perform vital functions.

COLLECTIVE BARGAINING: SOME KEY DIFFERENCES

The unions then are independent and have as *their* main sphere *industrial action* and *representation* on behalf of the working class. In this sense, of course, they resemble American unions. Furthermore, in the broad structural sense, there are many similarities, such as the existence of national unions along industrial or craft lines or both, a central federation, and some form of local organization.[5]

It is fair to say, however, that in their bargaining and industrial activities they do have a different attitude toward government action and political action than do American unions. Typically, for example, in many of these countries the unions accept government legislation as the regulator of such items as paid vacations and paid holidays. They also look to the government almost exclusively for social security items such as pensions, health, and welfare in contrast to American unions which also bargain "privately" on many of these items. In some

---

[4] Donald J. Blake, "Swedish Trade Unions and the Social Democratic Party: The Formative Years," *The Scandinavian Economic History Review,* 8, *1,* (1960), p. 43.

[5] In the matter of local organization in some countries there are patterns considerably different from ours, but space limitations preclude further discussion of this. Similarly, in Europe the central labor federations, or confederations as they are called (the equivalents of our own AFL-CIO), often exercise greater power and influence over the labor movement as a whole than does the AFL-CIO.

European countries such as France, Belgium, and Austria, the system of shop stewards owes its existence not to union agreements but to a state-sponsored series of plant elections. The rights and functions of these stewards are generally defined by legislation and only occasionally supplemented by union agreements.

NEW TRENDS IN UNION BARGAINING STRUCTURES AND POLICIES

With respect to wages and hours, bargaining in Western Europe is usually done by industry on a regional or even a national basis. Unlike the industrial-relations pattern in the United States, there is much less emphasis upon bargaining with particular employers and enterprises. Union devotion to ideals of class solidarity and class equality coupled with employers traditions of operating through strong associations tend to deter bargaining at the plant or firm level. One of the concomitants of this has been that, in comparison with American unions, European unions are less influential and less active at the plant level.

The enormous industrial changes and the great growth of the European economies in the past decade are causing some changes in traditional European union bargaining attitudes and structure. Confronted with complex problems of automation, as well as with the opportunity for economic advances on a scale hitherto unknown, some European unions have found that nation-wide, industry-wide, or region-wide bargaining is not entirely adequate. Bargains struck this way tend to be set in terms of what the marginal or relatively less efficient producer in a given industry can afford to pay.

Actually, in a number of European countries, especially in the highly prosperous large metal companies, the wage rates and earnings of workers today are often far above the rates negotiated in industry-wide agreements on a national or regional basis. As a consequence, rate setting in many major firms in a few countries has passed largely into the hands of the employers.

The so-called shop stewards' revolt in Great Britain in the past decade stems in part from certain structural weaknesses in the British trade union movement and the need to exercise greater worker control over wages and working conditions at the plant level.

Some of the European unions are responding to these challenges by placing new emphasis upon bargaining at the plant and firm level. The old union notion of working-class solidarity is being distorted in the context of the European "economic miracle." These unions may, however, run up against the problem of reconciling more energetic wage bargaining with price stability in the face of the strong and sustained full employment, which most European countries have successfully achieved in the past decade.

EUROPEAN LABOR AND THE ISSUE OF WORKERS' CONTROL OF INDUSTRY

Most European unions have not been content to limit their plant objectives to wages, hours, and working conditions. Socialist influence and tradition have led most of the labor movements to inscribe high on their platforms the doctrine of workers' control over industry, in the sense of industrial decisions on production, investment, and marketing. On the other hand, the doctrine that workers must have a *share* and *co-responsibility* in the management of enterprise has also had firm standing in European Catholic social doctrine since the latter part of the nineteenth century.[6]

[6] Syndicalist and guild socialist influences, which have since largely disappeared from Western Europe, also helped develop workers' interest in the issue of participating directly in management, around World War I.

These two different streams of social doctrine, as Frederic Meyers has commented, led to the establishment by legislation of systems of worker "representation," or at least worker consultation in the management of enterprise in a number of European nations.[7] There has been considerable American interest in the operation of the German co-determination laws; but forms of worker participation in, or consultation with, management also exist in some other countries in Europe.

To date these "experiments" have not had a serious impact. The real business of running the enterprise remains in management's hands. In some countries, however, these devices have helped to increase the workers' power to influence many of the working conditions that we normally take for granted as within the province of collective bargaining in the United States, as opposed to managing the enterprise in the broader sense of that term.

This tradition of workers' control and participation in management is, however, a deep one.

EVALUATING UNITED STATES AND EUROPEAN MOVEMENTS

. . . Sharp and direct comparisons between American unionism and the European labor movements are obviously impossible. Different conditions produce different movements. It can be said, however, that in some respects European movements have been more effective than our own. They have succeeded in building a greater degree of security on the part of European workers. This is reflected in more comprehensive social security and medical care systems, greater protection against layoff, longer paid vacations, and union cooperative

[7] Frederic Meyers, "Workers' Control of Industry in Europe," *Southwestern Social Science Quarterly* (September 1958).

travel and recreation programs which have tended to enlarge the lives of European workers. Workers' housing is commonly a product of union cooperatives. This whole range of activities tends to create unity and a sense of allegiance between workers and their movements which is much stronger than in the United States.

In contrast, however, the European movements are considerably weaker than the American at the factory floor or the enterprise level, and they have given workers much less control over their day-to-day working conditions. Again, while it is hard to generalize in terms of sheer economic achievement, the advantage must be given to the greater bargaining power of the American labor movement.

It cannot be denied, however, that a number of European labor movements (encompassing labor parties and unions) are a broader and more powerful social force in their own countries than the American labor movement. In some of these societies (for example, in the United Kingdom, Austria, the Low Countries, or Scandinavia) the European labor movement has even assumed a full or a large measure of national governmental power.

Some of the evolutionary forces at play in the United States and in Western Europe seem to be bending the respective lines of union development closer together. Note, for example, that whereas some European unions have had to take more action at the plant level, American labor finds itself drawn into a new government-sponsored national labor-management committee. Again, United States labor has also increased its political activities sharply in the past decade, as it has become painfully clear that the attainment of full employment and a more just society are to a considerable extent beyond the competence of collective bargaining, important as the latter is.

36

American Unionism: Taking Stock and Looking Ahead

George H. Hildebrand

George H. Hildebrand, "Taking Stock and Looking Ahead," from Hildebrand, *American Unionism: An Historical and Analytical Survey,* © 1979, Addison-Wesley Publishing Company, Inc., Chapter 8, pages 113, 114, 116, 117, 118, 120, 124. Reprinted with permission.

THE GROWTH OF UNIONISM

The Overall Growth of Membership since 1945

In 1945, the total membership of American unions, excluding Canadian affiliates, stood at 14,322,000, or 35.5 percent of all employees in nonagricultural establishments. Table 1 provides a summary of the period since that time. Taking the nonagricultural employee group as comprising those most likely to join unions, the most startling fact is the sharp drop in the percentage share of organized labor in the total—from 35.5 percent at the end of World War II to only 24.5 percent 31 years later.

Looking at the unions' shrinking relative importance in a little different way, we can say that over the entire period union membership grew by 5.1 million, or by 35.7 percent, while the employee pool from which that membership is drawn soared by 39 million, or by 96.5 percent. The sluggishness of union growth stands out even more clearly when it is noted that less than one out of every eight new workers (13.1 percent) actually joined a labor union during these three decades.

Concentrating upon the most recent period, we find that between 1970 and 1976 union membership rose by only 51,000, while the number of nonagricultural employees jumped by 8.5 million. In other words, for the

TABLE 1

U.S. Union Membership, 1945–1976

Year	Total Membership[a] (thousands)	Total Labor Force		Total Nonagricultural Employees	
		Number (thousands)	Union Members (%)	Number (thousands)	Union Members (%)
1945	14,322	65,300	21.9	40,394	35.5
1960	17,049	72,142	23.6	54,234	31.4
1965	17,299	77,178	22.4	60,815	28.4
1970	19,381	85,903	22.6	70,920	27.3
1975	19,473	94,793	20.5	77,051	25.3
1976	19,432	96,917	20.1	79,443	24.5

[a] Excludes Canada.

Source: For 1945, U.S. Department of Labor, Bureau of Labor Statistics, *Directory of National Unions and Employee Associations, 1975,* Bulletin 1937. For 1960–76, *ibid.,* "Directory of National Unions and Employee Associations, 1977," as published in *Daily Labor Report* (September 2, 1977), pp. D-14–17.

six years in question, total union membership was virtually stationary.

This recent stagnation also shows up when we look at the private sector alone. In 1970, there were 18.4 million union members in this branch of the economy, and they were about evenly divided between manufacturing and nonmanufacturing. By 1976, the total membership in the private sector had actually dropped to 18.0 million, while the manufacturing component was shrinking by a little over 700,000 members and nonmanufacturing was expanding modestly by 335,000. By contrast, the government sector jumped in membership by almost 1.7 million, almost entirely at the state and local levels.

Before we leave the subject of overall growth, we should note that if we consolidate the figures for union members with those who belong to bargaining associations such as the National Education Association (NEA), it turns out that aggregate membership stood at 21.2 million in 1970 and rose slightly to 22.5 million, or by 6.1 percent, by 1976.

Finally, if we confine ourselves to the years 1974–1976, it turns out that total *union* membership alone fell by 767,000, while total membership in unions and associations together dropped by 346,000. Clearly, the verdict has to be that the American labor movement has entered a period of stagnation as far as total membership is concerned. . . .

This disappointing recent record of overall growth requires further comment and interpretation. First, because organized labor in the United States remains so deeply committed to the principles of business unionism, overall growth is of considerably less importance to the individual organizations than it might be to an outside observer. Any particular union is most concerned about its negotiating and strike effectiveness relative to the employers in its own jurisdictional territory. If there are no major gaps in this zone, there is little incentive and actually no need to expand merely for the sake of growth as such.

Second, the declining *relative* position of organized labor since the last war is far more the product of a weight shift in employment patterns and in the composition of the work force than of an absolute decline in total union membership. On the employment side, there has been an explosive growth in the so-called knowledge and service industries and occupations (for example, higher education and computer services). In result, the manufacturing sector, which accounted for nearly 50 percent of the nonagricultural work force in 1955, has dropped to below 25 percent today—not through an absolute decline in employees but through much faster growth in other sectors typically less amenable to unionization. Furthermore, in the recent period the substantial increase in employment in the nonfarm sector has been concentrated among women, teenagers, and part-time employees—groups that have not been easy to organize.

Thus the overall membership figures do not tell the whole story, and while to those who look for a growing labor *movement* rather than growth of particular unions, the postwar record suggests decline; nonetheless, to those concerned with unions as such, the outlook will seem less pessimistic.

Present Centers of
Strength and Weakness

Today, American unionism has two kinds of organizational strength: its entrenched positions in manufacturing, construction, mining, transportation, and public utilities; and its already substantial and still expanding wedge in the government sector, particularly at the state and local levels.

In the first category, however, overall membership growth has turned into a small but worrisome decline within the last three years. Partly this reversal reflects the still lagging position of the capital goods industries, despite nearly three years of business recovery. Partly, too, it may be influenced by the migration of industry from the Northeast and Midwest to the Sun Belt and even to the emerging areas of Southeast Asia. In addition, it seems safe to say that the hard goods segment of the American economy may have reached its ultimate limit and thus no longer represents the cutting edge of growth. Finally, there are some signs of employee disillusionment with—or a skepticism about—unionism, although these indications may be dominated by the views of nonunion workers, and hence need to be interpreted with care. A recent poll placed organized labor just above Congress, which stood at the bottom of the list in public opinion regarding leading American institutions. Moreover, the unions have been losing more than half of recent representation elections and of elections over the decertification of bargaining representation by incumbent unions. And finally, the surge of imports in recent years has brought in its wake a wave of layoffs and plant closures. Very large unions such as the Machinists and the Steelworkers have suffered severe losses in membership from the combined effect of these forces.

By contrast, among union members the disillusionment seems to be directed not against unions as such but against a leadership that is seen as lacking in militancy—a view that partly reflects the increased role of young workers in the membership.

Because government has been a growth factor for unionism for nearly twenty years, it is not surprising that the NEA was the fastest growing organization during 1974–76, and that it is now the second largest labor group in the United States, next to the Teamsters. Equally interesting, among the government unions, the American Federation of State, County, and Municipal Employees (AFSCME) increased by 469,000 members during those years, to reach a total of 750,000, while the American Federation of Teachers (AFT) expanded by 321,000, to total 446,000.

For the future, it is unlikely that the growth of organizations of government employees can be sustained at the high levels prevalent since 1960, at any level of government. The fundamental reason is that the demand for the services of public workers is unlikely to expand at the high rate characteristic of the last 17 years. For the nation as a whole, public-school enrollment has now reached its peak and may be expected to decline substantially over the next several years. The overall population growth rate is also slowing down, which retards the rate of formation of new local governments as well as the expansion of existing public services provided by local governments already in being. In addition, there is some reason to believe that the creation of new government programs and the imposition of new and higher taxes and bond issues are meeting with increasing resistance from voters. Because of these changes in trend, the best prospects for the government employee organizations would seem to lie in winning recognition in the several states and many local governments where unions and associations so far are hardly even known.

But the task will be difficult, in good part for reasons similar to those that have restricted the ability of unionism in the private sector to move outward extensively from its traditional base in manufacturing, extractive industry, construction, transportation, and public utilities. As in the unorganized private sector, the targets are usually numerous and relatively small, organizing is much more costly, opposition is often intense, the employees are often indifferent or even hostile, facilitating legislation often is nonexistent, and the politicians may see no advantage in helping the union cause.

Patterns of Growth in the Past

The growth of membership has been predominantly centered in the national unions and to a much smaller extent in new local unions. Viewed as a whole, growth can occur in three major ways. The first involves the organization of additional plants or firms in industries that are already largely organized. The second concerns breakthroughs into new industrial territory, followed by further expansion. And the third is simply the passive process of expanding through natural increase in the labor force of the establishments in which the union already has a foothold.

Looking at the history of the national unions can be valuable for understanding the process of growth. For example, consider the Plumbers. Here is an organization built literally from the ground up, through city-by-city formation of independent locals of pipe fitters. By 1889 these locals had joined together to form a national union that affiliated with the AFL in 1897 and had eliminated all rivals by 1914. From thereon, the growth of the union was entirely through natural increase. In recent years, a revived open-shop movement has cut into total membership to some extent.

For a second case, consider the United Steelworkers (USW), a classic instance of what Ulman calls "organizing from the top down" initially by breakthroughs into new industrial territory, then by mopping up the still organized plants in the territory, and finally by invading other industries, chiefly by absorbing other unions through merger.

The USW began in 1936 as the Steelworkers Organizing Committee (SWOC). Its founders, John L. Lewis and Philip Murray, had come from the old United Mine Workers. As such they were strong advocates of centralized power and uniform contracts, as in the old Appalachian Agreement as the prototype in bituminous coal. Over its first six years, the SWOC grew through organizing strikes, representation elections, and the capitulation of Myron Taylor of U.S. Steel through his decision to recognize the union. After 1942, the USW grew through natural increase in the steel industry. However, two years later Murray abandoned his cherished principle of one union to an industry by allowing the Aluminum Workers to affiliate with the USW. By 1957, the union began raiding the nonferrous metals industry. In this way it ultimately absorbed the independent Mine, Mill and Smelter Workers (1967), following by taking in the United Stone Workers and the International Union of District 50. In consequence, the USW as a national union has grown in all three ways: through organization after breakthrough, by invasion of new industries, and through natural increase. Mergers also expanded the union and its influence, although obviously they added nothing to total membership of all unions together.

Our last illustration is the International Brotherhood of Teamsters (IBT). Today the IBT has become a rogue elephant in the American labor movement—a huge, powerful, and isolated organization, existing under constant and growing legal threats, and in reputation accurately perceived as unpredictable and dangerous to encounter.

It was not always this way. In its beginnings, the IBT was as humble and unobtrusive as the Plumbers. Both started from a key occupation, and both began through independent city locals. But the Plumbers stuck to their craft throughout their 90-year history, while the Teamsters were to experience explosive growth, spreading out in so many directions that by 1961 they officially had proclaimed their jurisdiction to be "all workers, without limitation," a variant of the one big union idea.

The IBT was inspired to become a national union and affiliate of the AFL in 1899, at the instigation of Samuel Gompers. But the new organization did not prosper until Daniel J. Tobin began his 45-year presidency in 1909. Until the early 1920s its business was local cartage, drayage, and livery stables. Then the great highway boom got under way, creating a whole new organizing opportunity for the union. In Farrell Dobbs, a brilliant but now forgotten organizer, the IBT found the right man to unionize the over-the-road drivers in the North Central states in 1937. At this stage, the growth of Teamster membership reflected the initial breakthrough, the subsequent mopping up, and then the creation of a rich and powerful base for extending unionization into an incredible variety of fields, from dry-cleaning shops to pallbearing.

These three cases indicate rather well how membership growth has taken place in the past. The next question is: What are the prospects for the expansion of unionism today?

The Challenge of Future Growth

. . . The AFL-CIO has recently declared that the organization has no plans for an organizing drive at the present time. Taken at its face value, this would suggest that the federation is not concerned at the recent decline in overall membership. However, to some extent this inference is belied by the current efforts of the AFL-CIO to obtain substantially increased protectionist measures to restrict imports, and to secure changes in the Taft-Hartley Act to make organizing somewhat easier under NLRB procedures.

Nevertheless, the real problem goes much deeper. Except for pockets of nonunion industry in the South and in small towns, manufacturing offers little organizing potential today. This prompts the question, Where is that potential to be found?

The answer seems to lie mainly in the so-called service and knowledge industries, in wholesale and retail trades, and in banking, finance, and insurance. According to each case, the obstacles are many. Many of the jobs call for professional or technical skills held by persons typically not susceptible to the appeal of unionism, particularly of the blue-collar sort. Many of their enterprises are small and therefore do not set manager and managed far apart, with a large and inflexible hierarchy in between. Many of the employees in these fields are young, moved by different values, and unreceptive to the union idea. And, finally, it would probably be far more expensive in organizing and servicing costs per each 100 members for a union to function in these fields.

Thus, while it is too early to formulate firm conclusions about the prospects for renewed overall union growth, it is clear that the outlook is by no means reassuring—at least until new leaders with new organizing techniques appear on the scene. But in saying this, it must be noted at the same time that American unionism remains strong in its present territory, and with its continued emphasis on collective bargaining this strength is what really matters.

FUTURE POSSIBILITIES FOR AMERICAN UNIONISM

Some Contemporary Characteristics of American Unionism

Looking back over the long history of the American labor movement, a few major observations stand out.

One of them is that, to this day, the unions have built their permanence and their success upon their role as market-oriented organizations. In other words, their primary goal has been to improve conditions at the workplace for their members by regulating the employer through contracts negotiated in collective bargaining. In this way, essentially by a process of representative "government" in the unionized industries, workers have acquired a substantial voice regarding the manner in which firms conduct the employment relationship. More than this, the control won through collective bargaining embraces many dimensions besides straight pay rates for the jobs in the bargaining unit. For example, they

also include fringe benefits, overtime opportunities, promotions, layoffs, recalls, transfers, premium pay for undesirable hours, disciplinary policies and procedures, union security arrangements; and perhaps most important of all, grievance procedures and arbitration for resolving contested interpretations and applications of rights or obligations contained in the collective agreement. In the large, collective bargaining introduces a system of privately negotiated rules for the joint control of the employment relationship. There are obvious benefits to the employers as well when joint control exists.

Precisely because these contracts, which number now in excess of 150,000 in American industry, are private documents negotiated by persons usually well informed about conditions in the particular firm and its industry and about the problems and interests of both sides, it can be said that, on the whole, this regulatory system has the considerable virtue of being both realistic as well as responsive to the interests of those most closely affected by it. In this respect it differs rather sharply from legislation, which is prepared typically at a distance from its locus of impact and drafted by those who are often uninformed about vital details, in a form made rigid by the necessities of the law itself. Admittedly, collective agreements at times and in part do reflect similar inflexibility, for example, in the wage doctrine implicit to the prototype contract in steel. Still, for the most part labor agreements are drafted mainly with an eye to the local situations from which the bargainers come. In consequence, they are shaped strongly by the environments of their application.

At the present time, there has emerged a broad interest in the Western countries concerning the participation of employees and their unions in the management of the enterprise. The proposals extant range from works committees to seats on the board of directors to profit-financed provision of common shares to the union; at one extreme is "self-management" in the sense of the old proposal of guild socialism in which the employees actually own and manage the firm themselves.

Aside from sporadic attempts at producers' cooperatives from time to time, none of these ideas so far has ever attracted extensive attention in the American labor movement. . . .

The explanation for this seeming lack of interest in labor participation is probably no more than the simple fact that collective bargaining itself is a system of participation of a specialized type. So far, it has worked so well for so long that little need has been felt to explore alternatives. At the same time, however, the *caveat* must be added—and it is a very important one—that the basic reason for the success of the system of collective bargaining lies in the collateral success of the American system of enterprise itself. After all, collective bargaining is at least in part a peculiar kind of profit-sharing system. It works when there are profits to share. Over the lengthy history of American capitalism, generally there have been ample profits available, and so the bargaining system has displayed a continuing vitality. And beyond this, of course, it has executed its regulatory functions with similar effectiveness.

This brings us to a second main observation: Until the advent of the great monetary collapse of 1931–33, American unionism from the inception of the AFL had practiced a peculiar kind of politics—it might well be called the politics of necessity. During this long preceding period, organized labor was a very small minority within the labor force and the larger community—a minority that had to function in an environment that was at best indifferent and more usually hostile. This was no setting in which to undertake a campaign even for the welfare state as viewed in Europe in those days, let alone for some brand of socialism. At the same time, what was the need

for such an unpromising endeavor when the system of collective bargaining itself continued to work more than tolerably well already—at least for those employees who were able to enjoy the benefits of unionism?

The answer is obvious: The emphasis continued to be placed upon control of the labor market, because here was an institutional arrangement that worked, and worked well. As for politics and politicians, the rule in those days was simple. Reward your friends, punish your enemies, avoid entangling party alliances, and limit political objectives to narrow supportive legislation such as the restriction of immigration, prevention of sale of prison-made goods, and keeping children off the labor market. Leave the rest to self-organization, the doctrine ran, using collective bargaining to control the labor market and the employers. "Organizational laissez-faire" was the result, in other words, a society dominated by relatively unregulated private organizations consisting mainly of business corporations, with some craft unions sprinkled here and there, and with all of it tied together by an economy of self-regulating markets.

The Great Depression changed all this by forcefully demonstrating the inability of collective bargaining to deal with certain problems of vital interest to working people, in particular, massive unemployment. With the election of 1932, the Democratic party found opportunity to commit the government to active policies for dealing with economic expansion and job creation, and thus to lay the groundwork for an informal alliance with organized labor. Over the ensuing years, this partnership has come to embrace almost the entire labor movement and to display itself repeatedly through candidates, elections, legislation, appointments, and administrative policies. Yet the fact should not be overlooked that the AFL-CIO and its political arm, COPE, always have been most careful to preserve their organizational independence from the Democratic party throughout. To this extent, Gompers's ancient doctrine of nonaffiliation still survives although in truncated form—precisely because such independence provides room and opportunity for bargaining over matters of critical interest to organized labor.

Indeed, there is a parallel here with bargaining with employers as well. By avoiding outright and unconditional identification with the Democratic party, the labor movement retains its independence and increases its ability to extract political concessions. In the case of employers, by limiting themselves to collective bargaining and at the same time avoiding schemes for other forms of participation in the enterprise, the unions elude any responsibility for the profitability of the business. This, too, has its obvious advantages when it comes to making demands and extracting concessions.

In the contemporary scene, then, organized labor stands firmly committed to the politics of the new welfare state, but as for its still central institution—collective bargaining—the outlook remains dominated by an ethic of immediate ends, to be sure, a more complex and a more sophisticated ethic than that expressed by Gompers' famous declaration of "more, and then still more" of 60 years ago, but still a policy of particular pragmatic objectives rather than the pursuit of an overriding and unitary ideology. Thus organized labor still chooses not to undertake a frontal challenge to private business enterprise and sounds no clarion call for a labor party to take the movement into socialism. But will things stay this way?

Permanence or Change
in Outlook and Policy

A great part of the answer, I think, will depend upon the future of the American business economy itself. If it can continue to grow according to the trends of the past, then the number of jobs will also increase and real wages will rise, because capital formation has never brought about a rate of labor displacement unacceptable to American unionism as a whole. In other words, most investment has created new jobs and added to productivity. Under these circumstances, the bargaining system can continue to yield the fruits that have entrenched its position for so long. These same conditions would also favor an essentially conservative type of labor leadership, more typical of George Meany and his close associates than, say, of Walter and Victor Reuther, or of Eugene V. Debs at an earlier time.

Also favorable to this view are the differences that still sharply distinguish the American from the British case. For decades, the British unions have had their own political arm in the Labour party, with its now unequivocal dedication to a fully socialist form of society. Buttressing these ambitions is a bitter degree of class consciousness that is the special legacy of British history. At the same time we must not overlook one of the principal sources of that dedication—the overwhelmingly socialist central tradition of the British intelligentsia that has been manifest from the founding of the Fabian Society in 1884. The influence of this powerful group on policy as well as thinking in the union movement, the Labour party, the government, and the civil service is not be overestimated. And finally, socialism is already a fact in Britain, with the nationalized industries accounting for more than half of the gross national product.

On the surface, at least, the American case appears different in decisive respects. The Democratic party is not a close counterpart to the Labour party. Although the socialist tradition probably predominates among American intellectuals, it by no means has gone unchallenged, and it has never conquered the civil service to the extent typical of Britain.

And most important, government-operated industry is still comparatively unimportant, with 85 percent of the GNP still originating from the private sector.

However, the basic question concerns the future of American capitalism itself, for if it should falter and fail, extensive and ever-enlarging measures of state intervention and control would quickly be forthcoming. In the process, our party politics would then become socialist in fact without bother of accepting the name. With seismic developments of this kind, the labor movement could not escape a parallel involvement and commitment, and a new set of leaders as well.

The way that this could all come about would be through a failure of private capital formation—a failure that would bring in its train a fall or even disappearance of the rate of improvement in labor productivity, a consequent rise in unit labor costs and prices, a decline in the rate of innovation, a retardation in the rate of formation of new jobs, and a continuing, even accelerating, rate of inflation.

The mechanism by which all of this might come about can be considered only briefly here. At the present time, the nation suffers from an unhappy combination of chronic unemployment and chronic inflation; it has now lasted long enough to be termed stubborn and persistent. In consequence the pressures are growing for attacking unemployment through a much larger program of public jobs, to be financed by still larger federal deficits, both on the venerable theory that larger public spending is still the key to the solution of the unemployment problem, because large-scale unemployment can only come from a deficiency of effective demand. Once a program of this form were adopted, say, with a goal of 3 percent unemployment within four years, it would impose a still much greater load of permanent federal financing upon the capital market, and before long an acceleration of inflation would follow. Unemployment would soon arise with this unexpected change in the behavior of the price level. At the same time, increased deficit financing would deprive the private-enterprise sector of the saving essential for continued growth at a time when adjusted real corporate profits after taxes are already below the level of 1966.

In turn, the acceleration of inflation could well bring forth irresistible demands for price controls, which if introduced would make wage controls also inevitable. Once all markets are shackled by controls, rationing and *de facto* government allocations of resources would also become necessary. In such circumstances there can be no collective bargaining. The unions would become wards of the government, along with private business as well. Both would become politicized as the market gives way to decisions by the state.

All this is only a paradigm at the present time. But it does suggest that the destinies of the traditional American labor movement and the American business system are closely bound together, despite the adversary positions of their representatives when they meet at the bargaining table.

37

How American Workers
View Labor Unions

Thomas A. Kochan

Thomas A. Kochan, "How American Workers View Labor Unions," *Monthly Labor Review,* April, 1979.

The American trade union movement has been characterized by theorists, social critics, and union practitioners alike as following a "business unionism" philosophy. That is, American unions are seen as very pragmatic organizations that seek to improve the economic and social conditions of their members, focusing on improving the conditions of employment in the short run, primarily through collective bargaining.

However, until recently, surprisingly little work has probed systematically the views of American workers toward trade unions.[1] Even less empirical evidence was available for measuring union members' assessments of the performance of their own unions.

The 1977 Quality of Employment Survey, conducted for the U.S. Department of Labor by the Survey Research Center at the University of Michigan, provides a first step toward changing this state of affairs.[2] Attitudes and ex-

[1] For a discussion of opinion polls covering selected views of trade unions between 1940 and 1966, see Derek C. Bok and John T. Dunlop, *Labor and the American Community* (New York: Simon and Schuster, 1970), pp. 11–19.

[2] This article is condensed from a report submitted to the Assistant Secretary of Labor for Policy, Evaluation, and Research under contract No. B-9-e-8-2899. For a general discussion of the survey results, see Graham L. Staines and Robert P. Quinn, "American workers evaluate the quality of their jobs," *Monthly Labor Review* (January 1979), pp. 3–12.

periences of a representative sample of the labor force were surveyed on a variety of questions related to the respondents' working lives.[3] Three sets of questions pertaining to unions were included in the survey. First, all respondents were asked about their beliefs about trade unions in general. Second, the nonunion respondents were asked about their voting preference if a union representation election were held where they work. Third, the union members in the survey were asked to report their satisfaction with their unions, priorities for what their unions ought to be doing, and views of what their unions actually were doing and to indicate the extent of their participation in their unions.

Results of the survey show that workers generally viewed unions as large, powerful bodies, which are highly effective. Of the nonunion workers, almost one-third said they would vote to unionize; and, although union members were mostly satisfied, they placed highest priorities on improving their unions' internal administration, while also emphasizing the importance of traditional collective bargaining issues, such as wages and fringe benefits.

PERCEIVING UNIONS

In the questions on what workers believe trade unions are doing, respondents were asked to rate on a five-point scale the extent to which they agreed or disagreed with the statements listed in Table 1.

"Big-Labor" Image

The first six questions in the table are clustered in something that might be labeled a "big-labor-image" dimension.[4] These questions measure the extent to which respondents agree or disagree with statements that the labor movement exerts a powerful influence over others in society. For example, those who generally agreed with these statements saw unions as exerting considerable influence over (1) who gets elected to public office, (2) what laws are passed, (3) how the country is run, (4) employers, and (5) union members. A final question in this cluster asked the extent to which the respondents saw union leaders as out to do what is best for themselves rather than what is best for their members. Between 70 and 80 percent of the respondents agreed with the statements that unions exert influence over who gets elected to public office, what laws are passed, how the country is run, and union members. Approximately two-thirds of the respondents agreed that unions are more powerful than employers and that leaders are more interested in what benefits themselves than in what benefits union members. Thus, a strong majority of workers saw unions as big, powerful institutions in society.

These results are consistent with earlier opinion poll data summarized by Derek C. Bok and John T. Dunlop. A 1941 survey found 75 percent of the public believed union leaders had accumulated "too much power," 62 percent agreed with this same question in 1950. Questions about union leaders asked in four polls between 1962 and 1965 consistently showed that the public held union leaders in very low esteem relative to business leaders, religious leaders, government officials, and college professors.[5] However, because the wording and specificity of the questions in the 1977 survey differ from these earlier polls, it is not possible to make exact comparisons.

---

[3] Information on the sample drawn for this survey is contained in Robert P. Quinn and Graham L. Staines, *The 1977 Quality of Employment Survey* (University of Michigan, Survey Research Center, 1978), Section Two.

[4] The clusters reported here and in Table 3 were derived from factor analyses that are available from the author upon request.

[5] Bok and Dunlop, *Labor*, pp. 13–18.

TABLE 1

American Workers' Beliefs About Trade Unions*
(in percent)

Beliefs	Strongly Agree	Agree	Neither Agree nor Disagree	Disagree	Strongly Disagree
Big-labor-image beliefs:					
Influence who gets elected to public office	37.5	46.0	1.8	12.7	1.1
Influence laws passed	24.0	56.6	3.8	14.4	1.2
Are more powerful than employers	24.8	41.6	6.2	25.4	2.0
Influence how the country is run	18.1	53.4	4.8	21.7	1.9
Require members to get along with decisions	18.5	56.0	3.9	20.1	1.6
Have leaders who do what's best for themselves	22.8	44.7	6.4	24.0	2.1
Instrumental beliefs:					
Protect workers against unfair practice	20.5	63.0	3.4	11.2	2.0
Improve job security	19.2	61.0	2.8	14.5	2.5
Improve wages	18.9	67.6	3.2	8.7	1.7
Give members their money (dues) worth	6.9	38.5	6.3	36.9	11.3

*In the survey, 1,515 workers were polled.

A regression analysis in which the dependent variable was an index composed of the average responses to these big-labor-image questions showed that those who were most likely to agree with these statements were older and white-collar workers, while those most likely to disagree with these statements were union members, Southerners, women, nonwhites, and workers employed in public sector occupations. Overall, however, only a very small proportion of the variations in these responses ($R^2 = .07$) was explained by the regression equation, indicating that this big-labor image was generally shared by a majority of the workers in all the demographic, industrial, regional, and occupational categories examined.

High Ratings for Effectiveness

The remaining four questions are clustered in a separate factor in the bottom half of Table 1. These questions appear to measure the extent to which respondents viewed unions as "instrumental" in improving the working lives of their members. Those who agreed with these questions saw unions as (1) protecting their members against unfair practices of employers, (2) improving members' job security, (3) improving the wages of their members, and (4) giving their members their money's (dues) worth. More than 80 percent of the respondents agreed that unions improve the wages and job security of their members and [protect] their members against unfair labor practices of employers. The respondents were almost equally divided over the question of whether the unions provide members their money's worth. Again these data are consistent with previous polls that show, despite the negative images of the political and economic power of unions, between 60 and 70 percent of Americans approve of unions in general and of the rights of workers to join unions. Bok and Dunlop interpreted these ratings (in conjunction with the negative public image of the power of unions) as support for the collective bargaining functions of unions.[6]

When a regression analysis was performed on the average responses to this "instrumental" dimension, it was found that those who were most likely to agree with these statements were members of trade unions, higher educated, and living in the South. White-collar workers, especially managerial employees, workers in the North-Central region of the country, and those in the manufacturing, transportation, and utility industries were less likely to agree with these statements. Although nonwhites and older workers also scored higher on this dimension than their white and younger counterparts, the relationships here were not statistically significant.

Those who scored high on the big-labor-image dimension were somewhat less likely to score high in the instrumental dimension (the correlation between the scores on these two dimensions is −.19). However, these are by no means mutually exclusive images. Instead, the majority of the workers surveyed apparently were somewhat skeptical of the political roles that unions play and of their power in society *and also* held positive views of union performance in collective bargaining.

[6] Bok and Dunlop, *Labor*, p. 13.

Workers Divided on Union Function

In addition to responding to multiple-choice questions, the respondents were asked in an open-ended question to describe what they believed labor unions in this country are trying to do. The responses to this question then were coded into a set of positive or negative categories depending on the nature of the responses. Overall, 51 percent of those responding mentioned only positive things that unions are doing. Twenty-four percent described only negative functions. Fourteen percent mentioned both positive and negative things, and the remaining 11 percent of the responses were not amenable to classification. The most common positive function mentioned was improving the wages and benefits of the union members. Twenty-nine percent of those giving a reason listed this as their primary view of what unions do. An additional 18 percent described unions as improving the working conditions of their members. Although the remaining responses on the positive side were scattered across a wide variety of categories, none of the reasons given were listed by more than 5 percent of the respondents.

Those describing unions as doing negative things had a more difficult time specifying exactly what they meant. Of the primary reasons given, the most frequent was the view that unions were out more for their own self-protection than for the good of society in general. Six percent of those responding gave this view of unions. The remaining negative views were, again, scattered across a wide array of categories. None of the reasons were given by more than 3 percent of the sample. Thus, the negative image workers have of unions appears to reflect a generalized stereotype, rather than a specific identifiable or easily expressed criticism.

VOTING ON UNIONIZATION

One of the key questions asked of the nonunion respondents in the survey was whether they would vote for union representation if an election were held in their workplace. Of the 983 that responded, 295, or 30 percent, indicated they would vote for unionization. When managers and the self-employed were excluded from the sample, the rate of support for unionization rose to 33 percent. Further breakdowns show that 39 percent of the blue-collar workers would support unionization, compared to 28 percent of the white-collar workers, excluding the self-employed and managers. Perhaps the most striking finding was the 67 percent of all black and other minority workers would vote to unionize. Also, 40 percent of all women and 35 percent of workers in the South would support unionization.

Dissatisfaction a Factor

The following statement by E. Wight Bakke is still perhaps one of the best propositions for guiding an analysis of how individual workers approach the decision to join or not join a union:

> The worker reacts favorably to union membership in proportion to the strength of his belief that this step will reduce his frustrations and anxieties and will further his opportunities relevant to the achievement of his standards of successful living. He reacts unfavorably in proportion to the strength of his belief that this step will increase his frustrations and anxieties and will reduce his opportunities relevant to the achievement of such standards . . . [7]

[7] E. Wight Bakke, "Why Workers Join Unions," *Personnel* (July 1945), p. 2.

In short, if we are to distinguish between individuals who would support unionization in 1977 versus those who would not, we must first identify the current job-related concerns of workers, their evaluation of their current conditions and their views of the instrumentality of unionization as a strategy for improving their well-being versus the perceived costs or negative consequences of unionization. [8]

The findings of several recent empirical studies suggest that dissatisfaction over the economic or traditional bread and butter issues of wages, fringe benefits, and working conditions is more strongly related to the desire to join a union than is dissatisfaction with other aspects of a job, such as relations with supervisors and the content of the job itself. [9] Thus, the initial proposition tested with these data was that those workers who are more dissatisfied with the economic or traditional bread and butter aspects of their job or those who report more problems with such aspects are more likely to be union supporters than those who are more satisfied or experience fewer problems with the aspects of their job.

The correlations and regression equations relating characteristics of the respondents, their jobs and their attitudes toward their jobs to the

[8] Note that the question being asked of the workers in this sample is whether they would vote for union representation, not whether they would join a union. Thus, the argument that union benefits are public goods that can be obtained without actually becoming a member and paying union dues need not be addressed here. For a discussion of this problem, see Mancur Olsen, *The Logic of Collective Action* (Cambridge, Mass.: Harvard University Press, 1971).

[9] See for example Julius Getman, Stephen Goldberg, and Jeanne Herman, *Union Representation Elections: Law and Reality* (New York: Russel Sage, 1977); Chester A. Schreisheim, "Job Satisfaction, Attitude Toward Unions, and Voting in a Union Representation Election," *Journal of Applied Psychology* (1978).

TABLE 2

Regressions of Workers' Propensity to Join Unions, by Occupational Group

Independent Variables	Overall Sample[a]			Blue-Collar Workers[d]		White-Collar Workers[e]	
	Correlation Coefficients	Standardized Regression Coefficients		Standardized Regression Coefficients		Standardized Regression Coefficients	
		Run 1[b]	Run 2[c]	Run 1[b]	Run 2[c]	Run 1[b]	Run 2[c]
Job satisfaction[f]							
Bread and butter	$-.297^g$	$-.135^g$	—	$-.061$	—	$-.127^i$	—
Supervision	$-.206^g$	$-.033$	—	$-.111^i$	—	$.004$	—
Nature of work	$-.299^g$	$-.112^h$	—	$-.095$	—	$-.160^h$	—
Desired on-the-job influence[j]	$.160^g$	—	$.104^g$	—	$.069$	—	$.150$
Difficulty exerting influence[j]	$.150^g$	—	$.057^i$	—	$.112^h$	—	$.022$
Job insecurity[j]	$.056$	—	$.007$	—	$-.015$	—	$-.012$
Severity of job dangers[j]	$.164^g$	—	$.141^g$	—	$.156^g$	—	$.081^i$
Travel to work difficulties[j]	$.041$	—	$.020$	—	$.038$	—	$.019$
Desirability of working conditions[j]	$.100^i$	—	$.005$	—	$.012$	—	$.030$
Inadequate income[j]	$.209^g$	—	$.067^i$	—	$.150^g$	—	$.002$
Inadequate fringes[j]	$.211^g$	—	$.087^h$	—	$.092^i$	—	$.097^h$
Pay equity perceptions[j]	$-.210^g$	—	$-.126^g$	—	$-.047$	—	$-.158^g$
Age	$-.090^i$	$-.014$	$-.026$	$-.044$	$-.053$	$-.044$	$-.016$
Education	$-.029$	$-.018$	$-.001$	$-.008$	$.022$	$.026$	$.025$
Sex: Female	$.118^h$	$.004$	$.035$	$-.011$	$.001$	$.064$	$.094$
Race: Nonwhite	$.244^g$	$.143^g$	$.148^g$	$.176^g$	$.180^g$	$.117^h$	$.130^g$
Big-labor-image beliefs	$-.167^g$	$-.076^h$	$-.091^g$	$-.116^j$	$-.120^i$	$-.060^i$	$-.079^i$
Instrumentality beliefs	$.329^g$	$.262^g$	$.273$	$.301^g$	$.301^g$	$.230^g$	$.261^g$
Region:							
North Central	$-.077^i$	$-.108^h$	$-.103^h$	$-.126^i$	$-.126^i$	$-.132^h$	$-.116^h$
South	$.043$	$-.061$	$-.073^h$	$-.043$	$-.058$	$-.117$	$-.105^i$
West	$-.020$	$-.038$	$-.047$	$-.040$	$-.038$	$-.046$	$-.057$
Size of establishment							
1 to 10 employees	$-.095^i$	$-.090^i$	$-.112$	$.136^i$	$-.215^h$	$-.091$	$-.068$
11 to 499 employees	$.057$	$-.004$	$-.121$	$-.002$	$.058$	$-.044$	$-.038$
Over 2000 employees	$-.021$	$-.016$	$-.011$	$-.065$	$-.059$	$.003$	$.016$
Industry:							
Secondary	$.048$	$.016$	$.021$	$.035$	$.017$	$.079$	$.082$
Government	$.015$	$-.031$	$-.035$	$.065$	$-.105^h$	$.022$	$.031$
Occupation[k]							
Professional/technical	$.020$	$.018$	—	—	—	—	—
Managerial/administrative	$-.116^h$	$-.023$	—	—	—	—	—
Clerical	$.031$	$-.002$	—	—	—	—	—

TABLE 2 (Continued)

Regressions of Workers' Propensity to Join Unions, by Occupational Group

Independent Variables	Correlation Coefficients	Overall Sample[a]		Blue-Collar Workers[d]		White-Collar Workers[e]	
		Standardized Regression Coefficients		Standardized Regression Coefficients		Standardized Regression Coefficients	
		Run 1[b]	Run 2[c]	Run 1[b]	Run 2[c]	Run 1[b]	Run 2[c]
Craftsman	$-.091^{[i]}$	$-.042$	$-$	$-$	$-$	$-$	$-$
Service	$-.110^{[h]}$	$-.047$	$-$	$-$	$-$	$-$	$-$

Measures of Regression Accuracy

F	$-$	$12.14^{[g]}$	$10.61^{[g]}$	$7.35^{[h]}$	$6.81^{[h]}$	$8.05^{[h]}$	$5.97^{[h]}$
R^2	$-$	.271	.261	.300	.313	.262	.226
$\bar{R}^2$	$-$	.249	.237	.265	.267	.229	.188

[a] N=604

[b] These regressions include indexes of job satisfaction.

[c] These regressions include measures of workers' perceptions of problems with different aspects of their jobs.

[d] N=335.

[e] N=469.

[f] Not included in Run 2.

[g] Significant at .01.

[h] Significant at .05.

[i] Significant at .10.

[j] Not included in Run 1.

[k] Not included in blue-collar and white-collar regressions.

propensity to join a union are presented in Table 2. For the overall sample, bread and butter aspects of the respondents' jobs were consistently significantly related to willingness to join unions, both before and after controlling for all of the other variables. Likewise, those respondents who reported more problems with inadequate income, fringe benefits, and problems with health and safety hazards on the job were also more likely to support unionization on their jobs than were workers not experiencing these problems (or experiencing them in lesser magnitudes). Examination of the distribution of these responses between union and nonunion supporters further indicated that only when the problems became most severe or the highest level of dissatisfaction was reported did a majority of respondents indicate a willingness to support unionization. Thus, it would appear that, while dissatisfaction with wages, fringes, and working conditions provides the initial stimulus to unionization, concern for this must be quite severe before a majority will support unionization as an option for improving these conditions.[10]

For white-collar workers, dissatisfaction with the content of their jobs exerted a somewhat greater effect on propensity to unionize than did dissatisfaction with the bread and butter aspects of the job. Still, however, dissatisfaction with bread and butter aspects of the job was significant in the white-collar equation. This implies that the motivation to unionize for both white-collar and blue-collar workers is influenced by their economic conditions, but that white-collar workers are also more motivated to support unionization when dissatisfied with the content, scope, and organization of their jobs.

Dissatisfaction with wages and economic benefits can arise both because their absolute levels are perceived to be below some acceptable standard or because of inequities that are perceived in one's wages or in the way in which working conditions are administered. Workers normally have some comparison in mind when evaluating their own conditions. However, we can also directly assess the effects of perceptions of inequitable wages, as workers were asked the extent to which they perceived their wages to be equitable relative to others doing the same type of work. A significant negative correlation was found between perceptions of equity and

[10] A satisfaction squared term was entered into the regression equation to test whether it outperformed or added to the explanatory power of the additive specification of this variable. The results did not significantly differ when the squared term was used as a substitute for the additive term. Including both terms in the equation did not significantly increase the explanatory power of the model.

propensity to unionize for the overall sample and for white-collar workers. Thus, it is not only the level of wages and other terms and conditions of employment that influence workers' willingness to unionize but also, in at least the case of white-collar workers, the extent to which workers' wages are perceived to be inequitable relative to others doing similar work.

Desire for Influence

While dissatisfaction with job conditions may provide the initial stimulus for unionization, not all workers are likely to turn immediately to unions as a way of coping with these problems. Workers have alternatives for influencing unsatisfactory working conditions. Not all workers believe it is their right or desire to have greater participation on their jobs. Furthermore, among those who believe it is their right or are interested in having greater influence, only those who are unable to influence their work environment through other, more informal, individualistic, or employer-initiated participation programs are likely to turn to unions as an alternative.

The correlations between the variables measuring the desire for participation and the difficulty of introducing changes on the job provide support for these propositions, though the correlations between these characteristics and the propensity to unionize are somewhat lower than the correlation on job dissatisfaction. However, the correlations do indicate that workers interested in unionization see it as both a means of introducing greater participation on the job and for overcoming employer resistance to change or to dealing with job related problems. In fact, a majority of the respondents who both desired greater participation *and* reported experiencing difficulty in getting em-

ployers to make changes on their jobs supported unionization.[11]

Again, differences betweem white-collar
and blue-collar workers were found with these
two measures. For the white-collar workers, a
belief about the rights of workers to participate
exerted srtonger effects on their propensity to
unionize than did the difficulty they experienced
in making changes on their jobs. For blue-
collar workers, the opposite was true; difficulty
of change outweighed beliefs about participation.

Beliefs Versus Costs

Workers who are dissatisfied with their present
conditions and seek greater participation and
influence still must decide whether the benefits
of unionization in their particular situation outweigh the costs associated with it. Here is
where the general beliefs workers hold about
unions enter into the process of deciding
whether to vote for unionization. Workers who
are more ideologically predisposed toward
unions or have more favorable images of unions
could be expected to support unionization in
their particular situations. The recent empirical
studies of representation elections cited earlier
in this article have found very strong relationships between the general images of unions and
workers' voting behavior.

In this study, the coefficients on the
instrumentality index tended to be approxi-

[11] An interaction term measuring the combined
effects of a high desire for participation and a high
perceived difficulty of achieving changes on the job
was tested in several regression runs. The explanatory
power of this interaction term was approximately
equal to the combined effects of desire for influence
and difficulty of change when entered in their additive
form. The interaction term did not add significant
explanatory power when included with the additive
form of these two variables.

mately three times as large as those on the big-
labor-image index, reinforcing the view that
American workers approach the decision to
unionize in very pragmatic terms. They are
apparently less influenced by their general
image of labor in society or by their general
views of the labor movement than they are by
their judgments about what unions actually do
for their members.

Demographic Determinants

A common theme running through much of
the popular speculation about the future of
the labor movement is that unions will have a
difficult time organizing because of the changing demographic, industrial, occupational, and
regional characteristics of the labor force. Consequently, the relationship between each of
these characteristics and the propensity to join
unions was examined again both before and
after controlling the psychological or attitud-
inal characteristics summarized in the previous
section.

In general, findings concerning the demographic characteristics suggest there are no
specific subgroups in the population that are
consistently unwilling to join a union if their
job conditions warrant unionization. At the
same time, there were no specific subgroups,
with the exception of nonwhite workers, that
appeared to be willing to join unions as a
matter of course. That is, holding job conditions constant, younger workers were as willing
(or unwilling) to join unions as older workers,
women at least as willing as men, and white-
collar workers apparently as willing as blue-
collar workers. . . .

Including regional variables in the analysis
also provided somewhat surprising results. Although it has often been argued that Southern
workers are less interested in joining unions

than their Northern counterparts, the negative coefficient on the Sourthern variable was significant only for white-collar workers. Southern blue-collar workers were, therefore, just as willing to join unions when their job conditions warranted unionization as were workers in the Northeast.

However, there appeared to be a more negative nonunion effect found among both blue- and white-collar workers in the North Central region of the country. Workers in the West appeared insignificantly different from the workers in the Northeast in their willingness to join trade unions. The North Central effect remained significant, even when the sample was broken down into white-collar and blue-collar subgroups.

The last variable examined was the size of the establishment in which the worker was employed. Size was measured by a series of categorical variables, because initial examination of the distribution of responses showed that the workers in the smallest (fewer than 10 workers) and the largest (1,000 workers or more) establishments were least willing to join trade unions. Those in the intermediate categories were somewhat more prone to unionization. Relative to the smallest establishments, workers in the intermediate size organizations were most likely to be willing to support unionization. These results may reflect the close interpersonal relationship between workers and employers in the very small organizations and the effectiveness of the very large nonunion employers in reducing the incentives to join unions by paying higher wages and benefits and by using sophisticated personnel techniques and policies.[12]

[12] A discriminant analysis also was performed on these data as a supplement to, and a check on, the regression results. The same profile of coefficients was obtained in both procedures. The discriminant model was able to accurately classify 73 percent of the "no" voters and 72 percent of the "yes" voters.

Benefits the Main Factor

When nonunion respondents were asked why they would vote for or against unionization, the most frequently cited reason for supporting unionization was that unions would improve wages and fringe benefits. Twelve percent of the union supporters cited this as the major reason for preferring unionization. The second most important reason, cited by 6 percent of the union supporters, was that unions would represent the workers' interests in dealing with their employer. Other reasons cited include unions' ability to improve working conditions, provide job security, ensure fair treatment, improve working hours, improve safety and health, and handle workers' grievances. Clearly, these verbal responses reinforce the concerns workers have for the economic and other traditional aspects of their jobs.

The major reason workers gave for voting *against* unionization was that a union was not needed on their job—the job was satisfactory as it now was. Twenty percent of those opposed to unionization gave this response. The second most common reason cited for opposing unions was that the worker preferred to handle problems individually with the employer. Ten percent of the union opponents gave this response. The next most common response reflects a negative image of labor unions; the respondent didn't approve of unions (8 percent). Finally, only 1 percent of the workers indicated that the primary reason for opposing unionization was a fear of employer retaliation or closure of the plant resulting from unionization.

EVALUATING UNION PERFORMANCE

What do American union members expect their trade unions to be doing? How well are unions fulfilling these expectations? These are perhaps two of the most critical questions for evaluating the responsiveness of trade unions to their members. Information on workers' views can be useful for tracing trends or changes in the responsiveness of the American trade union movement over time and for identifying the directions union members would like to see their organizations move in the future.

Greater Expectations

Workers were asked two sets of questions concerning their expectations from their unions and their evaluations of union performance. The first set of questions asked members to rate on a four-point scale how much effort they felt unions should be putting into various areas. The second question asked how well their unions actually were doing in the same areas. The list of issues included in these questions can be grouped into three categories: First, the traditional bread and butter issues of wages, fringe benefits, job security, and safety and health; second, the quality of work; third, the internal administration of the union.

The responses of the union members to these questions are presented in Tables 3 and 4. The greatest concern of the union members was for increasing the responsiveness of the union's internal administration. The highest priority rating was given to the concern for improving the handling of member grievances. The second highest was given to increasing the amount of feedback the union provides its members. In addition, the need to increase the influence that members have in running the union was rated as

TABLE 3

Union Member Priorities for Union Issues[a]

(in percent)

Issues	No Effort	A Little Effort	Some Effort	A Lot of Effort	Mean[b]
Wages	2.4	6.0	34.7	56.9	3.46
Fringes	1.1	4.2	30.9	63.8	3.57
Job security	3.4	7.8	34.4	54.4	3.39
Safety/health	4.3	13.1	34.9	47.6	2.87
Say on job	5.2	19.0	45.1	30.5	3.01
Interesting jobs	14.7	24.7	30.3	30.1	2.76
Say in union	3.2	4.9	31.8	60.0	3.49
Say in business	17.1	18.1	39.7	25.2	2.73
Feedback from union	2.0	5.9	22.1	69.7	3.60
Handling grievances	1.5	2.3	17.1	78.5	3.74

[a]Union members were asked how much effort they thought their unions should be putting into various issues.

[b]Degrees of effort were valued from 1 to 4 points with "little effort" equaling 1 and "a lot of effort," 4. The mean is the average value of response.

TABLE 4

Evaluation of Union Performance[a]

(in percent)

Issues	Not Good At All	Not Too Good	Somewhat Good	Very Good	Mean[b]
Wages	4.7	19.8	42.5	32.9	3.04
Fringes	7.7	21.8	41.9	28.6	2.91
Job security	7.6	18.0	50.8	23.6	2.90
Safety/health	6.5	21.5	50.7	21.3	2.87
Say on job	15.2	34.3	41.9	8.6	2.44
Interesting job	22.5	43.1	29.5	4.9	2.17
Say in union	16.2	27.9	37.3	18.7	2.58
Say in business	25.8	37.7	30.1	6.3	2.16
Feedback from union	10.5	23.3	36.5	29.6	2.85
Handling grievances	3.7	15.7	40.9	4.7	3.02

[a]Union members were asked how good a job their unions were doing in addressing various issues.

[b]Ratings were valued on a 4-point scale with "Not good at all" worth 1 point and "Very good" worth 4. The mean is the average value of response.

the fourth most important priority. Thus, three of the top four concerns of the union members reflected their interest in improving the governance of their union. The second major area of concern was in the traditional issues—wages, fringe benefits, job security, and working conditions. The concern for fringe benefits, in fact, was the third most important issue, while wages, job security, and safety and health issues ranked fifth through seventh, respectively. Issues concerning the quality of work were given the three lowest priorities.

The data pose somewhat of a dilemma for unions, however, for between 60 and 75 percent of all respondents wanted their unions to exert some or a lot of effort in improving the quality of work aspects of their jobs. Thus, while workers expected their union to give the highest priority to the internal administration and traditional issues, a majority also wanted their unions to exert an effort to improve the quality of work. Consequently, while workers

still viewed their unions as representatives of their economic interests, they also were looking for an expansion of the domain of union activity into these more uncharted areas.

The central determinant of workers' ratings of their unions' performance is their degree of job dissatisfaction with bread and butter issues or the existence of problems with these issues. Union performance was rated higher and members were more satisfied with union performance when these problems had been effectively addressed and when workers were satisfied with these aspects of their jobs. Older members and members in the South rated their unions significantly higher than did younger and non-Southern respondents.

Three major finding emerge from a comparison of data on what union members expect their unions to do with the data on how well unions are actually doing. First, there is a strong positive (r = .70) rank order correlation between the ratings of union priorities and union performance.[13]   This indicates that unions were perceived to be performing best on the issues of highest priority to their members. Second, the data further confirm the centrality of the traditional economic issues to union members. Third, the results indicate that members' expectations for their unions exceeded current union performance. On average, there was approximately a 0.5- to 0.7-point difference or gap (on a four-point scale) between the expectations members had for their unions and their perceptions of union performance.

When the gap between expectations and performance on each issue was examined (by subtracting from the percentage of the respondents who indicated they would like to see their unions exerting a lot of effort on a dimension the percentage of respondents who indicated their union was actually doing very well on that dimension), the importance of improving the internal administrative aspects of trade unions again was observed.   These differences are shown in Table 5.

In general, however, [our] analysis [detected] few significant differences in the priorities of the individual respondents or in the extent to which they perceived their union as effectively responding to their needs. Consequently, while these data are useful for giving us an overall view of the priorities of union members in general and their views of the performance of their unions, they do not provide much insight into the conditions under which unions are responding more or less effectively to their members' intersts.

[13] This correlation is almost identical to the one reported in a similar study of the relationship between the importance of alternative dimensions of union activists' jobs and the effectiveness of collective bargaining on these job dimensions. In the earlier study, the rank order correlation was .71. Thomas A. Kochan, David B. Lipsky, and Lee Dyer, "Collective Bargaining and the Quality of Work: The Views of Local Union Activists," *Proceedings of the 27th Annual Meeting of the Industrial Relations Research Association* (Madison, Wis.: IRRA, 1975), p. 159.

TABLE 5

Differences between Expectations and Performance

Issue	Size of Differences
Handling members' grievances	43.8
Providing more say in union	42.3
Providing more feedback from union	40.1
Getting better fringe benefits	35.2
Improving job security	30.8
Improving safety and health	26.3
Make jobs more interesting	25.2
Getting better wages	24.0
More say in how to do their jobs	21.9
More say in how business is run	18.9

General Satisfaction Prevails

The final question asked of the respondents was "How satisfied are you with your trade union?" The responses showed a trade union membership that was relatively well satisfied with its unions. Twenty-five percent of the respondents indicated that they were very satisfied with their union, 48 percent indicated they were satisfied, 17 percent indicated they were dissatisfied, and 10 percent indicated they were very dissatisfied. Thus, just under three-fourths of all of the union members surveyed indicated a general degree of satisfaction with their union. Subsequent regression analysis again confirmed that the only significant correlate of union satisfaction was satisfaction with the traditional economic or bread and butter aspects of workers' jobs. Beyond this, there were no consistent significant demographic, regional, or occupational groups that differed significantly on this satisfaction score.

IMPLICATIONS FOR ORGANIZED LABOR

Although the survey data do not provide [any] specific detailed suggestions for what unions need to do to improve their administration, they clearly show that this concern outweighs even members' concerns for substantive improvements in their conditions of employment. The data document that union members expect their unions to maintain their historical focus on seeking better wages, fringe benefits, jobs security, and working conditions. It is clear, therefore, that no shift in the focus of union priorities would be tolerated by the majority of union members. Any efforts made to improve the quality of work must be a supplement to, not a replacement for, efforts in the traditional areas of union concern. . . .

[The] data suggest several [implications concerning] the ability of unions to attract new members. On the positive side, extrapolating these sample results to the entire labor force indicates that if all workers who prefer to unionize (one-third of the unorganized work force[14]) were organized, the size of the labor movement would nearly double. The greatest source of potential growth appears to be among nonwhites; a two-thirds majority of

[14] Approximately 79 million employees are in the nonagricultural labor force, of which approximately 22 million are already members of labor organizations. Thirty-three percent of the remaining 57 million unorganized workers provide an estimated 19 million potential union members.

nonwhite workers prefers to unionize. In addition, none of the growing segments of the labor force exhibits an inherently negative view of trade unions or to the prospects of joining a union. Younger workers, women, and higher educated workers are no less willing to join a union when their job conditions warrant it than their older, male, or less educated counterparts. Even the common stereotype of the anti-union Southern worker does not show up in these data. Therefore, the changing regional and demographic composition of the labor force should pose no new barriers to organizing.

On the negative side, the majority of workers apparently only turn to a union when (1) greatly dissatisfied with their job and economic conditions, (2) they desire more influence over their job conditions, and (3) other forms of influence do not work. Unions are seen by a large number of workers as a strategy of last resort rather than as a natural or preferred means of improving job conditions. White-collar workers are especially concerned with the threats unionization might pose to their individual autonomy and independence. This suggests that potential members will have to be convinced that a union can respond to their specific sources of dissatisfaction and provide channels for effective participation and organizational change.

Collective Bargaining

Collective bargaining is a continuing relationship between one or more unions and one or more employers, for the purpose of reaching joint decisions on employee compensation, job tenure, and other conditions of employment. Harry Shulman and Neil Chamberlain point out that, although the content of collective agreements differs widely from industry to industry, the basic aims are largely the same. They emphasize the quasi-compulsory nature of the relationship, in which neither party is free to break off relations and contract with somebody else; the benefits that the parties can expect to gain from the agreement; and the continuity of bargaining. The day-to-day adjustment of differences through the grievance procedure may be as important as the more dramatic contract negotiations.

What are the parties to collective bargaining really after? What are the central objectives of the union? What areas of responsibility and initiative does management wish to retain? Frederick Harbison and John Coleman explain the main objectives on each side of the table, which they argue are similar in all collective bargaining relationships. They then ask why in some cases labor and management are able to reconcile conflicting objectives and to live in relative harmony, whereas in other cases they live in an armed truce with continuing tension.

For more than a century, ground rules for union and employer behavior in collective bargaining were laid down by court decisions. Beginning with the National Labor Relations Act of 1935, however, Congress and state legislatures have regulated in increasing detail the internal operation of trade unions, bargaining units and procedures, the content of collective agreements, and the use of strikes and other economic weapons. A major administrative agency, the National Labor Relations Board, was created to monitor the new ground rules. Charles Gregory outlines the long evolution of legal controls that has brought us to the present stage.

What a union can gain through collective bargaining depends partly on its ability to inflict economic damage on the employer in the event of disagreement. Albert Rees emphasizes the primacy of the strike as a source of union power and analyzes union policy in using the strike weapon. Other sources of union power, such as consumer boycotts and control of labor supply, are—in practice—of secondary importance.

Collective bargaining can lead either to an agreement or to a strike, which is costly to the parties and sometimes to the public. The United States and many other countries maintain a staff of government mediators, whose function is to intervene as neutral third parties in deadlocked negotiations in an effort to break the deadlock and achieve a voluntary settlement. What does a mediator actually do, and what determines whether his or her efforts will prove successful? Clark Kerr analyzes this question, drawing an interesting distinction between tactical mediation, involving intervention in a conflict that has already occurred, and strategic mediation, involving restructuring the bargaining situation so that conflicts are less likely to occur in the future.

Recent changes in the economy may significantly alter traditional collective bargaining arrangements. Everett Kassalow discusses three important areas of change: (1) the decline of the steel and auto industries, thus weakening the national leadership position of their unions; (2) the potential effects of government policies to control wage increases; and (3) the increasing role of the federal government in such areas as occupational health and safety, pension protection, and equal employment opportunity. Despite the efforts of the Reagan administration, Kassalow believes that in the long run the influence of the federal government will continue to increase.

What are the effects of unions and collective bargaining? The traditional opinion of many economists has been that unions are a monopoly, with negative effects on both productivity and resource allocation. In contrast, Richard Freeman and James Medoff develop the view that, by providing workers with a voice both at the workplace and in the political arena, unions improve the performance of the economy and of our political system. Specifically they show that, in the economic sphere, unions frequently increase productivity, improve the allocation of resources, and reduce both income inequality and racial discrimination.

38

The Process of Bargaining

Harry Shulman and Neil W. Chamberlain

Harry Shulman and Neil W. Chamberlain, "The Process of Bargaining," *Cases on Labor Relations* (Mineola, N.Y.: The Foundation Press, 1949). Reprinted with permission.

Collective bargaining is a concept, like law or government, which denotes some fundamental characteristics, but permits great variety in adaptation to specific needs and situations. Wage negotiations in the ... coal industry ... hardly resemble the ... negotiations with a ... shirt manufacturer in New Haven. The representation of employees and the nature of the process of adjustment of "grievances" on a building construction site present different problems requiring different methods from those in an automobile assembly plant. The detailed provisions of a collective agreement in a manufacturing plant are hardly transferable to an agreement covering hotel waiters, newspaper or magazine writers or university stenographers.

But the basic conditions and aims are largely the same. And the primary approach—the effort to consider and understand each other's needs, desires, fears and to inquire, negotiate and adjust jointly—that is also largely the same.

Theoretically, collective bargaining does not require a comprehensive collective agreement for a stated period of time. It requires only the recognition of the bargaining agency and of the principle of action that mutual problems be jointly considered and jointly decided. But while each party, if it were in full control, might wish to retain its freedom to deal with problems as it deems best when confronted by them, the fact of joint participation makes commitment for the future almost inevitable.

351

The desire of each party to be assured about the other's future conduct—that is, the desire for stability and security—makes the comprehensive collective agreement for a term the normal concomitant of collective bargaining. This reduces the possiblity of solving problems on the basis of spot judgments without formulated policies. It requires each party to think into the future, to anticipate situations and to determine solutions before the situations arise. It requires the making of policy—which, when agreed upon, becomes the collective agreement.

Typically, then, collective bargaining involves first, the negotiation of a general agreement as to terms and conditions of employment, and second, the maintenance of the parties' relations for the period of the agreement. The first process is the dramatic one which catches the public eye and which is sometimes mistaken to be the entire function of collective bargaining. But in fact, it is to labor relations approximately what the wedding is to domestic relations. It launches the parties on their joint enterprise with good wishes and good intentions. The life of the enterprise then depends on continuous, daily cooperation and adjustment. . . .

From this point of view, the heart of the collective agreement—indeed, of collective bargaining—is the process for continuous joint consideration and adjustment of plant problems. And it is this feature which indicates the great difference between the collective labor agreement and commercial contracts generally. The latter are concerned primarily with "end results"; the former, with continuous process.

The legal status of collective labor agreements has been the subject of much discussion in the legal literature and of considerable development in the courts. The early notion, still dominant in England, is that the collective labor agreement is not a legally enforceable transaction, that it is a statement of principles and purposes which must depend on good faith and self help and does not of itself create legal rights and obligations. In American courts this notion has given way to the conception of the collective labor agreement as a legally enforceable contract. But the practical significance of this newer conception has been only slightly illustrated. . . .

Whatever the legal status of the collective labor agreement may be, however, it is entirely clear that court enforcement can play only a relatively minor role in labor relations under such an agreement, just as in domestic relations. The nature of the agreement and of the parties' relations makes resort to the courts a theoretical and unsuitable remedy—except only in extreme cases and in those in which disruption has already taken place. For it must always be remembered that performance of the agreement is not the entire aim or object of the parties' relation. Their object is the operation of the enterprise in which each has indispensable tasks. And the agreement is a means of aiding them in their performance of those tasks and in the operation of the enterprise for their joint benefit.

The labor agreement is not made between parties who seek each other out for the purpose of entering into a business transaction and who can shop around among competitors for the most favorable connection. It is made, rather, between parties who find themselves already in a joint enterprise and who have little or no choice in selecting each other for the relationship. The union hardly chooses the employer; and the employer does not choose the union. Both are dependent on the same enterprise; and, as a practical matter, neither can pull out without destroying it. Even when a dispute between them results in suspension of operations (a strike or lockout), they must strive so to adjust the dispute as to resume their relationship.

Of necessity and quite independently of the agreement, the parties must live and work together daily and continuously. Their differences and frictions require adjustment not merely in terms of redress for past wrongs but more importantly in terms of facilitating today's and tomorrow's cooperation. While conformance with the collective agreement is intended as a means to that end, it is not the only means and is not a guaranteed cure-all.

The collective agreement applies to the relationships of a large number of people with various personalities, temperaments, ambitions, fears and tensions. While we speak of "the employer" and "the union" as entities, the agreement deals not merely with the relationships between numerous people—machine hands, laborers, craftsmen, rate checkers, plant policemen, several ranks of foremen, labor relations men, superintendents and so on. To think merely in terms of "employer" and "employees" or "management" and "union" is to miss a very important fact in labor relations—the fact that the relationships involve numerous people whose interests, needs, jobs and performances cannot be compressed, without distortion, into two general rubrics.

This means that what is sought is the satisfaction or adjustment of the needs, desires, or expectations of numerous people, rather than of certain officials on each side. And the adjustment is needed in numerous situations and under dynamic conditions. Even in the most stable enterprise there may be almost daily changes in details of operation and perhaps also in personnel. Each change may be of trifling significance to the enterprise as a whole; but to the individuals immediately affected it may appear of major importance.

The collective agreement cannot prescribe an indisputable rule of thumb for every dispute, difference, dissatisfaction or situation that may arise during its term. This is true for a number of reasons. First, it is humanly impossible to anticipate all the situations with all their variations and all the pressures that attend them when they do arise. But even if it were possible

thus to anticipate, it would be undesirable to lay down absolute, advance prescriptions in detail. For, by common paradox, while the parties want and need security, they also want and need freedom to act as occasion requires. Moreover, attempts at such advance prescription in detail would tend to prevent adoption of an agreement—first, because the negotiations would be endlessly protracted, and second, because agreement on the application of a principle in numerous hypothetical cases is infinitely more difficult than agreement on the principle itself. Again, the collective agreement must be susceptible of comprehension and administration by ordinary workers and supervisors; and it normally requires ratification by the union membership. Abundance of detail and minutiae may discover independent, individual objections of minor importance which may be aggregated (intentionally or otherwise) into a quite unwarranted total hostility. Like a political platform, a collective agreement may need to avoid "red flags."

For a number of reasons, then, the collective labor agreement must leave much to silence, to inference or to general statement. Like modern legislation in complex affairs, it must rely on administration to fill in the details and provide the needed adjustments. This requires continuous joint consideration of problems with the collective agreement as one aid to their solution.

But paradoxically again, the collective agreement also looses forces tending toward rigidity and unreasonableness. These are the temptations to refer all questions to the agreement; to argue about what the agreement provides and not about what the problem is and how it can best be met; to insist upon literal compliance without proper consideration of need, purpose and spirit; to couch requests and answers in terms of the agreement even when doing so conceals the parties' real concerns; in short, to think in terms of the agreement alone and not in terms of the problems or needs of the enterprise and of those engaged in it.

Remembering that the purpose of the parties' relationship is mutual benefit from the operation of their enterprise, the test of their success and maturity is not the rigidity of their compliance with the agreement, but rather the extent of their readiness sympathetically to understand and consider each other's needs and cooperate in efforts at adjustment—even by modification of prior agreement. The mechanism is normally the grievance procedure—either alone or in combination with other practices of joint meetings for discussion of general problems.

Like the rest of the collective agreement, the grievance procedure may be tailored to meet the requirements of the particular enterprise. In a small plant a single provision for a conference between the union representative and the "boss" may suffice. In larger plants, a series of steps or appeals may be required, each calling upon a different or higher level of authority. This assures participation by top authority when really necessary, but saves it from being swamped by minor grievances. It also affords opportunity to subordinate authorities to participate and effect adjustments within their special competence and concern. Various details may or may not be made parts of the procedure: time limits for the filing of grievances, appeals, or answers, requirements as to writing and employee signatures, limitations on the subject matter, and so on. Limitations and formalities have undoubted values; but their adoption or enforcement requires an appraisal of their values in relation to the cost of leaving frictions and dissatisfactions to fester without remedy. In any event, the adequacy of the grievance procedure for the maintenance of good relations depends less upon its structure than upon the spirit with which the individuals involved use it. If they are impatient, resentful,

petty, arrogant, misanthropic, legalistic, non-understanding or unwilling to understand, the best procedure will fail.

Even under ideal conditions, however, agreement in all instances can hardly be expected. In the past, unadjusted grievances and claims of contract violation were left to the parties' own power and to self-help. Resort to the courts was, and is, hardly a practical remedy. This is due only in minor part to the uncertain status in law of suits for enforcement of collective labor agreements. The major reason is that court litigation is an inappropriate method of securing harmonious cooperation in an enterprise involving continuous, daily, joint performance. The expense is too great for most of the disputes; the inevitable delay in securing final adjudication prolongs conflict; the spirit of litigation bolsters antagonism; the proceedings require professional representation and technicality beyond the competence of the clients; the emphasis is upon winning a case rather than restoring or maintaining a desired relationship; and the simple alternative of judgment for the plaintiff or defendant excludes the possibilities of intermediate adjustments which might be more appropriate and more helpful.

Accordingly, in recent years arbitration has been increasingly resorted to as the terminal step in grievance procedures. In some cases, separate consent to arbitrate is required for each dispute; in others, there is general advance agreement to arbitrate future disputes not satisfactorily resolved by the parties themselves. In some, the tribunal consists of several individuals; in others it consists of one. In some the composition of the tribunal is tri-partite either in the sense that, in addition to the impartial chairman, each party designates a member or in the further sense that the member designated is actually a representative of the party; in others, the tribunal is wholly non-partisan. In some cases, a separate tribunal must be constituted for each dispute; in others a standing tribunal is constituted to serve for a stated term or so long as it continues to be satisfactory to both parties. And in some cases the arbitrator is appointed by the parties upon their own nomination and investigation; in others, the parties delegate to a third body the nomination or appointment of the arbitrator.

Arbitration, in other words, like collective bargaining, is a flexible procedure which can be suited to different needs or desires. In some circumstances, it tends to become quite formal, rigid and legalistic. It then serves only the function of final adjudication—even as court litigation. But court litigants normally do not have to live together; their disputes generally relate to past events; the welfare of neither is dependent on that of the other; and a victory in the litigation is just as sweet whether it is the product of wisdom and understanding, or of confusion, misapprehension, or seduction by a witness or counsel. A labor dispute is wholly different. Though the dispute may formally relate to past events, the parties' major concern is with the present and the future; the parties must continue their relationship and work together during the dispute and after its determination; while the parties are in adversary positions, neither can disclaim interest in the other and neither can afford unduly to embitter the other; and a determination which is not wisely addressed to the problem and which does not contribute to greater harmony and understanding for the parties may be only a temporary victory which a little time may uncover as a serious loss. Arbitration employed with these differences in mind may be a powerful factor in promoting investigation, diagnosis and education for cooperation by the parties in their joint venture.

39

Goals and Strategy in Collective Bargaining

Frederick A. Harbison and John R. Coleman

OBJECTIVES OF COMPANY AND UNION LEADERS

We begin by asking: What are management and union leaders striving for in collective relations? This question deserves some careful thought because it is confusing to talk in generalities about "conflict of interests" or "harmony of interests" without a precise understanding of what such interests are. Although neither company executives nor labor leaders make a practice of sitting down and spelling out their objectives, it is possible for the observer to get a rough outline of these goals by analyzing their statements and actions over a period of time.

In this study we have not made use of the psychiatrist's couch or the poll-taker's multiple choices. We have simply talked with a great many persons in both companies and unions and tried to extract the more cogent implications of what they were saying. Then we "played back" our analysis to many of the persons interviewed. When they said, "Yes, of course, that's what I meant to say," we felt we were on the right track.[1]

[1] We have assumed throughout that men have objectives, for themselves, and for the institutions with which they identify themselves. As long as one looks at this or that man, the personal objectives may take precedence. But when one looks at the actions of a group of men, he is confronted with something more than the sum of the objectives of the group's members. There are institutional objectives which may at any time be just as important as the goals of the individuals in determining what sort of adjustment will be made between groups.

Management's Objectives

What does management try to achieve in its bargaining relationships with a union? An analysis of the cases we studied suggests that management's objectives in collective relations may fall into five broad categories: *first*, the preservation and strengthening of the business enterprise; *second*, the retention of effective control over the enterprise; *third*, the establishment of stable and "businesslike" relationships with the bargaining agents; *fourth*, promotion of certain broad social and economic goals; and *fifth*, advancement of personal goals and ambitions. In combinations of various kinds and with varying emphasis from case to case, these objectives become in essence the driving forces behind managerial policy and actions. Taken as a whole, they help to explain what management is striving for in collective relations.

Preservation and strengthening of the business enterprise. Management is first of all concerned with the institutional well-being of the business it is running. In order to survive and grow, a business must in the long run produce and sell goods or services at a profit. It must be able to compete successfully with other enterprises in the same line of activity. In more specific terms, management is concerned with the *financial* and *organizational* well-being of the enterprise. From the financial point of view, management strives to produce earnings which are sufficient to finance necessary expansion of the enterprise, to provide the owners with a "fair return," to attract additional capital funds if necessary, and to provide some reserves for contingencies. Thus, a healthy business must provide at least a modest return to its owners and plough back into the enterprise money to insure its long-run strength.

Closely associated with a firm's financial well-being is the organizational health of the enterprise. As a going concern, a business is primarily an organization of men whose ac-

tivities must be coordinated for a common purpose. This calls for teamwork and the development of morale in the working force. The importance of this aspect of the firm's health is well indicated by the fact that, when executives talk with each other, questions besides that of the profit record come into the discussion in evaluating the success of a particular business. The development of a "good organization" in which there is high morale among all employees frequently becomes, in the minds of the managers, an end in itself as well as a means for achieving the firm's financial objectives.

The union may threaten the survival and growth of the enterprise in several ways. It may press demands which impair the financial health of the business or it may undermine management's efforts to build a loyal organization. Management, for its part, may react in different ways. It may try to erect defenses against the union and to hold it at arm's length; or it may try to use the union as a means of helping to build a better organization and even try to enlist its support in improving the financial condition of the firm. In short, though the institutional objective of management is fairly constant, the *means* of achieving that objective in relations with organized labor can be quite varied.

Retention of effective control over the enterprise. In order to achieve the institutional objective set forth above, management is constantly striving to retain its control over the enterprise and its freedom to exercise its central managerial functions. If management is held responsible for the success of the business, then it must have the authority to direct its activities and to make fundamental decisions in the operations of the enterprise. In specific terms, management seeks to retain control in such areas as the financing of the business, the sale of its product, the setting of production standards, the lay-out of the plant, the selection,

promotion, transfer, and discipline of employees, and the general direction of the working forces. At almost every turn, however, the
union usually challenges unilateral managerial
exercise of such functions; it seeks to limit
management's discretion and to police management's actions. To most executives, consequently, the union constitutes an actual or
potential interference with the proper exercise
of managerial responsibilities. A major objective
of management in collective relations, therefore, is the minimization of union interference
with managerial functions.

Here again, a company may employ different means to achieve the same ends. It may
try to stake out areas of exclusive managerial
prerogatives, to draw lines between matters subject to unilateral determination and matters
subject to joint management-union determination, or to erect defenses to keep the union out
of the areas of vital control over the enterprise.
On the other hand, it may look upon the union
as an instrument to aid in implementing managerial policies and actions, and thus will share
decision-making with the union. The first of
these approaches is essentially a negative,
defensive action. The second seeks to minimize
the union's interference by accenting the positive contribution which the union can make in
certain areas.

Stable and businesslike relations. Another objective of management is the establishment of "businesslike" relations with the union
with which it deals. It usually attempts to
develop an orderly process of settlement of
grievances and complaints. It wants the union
leaders to live up to the contract and to take
some responsibility for making the union members abide by it as well. Management signs a
labor agreement to eliminate uncertainties in its
labor relations, to buy industrial peace at least
during the life of the agreement, and thus to
bring about a measure of stability in its formal

relationships with employees. Though there is
sometimes a great deal of talk about the need
for membership participation in union affairs,
management is primarily interested in dealing
with "responsible" union officers who can exercise some measure of control over the unruly
members in the organization. Management also
wants to deal with "responsible" union leaders
who recognize the problems faced by the
company and who thus refrain from making
"unreasonable" or "irresponsible" demands
which might seriously jeopardize the enterprise.

Management may try to build up stable
and businesslike relations in several ways. It
may demand a "management security clause"
in the contract; it may insist on prompt disciplining of all union officers or members who
violate the terms of the contract; it may seek
in many different ways to build up the prestige
of "responsible" union leaders; it may agree to
the union shop; or it may resort to undercover
deals with labor officials to achieve its ends. In
the course of appraising and re-appraising its
position *vis-a-vis* the union, it will choose that
course of action which holds the best promise
of making relationships stable, predictable, and
"businesslike."

Broad social and economic goals. In
many cases management is deeply concerned
with goals broader than the preservation and
strengthening of a particular business. It seeks
to defend the system of private enterprise as
the very basis of general economic progress and
individual liberty. It fears and deplores whatever it interprets as encroachments upon individual initiative, freedom to venture, and the
theory of the competitive market. In many
cases the union is looked upon as a threat to
the free enterprise idea, particularly when allied
politically with a greater potential threat to the
system—government. To other leaders in
management a responsible union is a potential
bulwark of free enterprise. But whatever their

view, men in management's ranks like to feel that their own approach to the union helps to promote the kind of collective bargaining which is most consistent with the goals of an economy of free enterprise.

Advancement of personal goals and ambitions. The objectives of management, however, do not stop with building the business or preserving the free enterprise system. As human beings, the members of management have purely personal goals and ambitions as well. In collective relations as in other phases of business management, executives like to establish a reputation. They may strive to be "firm, but fair," to "command the respect of the employees," to be "sympathetic but at the same time practical," or simply to be known as "good, sound businessmen with reasonable and practical judgment."[2]

In relations with unions, reputations can be built in many ways. One employer may pride himself on refusing to "appease power-hungry labor leaders," while another may get a real sense of achievement by finding ways of "working in harmony with organized labor." Regardless of the means employed, however, individual managers are anxious to harmonize their policies and actions in collective relations with their personal goals, ambitions, and their own concepts of the behavior appropriate for an enlightened, successful, and socially conscious business leader.

---

[2] From a somewhat different approach Professor E. Wight Bakke puts the personal goals of managers in these categories: (1) the society and respect of their fellows; (2) economic well-being comparable with that of their customary associates; (3) independence in and control over their own affairs; (4) an understanding of the forces which affect them; and (5) integrity within themselves and with respect to their relationship with the world and the peoples about them. "The Goals of Management," (pp. 141–42) in *Unions, Management, and the Public*, edited by Bakke and Clark Kerr (New York: Harcourt, Brace & Co., 1948).

Objectives of the Union

What does the union leadership try to achieve in collective bargaining with the employer and what are the principal driving forces which explain the policies and actions of union leaders? We can abstract from our interviews and contacts with labor leaders a set of objectives parallel to those pursued by management. The objectives of the union leadership fall into five broad categories: *first*, the preservation and strengthening of the union as an institution; *second*, the carrying out of the formal purpose of the union to get "more" for the membership; *third*, the acquisition of a greater measure of control over jobs to implement the first two objectives; *fourth*, the pursuit of certain broad social and economic goals; and *fifth*, fulfillment of personal goals and ambitions of the leadership.

Preservation and strengthening of the union as an institution. The first concern of the union leadership is, of necessity, the building of the union as an institution and the promotion of its security and stability as an organization. To most union leaders this is an end in itself, just as to management the preservation and strengthening of the enterprise is an end in itself. Professor Arthur Ross has observed that the "formal rationale of the union is to augment the economic welfare of its members; but a more vital institutional objective—survival and growth of the organization—will take precedence whenever it comes into conflict with the formal purpose.[3] This perhaps overstates the case. But few first-hand observers of the unions included in this study would deny that labor leaders do place very heavy emphasis upon the well-being of the organization as such and may occasionally give that well-being preference

---

[3] Arthur M. Ross, *Trade Union Wage Policy* (Berkeley: University of California Press, 1948), p. 43.

over the immediate economic advantages for the membership. The union leadership is continuously concerned with the institutional survival and growth of the organization in the face of management opposition, the apathy of much of the membership, the potential inroads of rival unions, the possible weakness of the union treasury, and the potential threats of adverse government legislation and community sentiment.

The union leadership may achieve this end in different ways. It may try to build the members allegiance by attacking management; in other cases, it may be forced to cooperate with management to keep the business prosperous as the only means of insuring the institutional survival of the union. It may build support in one case by creating issues and calling strikes, whereas in another case it may feel the necessity of avoiding conflict. One factor which will have an important bearing upon the course of action pursued by the union will be the internal political situation and hence the relative security of the incumbent leadership. In every situation, however, the union leaders must weigh the effects of their contemplated actions in terms of the effects they will have on the organization.

Promotion of the economic welfare of the members. The stated reason for the existence of a union is to protect and advance the general well-being of the workers it represents. Its mission is, in times of prosperity, to get "more" for the members in terms of wages, better working conditions, and "fringe benefits" of all kinds. In times of recession, it must protect what the workers have already secured. It must also seek under all circumstances to protect the individual job interests of the workers. A union which fails to "deliver" in these respects may not be able to survive as an organization in the long run no matter how lofty its aims may be.

Some union leaders are in a position to force concessions from an employer by brute force; others may reason that they can get more by the conciliatory approach. Some may proceed in their bargaining tactics without particular attention to management's needs; others must pare down their settling terms to conform to the company's "ability to pay"; still others may be forced to induce the members to give more production in order to get more pay.

The acquisition of control over jobs. In order to implement the twin objectives of building the organization and promoting the economic well-being of the members, union leaders are constantly driven to acquire more and more control over jobs, and are thus impelled to encroach upon what company executives conceive to be the areas of vital managerial functions. In order to keep their organization together and to protect the workers' interests, union leaders feel that they either have to protest company actions, police them, or actually participate with management in making important decisions which will affect individual jobs and employment opportunities as a whole.

The means of acquiring job control are diverse. To mention only a few which are utilized in these industries, they range from making seniority rules more rigid to outright limitations on the employer's freedom to hire; from informal discussions about the introduction of new machinery and processes to outright opposition to technological improvements; or from policing management's disciplining of hourly workers to telling the company whom to select as foremen.

Promotion of broad social and economic goals. Most labor leaders are concerned to some extent with goals which are much broader than building their particular unions and getting more for the workers. By and large, they hold to the philosophy of the primacy of human needs—that human welfare must be placed before profits, that men are more important than machines, and that the preservation of the dignity of the individual workingman is more important than the preservation of any particular economic system. Most of them believe in "more equal distribution of wealth" as a general principle, and they are also in favor of curbing the economic power of employers. In nearly all cases, they look upon collective bargaining as one of the means for the achievement of those ends. As a matter of practical expediency, this almost always means a here-and-now acceptance of the existing enterprise system even by union leaders who seek to modify it by making it "more responsive to human needs" or to supplant it entirely at some future date by a different economic system.

The position of most labor leaders on the matter of social goals might be summarized as follows: first, get what you can within the sphere of collective bargaining as one means of advancing the welfare of labor, and second, turn to political action as a way of supplementing what you get through negotiating with private employers.

Pursuit of personal goals and ambitions. The actions and policies of union leaders are also explained in part by their personal goals and ambitions. Union leaders are usually interested in their own personal position within the union as well as in the development of the organization as an institution. They strive to acquire personal status and power and to build reputations as "good fighters for labor," "respected citizens in the community," and "competent bargainers." In collective relations with management, there are many ways of building prestige and satisfying such personal goals, ranging all the way from baiting the employer to playing the role of a "labor statesman."

In comparing management's objectives in collective relations with those of union leaders,

however, an important distinction must be made. Relationships with unions are only one of the many problems which face the employer. Most of the energies of management are directed to the other activities of operating a business, such as procurement of materials, engineering, production planning, financing, and sales promotion. Management-union relations in most companies is not the central problem in operating the business. In the case of the union, however, collective bargaining is the central problem; it is the area in which most of the energies of union officers must be concentrated. To be sure, there is an increasing tendency for union leaders to devote more attention to community relations and political action, but these matters seldom overshadow the core function of collective bargaining.

Determinants of Conflict and Cooperation

Simply placing management's objectives alongside those of the union gives us a partial explanation of why modern labor-management relations in the mass production industries often involve a struggle for power. The union's quest for "more" appears to be in conflict with management's desire to protect the financial well-being of the firm. Management's concern for retaining its prerogatives must often be in basic conflict with the union's objectives of acquiring control over jobs. In building its institutional structure, the union may compete for the allegiance of workers with a management which is trying to build loyalty within the business organization. The labor leader's notions of human welfare often conflict with management's picture of "the economic facts of life." And finally, the concern of both labor leaders and company executives over their own personal goals and ambitions may lead to a bitter struggle for personal prestige. To a large extent, management and union leaders are simply after different things when they face each other at the bargaining table. Theoretically, at least, they have little in common and a great deal to quarrel about. There is no doubt that this is the pattern in many collective bargaining situations today.

Yet in many other cases employers and labor leaders appear to get along very well together. In some cases, moreover, they work hand-in-hand to increase output and improve efficiency. What then is the explanation of the existence of such relatively harmonious or cooperative relationships? Where harmony prevails, do labor and management have a different set of objectives from those situations where conflict is the rule? We think not. Our examination of many different labor-management relationships leads us to believe that management and labor leaders have roughly the same objectives in all kinds of relationships. We hold that the explanation of relative compatibility in each case is to be found in the different ways the parties view their objectives and in the different policies followed in pursuing them. *In other words, the different types of labor-management relationships are explained not so much by the ends sought by the parties as by the means employed to achieve these ends.*

40

Government Regulation or Control of Union Activities

Charles Gregory

Excerpted from Chapter 17, "Government Regulation or Control of Union Activities," by Charles Gregory in *Labor in a Changing America*, edited by William Haber, ©1966 by Basic Books, Inc.

EARLY JUDICIAL CONTROL OF LABOR UNIONS

Before 1910, the regulation and control of American labor unions was chiefly by judge-made law. Workers who used economic pressure to spread union organization in the early 1800's were held guilty of common-law criminal conspiracy. But this device for controlling unions was abandoned around 1850. Courts soon began to allow peaceful strikes for immediate benefits. But most judges thought that campaigns to extend union organization were unlawful. Actions for damages had become the only recourse in these cases. Then around 1880, state courts developed a far move effective de-

vice—the labor injunction. This remedy protected only against the tortious invasion of property rights. But our state courts soon invented theories making most peaceful union self-help pressures unlawful.

The courts had always allowed business combinations to eliminate trade rivals and control markets. No legal wrong was done if they were pursuing self-interest and gain. But if *unions* sought to protect *their* standards by eliminating nonunion employers and workers, the courts held this to be wrongful for the spread of unionization led to monopoly. And though monopoly was not tortious according to common law, the courts declared it to be an illegal purpose for union self-help. This was enough to support the labor injunction. More-over, peaceful secondary boycotts and organizational picketing were made torts in themselves. Thus the courts applied a double standard by denying to unions what they let business groups do.

THE LABOR INJUNCTION

The labor injunction was the most ruthless anti-union weapon ever devised. It was used to protect business only when unions threatened employers with organizing pressures. This remedy was far more effective than other legal sanctions. Criminal prosecutions and damage suits required extensive pleadings, months of waiting, and jury trials. But a judge could issue an injunction without a jury trial. And he could issue a temporary injunction without any trial at all. Thus strikes, picket lines, and boycotts could be smothered before they really got started. Anyone disobeying an injunction was summarily thrown into jail for contempt of court, again without jury trial.

SHERMAN ANTI-TRUST ACT—1890

As industry grew larger, employers began to produce for markets in other states and buy materials from outside. Then the Sherman Anti-Trust Act was passed in 1890. It was believed to be designed to apply to business organizations as an anti-trust measure. This act was enforced by indictments, triple damage suits, and injunctions. Under its terms, federal courts soon began to apply it to labor unions and to regard most union interferences with the movement of goods in interstate commerce as unlawful restraints of trade. Unions exerted organizational pressures on nonunion employers by peaceful secondary boycotts. Because they disrupted the interstate move-

ments of goods, the Supreme Court ruled that these boycotts violated the Sherman Act. But clearly they were not restraints of trade at all. The unions were simply trying to improve their conditions of work—not to monopolize the market for goods. They obstructed the transit of goods; but so did train robbers. And nobody would think of suing *them* under the Sherman Act.

But the Supreme Court refused to declare simple strikes unlawful under the Sherman Act merely because they disrupted the flow of goods in commerce. To show a violation in this area required proof that the strike was intended to unionize the employer—and for the purpose of eliminating competition between union-made and nonunion-made goods in interstate markets. Thus bargaining strikes which also obstructed the flow of goods in commerce would never be violations. Clearly the Supreme Court was using the Sherman Act merely as a device to stop the spread of union organization. And its concern over the movement of goods in commerce was only *incidental*.

ANTI-INJUNCTION MEASURES: THE CLAYTON ACT OF 1914 AND THE NORRIS-LA GUARDIA ACT OF 1932

At the same time, the labor injunction flourished in common law in federal and state courts. In 1914, Congress passed the Clayton Act to limit use of the injunction against union self-help pressures in labor disputes. Section 6 of the Act declared that the labor of a human being was not a commodity. Section 20 seemed to offer some relief from the court's injunctive process. But this measure was so narrowly construed that injunctions against union organizational drives continued. All that the Clayton Act *actually* did was to allow further injunctive relief against unions under the Sherman Act. In the 1920's, Professor Felix Frankfurter headed an attempt to promulgate a *really* effective anti-injunction law. The result was the Norris-La Guardia Act of 1932. This act defined permissible labor disputes broadly enough to include organizational drives against nonunion employers. It required only that the union have an economic interest in employment conditions at the nonunion plant. Then it described the permissible union self-help techniques—the strike, the secondary boycott, and picketing. Such devices when used in a labor dispute as defined were nonenjoinable in federal courts.

CHANGING FEDERAL POLICY—NATIONAL LABOR RELATIONS ACT OF 1935

While this act did not legalize organizational pressures, it removed the injunction, employers' only effective defense against unions. Certainly it meant congressional approval of union expansion throughout entire industries by economic self-help. But it left employers free to fight back with economic weapons by discriminating against employees who supported unionism. The National Industrial Recovery Act of 1933 and the amended Railway Labor Act of 1934 had introduced the principle that employees could join unions without employer interference. But in 1935, Congress pass the National Labor Relations Act, or Wagner Act, to replace the NIRA which was ruled unconstitutional. That statute prohibited anti-union conduct by most employers. If an employer interfered with his employees' attempts to organize unions or tried to dominate such unions, if he discriminated against employees for their union interest or refused to bargain with newly formed unions, he was committing unfair labor practices. The National Labor Relations Board, set up under the terms of the Wagner Act, ordered these unfair practices stopped and granted remedies such as reinstatement of employees with back pay. And the federal courts enforced these orders. Thus, Congress proclaimed the national policy of strong affiliated labor unions organized throughout entire industries. In upholding this statute, the Supreme Court greatly expanded the commerce power of Congress to cover virtually all important units of industry and production. Thereafter unions began to form and grow rapidly.

REPRESENTATIONAL FUNCTIONS OF THE NATIONAL LABOR RELATIONS BOARD

The Labor Relations Board administers an elaborate procedure enabling workers to select or reject unions. Many employers voluntarily recognize unions formed or chosen by their employees. The Board conducts elections when necessary, especially where two or more unions are competing for representational rights. The Board has strict rules governing attempts by outside unions to displace already recognized unions. It will protect an established employer—union contract relationship for three years. Then an outside union may call for an election. To avoid needless conflict, the AFL-CIO has developed no-raiding pacts, administered by an impartial arbitrator. The Board's enormously complicated task of handling these representational matters is a most important aspect of regulating and controlling unions today.

UNION IMMUNITY
FROM ANTI-TRUST LAWS

The anti-injunction and Wagner acts clearly made the expansion of union strength the prevailing national policy. At the same time, the interpretations of the Sherman Act remained unchanged. . . . The Supreme Court should have recognized this contradiction and have

overruled its earlier decisions, making organizational strikes and boycotts illegal under
the Sherman Act. But what it did in the 1941
Hutcheson Case was to indulge in some judicial
sleight of hand. It said that since peaceful union
self-help conduct in a broad labor dispute context is no longer enjoinable, it is lawful for all
purposes—even under the Sherman Act. It
based this incredible inference on Section 20 of
the Clayton Act which was rejuvenated by the
later Norris-La Guardia Act. In effect, the
Hutcheson doctrine removed labor unions from
the jurisdiction of the Sherman Anti-Trust Act.
However, it could still be applied if the unions'
conduct was violent or if they connived with
employers to restrain trade. . . .

RAILWAY LABOR ACTS
[AND THE WAR LABOR BOARD]

After decades of bitter strikes, the railroad
brotherhoods were firmly established. In the
1926 Railway Labor Act, Congress provided
mediation and voluntary arbitration of bargaining disputes, with emergency powers vested in
the President. This was unsatisfactory since the
carriers still interfered with the union organization of their employees. The amended Railway
Labor Act of 1934 created boards of adjustment to dispose of grievances and the National
Mediation Board to handle all unsettled bargaining and representational disputes. It clarified and enforced the rights of employees and
unions to organize and bargain collectively,
introducing the principle of majority rule.
Moreover, in 1951, Congress permitted the carriers and brotherhoods to contract for the
union shop.

[The War Labor Board]

Changes in labor relations laws and policies
were constant from 1935 to around 1950.

But World War II dominated this period.
Thus, although there were many strong unions
by 1941—unions maintaining a tremendous
pressure for higher wages and other concessions—in industries that had never been organized before, and this continued during the war,
a war economy could not afford to have
strikes. The War Labor Board was created to
handle the constantly recurring disputes between
unions and employers. Although strikes never
were prohibited, the unions made voluntary
no-strike pledges that were honored almost
100 percent.

War Labor Board tripartite panels held
hearings on bargaining demands. Sometimes
they persuaded the parties to settle. Usually
they made recommendations on issues that
remained unsettled. The War Labor Board
affirmed or modified these, in the end promul-
gating final contracts. The War Labor Board
kept wages at a reasonably stable level, made a
sensible compromise on the issue of union
security, and refused to include novel items in
collective agreements. But most important for
the future of labor relations, it added grievance
arbitration to thousands of contracts.

POST-WORLD WAR II CHANGES

After the war, the big unions sought wage
increases, union security, stronger seniority
provisions, vacations, and paid holidays, as well
as pensions and insurances of all kinds. With
wartime restrictions off, they conducted in-
dustry-shaking strikes. Simultaneously, the
National Labor Relations Board expanded the
employer's duty to bargain, including many
new items. These great strikes provoked widespread demands for compulsory arbitration.
Australia and New Zealand have long arbitrated
their bargaining disputes; but early experiments
in the United States were declared unconstitutional by the Supreme Court. At present, in-

dustry and organized labor would both rather continue free collective bargaining with strikes than share the dismal experience of countries having compulsory arbitration. . . .

TAFT-HARTLEY ACT—1947

The intensive strikes for money items and the closed union shop immediately after World War II contributed to Congress' passage of the Taft-Hartley Act in 1947. Title I of this statute is the amended National Labor Relations Act. The original National Labor Relations Act designated only unfair labor practices of employers. Unions were free to exercise any organizational and bargaining pressures. Unions were guaranteed the right to strike, and employees the right to engage in concerted activities. The National Labor Relations Board protected most of this conduct from employers' reprisals. When labor organizations had become very strong, extreme union self-help tactics were regarded as intolerable. This conduct included pressures against employers to force their employees to organize, pressures direct[ed] against employees themselves, secondary picketing and boycotting which implicated neutral employers and their employees, and even pressures against employers to ignore National Labor Relations Board certifications of other unions. Most unions sought the closed or union shop.

. . . Congress amended the National Labor Relations Act by defining six unfair labor practices of unions. The first made it unfair for unions to restrain or coerce employees. The second prohibited unions from trying to make employers discriminate against nonunion employees. The third was a union's refusal to bargain in good faith with the appropriate employer. But the fourth was the most elaborate: Subsection A outlawed union secondary labor boycotts; whereas, Subsection B allowed secondary tactics if the union was certified to the employer against whom the pressure was aimed. Subsection C outlawed union attempts to make an employer deal with a union when another union had been certified to him by the National Labor Relations Board. Subsection D made it an unfair practice for unions to engage in work-jurisdiction disputes, where two unions claim the right to do certain work, and each strikes if the employer gives the work to members of the other union.

The fifth unfair labor practice was to prevent excessively large initiation fees under a valid union-shop agreement. In a union shop, an employer is free to hire anyone he pleases, but he must agree to discharge an employee who refuses to join the union or who does not pay his dues. Under the Wagner Act, federal policy accepted the closed union shop if the employer agreed to hire only union members. This is forbidden by the 1947 statute. But employers, now free to hire anybody they please, may make and enforce agreements requiring both new and old employees to join the union. However, Congress deferred to the states in 1947 by specifying that any state was free to forbid agreements making employment conditional on union membership. Now there are about twenty of these so-called right-to-work statutes. A corporation with plants in forty states may have a master contract with one union covering all these plants; but half of these plants might be union shops and half of them not because of local right-to-work laws.

Whether to have union security or right-to-work statutes is a contentious issue. Supporters of right-to-work laws say that they allow employment without paying tribute to unions. Opponents of these acts say they are meant to keep unions weak by denying them financial support from workers who profit by union bargaining gains. They call such nonunion workers free riders. A compromise is the so-called agency shop where an employee pays the equivalent of union dues without actually joining the union. The National Labor Relations Board finds this compromise acceptable; but right-to-work states are in disagreement about the agency shop. Unions want Congress to permit union shops throughout industry as it did on the railroads in 1951. . . .

NATIONAL EMERGENCY STRIKES

In the Taft-Hartley Act, Congress provided a method of controlling national emergency strikes, except those handled under the Railway Labor Act. Whenever the President thinks an industry-wide strike imperils the national health or safety, he sets up an emergency board to investigate and report to him. The President may then direct the Attorney General to have the strike or lockout enjoined. Federal mediators undertake to secure agreement between the parties. If the dispute is not settled in sixty days, the National Labor Relations Board files a supplemental report containing the employer's last offer to the union. The National Labor Relations Board then conducts a secret ballot among the employees to see if they wish to accept the offer. The injunction is then dissolved. If settlement has not been reached, the strike may be resumed. By that time, the President has made a complete report to Congress.

This device has been invoked twenty-four times, and the Supreme Court upheld this procedure in the steel strike of 1959. It declared that by "national health" Congress meant that of the economy as a whole and the general well-being of the country. Another technique used during the war was seizure and public operation of strike-bound plants. The Supreme Court declared that the President has no such power of seizure, however, in the absence of specific legislation granting him such authority. The President has appointed groups to handle disputes between unions and employers under

contract with the Atomic Energy Commission or engaged in missile construction. When mediation fails, the appropriate panel takes jurisdiction, requesting the parties to appear and submit their claims. After hearings, the panel makes recommendations disposing of the various demands presented. The parties' submission to this procedure is entirely voluntary, but it has been effective in avoiding disruptive strikes.

ENFORCEMENT OF COLLECTIVE BARGAINING

Since 1935, a kind of self-government, far more effective than any imposed control or regulation, has evolved in collective bargaining. This is chiefly a result of increased union responsibility. A generation ago, labor unions generally could not sue or be sued. The Wagner Act greatly increased the number of unions and resulting collective agreements, but provided no means for their enforcement. Finally in 1947, Congress provided that the parties might sue each other in the federal courts if the employer operated in interstate commerce. Under this vague provision, the Supreme Court would not let unions directly sue to enforce promises dealing with the terms and conditions of individual employment. Federal courts could enforce promises to unions, however, including commitments to arbitrate unsettled grievances arising under contracts.

GRIEVANCE ARBITRATION

Since World War II, thousands of collective agreements provided for such arbitration. Now that unions could compel employers to comply with promises to arbitrate, it became possible to enforce provisions dealing with individual terms and conditions of employment. This whole development of grievance arbitration has become one of the most stabilizing controls in modern labor relations. Strikes seldom occur now, except when new agreements are bargained. With longer and longer contract terms, arbitration of unsettled matters arising under them will greatly minimize wasteful disputes.

The largest single issue in grievance arbitration is the discipline and discharge of employees for just cause. To justify a discharge, an employer must show that the penalized employee was guilty of something like theft, insubordination, or fighting, or was in violation of a plant rule meriting this extreme penalty. This power of the employer to impose discipline in proper cases is an effective method of controlling employees and even unions themselves. The privilege of employers to hire permanent replacements in bargaining strikes affords another control over unions. Moreover, unions may not terminate collective agreements and call bargaining strikes without a sixty-day notice to mediation officials. The Taft-Hartley Act also lets employers recover damages from unions for harm caused by specified unfair labor practices. In such cases, Congress requires the National Labor Relations Board to seek injunctions. Unions violating no-strike pledges still remain free from injunctions; but they are subject to damage suits, and employers may discharge employees who participate in such strikes. . . .

REGULATION OF INTERNAL UNION AFFAIRS

Traditionally, courts refused to interfere with the internal affairs of labor unions, treating them like clubs and lodges. They would protect vested property rights of members, but only when remedies within the organization were exhausted. [Prior to the Landrum-Griffin Act of 1959 and the Civil Rights Act of 1964, many] unions would not admit Negroes or would only let them join auxiliaries, with no voting rights. But some courts now regard this as a denial of equal protection under the Constitution. The National Labor Relations Board [also] revoked the certification of a union that refused to admit or represent Negroes. . . . [I]n the Landrum-Griffin Act, Congress has required unions to file elaborate reports with the government concerning their internal affairs. This statute also grants redress to employees against union officials who deny them the right to participate in union meetings and elections. But its chief concern is to prevent union officials from misappropriating funds. As unions have become more powerful, a greater measure of control has been necessary to insure their fiduciary responsibilities. Furthermore, unions are now sufficiently public in nature so that disclosure of their internal affairs is essential. . . .

41

The Sources of Union Power

Albert Rees

Albert Rees, "The Sources of Union Power," in Rees, *The Economics of Trade Unions,* 2nd ed. (Chicago: University of Chicago Press, 1977).

THE STRIKE

The strike is by far the most important source of union power, and the union is now virtually the sole organizer of strikes. This last was not always true; at one time spontaneous strikes among unorganized workers were frequent. However, in 1974, strikes that did not involve any union were only 1 per cent of recorded strikes and accounted for only 0.1 per cent of man-days lost from strikes. Some unauthorized strikes of union members are still immediate expressions of worker discontent, but collective bargaining provides other channels for handling most grievances.

The strike is a planned withholding of labor designed to impose union demands on the employer or to prevent the employer from imposing his demands on the union. It is traditional to divide work stoppages into strikes and lockouts, the former occurring where the workers walk off the job, the latter where the employer withholds employment from them. But the employer almost never needs to do this. At the expiration of an agreement he can always announce his terms unilaterally and allow the union the choices of striking, reaching an agreement, or working without an agreement during further negotiations. Almost the only occasion for a true lockout arises when a union calls a strike against one member of an employers' association; the other employers may then close down to make common cause with the struck employer. In this article, I shall use the word "strike" to cover all work stoppages, including the few that fit the traditional definition of the lockout.

The strike is the most conspicuous and dramatic aspect of labor relations and provides the labor movement with its heroes, martyrs, and folklore. To the general public, the prevention of strikes seems to be the chief problem in industrial relations and industrial peace is considered the chief goal. The economist is likely to be somewhat less concerned with the direct losses from strikes, and more concerned with the consequences as expressed in the terms of settlement. The strike keeps resources idle for days or months, but the settlement can determine the way in which resources are used for many years.

In the period 1960–1974 there were roughly 3,000 to 6,000 recorded strikes each year, with a generally rising trend over the period (see Table 1). In 1973, a relatively peaceful year, there were 5,353 recorded strikes involving more than 2 million workers and almost 28 million man-days of idleness. But this idleness was only 0.14 per cent of the estimated working time of all workers. The range of such estimates since 1960 is from 0.11 per cent in 1961 and 1963 to 0.37 in 1970.

The available statistics are of limited value in assessing the cost of strikes. On the one hand, strikes also cause secondary idleness not included in the statistics. For example, a steel strike can cause railroad workers to be laid off for lack of traffic or automobile workers to be laid off for lack of materials. On the other hand, there are very important offsets to strike losses. Most strikes cause production to be displaced in time or location rather than to be lost altogether. A strike against one producer in a large industry may be completely offset by the increased output of his competitors.

When an entire industry faces a threat of strike, it will often increase its output in anticipation; if the strike occurs, it may again produce at higher than normal levels for some time after the strike is over. If the industry struck is a supplier of materials to other industries, these industries can draw on inventories during the strike and replenish them afterward, so that there may be little effect on the output of final products.[1]

The possibility of offsets in time depends, of course, on the durability of the product. They are not possible for highly perishable goods or for services, and for many services offsets in location are also impossible. Since America has a large stock of automobiles and abundant facilities for keeping them in repair, a strike against automobile manufacturers could go on for months with little inconvenience to consumers. In contrast, a strike against a local bus line has an immediate impact. Moreover, if a bus strike prevents people from getting to work today, they will not be compensated by the possibility of going back and forth twice tomorrow. However, unions and management go to great lengths to avoid strikes that would cause severe hardships to the public, and strikes that create real emergencies are fortunately rare.

In considering the costs of strikes, some non-economic factors should also be taken into account. A strike can have a cathartic effect, cleansing away accumulated tensions and making possible new approaches to stubborn problems. It can provide a release from the monotony of routine work and a sense of excitement not present in a mere vacation. Frequently such factors improve productivity when the strike is over. Of course, the costs of a prolonged

[1] For an excellent analysis of the costs of steel strikes in terms of production of final products, see E. Robert Livernash, *Collective Bargaining in the Basic Steel Industry* (Washington, D.C.: U.S. Department of Labor, 1961), Chapter III.

TABLE 1

Number of Strikes, Workers Involved, and Man-Days Idle, 1960–1974

Year	Number of Strikes Begin- ning in Year	Workers Involved (1,000)	Man-Days Idle	
			Number (1,000)	Percent Estimated Working Time
1960	3,333	1,320	19,100	0.14
1961	3,367	1,450	16,300	0.11
1962	3,614	1,230	18,600	0.13
1963	3,362	941	16,100	0.11
1964	3,655	1,640	22,900	0.15
1965	3,963	1,550	23,300	0.15
1966	4,405	1,960	25,400	0.15
1967	4,595	2,870	42,100	0.25
1968	5,045	2,649	49,018	0.28
1969	5,700	2,481	42,869	0.24
1970	5,716	3,305	66,414	0.37
1971	5,138	3,280	47,589	0.26
1972	5,010	1,714	27,066	0.15
1973	5,353	2,251	27,948	0.14
1974	6,074	2,778	47,991	0.24

Source: U.S. Bureau of Labor Statistics, Bulletin No. 1902, p. 2.

strike can more than offset gains of this kind.

It is a favorite calculation of newspapers to compute the wage increases won in a strike and compare them with the wages lost during it, a calculation which often shows that workers have lost more wages than they will regain during the life of the agreement. Such calculations misjudge what is at stake. The strike is part of a long-range strategy for both parties. Union gains won without a strike are usually won through the threat of a strike, stated or implied. Such threats cannot retain much force if they are never carried out. Then too, in attempting to push gains just to the point at which a strike is averted, a union will sometimes misjudge its opponent. Once a strike is begun, whether through design or miscalculation, its settlement is not wholly a rational matter, but one that involves subtle questions of organizational and personal prestige. Union members can easily come to believe that the continued existence of their union is at stake, and they will then no longer reckon the outcome in cents per hour. It is no more possible to understand the causes or consequences of a strike by setting up a balance sheet than it would be for a dispute between nations.

Until about 1940, it was common for employers to attempt to operate struck plants, using non-striking employees or new employees recruited for the purpose. Unions engaged in mass picketing to prevent the strikebreakers or "scabs" from entering the plant. . . . Violence often occurred in such circumstances—fighting on the picket line, cars overturned, windows broken, and even shooting and dynamiting. The unions tended to be blamed for violence, though there were undoubtedly cases in which strikebreakers or employers were at fault. The outcome of such a strike depended critically on the position of the police and the courts. Injunctions against picketing and ample police protection for non-strikers could break the strike, and usually did. In a few more recent cases, police have prevented violence by forbidding strikebreakers to cross picket lines, an action that forces the employer to discontinue operations. Often the police or the courts now take a more lenient attitude toward strike violence than toward violence under most other circumstances.

Since World War II it has been unusual for employers in labor-intensive industries to attempt to operate during a strike. However, employers in some capital-intensive industries, such as petroleum refiners, telephone companies, and electric utilities, can maintain production or service during a strike by having supervisors or managers replace striking workers.

The use of nonstriking production workers during a strike still can cause great bitterness, especially in a small community. Friendships, social organizations, even families shatter as the community divides into strikers and strikebreakers, and the wounds may take years to heal.

Where the employer does not try to operate, the strike becomes a war of attrition. Around the silent factory, a few token pickets may chat with a lone policeman while their neatly painted signs lean against a fence. Maintenance crews may enter by prearrangement to keep equipment in good shape; sometimes the employer furnishes coffee and doughnuts to the pickets.

An effective strike imposes on both parties losses whose nature depends in large part on the scope of the strike. The employer must continue to meet fixed charges while receiving no revenues. If only one employer is struck in an industry, he may lose both customers and workers to competitors and he is not assured of getting all of them back when the strike ends. Customers often turn to more dependable suppliers or decide to produce their own requirements. At the same time, those strikers who cannot find other work are losing their wages. In some cases the union provides regular strike benefits, but these are possible chiefly in small strikes conducted by large unions.

The union strategy of striking one employer at a time, thus putting the struck employer at a competitive disadvantage, can be met by the formation of a united front among employers. This will usually force the union to strike a whole industry at once. If any competitive forces pressing employers toward settlement remain, they arise from other industries or from imports, and their pressures are usually weak. The dues of working union members cannot, in an industry-wide strike, provide benefits for the strikers. Benefits taken from accumulated strike funds or contributions from other unions will usually be reserved for cases of severe hardship. The ability of strikers to find work elsewhere will be sharply restricted. However, a strike against a whole industry can cause secondary unemployment on a large scale, or halt the flow of final products to consumers. The pressure of public opinion or the intervention of government may then force a settlement.

The ability of a union to win a strike depends on a number of factors. These are related to but not identical with the factors determining its ability to raise wages.... A union can be said to win a strike when it gains concessions that the employers were unwilling to make before the strike, and when these meet, in whole or in large part, the union's true demands (as distinguished from demands made for tactical purposes).

A strike hurts an employer most if the demand for his product is strong and profits are high. If demand is weak, he may lose little by shutting down, and can more easily regain lost production when the strike is over. Perhaps in part for this reason, chronically depressed industries like apparel have had low strike rates. Similar forces produced a high correlation between the number of strikes and the level of business activity for the period 1915–1938.

Another major determinant of the union's ability to win is the degree of skill and specialization of the members. The more skilled and specialized they are, the more difficult it is for management to carry on production by using strikebreakers or non-striking supervisory employees.

The ability of unions to win strikes does not necessarily govern the frequency with which they strike. If their power is great, mere threat of a strike may be all that is necessary. The propensity of a union to strike also depends in part on the philosophy and attitudes of its leaders and members. A high propensity to strike by unions of miners, seamen, and longshoremen has been noted for several countries. A well-known study of this phenomenon suggests that the isolation of miners and maritime workers from the larger society contributes to this high propensity,[2] though this interpretation has been disputed by other scholars.

GOVERNMENT INTERVENTION IN STRIKES

When a strike inflicts serious damage on neutral parties or on the general public, government is sooner or later forced to intervene. The party to the strike that considers itself least likely to win in the absence of intervention will encourage intervention by its statements or its behavior, while the other party will of course discourage it. The outcome of the strike will almost always be influenced by any forceful government intervention; only by the sheerest accident could strong intervention

[2] See Clark Kerr and Abraham Siegel, "The Interindustry Propensity To Strike," in A. Kornhauser, R. Dubin, and A. Ross, eds., *Industrial Conflict* (New York: McGraw-Hill Book Co., 1954).

produce the result that would have occurred without it.

The intervention of government in many major strikes is an important reason why unions seek to develop political power even where they have little or no political program. The power to influence elections is a valuable adjunct to the power to strike. The role of government in strikes may also help to explain why American unions have largely avoided formal alliances with political parties. The more an elected official can be certain of the support of one party to an industrial dispute come what may, the more he may lean toward the other in an attempt to gain added political strength. Thus we observe, ironically, conspicuous instances of intervention favorable to unions by conservative elected officials, and of adverse intervention by officials with labor support. . . .

WILDCAT STRIKES AND SLOWDOWNS

A wildcat strike is one conducted in violation of an agreement or without proper authorization from higher union bodies—by a department or unit without authorization from the local union or by a local union without authorization from the national union. (In most unions such authorization is required.) Many wildcat strikes, especially spontaneous ones, arise from dissatisfaction with union policies and thus cannot be considered a source of union strength. At other times, however, a union may tacitly condone or encourage strikes that it officially disowns. Wildcat strikes sometimes occur during negotiations for a new agreement, when they may exert pressure for a quicker settlement.

It may seem odd that although spontaneous strikes of non-union workers are now rare, wildcat strikes by unionists are fairly common. One explanation is that the penalty for striking is less severe in the latter case. Unions will usually agree to employer discipline of workers who strike in violation of an agreement, but they will oppose penalties they regard as excessive. Some wildcat strikes occur when workers feel there is an immediate threat to their health or safety. If they cannot convince their supervisors of the danger, a wildcat strike is their only recourse. Union opposition to severe or automatic penalties for wildcat strikers is based in part on cases of this kind.

Most observers of industrial relations report a decreasing frequency of wildcat strikes in recent years. In part this may result from the maturing of union organizations and greater control of union members by their leaders. In part, it is reported to result from more severe and consistent use of discipline by management, since management often found that to settle a wildcat strike by making concessions invited the use of similar tactics in the future.[3]

We can regard the authorized strike as the heavy artillery of the trade union, and the wildcat strike and the slowdown as its small arms—weapons suited for limited engagements and local objectives. The slowdown is a temporary slackening of the normal pace of work designed to put pressure on management to gain some objective. The workers remain on the job and appear to be engaged in their usual activities.[4] "Slowdown" is a narrower term than restriction of output, which may be permanent. The ability to restrict output permanently is a consequence of having power to begin with, and not a source of additional

power. For the slowdown to be effective as a pressure tactic, management must be aware of it. In contrast, restriction of output undertaken to prolong a job may be most successful if management is unaware of it.

The most frequent source of slowdown is dissatisfaction with incentive wage rates, and grievances of this kind give rise to slowdowns in non-union as well as union plants. A slowdown is almost never formally authorized by a union but may be conducted with tacit union consent. Its advantage over the wildcat strike is the protection from discipline afforded the participants. In a well-run slowdown, management observed the reduction in output but cannot detect the subtle changes in work behavior that cause it and therefore cannot identify the individual participants.

CONSUMER BOYCOTTS AND UNION LABELS

The consumer boycott and the union label are opposite sides of the same coin. A boycott urges consumers not to buy products made by non-union labor, whereas a union label on consumer goods encourages sympathetic shoppers to choose products made under union conditions. In general, these are weak weapons. However, the consumer boycott is sometimes effective against retail establishments in localities where union membership is concentrated. The most successful recent use of the consumer boycott has been in helping the United Farm Workers organize vineyards and lettuce fields in California. Resort to the boycott was needed because farm workers are excluded from the scope of the National Labor Relations Act.

The union label has helped to organize industries such as work clothing whose products are heavily consumed by manual workers. Where union strength rests largely on the power

[3] See Sumner H. Slichter, James J. Healy, and E. Robert Livernash, *The Impact of Collective Bargaining on Management* (Washington, D.C.: Brookings Institution, 1960), pp. 663–91.

[4] See R. S. Hammett, Joel Seidman, and Jack London, "The Slowdown as a Union Tactic," *Journal of Political Economy,* Vol. LXV (April, 1957).

to strike, the label can be of more value to the customer than to the union. Thus in most union print shops, the label or "bug" is used only at the request of the customer, yet little political campaign literature appears without it.

The proper public attitude toward the union label would be an important and difficult question if the weapon were more powerful. The principle that workers should be free to join or not to join unions of their own choosing would seem to require that they be free from consumer pressures as well as from management pressures. On the other hand, it can be argued that consumer freedom extends to knowledge about the working conditions under which products are made. On this view, the union label on a loaf of bread stands on the same footing as the label that it contains artificial preservatives—each may be of intense interest to some buyers and be totally ignored by others.

SECONDARY BOYCOTTS

The secondary boycott is a strike or threat of strike in which the union's complaint is not against the employer struck but against someone with whom he does business. For example, the workers in a retail store may refuse to handle the products of a struck manufacturer. If their employer directs them to do so, they may walk out altogether in an effort to force him to buy from another supplier.

The use of the secondary boycott is now severely restricted by law. The secondary boycott is one of a group of related devices that include organizational picketing, sympathetic strikes, "hot cargo" clauses, and the respecting of picket lines set up by other unions. All these devices may now be illegal in interstate commerce under most circumstances. The meaning of some of the terms used above can be conveyed by the example that follows.

Perhaps the simplest form of secondary boycott is the refusal to do struck work; thus if the molders' union strikes a job foundry, union molders at other foundries would refuse to fill orders for the struck employer. This example differs from the retail store example given above because the relation between the two employers is horizontal rather than vertical.

Secondary boycotts and hot cargo clauses can also be used for organizational purposes. If the employees of a certain trucker cannot be organized, hot cargo clauses in union agreements with other truckers are used to prevent them from handling transfer shipments to or from the non-union firm. Since such action could often force the non-union firm out of business, its employees are forced to change their minds and join the union to preserve their jobs. This union action interferes with the right of workers to organize or not to organize as they see fit if the individual employer is considered to be the proper unit for employee selection of a bargaining agent.

In perhaps the most objectionable case, a union will refuse to handle products made by members of another union. Thus the sheet metal workers' union has refused to install products made by members of the steelworkers' union. Here the object is not to force the steelworkers to change unions, but to get more work for another group of workers already organized by the sheet metal workers.

It is sometimes hard to distinguish between a secondary boycott and a consumer boycott. If pickets appear before a non-union service station with signs urging customers not to buy, these signs may have little effect on the customers. However, union teamsters may refuse to deliver gas and thus can force the station to close. The definition of a secondary boycott should not depend on externals like the wording of the picket sign, but on the consequences of the picketing. Although there is a tradition in the labor movement against crossing picket lines, most union members follow the instructions of their leaders in such matters. If teamsters all refuse to cross a certain picket line, there has probably been an arrangement between their local and the striking union. It then seems reasonable to conclude that the teamsters' local as an organization is engaged in a secondary boycott.[5]

A horizontal secondary boycott is one in which the primary and secondary employer are engaged in the same type of activity, as in the "hot cargo" and foundry examples above. The purpose of such boycotts is reasonably clear. Low wages in one plant in an industry may give it a competitive advantage. The union will seek to raise these wages if the plant is organized and to organize it if it is not. This action will be of direct benefit to union members elsewhere in helping to preserve their jobs and their wage levels, and their participation in the boycott can be explained by self-interest.

Where the relation between the primary and secondary employer is vertical—if, for example, the latter buys supplies from the former—the purpose of the secondary boycott is more complex. In some cases, the boycott may be entirely sympathetic, arising out of a feeling of solidarity among workers. If the union seeks to raise the costs of the primary employer, the boycotting workers of the secondary employer are acting against their economic self-interest. Higher costs of materials to their employer will tend to reduce his sales and his ability to offer employment or wage increases. The action of the boycotting unionists might then be affected by one or more of the following considerations: (1) They may not understand the way in which higher costs of materials are detrimental to them. (2) They or their leaders may consider that having a large union or a large labor movement is worth the possible costs of shorter hours or smaller wage increases. (3) They may benefit from some financial device within the union by which employees of the supplier pay more than their fair share of a pension or welfare fund that benefits employees of the purchaser. For example, workers who install sheetmetal work might benefit from a welfare fund to which manufacturing workers in the same union contribute heavily. This last consideration is appealing if we seek to explain behavior entirely in economic terms, but I know of no evidence supporting it.

CONTROL OF THE LABOR SUPPLY

The control of the labor supply is often considered to be a source of union power. The term can have several meanings. Most of those that apply to true unions, as distinguished from union-like organizations, have already been covered under other headings.

The most effective type of control of the labor supply is control over the number of people who can be trained for an occupation or profession. By limiting the number trained, the organization can protect or raise the earnings of its members. There is strong evidence that the American Medical Association has had such power,[6] but it is doubtful whether any organization ordinarily considered a union possesses similar power. Craft unions often operate apprenticeship programs in co-operation with employers and require employers under most circumstances to give preference in employment to those who complete such programs. However, union apprenticeship pro-

---

[5] Following the passage of the Landrum-Griffin Act in 1959, the teamsters' union instructed its locals not to respect the picket lines of other unions.

[6] See Milton Friedman and Simon Kuznets, *Income from Independent Professional Practice* (New York: National Bureau of Economic Research, 1945), pp. 8–21 and 118–37.

grams do not by any means train all of the journeymen in the skilled trades. Many workers pick up their skill on the job in non-union employment, especially in smaller communities. They may later move into union employment, for few unions will deny membership to all those not trained in union apprenticeship programs. While such a source of supply exists, the union cannot effectively limit entry to the trade by limiting the number of apprentices of union employers or unduly lengthening the period of apprenticeship.

The closed shop, which requires employers to hire only union members, is sometimes considered to be a control of the labor supply, but this view seems forced where qualified non-union members are available. It would be better to say that the union, by its power to strike, denies the employer access to part of the supply so that he is forced to choose between operating solely with union labor and solely with non-union labor. Of course, the union's power to strike is increased if there are few non-union workers in a trade and if these are reluctant to work for struck employers. . . .

42

Industrial Conflict and Its Mediation

Clark Kerr

Clark Kerr, "Industrial Conflict and Its Mediation," *The American Journal of Sociology,* Vol. 60, No. 3 (November, 1954). © 1954 by the University of Chicago Press.

TACTICAL MEDIATION

Guidance by a third party to an acceptable accommodation is the essence of mediation, which thus stands midway between conciliation, that is, adjustment of a dispute by the parties themselves, and arbitration, that is, decision by a third party. Mediation, in its traditional sense, involves the intervention of a third party into a particular dispute, and this participation of a third party in a situation which is already given will be called "tactical mediation. "Strategical" mediation consists, instead of the structuring of the situation itself, of the creation of a favorable environment within which the parties interact. The purpose of tactical mediation is to bring existing nonviolent conflict between the parties to a mutually acceptable result so that there will be no need for it to become violent or to end violent conflict by agreement or by transfer to nonviolent means. Strategical mediation aims instead at reducing the incidence of conflict and channeling it along nondestructive lines of development.

Tactical mediation is a particularly appealing method of reducing industrial conflict. It is simple to apply. It relies on persuasion rather than on force. It is almost universally supported, at least at the verbal level. But what contribution, in fact, can a tactical mediator make to the resolution of a conflict which the parties cannot provide for themselves? The parties will usually be more familiar with the situation and will have the greater incentive. Viewed analytically, the following are the major potential contributions.[1]

Reduction of irrationality. The mediator can bring the parties toward a more rational mood by giving the individuals involved an opportunity to vent their feelings to him, by keeping personal recriminations out of joint discussions, and by drawing the attention of the parties to the objective issues in dispute and to the consequences of aggressive conflict.[2]

Removal of nonrationality. The mediator can aid the parties in reaching a full appreciation of reality by clarifying the intentions of the parties toward each other, the issues in controversy, and the pertinent facts and by leading each party to accurate calculations of the cost of aggressive conflict and of the prospective results of such conflict. Quite commonly, each party, particularly when collective bargaining is new to it, underestimates these costs and overestimates the potential gain. The mediator can often bring a truer estimate of the strength of the opposite party and a truer expectation of the outcome than is available

initially.[3] While it is not normally too difficult to assist the leaders in these realizations, the task of reaching the constituencies on both sides is often an impossible one. The constituencies may come to recognize reality only through the fire of combat, for the endurance of a strike often serves an educational purpose. It is one of the functions of a strike to raise the calculation of cost and reduce the prospect of gain. The intervention of a mediator is sometimes timed to correspond with the growing recognition of true costs and realistic prospects.

Exploration of solutions. Not only can a skilled mediator help the parties explore solutions which have occurred to them independently, but he can create new solutions around which positions have not yet become fixed.[4] In collective bargaining, as elsewhere, there are several means to the same end, and some of these means will be less abhorrent than others to the opposite party. The mediator can assist in finding those solutions in which, for a given cost to one party, the advantage of the other is maximized or, phrased reversely, in which a certain gain for one party can be secured at the minimum cost to the other. The exploration

---

[1] This discussion will deal with an analysis of the mediation process. It will not describe legal mechanisms or actual techniques. A particularly helpful recent discussion of mechanisms and techniques is found in Elmore Jackson, *The Meeting of Minds* (New York: Harper & Bros., 1952). For a discussion of techniques see also Rose, *op. cit.;* E. L. Warren and I. Bernstein, "The Mediation Process," *Southern Economic Journal,* XV, 4 (April, 1949), 441–57; F.H. Bullen, "The Mediation Process," *Proceedings of the New York University Annual Conference on Labor,* 1948, pp. 105–43; and John T. Dunlop and James J. Healy, *Collective Bargaining,* rev. ed. (Homewood, Ill.: Richard D. Irwin, 1953), chap. iv.

For a study relating the mediator's personality and background to the mediation process see Irving R. Weschler, "The Personal Factor in Labor Mediation," *Personnel Psychology* (Summer, 1950).

[2] Sometimes, however, the mediator may encourage settlement by inducing an irrational desire on the part of the representatives for agreement through the use of all-night sessions or of liquor, for example.

[3] The mediator, however, is unlikely to be interested in removing nonrationality in those cases in which one or both parties has overestimated the strength of the opponent or has underestimated the potential result. Furthermore, he normally wishes to encourage an exaggerated estimate of costs and a minimal estimate of gains. In other words, his goal is a peaceful settlement, not the removal of a nonrationality in the parties, although the latter, in the standard situation, conduces to the former.

[4] George W. Taylor has emphasized the "art of proposing the alternate solution" as the crucial part of the mediation process. The skillful application of this art also involves assistance in the "graceful retreat" (see below), which Taylor has termed bringing about a "consent to lose." (See "The Role of Mediation in Labor-Management Relations," address at a conference of regional directors of the Federal Mediation and Conciliation Service, Washington, D.C., June 23, 1952, pp. 15 ff., and "Instead of Strike-bargaining," *New York Times Magazine,* July 6, 1947, p. 27.)

of solutions is generally most effective before the positions of the parties have become strongly solidified. It is particularly difficult to mediate disputes when the parties have rationalized or theorized their positions or have tied them in with a general ideological orientation. They are then not practical problems but matters of principle.

Assistance in the graceful retreat. All, or almost all, collective bargaining involves some retreat by both parties from their original positions. The union normally asks for more than it expects ultimately to receive, and the employer offers less than he expects ultimately to concede. There are at least two major reasons for this. First, neither party is likely to know exactly what the best offer of the other party will be. Thus it is only prudent to make one's own original demand well below or well above the most likely level of concession of the opponent to avoid any chance of having foregone a possible gain. Second, to insist to the end on the original proposal is almost an unfair labor practice, under the rules of the game, for it denies the other party the opportunity of forcing some concession and thus claiming a victory of sorts.

Normally both parties must retreat from their original positions, and much of the fascination of collective bargaining is in the tactics of retreat. Each party seeks to discover and profit from the best offer of the other without disclosing and having to concede his own. The mediator can assist the retreat in at least three ways. First, he can call the parties together. Particularly when a strike is in process, neither side may wish to request negotiations for fear it will betray a sense of weakness. The mediator can help avoid such embarrassment by issuing the call.

Second, the mediator can act as a go-between on the making of offers. Not only is it unwise to retreat a step without getting the other party to retreat a step also, but any open retreat at all may be unwise if it appears that no agreement may be reached, for then the parties may wish to resume their original positions unencumbered by face-to-face concessions. The mediator can help control the pace of retreat, for, if one party initially retreats too rapidly, the other may miscalculate the ultimate stopping point, and, in trying to push too far, cause aggressive conflict. Moreover, the mediator can speed up the retreat for both sides by making it more revocable, since he, rather than the parties themselves, seems to be making the suggestions. The more revocable a concession, the easier it is to make. The mediator makes it possible for the parties to yield without seeming to yield and thus to disclose their true positions to each other without being eternally committed to them. Each offer, after all, is presented as the "last offer," not as the "next to last" offer, and there is no point in prematurely becoming committed to the truly last offer unless it is necessary and will settle the controversy.

Third, he can help "save face." The mere entrance of a mediator is a face-saving device. In collective bargaining there are no really objective tests of the performance of the representatives of each side, yet their constituencies seek to test them, and they seek to justify their stewardship. Appearances thus are important. One proof of capable stewardship in negotiations is that the results are as good as or better than those achieved in similar situations elsewhere; another is that concessions were wrung from the opposite party; another is that an elected negotiating committee participated in the negotiations; and another is that the controversy was so hard fought that a mediator had to be brought in.

But a mediator may do more than put in an appearance: he may make recommendations, perhaps even public recommendations (as in the case of a so-called "fact-finding board").[5] A party can sometimes accept such recommendations, particularly if they come from a person of prestige, when it could not make a similar offer itself or accept such an offer from the other party.[6] The mediator shoulders some responsibility for the result, and the responsibility of the representatives is consequently lightened. The bargaining positions and arguments of the parties are preserved more intact for the next conflict. The public normally lends its support to third-party recommendations, and this makes their acceptance also more accountable. Such recommendations may even be privately handed to the mediator by one or both parties, with the comment that they will be acceptable if the mediator will take public responsibility for their suggestion. Defeat or partial defeat at the hands of a third party is more palatable than a similar surrender to the second party.

Raising the cost of conflict. A mediator may also raise the cost of conflict to one or both parties as an inducement to settle by bringing or threatening to bring public wrath down on their heads, by persuading their allies to withdraw their support, by threatening retribution (or reward) from government or customers or some other source, by going behind the backs of the representatives to reach and influence the principals in favor of a settlement. But these tactics are not normally pursued and are usually reserved for only the most crucial cases of great public concern. The mediator masquerades as a friend of the parties, and particularly of their representatives, with whom he has face-to-face dealings, and these are the acts of an enemy. Moreover, no mediator who employs such tactics is long acceptable as a mediator.

Some disputes are not subject to a mediation settlement short of aggressive conflict, regardless of the skill of the mediator. There are situations where aggressive conflict has positive values in itself—where there is some institutional gain from such conflict, such as a larger or more devoted membership; where the leaders need an external war to improve their internal positions; where one or both parties want to "burnish the sword"; where, as Pigou notes,[7] an employer may wish to use a strike to get rid of excess stocks or may encourage a strike during slack period so that one during a peak period will be less likely; where an employer uses a strike as an excuse for raising prices or for withholding production until a more favorable tax period arrives; where one or the other party seeks to further some end external to the relationship—it might be political, or it might be the union leader's need for an occasional strike to encourage the sale of "strike insurance"; or where a strike is desired as a relief from tension. A strike for strike's sake must run its course.

A particularly difficult controversy to mediate, strangely enough, is one in which the costs of aggressive conflict to each party are enormous.[8] Then any one of many solutions is better than a strike, and the process of narrowing these possible solutions to a single one is an arduous task.

While several important types of dispute are not susceptible to effective mediation at all,

---

[5] Advanced forms of mediation approximate arbitration, just as arbitration of disputes over new contractual arrangements (as contrasted with grievance disputes) often takes on many of the aspects of mediation.

[6] "Agreement" requires that both parties reach the same point in their concessions to each other. "Acceptability" only means that they are close enough to a point set by a third party so that they will not revolt against it. The range of "acceptability" may, of course, be wide or narrow.

[7] A.C. Pigou, *The Economics of Welfare*, 4th ed. (New York: Macmillan Co., 1950), p. 454.

[8] *Ibid.*, pp. 460–61.

short of aggressive conflict, mediation does undoubtedly settle some controversies peacefully.

THE CONTRIBUTION
OF TACTICAL MEDIATION

Mediation, undoubtedly, does make a substantial net contribution to the reduction of aggressive industrial conflict, but this does not mean that it does so in every case: indeed, it may even increase the propensity to strike. It may encourage a strike, of course, where an unskilled mediator serves only to turn the parties more against each other or to obscure solutions; but it may do so also when the mediator is skilled, for he may aid the parties to fight, as well as to retreat, gracefully. (The sophisticated negotiator is more likely to need help to fight gracefully under certain circumstances than to retreat gracefully under the same circumstances.) If the public is opposed to strikes and may take action against them, the participation of a mediator in a dispute may convince it of the good faith of the parties' attempts to reach a settlement, making the public more tolerant of a strike and thus making it easier for the parties to strike; or, if a strike is in process, the entrance of a mediator may forestall more drastic public intervention and thus make it possible to strike for a longer period.

Likewise, if a strike serves a leadership but not a membership purpose,[9] the use of a mediator may help convince the membership that the leaders made a determined effort to reach a settlement, when in fact they did not, and thus ease membership acceptance of strike costs. This ruse will not be successful if the

membership is sufficiently sophisticated, but this is very seldom the case.

The mediator has been employed in both these situations as a device to make the situation appear different from what it really is, to camouflage true intentions, to mislead the public or the members. This is "for-the-record" mediation. (See cases 1 and 2 below.)

The mediator may be an unwitting party, in the hands of skilled practitioners, to this deception, but he may also participate willingly, for basically he works for the representatives of both sides, not for the principals or for the public. It is the representatives with whom he associates and from whom he expects acceptance. But in some cases, particularly those of vital public concern, the mediator may go behind the backs of the representatives to reach the principals (or, in the case of the union, also to higher levels of the union organization) and encourage them to press their representatives for a peaceful settlement; or he may go over their heads to the public to exert pressure for settlement, by, for example, attacking the stubbornness of the representatives of one or both parties. (See cases 5 and 6 below.) The former is particularly difficult, however, for it involves a partial or complete repudiation of the representatives. The latter is especially effective in a culture, such as that of Germany, which places great stress on law and order and great reliance on public authority, and, conversely, it is less effective in the United States.[10] Where the public is unconcerned about a strike or is concerned but is unable to take effective action or where the membership has no control over its representatives, the mediator, of

---

[9] This assumes, of course, that there is a "membership purpose," but the membership may be and sometimes is so divided in its desires or interests that no single membership purpose can be said to exist.

[10] Mediation occurs at four levels of intensity: (1) where the mediator convenes the parties and transmits their offers back and forth (often called "conciliation"); (2) where the mediator makes suggestions and raises considerations on his own; (3) where the mediator makes public recommendations; and (4) where the mediator tries to manipulate the situation against the wishes of the representatives.

course, has no recourse beyond the representatives themselves. (See cases 3 and 4 below.)

More common are the situations in which the mediator can aid the leaders or members or both toward a more rational position or can bring skill beyond that available to the parties in making proposals or in aiding the retreat. (See cases 7, 8, and 9 below.)

Table 1 sets forth analytically these various situations.[11] It does not exhaust all the possible combinations, for reality is immensely complex, although other combinations not specifically set forth may be suggested. Particularly, the table abstracts from reality in giving only two alternatives ("Yes" and "No") to such questions as membership control of leaders, when, in fact, there is an infinite number of degrees of control.

Case 1 is the "pure" situation of full rationality, representativeness, and skill all around. Here the mediator can help the parties reach a settlement, if they want to agree, but he is not really necessary. If the parties do not wish to agree, however, his presence can only serve to fool the public about intent to settle and thus increase the propensity to strike. The public, of course, may not care whether a strike occurs or not, and then the mediator's

[11] This table assumes, as does the general discussion, that irrationality and nonrationality, misrepresentation of membership interests by leaders, and lack of skill conduce toward aggressive conflict, and this is normally true. But there are contrary situations —the leaders or members or both may overestimate the cost of a strike; the leaders may be too lazy and bureaucratic to want to manage an otherwise desirable strike, or they may "sell out" to the other party; or, through lack of skill, representatives may stumble into an agreement they never wanted. Generally, nevertheless, there is less peace, rather than more, because of lack of rationality, skill, and representativeness. When the leadership misrepresents the membership in favor of peace, unauthorized or "wildcat" strikes may occur, and they are particularly difficult to mediate because the conflict is a three-way affair— membership versus leadership versus employer. Generally, cessation of the membership versus leadership controversy is a prerequisite to effective mediation of the leadership versus employer conflict.

influence is neutral (case 3); or, if the public does care enough, the mediator may turn against the parties and bring public pressure to bear on them (case 5).

Case 2 is one of misrepresentation in a context of leader-membership responsiveness. The representatives of one or both parties want a strike which will not benefit the members. Here the mediator serves only to hoodwink the members, unless he is willing to go behind the backs of the representatives (case 6). The membership may not be able to control the representatives, however, and here the mediator serves no or little purpose, one way or the other, if the representatives desire a strike (case 4).

Cases 7, 8, and 9 show, respectively, where the mediator adds to the rationality of the leaders and the members, to the rationality of the members where the leaders are already rational, and to the skill available to the leaders on one or both sides.

The nine cases may be described in order, as follows:

1. *The case of the hoodwinked public.* The servant-of-the-parties mediator helps the parties to fool an agitated public into thinking that all is being done which can be done to encourage a peaceful solution, even though the parties are intent on warfare.

2. *The case of the hoodwinked membership.* The servant-of-the-parties mediator helps the leaders to fool the ignorant members into thinking that the maximum effort toward settlement is being made, when, in fact, the leaders want a strike for their own purposes.

3. *The case of the indifferent public.* The public does not care one way or another whether there is a strike or not, and so there is no point in trying to fool it through introducing a mediator into the situation.

4. *The case of the impotent members.* The members have no control over their

TABLE 1

Tactical Mediation—The Structure of Individual Case Situations

	Certain Type Situations and the Effect of Mediation on Propensity Toward Aggressive Conflict								
	Increase		Neutral		Decrease				
Situational Factors	1	2	3	4	5	6	7	8	9
Leaders (on both sides):									
Are they rational?	Yes	Yes	Yes	Yes	Yes	Yes	No*	Yes	Yes
Are they skilled?	Yes	Yes	Yes	Yes	Yes	Yes	Yes	Yes	No*
Do they represent their members?	Yes	No*	Yes	No	Yes	No*	Yes	Yes	Yes
Members (on both sides):									
Are they rational?	Yes	No*	Yes	Yes	Yes	No*	No*	No*	Yes
Do they control their leaders?	Yes	Yes	Yes	No*	Yes	Yes	Yes	Yes	Yes
Public:									
Does it dislike a strike, and is it able to penalize the parties?	Yes*	Yes	No*	Yes	Yes*	Yes	Yes	Yes	Yes
Mediator:									
Is he responsive to the wishes of the leaders rather than to those of the members and the public?	Yes	Yes*	Yes	Yes	No*	No*	Yes	Yes	Yes

Definitions: (1) "Propensity toward aggressive conflict" includes both the proneness to strike and the duration of the strike. (2) "Rational" means full and accurate knowledge of costs and results of aggressive conflict. (3) "Skilled" means ability to retreat gracefully, if so desired, without third-party assistance or gracefully to avoid a retreat, if so desired, with third-party assistance. (4) Leaders may "represent their members" either by working solely for membership goals (such as "burnishing sword") or by working for leadership goals (impeding the rise of a rival) where the latter calls for the same action as the former. (The representative of the single employer may be the employer himself, although on the employer side, as well as on the union side, the principles do not usually directly represent themselves.) (5) "The members control the leaders" when the members are able to prevent leadership action contrary to membership desires.

Basic assumptions: (1) There is a rational basis for some aggressive conflict in that conflict pays one or both parties, and the parties do not wish to avoid it. (2) Nonrationality, irrationality, and lack of skill of leaders or members and action flowing from leadership, as contrasted with membership interests, all increase the propensity toward aggressive conflict. (3) The membership, or at least a majority of it, is relatively homogeneous in its interests. (4) The mediator is skilled.

*Asterisks denote the particularly significant factors in each case.

leaders, and so nothing is to be gained by a pretense of a bona fide effort at settlement through mediation.

5. *The For-God-and-Country case.* The public servant mediator takes the side of an agitated public and puts pressure on the parties against their will toward a peaceful settlement.

6. *The For-God-and-the-Common-Man case.* The public servant mediator turns against the leaders in order to achieve a settlement where he believes the leaders are, for their own selfish reasons, choosing a strike against the interests of an ignorant membership.

7. *The case of general lack of appreciation of the situation.* The mediator introduces rationality to both leaders and members.

8. *The case of selective lack of appreciation of the situation.* The mediator helps the leaders bring rationality into the views of the members.

9. *The case of awkwardness.* The mediator supplies negotiating skills which the leaders lack.

Cases 7, 8, and 9 are certainly the most common of all, and they occur most frequently where small employers and local unions are involved and the members and the leaders are inexperienced; cases 3 and 4 are probably the next most common and arise chiefly when there is sophisticated leadership of well-established organizations in industries of no special concern to the public; cases 1 and 2, which come next in order of probable importance, develop when the leadership is highly sophisticated but must be careful of the sensitivities of the public and the members; and cases 5 and 6 are the least common and take place only where the conflict is of enough concern for the mediator to sacrifice his standing by taking action contrary to leadership interests. Historically, as collective bargaining moves, albeit quite slowly, from cases 7, 8, and 9 to cases 1, 2, 3, and 4, with the growth in size of organizations and the gain in sophistication of leaders, mediation can serve less and less of a positive purpose, except as it undertakes the disagreeable tactics implicit in cases 5 and 6. Compulsory mediation, as practiced in some countries, is no more effective than voluntary mediation unless such tactics are employed.

When a member joins an organization, he does so, in part, to purchase rationality and skill not otherwise available to him. If this purchase were always a successful one, mediation would be largely unnecessary. It finds its justification basically in the failings in this act of purchase—leaders are not skilled or are not rational or are not representative, or the members do not believe them if they are.[12]

There is no convincing evidence that tactical mediation has had much of an effect in reducing the totality of aggressive industrial conflict. Strikes seem to go their own way, responsive to other, more persuasive forces. To understand the role of tactical mediation, we must thus examine not only the internal characteristics of situations but also the external environments within which they arise.[13]

STRATEGICAL MEDIATION

A strike is not an isolated event, a solitary episode. It occurs within a given social context, a surrounding economic and political environment. The major variations in the incidence of such conflict relate not to the efficacy of the direct ministrations to the conflict, such as tactical mediation, but to the total milieu within which it arises. Fewer strikes are experienced in Sweden than in the United States, and fewer in the garment industry than in coal-mining, not because tactical mediation is more skilled in Sweden than it is in the United States or is more skilled in one industry than in another, but rather because of the differing surrounding

---

[12] This leadership-membership relationship is a difficult one, at best, for, if the members are not themselves rational, they can hardly know whether they did, in fact, purchase rationality, and, if they are rational, the purchase may be unnecessary. The former is the more common case and helps explain the usual skepticism and cynicism of the members vis-à-vis their representatives.

[13] Proposals for strengthening the effectiveness of the mediation process have generally been concerned with recommendations which are confined within the tactical-mediation orbit. Establishing orderly organized-procedure arrangements or fixing a definite time period as appropriate for mediation ("after collective bargaining has ended in disagreements and before a work stoppage has begun"), as Leiserson, for example, has suggested, could at best reflect in the efficacy of tactical mediation but could not circumvent the inherent limitation of tactical mediatory practice per se. (See William M. Leiserson, "The Role of Government in Industrial Relations," in *Industrial Disputes and the Public Interest,* Berkeley and Los Angeles: Institute of Industrial Relations, University of California, 1947, and his presidential address before the Industrial Relations Research Association, "The Function of Mediation in Labor Relations" in L. Reed Tripp, ed., *Proceedings of the Fourth Annual Meeting of the Industrial Relations Research Association,* 1951.)

environments. Aggressive industrial conflict varies greatly from nation to nation, industry to industry, firm to firm, and time to time. Which situations are most conducive to nonviolent, and which to violent, conflict?

Strategical mediation is concerned with the manipulation of these situations and thus with factors quite external to the parties themselves.[14] From one point of view, society is a huge mediation mechanism, a means for settling disagreements between rival claimants—taxpayers and recipients of benefits, buyers and sellers, proponents of opposing political ideologies—so that people may live together in some state of mutual tolerance. Some societies mediate their disagreements, through their markets, their courts, their political processes, more effectively than do others. Society in the large is the mediation machinery for industrial as well as other forms of conflict.

Two recent studies demonstrate the crucial relationship of the environment to the industrial conflict. The first[15] investigated the strike proneness of industries in eleven nations and found that some industries (like mining and longshoring) universally evidenced a high propensity to strike and others (like clothing and trade) a low propensity. The second study[16] summarized the environmental characteristics of a series of industrial plants in the United States noted for their industrial peace and concluded that these plants all fell within a definable environmental setting. Drawing on these two studies and, among others, on recent ones by Ross and Irwin[17] and by Knowles,[18] the social arrangements which seem in the long run generally most favorable to nonviolent industrial conflict, within the cultural context with which we are here concerned, may be set forth as follows:

Integration of workers and employers into society. To the extent that workers and employers consider themselves primarily citizens with roughly equal status, privileges, and opportunity, the sting is taken out of their relationship. The greater the social mobility, the more mixed in membership the various social associations, the more heterogeneous the community's occupational composition, the more accepted the institutions of workers and the greater their participation in general community life, the more secure the worker in his job and the higher his skill—the less violent will be the industrial conflict in the long run.

---

[14] Intermediate between tactical mediation and strategical mediation lies "preventative tactical mediation." It takes for its province more than the individual dispute but less than the total relevant environment. It deals with the relationships of the parties in general. It may be concerned with a long-run change in the attitudes of the parties toward each other or toward their mutual problems, with the nature of the leadership on one side or another, with the pressures to which the parties may be subject, with the timing of contract expiration dates, or with the alliances of the parties. It seeks to manipulate the parties and their relationships in advance in favor of nonviolent conflict.

[15] Clark Kerr and Abraham Siegel, "The Interindustry Propensity To Strike—An International Comparison" (published by the Society for the Psychological Study of Social Issues, in a volume on *Industrial Conflict,* edited by Robert Dubin, Arthur Kornhauser, and Arthur Ross, New York: McGraw-Hill, 1954).

[16] Clark Kerr, "Industrial Peace and the Collective Bargaining Environment," published by the National Planning Association as part of its final report in its series on "Causes of Industrial Peace."

[17] Arthur M. Ross and Donald Irwin, "Strike Experience in Five Countries, 1927–1947: An Interpretation," *Industrial and Labor Relations Review* (April, 1951), pp. 323–42. See also comment by Adolf Sturmthal (pp. 391–94) and rejoinder by Ross (pp. 395–98) in the April, 1953, issue of the same journal.

[18] *Op. cit.* See also his paper presented to the Second Congress of the International Sociological Association, Liege, Belgium, August, 1953, "Strike-Proneness and Its Determinants." Another paper presented to the same congress by Harold L. Sheppard, "Approaches to Conflict in American Industrial Sociology," suggests that only those studies of industrial conflict which take account of the broader environmental milieu can be productive of fruitful generalization.

Stability of the society. The incidence of strikes is directly related to major changes in the operation of the society—particularly to the business cycle and to wars.[19] Each major economic or political change creates a new situation for the parties, and they must adjust their relationship to it, often in a trial of strength. Similarly, unusually rapid growth or decline of an industry or technological change in it is likely to raise problems in a form which invites a violent solution. The parties normally can adjust more peacefully to gradual than to precipitous change.[20]

Ideological compatibility. The attitudes of people and groups toward each other and their over-all orientation toward society affect industrial relationships. Where people believe in brotherly love or the equality of man, for example, their disagreements will be fewer, less sharp, and more amenable to easy compromise. Where, however, they believe in the inevitable opposition of classes, in the rapacity of other men, then violent industrial conflict is more likely. The perspectives of men, it should be noted, are not unrelated to their actual experiences in their social environments. The close co-operation of leaders of industry and labor in the Netherlands during the German occupation in World War II, for example, has been a source of their intimate relations since then.

Secure and responsive relationship of leaders to members. For the minimization of violent industrial conflict, it is desirable that leaders be (a) relatively secure in their positions and (b) responsive to their constituencies. Security of position, on the union side, for example, means lack of intense rivalry for leadership and solidarity of the organization against defection of its members or attack by a rival group. When the leaders are under pressure directly or indirectly, they may respond by encouraging an external war. Vested interests in conflict may be particularly damaging when the leaders make the decisions but the members pay the costs. Under these conditions the leaders will seek to assure the irrationality or non-rationality of the members.

At the same time, leaders should be responsive to their constituencies; otherwise, they may make aggressive use of the organization as a means to an end external to the life of the organization, or by their neglect they may encourage internal revolt with its repercussions. It is relatively easy in many mass organizations for the leadership to exploit the membership in one fashion or another. The proper combination of security and responsiveness of leadership is not always readily attainable, for these two requirements point in somewhat contrary directions.

The dispersion of grievances. The mass grievance, one which is held by many people in the same place at the same time against the same antagonist, grows and feeds on itself. Society can more readily accommodate and adjust the small grievance.[21] Thus it is helpful

[19] See Sheila V. Hopkins, "Industrial Stoppages and Their Economic Significance," *Oxford Economic Papers* (new ser.) (June, 1953), pp. 209–20, for one of the more recent of the many studies which note the tendency of fluctuations in business activity to affect the frequency and duration of industrial unrest.

[20] See Robin M. Williams, Jr., *The Reduction of Intergroup Tensions* (Social Science Research Council Bulletin No. 57), pp. 56–58, where the propositions that "intergroup conflict" is the more likely the more rapid and far-reaching the social changes to which individuals have to adjust" and that "conflict is especially likely in periods of rapid change in levels of living" are singled out as significant factors in the incidence of hostility and conflict.

[21] A society riven by many minor cleavages is in less danger of open mass conflict than a society with only one or a few cleavages. . . . In the most extreme case of mass violence: "An essential step in the development of revolution is the gradual concentration of public dissatisfaction upon some one institution and the persons representing it" (quoted from L. P. Edwards, *The Natural History of Revolution,* Chicago: University of Chicago Press, 1927, p. 46, in Robin M. Williams, Jr., *op. cit.,* p. 59. Williams points out further that "the reduction of intergroup conflict depends upon. . . . proper canalization of existing hostilities, through sanctions, diversions, redefinition of situations, etc." (p. 62).

if discontent can find several outlets—individual quitting of jobs and political expression, for example, as well as organized economic action; if it is directed against several individuals and groups—the merchant, the landlord, the state, for example—rather than against an employer who also provides housing, retail facilities, and law enforcement; if it coagulates into small lumps by craft, by firm, by industry, rather than over the whole society; if it finds expression a little at a time, rather than in a single explosion; if it can be blunted by the imposition of relatively impersonal laws and rules standing between the parties on the basis of which decisions can be made which flow not alone from the parties in controversy but from less volatile sources; if it finds expression in several stages through appeal or through periodic reopening of questions and if it seldom encounters a final barrier to its voicing; if freedom to act and react is constantly preserved. At the opposite extreme is the mass grievance against a single source of power, subject to a single personal decision.

Structuring the game. As we have seen above, rules which reduce the risks of the parties and limit the means they may employ, without unduly stifling the conflict, can make a substantial contribution to non-violent resolution of controversy or can mitigate the destructive consequences of violent conflict. Rules which guarantee the independent sovereignty of each party, which raise the cost of fighting (as does multiemployer bargaining),[22] which set some fairly precise norms for the settlement (as does the "pattern bargain"), which prohibit use

---

[22] A high degree of horizontal and vertical integration of worker and employer interests does not, however, prevent strikes. Witness, for example, the largest strike in Swedish history—the metal-workers' strike of 1945.

of certain provocative means of combat, which limit conflict to intermittent periods, which confine the subjects for disagreement to some reasonable area at any one time—all aid the nonviolent settlement of industrial disputes. The rules of the game aid rationality—knowledge of costs and consequences—and thus diplomatic resolution of controversies. Fortunately, in industrial relations, contrary to international relations, these rules are enforcible by society if not accepted by the parties voluntarily.

These are not easy prescriptions, although all of them are potentially subject to some utilization—not, however, in totality by any single "third party" or even by a single institution. Strategical mediation relates to an over-all community approach to its organization and to the handling of its problems, and to a general philosophical orientation toward the management of the affairs of men.

CONCLUSION

Industrial conflict, then, may be affected in three crucial ways: (1) by reducing the sources of mutual discontent; (2) by affecting the process by which decisions to act are made, either (a) by reducing the power to make such decisions (through control of one party by the other or of both by the state) or (b) by facilitating the making and implementing of decisions to act nonviolently; and (3) by channeling the conflict along the least destructive lines. Tactical mediation is concerned with 2b; strategical mediation, with 1 and 3. It is suggested that the latter, by the advance creation of favorable situations, can make the greater contribution to the minimization of aggressive industrial conflict and particularly of its most socially harmful aspects.

43

Collective Bargaining: In the Grip of Structural Change

Everett M. Kassalow

Everett M. Kassalow, "Collective Bargaining: In the Grip of Structural Change," *Proceedings of the Annual Meeting of the Industrial Relations Research Association*, 1980.

We know that way down the road we may be a union of much smaller membership than we now have. But I think if we make a contribution to the social good and economic health and welfare of this country, we would make that sacrifice.... Now, they [the Japanese] use more [robots].... The president of Nissan [Datsun automobiles and trucks] told me ... he was in our Oklahoma City plant, a new GM plant, the newest assembly plant [opened in 1979] in the United States, and they build X cars there. And he said he was surprised about the lack of technology. This is not because we don't know how to do it ... when they [GM] built the plant for X cars, they thought to themselves,

"Look, we might be converting this plant from small cars to big cars" and you are not going to invest in fixtures and jigs and technology that you can't easily convert when you go from a small car to a large car....

Douglas Fraser, President, UAW, before the Joint Economic Committee Hearing on Auto Imports, March 19, 1980

It is my intent to indicate a few of those deeper and enduring forces that are significantly altering our industrial relations system. There is almost always the temptation to highlight the changes and understate the powerful elements of continuity in any system. Those few analysts who have stressed continuity rather than change have generally had a better track record in forecasting industrial relations futures.[1]

The tendency to overstate the possibility of change in IR systems springs from an underestimation of the inertial elements in such systems. For example, in the last decades of the twentieth century it is impossible to understand the differences between the U.S. IR system and those of Western Europe without reference to developments of one hundred years ago, and in several respects a century or two before then! Institutional forms and forces, once well rooted, can be even more powerful than economic and political factors when it comes to shaping IR systems.[2] Indeed, one of the strengths of IR systems in advanced, industrialized societies is often this very conservatism in resisting or adapting only slowly to changes in other institutions.

In the long run, however, IR institutions do tend to adapt to major economic and social forces. I am reminded of the fact that in 1960, several analysts called attention to the great growth in service employment and the decline of the blue-collar workforce when compared to total employment. Their analysis also indicated this trend was already reducing union membership (then largely concentrated among blue-

collar workers) as a percentage of the labor force, but not much attention was addressed to what seemed to be a slow moving change. Twenty years later, articles on the shrinkage of the unions (as a percentage of the labor force) have become commonplace, and the union movement itself has become much more sensitive to this trend.[3]

I now turn to three sets of change already occurring, and likely to persist in the decade ahead, and the impact of these changes on collective bargaining. These are: (1) stagflation and incomes policies; (2) the restructuring of American manufacturing, and particularly the steel and auto industries, and (3) the rise of articulate, "outside" groups and government agencies representing their interests. I shall place major stress on the impact of changes in industrial structure, since this has been a less explored area.

STAGFLATION AND ITS IMPACT ON INDUSTRIAL RELATIONS

The persistent stagflation of recent years, including rising prices and high unemployment, has intensified government's efforts to do "something" about wages and prices to try to fashion some sort of an incomes policy. At the heart of any IR system in a modern, democratic, industrialized society are union-management negotiations over wages and related matters. Any incomes policy vitally affects this central union function.

. . . Every [previous] administration in the

---

[1] See, for example of cautious, successful extrapolation from the recent past, John T. Dunlop, "The American Industrial Relations System in 1975," in *U.S. Industrial Relations: The Next Twenty Years*, ed. Jack Stieber (East Lansing: Michigan State University Press, 1958); and Dunlop, "Past and Future Tendencies in American Labor Organizations," *Daedalus* (Winter 1978).

[2] By institutional forces and forms I mean here primarily the structures and basic outlook of unions and employers in IR systems as well as the nature and character of the collective bargaining system they share. (That system, of course, has been shaped by government as well, but once in place it is not easily modified by government in an advanced democratic society.)

[3] See Lane Kirkland, "Labor's Outlook—Building on Strength," *The AFL-CIO American Federationist*, 87 (March 1980). Downward changes in the relative position of the union movement have too often been equated with their strength in the economy and the society. Unions' economic strength has varied less than the relative decline in numbers might suggest.

postwar era save for that of President Eisenhower has tried its hand at an incomes policy or something approaching it. . . .

Curiously, one reason why these efforts persist is that key union leaders have been accepting of incomes policies, in one form or another. Why this situation wherein at least important parts of the top union leadership accept incomes policies, even though the unions are often the first to feel the restrictions of such policies? I suspect it is because union leaders are really much less ideological than economists in judging the way in which wages and prices are set in the U.S. economy. A union leader could hardly share typical economics textbook assumptions that price-setting, either by individual corporations or by unions, has little real effect on the economy, that they are fundamentally transcended by anonymous market forces, or that "money" alone matters.

Under these circumstances it is not all that hard to persuade top union leaders that when inflation persists, some forms of government control—or coordination in the wage- and price-making process—are in order if inflation is to be checked. It is particularly those union leaders who operate at the national level, those who bargain with large oligopolistic corporations (whose price-making power looks especially "real"), and through them for virtually an entire industry, who tend to this more macro policy view.[4] Lower level union leaders are less likely to share or accept this view.

Management executives by the nature of their single-company settings are less likely to have this macro view than is the case of many national union leaders. Company leaders may, therefore, be less accepting of incomes policies. The way in which a number of top corporate leaders, in the past, have seemed almost eager

to accept devices like the Dunlop labor-management committee (I am not referring to the present government-supported body) suggests that they, too, are aware of the impact of large corporations and key unions on the path of the economy.

Looking to the decade of the 1980s, . . . the likely persistence of high inflation suggests that we shall have further efforts at incomes policies—programs to influence systematically wage and price movements, and with them profits and other incomes. The recent change in the political complexion of the federal government may delay these efforts, since the new administration of President Reagan has indicated its opposition to incomes policies. The experience of the Nixon administration which began in dead opposition to wage and price control may, however, be illustrative. One should also not overlook the symbolic, political-gesture value to any government of some formal policies aimed at influencing wages and prices, even if the results are not impressive. Seeming to do something about inflation, in the short run at least, can be almost

---

[4] Personal experiences of these leaders may also enter into the influences acting upon them. To speak of only two distinguished, departed labor leaders: George Meany gained his first, prominent national experience as an AFL member on the World War II National War Labor Board which, all things considered, helped the union movement to make many advances, despite labor's no-strike pledge. A less happy experience might have left Meany with a less favorable view of incomes policies, policies which he was to accept without great demur several times in succeeding decades. Walter P. Reuther, the other major postwar union leader, rose to the presidency of the United Automobile Workers on the heels (the wings?) of a major strike conducted against the General Motors Corporation in 1945–1946. At the heart of Reuther's appeal in that strike was a call for a look at the company's books—with the assumption then, and in some later wage movements in the automobile industry, that company prices and profits were artificially high, set by excessive market power. Reuther's response to such power was his consistent support, in succeeding decades, for the establishment of some sort of public review board to have surveillance over, and to help monitor, major companies' prices and related wages.

as important politically as actually doing something.

Whether at some time in the future we shall move on to a more formal social contract remains to be seen. This would entail, among other things, extensive reorganization and strengthening of American employer organizations at the expense of individual companies, the spread of tripartite bodies, and some further centralization of unionism, especially at the federation level. In the long run, an effective social-contract arrangement would also seem to require a wider acceptance of unionism by American employers. Without such an acceptance, a durable and equitable incomes policy is probably an impossibility.

RESTRUCTURING AMERICAN INDUSTRY: THE IMPACT ON COLLECTIVE BARGAINING

Related to the stagnation of recent years are the tremendous structural adjustments barely under way in a number of American industries: These adjustments are likely to have a major impact on collective bargaining in the United States. This is particularly true of developments in the steel and auto industries.

Many major innovations in bargaining in the postwar era often had their origin in the steel and auto industries. Complementary company pensions, early retirement, supplementary unemployment benefits, the persistent use of escalator clauses—these practices, as well as wage leadership in manufacturing, were largely pioneered by the auto and steel unions and companies in these industries.[5]

It would not seem that a steel industry that has become increasingly dependent on

government support, with trigger point and tariff-related devices, can continue to be a wage and fringe benefit leader. Indeed, before the steel industry can be reconstructed and made truly competitive, there will have to be large infusions of government aid in the forms of either special investment tax credits and/or depreciation allowances, and lines of federal credit that could make the Chrysler case seem almost modest. Of the 17 leading deepwater world-scale steel complexes (excluding the USSR) at the beginning of 1980, the first eight, with projected capacities ranging from 10 to 16 million metric tons were Japanese, and the 11th and 13th were also in that country. The only U.S. plant on the list—Burns Harbor—was tied for 14–17th place (6 million metric tons). This is an industry where (in basic steelmaking) unit cost "declines systematically with increasing volume. . . . In 1977, Japan had twenty-five blast furnaces capable of producing over two million annual tons in volume; the U.S. had none. . . ."[6]

It seems unlikely that as large-scale aid is forthcoming in the 1980s, the government will let the steel union and industry continue to be the leader in innovating significant new benefit and wage advances. The Chrysler roll-back looks like a more plausible precedent for what may come in the form of government pressure. (The continuing pressure on New York City

---

[5] I am aware that the United Mine Workers and the garment unions, among others, had made some steps in pensions and supplementary insurance benefits

before these occurred in auto and steel. But it was only after the powerful and highly publicized successful efforts undertaken by the auto and steel unions in the late 1940s and in the 1950s that programs like these became more generalized in rubber, glass, and elsewhere.

[6] See Ira C. Magaziner and Thomas M. Hout, *Japanese Industrial Policy* (London: Policy Studies Institute, 1980), pp. 13–16. The United States, with large regional markets and internal raw material sources and transport, need not duplicate the scale of Japanese deep-water steel operations, but there is general acknowledgement that our industry is lagging in comparison to Japan.

and its unions, tacit or overt, by the federal government has certainly been a spectre at their bargaining table ever since Congress granted the city financial aid.)

It's difficult to see even as far as the next negotiation in automobiles, but surely the government will again exercise considerable pressure against any lead or bellwether auto settlement which might encompass Chrysler— only this time it may be done in advance of negotiations.

The industrial situation in autos is less clear than in steel; the latter has fallen drastically behind Japanese competitors in technology and will need more time to catch up. In autos there appear to be no great technological lags, but rather retarded market responses on the part of the leading companies; but even if most of the auto companies make the transition by the mid-eighties, the UAW may not be the innovative force for new economic benefits that it was in past decades. A union which is leading the call for relief from imports, an industry which requires special depreciation regulations, and one of whose major producers has had to resort to the government for immense financial assistance—these don't look like prime candidates for great new bargaining advances.

Both auto and steel workers should continue to hold fairly high positions in the total wage and compensation league. This, after all, was the case with both railroad workers and coal miners even when their industries were in a kind of doldrum through the sixties. . . . But, to repeat, by and large major bargaining innovation on wages and fringe benefits would seem to be beyond these unions in the decade ahead.

However, the national task of restructuring these industries may draw the steel and auto unions into new decision-making areas on plant location, technology choice, and the like.

There already are indications how large the role of union leadership may be in these areas—if the unions can position themselves to face these difficult industrial decisions more directly. An example is provided by the important role of the steel workers' union in the national steel industry tripartite committee which negotiated the recent aid package for the steel industry with the Carter Administration. Another harbinger of some wider future change may be the UAW's recent negotiation of its right to nominate one of its officers for a seat on the respective boards of directors of the Chrysler and American Motors Companies. This, too, took place in the context of joint efforts to "rescue" these struggling corporations. Union ingenuity in steel and autos will also be taxed in more conventional areas, as plants are shut down and there is need to improve plans for transferring some employees, for extending early retirement for others, and for reinforcing supplementary unemployment benefits funds.

Generally speaking, the gravity and complexity of the structural problems in these two industries may tend to lock top union and management leaders into a more cooperative relationship than has been true in the past. It may be somewhat more difficult for top union leaders to work up to a national strike movement against companies with whom they have been cooperating extensively on legislation and related matters. Correspondingly, company managers are likely to be more flexible in dealing with these same unions.

The steel unions and the major steel companies will have gone at least nine years under the Experimental Negotiating Agreement (ENA) before there is even the possibility of a national strike in the industry. With the first renewal of the 1974 ENA, in 1977, the parties agreed to continue the binding arbitration clause that then, in effect, ran until 1983. This April, while the rest of the contract was renegotiated, action on the ENA part, which would have extended the no-national-strike clause to 1986, was deferred and the issue has not yet been resolved.[7] (Under the ENA, local unions at individual plants are free to strike under certain circumstances.)

In the case of autos, no such long formal period without the possibility of a major strike lies behind or ahead of them, but close cooperation on trade and industrial matters could also modify the quality of relationships. The negotiation of the accretion clause (which would extend UAW jurisdiction to some newly opened auto plants, by joint agreement) in the collective agreements late in 1979 and the extension of quality-of-work circles with the cooperation of management and the UAW in many auto plants seem to suggest greater cooperation and a reduced level of conflict.[8]

Equally difficult structural transitions are under way in some other important sectors. The rubber industry has, for some years, been faced with a breakdown in its national bargaining patterns, as settlements in tire plants diverge more and more from those in so-called nontire establishments. The rise of nonunionized tire plants is also a serious threat to the structure of collective bargaining in that industry. One could cite other cases, but none of these seems to be as important for national patterns as what occurs in steel and auto.[9]

DECLINE OF METAL BARGAINING NOT CONFINED TO THE U.S.

For several decades metal unionism, usually in the basic steel and auto industries, has been the labor standards pattern-setter in advanced democratic industrial societies. The decline of this role in the U.S. also has its counterpart in most other advanced societies.

The steel industries of Germany, France, and England are all in the throes of a great employment shakedown. The German steel union had a less-than-successful strike almost two years ago, and the British steel union has lagged behind some other settlements. Japanese steel increases no longer are at the top of the wage parade in that country's annual Spring wage drives (Shuntō), as they often were in the past. In almost all countries special programs to ease layoffs have come to the fore in the steel industry. What we are witnessing is the development of excess capacity and with it some

---

[7] *Daily Labor Report* (Bureau of National Affairs), April 16, 1980, p. A-11. The ENA originally reflected a growing joint concern about the precarious economic state of the steel industry, but management has been increasingly worried about the high level of settlements under this agreement.

[8] Common concern about trade and related matters does not *necessarily* enhance union-management mutual acceptance and their relations. The decline of unionism in the textile and electrical-electronics manufacturing industries, and the resistance to unionism of employers in those industries, even in the face of their common concerns about imports, is a case in point.

[9] See the articles by Arnold R. Weber in *The New York Times*, April 19 and 21, 1979, which deal with some examples of strain in "old labor ties," especially in rubber manufacturing, as a result of economic-structural change. The steel union has also been beset by demands from major steel companies for special treatment for nonbasic steel plants—treatment which would diverge from the wage and benefit pattern of the basic industry. See *Wall Street Journal*, April 9, 1980. An analysis of bargaining structure change in construction, especially in response to the threat of nonunion construction, is to be found in Paul T. Hartman and Walter H. Franke, "The Changing Structure of Bargaining in Construction: Wide-Area and Multicraft Bargaining," *Industrial and Labor Relations Review*, 33 (January 1980).

reduction of the all-central role of steel manufacturing in the economic lives of advanced
industrial societies. A somewhat similar fate
also seems to be overtaking sections of the
European auto industry.[10]

IN SEARCH OF REPLACEMENTS
FOR STEEL AND AUTO UNIONISM

Are there likely candidates to replace these two
unions (and industries) as change agents in the
IR system? Most industry specialists look to the
electronics sector to lead the way in industrial
innovation and sales growth in the coming
decade. If this is borne out, economically this
industry's labor sector begins with a very
fragmented union base and what appears to be
a growing nonunion area. Moreover, it has
never been an industrial wage leader. To the
extent that nonunion companies like IBM have
pioneered some innovative personnel practices,
this has been of interest, but these have not
spilled over very much to the newer, smaller
electronics areas. Whether they will remains to
be seen. Perhaps the communications industry
may prove to be one of the new sources for
labor innovation.

The great growth sector of unionism in
the past decade has, of course, been in the
public area. The catch-up nature of bargaining
there to date and increasing public resistance to
higher wages and benefits for public employees
make the emergence of innovative collective
bargaining leadership unlikely in this area.

Let me not seem to be too bleak in outlook, I hasten to add. There is always a tendency
to be overwhelmed by an era of stagnation
(shades of Alvin Hansen and Kondratieff in the

thirties). It doesn't always pay to extrapolate
the recent past! The real game for IR forecasters
may be picking out the sharply advancing
sectors of the modernized, more planned
capitalism of the future. Moreover, it is possible
that social advances in that new economy
might come in a more generalized pattern, in
the form of social *legislation* as distinguished
from bargaining gains.

EMERGING INTEREST GROUPS
EXPAND GOVERNMENT ROLE
IN COLLECTIVE BARGAINING

Let me, finally, mention one other area or set
of forces which is sharply altering the nature of
labor-management relations. I refer to the rise
of powerful interest groups whose efforts to
realize their fuller potential in economic life
is impinging sharply on bargaining structures
and reducing its "private" character.

As Jack Barbash has suggested, the Civil
Rights Act of 1964 set into motion the development of a new body of law attacking discrimination and calling for "affirmative action" against
employers and unions.[11] Bilateral bargaining on
hiring procedures, promotions, and retentions
has had to yield significant ground to this new
trend. The result has been to bring government
into the process as an important participant.
As the civil rights struggle has increasingly
caught up women, this process has been deep-
ened. It would be going too far to say the
bargaining process, even in large companies,
has become tripartite, but government's influence and role have grown significantly as a
result of its intervention on behalf of minority
and women's rights.

Some basic demographic trends are likely

---

[10] The chronic IR difficulties in Britain for
nearly two decades have stemmed, in considerable
part, from the stagnant state of its engineering (metal
fabricating) industry.

[11] Jack Barbash, "The Changing Structure of
Collective Bargaining," *Challenge Magazine* (September–October 1973).

to make even more difficult the satisfaction of minorities' and women's job claims in the coming decade. The great teenage cohort is now passing into the middle years of the labor force. Ordinarily it is in those middle years, 25–44, that most workers make their greatest wage and promotion gains. The extraordinary size of that age cohort will intensify competition within it and make promotions relatively hard to come by. (It is well to remember, too, that the entering labor force cohort, the teenagers, will be fewer to supervise, and this too will limit supervisory promotion opportunities.) This could lead to greater feelings of discrimination on the part of women and minorities. Having called upon the Equal Employment Opportunity Commission to help break open jobs in the 1970s, they may [seek further assistance] with upgrading and promotions in the 1980s.

It has not only been in the area of discrimination that government has been drawn into the labor system. Its role has also dramatically expanded in the area of safety regulation (OSHA). In the administration of private company pension plans, the government has also been called upon as a major regulator (ERISA).

In this latter field at least, the prospect seems to be for a widening of this role as many small company pension plans fall into difficulty. The great financial difficulties of a number of steel and auto companies may also lead to calls for assistance from the federal Pension Benefit Guarantee Corporation (set up under Title IV of ERISA) to prop up their pension plans. Government assistance is likely to be accompanied by more control. . . .

Taken together, EEOC, OSHA, and ERISA are having a wide and lasting effect on the bargaining system. The latter is less and less a private process.

Such then are some of the deeper social and economic structural changes that will continue to alter the structure of bargaining in the years ahead. It would be nice to end with a tidy integration of these forces, but although they all mirror profound economic and social change, I find no clear, integrating force among them. [In the long run, however, all] do seem to bespeak a passage to a new, more state-interventionist form of capitalism. . . .

44

The Two Faces of Unionism

Richard B. Freeman and James L. Medoff

Richard B. Freeman and James L. Medoff, "The Two Faces of Unionism," *The Public Interest,* No. 57 (Fall 1979).

Trade unions are the principal institution of workers in modern capitalist societies, as endemic as large firms, oligopolistic organization of industries, and governmental regulation of free enterprise. But for over 200 years, since the days of Adam Smith, there has been widespread disagreement about the effects of unions on the economy. On the one side, such economists as John Stuart Mill, Alfred Marshall, and Richard Ely (one of the founders of the American Economic Association) viewed unions as having major positive effects on the economy. On the other side, such economists as Henry Simons and Fritz Machlup have stressed the adverse effects of unions on productivity. In the 1930's and 1940's, unions were at the center of attention among intellectuals, with most social scientists viewing them as an important positive force in society. In recent years, unionism has become a more peripheral topic and unions have come to be viewed less positively. Less and less space in social-science journals and in magazines and newspapers is devoted to unions. For example, the percentage of articles in major economics journals treating trade unionism dropped from 9.2 percent in the 1940's to 5.1 percent in the 1950's to 0.4 percent in the early 1970's. And what is written is increasingly unfavorable. The press often paints unions as organizations which are socially unresponsive, elitist, nondemocratic, or ridden with crime. In the 1950's, 34 percent of the space devoted to unions in *Newsweek* and *Time* was unfavorable; that has risen to 51 percent in the 1970's. Economists today generally treat unions as monopolies whose sole function is to raise wages. Since monopolistic wage increases are socially deleterious—in that they can be expected to induce both inefficiency and inequality—most economic studies implictly or explicitly judge unions as having a negative impact on the economy.

Our research demonstrates that this view of unions as organizations whose chief function is to raise wages is seriously misleading. For in addition to raising wages, unions have significant non-wage effects which influence diverse aspects of modern industrial life. By providing workers with a voice both at the workplace and in the political arena, unions can and do affect positively the functioning of the economic and social systems. Although our research on the non-wage effects of trade unions is by no means complete and some results will surely change as more evidence becomes available, enough work has been done to yield the broad outlines of a new view of unionism.

UNIONS AS COLLECTIVE VOICE

One key dimension of the new work on trade unionism can best be understood by recognizing that societies have two basic mechanisms for dealing with divergences between desired social conditions and actual conditions. The first is the classic market mechanism of exit and entry, individual mobility: The dissatisfied consumer switches products; the diner whose soup is too salty seeks another restaurant; the unhappy couple divorces. In the labor market, exit is synonymous with quitting, while entry consists of new hires by the firm. By leaving less-desirable jobs for more-desirable jobs, or by refusing bad jobs, individuals penalize the bad employer and reward the good—leading to an overall improvement in the efficiency of the social system. The basic theorem of neoclassical economics is that, under well-specified conditions, the exit and entry of persons (the hallmark of free enterprise) produces a "Pareto-optimum" situation— one in which no individual can be made better off without making someone worse off. Economic analysis can be viewed as a detailed study of the implications of this kind of adjustment and of the extent to which it works out in real economies. As long as the exit-entry market mechanism is viewed as the only efficient adjustment mechanism, institutions such as unions must necessarily be viewed as impediments to the optimal operation of a capitalist economy.

There is, however, a second mode of adjustment. This is the political mechanism, which Albert Hirschman termed "voice" in his important book, *Exit, Voice, and Loyalty.* "Voice" refers to the use of direct communication to bring actual and desired conditions closer together. It means talking about problems: complaining to the store about a poor product rather than taking business elsewhere; telling the chef that the soup had too much salt; discussing marital problems rather than going directly to the divorce court. In a political context, "voice" refers to participation in the democratic process, through voting, discussion, bargaining, and the like.

The distinction between the two mechanisms is best illustrated by a specific situation —for instance, concern about school quality in a given locality. The exit solution to poor schools would be to move to a different community or to enroll one's children in a private school, thereby "taking one's business elsewhere." The voice solution would involve political action to improve the school system, through school-board elections, Parent Teacher Association meetings, and other direct activities.

In the job market, voice consists of discussing with an employer conditions that ought to be changed, rather than quitting the job. In modern industrial economies, and particularly in large enterprises, a trade union is the vehicle for collective voice—that is, for providing workers as a group with a means of communicating with management.

Collective rather than individual bargaining with an employer is necessary for effective voice at the workplace for two reasons. First, many important aspects of an industrial setting are "public goods," which affect the well-being (negatively or positively) of every employee. As a result, the incentive for any single person to express his preferences, and invest time and money to change conditions (for the good of all), is reduced. Safety conditions, lighting, heating, the speed of a production line, the firm's policies on layoffs, work-sharing, cyclical-wage adjustment, and promotion, its formal grievance procedure and pension plan—all obviously affect the entire workforce in the same way that defense, sanitation, and fire protection affect the entire citizenry. "Externalities" (things done by one individual or firm that also affect the well-being of another, but for which the individual or firm is not compensated or penalized) and "public goods" at the workplace require collective decision-making. Without a collective organization, the incentive for the individual to take into account the effects of his or her actions on others, or express his or her preferences, or invest time and money in changing conditions, is likely to be too small to spur action. Why not "let Harry do it" and enjoy the benefits at no cost? This classic "free-rider" problem lies at the heart of the so-called "union-security" versus "right-to-work" debate.

A second reason collective action is necessary is that workers who are not prepared to exit will be unlikely to reveal their true preferences to their bosses, for fear of some sort of punishment. The essence of the employment relationship under capitalism—as Karl Marx, Ronald Coase, Herbert Simon, and numerous other analysts have recognized—is the exchange of money between employer and employee in return for the employer's control over a certain amount of the worker's time. The employer seeks to use his employee's time in a way that maximizes the value of the output the employee produces. Even in the case of piece rates, employers monitor employee activity to assure the quality of output. As a result, the way in which the time purchased is utilized must be determined by some interaction between workers and their boss. Since the employer can fire a protester, individual protest is dangerous; so a prerequisite for workers' having effective voice in the employment relationship is the protection of activists from being discharged. In the United States this protection is granted in a section of the National Labor Relations Act which states: "It shall be an unfair labor practice for an employer by discrimination in regard to hire or tenure or employment or any term or condition of employment to encourage or discourage membership in any labor organization." Indeed, court interpretation of U.S. labor law makes a sharp distinction between collective and individual actions at the workplace: Workers acting collectively are protected from managerial retaliation, but an individual acting alone is not.

The collective nature of trade unionism fundamentally alters the operation of a labor market and, hence, the nature of the labor contract. In a nonunion setting, where exit and entry are the predominant forms of adjustment, the signals and incentives to firms depend on the preferences of the "marginal" worker, the one who will leave (or be attracted) by particular conditions or changes in conditions. The firm responds primarily to the needs of this marginal, generally younger and more mobile worker and can within some bounds ignore the preferences of "infra-marginal," typically older workers, who—for reasons of skill, knowledge, rights that cannot be readily transferred to other enterprises, as well as because of other costs associated with changing firms—are effectively immobile. In a unionized setting, by contrast, the union takes account of the preferences of *all* workers to form an average preference that typically determines its position at the bargaining table. Because unions are political institutions with elected leaders, they are likely to be responsive to a different set of preferences from those that dominate in a competitive labor market.

In a modern economy, where workers tend to be attached to firms for eight or more years, and where younger and older workers are likely to have different preferences (for instance, regarding pension or health-insurance plans versus take-home pay, or layoffs by inverse seniority versus work-sharing or cuts in wage growth), the change from a marginal to an average calculus is likely to lead to a very different labor contract. When issues involve sizeable fixed costs or "public goods," a calculus based on the average preference can lead to a contract which, ignoring distributional effects, is socially more desirable than one based on the marginal preference—that is, it may even be economically more "efficient."

As a voice institution, unions also fundamentally alter the social relations of the workplace. Perhaps most importantly, a union constitutes a source of worker power in a firm, diluting managerial authority and offering members a measure of due process, in particular through the union innovation of a grievance and arbitration system. While 99 percent of major U.S. collective-bargaining contracts provide for the filing of grievances, and 95 percent provide for arbitration of disputes that are not settled between the parties, relatively few nonunion firms have comparable procedures for settling disagreements between workers and supervisors. More broadly, the entire industrial jurisprudence system—by which many workplace decisions are based on negotiated rules (such as seniority) instead of supervisory judgment (or whim), and are subject to challenge through the grievance/arbitration procedure—represents a major change in the power relations within firms. As a result, in unionized firms workers are more willing and able to express discontent and to object to managerial decisions.

Thus, as a collective alternative to individualistic actions in the market, unions are much more than simple monopolies that raise wages and restrict the competitive adjustment process. Given imperfect information and the existence of public goods in industrial settings, and conflicting interests in the workplace and in the political arena, unionism provides an alternative mechanism for bringing about change. This is not to deny that unions have monopolistic power nor that they use this power to raise wages for a select part of the workforce. The point is that unionism has two "faces," each of which leads to a different view of the institution: One, which is at the fore in economic analysis, is that of a monopoly; the other is that of "a voice institution," i.e., a socio-political institution. To understand fully what unions do in modern industrial economies, it is necessary to examine both faces.

THE RESPONSE TO UNIONS

Another crucial point about unions is that their effects will depend upon the response of management. This was stressed by Sumner H. Slichter, James J. Healy, and E. Robert Livernash in their classic volume, *The Impact of Collective Bargaining on Management*. If management uses the collective-bargaining process to learn about and improve the operation of the workplace and the production process, unionism can be a significant plus that improves managerial efficiency. On the other hand, if management reacts negatively to collective bargaining or is prevented by unions from reorganizing the work process, unionism can have a negative effect on the performance of the firm. The important point is that just as there are two sides to the market, demand and supply, there are two forces determining the economic effects of collective bargaining, managements and unions. The economic impact of bargaining and the nature of industrial relations depend on the policies and actions of both. It is for this reason that we use the two terms "collective voice" and "institutional response" to refer to the second view of unionism under consideration.

The monopoly and collective-voice/institutional-response views of the impact of unionism are strikingly different, as Table 1 demonstrates. While no sophisticated adherent of the monopoly model would deny the voice aspects of unionism, and no industrial-relations expert would gainsay the monopoly effects, the polar dichotomization usefully highlights the facets of unionism stressed by the two views. The monopoly and collective-voice/institutional-response views of unionism in many instances give completely opposite pictures of the institution. According to the former, unions are by nearly all criteria undesirable impediments to the social good; in the latter view, unions have many valuable features that contribute to the functioning of the economy. In the monopoly view, the current dwindling in the percentage of private-sector wage and salary workers who are unionized (from 37 percent in 1958 to 29 percent in 1974) is a desirable development and should be associated with increased productivity and reduced inequality— and thus ought perhaps to be encouraged. From the collective-voice/institutional-response point of view, the

dwindling of private-sector unionization has serious negative economic and social consequences and should be an issue of public concern.

Since, in fact, unions have both monopoly and collective-voice/institutional-response components, the key question for understanding unionism in the United States relates to the relative importance of these two faces. Are unions primarily monopolistic institutions, or are they primarily voice institutions that induce socially beneficial responses? What emphasis should be given to these two extreme views for one to obtain a realistic picture of the role trade unionism plays in the United States?

To answer these important questions, we have studied a wide variety of data that distinguish between union and nonunion establishments and between union and nonunion workers, and we have interviewed representatives of management, labor officials, and industrial-relations experts. Although additional work will certainly alter some of the specifics, our research has yielded several important results which suggest that unions do a great deal more than win monopoly wage gains for their members.

EFFECTS ON EFFICIENCY

In the monopoly view, unions reduce society's output in three ways. First, union-won wage increases cause a misallocation of resources by inducing organized firms to hire fewer workers, to use more capital per worker, and to hire higher quality workers than is socially efficient. Second, union contract provisions—such as limits on the loads that can be handled by workers, restrictions on tasks performed, featherbedding, and so forth—reduce the output that should be forthcoming from a given amount of capital and labor. Third, strikes called to force management to accept union

TABLE 1

Two Views of Trade Unionism (Not Polar)

	Union Effects on Economic Efficiency	*Union Effects on Distribution of Income*	*Social Nature of Union Organization*
Monopoly View	Unions raise wages above competitive levels, which leads to too little labor relative to capital in unionized firms.	Unions increase income inequality by raising the wages of highly skilled workers.	Unions discriminate in rationing positions.
	Union work rules decrease productivity.	Unions create horizontal inequities by creating differentials among comparable workers.	Unions (individually or collectively) fight for their own interests in the political arena.
	Unions lower society's output through frequent strikes.		Union monopoly power breeds corrupt and nondemocratic elements.
Collective-Voice/ Institutional-Response View	Unions have some positive effects on productivity—by reducing quit rates, by inducing management to alter methods of production and adopt more efficient policies, and by improving morale and cooperation among workers.	Unions' standard-rate policies reduce inequality among organized workers in a given company or a given industry.	Unions are political institutions that represent the will of their members.
	Unions collect information about the preferences of all workers, which leads the firm to choose a "better" mix of employee compensation and a "better" set of personnel policies.	Union rules limit the scope for arbitrary actions concerning the promotion, layoff, recall, etc., of individuals.	Unions represent the political interests of lower-income and disadvantaged persons.
	Unions improve the communication between workers and management, leading to better decision-making.	Unionism fundamentally alters the distribution of power between marginal (typically junior) and inframarginal (generally senior) employees, causing union firms to select different compensation packages and personnel practices than nonunion firms.	

demands cause a substantial reduction in gross national product.

By contrast, the collective-voice/institutional-response model directs attention to the important ways in which unionism can raise productivity. First of all, unionism should reduce "quits." As workers' voice increases in an establishment, less reliance need be placed on the exit and entry mechanism to obtain desired working conditions. Since hiring and training costs are lowered and the functioning of work groups is less disrupted when "quit" rates are low, unionism can actually raise efficiency.

The fact that senior workers are likely to be relatively more powerful in enterprises where decisions are based on voice instead of exit and entry points to another way in which unions can raise productivity. Under unionism, promotions and other rewards tend to be less dependent in any precise way on individual performance and more dependent on seniority. As a result, in union plants feelings of rivalry among individuals are likely to be less pronounced than in nonunion plants and the amount of informal training and assistance that workers are willing to provide one another is greater. (The importance of seniority in firms in Japan, together with the permanent employment guaranteed many workers there, have often been cited as factors increasing the productivity of Japanese enterprises.) It is, of course, also important to recognize that seniority can reduce productivity by placing individuals in jobs for which they are not qualified.

Unionism can also raise efficiency by pressuring management into tightening job-production standards and accountability, in an effort to respond to union demands while maintaining profits. Slichter, Healy, and Livernash wrote in 1960, "The challenge that unions presented to management has, if viewed broadly, created superior and better-balanced man-agement, even though some exceptions must be recognized." Their conclusion means that with a unionized workforce management is able to extract more output from a given amount of inputs than is management that is not confronted with a union. This appears to occur largely because modern personnel practices are forced on the firm and traditional paternalism is discarded. Management's ability to make such improvements is a function of the union's cooperation, since the union can perform a helpful role in explaining changes in the day-to-day routine. One recent study supportive of this view reports that while union workers spend more time on formal breaks, they spend *less* time on informal ones and report working harder than nonunion workers.[1]

Finally, under the voice view, the collective bargaining apparatus opens an important communication channel between workers and management, one likely to increase the flow of information between the two, and possibly improve the productivity of the enterprise. As Lloyd G. Reynolds has observed, "Unions can do valuable work by pointing out improvements that perhaps should have been obvious to management but were not, and that, once discovered, can be installed with a net gain to the company as well as the workers."

What does the evidence reveal on these points? Most of the econometric analysis of unions has focused on the question of central concern to the monopoly view: How large is the union wage effect? In his important book,

---

[1] It is important to recognize that productivity gains, from improved methods of management in the face of unionism, run counter to the standard assumption of neoclassical economics that all enterprises operate at peak efficiency. It is, however, consistent with the "satisficing" models of firms developed by the recent Nobel prize winner Herbert Simon and other analysts and with the model of X-inefficiency put forth by Harvey Leibenstein. In these models, firms strive for maximum efficiency only when they are under severe pressure from competitors, unions, or other external forces.

Unionism and Relative Wages, H. Gregg Lewis summarized results of this analysis through the early 1960's, concluding that, while differing over time and across settings, the union wage effect averages on the order of 10 to 15 percent. That is, as a result of collective bargaining. a union member makes about 10 to 15 percent more than an otherwise comparable worker who is not a member. Later work, using larger data files which have information permitting more extensive controls and employing more complex statistical techniques, tends to confirm Lewis's generalization. While unions in some environments raise wages by an enormous amount, the average estimated union wage effect is by no means overwhelming.

As predicted by the monopoly wage model, the capital-labor ratio and average "quality" of labor both appear to be somewhat greater than "optimal" in union settings. However, the total loss in output due to this misallocation of resources appears to be miniscule; an analysis done by Albert Rees suggests that the loss is less than 0.3 percent of the gross national product. For 1975, that would have amounted to $21.00 per person in the U.S. Even this estimate may be too high if one considers the other important and relevant distortions in the economy.

THE EVIDENCE ON QUITS AND PRODUCTIVITY

One of the central tenets of the collective-voice/institutional-response model is that among workers receiving the same pay, unions reduce employee turnover and its associated costs by offering "voice" as an alternative to exit. Our own research, using newly available information on the job changes and employment status of thousands of individuals and industry-level turnover rates, shows that, with diverse factors (including wages) held constant, unionized

workers do have significantly lower quit rates than nonunion workers who are comparable in other respects. As Table 2 shows, the differences between organized and unorganized workers are very large. Moreover, consistent with the claim that unions provide better representation for workers with greater seniority, the evidence suggests a larger reduction in exit and a larger increase in job tenure for older male workers than for younger male workers.

As noted earlier, unionism can affect productivity in ways other than reducing turnover, thus leaving uncertain the net effect of unions on productivity. Traditional analyses of unionism and productivity based on case studies of particular establishments have cited examples in which positive effects dominate and others in which negative effects dominate. By their very nature, however, case studies cannot give a broad quantitative assessment of the net effect of unionism on productivity.

Our analyses of newly available data on unionism and output per worker in many establishments or sectors suggest that the monopoly view of unions as a major deterrrent to productivity is erroneous. In some settings, unionism leads to *higher* productivity, not only because of the greater capital intensity and higher labor quality, but also because of what can best be termed institutional-response factors.

Table 3 summarizes the available estimates of the union productivity effect. The calculations in the table are based on statistical analyses that relate output per worker to unionization, controlling for capital per worker, the skill of workers (in some of the analyses), and other relevant factors. While all of the studies are subject to some statistical problems and thus must be treated cautiously, a general pattern emerges. In manufacturing, productivity in the organized sector appears to be substantially higher than in the unorganized

TABLE 2

Estimates of the Effect of Unionism on Quits and Tenure with Firm*

Sample	Approximate Percentage Amount by Which Quits Are Reduced by Unionism (with wages fixed)	Approximate Percentage Amount by Which Tenure Is Increased·by Unionism (with wages fixed)
All workers (Michigan Panel Study of Income Dynamics)	45%	36%
All workers (May Current Population Surveys, 1973–75)	86	—
Male workers (National Longitudinal Survey)		
Older men (48–62 in 1969)	107	38
Younger men (17–27 in 1969)	11	15
Manufacturing workers (Industry-level Turnover Rates from Bureau of Labor Statistics)	34 to 48	—

Source: Figures are based on multivariate regression analyses reported in R. B. Freeman, "The Exit-Voice Tradeoff in the Labor Market: Unionism, Job Tenure, Quits, and Separations," *Quarterly Journal of Economics,* (June 1980), and in "Why Do Unions Increase Job Tenure?" National Bureau of Economic Research Working Paper.

sector, by an amount that could roughly offset the increase in total costs attributable to higher union wages.

In the typical manufacturing industry, the substantially lower quit rates under collective bargaining can explain about one-fifth of the estimated positive union productivity effect. Kim Clark, in his study of the cement industry, noted that from his discussions with individuals at recently organized plants, it appeared that the entrance of a union was usually followed by major alterations in operations. Interestingly, the enterprise typically changed plant management, suggesting that the union drive was an important signal to top management of ineffective lower-level man-

agement personnel: The drive thus provided valuable information or shock of a distinctive kind. Perhaps most importantly, the discussions with union and management officials in the cement industry indicated that firms often adopted more efficiency-oriented and less paternalistic personnel policies in response to unionism in order to raise productivity and meet higher wage demands.

On the other side of the picture, our analysis (with Marguerite Connerton) of productivity in organized and unorganized underground bituminous coal mines indicates that as industrial relations in the union sector deteriorated in the late 1960's and 1970's, unionism became associated with negative

TABLE 3

Estimates of the Impact of Unionism on Productivity*

Setting	Estimated Increase or Decrease in Output per Worker Due to Unionism
All 2-digit Standard Industrial Classification (SIC) manufacturing industries[a]	20 to 25%
Wooden household furniture[b]	15
Cement[c]	6 to 8
Underground bituminous coal, 1965[d]	25 to 30
Underground bituminous coal, 1975[d]	−20 to −25

[a] From C. Brown and J. Medoff, "Trade Unions in the Production Process," *Journal of Political Economy,* June 1978, pp. 355–378.

[b] From J. Frantz, "The Impact of Trade Unions on Productivity in the Wood Household Furniture Industry," Senior Honors Thesis, Harvard University, March 1976.

[c] From K. Clark, "Unions and Productivity in the Cement Industry," Doctoral Thesis, Harvard University, September 1978.

[d] From R. B. Freeman, J. L. Medoff, and M. Connerton, "Industrial Relations and Productivity; A Study of the U.S. Bituminous Coal Industry," in progress.

*Sources: All calculations are based on the analyses cited above, which control for capital-labor ratios and diverse other factors that may influence productivity.

productivity effects. As the internal problems of the United Mine Workers have grown and the ability of management to deal effectively with labor issues seems to have deteriorated (most likely because the industry's rapid growth has yielded supervisors who are on average younger and less experienced in labor relations than was typical prior to the late 1960's), the factors that lower productivity have come to dominate underground bituminous coal mining. The striking change in the estimated impact of unionism on productivity in this industry during the past decade highlights an important fact: The effects of unionism are not universal constants but rather depend on specific industrial-relations settings. An important, and as yet uncompleted task is to determine the dif-ferential impact of various industrial relations practices on productivity and to discover, as far as is possible, the reasons for these differing impacts.

To repeat, unionism may increase productivity in some settings and decrease it in others. If the increase in productivity is greater than the increase in average unit costs due to the union wage effect, then the profit rate will increase; if not, the rate of profit will fall. There is limited tentative evidence that, on average, net profits are reduced somewhat by unionism, particularly in oligopolistic industries, though there are notable exceptions. At present, there is no definitive accounting of what proportion of the union wage effect comes at the expense of capital, other labor, or consumers, and what portion is offset by previously unexploited possibilities for productivity improvements.

Finally, it is important to note that despite what some critics of unions might claim, strikes do not seem to cost society a substantial amount of goods and services. For the economy as a whole, the percentage of total working time lost directly to strikes during the past two decades has never been greater than 0.5 percent and has averaged about 0.2 percent. Even "national emergency" disputes—those that would be expected to have the largest repercussions on the economy—do not have major deleterious impacts. Though highly publicized, the days idle because of the direct and indirect effects of strikes represent only a miniscule fraction of the total days worked in the U.S. economy.

PERSONNEL PRACTICES AND EMPLOYEE BENEFITS

Under the monopoly view, the exit and entry of workers permits each individual to find a firm offering the mix of employee benefits and personnel policies that he or she prefers. As noted earlier, however, the efficiency of this mechanism breaks down when there are public goods at the workplace and when workers are not able to change firms easily. In the voice view, a union provides management with information at the bargaining table concerning policies affecting its entire membership (e.g., the mix of the employee-compensation package or the firm's employment practices during a downturn) which can be expected to be different from that derived from the movements of marginal workers. It is likely, then, that the package of employee benefits and employment-adjustment policies will be different in firms covered by collective bargaining than in those that are not. To what extent does the mix of goods at the workplace differ between union and nonunion firms?

Data on the remuneration of individual workers and on the expenditures for employees by firms show that the proportion of compensation allotted to fringe benefits is markedly higher for organized blue-collar workers than for similar nonunion workers. Within most industries, important fringes such as pensions, and life, accident, and health insurance are much more likely to be found in unionized establishments. While some of the difference is attributable to the higher wages paid to union workers (since higher-wage workers generally "buy" more fringes), Table 4 reveals that much of the difference is in fact due to the effect of unionism. The table also indicates that the greatest increases in fringes induced by unionism are for deferred compensation, which is generally favored by older, more stable employees. This is consistent with the view that unions are more responsive to senior, less-mobile workers.

Studies concerning workers' preferences for fringes, and managers' awareness of these preferences, provide support for the claim that

TABLE 4

Estimates of the Effect of Unions on Major Fringe Benefits with the Total Compensation of Workers Held Fixed*

Fringe Benefit	Cents per Manhour on Fringes, All Establishments	Percentage of all Establishments with Specified Fringes	Percentage Amount by Which Dollars Per Manhour Spent on Fringes Is Increased or Reduced by Unionism
Total fringes	40.9	—	14%
Life, accident, health insurance	10.1	85.0%	48
Pensions	9.4	62.6	21
Vacation pay	8.3	83.6	19
Holiday pay	5.2	77.8	15
Bonuses	1.8	27.1	−49

*Source: R. B. Freeman, "The Effect of Trade Unionism on Fringe Benefits," National Bureau of Economic Research Working Paper No. 292, October 1978.

a union can provide management with information that affects the composition of the pay package. For instance, Richard Lester's 1967 review of surveys of managerial perceptions of worker preferences found "limited data . . . that workers value benefits more highly compared to wages than employers believe their workers do." Equally important is the apparent role of unions in evaluating the complex costs and prospective advantages of modern fringe benefits and transmitting these facts to their members. It is unlikely that an individual worker will invest the time required to evaluate alternative compensation packages. Unions, however, can hire the lawyers, actuaries, and other experts necessary to perform these analyses.

The fact that many nonunion firms have imitated several of the provisions of union contracts is indicative of the better information available about workers' preferences in union settings. There is no reason for a nonunion firm to copy what union firms do unless union contracts offer forms of compensation that are also preferred by the average nonunion worker, since the satisfaction of the average (not the marginal) is what matters in a union-representation election. It is also important to note that to the extent that non-union firms adopt union-initiated practices, estimates of the impact of unionism on the prevalence of such practices will be understated.

Finally, it should be pointed out that knowledgeable representatives of both labor and management agree that one of the major functions performed by American trade unions is determining a division of the compensation package that will be acceptable to workers. They recognize that some of the most important bargaining under unionism goes on *inside* the union, where the desires of workers with disparate interests are weighed in a political process that decides the union's positions at the bargaining table.

One of the most important personnel decisions made by a firm is how to adjust its employment and wages in response to swings in economic demand: by temporary layoffs, cuts in wage growth, reduced hours, or voluntary attrition. The evidence indicates that the layoff mechanism is used to a much greater extent in unionized than in nonunion establishments. It is important to note, however, that the vast majority of these layoffs are temporary, in that the laid-off members await rehire and are recalled after a short spell of unemployment.

By contrast, evidence on the effect on wages of swings in the demand for products shows that the responsiveness of wage rates is smaller in union than in nonunion firms. For example, within the typical manufacturing industry during the very severe economic downturn from May 1973 to May 1975 the fraction of hourly blue-collar union members unemployed due to layoffs grew more than twice the comparable fraction for otherwise similar nonmembers, but the wages of the unionized workers grew by 18.1 percent versus 16.6 percent for nonunion workers. More generally, analysis of monthly data covering the 1958-to-1975 period for manufacturing industries indicates that the hourly wages of production workers vary with shipments in such a way as to reduce the need for layoffs to a greater extent in firms that are nonunion than in those that are unionized, while there is virtually no such linkage in union settings. These findings reflect the fact that since the late 1950s about two-thirds of the major contract manufacturing workforce has come to be covered by agreements of three years or more, and nearly all have provisions for automatic wage increases.

Why do temporary layoffs dominate alternative adjustment mechanisms to a much greater extent in firms that are unionized than in those that are not? The most reasonable explanation is that under the provisions of most union contracts—which specify that junior workers will be layed off before those with more company service—senior workers, who can be expected to have greater power in organized firms, will generally prefer layoffs over the alternatives.

THE DISTRIBUTION OF INCOME

One of the striking implications of the monopoly view, which runs counter to popular thought, is that union wage gains increase inequality in the labor market. According to the monopoly model, the workers displaced from unionized firms as a result of union wage gains raise the supply of labor to nonunion firms, which can therefore be expected to reduce wages. Thus in the monopoly view unionized workers are likely to be made better off at the expense of nonunion workers. The fact that organized blue-collar workers would tend to be more skilled and higher paid than other blue-collar workers even in the absence of unionism implies further that unionism benefits "labor's elite" at the expense of those with less skill and earning power. Since many people have supported unions in the belief they reduce economic inequality, evidence that unions have the opposite effect would be a strong argument against the union movement.

In fact, the collective-voice/institutional-response model suggests very different effects on equality than does the monopoly view. Given that union decisions are based on a political process, and given that the majority of union members are likely to have earnings below the mean (including white-collar workers) in any workplace, unions can be expected to seek to reduce wage inequality. Union members are also likely to favor a less-dispersed distribution of earnings for reasons of ideology and organizational solidarity. Finally, by its nature, collective bargaining reduces managerial discretion in the wage-setting process, and this should also reduce differences among similarly situated workers.

Two common union wage policies exemplify unions' efforts to reduce economic inequality. The first is the long-standing policy of pushing for "standard rates"—uniform rates for comparable workers across establishments, and for given occupational classes within establishments. While many large nonunion enterprises today also employ formal wage-setting practices, personal differentials based on service, performance, favoritism, or other factors are more common in the nonunion than in the union sector. For example, so-called "merit" plans for wage adjustment appear to be less prevalent in the union sector. In the 1970's, while about 43 percent of all companies offered plant employees "wage adjustment based on a merit plan," only 13 percent of major union contracts mentioned these plans. Overall, according to Slichter, Healy, and Livernash, "the influence of unions has clearly been one of minimizing and eliminating judgment-based differences in pay for individuals employed on the same job" and of "removing ability and performance judgments as a factor in individual pay for job performance." One important potential result of these policies is a reduction of inequality, possibly at the expense of efficiency, which may be lessened because the reward for individual effort is reduced. Another important potential result of this policy is that wage discrimination against minorities is likely to be less in unionized than in nonunionized settings.

Union policies favoring seniority in promotion, and job-posting and bidding systems in which workers are informed about new openings and can bid for promotions, can also be expected to have egalitarian consequences. The possibility that arbitrary supervisory judgments will determine the career of a worker is greatly reduced by the development of formal rules which treat each worker identically.

Thus, according to the monopoly model, trade unionism raises inequality, whereas according to the collective-voice/institutional-response model, it reduces inequality. What are the facts?

Our empirical estimates, based on new data, show that standardization policies have substantially reduced wage inequality, and that this effect dominates the monopoly wage effect. When, for instance, the distribution of earnings for male blue-collar workers is graphed, the results for unionized workers in both the manufacturing and nonmanufacturing sectors show a much narrower distribution, compressed at the extremes and radically peaked in the middle. For nonunion workers, by contrast, the graphs show a much more dispersed pattern of earnings.

In addition to reducing earnings inequality among blue-collar workers, union wage policies contribute to the equalization of wages by decreasing the differential between covered blue-collar workers and uncovered white-collar workers. In manufacturing, though white-collar workers earn an average of 49 percent more than blue-collar workers, our estimates indicate that in unionized enterprises this premium is only 32 percent; in the nonmanufacturing sector, where white-collar workers average 31 percent more in earnings than blue-collar workers, the estimated differential is only 19 percent where there are unions.

But to obtain the net effect of unionism on earnings inequality it is necessary to add the *decrease* in inequality due to wage standardization and the *decrease* due to the reduction in the white-collar/blue-collar differential to the *increase* due to the greater wages of blue-collar union workers. Our calculations show clearly that the *dominant* influence affecting earnings inequality is the standardization of rates within the union sector. As a result of the large reduction in inequality attributable to standard-rate policies, the variance in the natural logarithm of earnings (a common measure of inequality) is reduced by 21 percent in manufacturing and by 27 percent in the nonmanufacturing sector. Since the distribution of income is, as Christopher Jencks and others have shown, relatively stable in the face of dramatic changes in such important social factors as the distribution of schooling, these effects must be considered large. Unionism thus appears to *reduce* wage dispersion in the United States, which implies that the voice/response effects of the institution dominate the monopoly wage effect on this front.

RACE AND UNIONISM

There is a history of conflict between trade-union seniority rules and affirmative-action programs and of discrimination by craft unions. But empirical evidence, as Orley Ashenfelter was first to note, shows clearly that on average, unions aid black workers and reduce differences based on race. Unions affect the distribution of earnings between blacks and whites in at least three ways.

First, because blacks are actually more likely than whites to be union members, they are more likely to benefit from union wage gains. In the 1973-to-1975 period, 30 percent of black workers were organized compared to 24 percent of white workers. The greater degree of organization among blacks reflects the fact that they are overrepresented among blue-collar factory workers and underrepresented among the less organized white-collar workers. (While minorities are still not proportionately represented in some important craft unions, the latest apprenticeship data show that 18.1 percent of apprentices in 1976 were minorities; 9.4 percent of all apprentices were blacks, while

8.7 percent were members of other minority groups.)

Second, unionization reduces discriminatory differences within organized firms through the standard-rate and promotion-by-seniority policies described earlier. While organized black workers make less than organized white workers, the differential is smaller than among unorganized workers. Estimates using data from the 1973 to 1975 May *Current Population Surveys* show that among all unionized blue-collar workers in the private sector, the hourly wage for blacks was about 9 percent lower than for whites. Among comparable nonunion workers, the figure was about 15 percent. Seniority rules, which are often regarded as inimical to the interests of black workers because they conflict with affirmative-action programs, should in the long run be beneficial to blacks. When promotion depends on seniority, discrimination on the basis of race is impeded.

Third, an analysis by Duane Leigh of the effect of unionism on the quit rates of black and white workers shows that, with wages held constant, the turnover of blacks is as much reduced by unions as is the turnover of whites. This implies that the non-wage benefits associated with unionism improve conditions as much for blacks as for whites.

In sum, while there is discrimination in the union sector (as elsewhere in the economy) trade unions raise black earnings relative to white earnings and thus, on the whole, help reduce differences based on race.

THE CORRUPTION ISSUE

Under the monopoly view, the potential to use union monopoly power to raise wages and to extort funds from firms—particularly small, weak firms—fosters a significant amount of corruption and undemocratic behavior in the union movement. Many unions are alleged to be run by bosses or racketeers. But while the monopoly view has been highly publicized, the vast majority of evidence appears to support the voice view that unions generally are democratic political organizations and are responsive to the will of their members.

There are, to begin with, internal and external forces that push unions—both locals and internationals—toward being responsive to the wishes of their members. Union constitutions typically mandate democratic procedures and require conventions or referenda to discern the membership's sentiment on important issues, and fair and frequent elections to assess the members' satisfaction with their leadership. While at one time U.S. labor law dealt only peripherally with the internal workings of unions, the Landrum-Griffin Act of 1959 provides strong federal sanctions against corruption and undemocratic practices inside unions. It contains provisions that require local, intermediate, and international unions to hold elections at fixed, reasonably short intervals, that guarantee members a reasonable opportunity to nominate candidates, run for office, and freely criticize union leaders and their policies, that prohibit incumbents from using union funds to support the election of a given candidate for office in the union and from disseminating propaganda for one candidate without doing as much for his or her opponent, and that require officials to file information on the financial affairs of the union and its leaders and on its constitutional provisions. Moreover, the country's labor law provides an election procedure under which a group of workers can decertify its union and become unorganized, replace one union with another, or attempt to change the boundaries of an existing bargaining unit.

The evidence strongly suggests that the vast majority of local and international unions in the U.S. are quite democratic and suffer only rare breaches of internal democracy. From fiscal years 1965 to 1974, only 239 charges of improper conduct affecting the outcome of a union election were judged to have merit, according to information issued by the Department of Labor. Since approximately 200,000 elections were held by local, intermediate, and international unions during this period, the percentage of elections in which there were proven violations is approximately 0.1 percent. Moreover, it is probably true that in a fair number of these cases the violation was due to ignorance of the details of labor law on the part of union officials rather than to an explicit attempt to affect an election's outcome. And while surely there were some improper actions that were either not reported or not proved, the miniscule number of those which were suggests that number must also have been extremely small.

While many national union leaders tend to remain ensconced in office for years, at the local level a fair number of incumbents regularly get unseated, as would be expected in a well-functioning democracy. One pertinent study by Leon Appelbaum analyzed data on the turnover of union leaders in 94 locals in the Milwaukee, Wisconsin area between 1960 and 1962: 40 percent of the officials in office at the beginning of the period were not in office two years later.

The fact that the majority of members in most unions are satisfied with their union's internal operations is shown by the results of union-decertification elections conducted by the National Labor Relations Board. In each year during the past decade, only about 0.1 percent of all union members were in bargaining units that voted to decertify the union representing them.

Finally, recent surveys of members' views of the internal affairs of their unions indicate that the vast majority are satisfied with union operations. About 70 percent said they had "no problems" with their union in 1972-73, while about 80 percent had no problems in 1969-70. Roughly half of those who had problems in 1972-73 regarded them as "slight" or as "not really a problem at all." In both surveys, less than 10 percent of union members were dissatisfied with how democratically their unions were run, the conduct of their union's leadership, or the officials' policies.

The internal operation of unions aside, the collective-voice/institutional-response analysis stresses the role of unionism in increasing democracy at the workplace by providing workers with a channel for expressing their preferences to management and increasing workers' willingness to complain about undesirable conditions. Evidence from surveys of workers' job satisfaction tends to support this view. In these surveys the reported job satisfaction of unionized workers is less than the reported satisfaction of comparable nonunion workers. However, the union members are also more likely to state that they are "unwilling to change jobs under any circumstance" or "would never consider moving to a new job," than are their "more satisfied" nonunion counterparts. The most direct interpretation of the puzzle is that collective organization provides support that encourages the voicing of dissatisfaction. In contrast to most economic benefits, which increase both utility and stated satisfaction, "voice" increases utility while increasing stated dissatisfaction. In addition, because a union will collect more information than an individual and then disseminate it to every member, though union members know that their jobs are significantly better than the alternatives, they will also know that they are far from ideal. And since voice is also a tool of conflict, good strategists, unlike Voltaire's Pangloss, will not proclaim their workplaces as "the best of all possible worlds."

What about the view that unions are

corrupt institutions? The evidence from the surveys clearly runs counter to this stereotype. Ninety-nine percent of union members in both 1969-70 and 1972-73 stated that they had "no problems" with graft or corruption among their leaders. Moreover, after a careful analysis of the extent of corruption in the American labor movement, Derek Bok and John Dunlop, writing in 1970, stressed the honesty of most labor leaders:

> Although the record in this country compares unfavorably with that of many other nations, legal safeguards now go far to curb dishonesty and encourage democratic behavior. Probably only a tiny fraction of all union officials in America would stoop to serious abuse. The overwhelming majority of labor leaders are honest men who take seriously their obligation to represent the interest of the members who have elected them to office.

Finally, in what ways has organized labor affected outcomes in the American political arena? Have unions had greater success supporting "special-interest" legislation or "social" legislation that benefits lower-income persons and workers in general? Despite the bad press given some union efforts to obtain "special-interest" benefits from lawmakers, much union political muscle has been devoted to promoting legislation that would be of no obvious material gain to unionized workers—except as members of the overall working population. For instance, organized labor was quite active in pushing for the passage of the Public Accommodation Act of 1964, the Voting Rights Act of 1965, equal-employment-opportunity legislation, anti-poverty legislation, and the Occupational Safety and Health Act of 1971.

On the other hand, most union-favored special-interest legislation has failed to pass Congress, though important legislation opposed by unions as detrimental to their power or even their survival has been passed. The last major piece of legislation regulating collective bargaining and unionism, the Landrum-Griffin bill, was enacted in 1959 over the vociferous opposition of unions, while a mild 1977 labor-law-reform bill strongly favored by unions failed to clear the Congress. Typically, only when unions and management in a particular sector have united in favor of legislation to benefit that sector have unions had much success in gaining support for their "special-interest" legislative proposals.

All in all, though unions fight for self-interest legislation—as do other groups in our pluralist society—they have scored their greatest political victories on more general social legislation. In terms of actual outcomes, unions have been more effective as a voice of the whole working population and the disadvantaged than they have been as a monopoly institution seeking to increase its monopoly power.

EXPLAINING MANAGERIAL OPPOSITION

If, in addition to its negative monopoly effects, trade unionism is associated with substantial positive effects on the operation of the economy and on the performance of firms, why do so many U.S. firms oppose unions so vehemently? There are in fact several reasons.

First, the bulk of the economic gains that spring from unionism accrue to workers and not to owners or managers. Managers are unlikely to see any personal benefits in their subordinates' unionization, but are likely to be quite aware of the costs: a diminution of their power, the need to work harder, the loss of operating flexibility, and the like.

Second, though productivity might typically be higher in union than in otherwise comparable nonunion work settings, so too are wages. It would seem, given the objectives and actions of most unions, that the rate of return on capital would be lower under collective bargaining, although there are important exceptions. Thus, there is risk in unionization; the firm may be able to rationalize operations, have good relations with the union, and maintain its profit rate—or it may not. In addition, while the total cost of strikes to society as a whole has been shown to be quite small, the potential cost to a particular firm can be substantial. Since managers—like most other people —dislike taking risks, we would expect opposition to unions even if on average the benefits to firms equal the costs. Moreover, given the wide-ranging differences in the effects of unions on economic performance, at least some managerial opposition surely arises from enterprises in which the expected benefits of collective bargaining are small but the expected costs high. Even the most vocal advocate of the collective-voice/institutional-response view of unionism would admit that, though functional in many industrial settings, unions are not functional in others—and one must expect greater managerial opposition in the latter cases.

Third, management may find unionism expensive, difficult, and very threatening in its initial stages, when modes of operation must be altered if efficiency is to be improved. New and different types of management policies are needed under unionism, and these require either changes in the behavior of current management, or—as appears to be the case in many just-organized firms—a new set of managers.

Finally, U.S. management has generally adopted an ideology of top-down enlightened control, under which unions are seen as both a cause and an effect of managerial failure. In this view, unions interfere with management's efforts to carry out its social function of ensuring that goods and services are produced efficiently. In addition, because unions typically come into existence as a result of management's mistakes in dealing with its workforce, managers frequently resent what unionization implies about their own past performances.

We believe that our analysis of unionism has opened up a host of neglected issues regarding the key worker institution in the American capitalist system. While some of our findings will surely be altered by additional research and some may even be proven wrong, we do believe that our findings present a reasonably valid picture of modern unionism in our country. It stands in sharp contrast to the monopoly view of trade unions and to many popular opinions about them. And if, as we have found, the positive effects of unions are in many settings more important than their negative effects, then the on-going decline of private-sector unionism—a development unique to the U.S. among Western developed countries —deserves serious public attention.

Public Employee Bargaining

In the past two decades, collective bargaining has become important in the public as well as in the private sector—a development that has coincided with an increase in the number of public employees, especially at the state and local levels. Harry Wellington and Ralph Winter analyze the relative merits of collective bargaining in the public and private sectors. They argue that the social cost of collective bargaining is small in the private sector because firms are generally under considerable economic pressure to resist wage demands by unions that would lead to large cost increases. On the other hand, local government officials are said to be under much less economic pressure to resist union demands. Moreover, Wellington and Winter argue that voters (and thus public officials) are concerned primarily with the inconveniences resulting from a strike. Thus the strike is a particularly potent weapon for government employee unions and gives them an unfair advantage over other interest groups with competing claims on municipal government.

This analysis by Wellington and Winter is disputed in the selection by John Burton and Charles Krider, who argue that it may often be more equitable for public employee organizations to pursue their objectives through collective bargaining rather than by lobbying in the political arena. Thus Burton and Krider would allow strikes by most government employees. However, they would still prohibit strikes by policemen and other public employees who provide essential services. For such workers, they agree with Wellington and Winter that disputes must be settled by some nonstrike procedures, such as compulsory arbitration.

The future of public sector bargaining is discussed by Benjamin Aaron. In his view, organization of public employees will continue to increase, but at a greatly reduced rate. He concludes that the admonition to "lower our expectations in an era of limits" is irrelevant to workers demanding a voice in the determination of the terms and conditions of their employment. If government managers stop resisting the concept of collective bargaining, Aaron believes that public employee unions will become more conscious of their responsibilities to the general public.

45

The Limits of Collective Bargaining in Public Employment

Harry H. Wellington and Ralph K. Winter, Jr.

Harry H. Wellington and Ralph K. Winter, Jr., "The Limits of Collective Bargaining in Public Employment," reprinted by permission of The Yale Law Journal Company and Fred B. Rothman & Company
from *The Yale Law Journal*, Vol. 78 (1969), pp. 1111, 1112–24, 1126–27.

THE CLAIMS FOR COLLECTIVE BARGAINING IN THE PRIVATE SECTOR

Those who deny the validity of the claims for collective bargaining in the private sector will surely not find those claims to have merit in the public. We do not intend to debate the merits of these claims. We must, however, if we are fully to test our thesis that a full transplant of collective bargaining to the public sector is inappropriate, presume a minimal validity of the claims that are made for it in the private.

Four claims then, are made for a private-sector collective bargaining. First, it is a way to achieve industrial peace. The point was put as early as 1902 by the Industrial Commission:

The chief advantage which comes from the practice of periodically determining the conditions of labor by collective bargaining directly between employers and employees is that thereby each side obtains a better understanding of the actual state of the industry, of the conditions which confront the other side, and of the motives which influence it. Most strikes and lockouts would not occur if each party understood exactly the position of the other.[1]

Second, collective bargaining is a way of achieving industrial democracy—that is, partici-

[1] *Final Report of the Industrial Commission* (1902), p. 844.

pation by workers in their own governance. It is the industrial counterpart of the contemporary demand for community participation.[2]

Third, unions that bargain collectively with employers represent workers in the political arena as well. And political representation through interest groups is one of the most important types of political representation that the individual can have. Government at all levels acts in large part in response to the demands made upon it by the groups to which its citizens belong.[3]

Fourth, and most important, as a result of a belief in the unequal bargaining power of employers and employees, collective bargaining is claimed to be a needed substitute for individual bargaining.[4] Monopsony—a buyer's mo-

nopoly,[5] in this case a buyer of labor—is alleged to exist in many situations and to create unfair contracts of labor as a result of individual bargaining. While this, in turn, may not mean that workers as a class and over time get significantly less than they should—because monopsony is surely not a general condition but is alleged to exist only in a number of particular circumstances[6]—it may mean that the terms and conditions of employment for an individual or group of workers at a given period of time and in a given circumstances may be unfair. What tends to insure fairness in the aggregate and over the long run is the discipline of the market.[7] But monopsony, if it exists, can work substantial injustice to individuals. Governmental support of collective bargaining represents the nation's response to a belief that such injustice occurs. Fairness between employee and employer in wages, hours, and terms and conditions of employment is thought more

[2] See, for example, testimony of Louis D. Brandeis before the Commission on Industrial Relations, Jan. 23, 1915, S. Doc. No. 415, 64th Cong., 1st Sess. 8, 7657-81 (1916).

[3] See generally H. Wellington, *Labor and the Legal Process* (New Haven: Yale University Press, 1968), pp. 215–38.

[4] See, for example, *Final Report of the Industrial Commission* (1902), p. 800.
It is quite generally recognized that the growth of great aggregations of capital under the control of single groups of men, which is so prominent a feature of the economic development of recent years, necessitates a corresponding aggregation of workingmen into unions, which may be able also to act as units. It is readily perceived that the position of the single workman, face to face with one of our great modern combinations, such as the United States Steel Corporation, is a position of very great weakness. The workman has one thing to sell—his labor. He has perhaps devoted years to the acquirement of a skill which gives his labor power a relatively high value, so long as he is able to put it to use in combination with certain materials and machinery. A single legal person has, to a very great extent, the control of such machinery, and in particular of such materials. Under such conditions there is little competition for the workman's labor. Control of the means of production gives power to dictate to the workingman upon what terms he shall make use of them.

[5] Our use of the term monopsony is not intended to suggest a labor market with a single employer. Rather we mean any market condition in which the terms and conditions of employment are generally below that which would have existed if the employers behaved competitively.

[6] There is by no means agreement that monopsony is a significant factor. For a theoretical discussion, see F. Machlup, *The Political Economy of Monopoly* (Baltimore, Md.: Johns Hopkins University Press, 1952), pp. 333–79; for an empirical study, see R. Bunting, *Employer Concentration in Local Labor Markets* (Chapel Hill, N.C.: University of North Carolina Press, 1962).

[7] See, for example, L. Reynolds, *Labor Economics and Labor Relations*, 3rd ed. (1961), pp. 18–19.
To the extent that monopsonistic conditions exist at any particular time one would expect them to be transitory. For even if we assume a high degree of labor immobility, a low wage level in a labor market will attract outside employers. Over time, therefore, the benefits of monopsony seem to carry with them the seeds of its destruction. But the time may seem a very long time in the life of any individual worker.

likely to be ensured where private ordering takes the collective form.[8]

There are, however, generally recognized social costs resulting from this resort to collectivism.[9] In the private sector these costs are primarily economic, and the question is, given the benefits of collective bargaining as an institution, what is the nature of the economic costs? Economists who have turned their attention to this question are legion, and disagreement among them monumental.[10] The principal concerns are of two intertwined sorts. One is summarized by Professor Albert Rees of Princeton:

> If the union is viewed solely in terms of its effect on the economy, it must in my opinion be considered an obstacle to the optimum performance of our economic system. It alters the wage structure in a way that impedes the growth of employment in sectors of the economy where productivity and income are naturally high and that leaves too much labor in

low-income sectors of the economy like southern agriculture and the least skilled trades. It benefits most those workers who would in any case be relatively well off, and while some of this gain may be at the expense of the owners of capital, most of it must be at the expense of consumers and the lower-paid workers. Unions interfere blatantly with the use of the most productive techniques in some industries, and this effect is probably not offset by the stimulus to higher productivity furnished by some other unions.[11]

The other concern is stated in the 1967 Report of the Council of Economic Advisors:

> Vigorous competition is essential to price stability in a high employment economy. But competitive forces do not and cannot operate with equal strength in every sector of the economy. In industries where the number of competitors is limited, business firms have a substantial measure of discretion in setting prices. In many sectors of the labor market, unions and managements together have a substantial measure of discretion in setting wages. The responsible exercise of discretionary power over wages and prices can help to maintain general price stability. Its irresponsible use can make full employment and price stability incompatible.[12]

And the claim is that this "discretionary power" too often is exercised "irresponsibly."[13]

---

[8] See, for example, Labor-Management Relations Act §I, 29 U.S.C. §151 (1964).

[9] The monopsony justification views collective bargaining as a system of countervailing power—that is, the collective power of the workers countervails the bargaining power of employers. See J. K. Galbraith, *American Capitalism* (1952), p. 121 *et seq.* Accepting the entire line of argument up to this point, however, collective bargaining nevertheless seems a crude device for meeting the monopsony problem, since there is no particular reason to think that collective bargaining will be instituted where there is monopsony (or that it is more likely to be instituted there). In some circumstances collective bargaining may even raise wages above a "competitive" level. On the other hand, the collective bargaining approach is no cruder than the law's general response to perceived unfairness in the application of the freedom of contract doctrine. See H. Wellington, *supra* note 3, at 26–38.

[10] Compare, for example, Simons, "Some Reflections on Syndicalism," *J. of Pol. Econ.,* 52 (1944), p. 1, with, for example, Lester, "Reflections on the 'Labor Monopoly' Issue," *J. of Pol. Econ.,* 55 (1947), p. 513.

[11] A. Rees, *The Economics of Trade Unions* (Chicago: University of Chicago Press, 1962), pp. 194–95.

[12] Council of Econ. Advisors, *1967 Annual Report* (Washington, D.C.: U.S. Government Printing Office, 1967), p. 119.

[13] See ibid. at 119–34. See generally J. Sheahan, *The Wage-Price Guideposts* (Washington, D.C.: The Brookings Institution, 1967).

Disagreement among economists extends to the quantity as well as to the fact of economic malfunctioning that properly is attributable to collective bargaining.[14] But there is no disagreement that at some point the market disciplines or delimits union power. As we shall see in more detail below, union power is frequently constrained by the fact that consumers react to a relative increase in the price of a product by purchasing less of it. As a result any significant real financial benefit, beyond that justified by an increase in productivity, which accrues to workers through collective bargaining, may well cause significant unemployment among union members. Because of this employment-benefit relationship, the economic costs imposed by collective bargaining as it presently exists in the private sector seem inherently limited.[15]

THE CLAIMS FOR COLLECTIVE BARGAINING IN THE PUBLIC SECTOR

In the area of public employment the claims upon public policy made by the need for industrial peace, industrial democracy and effective political representation point toward collective bargaining. This is to say that three of the four arguments that support bargaining in the private sector—to some extent, at least—press for similar arrangements in the public sector.

Government is a growth industry, particularly state and municipal government. While federal employment between 1963 and 1968 has increased from 2.36 million to 2.73 million, state and local employment has risen from 6.87 to 9.42 million,[16] and the increase continues apace. With size comes bureaucracy, and with bureaucracy comes the isolation and alienation of the individual worker. His manhood, like that of his industrial counterpart, is threatened. Lengthening chains of command necessarily depersonalize the employment relationship and contribute to a sense of powerlessness on the part of the worker. If he is to share in the governance of his employment relationship as he does in the private sector, it must be through the device of representation, which means unionization.[17] Accordingly, just as the increase in the size of economic units in private industry fostered unionism, so the enlarging of governmental bureaucracy has encouraged public employees to look to collective action for a sense of control over their employment destiny. The number of government employees, moreover, makes it plain that those employees are members of an interest group which can organize for political representation as well as for job participation.[18]

The pressures thus generated by size and bureaucracy lead inescapably to disruption—to labor unrest—unless these pressures are recognized and unless existing decision-making procedures are accommodated to them. Peace in government employment too, the argument runs, can best be established by making union recognition and collective bargaining accepted public policy.[19]

[14] See, for example, H. G. Lewis, *Unionism and Relative Wages in the United States* (Chicago: University of Chicago Press, 1963), and earlier studies discussed therein.

[15] See generally J. Dunlop, *Wage Determination under Trade Unions* (New York: Macmillan, 1944), pp. 28–44; M. Friedman, "Some Comments on the Significance of Labor Unions for Economic Policy," in *The Impact of the Union*, ed. D. Wright (New York: Harcourt Brace Jovanovich, 1951), p. 204

[16] *Labor Relations Yearbook–1968*, (1969), p. 451.

[17] See *Final Report of the Industrial Commission* (1902), p. 805; Summers, "American Legislation for Union Democracy," *Mod. L. Rev.*, 25 (1962), pp. 273, 275.

[18] For the "early" history, see S. Spero, *Government as Employer* (New York: Remser Press, 1948).

[19] See, for example, *Governor's Committee on Public Employee Relations, Final Report* (State of N.Y., 1966), p. 9.

Much less clearly analogous to the private model, however, is the unequal bargaining power argument. In the private sector that argument really has two aspects. The first, which we have just adumbrated, is affirmative in nature. Monopsony is believed sometimes to result in unfair individual contracts of employment. The unfairness may be reflected in wages, which are less than they would be if the market were more nearly perfect, or in working arrangements which may lodge arbitrary power in a foreman, i.e., power to hire, fire, promote, assign or discipline without respect to substantive or procedural rules. A persistent assertion, generating much heat, relates to the arbitrary exercise of managerial power in individual cases. This assertion goes far to explain the insistence of unions on the establishment in the labor contract of rules, with an accompanying adjudicatory procedure, to govern industrial life.[20]

Judgments about the fairness of the financial terms of the public employee's individual contract of employment are even harder to make than for private sector workers. The case for the existence of private employer monopsony, disputed as it is, asserts only that some private sector employers in some circumstances have too much bargaining power. In the public sector, the case to be proven is that the governmental employer ever has such power. But even if this case could be proven, market norms are at best attenuated guides to question fairness. In employment as in all other areas, governmental decisions are properly political decisions, and economic considerations are but one criterion among many. Questions of fairness do not centrally relate to how much imperfection one sees in the market, but more to how much imperfection one sees in the political process.

"Low" pay for teachers may be merely a decision—right or wrong, resulting from the pressure of special interests or from a desire to promote the general welfare—to exchange a reduction in the quality or quantity of teachers for higher welfare payments, a domed stadium, etc. And we are limited in our ability to make informed judgments about such political decisions because of the understandable but unfortunate fact that the science of politics has failed to supply us with either as elegant or as reliable a theoretical model as has its sister discipline.

Nevertheless, employment benefits in the public sector may have improved relatively more slowly than in the private sector during the last three decades. An economy with a persistent inflationary bias probably works to the disadvantage of those who must rely on legislation for wage adjustments.[21] Moreover, while public employment was once attractive for the greater job security and retirement benefits it provided, quite similar protection is now available in many areas of the private sector.[22] On the other hand, to the extent that civil service, or merit, systems exist in public employment and these laws are obeyed, the arbitrary exercise of managerial power if substantially reduced. Where it is reduced, a labor policy that relies on the individual employment contract must seem less unacceptable.

The second, or negative aspect of the unequal bargaining power argument, relates to the social costs of collective bargaining. As we have seen, the social costs of collective bargaining in

---

[20] See, for example, N. Chamberlain, *The Union Challenge to Management Control* (New York: Harper & Row, 1948), p. 94.

[21] This is surely one reason which might explain the widely assumed fact that public employees have fallen behind their private sector counterparts. See Stieber, "Collective Bargaining in the Public Sector," in *Challenges to Collective Bargaining*, ed. L. Ulman (Englewood Cliffs, N.J.: Prentice-Hall, Inc., 1967), pp. 65, 69.

[22] See Taylor, "Public Employment: Strike or Procedures," *Ind. & Lab. Rel. Rev.*, 20 (1967), pp. 617, 623–25.

the private sector are principally economic, and seem inherently limited by market forces. In the public sector, however, the costs seem to us economic only in a very narrow sense and are on the whole political. It further seems to us that, to the extent union power is delimited by market or other forces in the public sector, these constraints do not come into play nearly as quickly as in the private. An understanding of why this is so requires further comparison between collective bargaining in the two sectors.

THE PRIVATE SECTOR MODEL

While the private sector is, of course, extraordinarily diverse, the paradigm case is an industry which produces a product that is not particularly essential to those who buy it and for which dissimilar products can be substituted. Within the market or markets for this product, most—but not all—of the producers must bargain with a union representing their employees, and this union is generally the same through the industry. A price rise of this product relative to others will result in a decrease in the number of units of the product sold. This in turn will result in a cutback in employment. And an increase in price would be dictated by an increase in labor cost relative to output, at least in most situations.[23] Thus, the union is faced with some sort of rough trade-off between, on the one hand, larger benefits for some employees and unemployment for others, and on the other hand, smaller benefits and more employment. Because unions are political

organizations, with a legal duty to represent *all* employees fairly,[24] and with a treasury that comes from per capita dues, there is pressure on the union to avoid the road that leads to unemployment.[25]

This picture of the restraints that the market imposes on collective bargaining settlements undergoes change as the variables change. On the one hand, to the extent that there are non-union firms within a product market, the impact of union pressure will be diminished by the ability of consumers to purchase identical products from non-union and, presumably, less expensive sources. On the other hand, to the extent that union organization of competitors within the product market is complete, there will be no such restraint and the principal barriers to union bargaining goals will be the ability of a number of consumers to react to a price change by turning to dissimilar but nevertheless substitutable products.

Two additional variables must be noted. First, where the demand for an industry's product is rather insensitive to price—i.e., relatively inelastic—and where all the firms in a product market are organized, the union need fear less the employment-benefit trade-off, for the employer is less concerned about raising prices in response to increased costs. By hypothesis, a price rise affects unit sales of such an employer only minimally. Second, in an expanding industry, wage settlements which exceed increases in productivity may not reduce union employment. They will reduce expansion, hence the employment effect will be experienced only by workers who do not belong to the union. This

---

[23] The cost increase may, of course, take some time to work through and appear as a price increase. See A. Rees, *The Economics of Trade Unions*, pp. 107–9. In some oligopolistic situations the firm may be able to raise prices after a wage increase without suffering a significant decrease in sales.

[24] *Steele* v. *Louisville & N.R.R.*, 323 U.S. 192 (1944).

[25] The pressure is sometimes resisted. Indeed, the United Mine Workers has chosen more benefits for less employment. See generally M. Baratz, *The Union and the Coal Industry* (New Haven: Yale University Press, 1955).

means that in the short run the politics of the employment-benefit trade-off do not restrain the union in its bargaining demands.

In both of these cases, however, there are at least two restraints on the union. One is the employer's increased incentive to substitute machines for labor, a factor present in the paradigm case and all other cases as well. The other restraint stems from the fact that large sections of the nation are unorganized and highly resistant to unionization.[26] Accordingly, capital will seek non-union labor, and in this way the market will discipline the organized sector.

The employer, in the paradigm case and in all variations of it, is motivated primarily by the necessity to maximize profits (and this is so no matter how political a corporation may seem to be). He therefore is not inclined (absent an increase in demand for his product) to raise prices and thereby suffer a loss in profits, and he is organized to transmit and represent the market pressures described above. Generally he will resist, and resist hard, union demands that exceed increases in productivity, for if he accepts such demands he may be forced to raise prices. Should he be unsuccessful in his resistance too often, and should it cost him too much, he can be expected to put his money and energy elsewhere.[27]

What all this means is that the social costs imposed by collective bargaining are economic costs; that usually they are limited by powerful market restraints; and that these restraints are visible to anyone who is able to see the forest for the trees.[28]

THE PUBLIC SECTOR MODEL

The paradigm case in the public sector is a municipality with an elected board of aldermen, and an elected mayor who bargains (through others) with unions representing the employees of the city. He bargains also, of course, with other permanent and *ad hoc* interest groups making claims upon government (business groups, save-the-park committees, neighborhood groups, etc.). Indeed, the decisions that are made may be thought of roughly as a result of interactions and accommodations among these interest groups, as influenced by perceptions about the attitudes of the electorate, and by the goals and programs of the mayor and his aldermanic board.[29]

Decisions that cost the city money are generally paid for from taxes and, less often, by borrowing. Not only are there many types of taxes, but also there are several layers of government which may make tax revenue available to the city; federal and state as well as local funds may be employed for some purposes. Formal allocation of money for particular uses is made through the city's budget, which may have within it considerable room for adjustments.[30] Thus, a union will bargain hard for as

---

[26] See "Trends and Changes in Union Membership," *Monthly Lab. Rev.*, 89 (1966), pp. 510–13; Bernstein, "The Growth of American Unions 1945–1960," *Lab. Hist.*, 2 (1961), p. 131.

[27] And the law would protect him in this. Indeed, it would protect him if he were moved by an anti-union animus as well as by valid economic considerations. See *Textile Workers Union* v. *Darlington Mfg. Co.*, 380 U.S. 263 (1965).

Of course, where fixed costs are large relative to variable costs, it may be difficult for an employer to extricate himself.

[28] This does not mean, of course, that collective bargaining in the private sector is free of social costs. It means only that the costs are necessarily limited by the discipline of the market.

[29] See generally R. Dahl, *Who Governs? Democracy and Power in an American City* (New Haven: Yale University Press, 1961). On interest theory generally, see D. Truman, *The Governmental Process* (1955).

[30] See, for example, W. Sayre and H. Kaufman, *Governing New York City* (1960), pp. 366–72.

large a share of the budget as it thinks it possibly can obtain, and beyond this to force a tax increase if it deems that possible.

In the public sector too, the market operates. In the long run, the supply of labor is a function of the price paid for labor by the public employer relative to what workers earn elsewhere.[31] This is some assurance that public employees in the aggregate—with or without collective bargaining—are not paid too little. The case for employer monopsony, moreover may be much weaker in the public sector than it is in the private. First, to the extent that most public employees work in urban areas, as they probably do, there may often be a number of substitutable and competing private and public employers in the labor market. When that is the case, there can be little monopsony power.[32] Second, even if public employers occasionally have monopsony power, governmental policy is determined only in part by economic criteria, and there is no assurance, as there is in the private sector where the profit motive prevails, that the power will be exploited.

As we have seen, market-imposed unemployment is an important restraint on unions in the private sector. In the public sector, the trade-off between benefits and employment seems much less important. Government does not generally sell a product the demand for which is closely related to price. There usually are not close substitutes for the products and services provided by government and the demand for them is inelastic. Such market conditions are, as we have seen, favorable to unions in the private sector because they permit the acquisition of benefits without the penalty of unemployment, subject to the restraint of non-union competitors, actual or potential. But no such restraint limits the demands of public employee unions. Because much government activity is, and must be, a monopoly, product competition, non-union or otherwise, does not exert a downward pressure on prices and wages. Nor will the existence of a pool of labor ready to work for a wage below union scale attract new capital and create a new, and competitively less expensive, governmental enterprise. The fear of unemployment, however, can serve as something of a restraining force in two situations. First, if the cost of labor increases, the city may reduce the quality of the service it furnishes by reducing employment. For example, if teachers' salaries are increased, it may decrease the number of teachers and increase class size. However, the ability of city government to accomplish such a change is limited not only by union pressure, but also by the pressure of other affected interest groups in the community.[33] Political considerations, therefore, may cause either no reduction in employment or services, or a reduction in an area other than that in which the union members work. Both the political power exerted by the beneficiaries of the services, who are also voters, and the power of the public employee union as a labor organization, then, combine to create great pressure on political leaders either to seek new funds or to reduce municipal services of another kind. Second, if labor costs increase, the city may, even as a private employer would, seek to replace labor with machines. The absence of a profit motive, and a political concern for unemployment, however, may be a deter-

[31] *Cf.*,M. Moskow, *Teachers and Unions* (Philadelphia: University of Pennsylvania, Industrial Relations Unit, 1966), pp. 79–86.

[32] This is based on the reasonable but not unchallengeable assumption that the number of significant employers in a labor market is related to the existence of monopsony. See R. Bunting, *Employer Concentration in Local Labor Markets* (Chapel Hill, N.C.: University of North Carolina Press, 1962), pp. 3–14. The greater the number of such employers in a labor market, the greater the departure from the classic case of the monopsony of the single employer. The number of employers would clearly seem to affect their ability to make and enforce a collusive wage agreement.

[33] Organized parent groups, for example.

rent in addition to the deterrent of union resistance. The public employer which decides it must limit employment because of unit labor costs will likely find that the politically easiest decision is to restrict new hires, rather than to lay off current employees.

Even if we are right that a close relationship between increased economic benefits and unemployment does not exist as a significant deterrent to unions in the public sector, might not the argument be made that in some sense the taxpayer is the public sector's functional equivalent of the consumer? If taxes become too high, the taxpayer can move to another community. While it is generally much easier for a consumer to substitute products than for a taxpayer to substitute communities, is it not fair to say that, at the point at which a tax increase will cause so many taxpayers to move that it will produce less total revenue, the market disciplines or restrains union and public employer in the same way and for the same reasons that the market disciplines parties in the private sector? Moreover, does not the analogy to the private sector suggest that it is legitimate in an economic sense for unions to push government to the point of substitutability?

Several factors suggest that the answer to this latter question is at best indeterminate, and that the question of legitimacy must be judged not by economic, but by political criteria.

In the first place, there is no theoretical reason—economic or political—to suppose that it is desirable for a governmental entity to liquidate its taxing power, to tax up to the point where another tax increase will produce less revenue because of the number of people it drives to different communities. In the private area, profit maximization is a complex concept, but its approximation generally is both a legal requirement and socially useful as a means of allocating resources.[34] The liquidation of tax-

ing power seems neither imperative nor useful.

Second, consider the complexity of the tax structure and the way in which different kinds of taxes (property, sales, income) fall differently upon a given population. Consider, moreover, that the taxing authority of a particular governmental entity may be limited (a municipality may not have the power to impose an income tax). What is necessarily involved, then, is principally the redistribution of income by government rather than source allocation,[35] and questions of income redistribution surely are essentially political questions.[36]

For his part, the mayor in our paradigm case will be disciplined not by a desire to maximize profits, but by a desire—in some cases at least—to do a good job (to effectuate his programs), and in virtually all cases either to be reelected or to move to a better elective office. What he gives to the union must be taken from some other interest group or from taxpayers. His is the job of coordinating these competing claims while remaining politically viable. And that coordination will be governed by the relative power of the competing interest groups. Our inquiry, therefore, must turn to the question of how much power public employee unions will exercise if the full private model of collective bargaining is adopted in the public sector.

[34] See generally R. Dorfman, *Prices and Markets* (Englewood Cliffs, N.J.: Prentice-Hall, Inc., 1967).

[35] In the private sector what is involved is principally resource allocation rather than income redistribution. Income redistribution occurs to the extent that unions are able to increase wages at the expense of profits, but the extent to which this actually happens would seem to be limited. It also occurs to the extent that unions, by limiting employment in the union sector through maintenance of wages above a competitive level, increase the supply of labor in the non-union sector and thereby depress wages there.

[36] In the private sector the political question was answered when the National Labor Relations Act was passed: the benefits of collective bargaining (with the strike) outweigh the social costs.

PUBLIC EMPLOYEE STRIKES
AND THE POLITICAL PROCESS

Although the market does not discipline the union in the public sector to the extent that it does in the private, the paradigm case, nevertheless, would seem to be consistent with what Robert A. Dahl has called the " 'normal' American political process," which is "one in which there is a high probability that an active and legitimate group in the population can make itself heard effectively at some crucial stage in the process of decision,"[37] for the union may be seen as little more than an "active and legitimate group in the population." With elections in the background to perform, as Mr. Dahl tells us, "the critical role . . . in maximizing political equality and popular sovereignty,"[38] all seems well, at least theoretically, with collective bargaining and public employment.

But there is trouble even in the house of theory if collective bargaining in the public sector means what it does in the private. The trouble is that if unions are able to withhold labor—to strike—as well as to employ the usual methods of political pressure, they may possess a disproportionate share of effective power in the process of decision. Collective bargaining would then be so effective a pressure as to skew the results of the " 'normal' American political process."

One should straightway make plain that the strike issue is not *simply* the essentiality of public services as contrasted with services or products produced in the private sector. This is only half of the issue, and in the past the half truth has beclouded analysis.[39] The services performed by a private transit authority are neither less nor more essential to the public than those that would be performed if the transit authority were owned by a municipality. A railroad or a dock strike may be much more damaging to a community than "job action" by teachers. This is not to say that governmental services are not essential. They are, both because the demand for them is inelastic and because their disruption may seriously injure a city's economy and occasionally the physical welfare of its citizens. Nevertheless, essentiality of governmental services is only a necessary part of, rather than a complete answer to, the question: What is wrong with strikes in public employment?

What is wrong with strikes in public employment is that because they disrupt essential services, a large part of a mayor's political constituency will press for a quick end to the strike with little concern for the cost of settlement. The problem is that because market restraints are attenuated and because public employee strikes cause inconvenience to voters, such strikes too often succeed. Since other interest groups with conflicting claims on municipal government do not, as a general proposition, have anything approaching the effectiveness of this union technique—or at least cannot maintain this relative degree of power over the long run—they are put at a significant competitive disadvantage in the political process. Where this is the case, it must be said that the political process has been radically altered. And because of the deceptive simplicity of the analogy to collective bargaining in the private sector, the alteration may take place without anyone realizing what has happened.

Therefore, while the purpose and effect of strikes by public employees may seem in the beginning merely designed to establish collective bargaining or to "catch up" with wages and fringe benefits in the private sector, in the long run strikes must be seen as a means to redistribute income, or, put another way, to gain a

---

[37] R. Dahl, *A Preface to Democratic Theory* (New Haven: Yale University Press, 1956), p. 145.

[38] *Ibid.*

[39] See, for example, S. Spero, *Government as Employer*, pp. 1–15.

subsidy for union members,[40] not through the employment of the usual types of political pressure, but through the employment of what might appropriately be called political force....

While there is increasing advocacy for expanding the scope of bargaining in public employment and in favor of giving public employees the right to strike—advocacy not just by unionists but by disinterested experts as well[41]—the law generally limits the scope of bargaining and forbids strikes. This is often done with little attention to supporting reasons. Ours has been an attempt to supply these reasons....

In the future, if strikes are to be barred, sophisticated impasse procedures must be established. If, on the other hand, some strikes are to be tolerated, changes in the political structure which will make the municipal employer less vulnerable to work stoppages must be developed....

---

[40] Strikes in some areas of the private sector may have this effect, too. See note 29 *supra*. The difference in the impact of collective bargaining in the two sectors should be seen as a continuum. Thus, for example, it may be that market restraints do not sufficiently discipline strike settlements in some regulated industries, or in industries that rely mainly on government contracts. If this is so—and we do not know that it is—perhaps there should be tighter restraints on the use of the strike in those areas.

[41] See, for example, Wollett, "The Taylor Law and the Strike Ban," in *Public Employee Organization and Bargaining*, ed. H. Anderson (Washington, D.C.: Bureau of National Affairs, 1968), p. 29.

46

The Role and Consequences of Strikes by Public Employees

John F. Burton, Jr. and Charles Krider

John F. Burton, Jr., and Charles Krider, "The Role and Consequences of Strikes by Public Employees," reprinted by permission of The Yale Law Journal Company and Fred B. Rothman & Company from *The Yale Law Journal*, Vol. 79 (1970).

Reason is the life of the law.

Sir Edward Coke

The life of the law has not been logic: it has been experience.

Oliver Wendell Holmes

The vexing problem of strikes by public employees has generated a number of assertions based largely on logical analysis. One common theme is that strikes fulfill a useful function in the private sector, but are inappropriate in the public sector, because they distort the political decision-making process. Another is that strikes in nonessential government services should not be permitted because it is administratively infeasible to distinquish among the various government services on the basis of

their essentiality. The present article attempts to evaluate these assertions in terms of labor relations experience at the local level of government. . . .

THE ROLE OF STRIKES IN THE PRIVATE SECTOR

Wellington and Winter have catalogued four claims which are made to justify collective bargaining in the private sector.[1] First, collective bargaining is a way to achieve industrial peace.

[1] Wellington and Winter, "The Limits of Collective Bargaining in Public Employment," *Yale Law Journal*, 78 (1969), pp. 1112–13. Hereinafter cited as Wellington and Winter.

Second, it is a way of achieving industrial democracy. Third, unions that bargain collectively with employers also represent workers in the political arena. Fourth, and in their view the most important reason, collective bargaining compensates for the unequal bargaining power which is believed to result from individual bargaining. Wellington and Winter recognize that the gains to employees from collective bargaining, such as protection from monopsony power, are to be balanced against the social costs resulting from the resort to collectivism, such as distortion of the wage structure. While noting that considerable disagreement exists among economists concerning the extent of the benefits and costs, they stress the fact that costs are limited by economic constraints. Unions can displace their members from jobs by ignoring the discipline of the market. These four justifications for private sector collective bargaining are presumably relevant to some degree whether or not strikes are permitted. Nonetheless, one can conceptualize two models of collective bargaining—the Strike Model, which would normally treat strikes as legal, and the No-Strike Model, which would make all strikes illegal—and evaluate whether, in terms of the above justifications, society benefits from permitting strikes. . . .

Use of the Strike Model instead of the No-Strike Model appears to enhance all but the third of the four claims for private sector collective bargaining offered by Wellington and Winter.[2] While they do not provide a claim by

claim analysis of the consequences of permitting strikes, their endorsement of strikes in the private sector must indicate that they believe the Strike Model preferable to the No-Strike Model. . . .

CONSEQUENCES OF STRIKES IN THE PUBLIC SECTOR

The best procedure for evaluating public sector strikes would be to investigate the respective impacts of the Strike Model and the No-Strike Model on each of the claims made for collective bargaining. Such an analysis should consider the economic, political, and social effects produced. An inquiry into these effects is particularly important since several authors who have implicitly endorsed the Strike Model in the private sector have done so more on the basis of noneconomic reasons than economic reasons.[3] Nonetheless, the attack on the Strike Model in the *public* sector has been based largely on the evaluation of the fourth claim for collective bargaining, that relating to unequal bargaining power. We will attempt to meet this attack by confining our discussion to the economic consequences of collective bargaining with and without strikes.

Even an examination confined to economic consequences is difficult. The most desirable economic data, which would measure the impact of unions on wages and other benefits, are unavailable. Our approach will be to review carefully the various steps in the analytical model developed by Wellington and Winter

---

[2] The first reason offered—it is a way to achieve industrial peace—appears to be inconsistent with the notion of permitting strikes as a method of increasing the employees' bargaining power. One possible resolution of this apparent contradiction is that the enhanced bargaining power of the employees will enable them to work out mutually satisfactory terms with their employer without having to resort to the strike, while workers with limited bargaining power will often engage in strikes as an expression of their futility. This explanation is not totally compelling, however, and one may therefore have to justify

collective bargaining among parties with equal power on grounds other than the diminution of strikes. The favorable consequences of the last three claims offered by Wellington and Winter for private sector collective bargaining presumably offset any possible increase in strikes.

[3] A. Rees, *The Economics of Trade Unions* (Chicago: University of Chicago Press, 1962), pp. 194–97.

by which they arrive at the notion of sovereignty. If we find that the evidence available on public sector strikes contradicts this model, we shall conclude that the differential assessment they provide for public and private strikes is unwarranted.

Benefits of Collective Bargaining

Wellington and Winter believe the benefits of collective action, including strikes, are less in the public sector than in the private sector since (1) the problem of employer monopsony is less serious, and (2) any use of monopsony power in the public sector which results in certain groups, such as teachers, receiving low pay may reflect, not a misallocation of resources, but rather a political determination of the desired use of resources.

Wellington and Winter assert that employer monopsony is less likely to exist or be used in the public than in the private sector.[4] But as they concede,[5] referring to Bunting, monopsony is not widespread in the private sector and, except in a few instances, cannot be used as a rationale for trade unions. They provide no evidence that monopsony is less prevalent in the public than in the private sector. Moreover, other labor market inefficiencies, common to the public and private sectors, are probably more important than monopsony in providing an economic justification for unions. For example, the deficiencies of labor market information are to some extent overcome by union activities,[6] and there is no reason to assume that this benefit differs between the public and private sectors.

Assuming there is monopsony power, Wellington and Winter believe that collective bargaining in the private sector can eliminate unfair wages "which are less than they would be if the market were more nearly perfect."[7] They assert, however, that low pay for an occupation in the public sector may reflect a political judgment which ought not to be countered by pressures resulting from a strike. To say, however, that the pay for an occupation would be higher if the employees had the right to strike than if they did not is not independent proof that strikes are inappropriate. The same criticism could be made of any activity by a public employee group which affects its pay. An independent rationale must be provided to explain why some means which are effective in raising wages (strikes) are inappropriate while other means which are also effective (lobbying) are appropriate. Whether the Wellington and Winter discussion of the politically based decision-making model for the public sector provides this rationale will be discussed in more detail subsequently.

Costs of Collective Bargaining

Wellington and Winter's discussion of the cost of substituting collective for individual bargaining in the public sector includes a chain of causation which runs from (1) an allegation that market restraints are weak in the public

---

[4] Wellington and Winter, "The Limits of Collective Bargaining in Public Employment," p. 1120.

[5] *Ibid.* p. 1113.

[6] "Under purely competitive conditions, it is assumed that perfect knowledge of existing wage rates in other firms, regions, and occupations, and mobility

of both labor and capital would tend to eradicate unnecessary wage differentials (i.e., differentials which did not truly reflect the marginal productivity of labor). Both knowledge and mobility, however, are very imperfect in the real market. The existence of trade unions to a large extent compensates for the lack of knowledge and represents a force tending toward wage standardization for similar work." A. Carter and F. Marshall, *Labor Economics: Wages, Employment, and Trade Unionism* (Homewood, Ill.: Richard D. Irwin, 1967), pp. 324–25.

[7] Wellington and Winter, "The Limits of Collective Bargaining in Public Employment," p. 1116.

sector, largely because the services are essential; to (2) an assertion that the public puts pressure on civic officials to arrive at a quick settlement; to (3) a statement that other pressure groups have no weapons comparable to a strike; to (4) a conclusion that the strike thus imposes a cost since the political process is distorted.

Let us discuss these steps in order:

Market restraint. A key argument in the case for the inappropriateness of public sector strikes is that economic constraints are not present to any meaningful degree in the public sector.[8] This argument is not entirely convincing. First, wages lost due to strikes are as important to public employees as they are to employees in the private sector. Second, the public's concern over increasing tax rates may prevent the decision-making process from being dominated by political instead of economic considerations. The development of multilateral bargaining in the public sector is an example of how the concern over taxes may result in a close substitute for market constraints.[9] In San Francisco, for example, the Chamber of Commerce has participated in negotiations between the city and public employee unions and has had some success in limiting the economic gains of the unions. A third and related economic constraint arises for such services as water sewage and, in some instances, sanitation, where explicit prices are charged. Even if representatives of groups other than employees and the employer do not enter the bargaining process, both union and local government are aware of the economic implications of bargaining which leads to higher prices which are clearly visible to the public. A fourth economic constraint on employees exists in those services where subcontracting to the private sector is a realistic alternative.[10] Warren, Michigan, resolved a bargaining impasse with an American Federation of State, County and Municipal Employees (AFSCME) local by subcontracting its entire sanitation service; Santa Monica, California, ended a strike of city employees by threatening to subcontract its sanitation operations. If the subcontracting option is preserved, wages in the public sector need not exceed the rate at which subcontracting becomes a realistic alternative.

An aspect of the lack-of-market-restraints argument is that public services are essential. Even at the analytical level, Wellington and Winter's case for essentiality is not convincing. They argue:

> The Services performed by a private transit authority are neither less nor more essential to the public than those that would be performed if the transit authority were owned by a municipality. A railroad or a dock strike may be much more damaging to a community than "job action" by teachers. This is not to say that government services are not essential. They are both because they may seriously injure a city's economy and occasionally the physical welfare of its citizens.[11]

---

[8] "It further seems to us that, to the extent union power is delimited by market or other forces in the public sector, these constraints do not come into play nearly as quickly as in the private." Wellington and Winter, *ibid.*, p. 1117.

[9] McLennan and Moskow, "Multilateral Bargaining in the Public Sector," *Ind. Rel. Res. Assn. Proceedings*, 21 (1968), p. 31.

[10] The subcontracting option is realistic in functions such as sanitation and street or highway repairs, and some white-collar occupations. Several other functions, including hospitals and education, may be transferred entirely to the private sector. The ultimate response by government is to terminate the service, at least temporarily. In late 1968, Youngstown, Ohio, closed its schools for five weeks due to a taxpayers' revolt. 281 *Gov. Emp. Rel. Rep.* B-6 (1969). In late 1969, 10 Ohio school districts ran out of money and were closed down. *Wall Street Journal*, Dec. 19, 1969, p. 1, col. 1.

[11] Wellington and Winter, "The Limits of Collective Bargaining in Public Employment," p. 1123.

This is a troublesome passage. It ends with the implicit conclusion that all government services are essential. This conclusion is important in Wellington and Winter's analysis because it is a step in their demonstration that strikes are inappropriate in all governmental services. But the beginning of the passage, with its example of "job action" by teachers, suggests that essentiality is not an *inherent* characteristic of government services but depends on the specific service being evaluated. Furthermore the transit authority example suggests that many services are interchangeable between the public and private sectors. The view that various government services are not of equal essentiality and that there is considerable overlap between the kinds of services provided in the public and private sectors is reinforced by our field work and strike data from the Bureau of Labor Statistics. Examples include:

1. Where sanitation services are provided by a municipality, such as Cleveland, sanitationmen are prohibited from striking. Yet, sanitationmen in Philadelphia, Portland, and San Francisco are presumably free to strike since they are employed by private contractors rather than by the cities.
2. There were 25 local government strikes by the Teamsters in 1965-68, most involving truck drivers and all presumably illegal. Yet the Teamsters' strike involving fuel oil truck drivers in New York City last winter was legal even though the interruption of fuel oil service was believed to have caused the death of several people.[12]

Public pressure. The second argument in the Wellington and Winter analysis is that public pressure on city officials forces them to make quick settlements. The validity of this argument depends on whether the service is essential. Using as a criterion whether the service is essential in the short run, we believe a priori that services can be divided into three categories: (1) essential services—police and fire—where strikes immediately endanger public health and safety: (2) intermediate services—sanitation, hospitals, transit, water, and sewage—where strikes of a few days might be tolerated; (3) nonessential services—streets, parks, education, housing, welfare and general administration—where strikes of indefinite duration could be tolerated.[13]   These categories are not exact since essentiality depends on the size of the city.   Sanitation strikes will be critical in large cities such as New York but will not cause much inconvenience in smaller cities where there are meaningful alternatives to governmental operation of sanitation services.

Statistics on the duration of strikes which occurred in the public sector between 1965 and 1968 provide evidence not only that public services are of unequal essentiality, but also that the a priori categories which we have used have some validity.   As can be seen from Table 1, strikes in the essential services (police and fire) had an average duration of 4.7 days, while both the intermediate and the nonessential services had an average duration of approximately 10.5 days.   It is true that the duration of strikes in the intermediate and nonessential services is only half the average duration of strikes in the private sector during these years.[14]   However, this comparison is somewhat misleading since all of the public sector strikes were illegal, and many were ended by injunction, while presumably a vast majority of the private sector strikes did not suffer

<hr>

[12] *N.Y. Times*, Dec. 26, 1968, p. 1, col. 1, and Dec. 27, 1968, p. 1, col. 5.

[13] We consider education a nonessential service. However, because our portion of the Brookings Institution study excludes education, our analysis in this article will also largely exclude education.

[14] U.S. Bureau of Labor Statistics, Dept. of Labor, *Analysis of Work Stoppages 1967, Bull. No. 1611*, p. 4 (1969).

TABLE 1

Duration of Strikes by Essentiality of Function*

	Average Duration in Days	*Standard Deviation** in Days*
Essential	4.7	7.9
Intermediate	10.3	18.5
Nonessential	10.6	20.1
Education	7.2	8.9

*Based on data collected by the Bureau of Labor Statistics on strikes during 1965–68 involving employees of local government.

**Standard deviation is a measure of dispersion around the average or the mean.

from these constraints. It would appear that with the exception of police and fire protection, public officials are to some degree, able to accept long strikes. The ability of governments to so choose indicates that political pressures generated by strikes are not so strong as to undesirably distort the entire decision-making process of government. City officials in Kalamazoo, Michigan, were able to accept a forty-eight day strike by sanitationmen and laborers; Sacramento County, California, survived an eighty-seven day strike by welfare workers. A three-month strike of hospital workers has occurred in Cuyahoga County (Cleveland), Ohio.

The strike as a unique weapon. The third objection to the strike is that it provides workers with a weapon unavailable to the employing agency or to other pressure groups. Thus, unions have a superior arsenal. . . . Conceptually, we see no reason why lockouts are less feasible in the public than in the private sector. Legally, public sector lockouts are now forbidden, but so are strikes; presumably both could be legalized. Actually, public sector lockouts have occurred. The Social Service Employees Union (SSEU) of New York City sponsored a "work-in" in 1967 during which all of the caseworkers went to their office but

refused to work. Instead, union-sponsored lectures were given by representatives of organizations such as CORE, and symposia were held on the problems of welfare workers and clients. The work-in lasted for one week, after which the City locked out the caseworkers.

. . . Wellington and Winter . . . claim that no pressure group other than unions has a weapon comparable to the strike. But this argument raises a number of questions. Is the distinctive characteristic of an inappropriate method of influencing decisions by public officials that it is economic as opposed to political? If this is so, then presumably the threat of the New York Stock Exchange to move to New Jersey unless New York City taxes on stock transfers were lowered and similar devices should be outlawed along with the strike.

Distortion of the political process. The ultimate concern of Wellington and Winter is that "a strike of government employees . . . introduces an alien force in the legislative process."[15] It is "alien" because, in the words of the Taylor Committee Report:

[15] State of New York, *Governor's Committee on Public Employee Relations, Final Report,* 15 (1966). Hereinafter cited as *Taylor Committee Report.* The committee chairman was George W. Taylor.

Careful thought about the matter shows conclusively we believe that while the right to strike normally performs a useful function in the private enterprise sector (where relative economic power is the final determinant in the making of private agreements), it is not compatible with the orderly functioning of our democratic form of representative government (in which relative political power is the final determinant).[16]

The essence of this analysis appears to be that certain means used to influence the decision-making process in the public sector—those which are political—are legitimate, while other—those which are economic—are not. For several reasons, we believe that such distinctions among means are tenuous.

First, any scheme which differentiates economic power from political power faces a perplexing definitional task. . . .

Second, even assuming it is possible to operationally distinguish economic power and political power, a rationale for utilizing the distinction must be provided. Such a rationale would have to distinguish between the categories either on the basis of characteristics inherent in them as a means of action or on the basis of the ends to which the means are directed. Surely an analysis of ends does not provide a meaningful distinction. The objectives of groups using economic pressure are of the same character as those of groups using political pressure—both seek to influence executive and legislative determinations such as the allocation of funds and the tax rate. If it is impossible effectively to distinguish economic from political pressure groups in terms of their ends, and it is desirable to free the political process from the influence of all pressure groups, then effective lobbying and petitioning should be as illegal as strikes.

[16] *Taylor Committee Report*, pp. 18–19.

If the normative distinction between economic and political power is based, not on the ends desired, but on the nature of the means, our skepticism remains undiminished. Are all forms of political pressure legitimate? Then consider the range of political activity observed in the public sector. Is lobbying by public sector unions to be approved? Presumably it is. What then of participation in partisan political activity? On city time? Should we question the use of campaign contributions or kickbacks from public employees to public officials as a means of influencing public sector decisions? These questions suggest that political pressures, as opposed to economic pressures, cannot *as a class* be considered more desirable.

Our antagonism toward a distinction based on means does not rest solely on a condemnation of political pressures which violate statutory provisions. We believe that perfectly legal forms of political pressure have no automatic superiority over economic pressure. In this regard, the evidence from our field work is particularly enlightening. First, we have found that the availability of political power varies among groups of employees within a given city. Most public administrators have respect for groups which can deliver votes at strategic times. Because of their links to private sector unions, craft unions are invariably in a better position to play this political role than a union confined to the public sector, such as AFSCME. In Chicago, Cleveland and San Francisco, the public sector craft unions are closely allied with the building trades council and play a key role in labor relations with the city. Prior to the passage of state collective bargaining laws such unions also played the key role in Detroit and New York City. In the No-Strike Model, craft unions clearly have the comparative advantage because of their superior political power.

Second, the range of issues pursued by unions relying on political power tends to be narrow. The unions which prosper by eschewing economic power and exercising political power are often found in cities, such as Chicago, with a flourishing patronage system. These unions gain much of their political power by cooperating with the political administration. This source of political power would vanish if the unions were assiduously to pursue a goal of providing job security for their members since this goal would undermine the patronage system. In Rochester, for example, a union made no effort to protect one of its members who was fired for political reasons. For the union to have opposed the city administration at that time on an issue of job security would substantially have reduced the union's influence on other issues. In Chicago, where public sector strikes are rare (except for education) but political considerations are not, the unions have made little effort to establish a grievance procedure to protect their members from arbitrary treatment.

Third, a labor relations system built on political power tends to be unstable since some groups of employees, often a substantial number, are invariably left out of the system. They receive no representation either through patronage or through the union. In Memphis, the craft unions had for many years enjoyed a "working relationship" with the city which assured the payment of the rates that prevailed in the private sector and some control over jobs. The sanitation laborers, however, were not part of the system and were able to obtain effective representation only after a violent confrontation with the city in 1968. Having been denied representation through the political process, they had no choice but to accept a subordinate position in the city or to initiate a strike to change the system. Racial barriers were an important factor in the isolation of the Memphis sanitation laborers. Similar distinctions in racial balance among functions and occupations appear in most of the cities we visited.

Conclusions in Regard to Strikes and the Political Process

Wellington and Winter. . . reject the use of the Strike Model in the public sector. They have endorsed the No-Strike Model in order "to ensure the survival of the 'normal' American political process."[17] Our field work suggests that unions which have actually helped their members either have made the strike threat a viable weapon despite its illegality or have intertwined themselves closely with their nominal employer through patronage-political support arrangements. If this assessment is correct, choice of the No-Strike Model is likely to lead to patterns of decision making which will subvert, if not the "normal" American political process, at least the political process which . . . Wellington and Winter meant to embrace. We would not argue that the misuse of political power will be eliminated by legalizing the strike; on balance, however, we believe that, in regard to most governmental functions, the Strike Model has more virtues than the No-Strike Model. Whether strikes are an appropriate weapon for all groups of public employees is our next topic.

DIFFERENTIATION AMONG PUBLIC SECTOR FUNCTIONS

The most important union for local government employees, The American Federation of State, County, and Municipal Employees (AFSCME), issued a policy statement in 1966 claiming the right of public employees to strike:

> AFSCME insists upon the right of public employees . . . to strike. To forestall this right is to handicap free collective bar-

---

[17] Wellington and Winter, "The Limits of Collective Bargaining in Public Employment," pp. 1125–26.

gaining process [sic]. Wherever legal barriers to the exercise of this right exist, it shall be our policy to seek the removal of such barriers. Where one party at the bargaining table possesses all the power and authority, the bargaining becomes no more than formalized petitioning.[18]

Significantly, AFSCME specifically excluded police and other law enforcement officers from this right. Any local of police officers that engages in a strike or other concerted refusal to perform duties will have its charter revoked.

Can a distinction among functions, such as is envisioned by AFSCME, be justified? In view of the high costs associated with the suppression of strikes, could each stoppage be dealt with, as Theodore Kheel suggests, only when and if it becomes an emergency?

Despite arguments to the contrary, we feel that strikes in some essential services, such as fire and police, would immediately endanger the public health and safety and should be presumed illegal. We have no evidence from our field work to support our fears that any disruption of essential services will quickly result in an emergency. But the events which occurred on September 9, 1919, during a strike by Boston policemen provide strong proof, those which occurred on October 7, 1969, following a strike by Montreal policemen would appear to make the argument conclusive. . . .

In the case of strikes by essential employees, such as policemen, the deterioration of public order occurs almost immediately. During the first few hours of the police walkout in Montreal, robberies occurred at eight banks, one finance company, two groceries, a jewelry store and a private bank.[19] In the case of the Boston police strike of 1919, outbreaks began within four hours after the strike had com-

menced. Such consequences require that strikes by police and other essential services be outlawed in advance. There is simply no time to seek an injunction.

Even if a distinction in the right to strike can be made among government functions on the basis of essentiality, is such a distinction possible to implement? The Taylor Committee based their argument against prohibiting strikes in essential functions but allowing them elsewhere on this difficulty:

> We come to this conclusion [to prohibit all strikes] after a full consideration of the views ... that public employees in non-essential governmental services, at least, should have the same right to strike as has been accorded to employees in private industry. We realize, moreover, that the work performed in both sectors is sometimes comparable or identical. When, then, should an interruption of non-essential governmental services be prohibited?
>   To begin with, a differentiation between essential and non-essential governmental services would be the subject of such intense and never ending controversy as to be administratively impossible.[20]

Despite the conclusion of the Taylor Committee it appears that in practice a distinction is emerging between strikes in essential services and strikes in other services. Employee organizations and public officials do in fact treat some strikes as critical, while other strikes cause no undue concern.

Our analysis of the Bureau of Labor Statistics strike data pertaining to the last four years suggests that it is possible to devise an operational definition of essential service. First, as we have indicated above, strike duration was considerably shorter in the essential services than in the intermediate or nonessential services (see Table 1). These data suggest that, except

---

[18] *International Executive Board AFSCME, Policy Statement on Public Employee Unions: Rights and Responsibilities*, 2 (July 26, 1966).

[19] *N.Y. Times*, Oct. 8, 1969, p. 3, col. 1.

[20] *Taylor Committee Report*, p. 18.

in police and fire services, public officials have some discretion in choosing to accept long strikes. Second, the statistics reveal that managers have been able to distinguish between essential and nonessential services in their use of counter sanctions. In strikes involving essential services, injunctions were sought more frequently and employees, because of their short run indispensability, were fired less frequently. Injunctions were granted in 35% of the essential strikes, and in 25% of the intermediate, but only in 19% of the nonessential strikes. Third, partial operation was attempted more frequently in essential services. By using nonstrikers, supervisors, replacements or volunteers, local governments were able to continue partial operation during 92% of the essential strikes, but in only 80% of the intermediate, and 77% of the nonessential strikes. Such data suggest that it may be administratively feasible to differentiate among public services so as to permit some, but not all, public employees to strike. Indeed, public administrators already seem to be making such distinctions. . . .

IMPLICATIONS FOR PUBLIC POLICY

We have expressed our views on the market restraints that exist in the public sector, the extent of the public pressure on public officials to reach quick settlements, the likely methods by which decisions would be made in the No-Strike Model, and the desirability and feasibility of differentiating among government services on the basis of essentiality. In this light, what public policy seems appropriate for strikes at the local government level?

In general, we believe that strikes in the public sector should be legalized for the same reasons they are legal in the private sector. For some public sector services, however—namely, police and fire protection—the probability that a strike will result in immediate danger to public health and safety is so substantial that strikes are almost invariable inappropriate. In these essential functions, the strike should be presumed illegal; the state should not be burdened with the requirement of seeking an injunction. We would, however, permit employees in a service considered essential to strike if they could demonstrate to a court that a disruption of service would not endanger the public. Likewise, we would permit the government to obtain an injunction against a strike in a service presumed nonessential if a nontrivial danger to the public could be shown.[21]

The decision to permit some, but not all, public employee strikes cannot, of course, take place *in vaccus publicum jus.* Mediation, fact finding, or advisory arbitration may be appropriate for those functions where strikes are permitted. Where strikes are illegal because of the essential nature of the service, it may be necessary to institute compulsory arbitration.

---

[21] The Labor Management Relations Act (Taft-Hartley Act) is a statute which presumes strikes are legal unless an emergency is involved. 29 U.S.C. §§176-180 (1969). The President may delay or suspend an actual or threatened strike which if permitted to occur or continue will constitute a threat to the national health or safety. The emergency procedures have been invoked 29 times since 1947. This experience should provide some guidance in formulating an operational version of our policy which would permit strikes in nonessential functions unless a nontrivial danger to the public could be shown. We realize that it may be more difficult to formulate an operational version of our policy for essential functions. We are not aware of any experience with a statute which permits the presumption of illegality for strikes to be rebutted under appropriate circumstances.

47

Future of Collective Bargaining in the Public Sector

Benjamin Aaron

Benjamin Aaron, "Future of Collective Bargaining in the Public Sector," from *Public Sector Bargaining*, Benjamin Aaron et al., eds. Industrial Relations Research Association Series, 1979.

Exercises in "futurology," as I have noted elsewhere,[1] are apt to be unrewarding in areas outside the physical sciences. . . . The foregoing essays in this volume provide ample evidence that our vision of the future of specific aspects of collective bargaining in the public sector[2] must necessarily be as through a glass, darkly.

EXTENT OF BARGAINING

This point is made perhaps most emphatically in John Burton's essay* on the extent of bargaining in the public sector. After extensive review and analysis of the relevant data, Burton concludes that the mushroomlike growth of bargaining-organization[3] membership in government employment in the 1960s was largely unanticipated before the fact and is not fully explainable after the fact. Even more surprising

---

[1] Benjamin Aaron, *Legal Framework of Industrial Relations*, in The Next Twenty-Five Years of Industrial Relations (Madison, Wis.: Industrial Relations Research Association, 1973), p. 101.

[2] By "public sector," I mean only government employment, whether at the federal, state, or local level.

*Editor's note: Burton's essay and the others mentioned in this article are included in *Public Sector Bargaining,* ed. Benjamin Aaron, et al. (Industrial Relations Research Association Series, 1979).

[3] Employees in the public sector are represented in some cases by unions and in others by associations. Although the differences between the two types of organizations, in respect of collective bargaining attitudes and tactics, are gradually disappearing, some associations still object to being called unions. The term "bargaining organizations" employed in this chapter is designed to overcome this difficulty.

is his judgment that public-policy changes were a relatively unimportant factor in the surge of membership in bargaining organizations. If Burton's conclusions are correct, there seems little reason to suppose that we can confidently forecast the future of the extent of collective bargaining in the public sector.

In the short term, however, there is at least the possibility of a rather anomalous development: continuing, steady, if not spectacular growth in the total membership of all public-sector bargaining organizations, accompanied by a diminution in the membership of some, together with an overall decline in bargaining effectiveness in the context of an unfavorable economic and political environment. For example, the American Federation of State, County, and Municipal Employees (AFSCME), having absorbed the 262,000-member Civil Service Employees Association of New York, has become the largest union affiliated with the AFL-CIO, paying a per capita dues for a membership of more than one million. At the same time, AFSCME's District 37 in New York is struggling to retain its 105,000 members in the face of New York City's work force reductions and hard-bargaining stance—part of the price of continued willingness by the federal government to rescue the city from its chronically desperate financial plight. Similarly, in California, the sharp reduction in local property taxes as a result of the adoption of Proposition 13 is already causing cut-backs in government employment; moreover, politically sensitive public employers will almost certainly stiffen their resistance to the bargaining demands of their employees. There is a substantial likelihood that these conditions will recur in an increasing number of other cities and states.

The question is, how will such developments affect the extent of bargaining in the public sector? Burton's study suggests the possibility of two quite different, and counter-

vailing results. On the one hand, bargaining organizations of public employees may pull themselves up by their own bootstraps by lobbying successfully to strengthen collective bargaining laws in states that already have them and to obtain enactment of such laws in states that do not presently have them; success in these efforts would, presumably, lead to increases in membership and further gains at the bargaining table. On the other hand, the legislative process is characteristically slow, and there is usually a considerable lag between enactment of new legislation and any tangible benefits to its intended beneficiaries; meanwhile, lack of immediate success in improving the lot of their members may lead to defections and consequent loss of membership by many public-sector bargaining organizations.

On balance, it appears that organization in the public sector will continue, but at a greatly reduced rate, for the foreseeable future. Much depends upon factors over which public employees have little or no control, including the general state of the economy, the rate of growth in public employment, and shifts in political power at both federal and state levels. A factor of particular significance is the current and rather pervasive rebellion against higher taxes, growing government employment, and greater centralization of power in the hands of the federal government. This rebellion is not new, but its present manifestation has been exploited more skillfully and seems better and more purposefully organized than at any previous time in the past 40 years. The term "government employee" has now joined "politician" and "bureaucrat" in the lexicon of opprobrium of many members of the general public who urge sharp reductions in government services and greater reliance upon the private sector to provide them. It is still too early to discern whether this new mood signals a major change in our society, or merely a temporary uprising, or, perhaps, something in between—a permanent, though more subdued than at present, countervailing pressure against the growth of government and expansion in the number, size, and power of employee bargaining organizations in the public sector.

UNIONISM IN THE PUBLIC SECTOR

Prospects for Growth

Despite the spectacular growth of AFSCME, the outlook in the next decade for public-employee bargaining organizations is not particularly sanguine, although, in the judgment of James Stern, total membership growth of such organizations, while tapering off, will probably not go into an absolute decline, as has the AFL-CIO in the past few years.[4]

Faced with the prospect of a declining growth rate at best, public-sector bargaining organizations may be expected to undergo certain changes in structure and in ideology. Once again, however, the anticipated changes are likely to offset each other. One may reasonably anticipate continuing mergers and consolidations among bargaining organizations, but, as Stern points out, there is a stronger emphasis on local decision making in the public-sector bargaining organizations than in those in the private sector. This is to be expected because the wide variety of state laws and local ordinances applicable to members of a national organization makes it impossible for such an organization to formulate a single national bargaining policy that will be applicable to all affiliates. Thus, the added economic power and administrative efficiency normally resulting

from a merger may be offset by the demand for autonomy in general policy-making by the constituent units of the new organization.

The Federal Executive Branch

Stern's essay indicates that the outlook for the principal bargaining organizations of employees in the federal executive branch is mixed, but generally not very promising. The substantive limitations (particularly the prohibition against compulsory payment of union dues) of the various executive orders governing labor-management relations between the executive departments and their employees, combined with administrative interference with arbitral decisions in rights disputes by the office of the Comptroller General,[5] have hampered effective collective bargaining and have resulted in a large percentage of "free riders" in some of the organizations.

The present situation was dramatically summed up by former Secretary of Labor W.L. Usery, during his tenure as Director of the Federal Mediation and Conciliation Service:

> The truth is that there is precious little real collective bargaining in the federal sector—and far too much collective begging. . . .
>
> The reason there is so little true collective bargaining . . . is because there is so little that can be bargained for.
>
> Congress preempts the economic issues. . . .
>
> Many of the primary noneconomic issues—seniority, job transfers, discipline, promotion, the agency shop, and the union shop, are nonnegotiable—because of a combination of law, regulation, management rights, and thousands of pages in the Federal Personnel Manual.
>
> The result, all too frequently, is a con-

---

[4] The latest (1977) membership figures available for the AFL-CIO reveal that since 1975 its membership has declined by about 500,000, and is now about 13.5 million. AFL-CIO Executive Committee Report, BNA Daily Labor Report, No. 235, December 6, 1977, E13–15.

[5] See John Kagel, "Grievance Arbitration in the Federal Service: How Final and Binding?" *Ore. L. Rev.*, 51 (1971), p. 134.

tract that simply restates what management says management will do—providing only the protection to grieve should management violate its own rules.[6]

Usery predicted that the executive orders "will one day be replaced by legislation,"[7] presumably transferring many substantive issues from management's exclusive domain into the arena of collective bargaining. That day seems at the moment, however, to be far removed—too far, indeed, to permit any reliable prediction as to when, or even if, it will come. The Carter Administration has pushed for a comprehensive reorganization of the federal Civil Service and improved collective bargaining mechanisms, but the mood of the Congress sitting in 1978 is typified by the heightened concern over the question of whether the armed services will become organized—a largely irrelevant issue.

The Postal Service

The system of collective bargaining in the federal service that most nearly approximates that in the private sector is, of course, the one established in the quasi-governmental Postal Service by the Postal Reorganization Act of 1970. The results so far have been mixed. Three national agreements between the Postal Service and the principal labor organizations have been negotiated, and the principle of joint decision making has been established. Contrary to the general situation in government employment, Postal Service management is far more skilled and much better organized than the representatives of the several labor organizations with which it deals—at least in respect to the day-to-day administration of the national

agreement. Indeed, the failure thus far of the postal unions to eliminate grievances that are obviously without merit and to present effectively those which appear to have some foundation has put great strains on the grievance-arbitration system established by the national agreement.

Under the Postal Reorganization Act, the employees are forbidden to strike; the ultimate means of resolving interest disputes is arbitration. As of September 1978, new contract negotiations had reached an impasse, the tentative agreement accepted by union officers had been rejected by their memberships, and the final process of mediation-arbitration had begun. Despite official denials, it seems clear that the federal government interfered actively in the negotiations in order to ensure that the Postal Service's wage proposal would not exceed a predetermined percentage compatible with the Administration's anti-inflationary policies. This government intervention caused considerable resentment on the part of the rank-and-file Postal Service employees and was a major factor leading to both rejection of the tentative agreement and sporadic wildcat strikes across the country.

The apparent inability of the leadership of the larger postal unions to control their members, the superior organization on the management side, and the unwillingness of the federal government to remain aloof from new contract negotiations suggest that labor-management relations in this sector will be somewhat unstable in the years immediately ahead.

Education

Among the larger specialized groups of government employees, the outlook for bargaining organizations of teachers seems the brightest. As Stern has observed, one of the major developments in public-sector labor relations has

[6] W. J. Usery, Jr., at the Collective Bargaining Symposium for Labor Relations Executives, Warrenton, Va., July 8, 1974.

[7] *Ibid.*

been the shift of teachers from a passive role to that of militant unionists. Continued rivalry between the American Federation of Teachers (AFT) and the National Education Association (NEA), and between their respective affiliates, has tended to increase organizational successes rather than to diminish them. In most communities, the economic welfare of teachers in the elementary and secondary grades, up through the first two years of college, is almost entirely dependent upon property taxes, which are currently under sustained attack, not only in California, but also in other parts of the country.

Here again, we may expect continued organizational gains by the AFT and the NEA, even while they may be suffering from reductions in jobs and little or no successes in negotiations over economic issues. In situations of this kind, the law of inertia seems to apply: once a certain degree of militancy has been achieved, it tends to continue in spite of various obstacles, unless it meets one that can be neither surmounted nor side-stepped. On the other hand, the tendency among unorganized teachers to remain apathetic toward organizational initiatives may well be broken by the shock of the latest assault on their jobs and their working conditions.

The same cannot be said, however, for faculty members of state colleges and universities above the junior-college level. The great organizing drives of the 1960s among teachers at the lower levels left the situation in higher education virtually unchanged. They did, however, have the belated effect of compelling the American Association of University Professors, as well as independent associations of faculty members in a number of four-year colleges and universities, to focus on the issue of collective bargaining for faculty members, and in some cases to enter the lists against affiliates of the AFT and the NEA for the right to represent units of faculty members. For the most part, however, college and university professors, especially those with tenure, have remained cool to the idea of collective bargaining, either because they are reasonably satisfied with things as they are, because they distrust the motives, the philosophy, or the competence of the organizations seeking their support, or because, although dissatisfied with their present lot, they prefer to seek to improve it in other, more traditional ways.

Yet there is at least the possibility that this mood may change to a more aggressive one.... If the prospects for tenure of junior faculty, the economic status of the entire faculty, and the opportunities for recruiting new faculty continue to deteriorate, those who favor collective bargaining may eventually gain the upper hand.

MANAGEMENT ORGANIZATION FOR COLLECTIVE BARGAINING IN THE PUBLIC SECTOR

Management Attitudes

In order for collective bargaining to endure in the public sector, government managers must establish their credibility as an effective countervailing force against the political and economic power of the employee bargaining organizations. This formidable task was at first made still more difficult by the attitude of managers at all levels of government; collectively, and with all too few exceptions, they presented in their behavior complete confirmation of the aphorism that those who pay no attention to the mistakes of the past are condemned to repeat them in the future.

Long after the portents of the approaching collective bargaining revolution in the public sector had become unmistakably clear, most government managers persisted either in pretending that the problem did not exist or in magisterially ordering the tidal wave about to engulf them to recede. When, finally, they were forced to confront reality, some of them acted as if the ship of state had been captured by pirates and that unconditional surrender was the price of survival; a somewhat greater number, however, still unwilling to abandon their fantasies and continuing to act as if nothing had happened, violated both the letter and the spirit of the new laws governing their relations with their employees, while neglecting to prepare for the day when those laws would be enforced against them.

This strange initial failure of government managers to adjust to the changing attitudes and patterns of behavior of their employees can, in retrospect, be attributed to two major factors. The first was their unshakable conviction that the differences between the public and private sectors were so great that no useful purpose would be served by studying the development of collective bargaining in the latter. The second was their belief, often proved to be correct, that even under the new dispensations they could successfully frustrate efforts by their employees to engage in genuine collective bargaining by drastically limiting the scope of bargaining and maintaining a broad area of undisturbed management rights.

The second factor, bolstered by some state statutes and local ordinances, as well as by the executive order governing federal employees, remains a major barrier to genuine collective bargaining in the public sector. The myth of the complete uniqueness of government employment is slowly eroding, however, although it is generally conceded that there are some genuine and important differences between employment in the public and private sectors. Thus, an increasing number of government managers are becoming aware of both the need to learn more about labor-management relations in the private sector and the benefits that can be derived from that knowledge.

Outside Pressures

The problems of developing an effective management organization that meets the responsibilities of a system of shared decision-making, while at the same time preserving management's right to ensure that the mission of a given agency will be carried out, are analyzed in detail by Milton Derber. Of growing significance is the role of various citizen groups, which, under the banner of participatory democracy, seek ways in which to advance their special interests. The pressures that these groups exert are directed primarily at management; employee organizations usually feel it indirectly. Thus, most state "sunshine laws" have been construed to require only that meetings of legislative bodies be held in public. It is doubtful that laws requiring active participation of outside groups in the collective bargaining process will prove feasible.

That the pressures upon public managers by special-interest groups have already, and will continue to be, effective in some situations seems clear. In relatively small communities, one may assume that the requirement that all negotiated collective bargaining agreements or "memoranda of understanding" be ratified by the voters in a special election[8] will continue to gain in popularity, at least during the period of widespread public revolt against any increase in the cost of government. I think

[8] See, for example, statements by David H. Rodgers, Mayor of Spokane, Wash., and A. Herbert Abshire, President, National Public Employer Labor Relations Assn., in *LMRS Newsletter,* 8 (September 1977), p. 2, and *LMRS Newsletter,* 8 (October 1977), p. 3, respectively.

it doubtful, however, that such a procedure will ever be adopted by many of the larger towns and cities; and it seems to me much more likely that as both public managers and the bargaining organizations become more skilled and sophisticated in bargaining techniques, both sides will take steps to neutralize what they regard as undue interference by outside pressure groups. The latter will thus have to confine themselves to the traditional practice of lobbying the appropriate legislative bodies rather than the bargaining parties.

Supervisors

The rapid sophistication of government managers in bargaining philosophy and techniques is a consummation devoutly to be wished. Despite a slow start, for the reasons previously mentioned, this process is now going forward at all levels of government, although not at a uniform pace and with many exceptions. Most government bodies are now aware of the need for a strong management team to represent them in contract negotiations. Derber notes that the majority of states with specific laws dealing with public-sector collective bargaining, as well as the federal executive branch, have opted to treat supervisors as they are treated under the National Labor Relations Act. This means that supervisors can be made key members of the management team. A number of states, however, permit supervisors to bargain collectively in units of their own. Thus, the pattern of future relationships of supervisors to higher management and to the employees they supervise is still unclear. For the short term, it appears that the present diversity of practice will continue. I think it likely, however, that in the relatively near future serious efforts will be made in states and communities now permitting supervisors to bargain separately, or as part of the bargaining unit they supervise, to remove the bargaining rights of supervisors and to incorporate them in the management group.

It should be borne in mind, however, that many, if not most, associations of government employees have traditionally accepted into membership not only supervisory employees, but also top managerial employees. This policy had much to do with the resistance within such organizations to the idea that they should switch their principal activities from lobbying to collective bargaining. Even now, after most of them have apparently accepted the inevitability of the latter development, supervisor-members continue to exercise considerable influence, of a relatively conservative character, on their policies.

In a few governmental services—notably those performed by the police, fire fighters, eduators, and social workers—the rank-and-file employees seem to prefer to retain their traditionally close relationship with first-line supervisors and to include the latter in their bargaining units. In most areas of public employment, however, particularly those in which unions have taken over employee association, the apparent dominant feeling is that supervisors should be excluded from the bargaining unit of employees whom they supervise, although this contention is usually accompanied by the argument that supervisors should be allowed to comprise a bargaining unit of their own.

The status of supervisors under applicable legislation in California, for example, has been among the most controversial issues raised every time proposals are made for new legislation covering labor-management relations in government employment. At least some of the bargaining organizations insisting upon bargaining rights for supervisors, however, have indicated a willingness to amend their constitutions to exclude supervisors from membership in return for a statutory provision for a compulsory agency shop. The rationale of that position is that the loss of dues paid by supervisory members would be considerable and would have to be offset by the payment of a compulsory "service fee" by all employees in the bargaining unit. The expulsion of supervisors, as Stern points out, could be expected to result in a more militant stance being taken by the bargaining organization in its dealings with the government employer. At the same time, this move might also lead to inclusion of the supervisors in the employer's management team and increase its effective resistance to the organization's demands.

Ultimately, the status of supervisors who are members of bargaining organizations in collective bargaining rests with legislative bodies or administrative agencies. My best guess, however, is that future attempts to organize groups of government employees not previously organized will probably not include supervisors.

Multi-Employer Bargaining Units

Derber has observed that there has been surprisingly little interest among local management groups in establishing multi-employer bargaining units with corresponding coordinating organizations. Such an alignment seems to me, however, to be virtually inevitable, if only in order to match similar developments among employee bargaining organizations. It is also required as an effective counter to strikes by particular groups of government employees, and as a means of reducing the number of what the late Arthur Ross termed "orbits of coercive comparison."[9]

[9] Arthur M. Ross, *Trade Union Wage Policy* (Berkeley: University of California Press, 1956), pp. 53–64.

Management Training

Experience has shown that properly conceived and executed training programs in collective negotiations and contract administration produce excellent results. Generally, managers have access to greater amounts of money for such training than do the employee bargaining organizations, but Derber has found that government managers have scarcely begun to take advantage of this opportunity. This situation, too, is likely to change rather rapidly. Once government management comes to understand that its relationship with employee bargaining organizations is a dynamic one, subject to constant pressures for change, it will also learn to appreciate the need for the continuous training of its supervisors and executives to keep pace with new developments and techniques.

I look for no major changes in the attitudes or practices of managers in the federal executive branch in the absence of more liberal legislation to replace the present executive order. Managers do only what they consider necessary, and the lack of a need to show a profit in dollars and cents makes those in government more indifferent than they might otherwise be to such aspects of employment as morale and productivity. Many state and local government managers are now required by law, however, to engage in some form of collective negotiations with representatives of their employees. They have been forced, therefore—often against their wishes—to come to grips with problems of labor-management relations that were previously ignored. A large number of government managers have already developed an awareness of their problems and acquired the skills to deal with them rather rapidly, and I expect this trend to continue at an accelerating rate. I do not mean to suggest, however, that the path of collective bargaining in state and local governments will therefore run smoothly. . . .

THE IMPACT OF COLLECTIVE BARGAINING ON COMPENSATION IN THE PUBLIC SECTOR

The same controversy over the impact of collective bargaining on wage rates that has continued for so long in the private sector exists also in the public sector. *Daniel Mitchell* deals with these and related questions in his essay and further comment on his major findings and conclusions is beyond both the scope of this chapter and my own professional competence. There are several points, however, that have particular significance for the future of collective bargaining in the public sector.

Public-Employee Bargaining and Urban Financial Problems

Mitchell notes that public-employee bargaining organizations have been widely blamed for the financial plight of the big cities. His analysis of the "New York City Syndrome" leads him to conclude that the New York City problem was the result of an unfortunate compounding of several factors, including erosion of an industrial base, a growing level of dependency on city services, and shortsighted budgeting, and that although collective bargaining may have speeded up the city's slide into bankruptcy, it was not the sole cause, and probably not the principal cause. Indeed, he finds that the chief source of pressure for more revenue for labor costs comes from the employment side rather than from the wage side.

These findings suggest that the financial plight of our big cities is likely to continue, regardless of the rise or decline of collective

bargaining in the public sector. On the other hand, they also suggest that if the general public can be persuaded to demand fewer government services, thereby slowing down appreciably the rapid growth in government employment (largely at state and municipal levels), the main cause of increased labor costs will be eliminated. . . .

Counterpressures Against Increased Labor Costs

Additional factors noted by Mitchell will exert greater counterpressure against increased labor costs in government employment in the future. The prevailing-wage provision in many city and county charters is under heavy attack and will, doubtless, be repealed in a number of instances. Moreover, unlike the employee bargaining organizations, government managers are not free to disregard budgetary information, but must use it as the principal basis for formulating their bargaining positions. As managers become more skilled in bargaining, they will be better able to convince the employee organizations that resistance to their demands has a factual, rather than a purely ideological, basis. In this regard, they will be able, at least in the short term, to exploit the prevailing mood of the country against any expansion of government services and in favor of cutting out "government waste"—a term that is varyingly defined, depending upon the points of view of the numerous, competing interest groups in any given community.

One hopes, however, that government managers will not misread this mood as favoring an all-out assault against the principle of collective bargaining in the public sector. As I shall explain at the conclusion of this chapter, it is either too early or too late for such an attempt.

DISPUTE RESOLUTION
IN THE PUBLIC SECTOR

It is unfortunate, but true, that popular attitudes toward collective bargaining in the public sector seem to be unduly influenced by the incidence of strikes by government employees, to which the great majority of the general public is opposed. But strikes, as Thomas Kochan reminds us in his essay, occur because of the absence or the failure of alternative methods for resolving collective bargaining impasses. In respect of this aspect of public-sector collective bargaining, therefore, the emphasis now and for the foreseeable future should be (1) on how to prevent impasses from arising and (2) on weighing the advantages and disadvantages of a number of methods, including the strike, for resolving those impasses which will inevitably occur.

Advantages of Pluralistic
Approaches to Strike Legislation

The country is fortunate, I think, in not having a single, uniform law governing the procedure of impasse resolution. In the absence of such a law, the individual states have engaged in a number of interesting experiments for resolving impasses, thereby adding substantially to the general knowledge about that problem. Kochan's conclusion, reached after an exhaustive review of the available evidence, deserves the same credence now generally accorded the economists's aphorism that there is no such thing as a free lunch; for it is equally true, as he says, that there is no "best way" for resolving all types of disputes. Perhaps, if that idea gains common acceptance, we may be spared, so far as the public sector is concerned, from the futility of the seemingly endless search by legislators and labor-law scholars for a single formula for dealing with "emergency disputes."

Some aspects of strikes by government employees are well known by now: the total number is increasingly annually; the existence of laws making strikes illegal has not been a significant deterrent; and punishment of strikers, more often than not, is inconsistent, unequal, and arbitrary. That many strikes have occurred only because of an absence of any credible alternative cannot be doubted. The task ahead, therefore, is not only to improve the quality of public-sector collective bargaining and continue to evaluate the experience under existing laws, but also to keep experimenting with new methods of impasse resolution for dealing with specialized types of disputes.

Choices of Impasse-Resolution
Techniques

The choice of an appropriate impasse-resolution mechanism obviously depends upon the nature of the dispute involved. It is important to keep an open mind concerning the advantages, as well as the disadvantages, that conventional wisdom has assigned to strikes and compulsory arbitration, as well as to the various procedures falling somewhere in between those polarities. A society that deplores strikes by government employees cannot afford to ignore the alternative of compulsory arbitration, despite the undesirable features of that procedure. Just as there is no best method for settling impasses, so is there no method that is without any undesirable aspect.

As of mid-1978, the ratio of states that have opted for compulsory arbitration of public-sector impasses to those that grant a limited right to strike is a little more than two to one. There does not seem much likelihood either that this ratio will change significantly in the near future, or that compulsory arbitration will be abandoned in favor of combinations of mediation and fact-finding that do not necessarily result in some resolution of the dispute. Indeed, states that have thus far authorized the use only of inconclusive procedures, and have experienced a larger number of strikes than is acceptable, may eventually conclude that the best way to control strikes, without resorting to compulsory arbitration, is to authorize the use of the strike within carefully defined limits.

Lockouts

I have predicted, on several previous occasions, that the use of the lockout by government managers is a potent weapon in collective bargaining and one that will very likely be used more frequently in the future. Not so many years ago, the possibility of strikes by government employees was viewed by most persons as simply unthinkable. When the unthinkable became a reality, the modified version of the former view was that strikes by employees in "essential services," such as police and fire fighters, were unthinkable. A number of strikes by these groups of employees have demonstrated that although they may result in temporary and severe hardship, government has not been paralyzed and the world has continued to turn. The knowledge that most government services can be temporarily discontinued without undue hardship to the citizen-consumers will, I believe, persuade government managers increasingly to attempt to resolve collective bargaining impasses on favorable terms by locking out their employees.

Essential Considerations

The one proposed solution that I feel sure will not work is that embodied recently in a proposed initiative to amend the California constitution by prohibiting both strikes by gov-

ernment employees *and* arbitration of interest disputes, even when agreed to by the government employer. Fortunately, this ill-conceived plan did not receive enough signatures to qualify it for a place on the ballot. The problem of eliminating strikes in such disputes can be solved only by providing one or more credible and workable options; it will merely be further complicated by outlawing not only strikes but also effective alternatives acceptable to the parties to a given dispute.

PUBLIC-SECTOR LABOR LEGISLATION

In her "evolutionary analysis" of public-sector labor legislation, Betty Schneider traces the gradual disappearance of statutory and judicial barriers to collective bargaining by government employees in the key areas of right to bargain, impasse resolution and the strike, scope of bargaining, and union security. She concludes that despite these developments, there remain tensions between the concept of government sovereignty and that of bilateral, or shared, decision-making authority.

Schneider also recognizes the strong, perhaps controlling, influences that the prevailing economic and political environmentalists have upon the continued development of public-sector collective bargaining. She believes that the reluctance of Congress to enact a federal statute covering the collective bargaining rights of all government employees, in the same way that the amended National Labor Relations and Labor Management Relations Acts cover those of employees in the private sector, is due more to the general feeling that government employees are now about as "equal" as they ought to be, rather than to doubts about the constitutionality of such legislation.

Federal Minimum Standards
Versus a Federal Preemptive Law

... In my view, the nation has benefited immeasurably from the experimentation with public-sector collective bargaining laws within what Justice Holmes called "the insulated chambers of the several states."[10] A substantial body of descriptive and analytical research provides ample evidence that the extreme variety of labor-management problems to be found in the different states is the result of the particular economic, political, and social climates in those states. To adopt a law for all government employees similar to those governing labor relations in the private sector, and administered by the National Labor Relations Board or some other agency in Washington, would be, in my judgment, the height of folly. What I[11] and others[12] have suggested as an alternative is a different kind of law designed merely to establish a minimum standard for all federal, state, and municipal employees. According to my proposal, the federal law would establish the following: (1) the absolute right of all government employees at state and local levels to organize and to engage in collective bargaining over wages, hours, and working conditions; (2) the right to an orderly procedure for dealing with all questions concerning representation, including determination of appropriate units, conduct of elections, and related matters; (3) the right to negotiate, but

not to compel, a provision for the final and binding arbitration of grievances by a neutral third party; (4) the right, in the absence of the legal right to strike, to an impasse procedure leading to specific settlements of interest disputes; (5) the right of access to an independent agency with the power and the means to administer adequately all provisions of the statute; and (6) the right of judicial review of any final orders of that agency. Finally, recognizing that the federal law would probably contain a statutory proscription against strikes by any government employees, I recommend a provision that would permit individual states to grant the right to strike to their own employees.

At least for the foreseeable future, this seems to me to be the only type of law that has much of a chance of enactment by the Congress, and that chance is a slim one. In any event, it would be better to have no federal legislation of any kind in this area than to subject the states to a single, preemptive statute that would put an end to the valuable experimentation now taking place.

JUDICIAL RESPONSE TO PUBLIC-SECTOR ARBITRATION

In the early stages of development of collective bargaining in the public sector, management's preoccupation with the concept of government sovereignty, and its paranoid fear of making the slightest concession to bilateral decision-making, resulted in widespread resistance to the idea of grievance arbitration, which is, of course, one of the key principles underlying our national labor policy for the private sector. The more daring managers were willing to experiment with "advisory arbitration," a meaningless and misleading term to describe what is no more than fact-finding with nonbinding recommendations. Genuine arbitration—a decision

[10] *Truax* v. *Corrigan*, 257 U.S. 312, 344 (1921) (dissenting opinion).

[11] See Benjamin Aaron, "Federal Bills Analyzed and Appraised," *LMRS Newsletter,* 5 (November, 1974), p. 4.

[12] See, for example, statement of Arvid Anderson, Chairman, New York City Office of Collective Bargaining, at Hearings on H.R. 12532, H.R. 7684 & H.R. 9324 Before the Special Subcommittee on Labor of the House Committee on Education and Labor, April 18, 1972.

by a third party or parties that is final and binding on both disputants—was eschewed primarily on the ground that it constituted an impermissible limitation on government sovereignty.

Government management's opposition to interest arbitration had a firmer foundation than the sovereignty concept; its most persuasive argument was, and is, that the submission of disputes over new terms and conditions of employment to an independent third party consitutes and unlawful delegation of legislative power.

The development of judicial doctrine in this area of public-sector collective bargaining is traced by Joseph Grodin. He finds that the courts have generally accepted the constitutional legitimacy of grievance arbitration in the public sector, but have been reluctant to defer to arbitration awards to the extent decreed by the Supreme Court in the private sector.[13] He also notes that in respect of the legality of interest arbitration, the courts are divided.

The first reaction of the courts to arbitration, in both the public and the private sector, has always been essentially hostile; the very existence of a procedure for the final settlement of disputes formerly within the exclusive jurisdiction of the courts has been perceived by judges as a threat to judicial supremacy. In the private sector, Section 301 of the Taft-Hartley Act, and the Supreme Court decisions in *Lincoln Mills*,[14] the *Steelworkers'* trilogy,[15] and their progeny, virtually removed grievance arbitration from the inital restraints and the power of substantive judicial

review formerly exercised by the courts. In the public sector, however, the battle has been fought all over again, and grievance arbitration has not won the conclusive victory it gained in the private sector. Indeed, Grodin characterizes as a "trend" recent judicial decisions which have ruled against the arbitrability of issues as to which it is not clear that the parties contemplated arbitration, or which call for the exercise of discretion not governed by explicit contractual criteria. Similarly, the courts have shown an increasing reluctance to enforce arbitral awards that have potential impact upon the level or quality of government services or upon financial resources.

It would be a mistake, I think, to attribute the current judicial attitude merely to jealousy of a rival authority and to assume that the precedents from the private sector will be gradually absorbed and will eventually control the issues of arbitrability of grievances and judicial review of arbitral awards in the public sector. There are, of course, important differences between the public and private sectors, and Grodin believes that the courts, influenced perhaps by the current public hostility toward government employees and collective bargaining, have seized upon those differences as the justification for not following private-sector precedents.

Presumption of Arbitrability

Like Grodin, I believe that the courts' preoccupation with certain differences between the public and private sectors is, in the case of grievance arbitration, excessive, and that the presumption of arbitrability and deference to the substance of arbitration awards are as justifiable in the public sector as they are in the private sector. Whether the courts will eventually come to that point of view, however, is problematical. The chances for that result seem to me somewhat better for the presumption of arbitrability than they are in respect of

---

[13] See *United Steelworkers* v. *Enterprise Wheel & Car Corp.*, 363 U.S. 593, 46 LRRM 2423 (1960); *United Steelworkers* v. *Warrior & Gulf Navigation Co.*, 363 U.S. 574, 46 LRRM 2416 (1960); *United Steelworkers* v. *American Mfg. Co.*, 363 U.S. 564, 46 LRRM 2414 (1960).

[14] 353 U.S. 448, 40 LRRM 2113 (1957).

[15] *Supra* note 13.

judicial deference to arbitral awards. Arbitrability usually invokes the "scope clause" of public-sector bargaining agreements, and restrictions on the scope of bargaining are frequently incorporated in state laws. Courts are more likely to uphold the arbitrability of issues not specifically precluded by statutory language than that of issues not specifically proscribed by collective agreements; for, as Grodin points out, the absence of midterm strikes in public employment renders irrelevant the Supreme Court's dicta that in the private sector, the agreement to arbitrate is a quid pro quo for the agreement not to strike.

Judicial Review

In the area of judicial review, however, I think the courts will continue to resist the private-sector precedents requiring virtually total deference to arbitral awards. . . . In the case of public employment, much of which is governed by statute and was, at least formerly administered by civil service commissions or personnel boards, it is by no means clear that the parties to a collective agreement had in mind that it be administered according to the "law of the shop," or that arbitrators are more qualified than "even the ablest judge"[16] to construe and apply collective agreements. If this prediction proves correct, then it is not beyond the realm of possibility that some federal judges will become emboldened by the example set by the state courts in public-sector cases to begin whittling away at the doctrine of deference to arbitral awards in the private sector.

Interest Arbitration

So far as the legality of interest arbitration in the public sector is concerned, I think the state legislatures rather than the courts will have the

[16] See *United Steelworkers* v. *Warrior & Gulf Nav. Co.*, 363 U.S. 574, 582 (1960) (opinion of Douglas, J.).

ultimate power of decision. The argument that interest arbitration is an unconstitutional delegation of legislative power can be almost completely undermined by a statutory delegation that is accompanied by a reasonably specific set of standards to which arbitrators must adhere. Therefore, it seems to me that the real battles ahead will be over the desirability of adopting a policy of voluntary or compulsory arbitration of interest disputes in the public sector, rather than over the constitutionality of a carefully drawn statute.

FOREIGN INFLUENCES

The indifference of American lawmakers, whether legislators or judges, to foreign laws and practices in both public- and private-sector labor law is well known. Because of the uniqueness of our society—the product of peculiar geographical, historical, economic, political, and social factors—they seem to have automatically assumed that the experience of other highly industrialized countries with roughly similar political and economic orientations is completely irrelevant to our concerns. That the labor laws in the Western European democracies for the private and public sectors are tending to merge into a single body of law applicable to both either is unknown, or, if known, is regarded with disapproval or alarm.

Hence, the increasing interest in this country in the various laws governing labor-management relations in the public sector enacted by the federal and provincial governments of our more advanced neighbor to the north is a welcome surprise. In her essay on the Canadian experience, Shirley Goldenberg traces developments in her country that deserve careful study by federal and state governments in the United States. A few of these are of particular interest. First, the federal government of Canada has been a leader in accepting collective bargaining as the basis of its relations with its own employees, in permitting employees to strike in some circumstances, and in introducing a choice of alternatives—either arbitration or compulsory conciliation followed by the right to strike, if necessary—as the means of resolving impasses in interest disputes. Second, in addition to the federal government, approximately one half of the provinces have granted government employees the right to strike, subject to the requirement that essential services be maintained; and although these arrangements have not been uniformly successful, none has seriously interfered with the functions of government. Third, some of the provincial courts have resisted the use of injunctions against illegal strikes, on the ground that the appropriate legislative bodies should not ask relief from the courts in dealing with what is primarily a political question. This has led to suggestions at the federal level that the Cabinet be empowered by legislation to postpone (not prohibit) a strike in cases in which it deems the public interest to be at stake. Finally, the Canadian experience reaffirms evidence in this country that, in Goldenberg's words, "the socioeconomic and political environment and the historical context of the bargaining relationship have at least as important an impact on the dynamics of dispute resolution as the procedures for dealing with an impasse provided in the law."

It seems to me both likely and desirable that state legislatures—aided and perhaps prodded by scholars—will turn increasingly to foreign experience in their search for improved policies and procedures applicable to collective bargaining in the public sector. I do not mean to suggest that foreign ways can be adopted wholesale, without change, in our different economic, political, and social climate; but a study of how different countries deal with problems similar to those we face is likely to cause us to view our own system from a different perspective which may, in turn, lead to new and better approaches.

CONCLUSION

In relative terms, collective bargaining in the public sector is in its infancy; moreover, it is still developing. It is, therefore, much too soon to pronounce it a success or a failure. On the other hand, collective bargaining in one form or another now affects probably a majority of state, county, and municipal government employees. It is, therefore, too late to reject it as a workable system for determining wages, hours, and working conditions for government employees. Indeed, the organization of the public sector and the spread of collective bargaining seems to many, including myself, to be an irreversible process.

It is possible, of course, that changing policies and practices may, in the still unforeseeable future, lead to the substitution of some other system of labor-management relations for collective bargaining. In my opinion, however, such a possibility is extremely remote, and should it be realized, it would affect both the private and public sectors.

In the meantime, some of the more interesting developments will involve the relationships between policies and practices in the public sector and those in the private sector. Thus far, the former has borrowed much from the latter, but as I suggested earlier in this essay, we may soon witness some significant reversals in that trend. In addition to principles of judicial review previously mentioned, I think the treatment by the courts of individual rights in the public-sector cases may have an increasing influence in similar cases in the private sector.[17]

Certainly, the underlying conditions that gave impetus to the great organizational wave in the public sector in the 1960s have not gone

[17] See Benjamin Aaron, "The Impact of Public Employment Grievance Settlement on the Labor Arbitration Process," in *The Future of Labor Arbitration in America* (New York: American Arbitration Assn., 1976), pp. 1, 30–44.

away; in many instances they have become aggravated. The current admonition to "lower our expectations in an era of limits," so beloved by politicians, is completely irrelevant to the natural and unquenchable demand by those who work for their living—whether in the public or the private sector—to have some voice in determining the terms and conditions under which that work shall be done. The sooner government managers stop resisting the idea of collective bargaining by their employees, the sooner the employee bargaining organizations will recognize their own responsibilities to the general public. Notwithstanding the very real differences between government and private employment, the collective bargaining *process* in both sectors is fundamentally the same: a cooperative sharing of decision-making responsibility within a carefully defined framework, with restrictions and exceptions specifically tailored to the functions and requirements of the activity involved.